Studies in Contemporary and Historical Archaeology 1

# The Historical Archaeology of Pottery Supply and Demand in the Lower Rhineland, AD 1400-1800

## An archaeological study of ceramic production, distribution and use in the city of Duisburg and its hinterland

David R. M. Gaimster

BAR International Series 1518
2006

Published in 2016 by
BAR Publishing, Oxford

BAR International Series 1518

Studies in Contemporary and Historical Archaeology 1
*The Historical Archaeology of Pottery Supply and Demand in the Lower Rhineland, AD 1400-1800*

ISBN 978 1 84171 952 8



Typesetting and layout: Monika Porsche



BAR Publishing is the trading name of British Archaeological Reports (Oxford) Ltd. British Archaeological Reports was first incorporated in 1974 to publish the BAR Series, International and British. In 1992 Hadrian Books Ltd became part of the BAR group. This volume was originally published by Archaeopress in conjunction with British Archaeological Reports (Oxford) Ltd / Hadrian Books Ltd, the Series principal publisher, in 2006. This present volume is published by BAR Publishing, 2016.

Printed in England

BAR
PUBLISHING

BAR titles are available from:

BAR Publishing
122 Banbury Rd, Oxford, OX2 7BP, UK
EMAIL info@barpublishing.com
PHONE +44 (0)1865 310431
FAX +44 (0)1865 316916
www.barpublishing.com

# Studies in Contemporary and Historical Archaeology

*Studies in Contemporary and Historical Archaeology* is a new series of edited and single-authored volumes intended to make available current work on the archaeology of the recent and contemporary past. The series brings together contributions from academic historical archaeologists, professional archaeologists and practitioners from cognate disciplines who are engaged with archaeological material and practices. The series will include work from traditions of historical and contemporary archaeology, and material culture studies, from Europe, North America, Australia and elsewhere around the world. It will promote innovative and creative approaches to later historical archaeology, showcasing this increasingly vibrant and global field, and celebrating its diversity, through extended and theoretically engaged case studies.

Proposals are invited from emerging and established scholars interested in publishing in or editing for the series. Further details are available from the series editors: Email Dan.Hicks@bristol.ac.uk or Joshua.Pollard@bristol.ac.uk

In this, the first volume in the series, David Gaimster presents a systematic analysis of important excavated late medieval and post-medieval ceramic assemblages from the German Rhineland. Because of the wide exportation of German stonewares across northern Europe and to North America during the period 1500-1800, the work will be of considerable value to those engaged in the archaeology of the late medieval and early modern world within these regions. As David Gaimster explains in his Forward, the text was completed in 1990 and submitted as a Ph.D. thesis to the University of London in 1991. As studies in contemporary and historical archaeology develop in the 2000s, we are delighted to be able to begin this new series with this important contribution to our understanding of the value of studying the development of European ceramics during the sixteenth, seventeenth and eighteenth centuries.

Dan Hicks and Joshua Pollard (University of Bristol)
Series Editors

# Abstract

This study of post-medieval ceramic production and consumption in the Lower Rhineland is prefaced by a survey of previous work and approaches in the field. With the initiation of large-scale urban excavations in the Lower Rhineland during the 1980s, particularly in the town of Duisburg, an extensive sequence of pottery has been recovered dating from *c.*1400 to 1800, enabling archaeologists for the first time to re-examine traditional chronologies, attributions and socio-economic interpretations. This survey comprises 95 individual assemblages of pottery from sites excavated in Duisburg and from towns and rural sites in the region.

Substantial emphasis is given to the establishment of a regional type-series of post-medieval ceramics. The methods of fabric characterisation are discussed along with the definition of form and functional-type categories used in the quantification of individual assemblages. These are followed by a problem-orientated programme of chemical analyses by Neutron Activation, which is designed to test and refine the archaeological type-series and to help clarify the geographical attribution of wares made in the region. The pottery classification proceedure and NAA programme form the basis of the subsequent survey of trends in postmedieval ceramic production and distribution in the Lower Rhineland.

Subsequent sections deal with the statistical composition of individual assemblages on an intra-, inter- and multi-site basis. Firstly, a series of representative contexts from Duisburg are investigated in detail. Developments in the regonal consumption of ceramics are reviewed through time with the aid of pie-charts showing the relative variation in ceramic frequencies in the towns of Duisburg and Wesel and at the rural hinterland site of Krefeld-Linn. In identifying the variable composition of ceramic groups in the region a series of conclusions regarding the functional, economic and socio-behavioural role of ceramics are drawn over a 400-year timespan. With the aid of contemporary pictorial sources showing pottery made and imported into the region, it is demonstrated that excavated ceramics may be employed as a prime historical source for the study of European post-medieval society.

# Table of contents

# List of illustrations

## Maps



## Plans



## Diagrams



## Graphs

## Pottery figures p. 199 ff.

## List of tables

# Acknowledgements

The stimulus to embark on this project was provided by Dr Günter Krause of the former Niederrheinisches Museum (now the Kultur- und Stadthistorisches Museum Duisburg) and director of the urban archaeology project in Duisburg, who was the first to recognise the research potential of the post-medieval ceramics being excavated in the town. I am enormously grateful to him both for his initial inspiration and for his constant support, encouragement and advice over the duration of the project. The success of this project has relied almost solely on his capacity to allocate precious Museum resources towards the rapid post-excavation processing, illustration and photography of the Duisburg ceramic finds.

Of the then Niederrheinisches Museum staff I am especially grateful to Erwin Kiel for advising on the line drawings and to Wulf Holtmann for providing information on the Duisburg excavation contexts. However, the project would not have been possible at all without the voluntary efforts of members of the Niederrheinische Gesellschaft für Vor-und Frühgeschichte who were heavily involved in the excavation and post-excavation of the ceramic finds from Duisburg. In particular, I would like to thank Peter Müller †, for his enormous contribution in both areas and for single-handedly supervising the ceramic restoration programme. The swiftness by which the Duisburg pottery groups were recorded testifies to his phenomenal work-rate and long-standing commitment to the project. Finally, I am grateful to Paul Fitscher who, in my absence, completed the pottery illustration programme between 1987–1989.

An understanding of regional ceramic trends would not have been possible without the cooperation of the following museum colleagues and excavators in the Rhineland and other parts of Germany who allowed me access to their collections of post-medieval pottery, and who supplied photographs and illustrations, some of which are reproduced here: Dr Baron Ludwig Döry (Historisches Museum, Frankfurt-am-Main); Dr Else Hähnel (Rheinisches Freilichtmuseum, Mechernich-Kommern); Ursula Francke (Rheinisches Amt für Bodendenkmalpflege); Wolfram Giertz (Roetgen); Dr Jochen Giesler (Rheinisches Landesmuseum, Bonn); Professor Dr Rainer Kahsnitz (Germanisches National-museum, Nürnberg); Lydia Kesselring-Poth (University of Bonn); Dorette Kleine (Keramikmuseum, Frechen); Dr Ekkart Klinge (Hetjens-Museum, Düsseldorf); Dr Michael Kohnemann (Töpfereimuseum, Raeren); Dr Andrea Korte-Böger and Dr Thomas Ruppel (Torhaus-Museum, Siegburg); Dr Ch. Reichmann (Museum Burg Linn, Krefeld-Linn); Dr Gisela Reineking-von Bock (Museum für Angewandte Kunst, Cologne); Dr Werner Schäfke (Kölnisches Stadtmuseum, Cologne); Dr Siepen Koepke (Gemeinde Grefrath); Dr Burghard Sielmann (Töpfereimuseum, Langerwehe); Dr Werner Sundermann (Verein für Heimatpflege, Bocholt); Dr Max Tauch and Dieter Hupka (Clemens-Sels Museum, Neuss); and Dr Matthias Untermann (Landesdenkmalamt Baden-Württemberg).

With the assistance of the following colleagues I was able to monitor the dating and distribution of post-medieval Lower Rhine pottery found outside Germany: Jan M. Baart (formerly Town archaeologist, Historical Museum, Amsterdam); drs. Hemmy Clevis (Town archaeologist, Zwolle & Kampen); Hazel Forsyth (Museum of London); Bieke Hillewaert and Hubert De Witte (Stedelijke Archeologische Dienst, Bruges); John G. Hurst † (formerly English Heritage, London); Professor drs. H.L. Janssen (University of Leiden); Tony Oost (Museum Vleeshuis, Antwerp); Alma Ruempol † and Alexandra van Dongen (Museum Boymans-van Beuningen, Rotterdam); Jan Thijssen (Stichting Stad-sarcheologie Nijmegen); Dr S. Vandenberghe (Gruuthusemuseum, Bruges); and Claes Wahlöö (Kulturen Museum, Lund).

I am particularly indebted to the following individuals for their willingness to discuss various aspects of methodology and post-medieval Lower Rhine pottery: Bernd Brinkmann, Mülheim (stoneware mineralwater bottles); Alfred Falk, formerly Amt für Vor- und Frühgeschichte der Hansestadt Lübeck; Wolfgang Hackspiel, Meerbusch (Haus Gelinde finds); John G. Hurst †; Dr Hans Peter Mielke, Niederrheinisches Freilichtmuseum, Grefrath (stove-tiles); Prof. Clive Orton, Institute of Archaeology, University College London; Dr Christoph Reichmann, Museum Burg Linn, Krefeld-Linn; Dr Hans-Georg Stephan, Seminar für Ur- und Frühgeschichte, University of Göttingen (Werra and Weser wares); Dr Ingeborg Unger, Kempen (Cologne stove-tiles); Jan D. van Dam, Rijksmuseum, Amsterdam (Dutch tin-glazed wares); Professor Frans Verhaeghe, Research Associate N.F.S.R., Belgium; and Alfred Zeischka, Oberhausen.

The programme of scientific analysis was carried out by Michael Cowell of the British Museum, Department of Scientific Research. His enthusiasm and efforts to complete the analysis in good time proved vital to the success of the project as a whole. I am indebted to the British Museum Research Laboratory for agreeing to establish a N.A.A. database for Lower Rhine post-medieval ceramics and for accepting the substantial costs involved. The following individuals provided samples on behalf of their respective institutions: Dr G. Krause (Niederrheinisches Museum, Duisburg); Dr Volker Arnold (Museum für Ditmarscher Vorgeschichte, Heide); Wolfram Giertz (Roetgen); Dieter Hupka (Clemens-Sels-Museum, Neuss); Lydia Kesselring-Poth (on behalf of Rheinisches Amt für Bodendenkmalpflege, Bonn); Dorette Kleine (Keramikmuseum Frechen); Dr Mark Redknap (on behalf of Landesamt für Denkmalpflege, Koblenz); Dr Christoph Reichmann (Museum Burg Linn, Krefeld-Linn); and Dr Werner Schäfke (Kölnisches Stadtmuseum, Cologne).

Before joining the British Museum as a curator in the Department of Medieval and Later Antiquities in 1986, I was in receipt of a Major State Studentship from the British Academy (1985–1986). Before taking up the post a grant from the Heinrich Hertz-Stiftung, Federal Republic of Germany, enabled me to complete the initial data collection phase of this survey between January and March 1986. I am grateful to Professor Dr Günther Binding of the Kunsthistorisches Institut, University of Cologne, for securing this funding for me. Thanks to a grant from the Central Research Fund, University of London, I was able to record the important cellar assemblages of pottery from Krefeld-Linn at the Museum Burg Linn during the Autumn of 1987.

Throughout the duration of the project I enjoyed the support of the British Museum, which was generous in allocating me periods of study leave both to prepare this final text and to attend a number of ceramics conferences in Germany. In particular I wish to thank my departmental colleagues Timothy Wilson (now Ashmolean Museum, Oxford) and John Cherry for their keen interest and encouragement. Advice on the preparation of my artwork from James Farrant and James C. Thorn, technical illustrators in the Department of Medieval and Later Antiquities, has proved invaluable. The British Museum kindly agreed to undertake the reduction of the pottery drawings. The work was sponsored by the Niederrheinisches Museum, Duisburg.

Finally, I wish to record my gratitude to Dr Helen Clarke, my doctoral supervisor, whose enthusiasm for the project and helpful advice were vital.

David Gaimster, London, 1991

*Postscript*

This text has been edited in advance of publication in 2005. There has been little revision. The data and its interpretation are as valid today as they were in the early 1990s.

For enabling this research to come to publication, I would like to express my sincere thanks to Dr Monika Porsche of Heidelberg and to Dr Günter Krause of Duisburg. Without their support and persuasion this work would never have seen the light of day.

David Gaimster, London, 2004

# Summary

## A survey of the production, distribution and use of ceramics in the Lower Rhineland c. 1400-1800: some methodological notes

Traditionally the study of late medieval and postmedieval ceramics in the Lower Rhineland has been the preserve of art- and folkhistorians, with a strong emphasis on the recording of the more highly decorated wares. At the same time the focus of archaeological research in the region has centred on the production sites, particularly the larger of the stoneware centres. The publication of excavations on these sites, however, remains a low priority with the State archaeological authorities. Little attention has been given, moreover, to the broader questions of how the Lower Rhine ceramic market functioned in the late medieval to post-medieval period. With the initiation of large-scale urban excavations in the region during the 1980s, primarily in Duisburg, the question of regional supply and demand in a wider range of materials has been given considerably more attention, particularly the ceramic products. The increasing availability of consumer assemblages, both in town and country, has led to a new interest in regional marketing patterns and the variations in ceramic status and function across time, space and social context. The changing archaeological situation and increasing opportunities for archaeological and collections-based comparative work led to the initiation of this project based at the Niederrheinisches Museum, Duisburg (now the Kultur- und Stadthistorisches Museum). The results have been presented in the form of a doctoral thesis and a series of interim discussion papers.

### *The Lower Rhine region (map 1–2, p.35 f.)*

Since 1980 the city of Duisburg, with its rolling programme of rescue excavation, has produced the core sequence of ceramics for inter-site comparative analysis in the region. A former Hanseatic trading station, situated on the confluence of the Rhine and Ruhr rivers, and later an important university town and administrative centre, the site has provided the optimal control material for regional archaeological comparison. The Duisburg sequence can also now be calibrated by comparison with contemporaneous assemblages from small-town, village, monastery and farm sites in the immediate hinterland of the town and across the region as a whole. Of particular interest to this project has been the differential consumption of ceramics on urban, rural and function-specific sites such as fortifications and monasteries. Invariably archaeological control varies from site to site across the region, but statistical comparability was possible on the majority of sites sampled. In all 27 sites were sampled within Duisburg and 36 outside. Within the city brick-lined latrines constituted the majority of contexts (26 %), followed by pit groups (22 %), middens (14 %), cellars (8 %) and brick- or stone-lined wells (7 %). 23 % of the material analysed came from artefact scatters (habitation levels) and unstratified contexts.

### *The establishment of a regional ceramic type-series*

In order to conduct comparative statistical ceramic analysis on an intra- or inter-site basis, it is necessary to develop a standard system of classification and characterisation, one which can be understood and used easily both within the region of study and outside. The ceramics collected during the course of the survey were classified in a multidimensional way, each dimension reflecting separate technological or behavioural information and thereby the interpretational potential of the quantification process. The primary categories selected for classification purposes were:

### *Quantification*

For the closed contexts such as rubbish pits, latrines and wells, the method of quantifying by minimum vessel count was adopted, largely due to the low fragmentation ratio of the assemblages. The technique was also found to be most appropriate for the multi-dimensional approach. In other words it enabled precise calculations to be made about the ratio of ware-types, forms and functional types to be found in individual contexts. This multivariate system aimed to provide more detailed data relevant to the questions being asked about household or community consumption patterns. The statistical analysis was presented in the following multidimensional manner:

1. Pie charts showing the relative frequency of Ware-types for different phases (i. e. at 50-year intervals) (graphs 1–10, p. 122–124)
2. Pie charts showing the relative frequency of forms within Ware-types for different phases (graphs 11–33, p. 124–130)
3. Stacked bar charts showing the relative proportions of functional categories from Duisburg and Wesel (graphs 34–36, p. 130–131)

*Scientific analysis*

Quantification and inter-site comparative analysis depend ultimately on the standardised classification of the material concerned. Most fabric characterisation is achieved through the macroscopic (visual) examination of ceramic bodies. Indeed it would be impractical to expect all identifications to be based upon the results of specialist scientific research. The chemical analysis of pottery fabrics conducted during the course of this project (neutron activation analysis) was undertaken principally as a means of objective verification and refinement of the existing fabric type-series. The nature of the sedimentary geology in the Lower Rhineland has made the visual characterisation and geographical attribution of the local ceramic products a difficult process, particularly in the case of untempered leadglazed earthenwares and fully fused saltglazed stonewares. Therefore, neutron activation analysis, which identifies the trace elemental composition of the clay-fabric, was selected as the primary method of ware differentation, as it does not rely on characterising inclusions or major elements. The analysis, based on 162 individual samples from sites across the region (Table 3, p. 71–73) was conducted by the British Museum Research Laboratory. Material was collected from both regional production and consumer sites across the region with the aim of attributing specific ware-types to their respective geographical source. The NAA sampling strategy can be summarised as follows:

1. Verification of the Ware-types
2. Attribution of marketed vessels to source, thereby indentifying regional variation in pottery distribution
3. Assessment of fabric variability within waretypes in order to clarify whether they share one or more sources of manufacture

The results of the analysis were presented in the form of a series of principal components plots showing the relative variations in traceelemental composition of selected Ware-types. In the case of 15th-century leadglazed whiteware for example (diagram 2, p. 74), the Langerwehe ware was represented by a well-clustered set of samples, whereas the diffuse nature of the Cologne readings suggest that the local potters exploited a number of separate clay sources (as opposed to one).

*The illustrated catalogue*

Each of the assemblages sampled by the survey were systematically illustrated. The full range of forms and decorative variations were recorded, providing a detailed overview of typological and functional character of each assemblage. The typology and chronological development of each of the main categories of Wares (I-V) were presented in a series of illustrated summary charts (diagrams 8a–8g. p. 101–107).

*Ceramic production, supply and demand in the Lower Rhineland: an interpretative strategy*

Four major themes are discussed in the context of interpreting the Lower Rhine ceramic evidence. Each illustrate the importance of archaeological ceramics as a primary historical source:

1. Organisation of the regional pottery supply, including the transportation of and marketing of pottery to, from and within the region
2. Ceramic form, function and decoration as indicators of increasing material comfort or economic hardship and dining habits
3. Ceramic frequency as an index of social emulation and changes in fashion
4. The question of socially 'curated' ceramics in post medieval society

*Recommendations*

It is essential that those working on medieval and later ceramics in the Lower Rhineland (both Germany and the Netherlands) work together to promote a regional perspective (as opposed to a site-specific one). More regional synthesis, i. e. inter-site comparisons, must be undertaken.

Extensive urban sequences of ceramics, such as that at Duisburg, must be regarded as control assemblages for regional comparative work. They should be curated as primary reference collections, and used as the basis for all future ware characterisation and classification. I recommend the creation of a regional ceramic reference collection, possibly at Duisburg.

There is an urgent need to formally establish a standard, internationally-recognised Lower Rhine ceramic type-series, with commonly acknowledged wares and forms. This is essential for regional synthesis, so that for the first time like could be compared with like. Finally, I would urge that outstanding kiln-site assemblages in the region be processed and published as a matter of urgency. This would significantly improve the possibility of attributing traded material to source.

# Zusammenfassung

Traditionell ist die Beschäftigung mit der spätmittelalterlichen und neuzeitlichen Keramik am Niederrhein eine Domäne der Kunsthistoriker und Volkskundler mit einer starken Bevorzugung der Erfassung der hoch dekorierten Waren gewesen. Zur gleichen Zeit hat sich das Hauptaugenmerk der archäologischen Arbeit in der Region auf die Töpfereizentren konzentriert, darunter besonders die größeren Steinzeugproduktionszentren. Die Veröffentlichung der Ausgrabungen auf diesen Fundplätzen ist jedoch von geringer Priorität innerhalb der Amtsarchäologie geblieben. Wenig Aufmerksamkeit wurde dazu den breiteren Fragen nach der Funktion des niederrheinischen Keramikmarktes im Spätmittelalter und der frühen Neuzeit entgegengebracht.

Mit dem Beginn von großangelegten Altstadtgrabungen in der Region in den 1980er Jahren, an erster Stelle in Duisburg, hat die Frage der regionalen Versorgung und Nachfrage auf einer größeren Materialbasis beträchtlich mehr Aufmerksamkeit gefunden. Das gilt besonders für die Töpferwaren. Die zunehmende Verfügbarkeit von Inventaren an Gebrauchskeramik, gleichermaßen aus Städten und vom Land, haben zu einem neuen Interesse an den regionalen Vermarktungsmustern und der Variationsbreite des Status der Keramik und deren Funktion in Zeit, Raum und gesellschaftlichem Kontext geführt. Die sich verändernde Situation innerhalb der Archäologie und bessere Möglichkeiten zu Vergleichsstudien an archäologisch gewonnenen und gesammelten Materialien führten zur Initiierung dieses Projekts mit dem Niederrheinischen Museum Duisburg (seit 1990 Kultur- und Stadthistorisches Museum Duisburg) als Ausgangsbasis.

*Die Niederrheinregion (map 1-2, S. 35 f.)*

Seit 1980 hat die Stadt Duisburg mit ihrem laufenden Programm von Rettungsgrabungen die Kernsequenz für eine vergleichende Keramikanalyse zwischen verschiedenen Fundorten in der Region geliefert. Als ehemalige Hansestadt, am Zusammenfluss von Rhein und Ruhr gelegen, später preußische Universitätsstadt, hat der Fundort das optimale Kontrollmaterial für einen regionalen archäologischen Vergleich geliefert. Die Duisburger Abfolge kann inzwischen mit gleichzeitigen Inventaren aus Kleinstädten, Dörfern, Klöstern und Bauernhöfen im unmittelbaren Hinterland der Stadt und aus der ganzen Region abgeglichen werden. Von besonderem Interesse für dieses Projekt waren die Unterschiede im Gebrauch von Keramik in städtischen, ländlichen und funktionsspezifischen Fundplätzen wie Festungen und Klöstern. Obwohl mit der Region die archäologische Überwachung von Fundplatz zu Fundplatz beständig wechselt, ist ein statistischer Vergleich bei der Mehrzahl der betrachteten Fundstellen möglich. Insgesamt wurden 28 Fundstellen in Duisburg und 36 außerhalb Duisburgs analysiert und mit einander verglichen. Innerhalb der Stadt bildeten Ziegellatrinen die Mehrzahl der Befunde (26 %), gefolgt von Grubenkomplexen (22 %), Abfallschichten (14 %), Kellern (8 %) und aus Ziegeln oder Natursteinen gebauten Brunnen (7 %). 23 % des untersuchten Material stammen aus Fundstreuungen (Siedlungsschichten) oder sind unstratifiziert.

*Die Aufstellung einer regionalen keramischen Typenserie*

Um eine vergleichende statistische Keramikanalyse innerhalb eines Fundortes oder zwischen verschiedenen Fundorten durchzuführen, sollte ein Standardsystem der Klassifikation und Charakterisierung der Keramik entwickelt werden, das gleichermaßen innerhalb der untersuchten Region und außerhalb verstanden und leicht genutzt werden kann. Die im Verlauf dieser Übersicht gesammelte Keramik wurde in einer multidimensionalen Weise klassifiziert, wobei jede Dimension unterschiedliche Informationen zur Keramiktechnologie oder menschlichen Verhaltensweise spiegelt und damit das Interpretationspotential des Quantifizierungsprozesses. Die primären Kategorien, die für Klassifikationszwecke gewählt wurden sind:

1. Warentypen (einschließlich Oberflächenbehandlung, Warenart, Verzierung usw.)( S. 52 ff.)
2. Formtypen (table 1, S. 62 ff.)
3. Gefäßfunktion (table 2, S. 64 ff.)

*Quantifizierung*

Für die geschlossenen Fundkomplexe wie Abfallgruben, Latrinen- und Brunnen wurde die Mengenbestimmung mit der Methode der Ermittlung der Minimalgefäßzahl durchgeführt. Die geringe Fragmentierung der Gefäße macht das möglich. Eine solche Vorgehensweise erwies sich auch als am besten geeignet für den multidimensionalen Zugang. Sie führte zu einer präzisen Berechnung des Verhältnisses der Waren-, Formen- und Funktionstypen in den einzelnen Kontexten. Dieses Multivarianzsystem war darauf ausgerichtet, detailliertere Daten zu liefern, die Auskunft über Fragen nach Verbrauchsmustern für Haushalte oder Gemeinschaften geben können.

Die statistische Analyse wird in der folgenden multidimensionalen Art vorgestellt:

1. Tortendiagramme für die relative Häufigkeit

der Warentypen in verschiedenen Zeitabschnitten (50-Jahr-Intervalle) (graphs 1–10, S. 122–124.).
2. Tortendiagramme mit der relativen Häufigkeit der Gefäßformen bezogen auf Warentypen in verschiedenen Zeitabschnitten (graphs 11–33, S. 124–130)
3. Balkendiagramme zum relativen Verhältnis funktionaler Kategorien in Duisburg und Wesel (graphs 34–36, S. 130 f.).

*Naturwissenschaftliche Analyse*

Die Mengenbestimmung und die vergleichende Analyse zwischen verschiedenen Fundorten hängen letztendlich von der standardisierten Klassifikation der behandelten Materialien ab. Die Warenartcharakterisierung wird überwiegend durch die makroskopische (visuelle) Untersuchung des keramischen Scherbens erreicht. In der Tat wäre es unangemessen zu erwarten, dass alle Identifizierungen auf den Resultaten spezieller naturwissenschaftlicher Untersuchung basierten. Die chemische Analyse von Keramikwaren, die im Laufe dieses Projekts durchgeführt wurde (Neutronenaktivierungsanalyse, abgekürzt NAA) diente prinzipiell als Mittel einer objektiven Überprüfung und Verfeinerung der bestehenden Warentypenserie. Die Natur der geologischen Sedimente am Niederrhein hat die visuelle Charakterisierung und geographische Zuordnung der lokalen Keramikprodukte zu einem schwierigen Prozess gemacht, dieses besonders bei ungemagerten bleiglasierten Irdenwaren und vollständig gesintertem salzglasiertem Steinzeug. Die Neutronenaktivierungsanalyse wurde als primäre Methode der Warendifferenzierung gewählt. Mit ihr bestimmt man die Zusammensetzung der Spurenelemente in der Tonmatrix, nicht die charakteristischen Einschlüsse oder Hauptbestandteile derselben. Die Analyse umfasst 162 einzelne Keramikproben von über die Region verteilten Fundplätzen (table 3, S. 71–73). Sie wurde vom Forschungslaboratorium des British Museum durchgeführt. Materialproben gleichermaßen von Produktionsstätten und Verbrauchsorten aus der Region wurden mit dem Ziel, spezifische Warentypen mit ihrer geographischen Herkunft zu verbinden, untersucht. Die Probenauswahlstrategie für die NAA lässt sich folgendermaßen zusammenfassen:
1. Bestimmung des Warentyps
2. Zuweisung von verhandelten Gefäßen zu ihrer Herkunftsquelle, wobei regionale Verschiedenheiten in der Keramikverteilung identifiziert werden.
3. Bestimmung von Unterschieden im Scherben innerhalb von Warentypen um zu klären, ob sie aus einer oder mehreren Quellen stammen.

Die Ergebnisse der Analyse werden in der Form einer Serie von Hauptkomponentendiagrammen dargestellt (Table 3–4 S. 71–73, Diagramme 2–6, S. 74–76.). Im Fall der weißtonigen bleiglasierten Irdenwaren des 15. Jahrhunderts (Diagram 2) bilden die Proben der Langerweher Ware ein deutliches Cluster, wohingegen das diffuse Bild der Ähnlichkeitsverteilung der Kölner Proben vermuten lässt, dass man dort unterschiedliche Tonvorkommen ausgebeutet hat (nicht nur ein einziges).

*Der Abbildungsteil*

Jede der behandelten Fundvergesellschaftungen ist vollständig abgebildet. Der volle Umfang der Formen und Dekorvariationen wurden aufgenommen, so dass ein detaillierter Überblick über den typologischen und funktionalen Charakter derselben gegeben ist. Die Typologie und die chronologische Entwicklung jeder der Hauptwarenkategorien (I-V) wird S. 101–107 in den Diagrammen 8a-g summarisch zusammengefasst.

*Keramikproduktion, Versorgung und Nachfrage am Niederrhein: Eine Interpretationsstrategie*

Vier Hauptthemen werden im Zusammenhang der Interpretation der niederrheinischen Keramikerzeugnisse besprochen. Sie illustrieren die Wichtigkeit archäologischer Keramikfunde als historische Primärquelle. :
1. Die Organisation der regionalen Keramikversorgung, einschließlich des Transports und der Vermarktung der Keramik aus der und innerhalb der Region
2. Keramische Form, Funktion und Dekoration als Indikatoren zunehmenden materiellen Komforts oder ökonomischer Schwierigkeiten und von Tischsitten.
3. Häufigkeiten im Keramikspektrum als Indikator für gesellschaftlichen Wettbewerb und Geschmacksveränderungen.
4. Die Frage nach Statusbezügen der Keramik in der frühneuzeitlichen Gesellschaft

*Empfehlungen*

Es ist wichtig, dass diejenigen, die sich am Niederrhein mit mittelalterlicher und nachmittelalterlicher Keramik beschäftigen (gleichermaßen in Deutschland und in den Niederlanden) zusammenarbeiten, um eine regionale Perspektive voranzutreiben (im Gegensatz zu einer fundortbezogenen). Mehr an regionaler Synthese, d. h. vergleichende Untersuchungen zu verschiedenen Fundorten muss durchgeführt werden.
Umfangreiche Keramikabfolgen wie in Duisburg müssten als Kontrollinventare für vergleichende regio-

nale Arbeiten angesehen werden. Sie sollten als primäre Referenzkollektionen unterhalten werden und als die Basis für alle kommenden Warenbeschreibungen und -klassifizierungen genützt werden. Ich empfehle die Schaffung einer regionalen Keramikreferenzkollektion, möglichst in Duisburg.
Es besteht die dringende Notwendigkeit, formell eine standardisierte niederrheinische Keramiktypenserie zu erstellen, mit allgemein anerkannten Warenbeschreibungen und Bezeichnungen. Dies ist wesentlich für regionale Synthesen, damit zum ersten Mal Gleiches mit Gleichem verglichen werden kann.
Zum Schluß möchte ich darauf drängen, dass herausragende Inventare von Töpferzentren in der Region bearbeitet und schnellstens publiziert werden. Das würde die Möglichkeiten, verhandeltes Material den Herkunftsquellen zuzuweisen, beträchtlich erhöhen.

# Foreword

This study of the historical domestic ceramic market in the Lower Rhineland was completed in 1990 and submitted as a PhD thesis at the University of London in 1991. It is certainly legitimate to ask why it should be published now some fifteen or more years since its original completion.
As former City Archaeologist for Duisburg, Günter Krause, explains in his preface, any delay in publication has been beyond the control of the author. However, it is refreshing to note that such a timelag between completion and final communication has not blunted the topicality and wider research value of this work. In fact, the opening up of Europe after 1990, particularly in eastern Germany and in the Baltic, has created a new relevance for this study of the manufacture and home market of wares that were traded across central, eastern and northern Europe from the 13th to 17th centuries. Besides its increasing comparative value for the study of regional supply and demand for Rhenish ceramics from the English Channel to the Gulf of Finland, no subsequent major synthetic study of the Lower Rhine ceramic marketplace has been undertaken since 1990. This study of ceramic production and consumption on the confluence of the Rhine and the Ruhr, with its chemical analysis, extensive catalogue and illustrated type series, may have more relevance today than even a decade and half ago. Such illustrated synoptic works are an invaluable resource in the modern rescue environment of western Germany, where few domestic site assemblages are published fully and are reported instead only by (unpublished) site reports containing footnoted cross-references to previously published corpora.
This study of regional manufacture and material consumption in the Lower Rhineland represents a small milestone in the evolution of historical archaeology in western and northern Europe. Firstly, it is interdisciplinary in intent and execution, combining the primary archaeological and historical evidence with material science testing and an iconographic examination of ceramics in their contemporary domestic context. Secondly, it deals with domestic consumption and competition across a broad cross-section of Lower Rhine urban and rural society, including, crucially, those communities not recorded in the documentary record in terms of their living conditions and lifestyle. Thirdly, it aims to examine a period of very profound social and economic change, that being the transition between the Middle Ages and early modern period, in which both the Lutheran Reformation and proto-industrialisation had a dramatic impact on everyday life and belief. And fourthly, this study attempts to place the Lower Rhine ceramic market within its wider international dimension, both simultaneously as a centre of production and long-distance export and of demand for luxury wares from neighbouring regions and from more exotic sources. Its proximity to Amsterdam and the first Chinese porcelain cargo auctions makes it a sensitive index of the popular taste for Far Eastern domestic goods from the turn of the 17th century onwards.
For the author his study of the Lower Rhine pottery sequence from 1400 to 1800 formed a platform for a subsequent more intensive investigation of the Rhenish and German stoneware industry 1200–1900, which was published by the British Museum in 1997. Much of the detailed quantitative data from Duisburg was employed as the basis for discussing the consumption of Rhenish stoneware in the western European mercantile communities. In consequence, the author has made a special study of the Hanseatic pottery market in northern Europe and the Baltic, focussing on domestic ceramics as an index of long distance acculturation and resistance. In each investigation the author has demonstrated the role of domestic ceramics from controlled excavations as a primary historical source, their mode of production and social distribution providing a measure of some of the key attributes of the medieval to modern transition in Europe, including the development of mercantile capitalism, increasing social stratification, Europeanisation and colonialism. Final publication of this discussion of the ceramic supply and demand in the Lower Rhineland 1400-1800 makes a timely contribution to the fast-emerging discipline of European historical archaeology and material culture studies.

David Gaimster, London
November 2005

# Preface

From 1980 to about 1995 a large-scale interdisciplinary urban archaeological research project took place in the Old Town of Duisburg, directed by the undersigned. About 1500 collaborators from four European countries, among them many students, were engaged. It was initiated by a phase of extensive development in the heart of Duisburg that has been unrelenting for almost twenty-five years.

The discovery of early Duisburg in the centre of the Old Town in 1980 promoted a strong interest amongst the city council and local community in saving the remains of Duisburg's important past which was being threatened by destruction. The archaeologists of the then Niederrheinisches Museum Duisburg, the largest regional archaeological museum in the Lower Rhine area, founded in 1902 in a city with a long tradition of archaeological research and collecting dating back to the 1840s (Krause 1990), were entrusted – as many times before – with rescue excavations in order to save the archaeological evidence of Duisburg's past and make this available for academic research and public view. Until the early 1990s, from the beginning, support of the Rheinisches Landesmuseum/Rheinisches Amt für Bodendenkmalpflege in Bonn, (Rhineland State Museum/Rhineland State Office for the Care of Monuments or RAB), represented from 1980 by the late Prof. Walter Janssen and his successors, was essential.

The project was preceded by an evaluation and publication of earlier excavations of the Duisburg museum as the basis for further work (Milz 1982). At the same time systematic training of volunteers began under the guidance of the writer in seminars, using the museum's library and collections, and in the field. The volunteers belong in the main to a regional archaeological society, founded in 1921. It has been directed by the undersigned since 1978 and was based in the museum. Over the years the volunteers became the only permanently qualified collaborators besides the director of the excavations, because the city denied skilled collaborators. This happened in spite of sufficient funding from the Federal government, the state of North Rhine Westphalia and the city of Duisburg.

The aim of the Duisburg research project was to connect the living people in the town with their past in tracing back the long history of their city as far as possible in all its facets and, moreover to use the potential of the archaeological archives of the city for an exemplary research in the history and development of early towns in western Europe for a better understanding of modern urban society. To reach this goal the Old Town of Duisburg was approached as a single coherent archaeological monument and all available basic data and materials related to endangered plots and places were collected systematically (Krause 1994b, 49–75). The evidence gathered spans the last 2000 years.

The extraordinary preservation of archaeological remains in Duisburg and the long history of the city gives these investigations a meaning far beyond the importance of the city itself. Already by the end of the 1980s the Rhenish State authorities for the care and protection of the archaeological monuments in Bonn (RAB) awarded the Duisburg urban excavation project "national status and international importance". In recognition for long lasting and outstandig services to the city and citizens because of his archaeological work the author was awarded in 1990 the arms of honour of the Civic Society of Duisburg.

Shortly after the First World War the members of the regional archaeological society in Duisburg began to excavate, collect and publish rich find groups from all prehistoric and protohistoric epochs in the Lower Rhine region for the first time. They continued this work in the early 1930s and after the Second World War. These finds formed the basic archaeological collections of the Niederrheinisches Museum Duisburg, directed then by prehistoric archaeologists. From 1980 onwards their successors succeeded in close co-operation with the Museum to tie the early history of the Old Town of Duisburg to prehistory. With the same care protohistoric, medieval and post-medieval contexts up to the 20th century were excavated in Old Duisburg. This was rather uncommon at that time in Germany because of the widespread belief that these younger epochs were much more the domain of art history and folk studies and that archaeology should at the latest deal with the study of the Middle Ages. But it is quite clear that even for the post-medieval period an appreciation of everyday material culture as an important historical source can only be reached through careful archaeological excavation. In Duisburg a complex interdisciplinary co-operation was built up, incorporating numerous disciplines, learned institutions and single specialists from various European countries, bringing a value to knowledge far beyond the purely archaeological questions (Krause 1992, 37 f.)

It was a stroke of luck that in 1984 with David Gaimster a young archaeologist from a country with a much longer tradition in medieval and post-medieval archaeology was found, where pottery studies covering these periods already had reached a high standard. He chose the late and post-medieval pottery contexts from Duisburg and its hinterland as theme of his doctoral dissertation at the University of London. David Gaimster was much more aware than any German scholar at that time that imported Rhenish medieval and post-medieval pottery were key type-fossils for the dating of domestic contexts not only in Great Britain but also in the whole of northern Europe and, moreover, were indicators of far reaching contacts and developments. From the 16th century onwards Rhenish Pottery spread over all five continents. It is not astonishing that the interest in the production, chronology and distribution of this pottery is much greater in these regions of the world than in the Rhineland, where there exist quite different focuses of interest. For a better understanding and evaluation of reliable medieval and post-medieval pottery dates from the Rhineland has long been a desideratum in these countries and regions. David Gaimster, with his wider view from the British Isles, perceived that Duisburg could furnish the material basis for these studies. His special interest in the Duisburg contexts was a great encouragement for the excavator and his staff, who saw the potential of extending the existing database as far as possible for his studies and further research, for displays in the museum and in temporary exhibitions in Duisburg and many other European urban centres.

For this endeavour the permanent engagement and support of well trained and highly motivated volunteers were essential. Besides at the *Alter Markt* site the excavations were carried out during construction activities without the opportunity for rigorous evaluation and excavation. The constant mobilisation of the volunteers helped to overcome these disadvantageous preconditions. Very often they were on site with the director of the excavations until midnight or even later and often during weekends.Only by these means it was possible to excavate and document the bulk of the latrines, wells, waster pits and settlement layers completely and in stratgraphical order. Moreover the volunteers participated widely in the post-excavation process. So newly excavated pottery complexes could be restored and drawn within days or only weeks in order to make them available for research and exhibition purposes. It is hardly surprising that by about 1990 the Duisburg urban archaeology unit was widely regarded as the most efficient in Germany in respect of scientific output and cost effectiveness.

Among the volunteers Paul Fitscher and the late Peter Müller must be mentioned first, and in addition the late Helene and Werner Lauppe, Hans Peter Arens, Wilhelm Stahlhacke, the late Rolf Falkenstein, Reinhold Stausberg und Heinz Zander, all from Duisburg. Especially helpful in connection with this study was Peter Müller, a grammar school teacher, professional archaeologist, historian and art historian who worked with the writer from the beginning of the urban excavations in 1980 until his early death in 1995 as an excellent and devoted excavator and restorer of the mass of the pottery from the urban excavations. Moreover, he did thousands of field and object drawings. His early death prevented him from contributing to the publication of major parts of the urban excavations. We owe to him together with the writer the meticulous stratigraphic excavation of many of the latrine pits and wells, most of them less than a metre in diameter and up to 8 metres deep. He did not omit recording a single pin in its stratigraphical position. Paul Fitscher joined the excavations in 1983/4 after his retirement as head of a housing company. He developed extraordinary skills as an excavator and in the field of object drawing. After David Gaimster's return to Britain to become a curator in the British Museum in 1987, it was mainly Paul Fitscher who created the preliminary drawings of the newly found and restored pottery from the urban excavations in Duisburg for his study until 1989. Besides the volunteers much of the valuable post-excavation work was done by numerous students, who cannot be named here.

Soon after David Gaimster had finished his doctoral dissertation in 1992 the Rheinisches Amt für Bodendenkmalpflege in Bonn (RAB) offered the opportunity for (a publication in German) in the series *Rheinische Ausgrabungen*, which was gratefully accepted by the author and the undersigned. The latter was asked for a proposal and a budget to translate the English text. In agreement with David Gaimster he proposed the translation through an experienced interpreter at a moderate price in close cooperation with the author and the undersigned, who offered his services for the appropriate translation of the specialist English terms into German. This proposal and the budget were highly praised by the Director of the RAB but not followed up at all. Without informing the author or the writer the translation was begun and eventually finished by an archaeologist, who was neither a native German speaker nor a translator, nor an expert in medieaval and post-medieval pottery. At the same time the text was revised and many passages changed and transposed. The correction of the German translation proved to be extremely difficult and to be an enormous sacrifice of time. Neither David Gaimster nor the writer could afford this. A costly complete new translation would have been the only way out and certainly less laborious. This mishandling brought the whole publication project to a standstill. The only chance to avoid further delays and large costs has been to publish an English version, the language most of the scholars interested in such a study, understand. But after more than 12 years the original text and diagrams on floppy disks from 1991 had to be transferred into modern digital form. This was done with the help of Prof. Matthias Untermann, of the University of Heidelberg. Subsequently the whole text was revised by the author and the writer took care of the necessary additions to the original bibliography from 1991, checked the inventory numbers and short descriptions of the contexts (Appendix 2), translated the summary into German and finished with a final proof-reading.

Monika Porsche from Heidelberg completed all the difficult and laborious editorial work on the text, figures and layout of this volume.

David Gaimster's recommendations and aspirations for a better inter-institutional cooperation and the establishment of a regional type series (see page 16 [engl.] / 18 [dt.] and Gaimster 1992, 338 ff.), are today far further from realisation than in 1992. The further publication of the excavations has been made impossible in Duisburg. This work includes, for instance, the contexts of the latrine- and well complexes, from houses and stratigraphic deposits, the abundant plant and animal remains, the textiles (see Knörzer 1983, 1991, 1992; Meurers-Balke *et al.*; Nobis and Ninov; Heinrich; Reichstein; Tegtmeier; Farke), the dendrodates, the evidence of environmental pollution from the latrine pits and deposits (Gerlach *et al.*), the water quality of the wells, the social topography of the town in the light of the findings and finally the historical evidence (see Milz 2005) etc.

Not only was Duisburg's urban archaeological project and Museum destroyed by the City's political masters, while the State monument authorities and the RAB in Bonn remained unconcerned. The latter institutions are no longer engaged to fulfil their responsibilities in line with monument legislation and modern archaeological standards, but act in the interest of the construction sector, give fraudulent evidence to hide their shortcomings to the public, the state parliament and even the public prosecutor to avoid prosecution, so abusing the credibility of their academic discipline and their institutions. All these events are the result of massive political pressure that began in the early 1990s (Krause 1994c, 1998, 2004, Dierkes and Jakobi 1998).

The head of the department for the protection and care of archaeological monuments in the responsible ministry in Düsseldorf , the highest monument authority in the State of NRW, whose duty has been to make the Rhineland follow the state monument legislation, wrote to the undersigned as early as 1992 that Hercules was the last to decapitate the Hydra as a single fighter and that he should wait for better times, leaving everything to market forces. He introduced contract archaeology, which resulted in a reliance on the interests of constructors and politicians to the utter detriment of the monuments. He became the founder of a second market to exploit archaeological monuments commercially, following the antiquities market, pretending to act in favour of the monuments. But the standards for this type of costly commercial archaeology lack any concept and interdisciplinary approach, and are so debased and poor that it cannot honestly be called archaeological fieldwork at all. It is fictitious, reduced to the business of earning money and a far cry from the potentials of modern archaeology. The main instrument of this type of excavation is the bulldozer. The obligatory standard excavation permits of the RAB follow a "one size fits all" approach for nearly every type of excavation. No qualification is required to run such a company, only the employment of an archaeologist with the minimum qualifications. As well no specialisation, no excavation reports are asked for. This shameless practice has become the workaday routine for field archaeologists and has made archaeology more and more irrelevant. All this happens on a systematic scale. Even monuments of European significance such as the last remains of Holy Roman Emperor Charlemagne's palace precinct in Aachen were not spared and were bulldozed in the summer of 2005 without proper documentation of the construction trenches (see Abschied vom Bodendenkmal Aachener Kaiserpfalz?, in Kunstchronik. Monatsschrift für Kunstwissenschaft, Museumswesen und Denkmalpflege, 58. Jahrg., Sept./Okt. 2005, Heft 11, Nürnberg 2005, 557–562). It was led and backed by the absurd pseudo-excavation permit of the RAB that denied, together with the responsible ministry, any mishandling to the public and the scientific community.

In Duisburg this new type of "archaeology" has caused the invention of archaeological monuments in a large building site to exploit the numerous house builders and make them pay for "necessary archaeological excavations", while existing monuments were deliberately destroyed in the same area and their documentation faked. A special company was founded in 1994 for these purposes, replacing the City Museum's archaeological unit, a tactic favoured by the civic administration, which offered personnel and equipment for nothing (see Krause, 1998, 92 ff., 102 ff.).

In 2000 the Duisburg city council began to deny the existence of important archaeological monuments by majority vote, backed up by the state monument authorities. Our knowledge related to these monuments today is entirely dependent on the writer's private opinion and free time commitment. On duty he has to follow the city council's ruling. After the intended destruction of one of these monuments it has even been sheduled as a monument by the city's cultural affairs committee.

The regional archaeological museum in Duisburg (in which more than 80% of the collections were regional archaeological finds), with its special facilities for excavations and post-excavation work including a modern conservation unit for the finds and an archaeological library as the basis for excavations and post-excavation research was remodelled and no longer exists. The gap in the show rooms of the museum caused by the removal of the regional archaeological finds has been filled by a large private collection of coins and archaeological objects from the antiquities market, which have no cultural context or provenance. Its care and publication creates enormous annual costs. Somewhat later the writer was released from his duties as deputy director, excavator and curator of the collections, because he was regarded as the main obstacle for that change in policy.

Most of the objects depicted in this volume, and which toured in the 1980s and early 1990s in numerous European countries, are no longer regarded as worth being kept. Together with the one and a half million finds from the urban excavations and many other archaeological objects from the museum it has been decided that they shall no longer form part of the cultural history of mankind. Since 1998 they have been transferred into the custody of the civic contruction department that took over the control of Duisburg's archaeological monuments still in place and most of the archaeological archives in order to make them disappear from public consciousness. Only "nice objects" shall be kept in the Museum. There no longer exists any interest in these collections nor facilities for their curation. They are stored in the town hall, in cellars poisoned by mould since 1997 (Dierkes and Jakobi 1998) and in disarray in the large hall of a former industrial compound, where it rains through the roof (Krause 2004, 135, note 21). The storerooms in the basement of the town hall are only accessible, when wearing protective clothes and a mask against mould, and it is forbidden to enter the hall in the former Industrial compound, because of the complete lack of safety provisions. Moreover there exists an extreme moist heat in summer, while in winter it is extremely cold and moist. It is easy for anybody to enter these stores and to steal nearly everything. Many valuable objects are already missing, others heavily damaged or already destroyed.

Since 1994 there has been no conservation care and no insurance for the more than two million objects, which were excavated at considerable public expense. The only persons to object constantly are the undersigned, his volunteers and the local archaeological society, who have been blocked from excavations for more than ten years. The city even wanted the dissolution of the archaeological society who were driven out of the museum in 1995, in order to prevent the writer from training new volunteers and from undertaking post-excavation work. When urged to vanish without causing further costs the writer was told as early as in 1992 that the state monument legislation had no currency in Duisburg. The lord mayor of Duisburg publicly called for the abolition of the state monument authorities in North Rhine Westphalia in December 1992, while the head of Duisburg's civic administration declared somewhat later that archaeology was out of time, stating that the archaeologists have nothing to seek in the urban environment because archaeology obstructs a better future of the town. By 1992 he had replaced state monument legislation by his own ruling in favour of the civic construction department. The undersigned lost the rests of his personnel, still about 60 collaborators in 1993 and all funds as early as 1994. At the same time the city began, backed by the RAB, to defame and prosecute the volunteers, so that a closed system of contract archaeology could be introduced. In 1983, in the presence of the President of the German Federal Republic, when the city celebrated its 1100th aniversary for a whole year, the volunteers were called "the avant-garde of Duisburg's citizens, who begin to seek for the roots of their city".

Since 1994 the writer has practically been taken hostage with his excavation archive, his international academic contacts and cooperations have been blocked, and his mail censored or held back. Meanwhile his name has disappeared from the directory of the civic administration and from the door of his office, he has been swamped with disciplinary actions and even his family was threatened. Guided tours in the Old Town were forbidden to him in 1992 and his publications halted or censored. Only his presence has prevented the civic planning and construction department and Duisburg's political masters to dispose of the bulk of the city's rich excavation materials and documents. The State Ministry and the RAB withdrew the very modest, but highly symbolic, State funds for urban archaeology in Duisburg in 2005, the only ones left as an alibi for the curation of the urban archaeological collections since 2000 because "there exists no urban archaeologist in Duisburg". So both the undersigned and the urban archaeological resource and results once regarded as of "international importance and of national status" by the above named state institutions have become a phantom. The monument authorities do not know any longer what urban archaelogy is, nor what is the meaning of archaeological research. In Duisburg a special museum for children has opened, funded by the State of NRW, which presents an artificial archaeological site for the children's entertainment,while existing archaeological monuments in Duisburg are denied and destroyed, together with the archaeological collections. This is quite an Orwellian situation.

After the writer's retirement in 2007 only David Gaimster's thesis provides an insight into the city of Duisburg's rich late medieval and post-medieval ceramic sequence. Obviously not only in war-torn countries like Iraq or Afghanistan our cultural heritage are threatened by vandalism. The cases from Duisburg and the state of North Rhine Westphalia illustrate that you can find offshoots of Taliban-like behaviour in too many other parts of the world for comfort.

Günter Krause Duisburg, October 2005

# 1. Introduction

## 1.1 The study of post-medieval ceramics in the lower Rhineland 1850–1990: an archeological review

### *1.1.1 The history and scope of changing approaches*

Trends in the study of post-medieval ceramics reflect many of the developments in the archaeology of the post-medieval period as a whole. The historiography of post-medieval ceramics in the Rhineland deserves attention not only as an index of changing academic approaches, but also as an essential background to the data which are used in contemporary research. Changing approaches to the study of medieval and later ceramics from the region reflect the interests and attitudes of the successive generations of antiquarians, collectors, museum curators and archaeologists. It is therefore necessary to consider these developments in order to understand the nature of the evidence from which conclusions are to be drawn.

The changing emphasis in the literature on Rhenish post-medieval pottery reflects the broader trends of European ceramic research. The nineteenth-century genesis of the subject can be characterized by an identifiable "antiquarian" phase resulting from the contemporary collectors' market. This was supplemented at the end of the century by the founding of museum collections of regional historical ceramics and the first attempts to define a reliable typochronology of Rhenish stoneware. The century between the 1870s and the 1970s witnessed numerous excavations on production sites in the region, usually resulting from the chance discovery of wasters. Successive monographs on individual production centres and ware-types have appeared alongside a number of museum exhibitions devoted to the ceramic history of the region. Specialized studies on ornament, iconography and the archaeological distribution of wares have added to the literature in recent years.

The value of pottery as a social and economic indicator has only become accepted comparatively recently, and problems of assimilating the data have hindered the widespread adoption of an integrated approach to the study of production and consumption. This situation is improving rapidly, however, with the initiation of large-scale urban excavations in the region, centred on the city of Duisburg, and the availability of sealed, quantifiable groups of ceramics for comparative and scientific analysis. The newly-generated material is providing important evidence for the refinement of established chronologies and attributions.

In order to understand the significance of these recent developments, a broadly thematic framework has been adopted for the survey of past approaches to the post-medieval ceramics of the Rhineland. It is not intended as a comprehensive history of research in this field but more as an insight into the changing nature of methodological and interpretative approaches through time. This short resumé covers not only the ceramics produced in the Rhineland itself (salt-glazed stoneware, lead-glazed earthenware/slipware), but also those main groups of pottery imported into the region during the post-medieval period (e.g. Netherlands tin-glazed earthenware, Oriental porcelain).

### *1.1.2 Salt-glazed stoneware*

Until relatively recently the subject of medieval and later ceramics in the Rhineland has been synonymous with the study of the regional salt-glazed stoneware industries (see Map 2 for situation of principal production centres). This is hardly surprising in view of their staggering productivity and the widespread export of their wares over a period of 600 years (Reineking- von Bock 1980). In terms of long-distance trade, this must rank as one of the most successful craft industries of the Late Middle Ages and pre-industrial period, involving producers, middlemen, shippers, wholesalers and retailers on an international scale (Haselgrove 1989). Fully fused stoneware had been developed through several prototype stages in the Rhineland by the end of the 13th century (Stephan 1983). Due to a combination of its non-porosity, durability, functional versatility and decorative quality, it remained in constant demand on a European scale until the beginnings of industrialisation, or in the case of Britain, until an indigenous stoneware industry emerged in the late 17th century.

In Britain finds of Rhenish stoneware are common on even the most modest rural site (e. g. Hurst 1979, Fig. 16, No. 53), and their excavation in many British towns and ports has helped to refine the chronology of site sequences and to provide evidence of trading mechanisms. The same is true in the Low Countries, Scandinavia and eastern Europe, where the identification of Rhenish stoneware exports has made a significant contribution to the social and economic history of the region.

Antiquarian interest in the historical stonewares of the Rhineland developed initially not through archaeology, however, but as a result of the nineteenth-century historicist movement. Renaissance and Baroque-style vases, jugs, tankards and bottles, with their applied grotesques, heraldry, strapwork, biblical or mythological scenes and figures, were collected as embellishments to the historicist Gründerzeit interior (Gaimster 1992; 1997, 335-338). By the middle of the century an international market for German ceramics of the Reanaissance had emerged, with dealers willing to pay high prices at auction for authentic specimens (Klinge 1972, note 3). At the same time public museums, in the realisation that stonewares were important as historical documents of ceramic technology and decorative styles, began to acquire representative examples. The origin of the British Museum collection, for instance, can be traced to the purchase in 1855 of 39 pieces at the sale of the collection created by Ralph Bernal (Gaimster 1997, Chap. 1).

An inevitable consequence of this surge in interest led stoneware potters in the Rhineland to reproduce vessels for the antique ceramics market. Much of the art-historical research conducted in recent years on German stonewares has concentrated on the identification of nineteenth-century replicas and pastiches (Reineking-von Bock 1970; Gaimster 1992). This crucial avenue of research is complicated by the knowledge that potters in the Rhineland of the nineteenth century had access to the same clay sources as their predecessors (Gaimster 1990a). Thus fabric and texture could be replicated accurately. Glaze effects and surface finish are equally unreliable indicators of repoduction as kiln technology had not changed significantly since the 16th century. Moreover, original positive and negative moulds or matrices for the applied ornament were still available from waster heaps surrounding the stoneware potting villages.

It was at the Siegburg and Raeren waster heaps in the 1870s that "excavations" by the early collectors and antiquarians such as Laurenz Hetjens and J.B. Dornbusch began. In 1906 Hetjens donated his collection of waster finds and whole pieces of Rhenish stoneware to the city of Düsseldorf, thereby laying the foundation of the present Hetjens-Museum (Deutsches Keramikmuseum; Klinge 1972, 7). In 1888 the Museum of Applied Arts (Kunstgewerbemuseum) was established in Cologne, one of the principal centres of stoneware production. A primary aim was to form a representative collection of Rhenish stoneware illustrating technical and artistic developments in German ceramic art (Reineking-von Bock 1986, 29). The first director of the Museum, Arthur Pabst, published his *Kunstvolle Thongefässe aus dem 16.–18. Jahrhundert* the following year (Pabst 1889), advertising the acquisition policy of the Museum in this field. The publication was followed by a steady flow of new acquisitions. The emerging international interest in German stoneware is illustrated by the publication by M. L. Solon in 1892 in London of *The Ancient Art of Stoneware of the Low Countries and Germany*.

The second director of the Cologne Kunstgewerbemuseum, Otto von Falke, realised the importance of monitoring the destruction of the production sites in the Maximinenstraße, Komödienstraße and Eigelstein, all within the city walls. A wide selection of vessels rescued from these developments appeared in his early articles on Cologne stoneware (von Falke 1898b, 1899) and was acquired by the Museum. Their respective provenances provide a detailed picture of the variation in products made by individual workshops of the same industry. The Kunstgewerbemuseum collection provided the framework for his seminal two volume monograph on Rhenish stoneware published in Berlin (von Falke 1908). This work provides to this day the most comprehensive comparanda of stoneware forms and decorative types from the main production centres.

Coinciding with developments in Cologne, sherds were being systematically collected from the waster heaps at Bouffioulx, near Chatalet, Belgium, an offshoot of the Rhenish stoneware industry. An impressive range of forms and decorated sherds appear in van Bastalaer's monograph of 1885. The detailed watercolour plates represent the first instance of archaeological recording techniques in this field.

Between the Wars the comparanda of Rhenish stoneware types was amplified by the publication of selected pieces from the Hetjens-Museum collection (Koetschau 1923), which was in turn extended in 1936 by the acquisition of the Eigel and Lückger collections of archaeological samples from Cologne and Siegburg. As an aid to dating specific form-types, Max Sauerlandt (1928) completed a study of Rhenish stonewares with dated English silver gilt mounts, and Joseph Hagen (1937) published a short catalogue of stoneware vessels found in the Rhineland containing coin hoards.

It was not until 1961 that the subject of Rhenish stonewares received detailed iconographic analysis (Lipperheide 1961). The study contained a vital resumé of graphical sources for the applied decoration of the Renaissance. A thorough survey of the range of ornamental motifs and forms from one production centre was supplied by Ekkart Klinge in his catalogue of the Siegburg stonewares held by the Hetjens-Museum (Klinge 1972). The publication remains an indispensible work of reference, particularly in its treatment of decorative details. It coincided in 1971 with the first edition of the catalogue of stoneware held by the Kunstgewerbe Museum, Cologne, by Reineking-von Bock. The catalogue has been reprinted twice (1976, 1986), until recently. Based on dated examples, it provides a strict typochronological scheme for the wide variety of forms and deorative motifs from all the major production sites.

At the same time Karl Göbels (1971) produced the

first edition of his monograph on the stoneware and earthenware potters of Frechen, situated immediately to the West of Cologne. It outlined the working practices and organisation of the potters at a major production centre and discussed the marketing and distribution of their wares along the Rhine. Documentary research provides an extensive list of potters, pottery dealers and shippers.

Archaeological activity on stoneware production sites in the Rhineland has increased dramatically since the Second World War, albeit at variable levels of intensity and competence. Between 1961 and 1966 Bernhard Beckmann excavated the last remaining waste dump in the Siegburg Aulgasse. The site was immense, measuring nearly 60 m in length, 23 m in width and 5 m in height. It contained millions of waster sherds dating from the 12th to 16th centuries. The subsequent publication (Beckmann 1975; 1974 for an English summary) identified the main fabrics and forms of the first four periods of production at Siegburg. The finds of the 16th and early 17th century, the period during which Siegburg reached its peak in terms of output and artistic achievement, remain unpublished.

In 1977 the Töpfereimuseum in Raeren issued a substantial resume of 25 years of research and excavations in the village and its outlying production sites (Hellebrandt et al. 1977). As a useful comparison to Göbels work at Frechen, the paper by Hellebrandt includes a study of the local potters' guild and the organisation of the industry. The volume also contains a summary of wares excavated during 1969 and 1970 at the offshoot industry at Aachen (Hugot in same volume). A wider spectrum of Aachen wares was published after rescue excavations by Janssen in the early 1970s (W. Janssen 1973). The products of one Raeren kiln dating from the 15th century were published in 1977 (de Ridder-Blenska *et al.* 1977).

Limited fieldwork was carried out at Langerwehe, Cologne and Frechen during the 1950s to late 1970s, although knowledge of kiln construction and technology was greatly improved by excavations at Langerwehe (Müller & Wentscher 1981; Jürgens & Bös 1983) and Frechen (Kleine 1982). The products of one mid-16th-century kiln in the Cologne Streitzeuggasse complemented von Falke's typology of fifty years before (Brill 1969).

Since the early 1980s a relative boom in excavations, museum exhibitions and research monographs has extended our knowledge of stoneware production in the Rhineland even further. Michael Kohnemann's corpus (1982) of matrices for applied ornament recovered from the Raeren waste heaps is of major importance, as it offers a graphical overview of the decorative repertoire at one production source. Knowledge of the typological range of Siegburg production has been amplified by Elsa Hähnel's exhibition and catalogue of the collection of kiln waste held by the Rheinisches Freilichtmuseum Kommern (E. Hähnel ed. 1987). The latest rescue excavations in the Siegburg Aulgasse have located the workshop of the Knütgen family, the most documented local potting family of the 16th and early 17th centuries, and recovered a representative sequence of their output (Ruppel 1991a). Refined dating of the sequence is possible by virtue of a destruction level dating from the torching of the town by Spanish troops in 1588. At long last a datum-point for late Siegburg production has been made available by this discovery.

At nearby Altenrath, rescue excavations in recent years have located the waste heaps of the industry which took over from Siegburg during the first half of the 17th century (Rech 1988; Francke 1999). The wares, decorated in the cobalt-blue manner of the Westerwald stonewares to the south, emphasizes the complexity of blue and grey stoneware attribution in the region. The discovery highlights the need for a systematic programme of fabric characterization in the Westerwald region itself in order to differentiate between the sherds of similar decoration found on consumer sites.

One minor class of Rhenish stoneware received a great deal of interest during the 1980s. Mineralwater bottles, made in the Westerwald region for filling at spas all over Germany between the 17th to 19th centuries have been the subject of extensive chronological and typological studies by Brinkmann (1982) and Nienhaus (1989a; 1989b). A formerly neglected form-type is now being recognized on excavations across Europe.

Our knowledge of stoneware distribution has also increased dramatically over the years, especially at an international level. In Britain J.G. Hurst has for over 20 years been engaged in the identification of imported Rhenish stoneware on archaeological sites (Hurst 1988). This vital groundwork has been complemented by the publication of extensive assemblages excavated in major ports and towns such as Southampton (Platt & Coleman-Smith 1975), Norwich (Jennings 1981; Evans 1985), Exeter (Allan 1984), Newcastle-upon-Tyne (Ellison 1981), Plymouth (Clark 1979), Portsmouth (Fox & Barton 1984) and London (Gaimster 1987a). The systematic quantification of sealed groups of pottery will enable comparative studies to take place between sites on both sides of the Channel.

The collection of Rhenish stoneware held by the Museum Boymans-van Beuningen, Rotterdam, originates primarily from findspots in the Netherlands. Its publication (Hurst *et al.* 1986, 176–225) offers an invaluable insight into the changing distribution of stoneware over the period 1350–1650 (see reviews by Stephan 1987c; Clarke 1988). The spectrum of export wares published here has been complemented by large groups of material excavated on town and castle sites in the Low Countries, notably Antwerp (van Vlieberghe & Dennissen 1982), Bruges (Swimberghe 1985; Hillewaert 1988; Hillewaert & Verhaeghe 1991), Mechelen (Vandenberghe & Raffo 1981), Bergen-op-Zoom (Vandenbulke & Groeneweg 1988), Maastricht (Panhuysen 1984), s'Hertogenbosch (H.L. Janssen 1983), Masseik (Heymans et al. 1989), Tilburg Castle (Stoepker 1986) Kessel Castle, Venlo (Clevis & Thijssen 1989); Deventer (Clevis & Kottman 1989) and Nijmegen (Thijssen ed. 1991). Many of them will provide the foundations for comparative studies of Rhenish pottery on an inter-site and inter-regional basis. Sealed groups with tight dating evidence are being published separately and cheaply for the purpose of rapid dissemination in the Corpus Middeleeuws Aardewerk series (see review by Davey 1987).

The overall picture of long-distance trade in Rhenish stoneware has been extended by the publication of significant groups of material in Scandinavia, including urban sequences from Sweden (Wahlöö 1976, Cat. 438-548; Billberg 1987, Cat. 95–120) and hoard finds from Denmark (Liebgott 1978), and by the notification of discoveries in eastern Europe (Reineking-von Bock 1980). The extensive trading network of the Hanseatic League accounted for the widespread distribution of stoneware in the North Sea and Baltic region (Gaimster 1997, chap. 3.3). Assemblages of stoneware from the Rhineland are known from Hamburg, Emden, Göttingen, Bremerhaven, and Elbląg (Poland) (Hamburg 1989b, Cat. 14.28–41). Excavations at Lübeck are revealing a detailed picture of the Hanseatic trade in Rhenish stoneware from the medieval to late post-medieval period (Falk 1987a; Schulz 1990).

A greater understanding of the mechanisms of distribution themselves has been achieved in recent years by the documentary research conducted by J. van Loo into the activities of Dutch stoneware dealers and shippers (van Loo 1984; 1986; 1989). Complementary work by Haselgrove (1989) has disentangled the complex documentary evidence for the export of stoneware to Britain and identified the chief personalities involved in the trade on both sides of the Channel.

As an aid to dating and assessing the lifespan of individual forms, the publication of stoneware vessels containing coin-hoards is proving invaluable. Notable corpora include Sarfatij's catalogue (1979) of medieval and later hoards from the Netherlands and Liebgott's monograph on Danish finds (1978). Despite the frequency of hoard finds in the Rhineland itself (Hagen 1937), no definitive regional assessment has yet appeared.

Finally, the vexed questions of fabric identification and characterisation (Gaimster 1987a; Hurst 1988) are beginning to be addressed by archaeologists and scientists alike. Following the textural analysis conducted by Strunk-Lichtenberg (1975) on the wasters from Siegburg, a programme of Neutron Activation Analysis (NAA) at all the major stoneware production sites in the Rhineland has been initiated at the British Museum, London (Gaimster 1990b; Gaimster & Hook 1995; Hook 1997). The aim of the programme is to establish the trace-elemental compositions of their respective products as an aid to the attribution of specific types. Selected examples from consumer sites or museum colections can then be linked to the source material once the database is fully established. Future work will address the question of characterising wares from individual workshops within the respective industries.

### *1.1.3 Lead-glazed earthenware and slipware*

Hans-Georg Stephan, in his survey of Renaissance Decorated Pottery in Central Europe (1987a), rightly identifies the relatively superficial level of archaeological research into the utilitarian lead-glazed earthenwares of the Rhineland in contrast to the historic bias of interest in the stonewares of the region. Until urban excavations began in the Lower Rhineland at the beginning of the 1980s there were few, if any, excavated groups of early post-medieval earthenware available for study (Stephan 1987a, note 72).

Traditionally the accent of research in this field has been on the decorative treatment and iconography of the commemorative slipwares (*Zierschüsseln*) made in the Lower Rhineland between the end of the 17th and beginning of the 19th century. Since the middle of the 19th century these wares have been avidly collected both by local museums and private collectors because of their documentary value (many are signed and dated by the potter). As surviving illustrations of regional folk art they are without parallel, their graphical sources the subject of intense interest today (Bartels 1982; 1988). The term *Niederrheinische Bauerntöpferei* ("Lower Rhine peasant pottery") has been used as a shorthand description for these slipwares since the beginning of the century (Bartmaan 1914). However, it is now clear, thanks to urban excavations, that this class of pottery was produced as much for the town as the rural market (Gaimster 1986a).

It was not until 1905 that the first public exhibition on the subject of Lower Rhine earthenware took place at the Kaiser-Wilhelm-Museum in Krefeld. This was followed by a catalogue of the Krefeld Museum's collection by its director Friedrich Deneken in 1914. The importance of local ceramics to the study of regional folk culture was further emphasised by the inclusion of 67 examples of Lower Rhine Slipware out of a total of 172 catalogue entries in Max Creutz's Deutsche Volkskunst (1924). In the following year Lower Rhine Bauernschüsseln formed a centrepiece to the section on "Rhenish folk art" at the Rhineland millennium exhibition held in Cologne. During the 1930s Karl Ritzerfeld, curator at the Hetjens-Museum in Düsseldorf, formed the first permanent display of the Museum's holdings.

In 1953 the Hetjens-Museum organised a special exhibition of their Lower Rhine slipwares entitled Niederrheinische Irdenware 17.–19. Jahrhundert, and in 1954 this class of pottery received particular emphasis in the exhibition *Mit Drehscheibe und Malhorn* at the Germanisches Nationalmuseum in Nuremberg (Meyer-Heisig 1955). The museological interest in the decorative slipwares of the region has continued in more recent times with specialist exhibitions at the Museum für Niederrheinische Volkskunde in Kevelaer (Kevelaer 1970), the Niederrheinisches Freilichtmuseum in Grefrath (Grefrath 1978) and at the Niederrheinisches Museum in Duisburg (Bartels 1982). They have also formed an important focus in exhibitions covering the entire range of Rhenish medieval and later ceramics at Frechen (Reineking-von Bock 1966), Düsseldorf (1967), and Kommern (1968).

Supported by the institutes of folk-history in the region, the subject was given full academic treatment by Mechthild Scholten-Neess and Werner Jüttner in their corpus of Lower Rhine Slipwares, Niederrheinische Bauerntöpferei, 17.–19. Jahrhundert (1971). The volume comprises an impressive catalogue of wares produced at nineteen of the main Lower Rhine production centres, concentrating on the design and iconography of commemorative dishes preserved in local museums, and a short section dealing for the first time with some of the more utilitarian forms used in the kitchen and cellar. The study also contains a wealth of documentary information concerning the organisation of the rural workshops and a list of over 500 potters' names and their working lifespans. This initial attempt at locating and mapping the main production sites in the Lower Rhine from documentary sources (see Map 1) has proved an invaluable basis for current archaelogical research concerned with the geographical source of material found on consumer sites.

With the documentary and art-historical groundwork well established, a shift of emphasis has occurred during the 1980s with the boom in excavation taking place in the towns along the Rhine (Krause 1990; Tromnau 1990). Increasingly, entire groups of domestic slipware and plain earthenware made by the same workshops which produced the commemorative vessels are coming to light from consumer sites. A preliminary overview of the Duisburg finds, which date from end of the Middle Ages to the early 19th century, has been provided by the author (1986a; 1988a; 1988b). The exhibition Volkstümliche Keramik vom Niederrhein organised by the Niederrheinisches Museum der Stadt Duisburg in 1986 (Duisburg 1986) attempted to set the chronology of Lower Rhine ceramics into an independent archaeological sequence in the light of the excavations in the town. Documentary evidence for local post-medieval earthenwares has also come to light at the rural production site of Sonsbeck, Kreis Wesel, where the accounts book dating from 1852–82 containing the names and prices of a wide variety of wares has survived (Wolters 1988a; 1988b).

An overview of the range of local plain earthenware and slipware in use in the Lower Rhine countryside has been supplied by the discovery of over 250 vessels at the farmhouse of Haus Gelinde, Rheinberg in 1970 (Soechting ed. 1976; Hackspiel 1982; 1993). The find provides a spectrum of household wares in use at the site between the early 18th and mid 19th century. A further household inventory of regional slipware and plain earthenware was recovered in 1981 from closely dated flood deposits of *c.* 1740 and 1784 at the village of Krefeld-Linn in 1981 (Reichmann 1988; see Appendix 3, Contexts 60, 61 in this study). The two assemblages from Haus Gelinde and Krefeld-Linn provide important evidence for town and country comparative studies in the region.

Excavated town and castle sites in the Low Countries are proving useful in the calibration of the Lower Rhine sequence of local pottery and in the charting of its long-distance distribution. Quantitative data is only available in a limited number of cases, of which the most notable are Amsterdam (Baart *et al.* 1986; 1988; Thijssen 1985), Nijmegen (Thijssen *et al.* 1984; 1991 ed.), Masseik (Heymans ed. 1989); Deventer (Clevis & Kottman 1989) and Kessel Castle, Venlo (Clevis & Thijssen 1989). Imports of Lower Rhine slipware have also been identified by the author along the southern and eastern coastline of Britain (Gaimster 1988c), although the location and frequency of finds suggest that they are more likely to represent vessels used on board ship as opposed to traded cargo.

The task of pinning down the new finds to their original source in the Lower Rhine hinterland has been hampered, however, by the virtual absence of production site material for comparison. Rescue work on the waste dumps at Issum (Scholten-Neess & Jüttner 1971, Cat. 323–324; Hurst *et al.* 1986, Cat. 393–395) and Kervenheim (Frankewitz & Koster 1982; Frankewitz 1988) have been reported on in brief, but full-scale catalogues of finds have yet to appear. Interim reports on the wasters from excavations in Frechen have simplified the task of identifying their counterparts on consumer sites in the region (Jürgens & Kleine 1988; Kleine 1989). The precise attribution of wares remains a principal research aim at the present time. In response to the problems of fabric characterisation the British Museum, in conjunction with local museums in the

Lower Rhineland, has embarked on a programme of scientific analysis (see Section 4 below).

The distribution of a small but important class of regional decorated earthenware still remains somewhat of a mystery. A group of polychrome-glazed wares or Hafnerware (the generic German term for polychrome lead-glazed tiles and pottery), often with applied designs in the contemporary Renaissance manner or with overall encrusted decoration, was identified among a number of Cologne casual finds by von Falke in 1898 (von Falke 1898a). Now in the Museum für Angewandte Kunst, Cologne (Reineking-von Bock 1966, Cat. 219–221; see Appendix 5 in this study), they provide evidence of a sophisticated earthenware manufacture in the city. According to Unger (1988 ed., 20–21), they were made as a sideline by stove-tile and stoneware potters in Cologne. Some of the vessels were commissioned by the local potters' guilds themselves (*ibid.*, Fig. 3).

The history of one silver-mounted ceremonial beaker has been documented in Vollenhove, the Netherlands, since the middle of the 16th century (Dubbe 1960). Further archaeological finds of Cologne Hafnerware have been made in the Netherlands (Hurst *et al.* 1986, Cat. 346–350, 354, 358, 361–2) and in Britain (unpublished; note 1); but to date only one polychrome bird-whistle has been found in Neuss (Hupka 1988, Pl. 7b). No other examples have come to light in the Lower Rhine outside Cologne. Further research and recognition of this class of slipware will no doubt help to clarify this geographically biased distribution pattern. A first priority, however, is a physical re-examination of the original finds from Cologne, as their exact forms and decorative details remain obscured by heavy museum restoration.

During the late 1980s there has been an explosion of archaeological and museological interest in the post-medieval slipware and associated earthenware of the region, precipitated by the recent availability of excavated material in Duisburg, Düsseldorf, Neuss, Wesel, Krefeld and in Cologne. To take stock of the new data, the Hetjens-Museum, Düsseldorf, hosted an international conference in 1988 (*Die Keramik vom Niederrhein und ihr internationales Umfeld insbesondere zur Renaissance- und Barockzeit*) (Endres 1989a). This was accompanied by exhibitions on different themes and finds at seven museums in the region (Naumann *et al.* 1988). The events coincided with a handbook containing 25 papers on the latest archaeological discoveries, the international distribution of finds and on ceramic iconography, among other themes (Naumann ed. 1988; review by Endres 1989b). The conference was followed in 1989 by the publication of its proceedings (Naumann ed. 1989). In the same year the Museum Burg Linn in Krefeld published a well-illustrated handbook dealing with the social meaning of images and mottos decorating Lower Rhine Slipware dishes and stove-tiles in its collections (Reichmann 1989). These recent developments serve to illustrate the now multidisciplinary nature of the subject, with researchers from folk-life studies, art-history and archaeology collaborating on publication and exhibition projects.

Finally the Rheinisches Freilichtmuseum in Kommern dedicated an exhibition, *Frühe Dekorierte Irdenware*, to the early development of decorated earthenwares in the Rhineland. The accompanying catalogue (Burhenne *et al.* 1991) contains a number of essays on the archaeological evidence for the beginning of slipware production in the region, including a review of the Duisburg sequence of the late 16th to 17th centuries (Gaimster 1991), and a discussion of the influence of the slipwares of the Werra region on developments in the Lower Rhine and Low countries during the Renaissance period (Stephan 1991). The link between regional ceramic production of the late Middle Ages and the early post-medieval period was being recognised.

### *1.1.4 Stove-tiles*

Ceramic tiles, used in the construction of wood-burning stoves, have been an integral component of earthenware manufacture in the Rhineland since the Middle Ages. Deep, conical tiles (*Topfkacheln*), such as those from the stoneware-producing centre of Siegburg (Beckmann 1975, Pl. 8–9), date from the 13th century. German woodcuts of the late 15th century (Strauss 1968) illustrate the development of the familiar tripartite stove, with its substantial plinth, large cuboid firing-box and free-standing upper tower (*Turmofen*). With the evolution of the stove form came the development of a range of tiles designed to fit the crest of the stove, cornices, corners, and ledges separating the three levels of the structure. The fashion for tile-stove heating spread rapidly over transalpine central Europe during the later Middle Ages; and by the early 16th-century tiles imported from Germany were in demand in Britain (Gaimster 1988f; 1989a; Gaimster *et al.* 1990), Scandinavia (Liebgott 1972; Wahlöö 1976, Cat. 602–654) and in the Low Countries (Dubbe 1966; 1980; 1987). As in the case of Rhenish salt-glazed stoneware there is a growing international interest in the typochronology of stove-tiles produced in the Rhineland for the export market.

Thanks to the publication of Dr Ingeborg Unger's catalogue of the stove-tile collection held by the Kölnisches Stadtmuseum, Cologne (Unger ed. 1988), the recognition of Cologne products on consumer sites in the region and abroad has increased significantly. The collection, dating from the 14th to late 16th centuries, consists almost entirely of tiles and fragments found in the city. Many pieces come directly from the sites of known tile workshops. The survey, although based on the survival of casual finds, provides an overview of the development of one specialist ceramic industry in the region. This essential groundwork will assist in the differentiation between Cologne tiles and the products of contemporary, as yet unidentified, workshops operating in the near vicinity (Mielke 1989) and in the Middle Rhine area immediately to the South (Mielke 1977; Döry 1978, Cat. 235). Nevertheless, differentiation on stylistic grounds between the products of the local industries, is problematic in the extreme. Waster finds from Raeren-Eynatten illustrate the stylistic uniformity of the regional stove-tile tradition (Mayer 1977, Fig. 21). It is now realised that the precise attribution of tiles is dependent on refined petrographic methods, such as Neutron Activation Analysis (see Section 4).

The question of geographical source is complicated by the evidence for the long-distance trade in stove-tile moulds (Mielke 1983; Gaimster 1989). Hence negative moulds of tiles produced in the Rhineland may have been used to produce tiles in North Germany and Scandinavia. Negative moulds of Rhenish type have been excavated in Lübeck (Metzger 1900, Pl. 2; Hasse 1969, Cat. 340) and Lund, southern Sweden (Blomquist 1936, Figs. 70–3; pers. comm. C. Wahlöö). The evidence suggests that any attribution based on stylistic features alone must proceed with extreme caution.

In 1986 a large group of imported green-glazed stove-tiles dating to around 1500 were discovered in the Dissolution deposits of St Mary Graces monastery, London (Gaimster 1987f, Fig. 15–18; Gaimster et al. 1990). It was decided to mount a programme of scientific analysis (NAA) on fabric samples at the British Museum with the aim of confirming or eliminating the Rhenish attribution based on stylistic analysis (Cowell 1990). Although no match could be made with the samples of kiln-waste material from Cologne, their trace-elemental compositions suggest that the tiles were originally made in the Rhine region, probably at an as yet unidentified source.

A combined stylistic and scientific approach to the identification of stove-tiles on consumer sites is projected for the future. The latest discoveries from Duisburg and Wesel (Section 4) have been sampled for neutron activation analysis by the British Museum with the view to establishing a database of Rhenish stove-tile compositions.

### *1.1.5 Tin-glazed earthenware*

Discoveries in the towns of Duisburg, Wesel, Cologne (Tietzel 1980) and Neuss (Giertz 1988), among others, suggest that the Lower Rhineland became a profitable market for Netherlands maiolica wares from the end of the 16th century onwards. So far no evidence for Italian or South Netherlandish (Antwerp) products have been found on local excavations. The dating of individual wares still relies on the monograph written by Dingeman Korf in 1981 (2nd edition). For the later faience wares from Holland the researcher is dependent on van Dam's chronology published in 1982 and Lunsingh Scheurleer's study of white faience (1970). As overviews these volumes offer only very general guides to the dating and attribution of tin-glazed pottery imported from The Netherlands. Baart *et al.*'s recent contribution on white Dutch and Italian faience found in Amsterdam (1990) has provided an independent dating framework for this class of ware (see review by van Dam 1991).

Evidence for the indigenous production of tin-glazed earthenware has been difficult to identify archaeologically. However, the documented faience manufactory established by Gottfried Becker in 1764 at Duisburg (Lehnemann 1982) was located by excavation in 1987 (Ruppel 1988). Becker's factory continued working until 1787, and it will be the task of future research to differentiate between the Becker material and the imported Dutch wares.

### *1.1.6 Oriental and native porcelain*

Apart from isolated finds of early 17th-century Chinese *Kraak* porcelain in recent excavation contexts at Duisburg (Gaimster 1986b, Fig. 4, Cat. 212), there does not appear to be any archaeological evidence for an identifiable demand for porcelain in the Rhineland before the end of the 17th century. Thereafter Chinese export porcelain becomes ubiquitous on both urban (e. g. Duisburg: Gaimster 1986a, Fig. 6.11–13) and rural sites (e. g. Haus Gelinde, Rheinberg: Hackspiel 1982, Cat. P.16). It owed its popularity in the main to the introduction of tea, chocolate and coffee drinking to the Rhineland during the 18th century. Porcelain made by German factories appears in archaeological contexts during the second half of the 18th century, although individual sources have not yet been identified.

### *1.1.7 Staffordshire finewares*

The remaining category of imported post-medieval pottery found in the Lower Rhineland is the fine tableware from Staffordshire, England (e. g. Duisburg: Gaimster 1986a, Fig. 6.9–10). Mainly teawares, they were shipped via London and Amsterdam down the Rhine during the mid to late 18th century (Treue 1973). To date, the most spectacular illustration of this trade was the recovery of a Black Basalt teapot on the Duisburg *Alter Markt* site in 1982 (Gaimster 1987b). The underside of the vessel bore the mark of Edmund

John Birch, who was working in Hanley, Staffordshire, between 1790 and 1810. So far Staffordshire red stoneware, blackware, Agate ware, and coloured and plain creamware are also represented in the regional ceramic sequence. Their presence reflects the increasing specialisation and formalisation of tablewares in use in the Lower Rhineland during the 18th century.

### *1.1.8 Bias in the archaeological sample*

It will be apparent from the above resumé that the vast bulk of post-medieval ceramics found in the Lower Rhineland, until the 1980s at least, has come from casual discoveries or from salvage excavations on production sites. Until full-scale excavations in Duisburg began in 1981 (Krause 1990a; 1990b) no stratified sequences of medieval and later pottery were available from any urban centre in the Lower Rhineland. Even in Cologne, where excavations have been constant since the Second World War, the investigations have concentrated almost entirely on the extensive Roman and Frankish remains (Hellenkemper 1990, 84). Only now are resources being channelled into the documentation of the city's later periods. Hence, no consumer assemblages have been available for comparative or synthetic analysis on a regional scale.

As we have seen, the emphasis has been on the examination of production sites, particularly at the stoneware centres. An overall picture of the relationship between ceramic production and distribution in the region is yet to emerge. The most severe problem is one of data assimilation. Due to the vast quantities of material found on production sites, very little has been processed, let alone published. Beckmann's 1975 report on the Siegburg Aulgasse waster-heaps is a rare exception, although only the pre-1500 finds were selected for publication. A post-excavation strategy, involving a carefully structured sampling programme, is desirable for the kiln waste assemblages still languishing in both federal and local museum stores.

Earthenware production of the medieval and later periods has been neglected almost entirely by professional archaeologists in the Rhineland (Stephan 1990), with the notable exceptions of salvage work at a late medieval greyware kiln in Xanten (Wegner 1981) and recent investigations in Frechen (Jürgens & Kleine 1988). Our knowledge of this field relies heavily on largely unrepresentative museum collections of highly decorated wares and the chance recovery of individual finds from town centres (see Appendix 5). The Traubert collection of post-medieval earthenware found in Cologne and given to the Rheinisches Freilichtmuseum Kommern (Burhenne *et al.* 1991) is one of the best examples of the latter source of evidence. The resulting picture is geographically, chronologically and statistically biased towards stonewares of the Middle Ages and their production sites.

With the dramatic increase in city-centre development and excavation since 1980 along the Rhine (Koschik 1990, 48), there has been an urgent need to tackle the documentation of medieval and post-medieval features, including wells, cellars, and latrines, and their associated artefactual assemblages. In the face of being overwhelmed by the ever-increasing quantity of finds, local museums and the federal archaeological institutions have now embarked on largescale post-excavation programmes. It is a sad fact, however, that the lack of a coherent post-excavation strategy for the region will prevent any organised synthetic analysis taking place for some years to come.

Finally, it is regrettable that no attention has been paid by the archaeological authorities to the potential of fieldwalking settlement and production sites in rural areas. The collection of field samples from the hinterland of Lower Rhine towns can provide important information about the rural movement of ceramics (Gaimster 1984). The technique could be employed to detect post-medieval production sites in the region, and where their location is already known, to collect representative type-series of waster-sherds. Available sites, such as Sonsbeck, an earthenware-manufacturing centre in the Lower Rhine hinterland (Wolters 1988a, note 18), provide excellent opportunities to supplement our distribution map of local production centres.

### *1.1.9 Limitations of methodology and interpretation*

Over the past hundred years the basic groundwork for the post-medieval ceramics of the Rhineland has been achieved. In terms of progress made on methodological and critical approaches the situation is comparable to that achieved in neighbouring Belgium (Verhaeghe 1988), where the need for problem-orientation has also been identified.

The broad characterisation of wares from the main centres of production has been established both by stylistic and archaeological evidence. There has, however, been far too great an emphasis on the highly decorated products. The bias is reflected in the selective nature of specialist museum exhibitions (e. g. Klinge 1979 on stoneware) and monographs (e. g. Scholten-Neess & Jüttner 1971 on slipware). There is a growing need to examine the range of contemporary utilitarian wares, especially from stoneware-producing centres. Recent displays of everyday tablewares at the Töpfereimuseum Raeren (Reineking-von Bock 1989) provide a welcome break from tradition. For Lower Rhine earthenwares the Sonsbeck accounts book (Wolters 1988a; 1988b) has provided a unique insight into the range and value of domestic products of the late post-medieval period. Current rescue excavations in the region are amplifying our knowledge of vessel forms at an ever increasing rate.

Traditionally the attribution of Rhenish stonewares and earthenwares to their source has been based on the stylistic characterisation of form details and decorative features. Often, however, these identifications can only be general, i. e. "Siegburg-type ware" or "Lower Rhine/Middle Rhine slipware". It is common to find in published reports that the variety of Siegburg ware, for instance, is not defined (is it proto-stoneware, earthenware or true stoneware?). It is well recognised that the macroscopic characterisation of post-medieval stoneware and earthenware fabrics in the area is problematic as the fabrics are predominantly refined, and without identifiable inclusions visible in the matrix. Scientific techniques, such as neutron activation analysis which establish the trace-elemental composition of the ceramic body, are urgently required to define the range of fabrics made by individual production centres (Section 4).

Until the results of recent excavations can be assimilated, the established ceramic typochronologies, based largely on stylistic analysis and the survival of "dated" vessels, will continue to be used. The danger of using stoneware vessels with applied dated ornament has not been stressed enough in the literature (Hausmann 1973). However, it is now clear that matrices remained in use for several generations and migrated with the resettlement of individual potters and potting communities on several occasions (Reineking-von Bock 1981, 236; Gaimster 1997, 166–167). As we have seen, 16th-century moulds were even available for re-use during the 19th century. Further work is needed to examine the longevity of ornamental mould-types in relation to vessel forms. In this regard, the dangers of dating stonewares by their hallmarked silver-gilt mounts has been stressed recently (Glanville 1989). Many of the mounts were applied long after the original production date of the stoneware.

It was realised during the course of this research programme that the lack of quantified assemblages of post-medieval pottery in the region had prevented any comparative work at an inter-site level taking place. The importance of a standardized approach to quantification procedures is crucial here. The other major obstacle to the comparability of ceramic assemblages in the Rhineland has been the absence of a publication standard and common terminology for the description of ceramic fabrics, forms and decorative features (Endres 1989b). As a response to this shortcoming, a working party at the Rheinisches Landesmuseum in Bonn published its *Vorschläge zur systematischen Beschreibung von Keramik* in 1986 (Bonn 1986). However, its applicability to the diversity of post-medieval ceramic fabrics and forms has proved inadequate (Gaimster 1988e). The chronologically more relevant *Leitfaden zur Keramikbeschreibung* (Bauer *et al.* 1986) may prove more useful in the long term, and has been employed to describe the objects in the catalogue section of the recent Kommern exhibition on early decorated slipwares (Schilling in Burhenne *et al.* 1991). It is hoped that the section on ceramic forms can be expanded to include a wider range of postmedieval vessel-types (for a full discussion of the problems see Sections 3.2 and 3.3).

It is only in the last decade that an identifiable multidisciplinary approach to the study of post-medieval ceramics in the Rhineland has emerged. Previously, folk-life exhibitions of ceramics and archaeological salvage operations had occurred in isolation and without mutual reference. Since then museum exhibitions at Duisburg in 1986 (Duisburg 1986), Düsseldorf and associated venues in 1988 (Naumann *et al.* 1988), Kommern in 1991 (Burhenne *et al.* 1991) and Siegburg in the same year (Korte-Boge ed. 1991) have been characterised by the collaboration of archaeologists, folk-life historians and art historians on a common theme. This is essential as no one discipline is able to assimilate the mountain of material and documentary evidence on its own. Ultimately this trend will lead to a more synchronic approach to the questions of ceramic production, disribution and use in the region.

The latest developments, and particularly the increasing rate of rescue excavation in the region, highlight the necessity of identifying research aims and objectives. The symposium *Zur Keramik des Mittelalters und der beginnenden Neuzeit im Rheinland*, held in Koblenz in 1988 (Gaimster *et al.* eds 1988), was organised in order to discuss the current rate of research. A strong feeling emerged that future archaeological investigation and research activities should be problem-orientated on a regional basis so that the duplication of effort could be avoided and so that the relatively scarce resources allotted to the medieval to later period could be utilised to maximum effect.

In view of the steadily growing quantity of excavated material, the coordinated sampling of both production and consumer site assemblages is a first priority. Sampling of material for scientific analysis must also be coordinated at a regional level so as to avoid duplication. It is hoped that in the future a regional pottery research group will emerge to identify priorities and maintain standard practices of post-excavation and publication under the auspices of the archaeological and museum authorities. By way of example, the regional groups of the Medieval Pottery Research Group operate such a system with some success in Britain. It is only through a more coordinated approach that some of the most pressing questions of methodology and research can be resolved. In this way archaeological interest may be directed towards the critical interpretative relationship between ceramic production and consumption in the region.

## 1.2 Nature and aims of the survey

### *1.2.1 A problem-orientated research strategy for the region*

It is a reflection of the administration of archaeology in the Lower Rhineland that ceramic research has tended to be based upon specific localities. The rapid accumulation of data over the past decade has no doubt accounted for the absence of a regional approach. This is regrettable as research on a regional scale, which incorporates the detailed assessment of specific sequences, is best suited to the appraisal of the economic aspects of ceramic production and distribution (Streeton 1982).

In this context there is a need both for the re-evaluation of information which is already available and for the systematic recording of new data. In this survey, which comprises published reports, extant museum collections and the archaeological dicoveries, the disparate sources of information have been brought together for the first time. Using the Duisburg ceramic sequence as a baseline for the definition and relative chronology of regional post-medieval ceramics, a wide range of urban and rural sites in the Lower Rhine hinterland has been sampled. A standard means of ceramic classification and quantification has been employed so that the proportional variability of assemblages can be compared and evaluated on an intra- and inter-site basis.

The aim of this study is to provide an objective body of data so that a more synchronic picture of post-medieval ceramic trends in the region can be built up. The decision to concentrate primarily on the evaluation of consumer assemblages during the course of this survey was taken with a view to assessing regional patterns in pottery marketing, fashion, status and function over a 400 year period (*c.* 1400–1800) of continuous social, economic and political change. The evolution of a problem-orientated approach to the collection, recording and analysis of ceramic data is outlined here.

### *1.2.2 A decade of rescue archaeology in the Duisburg Altstadt: the establishment of a ceramic sequence*

In 1929 the city of Duisburg, situated on the confluence of Rhine and Ruhr, became a metropolitan conurbation consisting of the old territory of Duisburg together with the barge-port of Ruhrort and the industrial centre of Meiderich. In 1929 the industrial centre of Hamborn and rural parts to the South and in 1975 the boroughs of Walsum to the North and Baerl, Homberg, Rheinhausen and Rumeln-Kaldenhausen on the left bank of the Rhine (from North to South) were added to the town. Today the population of the metropolitan borough numbers over half a million.

The modern extent of the town is misleading, however. Until the beginning of the 19th century, Duisburg was a small provincial centre with a population of only 4,000, merely a thousand more than its medieval counterpart. With the completion of the Rhine Canal scheme and regional railway connections, the city evolved rapidly with the introduction of heavy industry. The population in 1900 was over 100,000. Inspite of all the changes the structure of the Old Town survived until the Second World War. At the end of the war about 80 % of the medieval town wall, the old pattern of the streets and properties were still intact. But between 1950 and 1970 more than 50 % of the medieval town-wall was dismantled, most of the pre-waretime buildings disappeared and the pattern of the streets were changed (Krause 1994b, 51 ff.).

In the Duisburg Altstadt the topography of the original medieval town is still recognisable above ground, if only in the street plan and the survival of stretches of town wall (Plans 1 & 2). At the core, on the site of the current Rathaus and Salvatorkirche, stood the nucleus of the Carolingian and subsequent medieval settlement (Duisburg 1983). Its location on the bank of the Rhine and its proximity to the mouth of the Ruhr made this an advantageous position for riverine trade. The town enjoyed Imperial status as an important commercial centre and the site of a fortified enclosure and mint. The outline of the Imperial Burgplatz with its church can still be seen in the modern street plan of the Duisburg Altstadt (see Plan 2; Burg Marktplatz area). With the erection of town walls in the 1120s came a number of monastic communities to settle both within and on the edge of the town. The latter settlements were enclosed within the present circuit of urban defences by the end of the 13th century.

During the late to post-medieval period the town became the object of a series of struggles for control between regional powers. In 1290 Duisburg was ceded by treaty to the Duchy of Cleves (later Cleves-Julich-Berg), and became one of its principal administrative centres (Flink 1984). Imperial interests continued during this time and contributed to the occupations of the town that belonged to Brandenburg since 1614 by the Spanish in 1614–21 and 1625–1628, in 1629–31 and 1636–44 by the Dutch and after 1648 by the forces of Brandenburg. In 1672–73 Duisburg was occupied by the French in the war against Brandenburg and the Dutch and again in the seven years' war from 1757–63.

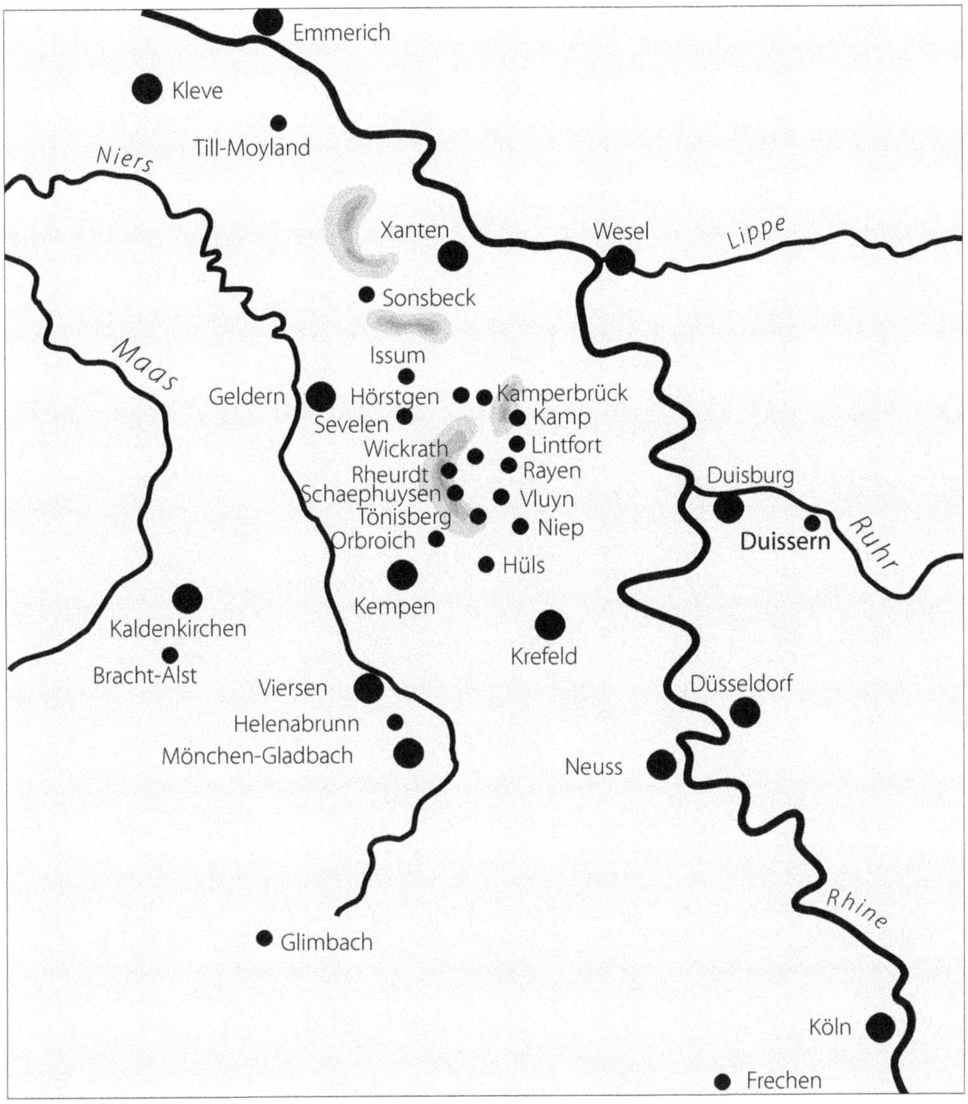


*Map 1*
*Principal earthenware production sites in the Lower Rhineland c. 1600-1900 (from M. Scholten-Neess & W. Jüttner 1971, 8)*

It became part of the French province in the Rhineland from 1805 until the end of the Napoleonic Wars. At the Congress of Vienna (1815) the Rhineland and Westphalia were ceded to Prussia. In 1823 the town of Duisburg became the administrative centre for the surrounding region. It is significant that it was not until the onset of industrialisation in the town during the 1820s that extra-mural development took place.

In 1407 Duisburg was accepted as a permanent member of the Hanseatic League along with the town of Wesel immediately to the north. Until 1668 the town was represented by traders in Lübeck, Rostock, Stralsund, Danzig, Visby, and Riga among other Baltic ports. Its position on the Rhine connected it to the riverine trade between Cologne and the Rhine-mouth port of Dordrecht in the Netherlands, where a permanent settlement of Duisburg merchants is recorded (von Roden 1984, 155). The settlement facilitated Duisburg's long-distance trading activities with Brabant, Flanders and England.

The first large-scale opportunity to investigate the below-ground archaeology of the Duisburg Altstadt occurred at the beginning of the 1980s. Redevelopment of the town centre with shafts for an extension to the urban underground railway system and the construction of multi-storey shopping centres took place throughout the decade causing the destruction of acres of historical strata. In collaboration with the town authorities, the local museum (Niederrheinisches Museum der Stadt Duisburg, now Kultur- und Stadthistorisches Museum Duisburg) was responsible for programme of rescue excavation under the direction of Dr Günter Krause (Krause 1992 & 1994b). The work has been supported by the Rheinisches Amt für Bodendenkmalpflege and the Federal Ministry for Urban Development (Ministerium fur Stadtentwicklung, Wohnen und Verkehr des Landes Nordrhein-Westfalen).

The initial excavations concentrated on the *Alter Markt* site, an open stretch of land to the south of the present-day Rathaus and on the periphery of the early medieval settlement (Plan 2, Nr.1). A branch of the Rhine flowed directly past this spot during the early Middle Ages. Successive layers of the original medieval market place were uncovered. The sequence of levels, dated by the

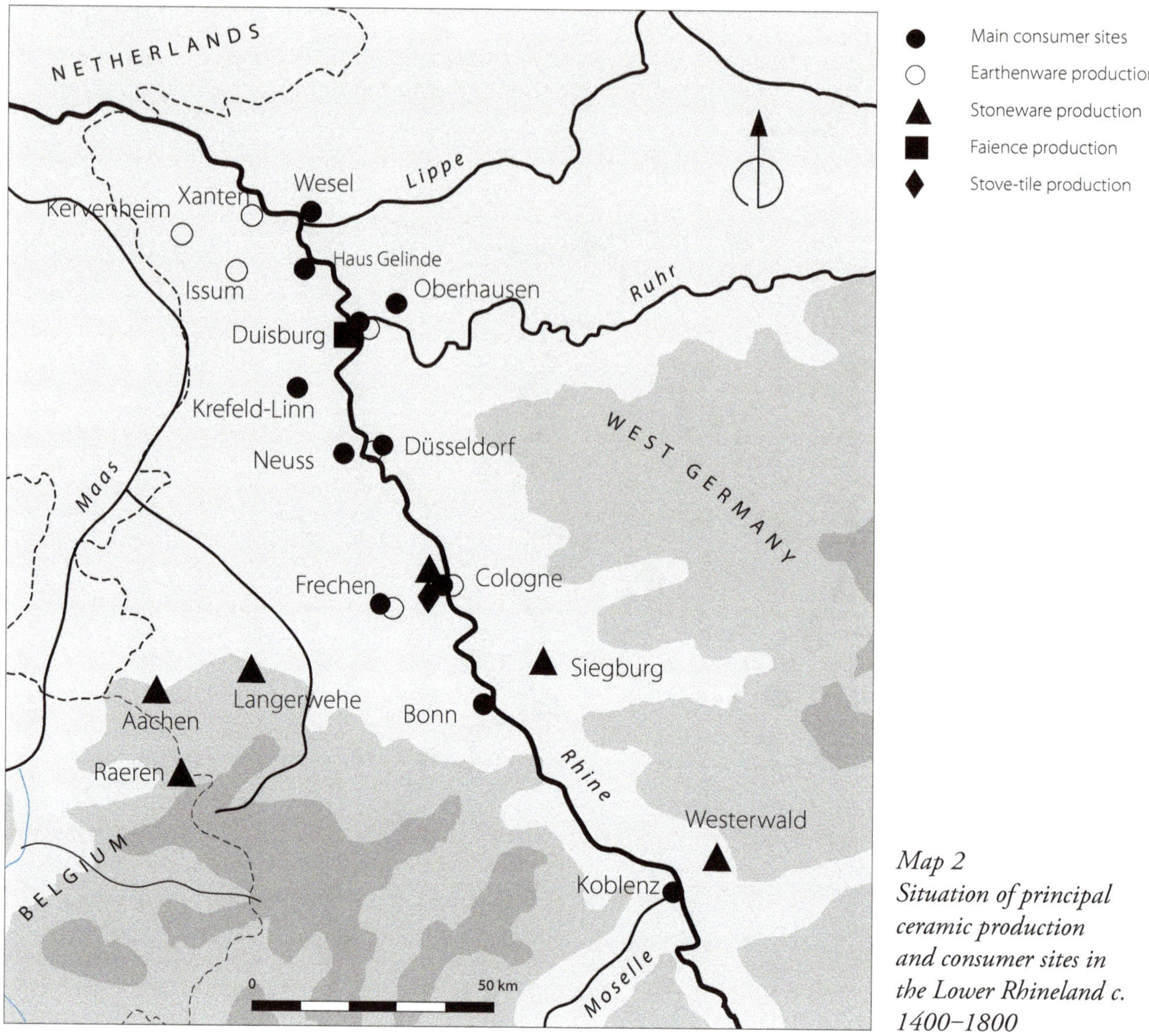


*Map 2*
*Situation of principal ceramic production and consumer sites in the Lower Rhineland c. 1400–1800*

pottery trapped between each layer of cobbling, began in the early 10th century and continued until the late 18th century (Context 45; Appendix 2). This 5 m depth of cultural strata provided the first clear sequence of medieval and later ceramics to be found in the town. Further excavation has extended the chronology of the sequence back to the 5th century (Krause 1992 & 1994b). Following the excavations on the market levels themselves, attention has turned to the associated market hall buildings of the 14th century, which contain deep cellars and large-scale artefactual assemblages (Untermann 1992). The *Alter Markt* complex has now been preserved in situ, and forms the focus of an open-air archaeological conservation area.

During the mid-1980s a continuous programme of rescue excavation took place in the vicinity of the *Alter Markt* zone. Brick-lined latrines, wells, rubbish pits, some associated with the cellars of medieval and post-medieval tenements, have been uncovered , notably along the line of an underground railway shaft being sunk in the Schwanenstraße (Plan 2, Nos. 18–30; Plan 3). Rescue work here was followed in 1987–9 by the investigation of similar sanitary and refuse deposits along the stretch of town wall bordering the Innenhafen canal, the site of the Duisburg trading settlement (Stapelviertel) in the Middle Ages and post-medieval period (Plan 2, Nos. 4,5,13–17; Ruppel 1989). This campaign of excavation also included the recording of town bastions and their internal fills (*ibid.*).

During the 1980s over 30 well-stratified and sealed contexts containing ceramics dating from the period *c.* 1400–1800 were excavated in the centre of Duisburg. They range from domestic latrine, well and midden groups to the interior fills of monastic buildings, house-cellars and bastions on the town wall. The combined evidence has enabled a calibrated sequence of regional ceramics to be established. Future excavations will serve to refine the sequence and supplement the type-series of wares on an on-going basis. These excavations at Duisburg provide a preliminary insight into the changing nature of distribution and consumption of a wide range of ceramics produced and imported into the region during the post-medieval period.

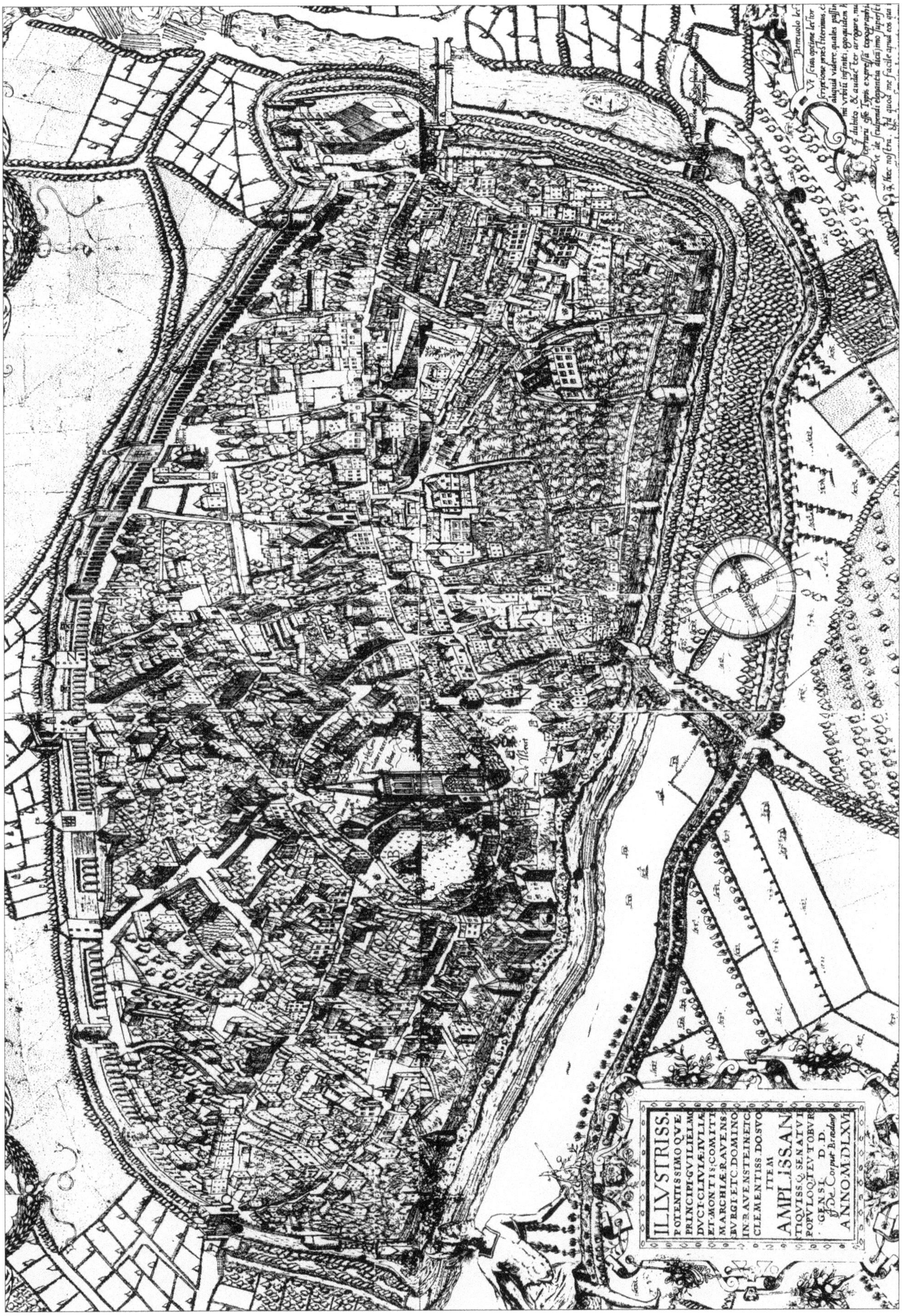

*Plan 1 Duisburg Altstadt in 1566; Town plan by Johannes Corputius*

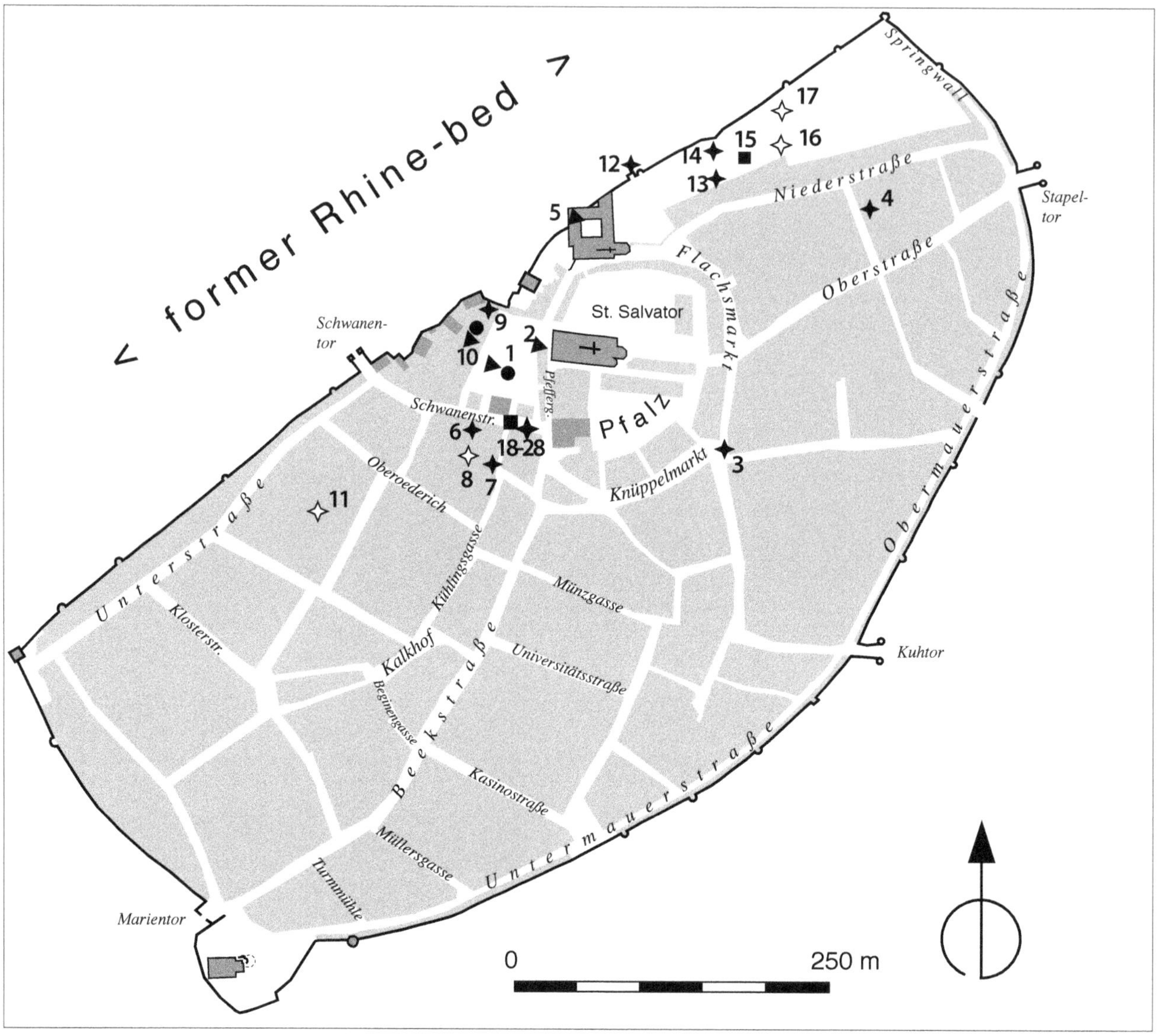


*Plan 2 Plot of principal ceramic assemblages from Duisburg on town plan of 1823–1825 (see Appendix 1)*

▲ *Cellars*

● *Rubbish levels / dumps*

■ *Wells*

✦ *Latrines*

✧ *Rubish pits*

| | |
|---|---|
| *1* | *Alter Markt, contexts 45, 28, 5, 45, 32, 25, 27* |
| *2* | *Salvatorkirche, contexts 26, 50* |
| *3* | *Alte Post, context 47* |
| *4* | *Dreigiebelhaus, context 46* |
| *5* | *Minoritenkloster, context 36* |
| *6* | *C & A, context 42* |
| *7* | *C & A, context 43* |
| *8* | *C & A, context 41* |
| *9* | *Innenhafen, context 37* |
| *10* | *Innenhafen, contexts 38, 39, 40* |
| *11* | *Abteistraße, context 44* |
| *12* | *Aachener Turm, contexts 23, 24* |
| *13* | *Niederstraße, context 20* |
| *14* | *Niederstraße, context 21* |
| *15* | *Niederstraße, context 22* |
| *16* | *Niederstraße, context 29* |
| *17* | *Niederstraße, context 30* |
| *18–28* | *Schwanenstraße, contexts 7–13, 1, 2, 19, 18, 17, 34, 15, 16, 31, 33, 35, 34* |

### *1.2.3 The chronological range of the survey*

The decision to examine ceramics in the Rhineland during the period 1400–1800 has been dictated by a combination of factors, consequent both on the nature of the surviving sample of finds and current research questions.

Until the urban excavations of the 1980s few assemblages of post-medieval pottery were available from controlled excavations in the region (Stephan 1987, note 72). The sheer quantity of post-medieval finds have dictated an urgent response to post-excavation and a comprehensive review of regional research needs.

In the past there has been an emphasis in the Rhineland on the ceramics of the period before 1500 (Beckmann 1975; Stephan 1983; 1990). The bias reflects trends in the regional archaeology of the historic period (e. g. Hellenkemper 1990). The compartmentalisation of research into the archaeology of the Middle Ages or that of the early modern period has blurred our understanding of the continuity of pottery industries and how they adapted to changes in habit or fashion. Of special interest is the "transitional" period of the 15th to 16th centuries, which has been identified as a crucial era of change in the regional pottery industries of Britain (Dawson 1979; Orton 1982a). According to Orton's model (1985), the phase can be characterised by the introduction of different fabrics, new forms, styles of decoration, advanced kiln technology and potting techniques. The impact of the European Renaissance on the typology and ornament of pottery and tiles at the beginning of the 16th century has been charted in detail by a number of recent studies on slipware (Stephan 1987), maiolica (Wilson 1987) and stove-tiles (Unger ed. 1988; Gaimster *et al.* 1990).

This "revolution" has also been evident in the changing technology and typology of pottery made in the Rhineland from the beginning of the 15th century onwards (Gaimster 1988a). However, an understanding of the tempo and geographical extent of these changes has not existed until now. The same lack of information has hampered the study of the regional ceramic transition between the end of the post-medieval period and the early phases of industrialisation. The timing of the introduction of mass-produced wares and their replacement of indigenous "craft" products has long been the subject of discussion in NorthWest Germany (Lehnemann 1978; Gaimster 1986a). The selection for study of the period 1400 to 1800, therefore, covers both the beginning and the end of a crucial phase of development in ceramic production and consumption in the Rhineland.

The rich archaeological sequence and type-series of ware-types established at Duisburg have enabled a regional survey of the period 1400 to 1800 to take place. The period of study has been selected with a view to discussing some of the most pressing questions of ceramic typochronology and interpretation in the Rhineland (Gaimster *et al.* eds 1988). International interest in the Rhenish ceramics of this period have also played a role in the chronological focus of the project (see Section 1.2.7).

### *1.2.4 Area of study: excavations and collections in the region*

The quantity of information available places a strict limit on the area which can be examined, but the region must be of sufficient size to highlight variations on an inter-site level. The very scale of such a survey, however, imposes limitations upon its scope. Methods of data collection must be tailored to the demands of a regional survey as opposed to the specifications of individual excavations.

The decision to expand the study of the Duisburg assemblages from the town itself to its hinterland originated from the need to interpret the Duisburg sequence in the context of regional ceramic trends. The emerging picture of pottery supply and demand in Duisburg required calibration by comparison with available sequences in the region. In turn the Duisburg type-series could be used to refine the chronology and define the wares found on hinterland sites. Thus, more advanced interpretational questions could be asked of the site specific data and refined by inter-site comparisons.

The situation of production sites and the location of excavations and casual finds has determined the extent of the region to be examined here (Maps 1 & 2). The core site of Duisburg is surrounded by a number of urban and rural consumer sites in its immediate hinterland. Immediately to the north-west lie the earthenware production sites of the Lower Rhineland. Upstream on the Rhine and to the West of Cologne lie the main stoneware centres. The geographical extent of the survey coincides in the main with the cultural boundaries of the Lower Rhine province identified by social geographers and folk historians (Creutz 1924; Scholten-Neess & Jüttner 1971).

Until the early 1980s, few if any major urban consumer assemblages were available for study. Perhaps the most important post-medieval ceramic collections outside Duisburg have come to light in the centre of Wesel (Weber 1988; 1989), which was the senior Hansa trading settlement in the Lower Rhineland (Prieur-Pohl 1989). The latrines, wells and refuse dumps from the *Magermannstraße* site have provided the basis of inter-site comparative studies (Müller 1988). The large-scale excavations in Neuss have proved equally useful for this purpose (Hupka 1988; 1989). The emerging trends are now being supplemented by rescue work in Düsseldorf

(Becker & Siegmund eds 1990) and Bonn (Kesselring-Poth 1988; 1989). At long last the systematic recording of kiln sites in Cologne (Neu 1990) is supplementing the collections of casual finds from the city. The above sites have all been sampled for the purpose of this study in accordance with a sampling strategy (Cherry *et al.* eds 1978) designed to yield the maximum of comparative data from a wide geographical area (Section 2.2).
Assemblages of post-medieval pottery from rural consumer sites have been provided by excavations at Haus Gelinde, Rheinberg, and Krefeld-Linn, outside Krefeld. Their analyses have enabled a comparative study of the variability of ceramic consumption in town and country to be attempted.
Thus regional and local trends can be identified by making comparisons between ceramic assemblages from consumer sites. Stratified groups are clearly important for the establishment of a chronological framework, but the Duisburg groups alone would be insufficient to define geographical distributions. Spatial trends, therefore, can only be identified by the mapping of evidence derived from smaller excavations or casual finds occurring over a wide area. Following the work of Jope (1962) and Streeton (1982) both the positive and negative evidence for regional ceramic distribution (in the form of presence and absence tables) are given equal emphasis here.
A full gazetteer of consumer sites sampled in this survey and their respective status and reliability (Sections 2.2.1 & 2.2.2) is provided by the following pottery information tables:

Appendix 1: Stratified and associated groups of pottery from the Duisburg Altstadt (Contexts 1–53)
Appendix 2: Stratified and associated groups of pottery from the Duisburg hinterland and the Lower Rhine sites (Contexts 54–84)
Appendix 3: Published excavation reports from the Lower Rhineland (Contexts 85–95)

### *1.2.5 The establishment of a regional ceramic type-series: macroscopic and chemical characterisation*

Classification is a broad term referring to the general process of ordering material or concepts by placing them in groups or classes. For archaeologists, classification is the procedure for deriving information about the past cultural system. The principle is best summed up by Redman (1978), *"...to describe or explain the archaeological record, we must categorize it into classes in order to recognise the empirical patterns that are reflections of past behaviour"*. Ceramic characterisation is to be regarded, therefore, as a means to an end, rather than as an end in itself. The classification strategy adopted here has been designed to provide the necessary objective data for regional comparative analysis.
A cursory examination of the few published reports of post-medieval pottery found on excavations in the Lower Rhineland (see Appendix 4) will reveal the absence of a standardised means of ceramic classification. This failure has severely restricted the task of assessing the variability of ceramic assemblages on an inter-site level within the region. As Orton (1979) and Moorhouse (1983) have stated, the consistent classification of pottery-types, often by different people spread over a long period of time, is fundamental to the mutual comparability of ceramic assemblages, *"Every medieval [and post-medieval] pot is unique and differs from other similar vessels in its details of shape, decoration and the peculiarities of hardness, texture and the colour imposed during firing. A detailed, individual pot description is therefore of limited value"* (Moorhouse 1983a, 84).
With the recovery of a stratified archaeological sequence in Duisburg (Krause 1989; 1992; 1994b) has come the opportunity to establish a chronologically-ordered type-series of Ware-types and associated forms based on a definable combination of common attributes (see Sections 3.2 & 3.3). The classification system has been employed to conduct a problem-orientated distibutional analysis of post-medieval ceramic variability in the Lower Rhine region.
Using the Museum of London (DUA) reference collection as a model (Rhodes 1977; Orton 1979), the type-series was designed to be consulted in both a descriptive and physical form. The system was designed to characterise regional Ware-types and facilitate the comparative assessment of pottery groups found both within the city of Duisburg and on sites across the Lower Rhineland. A combination of descriptive and physical classificatory systems ensured that maximum consistency in Ware-type identification and characterisation was maintained.
The initial type-series was based on the Duisburg assemblages alone, and has evolved over a period of five to six years to incorporate subsequent material excavated from regional sites. A model for this approach was provided by Cunninghams's regional type-series for the post-medieval pottery of Essex, England, which is based on the Colchester and Chelmsford finds (Cunningham 1985). Where possible the Ware-type definitions have been created with reference to published production-site reports (e. g. Beckmann 1975 on the range of Siegburg fabrics). It is hoped that, with future excavations in the region, the Duisburg type-series will be expanded and the details of individual definitions improved.
The technique of Neutron Activation Analysis (NAA) has been selected to systematise and refine the visual characterisation of fabric-types (Sections 2.3; 4). The sampling strategy was formulated to address specific

questions of Ware-type definition and ultimately to help define geographical sources. The analysis has been orientated from the outset towards tracing ceramic distributional and marketing patterns both in and outside the region.

### *1.2.6 Ceramic group composition: quantification on an intra-site and inter-site basis*

To date, the emphasis of virtually all previous research on the post-medieval pottery of the Rhineland has focussed on particular Ware categories in isolation. The interest in salt-glazed stoneware and native slipware has remained mutually exclusive to the present day (Section 1.1). There has been little, if any, attention paid to the functional and socio-economic relationship between the individual wares in domestic use at any given time. By investigating the proportional composition of archaeological assemblages, this survey seeks to examine the relative importance of pottery types and their respective roles as functional and symbolic media.
According to Blake (1980), *"Relative proportions of pottery types are the only meaningful indicators. Entire asemblages or genuine samples must be collected, studied and stored in both excavation and field survey."*
If ceramics are to be taken as an index of functional and socio-economic trends (*cf.* Redman 1986a; 1986b), then the relative proportions of individual wares, and their respective forms and functional types must be systematically recorded. The ratios of locally-produced wares to imported wares or coarse wares to finewares, are also required to generate socio-economic interpretation. From the detailed analysis of one context or one site (Section 6), the study seeks to examine these variables over a number of sites, both within the same town and on a regional basis (Section 7). Of course, the synthetic analysis can only be conducted if the groups selected for comparison are broadly contemporary, *"This type of synchronic, distributional analysis is at the heart of understanding the functioning of past communities"* (Redman 1986b,14).
All too often in the history of Rhenish ceramic studies evaluations of the social or economic value of individual vessels or groups of wares have been based on small, unrepesentative samples of material. Using the quantified evidence taken from a range of urban and rural sites, the study attempts to present a more objective picture of the changing proportions of pottery types across the region. In this way the diversity of ceramic group composition within and between sites may reflect contrasting habits of pottery consumption among particular households or communities.
The selection of a standard means of ceramic quantification for the purpose of intra-site and inter-site comparison is discussed in Section 2.2.4.

### *1.2.7 International significance of the study*

Thanks to the pioneering work of Gerald Dunning (e. g. Dunning 1968) and John G. Hurst (Hurst *et al.* 1986) the archaeological evidence for the movement of ceramics has become a feature of our understanding of the medieval and later commodity trade in North-West Europe (Davey & Hodges eds 1983). As Dunning has stated (1968, 1), if pottery was not the primary object of trade, at least it was an important component in the cargoes of general merchandise being carried by river and sea transport.
With the evolving complexity and sophistication of shape and ornament during the post-medieval era, the study of traded pottery provides an index of cultural contacts and influences between regions and across international boundaries (Wilson 1987; Gaimster *et al.* 1990). Moreover, the technological impact of the ceramic trade led to the indigenous adoption and adaption of new potting and firing techniques. Perhaps the most dramatic example of the latter was the production of brown stoneware at Fulham, London, by John Dwight in the 1670s (Haselgrove 1990). The forms and decorative repertoire produced by the factory were based squarely on imported stonewares from Frechen in the Rhineland.
Because of their relative distinction from the mass of locally-made wares, imported vessels are often viewed as a vital aid to dating artefactual assemblages. Their relatively longer lifespans as socially curated items (see Section 8.3.4) often leads to interpretational complications. Due to their relative scarcity, on say British excavations, they have also been regarded as indicators of status. As analytical tools, imported ceramics are, therefore, problematic in their own right (Evans 1987), and require urgent reassessment, particularly on a quantitative level.
Stoneware from the Rhineland was exported en masse throughout north-western Europe during the 14th to 18th centuries. In Britain analysis of Customs port books indicates that "stone potts" were imported in their millions from the Dutch and Flemish Channel ports (Haselgrove 1989, note 2). Their distribution in Britain is not confined to coastal ports, however, as examples are to be found on the most modest inland rural site. As we have seen, large assemblages of Rhenish stoneware have been recovered from major urban excavations in Britain, the Low Countries, Scandinavia and eastern Europe (Section 1.1.2). Nevertheless, as an examination of the London evidence has shown (Gaimster 1987a), the overall chronological sequence for Rhenish stoneware on consumer sites outside the core production area continues to depend on comparative, as opposed to independent, dating evidence. Few dated sealed groups of material are available for

study. The inherent bias of variable longevity of use coupled with depositional and post-depositional factors may have produced a somewhat distorted impression of stoneware chronology outside the Rhineland.

It is one of the aims of this study to calibrate the external picture with reference to trends within the core area of production. The data presented here will serve to test the reliability of the combined British, Low Countries and Scandinavian typochronologies and provide a quantitative and qualitative datum-point for questions regarding the economic and social value of Rhenish stoneware during the post-medieval period.

Although not so frequent, slip-decorated earthenware and relief-decorated stove-tiles were also exported from the Rhineland to the Low Countries (e. g. Baart 1988; Thijssen 1989; Dubbe 1963; 1966; 1980; 1987; Clevis & Kottman 1989), Britain (Gaimster 1988c; 1988d; 1989; *et al.* 1990) and Scandinavia (Liebgott 1972; Wahlöö 1976;). For the most part, the primary identification and chronology of these wares relies heavily on the development of a comprehensive type-series of ware-types and forms in the Lower Rhine region itself. Again analysis of their relative social and economic value as exports must be assessed with reference to quantitative analysis conducted in the region. As with the stonewares, the question of their comparative frequency on consumer sites both inside and outside the core production area is a fundamental one. Related to it is the question of differing typologies. Can a repertoire of products for the home market be identified, in contrast to a definable range of export wares?

Finally, one of the most significant aspects of this research project has been the initiation of a programme of Neutron Activation Analysis on samples from the ceramic type-series (see Sections 2.3 & 4). With the creation at the British Museum, London, of an extensive database of samples from the Lower Rhineland, specific attributional work may now be carried out on samples from extraneous locations. So far the database has been used to identify the possible sources of late-medieval to early post-medieval stove-tiles found in Britain (Gaimster 1989; Gaimster *et al.* 1990). This scientific aspect of the project will make a considerable contribution to the study of long-distance trade in post-medieval ceramics.

### *1.2.8 The use of pottery as a historical source*

One of the main objectives of this study is to assess and interpret the variable composition of post-medieval ceramic assemblages from consumer sites in the Lower Rhineland. The resulting information, it is hoped, will provide an insight into socio-economic developments and into the changes in the function of pottery in the region: consumer sites being more representative of past society than production sites which can only provide information about technological and commercial activities.

Ceramics are the most abundant human artefactual remain and, having taken into account a wide variety of intrinsic depositional and archaeological biases, are judged to be the most sensitive to cultural change (Le Patourel 1976; Blake 1980, 8). Variability in the composition of the ceramic record provides a window on the past activities that produced that deposit, *"That is to say, the archaeologist uncovers a single view of the past, and encoded in that image are the many different processes and the very nature of the society that produced it. The challenge to the archaeologist is to decode these very conplex messages from the past"* (Redman 1986a, 103).

The material inventory created by this survey is indeed rich, providing a substantial and quantifiable body of data for regional socio-economic analysis. Of primary interest here is the question of the changing demand for ceramics over time and space, *"Pottery is an elastic consumption commodity because it is inessential and its function can be performed by vessels made in other materials. Its degree of elasticity would depend on its relative price and on taste, custom and other socio-cultural factors, which may have made a necessity of want."* (Blake 1980, 5).

Thus ceramics, at least in the medieval to post-medieval era, perform a vital role as mirrors of material-culture change. With the systematic sampling, classification and quantification of excavated assemblages, questions regarding technological and functional developments, trading mechanisms, refinements in eating habits (*Esskultur*), individual or community wealth, and the general evolution of material comforts (*häusliche Wohnkultur*) may be addressed (Section 8).

Because of the traditional over-reliance on the documentary record in the post-medieval period, ceramics are often relegated to a secondary status and largely viewed as *"paraphernalia of the past"* (Redman 1986b, 11). Work published by ceramic researchers in the 1980s has brought about a transformation in this attitude, and established the pottery record as a key source of information on both everyday life and the organisation of past societies. Using ceramics as the prime information source, this survey aims to provide a contribution to the study of material culture in the Lower Rhine region over the post-medieval period. Selection of contemporary graphical sources provides a framework for the social and functional analysis of ceramics identified in this survey (Section 2.4; Appendix 7).

# 2. Methodology 1: a multi-disciplinary research strategy for the study of post-medieval ceramics in the Lower Rhineland

## 2.1 Introduction

As we have seen, the systematic study of excavated ceramics and associated cultural material can provide an invaluable source of information on many of the socio-cultural and economic aspects of past societies. However, the quality of our interpretations depends ultimately on the nature and reliability of our methodological approaches. The ability to compare archaeological assemblages on an inter-site basis and to identify variability in the data relies heavily on the employment of a standardized classification system and a uniform method of quantification. The procedure for both systems of analyses, designed to examine specific interpretive questions, is outlined below (Sections 2.2.3– 4).

In accordance with a strictly multivariate approach to ceramic analysis (Redman 1978), the basic classificatory and quantitative recording schemes have been supplemented by a series of qualitative systems of analysis designed to increase our understanding of the variability within and between ceramic types. Thus vessel forms have been systematically coded and recorded by illustration in order to identify the relationship between form and Ware-type (Section 2.2.5). A problem-orientated sampling programme by Neutron Activation Analysis was undertaken in order to assist in the chemical characterisation and geographical attribution of ware-types (Sections 2.3; 4). Finally contemporary graphical sources (woodcuts, engravings and paintings) have been employed to provide a historical context for our interpretation of changing ceramic value, function and social habits (Section 2.4; Appendix 7).

The combination of analytical systems described below represent a multidisciplinary approach to the archaeology of post-medieval ceramics in the Lower Rhineland, incorporating taxonomic, statistical, scientific and contextual evidence.

## 2.2 Recording and presenting the information

### *2.2.1 The nature of the sample: evaluation of the excavated evidence*

Before discussing the methodological approaches in detail, it is first necessary to evaluate the nature of the archaeological contexts containing post-medieval pottery in the Lower Rhineland. The total sample of material selected for study in the region comprised of the following related but discrete archaeological sources:

(1) Stratified and associated groups of pottery from the Duisburg Altstadt (51 contexts; Appendix 2)

(2) Stratified and associated groups of pottery from the Duisburg hinterland and Lower Rhine sites (32 contexts; Appendix 3)

(3) Published excavation reports of Lower Rhine sites (12 contexts; Appendix 4)

Total number of discrete contexts: 95

The recording of this material took place periodically between 1985 and 1989. Since 1989 several major assemblages of post-medieval pottery have been excavated in the town of Duisburg and in the Lower Rhine hinterland. Due to the constraints of time and necessary problem-orientation of this pilot study, this related material is being dealt with by another researchers.

Stratified sequences of pottery and sealed groups sampled by this survey (1 & 2 above) were recovered from the following archaeological contexts:

i. Brick-lined latrines 16 % of total of sites sampled

ii. Brick-lined wells 17 %

iii. Pit groups 22 %

iv. Cellar fills 8 %

v. Midden levels/dumps 14 %

vi. Artefact scatters/casual 16 % finds

vii. Others 7 %

A breakdown of the types of sites producing post-medieval pottery in Duisburg is provided by Appendix 1 and by Plan 2, which indicates the distribution of the principal deposits.

In order to assess the reliability of the above site categories for quantification and dating purposes it is appropriate to consider briefly the question of site formation processes in the Lower Rhine urban situation.

The site formation processes responsible for the composition of post-medieval ceramic assemblages in the region are for the most part culturally, as opposed to environmentally, derived (Schiffer 1987, 7), and require assessment before interpretation of the individual context can take place (Millett 1987, 101). The main categories of archaeological context producing reliable (quantifiable) groups of post-medieval pottery are summarised below. The usefulness of statistically unreliable groups of pottery of individual finds is also discussed.

(1) Brick-lined latrines and wells (33 % of sites)

As in other towns and cities of Continental Europe,

substantial assemblages of medieval and later artefacts have been preserved in the fills of disused well and latrine shafts uncovered in the Lower Rhine towns. By way of comparison, they provide one of the main sources of ceramic finds in Lübeck (Falk 1987a; Schulz 1990), Amsterdam (Baart *et al.* 1986) and Bruges (Hillewaert & Verhaeghe 1990). Full descriptions of the construction and dimensions of the Duisburg examples will appear in the final publication, but it is relevant to describe them briefly here. The circular shafts are predominantly of brick construction, using a combination of rectangular building bricks and compass bricks (usually for the well head). Occasionally the well head survives, either rectangular or circular in plan. In excavation they reveal a series of stratified levels containing domestic debris, cess deposits, building rubble and layers of sterile soil. Commonly waterlogged, their fills provide a *"natural preservation laboratory"* (Noel Hume 1989, 10) for a wide range of domestic refuse (organics, ceramics, glass).

The shafts were either built as wells or from the outset as latrines. Usually the well shafts are narrower, their original purpose to provide a water supply only. With a high water table due to the proximity of the Duisburg Altstadt to the Rhine, wells were sunk within the boundaries of the town's tenement blocks. Latrines were either disused well shafts or were purpose built, usually with a greater diameter. The spatial relationship of both features to the residential topography of the town make them an invaluable source of information about the social and domestic life of a particular community or household (*cf.* Lübeck situation in Falk 1987b).

In Duisburg, as in Lübeck (Hahn 1980; Falk 1983, 35), well shafts containing post-medieval pottery date from the Middle Ages. The earliest fill containing post-medieval pottery dates from the 15th century (Context 22; see Appendix 2). It is possble that the disuse of wells in the centre of the town coincided with the continuous displacement of the Rhine during the later Middle Ages (Krause 1990b), which in turn lowered the water level. When the wells ceased to serve their original purpose they became convenient repositories for household waste.

The sequences recovered from disused wells and purpose-built latrines in Duisburg cover a 400-year period, the uppermost fills dating to the late 18th century. However, the nature of the deposits suggest that the process of refuse disposal was carefully managed during this time (*cf.* Noel Hume 1989, 31). Many of the latrine and well levels contain virtually complete services of both finewares and coarseware pottery, which suggest the wholesale clearance of unwanted goods rather than the accumulation of day-to-day refuse (c. f. London situation: Vince 1981a). The resulting strata represent a series of discrete "episodes" of disposal, as the shafts appear to have been cleaned out on a regular basis, or at least on a number of occassions. The presence of redeposited material in the stratigraphical sequence provides evidence for the periodic excavation and refilling of the shafts (*cf.* the situation at Aldgate, London in Thompson *et al.* 1984; at Lübeck in Falk 1987b, 22). Thus the lower levels dating from the 15th century may not be completely representative of the original sample. Moreover, the relative scarcity of 16th-century finds from Duisburg (in comparison to the much larger 17th-century assemblages) possibly reflects a more rigorous policy of waste management at this time.

Nevertheless, the ceramic assemblages recovered from the Duisburg shafts are consistently well stratified and the discernible levels chronolgically homogeneous. During sorting and reconstruction of the vessels no ceramic "cross-fits" (Brown 1985) linking separate levels were observed. So far the contexts excavated have provided large samples of material, the individual strata representing a single phase of disposal (Noel Hume 1989, 31). Their survival in well and latrine shafts has prevented their further fragmentation and facilitated the reconstruction of a majority of vessel profiles. Crucially, the high degree of vessel completeness has enabled quantification to be undertaken by minimal vessel count (Section 2.2.3).

(2) Pit groups (22 % of sites)

Basic rubbish pits comprise the other major category of context for post-medieval pottery on Lower Rhine consumer sites. Pits were dug within tenement boundaries in Duisburg to fulfil the periodic need for domestic refuse disposal or were dug to facilitate the construction of well or latrine shafts. The latter are discernible as rubbish fills surrounding the surviving shaft heads.

The relatively small dimensions of the pits and their chronologically homogeneous fills suggest that the contents represent a single "episode" of disposal or at least a short phase of assemblage formation. Consequently the possiblity of contamination by redeposited material is limited. Many of the Duisburg groups represent the ceramic lifespan of a single generation (e. g. Context 14) or even shorter timespan (e. g. Context 41).

(3) Cellar groups (8 % of sites)

A less frequent, but no less reliable, source of post-medieval pottery were cellar fills of residential buildings. Usually the most convenient and accessible spot, domestic cellars were often filled with household rubbish.

In the case of the Innenhafen site in Duisburg (Context 38) the fill overlying the cellar floor represents the slow accumulation of domestic refuse over a 75 to 100-year period. At Krefeld-Linn (Contexts 60-61) the excavation of a sequence of sealed cellars in the basement of a residential house (Reichmann 1988) has revealed two entire ceramic inventories destroyed by separate floods in the 18th century.

(4) Midden levels/dumps (14 % of sites)

In any urban situation deliberate dumps of household rubbish or middens representing the slow accumulation of domestic debris are key contexts for ceramic finds. Frequently, however, their formation timespan is considerable, allowing for their contamination by successive phases of partial removal and redeposition.

Many of the Duisburg groups cover extended timespans; the dumping levels against the perimeter walls of the Minoritenkloster site (Context 36), for example, contain a sequence of pottery covering a century or more.

An associated problem is the relatively heavy fragmentation of the ceramic assemblages from these contexts. The breakage rate suggests the presence of substantial groups of redeposited material, and requires specific strategies for their quantification (Section 2.2.3).

(5) Artefact scatters/casual finds (16 % of sites)

Artefact scatters and provenanced casual finds have also provided useful comparative material from town sites. Even the positive or negative composition of small groups of material or individual chance discoveries can be of considerable significance for distributional studies within a region (Streeton 1982, 25).

### *2.2.2 Dating the groups*

An understanding of the changes in post-medieval ceramic production and distribution in the Lower Rhine region depends ultimately on the establishment of a workable chronology of wares. It has become increasingly clear that an understanding of ceramic chronology in this region particularly relies not on inferences drawn from typological or stylistic classification but on the systematic analysis of archaeologically derived groups of artefacts.

The need for a chronological framework applicable both to closely dated groups and other less clearly defined assemblages is paramount. The establishment of a regional typochronology of ware-types and associated vessel forms is the cornerstone of all comparative analysis and historical interpretation. In order that comparative analysis of ceramic variability can take place on an inter-site basis, it is essential to establish the broad contemporaneity of the relevant assemblages. The emphasis must be on dating groups of pottery rather than the component types in an assemblage (Blake 1980, 8; Millett 1987, 99).

With the absence so far of a regional dendrochronological curve and the inability of thermoluminescence dating to operate within the narrow timespan of the post-medieval period (Gaimster 1992), the methods used to date the ceramics collected during the course of this survey are based upon interpretation of their stratigraphical context, analysis of the composition of the assemblage, comparison with groups for which a date-range already exists and on the rigorous examination of the pottery sherds themselves. Thus the chronological sequence of post-medieval pottery found in the Lower Rhineland is essentially relative, and derived from intensive comparative analysis and cross-dating between a maximum number of groups both within the town of Duisburg and in the region as a whole. The result is an aggregate date range for individual ware types based on the combined evidence from several sites (see Diagram 1). Vital datum points in this process were provided by:

i. Coins
ii. Dated vessels
iii. Datable imports
iv. Comparable shipwreck finds (Appendix 6)
v. Marked vessels (factory marks etc.)
vi. Vessels containing coin-hoards
vii. Documentary site evidence
viii. Typological analysis

(1) Coins

Coins were recovered from only a small number of contexts during the course of the survey (Contexts 1, 78). They were easily identifiable and provided a useful *terminus post quem* date for their respective deposits. However, it is clear by looking at the pottery contained within the two pit groups concerned that the deposits began to form significantly earlier than the dates of the coins. In the case of Context 78 the coin date appears to coincide with the terminal date of the group. Thus the coins are employed more as confirmatory evidence for relative dating.

(2) Dated vessels

Dated examples of stoneware, slipware and tin-glazed earthenware, are much more frequent, providing another source of *terminus post quem* dating for individual deposits. In the case of clearly stratified latrine or well shafts, the presence of dated vessels within the individual levels has provided crucial *terminus ante quem* evidence for the stratigraphically earlier deposits. The dating potential of vessels bearing dates must be qualified, however. Their reliability depends on the nature of the ware concerned.

Applied relief moulded dates on Rhenish stoneware must be treated with extreme caution (Hurst *et al.* 1986, 5). The mould matrices used for the application of medallions, cartouches or decorative panels were used very often by several generations of potters working at the same workshops. The dates pressed into the individual matrices indicate the date of mould cutting itself and do not necessarily reflect the date of manufacture of an individual vessel. Dated matrices of the 16th century were still available for reproduction purposes during the 19th century (Section 1.1.2). The longevity of stoneware moulds is a problem which continues to hamper stylistic dating schemes (Hausmann 1973).

Recent excavations at Siegburg, however, have uncovered one of the main potting workshops in the town which was destroyed by fire in 1588. The matrices recovered from the destruction horizon bear dates covering the period 1567 to 1586, indicating that dated moulds were only in use at this workshop for a period of ten to twenty years. Statistical analysis shows that the majority of matrices were produced during the 1570s and 1580s (Ruppel 1991b; Gaimster 1997, 166-167). The overall impression from the site is that the relief decoration of products made by the workshop was kept relatively up-todate. Judging by the evidence it may be assumed that dated stoneware vessels have a fluid production date covering a maximum of twenty years. Nevertheless, the dated relief decoration is an important *terminus post quem* indicator for the production date of individual vessels. In other words, the pot could not have been made any earlier than the date on the applied relief.

Slipware dates are much more accurate indicators of vessel chronology as these dates could not be "reused" in this way and are much more likely to reflect a contemporary date of manufacture (Hurst *et al.* 1986, 5). Unlike the contemporary dated display wares (*Zierschüsseln*: see Scholten-Neess & Jüttner 1971; Bartels 1988), it is unlikely that the dates painted on utilitarian post-medieval slipware were historically commemmorative.

(3) Datable imports and shipwreck finds

The presence of Oriental porcelain and Netherlands tin-glazed pottery on consumer sites in the Lower Rhineland has also benefited the construction of the regional chronological sequence. Recent studies of the latter category by Korf (1981), van Damm (1982) and Baart *et al.* (1990) have assisted with the comparative dating of the Lower Rhine assemblages containing groups of tin-glazed earthenware. Moreover, of all the ware categories found in the region, Oriental porcelain has emerged as a key dating aid by virtue of its presence on dated shipwrecks (Appendix 6). The ubiquitous presence of Rhenish stoneware on shipwreck sites dating from the 16th to 18th centuries has also formed an important framework for estimating vessel lifespans (e. g. the Bartmann-type jug from Frechen; see Appendix 6; see Gaimster 1997, chap. 3.6).

(4) Vessels containing coin-hoards

A significant number of post-medieval vessels containing coin-hoards have been discovered in the Lower Rhine region (Hagen 1937; Gaimster 1987a, note 32), in the neighbouring Netherlands (Sarfatij 1979) and in Denmark (Liebgott 1978). They provide a valuable cross-section of dates for both Rhenish stoneware and lead-glazed earthenware forms, although it is necessary to realise that the end-date of the hoard is often unlikely to coincide with the production date of the vessel. A lengthy timelag is to be expected in view of the long-term accumulation of many of the hoards recovered from the Lower Rhine region (Hagen 1937, 177). In many cases a rough date of final deposition can be calculated from the extent of wear on the chronologically-latest coin. Near-mint coins suggest the contemporaneity of inclusion in the hoard and the episode of deposition.

Sarfatij has summarized the complexed problems of dating ceramics used to despose of coin hoards (1979, 492–495). It has been recognised for some time that the deposition date of a hoard provides a *terminus ante quem* date for its vessel container (Lobbedey 1968). However, this date is dependent on the close contemporaneity of the individual components of the hoard. The period of hoard accumulation is determined by the nature of the hoard itself: i.e. the "catastrophe hoard", "trading-hoard", "bullionhoard" or the "savings-hoard". The lifespan of the first two types of assemblage is likely to be shorter than the latter two hoard-types, and will therefore provide a more reliable dating indicator for the pot. However, the problem stll arises when a vessel is already of a considerable age when used to dispose of the hoard. In short, the dating of ceramics by their contents requires an intensive study of individual coin dates, wear and tear of coin surfaces, and an evaluation of the likely contemporaneity of the vessel concerned. The scope for error is substantial, with the result that ceramics containing coin hoards can be relied on to provide only the most general dating information about specific form-types.

(5) Marked vessels

Factory marks on post-medieval ceramics are rare in the region , but are a consistent feature of English (Staffordshire) export products, such as the Black Basalt teapot found in the centre of Duisburg (Gaimster 1987b). The painted marks on early 18th-century Dutch faience from Duisburg are equally significant, and specify which factory was responsible for their manufacture and when (e. g. Context 18).

(6) Documentary site evidence

Site-specific documentary information is also a rewarding source for context dating. The two cellar assemblages from Krefeld-Linn (Contexts 60–61) are dated to the periods 1700–1740 and 1740–1784 respectively by documented flooding episodes. Destruction levels, dated by documentary evidence are a vital source of chronological evidence in the region. The destruction of the potting communities at Siegburg during the Cologne War (Truchsessischer Krieg 1569-1605) in 1588 has enabled archaeologists to establish a terminus date for the substantial waster deposits recently excavated from the Knütgen family workshop in the town (Ruppel 1991b; Gaimster 1997, 166-167). The vessels, mainly with applied dates, will provide a datum point for the chronology of assemblages containing Siegburg wares throughout the region. The results of these latest discoveries have been assimilated into the chronological scheme attempted here.

(7) Typological analysis

Finally, with the large body of material available for study, the comparative framework for the dating ceramics in the region has relied to a large extent on typological analysis. In this way comparison of the variability of vessel profiles and decorative features have been used to establish the contemporaneity of specific wares found in different assemblages.

The relative chronology for post-medieval ceramics in the Lower Rhineland has enabled a majority of groups to be given an aggregate date-range which reflects both the period of manufacture and lifespan of individual vessel types. Thus the date assigned to the individual contexts are a reflection of the "active life" of the vessels which are contained within it, and do not take into account the "rubbish life" of the group covering the point of breakage to final deposition (Orton 1982). These site formation processes have been discussed in section 2.2.1, and it is clear that each context had a variable "rubbish life" prior to the final deposition or sealing episode. However, as we have already seen, the majority of latrine, well and pit group deposits contain a large number of nearly-complete vessls and display little evidence of degradation or long-term fragmentation. It may be assumed, therefore, that the "rubbish life" of the urban assemblages recorded in this survey was relatively short. The pottery evidence itself suggests that the final deposition of the majority of deposits was a single as opposed to a series of episodes.

Along with the expected problems of site formation processes, the assigned date-range of a group of pottery may also be influenced by the presence of culturally residual or socially curated items which enjoyed an artificially extended lifespan or "active life" (Brown 1988). The problem is particularly acute when using highly decorated wares, such as Netherlandish maiolica or Oriental porcelain, to provide dating evidence for an assemblage of coarse or local wares. The relative active lives of both types of pottery must therefore be evaluated before a combined date-range for the assemblage can be established. This factor will be discussed in more detail in Section 8.3.4.

### *2.2.3 Classification of the pottery*

From the very outset of the project it was clear that to conduct comparative ceramic analysis on an inter-site basis or even between assemblages from the same site, it would be necessary to develop a standard system of classification (*cf.* Orton 1977; 1979). It was essential that the procedure employed was consistent so that the data could be checked at a later date and so that researchers working on pottery in other parts of the region could compare their data using the same system of ceramic characterisation. The construction of a standardised system is also an automatic task to be undertaken before the quantitative analysis can take place and must be designed with this in mind (Redman 1986, 12).

In order to maximize the interpretational potential of the quantification analysis, the ceramics collected during the course of the survey were classified in a multidimensional way, each dimension reflecting separate technological or behavioural information. The process of classification has been designed from the outset to satisfy pressing research questions regarding the variability of ceramic attributes through time and space. The primary categories selected for classification were:

i. Ware-type (incorporating fabric, surface treatment and decoration among other variables);
ii. Form-type;
iii. Functional category.

The methods used in the construction of these classificatory schemes are described in detail in Section 3.2.-4.

### *2.2.4 Quantifying the groups*

The subject of quantification has generated a substantial methodological literature in recent years (Orton 1975; 1980; 1986; Vince 1977; Fletcher & Heyworth 1987 among others). The quantification of archaeological assemblages of pottery is carried out to *"assess the represented proportion, by each type, of the total poulation of the context or site, with a view to comparing proportions of different types between various contexts or sites"* (Fletcher & Heyworth 1987, 35). However, the methods used to quantify ceramic assemblages differ according to the nature of the group or excavational context. It is conducted on the assumption that the ratio of the various type groups within each context is representative of their relationship to the actual populations in the past.

The range of possible methods have been summarised by Blake & Davey (1983, 24) and their various advantages and disadvantages assessed by Orton (1975; 1986) and Fletcher and Heyworth (1987). They include:

i. Sherd count;
ii. Sherd weight;
iii. Minimum number of vessels;
iv. Vessel equivalents.

According to Orton (1986) "vessel equivalents" offer the greatest versatility for estimating the proportions of vessel types in large assemblages. However, it takes some time to record the information and it is essential that only the most significant groups are selected for comprehensive analysis (i.e. a minimum of 20 EVEs are required to support the complexity of analysis; see Orton & Pearce 1984, 35). This method of quantification would, therefore, be impracticable for a regional survey where the size of assemblages varies considerably from site to site.

Practical considerations dictate that a relatively simple method should be adopted for a regional survey where the data are required for both distributional mapping and statistical manipulation. Sherd counts offer a rapid means of quantifying assemblages irrespective of their size and without the need for sophisticated equipment (as with sherd weight). However, the technique is fundamentally flawed in the analysis of postmedieval ceramics as the primary ceramic body types (earthenware, stoneware, porcelain, creamware) are all characterised by differential breakage rates. Similarly, the weighing of post-medieval ceramics is also influenced by the differential weight ratios of the separate bodies (i.e. several large sherds of creamware may only weigh the same as a single small fragment of stoneware). The contrasting results of different quantification techniques on the same assemblage of post-medieval ceramics are best illustrated by a series of pie-charts showing the relative poroportions of pottery from pit groups in the City of London (Vince & Egan 1981). Here, due to its lightweight and fragile body, the ratio of Oriental porcelain was underrepresented by weight while being overrepresented by sherd count. A similar scenario has been identified among post-medieval pottery excavated in Nijmegen (Thijssen 1985).

For the purpose of this survey, therefore, the technique of estimating the minimal number of vessels was adopted. The method involves examining all the sherds objectively and placing similar sherds which may be from the same vessel together. The minimum number figure is free from bias caused by breakage factors, sherd size and thickness, and ensures that rare or minor ceramic types will also be represented. With the low fragmentation ratio and near-completeness of many of the vessels found within the Duisburg and Lower Rhine assemblages, the process was accomplished with the minimum of difficulty. To ensure the uniformity of the approach (DUA 1984), the author personally conducted the entire sorting process on all sites examined. Following Moorhouse's (1983a) technique of calculating minimal vessel counts, the pottery was laid out in the horizontal and vertical stratigraphical relationship in which it was found. This enabled dispersed sherds from individual vessels to be identified. The data is presented in Appendices 2–4, and analysed in Graphs 1–36.

The technique was selected to take account not only of the number of vessels representative of an individual ware within a context but also to make an accurate count of the vessel forms represented. This twodimensional approach to ceramic quantification (Redman 1986, 12) represents a core element of the survey strategy designed to measure the relative proportions of both wares and vessel forms on an inter-site basis (Brown 1988; Vince 1989). This dual approach was successfully employed by Hayfield (1988) in his survey of medieval ceramic trends in Humberside, England. The quantification of form-types by minimum vessel count within each ware category (Graphs 11–33) has led directly to an analysis of functional category trends (Graphs 34–36). This multivariate approach to ceramic quantification aims to produce a more detailed set of data relevant to the questions being asked and which "more closely reflect the procurement patterns the community" (Redman 1986, 15).

An even more detailed comparison can be made between selected groups using a combination of the minimum vessel count method and another technique. From the outset of the survey, sherd counts were also rigorously kept. According to Egloff (1973) this combination gives an accurate indication of the fragmentation ratio and an understanding of the processes of post-deposition. It also gives a measure of the differential breakage of robust or fragile wares. For the purposes of this study the sherd counts are not presented here, but will be published alongside the minimum vessel counts in the final Duisburg excavation reports.

The choice of minimum vessel counts as the primary means of ceramic quantification was made as a key element of the research strategy designed to examine specific interpretative questions. The nature of the Lower Rhine contexts examined here, with their low fragmentation rates, made it the most suitable method of statistical analysis. Some groups were either too small or too disturbed, however, to make full quantification worthwhile. A minimum vessel count of 10 vessels from each context or site with a running archaeological sequence was identified as a prerequisite for quantitative assessment. Where appropriate, therefore, presence and absence tables of the Ware and form-types recovered are given. The ceramic inventories of published sites, not examined by the author, are also listed by presence and absence tables (Appendix 4). Several midden deposits (e. g. Contexts 36, 45) were too fragmented for minimum vessel estimation, and were therefore subjected to quantification by the vessel equivalents method (EVEs). However, it was not possible using this technique to specifyy the form-types represented among each ware.

The pottery information tables (Appendices 2 & 3) contain the basic quantified data fom Duisburg and the Lower Rhine sites sampled during this survey. Ware-types are listed in their classification order (Section 3) alongside their minimal vessel count, form-types and relative proportions within the group (by % of the total minimum vessel count). The final column lists illustrations of the respective form-types.

### *2.2.5 Pottery illustration strategy*

(1) Conventions

The pottery selected for illustration is shown at 1:4 scale. The conventions used to record coloured decorated pottery are shown in Figure 73. In general the recognised methods of ceramic illustration were followed (Blake & Davey 1983, 42–3).

(2) Selection strategy

Representative examples of vessel types were selected for illustration from each context examined during the survey. They were chosen to illustrate the full range of forms, decoration, and methods of construction. The comprehensive system of pottery illustration conducted during the course of the project was designed to provide the maximum amount of information for detailed typological and functional analysis. The selection was systematic within each group, although the duplication of types from group to group was carefully avoided. The pottery from several contexts was not selected for illustration for this very reason. To ensure a standard approach to the pottery illustrations and a uniform style they were all drawn or supervised by the author.

(3) Layout

The drawings are arranged by ware-type within each context, giving an overview of the typological composition of the group. An attempt was made to identify the most common forms and profiles within each ware. A concordance of pottery illustrations (Appendix 8) contains details of each pot illustrated, including its respective ware-type and vessel form.

## 2.3 Scientific analysis

### *2.3.1 Neutron Activation Analysis: the establishment of a regional database*

It is important to stress that ceramic analysis should be seen as a means to an end, rather than as an end in itself. Pottery characterisation has not developed as a discipline merely in order to categorize a disparate range of material, but has emerged rather as the objective basis for regional marketing and distributional studies (Orton 1980, Chapter 4). Quantification and inter-site comparative analysis depend ultimately on the uniform characterisation of the samples concerned. Central to the economic aspects of production and distribution are the following principal applications of ceramic classification (Blake & Davey 1983, 13):

i. Definition of fabrics;
ii. Identification of kiln sources;
iii. Identification of geological and geographical sources of raw materials.

Most questions can be answered by visual (macroscopic) examination of a ceramic assemblage. Indeed, it would be impractical to expect that all identifications for the purposes of quantification could be based upon the results of specialist analysis. The scientific analysis of pottery fabrics is therefore undertaken principally as a means of objective verification for the groups identified by eye (Aspinall 1977; Streeton 1982). These include material found on consumer sites which has been attributed on macroscopic and stylistic analysis to known production sources.

The nature of the sedimentary geology in the Lower Rhineland has made the visual characterisation and geographical attribution of specific products difficult, particulary in the case of the regional lead-glazed earthenware fabrics (Ware-types Ia.-Id.). In the fabric-break, for instance, red earthenwares found in 15th and 18th-century contexts are optically almost indistinguishable from each other. Consequently much of the subclassification of the regional lead-glazed earthenware depends on the chronological context (3.2.1). Chronologically or geologically diagnostic inclusions are not observable in any of the regional earthenware products.

In view of the inherent problems of fabric differentiation by eye, the attribution of the bulk of Lower Rhine earthenware has relied on the study of decorative treatment (e. g. slip motifs, relief ornament on stonewares and stove-tiles). However, with the emerging evidence that slip motifs and moulds for applied decoration were exchanged or traded between production centres (Sections 5.2.4; 5.2.6; and 5.3 respectively), the ascription of specific products to a known source is becoming increasingly unrealistic. Only scientific analysis can ensure the categorical attribution of decorated wares made in the region.

Following a long period of visual characterisation of the Duisburg and Lower Rhine pottery assemblages (Section 3.1), the chemical technique of Neutron Activation Analysis (NAA) was selected as the most suitable to verify and refine the initial classification (Aspinall 1977). The British Museum Research Laboratory accepted the project as part of its current programme of analyses on Continental post-medieval ceramics (Hughes *et al.* 1991). The project was formulated to complement and exploit the database already collected on the chemical compositions of post-medieval Rhenish stove-tiles (Cowell 1988; 1989; 1990).

It is worth bearing in mind that the fundamental assumption in using such an analytical method for provenance studies is that the potters at one site used as raw material clay which has a "uniform" composition. To distinguish the compositional fingerprint of a particular production centre the variation across one clay source has to be considerably less than the variation between different sources. Assuming the basic consistency of use, the success of this analysis rests on being able to characterise the clay material with sufficient precision to produce an accurate chemical fingerprint. By measuring a fairly large number of trace elements it has been shown to be possible to characterise clay types more effectively than by concentrating on the major elements. With the definition of statistically defined values for pottery from one clay source, pottery with chemical compositions "outside" such a group would be judged to come from another source.

The sampling strategy was deliberately problem-orientated towards examining similarities and differences in the chemical compositions of the lead-glazed earthenwares (Ware-types Ia.-d) recovered during the course of the survey. A principal objective was the assessment of fabric variability within recognised Ware-types in order to clarify whether they come from one or a variety of sources. Material from both production and consumer sites was collected with the aim of attributing the latter finds to their respective origin. Finally, specific questions regarding the chronological development of certain Ware-types were addressed by comparing samples throughout the ceramic sequence. The Duisburg excavations provided the majority of samples but material was collected where possible from consumer sites across the region so that distributional patterns could be tested and refined. A detailed resumé of sample size and rationale behind the analytical strategy employed is provided by section 4.1.

The identification and attribution of stonewares found in the region did not present such an acute degree of difficulty, and were not analysed during the course of this programme of research. The chemical characterisation of Rhenish stoneware has formed the subject of a separate but complementary research programme underway at the British Museum (Gaimster & Hook 1995; Gaimster & Hook 1997).

### *2.3.2 NAA Methodology*

Adequate descriptions of the technique of Neutron Activation Analysis (NAA) are given elsewhere in the literature (Tite 1972; Aspinall 1977). Nevertheless, it is worth giving a brief summary of the particular method of analysis used by the British Museum Research Laboratory. Full details of the Museum's sampling and analytical proceedures are published elsewhere (Hughes *et al.* 1991). The same procedure has been used for previous analyses of medieval tiles (Leese *et al.* 1986), post-medieval Italian maiolica (Hughes 1991) and British finds of post-medieval Rhenish stove-tiles (Cowell 1988; 1989; 1990) and stoneware (Gaimster & Hook 1995; Hook 1997).

i. Sampling

Samples, weighing 50 to 100 mg are removed from the pottery by means of a tungsten-carbide drill bit, the nature of the metal sampling tool chosen to reduce the risk of contamination. The same tool is used throughout the project to ensure the uniformity of sampling. Prior to packaging for irridation the powdered samples are stored in glass vials and dried for several hours at 110° C. Included in each batch of ceramic samples are five samples of a pottery standard, and one or two samples of other standards treated as unknowns, which serve as a check on the analytical accuracy and ensure continuity between irradiation batches. Once the samples have been taken, the analytical technique then proceeds to activation, counting and spectrum processing.

ii. Activation

The samples are irradiated for about 24 hours with neutrons at a nuclear reactor. The neutrons, which interact with the atomic nuclei of the elements present in the sample, form radioactive isotopes.

iii. Counting

The radioactive isotopes decay, emitting gamma rays whose energies are characteristic of the particular element which has been activated. The values of these are counted and the resultant spectra transferred to magnetic disc storage for subsequent processing. Two counting cycles are employed: one of 3000 seconds for the short-lived isotopes immediately after the return from irradiation, and the second of 6000 seconds for the longer-lived isotopes about 18 days after irradiation.

iv. Manipulation & presentation of the data

Spectrum processing is carried out using a series of four computer programs which collect and deconvolute each spectrum and isolate peaks, calibrate and finally calculate concentrations. The results of the neutron activation analysis are run into a computer database file in preparation for multivariate statistical analysis. Values for 14 trace elements analysed in the spectrum are listed in Table 1.

In order to interpret the data, a number of samples are grouped according to a probabilistic matching strategy and their values subjected to cluster analysis using the CLUSTAN package (Wishart 1978; 1982). The rationale for analysing particular groups is discussed in Section 4.1. The general relationships of the analysed data are presented graphically in a series of two-dimensional principal components plots (Diagrams 2–6), recognised as the most convenient means of displaying multivariate data (*cf.* Cowell 1989; 1990). Each plot reduces the data to give an indication of of the degree of similarity between individual samples and clusters. Samples which plot closely together have similar compositions; those that plot futher away from each other suggest different trace-element values. In other words, pottery which is made of the same clay would be expected to cluster together, while pottery from a variety of sources would be expected to form separate clusters.

## 2.4 Contextual analysis

### *2.4.1 The use of contemporary graphical sources*

The use of contemporary graphical sources for providing additional information about historic pottery was first demonstrated in a major way by Rackham (1926; 1939) when he used illuminated manuscripts and paintings to identify and date Spanish Lustrewares and 15th-century South Netherlands maiolica. In recent years there has been a growing emphasis on the use of contemporary graphical sources, such as paintings, engravings and book illustrations, to provide a chronological, socio-behavioural and functional context for medieval and later ceramics, glass, metalwork and other media in North West Europe (Grimm 1984). The aim is to achieve a systematically more contextual approach to material culture studies in the historical period (Hodder 1986, 118–121, 141).

The primary sources available to us are (1) the 15th to 17th-century interiors from the Low Countries and Germany, (2) 16th to 17th-century genre painting (scenes of everyday life) from the Low Countries and (3) 16th to 18th-century still life paintings from the Netherlands and Germany. Very often the sources are dated by the painter and provide an additional insight into the respective lifespans of particular vessel types (*cf.* Brongers & Wijnmann 1968 for post-medieval glass studies). Some inherent problems exist, however, with the interpretation of historical graphical sources and with their validity as chronological indicators (Grimm 1984; Schneider 1989). These factors will be addressed in the general discussion in Section 8.

Over the past few decades a series of important studies, exhibition catalogues and monographs have appeared providing a rich resource for contextual archaeological research. This has been systematically consulted during the course of the research project to provide a historical basis for the socio-economic and functional analysis of the Lower Rhine pottery assemblages. Questions regarding the evolution of eating habits, domestic living standards, the status of ceramics within the household in relation to other materials and the nature of the link between social status and ceramic procurement have all been addressed with the aid of contemporary sources. Specific queries regarding ceramic function and the location of individual wares within the domestic interior (i.e. in the dining, kitchen or storage areas) have also been illuminated by referring to their respective graphical context.

The iconographical resource relevant to the post-medieval pottery of the Rhineland and its imported wares is immense, and it is beyond the scope of this survey to itemize every example. Therefore, only a selection has been cross-referenced here. The following studies of painting schools, genres and of individual artists have proved the most useful during the course of this project. Museum catalogues containing individual paintings were also consulted but are not listed separately. Individual paintings, prints etc. containing post-medieval pottery relevant to the study are listed in Appendix 7. Ware-types recognisable in the following sources include lead-glazed earthenware, salt-glazed stoneware, Netherlandish maiolica and Oriental porcelain.

(1) 15th to 17th-century interiors (inc. dining scenes, kitchen scenes, living interiors).

i. Sievers 1908 (on Pieter Aertsen)
ii Friedländer 1949; 1956
iii. Strauss 1968 (on stove-tiles)
iv. Thornton 1978
v. Schneider 1979
vi. Haedecke 1983
vii. Philadelphia 1984
viii. Munich 1986
ix. Ghent 1986; Peremens 1986 (on J. Beuckelaer)
x. Moulin 1988
xi. Chatelet 1988
xii. London 1988

(2) 16th to 17th-century genre paintings (inc. market, festival, tavern & peasant scenes).

- i Sievers 1908 (on Pieter Aertsen)
- ii. Grossmann 1973 (on Breughel)
- iii. London 1976
- iv. Klinge 1982 (on Adriaen Brouwer & David Teniers The Younger)
- v. Philadelphia 1984
- vi. Ghent; Peremans 1986 (on Joachim Beuckelaer)
- vii. Bosing 1987 (on Hieronymus Bosch)

(3) Still Life painting from the Netherlands & Germany, 16th to 18th centuries

- i. Bergström 1956
- ii. Spriggs 1966 (on Oriental porcelain)
- iii. Erichson-Firle & Vey 1973
- iv. Münster 1980
- v. Segal 1983; 1988
- vi. Dresden 1983
- vii. Grimm 1988
- viii. Schneider 1989

# 3. Methodology 2: a ceramic type-series for the Lower Rhineland

## 3.1 Introduction: the classification of wares

### *3.1.1 The characterisation of ware-types*

In all 60 discrete "wares" or pottery types were identified during the course of this survey of post-medieval ceramic assemblages in the Lower Rhineland. They have been grouped into the following primary ceramic body categories, reflecting the nature of their technology (Bauer *et al.* 1987, 100–101):

- I. Lead-glazed earthenware & slipware
- II. Stoneware (with or without salt-glaze)
- III. Tin-glazed earthenware (maiolica/faience)
- IV. Porcelain
- V. Creamware

Each main class of pottery (I-V) was then subdivided into its constituent "ware-types" (II.1, II.2 etc.). For the larger categories, such as the lead-glazed earthenwares, the wares have been further subdivided by century (Ia–Id) in order to take account of their evident chronological development. Individual "wares" were defined by a combination of fabric, form and decorative characteristics and other related indicators (Celoria 1980, 44). These were:

- i. Fabric characteristics
  Comprising hardness, colour, texture, surface treatment, glaze (see Orton 1979; DUA 1984)
- ii. Representative forms
  For glossary of form-types see Section 3.3
- iii. Decoration
  Slip-decoration, overpainting, stamps, incised patterns, applied relief ornament etc.
- iv. Date range
  Based on relative chronology & other indicators (see Section 2.2.2)
- v. Published comparable material
  References to previously published descriptions of the same ware-type

This scheme is similar in its approach to ceramic classification as a number of published pottery studies, namely by Moorhouse 1982; 1983a; and McCarthy 1979. The aim is to define regional types of pottery by common name, based on the above range of ceramic characteristics and archaeological indicators. These traits, according to Moorhouse (1983, 85), may be used in combination to identify the products of individual regional workshops. The primary objective is to devise a classificatory system which is both repeatable by the ceramic worker on a wide range of assemblages in the region and also reproducible by different workers describing the same charactertistics (Orton 1977; 1979; Blake & Davey eds 1983, 10). As far as possible the ware-type definitions have been constructed with reference to the following recent German and British recommendations for pottery descriptions (see review in Gaimster 1988e):

- i. Erdmann *et al.* 1984
- ii. Bonn 1986
- iii. Bauer *et al.* 1987
- iv. Blake & Davey eds 1983
- v. DUA 1984

The definitions presented in Section 3.2 are shown in their abbreviated form in the manner of McCarthy (1979) and Moorhouse (1982; 1983). Full fabric descriptions of the individual ware-types, including Munsell colour and Mohs hardness readings, will be published in the final Duisburg excavation reports. In the meantime reference sherds used in the formulation of this type-series are available for examination by pottery workers at the Kultur- und Stadthistorisches Museum Duisburg.

## 3.2 Ware-type definitions

### *3.2.1 Lead-glazed earthenware & Slipware*

Ia. 15th-century Groups

Type Ia.1
Siegburg-type earthenware
Fabric: Hard, yellow-buff fabric with unfused homogeneous matrix. Exterior surface with slightly darker tone or dipped in purple iron-rich wash. Unglazed.
Forms: tripod pipkins, pilgrim horns, deep bowls, bottles, jugs.
Decoration: none.
Date range: c. 1350–1500
Lit: Beckmann 1975, 11 ("weiche Ware"); Heide 1975, Fig. 33; Strunk-Lichtenberg 1975; E. Hähnel ed. 1987, Cat. 123–5,127–128, 343; Hauser 1990, Fig. 7.1.

Type Ia.2
Langerwehe-type whiteware
Fabric: Hard, fine off-white fabric with outer pale cream-yellow or yellowish-green glaze, with a large number of copper green and a few iron flecks.
Forms: tripod pipkins, feeding bottles, beakers, drinking jugs, pilgrim horns.
Decoration: none.
Date range: c. 1400–1475
Lit: Hurst *et al.* 1986, 227–229.

Type Ia.3
Rhenish whiteware
Fabric: Hard, fine to medium coarse chalky off-white fabric, with transparent (pale yellow) & occasionally green speckled glaze.
Forms: tripod pipkins, lids, deep bowls with footrings, small shallow bowls, dripping pans.
Decoration: none.
Date range: c. 1400–1500
Lit: Reineking-von Bock ed. 1966, Cat. 214–215; Mus. Boymans-van Beuningen 1973, Cat. 436 (Cologne find); Gaimster 1988a, Fig. 2, No. 1.; Hurst *et al.* 1986, Cat. 192.

Type Ia.4
Hard-fired whiteware
Fabric: Very hard, almost fused buff-grey fabric, with inclusions standing proud of surface. Interior surface with transparent (yellow) or green (copper-rich) glaze.
Forms: squat cups, porrigers, bowls.
Decoration: occasionally with dense concentric rilling around body.
Date range: c. 1450–1500
Lit: Gaimster 1988a, Fig. 2, No. 2.

Type Ia.5
Coarse whiteware
Fabric: Hard, coarse off-white fabric with quartz inclusions clearly visible in surface. Interior with green (copper-rich) glaze.
Forms: tripod pipkins, jars.
Decoration: single bands of concentric vertical notch rouletting around exterior.
Date range: c. 1400–1450
Lit: e. g. Soffner 1987, Cat. K3.

Type Ia.6
Greyware A
Fabric: Hard, medium coarse reduced fabric, with a uniform grey core and surfaces. Unglazed.
Forms: globular jars, tripod jars, bowls/pancheons with frilled bases and pouring lips, biconical jars with frilled bases.
Decoration: none.
Date range: c. 1400–1475
Lit: cf. for Netherlands: H.L. Janssen 1983a, 171–2; Gaimster 1988a, Fig. 3, Nos. 1–6.

Type Ia.7
Greyware B
Fabric: Hard, medium coarse reduced fabric, with surfaces blackened in contrast to grey core. Unglazed.
Forms: as Type Ia.6, with addition of small jugs with flat bases.
Decoration: none.
Date range: c. 1400–1475
Lit: cf. for Netherlands: H. L. Janssen 1983a, 171–2; Gaimster 1988a, Fig. 3.

Type Ia.8
Redware
Fabric: Hard, orange-red to red-brown fabric (occasionally overfired with reduced grey core), with fine quartz sand matrix. Thick, transparent (with iron flecks), iron-rich (dark brown to black) to copper-rich (olive green) glaze on interior surface.
Forms: tripod pipkins, pipkins/chamber pots with frilled bases, tripod skillets, deep bowls/pancheons with pouring lips and frilled bases, lids, baskets.
Decoration: tripod pipkins with arcs and blobs of white slip piped on to exterior surface.
Date range: c.1425–1475
Lit: Gaimster 1988a, Fig. 4.

Type Ia.9
Redware (with reduced core)
Fabric: Hard, reddish-brown fabric with rough texture and reduced grey core. Interior with pitted, copper-rich glaze. Bases heavily knife-trimmed.
Forms: tripod pipkins, biconical jars, dripping pans, lids.

Decoration: occasional deep concentric rilling.
Date range: c. 1400–1475
Lit: none.

Type Ia.10
South German (Franconian) earthenware
Fabric: Hard, medium coarse, buff-orange fabric with bright orange core. Unglazed.
Forms: tall biconical jars with flat bases.
Decoration: even concentric rilling around body. Unglazed.
Date range: c. 1400–1500
Lit: Endres & Loers 1981; Brandl 1984a.

Type Ia.11
Redware stove-tiles
Fabric: Hard, coarse, orange-red to light buff fabric (similar to Ib.1), with exterior green (copper-rich) glaze.
Forms: niche-tiles with tracery openings.
Decoration: relief-moulded flange, baldachin and niche ornament.
Date range: c. 1400–1500
Lit: Mielke 1977; 1989; Unger 1983a; 1983b; ed. 1988, Cat. 38–59.

Type Ia.12
Whiteware stove-tiles
Fabric: Hard, coarse off-white to pinkish-buff fabric, with exterior transparent (yellow) or green (copper-rich) lead glaze; quartz sand inclusions often visible on matrix surface.
Forms: niche-tiles with tracery openings.
Decoration: relief-moulded flange, baldachin and niche ornament.
Date range: c. 1400–1500
Lit: Mielke 1977; 1989; Unger 1983a; 1983b; ed. 1988, Cat. 22–29; 38–59.

Ib. 16th-century Groups

Type Ib.1
Redware
Fabric: Buff to pinkish-orange fabric with pronounced quartz inclusions visible on surface; transparent (iron speckled), black-brown (iron-rich) or green (copper-rich) glaze; concentric exterior rilling on hollow wares.
Forms: tripod & flat-based pipkins, pipkins with hollow handles, cauldrons, casseroles, chamber pots, cups, porringers, skillets, pancheons.
Decoration: none.
Date range: c. 1500–1580
Lit: Kommern 1968 Cat. 397; Rotterdam 1973, Cat. 437–8, 440–444; Gaimster 1988a, Fig. 5, Nos. 2–9; Ellison 1981, Fig. 29, Nos. 306–312.

Ib.1i
Polychrome-glazed earthenware
Fabric: as Ib.1
Forms: beakers and drinking jugs.
Decoration: applied decoration occasionally in white-firing clay (laurel-leaf medallions, oak-leaf tendrils) or with overall or zonal encrusted decoration.
Date range: c.1525–1550
Lit: von Falke 1898; Walcher von Molthein 1909; Reineking-von Bock ed. 1966, Cat. 219–221; Hurst *et al.* 1986, 229–337, 358–62 (for encrusted wares); Schilling 1991, Cat. 16–17.

Type Ib.2
Redware with incised decoration
Fabric: as Ib.1. with transparent (with iron speckling) or green (copper-rich) glaze.
Forms: dishes.
Decoration: combed underglaze decoration in concentric wavy bands around the face of the dish.
Date range: c. 1500–1580
Lit: Gaimster 1988a, Fig. 5, No. 1; Schilling 1991, Cat. 11,13,17.

Type Ib.3
Rhenish Whiteware
Fabric: Hard, off-white fabric with prominent quartz inclusions visible on surface; interior transparent (yellow with iron speckling) or green (copper-rich) glaze; occasional concentric exterior rilling & zonal yellow & green interior glaze.
Forms: bowls, porringers, cups, dishes, plates.
Decoration: dishes with combed decoration as Ib.2, bowls, porringers.
Date range: c. 1500–1580
Lit: von Falke 1898; Reineking-von Bock ed. 1966, Cat. 214–215; Hurst *et al.* 1986, 229–337; Schilling 1991, Cat. 9–10,12,14,15,17.

Type Ib.3i
Polychrome-glazed whiteware
Fabric: as Ib.3I
Forms: beakers, drinking jugs.
Decoration: as Ib.1i.
Date range: c.1525–1550
Lit: as Ib.1i.

Type Ib.4
Slipped earthenware
Fabric: Hard, chalky-white to pinkish-buff fabric; with interior white slip under transparent (bright yellow) glaze.
Forms: pipkins with flat bases, dishes.

Decoration: none.
Date range: c. 1550–1600
Lit: none.

Type Ib.5
Lower Rhine Slipware
Fabric: Hard, orange to red-brown fabric with prominent quartz inclusions visible on surface; exterior surface often a darker tone; transparent ironspeckled glaze over slip decoration.
Forms: dishes, porringers.
Decoration: trailed white slip decoration with overpainting in green; occasionally with slip scratched through to create series of dashes or a dotted effect. Motifs include simple botanical designs (e. g. tulips), zoological representations (e.g. cockerels) and geometric patterns (stars and chequer-pattern).
Date range: c. 1575–1600
Lit: Kommern 1968, Cat. 405–6; Gaimster 1988a, Fig. 7; 1991, Figs. 1–2, 3.3.

Type Ib.6
Netherlands Slipware
Fabric: Hard, orange to red-brown sandy fabric with transparent iron-speckled glaze over slip decoration.
Forms: dishes with pulled tripod feet.
Decoration: trailed concentric wavy bands of white slip on face of dish; blobs and dashes of slip on flange.
Date range: c. 1570–1700
Lit: Hurst *et al.* 1986, 154–175; van Gangelen & Lenting 1986; Stoepker 1986, Fig. 68.

Type Ib.7
Redware stove-tiles
Fabric: Range of hard, light to red-brown, orange sandy to light buff fabrics (similar to Ib.1) with transparent glaze over slipped and painted decoration. Most frequently a simple green (copper-rich) or dark brown (iron-rich) glaze. Often a thin white earthenware fabric or slip forming the surface of the decorative panel.
Forms: rectangular panel-tile types.
Decoration: motifs on front panel moulded in high relief; most commonly with a Renaissance-style architectural frame and a variety of allegorical, biblical or figurative subjects.
Date range: c. 1525–1600
Lit: Strauss 1972; 1983; Mielke 1981; Unger 1983a; 1983b; ed. 1988; Gaimster 1989; Unger 1991.

Type Ib.8
Whiteware stove-tiles
Fabric: Range of hard, coarse off-white to pinkish buff fabrics with transparent glaze over slipped and painted decoration; often with overall green (copper-rich) glaze.
Forms: rectangular panel-tile types.
Decoration: as Ib.7
Date range: c. 1525–1600
Lit: as Ib.7

Type Ib.9
Greyware
Fabric: Hard, fine sandy uniformly reduced fabric.
Forms: bowls, dishes, pancheons.
Decoration: none.
Date range: c. 1500–1600
Lit: Bocholt 1987, Cat. 45–46.

Ic. 17th-century Groups

Type Ic.1
Redware
Fabric: Hard, orange to red-brown sandy fabric with transparent iron-speckled, occasionally black (iron-rich) or dark olive green (copper-rich) glaze.
Forms: dishes, bowls, chamber pots, jugs, cauldrons, tripod pipkins (also with hollow handles), tripod colanders, cups, porringers, foot-warmers, lids, storage-jars, skillets, frying pans, lamps.
Decoration: cups and porringers occasionally with bands of horizontal concentric rouletting around upper body.
Date range: c. 1580–1680
Lit: Gaimster 1988a, Fig. 9, Nos. 1–4, 6–15.

Type Ic.2
Redware with incised decoration
Fabric: as Ic.1
Forms: dishes, plates.
Decoration: combed wavy band around interior flange.
Date range: c. 1580–1650
Lit: Gaimster 1988a, Fig. 9, No. 5.

Type Ic.3
Frechen-type Whiteware
Fabric: Hard, refined off-white fabric, with quartz inclusions of uniform size visible on surface. Hollow wares with interior transparent (yellow), and exterior with green (copper-rich) glaze; flat wares with interior green (copper-rich) glaze.
Forms: bowls, plates, dishes, dishes with hollow pedestal bases, tripod pipkins (also with hollow handles), porringers, ointment pots, tripod colanders.
Decoration: dishes and plates with concentric combed wavy bands on face, with lathe-turned spirals in centre.
Date range: c. 1580–1680
Lit: Gaimster 1988a, Fig. 6; 1991, Fig. 4; Jürgens & Kleine 1988, Figs. 10a & b (kiln waste); Clevis & Kottman 1989 29; Schilling 1991, Cat. 1–8.

Type Ic.4
Lower Rhine Slipware
Fabric; Hard, orange to red-brown sandy fabric with transparent ironspeckled glaze over slip decoration.
Forms: dishes, dishes with hollow pedestal bases, bowls with double horizontal handles, porringers, tripod pipkins.
Decoration: trailed white slip with overpainting in green; occasionally with slip scratched through to create series of dashes or a dotted effect. Motifs as for Ib.5.
Date range: c. 1600–1675
Lit: Kommern 1968, Cat. 425–26; Gaimster 1988a, Fig. 8; Gaimster 1991, Fig. 3.1, 3–7; Schilling 1991, 18–43.

Type Ic.5
Werra-type slipware
Hard, red-brown sandy fabric with interior transparent, slightly ironstained glaze over slip decoration.
Forms: dishes.
Decoration: trailed white slip designs with greenish-yellow tinge and sgraffito outlines, overpainted in green, blue and orange.
Date range: 1580–1650
Lit: Hurst *et al.* 1986, 242–248; Stephan 1981; 1986, 85–99; 1987b.

Id. 18th-century Groups

Type Id.1
Lower Rhine Slipware
Fabric: Hard, red-orange to red-brown sandy fabric with transparent glaze over slip decoration.
Forms: dishes, dishes with hollow pedestal bases, plates, tripod pipkins, colanders, jugs, cups, porringers.
Decoration: trailed white slip decoration with overpainting in green and orange. Central panels on dishes contain simple botanical, zoomorphic, figurative or geometric designs picked out in green. Some dishes with regular marbled and feathered slip designs. Flanges with concentric circles, spirals or blobs of white slip.
Date range: c. 1680–1800
Lit: Scholten-Neess & Jüttner 1971; Hackspiel 1982, Cat. Ir.1–9; Gaimster 1986, Fig. 3; Gaimster 1988a, Fig. 10, Nos. 2–5; Frankewitz 1988.

Type Id.2
Lower Rhine Sgraffito
Fabric: as Id.1
Forms: dishes, plates.
Decoration: slip decoration and motifs as Id.1 with outlines in sgraffito, and concentric notch rouletting around flange.
Date range: c. 1660–1700
Lit: Scholten-Neess & Jüttner 1971; Hackspiel 1982, Cat. Ir.10–12; Gaimster 1988a, Fig. 10, Nos. 1–2. Frankewitz 1988, Fig. 20–21; Reichmann 1989.

Type Id.3
Frechen-type Slipware
Fabric: Hard, refined to gritty off-white fabric, occasionally pinkish-buff in break, with transparent (yellow) glaze over slip decoration.
Forms: dishes, plates, chamber pots, jugs, bowls, basins, colanders.
Decoration: combination of trailed brown, orange and blue slip decoration with overpainting in green; interior with overall green (copper-rich) glaze and combed spiral decoration; or with interior overall red slip and trailed white & brown slip motifs. Motifs mainly botanical and geometric.
Date range: c. 1700–1800.
Lit: Gaimster 1988a, Fig. 10, No. 6; Jürgens & Kleine 1988, Fig. 11.

Type Id.4
Redware
Fabric: Fabric as Id.1 with transparent (occasionally with iron flecks), black (iron-rich), or olive-green (copper-rich) glaze.
Forms: jugs, bowls, basins, handled jars, colanders, storage jars, lids, flat-based cauldrons, tripod pipkins, porringers, cheese sieves, kettles, pancheons, baskets.
Decoration: none, but porringers occasionally with interior white slip.
Date range: c. 1680–1800
Lit: Hackspiel 1982, Cat. Ir.13–18, 21, 23, 31–35.

Type Id.5
Redware (reduced core)
Fabric: Hard, sandy fabric with reduced grey break; transparent glaze with patches of thin light green (copper) staining.
Forms: storage jars, cauldrons.
Decoration: none.
Date range: c. 1700–1800
Lit: none.

Type Id.6
Blackware
Fabric; Hard, sandy bright orange-red fabric with overall thick brownish-black to black (iron-rich) glaze.
Forms: jugs, teapots.
Decoration: none.
Date range: c. 1700–1800
Lit: none.

Type Id.7
Refined Blackware
Fabric: Hard, fine, sandy bright orange fabric with

overall lustrous black (iron-rich) glaze.
Forms: jugs, flat-based pipkins with hollow handles.
Decoration: none.
Date range: c. 1700–1800
Lit: Hackspiel 1982, Cat. Ir.22.

Type Id.8
Green-glazed redware
Fabric: Hard, orange-red sandy fabric with exterior green (copper-rich) glaze over white slip and interior transparent (yellow) glaze over white slip.
Forms: tripod pipkins, chamber pots.
Decoration: none.
Date range: c. 1700–1800
Lit: none.

Type Id.9
Staffordshire refined blackware (Jackfield-type)
Fabric: Very hard, refined reduced fabric with overall lustrous black glaze.
Forms: jugs, teapots, sugar-bowls, lids.
Decoration: none
Date range: 1750–1770
Lit: Barker & Halfpenny 1990, 34–35; Barker 1991, 273–4.

Type Id.10
Staffordshire red earthenware (Astbury-type)
Fabric: Very hard, refined red-brown fabric with overall transparent glaze.
Forms: jugs, cups, sugar-bowls.
Decoration: applied sprigging in white clay.
Date range: c. 1725–1760
Lit: Barker & Halfpenny 1990, 23–25; Barker 1991, 271–2.

Type Id.11
Staffordshire Agate ware
Fabric: Very hard, refined marbled red, brown and white fabric with overall transparent glaze.
Forms: sugar-bowls, cups, saucers.
Decoration: none.
Date range: 1730–1770
Lit: Barker & Halfpenny 1990, 31–33.

Type Id.12
Middle Rhine Slipware
Fabric: Hard, sandy pinkish-buff fabric with combination of slip designs under transparent glaze.
Forms: dishes, plates, small bowls.
Decoration: trailed white, brown red, and orange slip motifs (mainly botanical and geometric); or with overall red slip under trailed white, brown and orange slip designs.
Date range: c. 1700–1780
Lit: Döry 1978, Fig. 15; Döry 1988, Fig. 2–3; Kleine 1989, Figs. 5–8 (kiln site material from Eppertshausen, Hesse)

### *3.2.2 Stoneware*

Type II.1
Siegburg stoneware (with iron wash)
Fabric: Fine, fully fused yellowish-grey to light grey fabric with exterior overall purple iron wash.
Forms: drinking jugs (*Trichterhalskrüge*), bottles, jugs, bowls.
Decoration: none.
Date range: c. 1400–1475
Lit: Gaimster 1987a, Fig. 1, No. 4; E. Hähnel ed. 1987, Cat. 135–148, 344–347.

Type II.2
Siegburg stoneware (ash-glazed)
Fabric: Fine, fully fused fabric as II.1, with flamed ash glaze forming characteristic orange-brown patches.
Forms: jugs (inc. *Jacobakannen*), drinking-jugs (*Trichterhalskrüge*), beakers, mugs, drinking-bowls, globular costrels, marbles (games).
Decoration: applied rosette prunts and small medallions in high relief.
Date range: c. 1400–1500
Lit: Klinge 1972; Sarfatij 1979, Cat. 4–15; Stephan 1983; Hurst *et al.* 1986, Cat. 257–263; Gaimster 1987a, Fig. 1, Nos. 1–3,5; E. Hähnel ed. 1987; Ruppel 1991.

Type II.3
Siegburg stoneware (salt-glazed)
Fabric: as II.1, with overall exterior salt-glaze.
Forms: drinking jugs and beakers (*Trichterhalskrüge*), jugs, upturned beakers, costrels.
Decoration: applied and face-masks medallions in high relief, incised geometric and botanical motifs; occasionally with cobalt blue applied under the glaze.
Date range: c. 1500–1600
Lit: Klinge 1972; Reineking-von Bock 1986 (3rd ed.); Hurst *et al.* 1986, Cat. 264–290; Gaimster 1987a, Fig. 1, Nos. 6–9; E. Hähnel ed. 1987; Ruppel 1991.

Type II.4
Siegburg stoneware (unglazed)
Fabric: as II.1, but a uniform clear light buff-grey tone.
Forms: tankards (various), beakers.
Decoration: applied medallions and panels with motifs in high relief, incised geometric designs.
Date range: 1560–1625
Lit: Klinge 1972; Reineking-von Bock 1986 (3rd ed.); E. Hähnel ed. 1987; Ruppel 1991.

Type II.5
Langerwehe stoneware
Fabric: Coarse, gritty dark grey fabric with exterior iron wash under uneven brown speckled salt glaze.
Forms: large storage jars (*Baaren*).
Decoration: applied armorial medallions in high relief.
Date range: c. 1590–1750
Lit: Ohm et al. 1971; Schwarz 1984, Fig. 11; Sielmann 1980, Fig. 5.

Type II.6
Raeren stoneware
Fabric: Coarse to fine dark grey fabric with exterior iron wash under uneven brown to grey salt glaze. In second half of 16th-century wares with uniform exterior iron wash and lustrous salt glaze. End of 16th-century wares in grey stoneware with cobalt blue painted decoration.
Forms: mugs, jugs, chamber pots, spouted pitchers, bottles, ointment pots.
Decoration: applied armorial medallions.
Date range: c. 1475–1600
Lit: Kohnemann 1982; Hurst et al., 1986, 194–208; Gaimster 1987a, Fig. 3.

Type II.7
Cologne stoneware
Fabric: Coarse to fine mid to dark grey fabric, often with a pink or light coloured internal surface. Exterior commonly with overall iron wash and grey to brown salt glaze.
Forms: drinking jugs, tankards, bottles.
Decoration: applied bearded face masks, applied armorial medallions, and sprigged oak leaves or acorns and rose flowers and leaves.
Date range: c. 1500–1550
Lit: von Falke 1899; von Falke 1908; Hurst *et al.* 1986, 208–214; Gaimster 1987, Fig. 5.

Type II.8
Frechen stoneware
Fabric: as II.7; surface with pronounced pitted texture.
Forms: Bartmann-jugs, bottles, chamber pots, handled jars, ointment pots.
Decoration: jugs and bottles with grotesque bearded face masks, applied armorial medallions, occasionally with cobalt-blue painted decoration under the glaze.
Date range: c. 1550–1675
Lit: Göbels 1971; Hurst *et al.* 1986, 214–221; (see Appendix 6 for shipwreck finds).

Type II.9
Westerwald stoneware
Fabric: Fine light grey to cream fabric with uniform grey salt glaze.
Forms: tankards, mugs, chamber pots, jugs, storage jars, porringers, bowls with double horizontal handles, inkstands, ointment pots, terrines, jardinieres, feeding bottles.
Decoration: stamped, incised motifs, and applied medallions and panels. Designs mainly geometic, floral and armorial. Painted in cobalt blue and manganese under glaze.
Date range: c. 1590–1770
Lit: von Falke 1908; Spiegel 1980; Hurst *et al.* 1986, 221–225; Reineking-von Bock 1986 (3rd ed.); (see Appendix 6 for shipwreck finds).

Type II.10
Westerwald stoneware (monochrome teawares)
Fabric: Fine uniform grey fabric with clear salt glaze.
Forms: tea bowls, saucers, teapots, bowls.
Decoration: incised geometric and floral motifs.
Date range: c. 1725–1775
Lit: Reineking-von Bock 1986 (3rd ed.), Cat. 734–9; Spiegel 1980, Fig. 17.

Type II.11
Mineralwater bottles (Westerwald-type)
Fabric: Range of light grey, bluish-grey, grey-brown to buff fabrics with pitted exterior salt glaze.
Forms: mineralwater bottles.
Decoration: stamped medallions bearing initials of spa, ocassionally emphasised with ring of cobalt blue.
Date range: c. 1650–1780
Lit: Brinkmann 1982; Nienhaus 1989a & b; Vliermann & Kleij 1990, Cat. 05/003; (see Appendix 6 for shipwreck finds).

Type II.12
Staffordshire salt-glazed stoneware
Fabric: Fine creamy-white fabric with transparent lustrous salt glaze.
Forms: plates, dishes, bowls, saucers, cups, chamber pots.
Decoration: press-moulded geometric flange designs on plates.
Date range: c. 1740–1780
Lit: Gaimster 1986, Fig. 6, No. 10; Lockett 1982, Cat. 35–52; (see Appendix 6 for shipwreck finds).

Type II.13
Staffordshire Black Basalt ware
Fabric: Refined matt black fabric with extremely thin body; unglazed.
Forms: teapots.
Decoration: sprigged floral designs, engine-turned vertical fluting.

Date range: c. 1780–1810
Lit: Grant 1967; Gunson 1982; Gaimster 1987b.

Type II.14
Staffordshire Red Stoneware
Fabric: Refined matt red stoneware with thin body.
Forms: teapots, coffee-pots.
Decoration: sprigged floral designs
Date range: c. 1750–1770
Lit: Barker & Halfpenney 1990, Cat. 44–49.

### *3.2.3 Tin-glazed earthenware*

Type III.1
North Netherlands maiolica
Fabric: Fine buff fabric; flat wares with interior off-white tin glaze and exterior transparent lead glaze; hollow wares often also with interior tin glaze.
Forms: dishes, porringers, pharmacy jars, tiles.
Decoration: wide range of painted blue and white and polychrome zoomorphic, anthropomorphic, botanical and geometric designs in zones or medallions.
Date range: c. 1560–1660
Lit: D. F. Lunsingh-Scheurleer 1973; Tietzel 1980; Korf 1981; van Dam 1982; van Dam 1988.

Type III.2
Dutch white faience
Fabric: Fine buff fabric; overall plain white tin glaze.
Forms: jugs, tankards, salts, porringers, bowls, dishes (plain & lobed), plates, colanders.
Decoration: none.
Date range: c. 1640–1700
Lit: D. F. Lunsingh-Scheurleer 1970; Baart *et al.* 1990; van Dam 1991.

Type III.3
Delft-type blue & white/polychrome faience
Fabric: Fine buff fabric with overall bluish-wite tin glaze.
Forms: dishes (lobed & plain), plates, tea bowls, saucers, jugs, tankards, bowls, tiles.
Decoration: painted blue and white and polychrome zoomorphic, anthropomorphic, botanical and geometric designs.
Date range: c. 1640–1785
Lit: De Jonge 1970; Andersen 1974, Figs. 7-8; D. F. Lunsingh-Scheurleer 1975; Tietzel 1980; van Dam 1982; (see Appendix 6 for shipwreck finds).

Type III.4
Frisian tin-glazed wares
Fabric: Fine to coarse pinkish buff fabric with interior off-white tin glaze and exterior lead glaze.
Forms: dishes.
Decoration: painted blue and white and polychrome zoomorphic, botanical and geometric designs.
Date range: c. 1700
Lit: Tietzel 1980, Cat. 21–23; Tichelaar 1982.

Type III.5
N. German faience
Fabric: Fine buff fabric with overall off-white tin glaze.
Forms: tea bowls, saucers.
Decoration: painted blue and white and yellow botanical designs picked out in manganese outlines.
Date range: c. 1750–1800
Lit: Lehnemann 1976; 1982; Gaimster 1988, Fig. 11, No. 2.

Type III.6
Duisburg faience (biscuit, trial-piece & waster finds)
Fabric: Biscuit ware a fine pinkish-buff fabric; overall off-white tin glaze.
Forms: dishes, plates, tea-bowls, saucers.
Decoration: painted blue and manganese botanical designs.
Date range: c. 1764–1787 (factory of Johann Gottfried Becker).
Lit: Lehnemann 1982; Gaimster 1988a, Fig. 11, No. 1; Ruppel 1988.

### *3.2.4 Porcelain*

Type IV.1
Chinese *Kraak* porcelain
Fabric: Off-white porcelain body.
Forms: dishes.
Decoration: oriental zoomorphic, botanical, geometric and figurative motifs painted in underglaze cobalt blue.
Date range: c. 1575–1625
Lit: Harrisson 1981; van der Pijl-Ketel 1982; Sheaf & Kilburn 1988; Rinaldi 1989; Jörg 1990; (see Appendix 6 for shipwreck finds).

Type IV.2
17th/18th-century Chinese export porcelain
Fabric: Bluish-white speckled porcelain body.
Forms: tea-bowls, saucers, plates, bowls.
Decoration: oriental figurative, zoomorphic, botanical and landscape motifs painted in underglaze cobalt blue or white enamel; also overpainted with overglaze polychrome enamels (Imari type).
Date range: c. 1675–1775
Lit: Gabbert 1977; Jörg 1982; 1986; Howard 1984, Cat. A4,9,11,19; Sheaf & Kilburn 1988; Wastfelt *et al.* 1990; (see Appendix 6 for shipwreck finds).

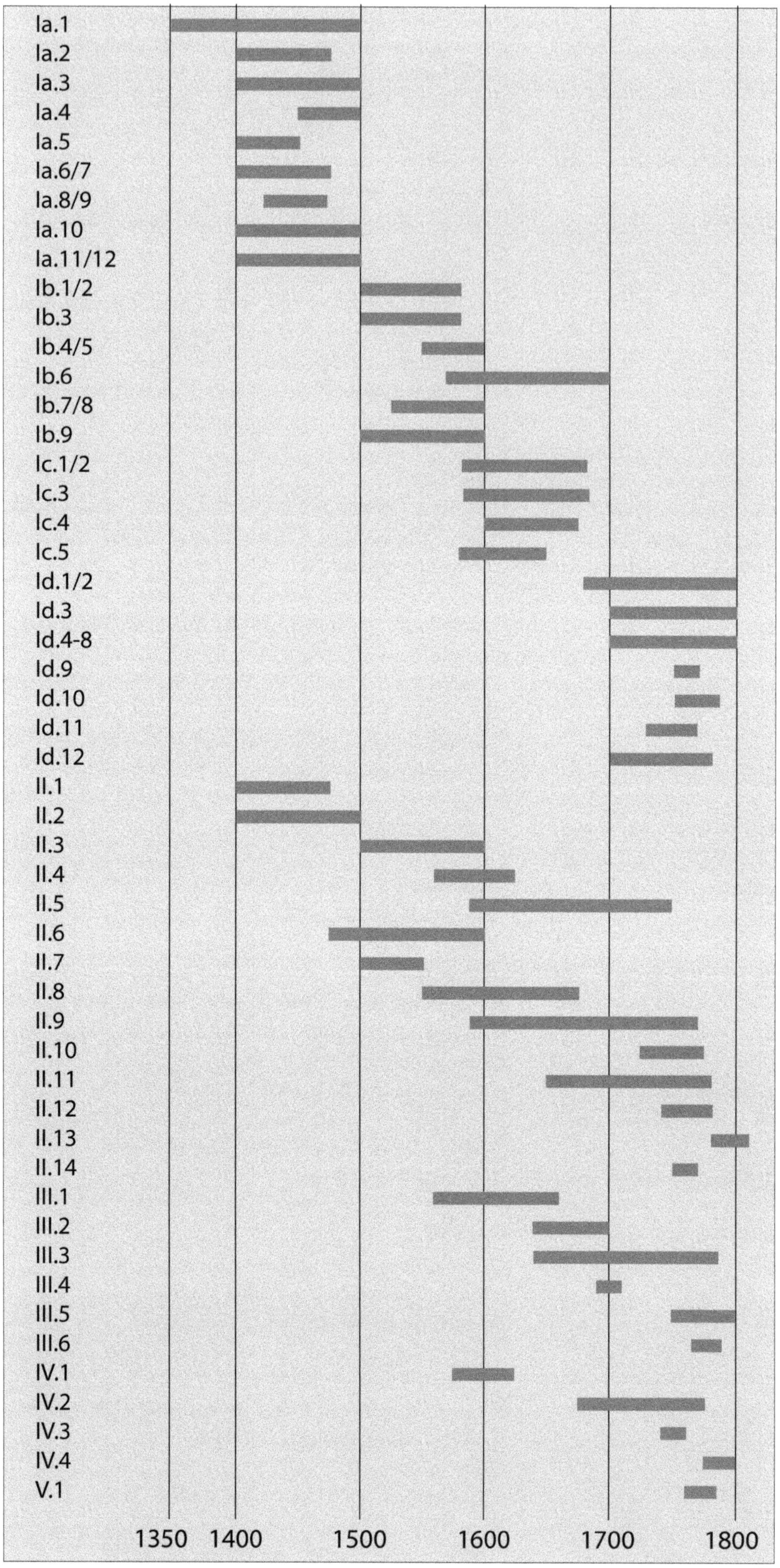


*Diagram 1 Date range of individual ware types*

Type IV.3
18th-century Chinese export porcelain
Fabric: Bluish-white porcelain body; the exterior with overall brown glaze (*Cafe au lait*).
Forms: small bowls, saucers (probably for drinking coffee).
Decoration: blue and white interior motifs as IV.2.
Date range: c. 1740–1760
Lit: Jörg 1986; Sheaf & Kilburn 1988, 144–147; Wastfelt *et al.* 1990; (see Appendix 6 for shipwreck finds).

Type IV.4
German Blue & White porcelain
Fabric: Off-white body.
Forms: cups, saucers.
Decoration: underglaze painted cobalt blue floral motifs (*Strohblumenmuster*)
Date range: c. 1775–1800
Lit: Hahn 1980; Gaimster 1986a, Fig. 7, No. 9; Hamburg 1989a; Röntgen 1989; Falk 1983, Fig. 9.4; 1987, Cat. 149,151–2.

### *3.2.5 Creamware*

Type V.1
Staffordshire creamware
Fabric: Very hard refined cream-coloured fabric with lustrous transluscent lead glaze.
Forms: plates, sugar bowls, saucers, dishes, punch bowls, tea bowls, cups, chamber pots, lids.
Decoration: flatwares with press-moulded floral borders; hollow-wares with flower & leaf handle terminals; colour-glazed wares, and hand-painted overglaze enamel painting.
Date range: c. 1760–1785.
Lit: Lockett & Halfpenny eds 1986; Barker 1984, Cat. 114–142; 1990; Barker & Halfpenny 1990, Cat. 31–70; Barker 1991, 166–262; (see Appendix 6 for shipwreck finds).

## 3.3 The classification of forms

### *3.3.1 Form typology*

The study of medieval and later ceramics continues to suffer from the absence of a standard glossary of vessel form types (Yentsch 1990, 30). The debate between those advocating a functional nomenclature system and those in favour of a more technical approach is familiar to pottery specialists of all periods (Celoria 1980). The problem is particularly acute in the treatment of post-medieval ceramics, where the range and variety of specialised forms expands dramatically through time. By the 18th century, moreover, an entire repertoire of teawares and dinner services had emerged to cater for the latest fashions in eating and drinking. Tradltionally, their terminology is based on individual function (e. g. „teapot“, „punch-bowl“), although this varies enormously from publication to publication and from country to country.
To be effective, a workable glossary must be undertaken at an international level so that the continuing discrepancies in European terminology can be resolved. The forthcoming diagramatic Glossary of ceramic forms in preparation by the Medieval Pottery Research Group (UK) (M.P.R.G. in prep.) will make a significant contribution towards the acceptance of an internationally recognised common reference system. It is also hoped that, once fully developed, the mathematically-based *Envelope* system (Orton 1987) will help to put the methodology of form definition on a more systematic and objective footing.
Until this time a wide range of published typologies for separate ware categories must be used (i. e. for lead-glazed earthenware, stoneware, tin-glazed earthenware, porcelain and creamware respectively). Listed below are the principal schemes employed in the definition of vessel forms at Duisburg and the Lower Rhine sites (3.3.2). The classification of form types (3.3.3 Table 1) is consistent throughout the quantification (Appendices 2, 3, 4) and in the concordance of pottery figure descriptions (Appendix 8).
The three principal German language guidelines for the publication of archaeological ceramics (Erdmann *et al.* 1984, Bonn 1986, Bauer *et al.* 1987) have been consulted here in order to establish a bilingual correlation of the primary form types (e. g. bowl, dish, jug etc.). However, the linguistic correlation of the specialised forms has relied on the individual post-medieval studies specified below (3.3.2)

### *3.3.2 Published typologies*

General systems:
- T. Dexel 1980
- S. Jennings 1981, 233–238 (Glossary of terms)
- DUA 1984; unpublished index of form-type definitions at DUA
- Erdmann *et al.* 1984
- Bonn 1986
- Bauer *et al.* 1987

Lead-glazed earthenware (N. Germany, NL):
- W. Lehnemann 1978, 76–124
- H.-G. Stephan 1980, 1987a
- J. G. Hurst *et al.* 1986, 117–175, 227–267
- W. Hackspiel 1988

Lead-glazed earthenware (Britain):
- F. Holling 1971
- C. Orton & J. Pearce 1984

Stove-tiles:
D. Gaimster, R. Goffin & L. Blackmore 1990

Salt-glazed stoneware:
E. Klinge 1972
G. Reineking-von Bock 1986
J. G. Hurst *et al.* 1986, 176–227
E. Hähnel ed. 1987
H.-G. Stephan 1987a

Tin-glazed earthenware:
C. Orton 1988, 308–318
J. Baart *et al.* 1990

Oriental porcelain:
C. L. van der Pijl-Ketel 1982
C. Sheaf & R. Kilburn 1988

Creamware:
D. Barker 1991

### *3.3.3 Correlation of principal form terms with published typologies*

Table 1 (Terms followed by respective Cat. numbers)

**Lead-glazed earthenware (I)**

| **Form type** | **Lehnemann 1978** | **Hackspiel 1988** | **Orton & Pearce 1984 after Holling 1971** | **Hurst et al. 1986** |
|---|---|---|---|---|
| Dish | *Schüssel* 7.1.4 | *Schüssel* 17-25 | Dish e. g. 42–44 | Dish e. g. 226–229 |
| Plate | | *Teller* 1–11 | | |
| Bowl | | *Kuppe* 52 | Bowl 40–42 | |
| Pancheon | *Aufrahmschüssel* 7.1.5 | *Kuppe* 53 | | |
| Colander | *Durchschlag* 7.1.6 | *Sieb* 35–37 | | Colander 200 |
| Chamber pot | *Nachttopf* 7.1.14 | *Nachttopf* 55 | Chamber pot 48–50 | Chamber pot 203 |
| Beaker | | *Becher* 89–92 | | Beaker 357–361 |
| Porringer | | *Breischüssel* 48–49 | Porringer 47 | |
| Cup | | *Tasse* 44–47 | Cup 67–69 | |
| Drinking bowl | | *Kümpchen* 42 | | |
| Cauldron | | *Grapen* 62 | | Cooking pot 178–187 |
| Casserole | | *Pastetentopf* 122 | | |
| Pipkin | | *Henkeltopf* 54 | Pipkin 4 | Pipkin 188–197 |
| Tripod pipkin | | *Grapen* 63 | Tripod pipkin 1, 10 | |
| Frying pan | | *Pfanne* 31 | | |
| Skillet | | | Skillet 5 | Skillet 198–199 |
| Dripping pan | | *Bräter* 158 | | Dripping pan 201 |
| Storage jar | *Aufbewahrungsgefäß* 7.1.12 | | Storage jar 51–52 | |
| Jug | | *Kanne* 104–112 | | Jug 202 |
| Basket | | *Essenträger* 50 | | |
| Basin | *Waschschüssel* 7.1.13 | | | |
| Oil-lamp | *Öllämpchen* 7.1.17 | *Öllampe* 127 | | Oil-lamp 207–210 |
| Brazier | *Gluttopf* 7.1.15 | *Gluttopf* 56 | | |
| Chafing dish | | *Komfor* 66 | | Chafing dish 104–107 |

## Stoneware (II)

| Form type | Klinge 1972 | Reineking-von Bock 1986 | Hähnel 1987 | Hurst *et al* 1986 |
|---|---|---|---|---|
| Jug | *Krug* 647–650 | *Krug/Kanne* p. 92-97 | *Krug* 82–107 | *Jug* e. g. 102–105 |
| Flagon | *Pulle* 631–642 | *Pulle* 179–182 | | *Pulle* 269–270 |
| Bottle | | *Flasche* p. 95 | *Fußflasche* 135–148 | |
| Beaker | *Becher* 590–607<br>*Trichterhalsbecher* 121–129 | *Becher* p. 94 | *Becher* 262–290<br>*Trichterhalsbecher* 300–307 | Beaker 258<br>*Trichterhalsbecher* Pl. 30 |
| Drinking jug | *Trichterhalskrug* 133–140 | *Trichterhalskrug* p. 101.3 | *Trichterhalskrug* 328–336 | *Trichterhalskrug* Pl. 30 |
| Drinking bowl | *Schale* 211–217 | *Schale* 128 | *Kleine Schale* 236–247 | Bowl 257 |
| Mug | | *Krug* 341<br>*Pinte* 311 | | Small jug 300–301 |
| Tankard | *Schnelle* 314–326<br>*Humpen* 608–617 | *Schnelle* p. 100.8<br>*Humpen* p. 100.10 | *Schnelle* 361–558<br>*Humpen* 589–736 | *Schnelle* 268 |
| Costrel | *Feldflasche* 255 | *Feldflasche* 121 | *Pilgerflasche* 154 | Globular costrel 295 |
| Storage jar | | *Baare* 337 | | |
| Chamber pot | | | | Chamber pot 339–340 |
| Teapot | | *Teekanne* 668–675 | | |
| Tea-bowl | | *Kleine Schale* 736 | | |
| Ointment pot | | *Apothekergefäß* 754–755 | | |

## Tin-glazed earthenware, Porcelain, Creamware (III, IV, V)

| Form type | Orton 1988 | Baart *et al* 1990 | Sheaf & Kilburn 1988 | Barker 1991 |
|---|---|---|---|---|
| Dish | Dish 1294–1302 | *Schotel* 41–50 | | |
| Plate | Plate 1305 | *Bord* 51–57 | Plate Pl. 160 | Plate Fig. 32–33 |
| Bowl | Bowl 1287–1288 | *Oorkom* 70 | | Bowl Pl. 82 |
| Porringer | Porringer 1275–1286 | *Papkom* 64–69 | | |
| Salt | Salt 1289–1293 | *Zouvat* 76–79 | | |
| Jug | | *Wijnkan* 81–84 | | |
| Tankard | | *Bierkan* 31, 85 | | |
| Colander | | *Vergiet* 108 | | |
| Ointment pot | Small jar 1248–1254 | | | |
| Drug jar | Large jar 1257–1264 | | | |
| Tea-bowl | Small bowl 1329 | *Kopje* 121 | Bowl Pl. 137 | Teabowl Pl. IX |
| Coffee-bowl | | | Coffee cup Pl. 150 | |
| Saucer | | | Saucer Pl. 150–151 | Saucer Pl. IX |
| Teapot | | | | Teapot Pl. XX |

## 3.4 The functional classification of form-types

### *3.4.1 Functional typology*

The arrangement of forms according to their presumed purpose (3.3.4 Table 2) is based on the functional classification of the Van Beuningen-de Vries collection of medieval and later pottery at the Boymans-van Beuningen Museum, Rotterdam (Ruempol & van Dongen 1991) and on the functional division of form-types at the Aldgate site, City of London (Orton & Pearce 1984). Functional attribution does not, however, preclude pottery forms being used for a variety of purposes. Jugs, for instance, were used both at the table and in the kitchen. Thus jug forms are listed in both categories. Form types are listed in English with their corresponding German terms (italics) taken from the reports and monographs listed in Section 3.3.2.

The classification has been used to examine the functional composition of pottery groups in Duisburg and a number of Lower Rhine sites (Graphs 34–36).

### *3.4.2 Principal form-types according to functional category*

Table 2

**Tableware**

| I.<br>**Lead-glazed Earthenware** | II.<br>**Stoneware** | III.<br>**Tin-glazed Earthenware** | IV.<br>**Porcelain** | V.<br>**Creamware** |
|---|---|---|---|---|
| A. Eating | | | | |
| Dish<br>*Schüssel* | | Dish<br>*Schüssel* | Dish<br>*Schüssel* | |
| Plate<br>*Teller* | Plate<br>*Teller* | Plate<br>*Teller* | | Plate<br>*Teller* |
| Bowl<br>*Schale* | | Bowl<br>*Schale* | Bowl<br>*Schale* | |
| Porringer<br>*Breischüssel* | Porringer<br>*Breischüssel* | Porringer<br>*Breischüssel* | | |
| Salt<br>*Salzschale* | Terrine<br>*Terrine* | Salt<br>*Salzschale* | | |
| B. Drinking & decanting | | | | |
| Jug<br>*Krug/Kanne* | Jug<br>*Krug/Kanne* | Jug<br>*Krug / Kanne* | | |
| Cup<br>*Tasse* | Flagon<br>*Pulle* | | | |
| Saucer<br>*Untertasse* | Saucer<br>*Untertasse* | Saucer<br>*Untertasse* | Saucer<br>*Untertasse* | Saucer<br>*Untertasse* |
| Feeding bottle<br>*Kinderflasche* | Bottle<br>*Flasche* | | | |
| Beaker<br>*Becher* | Beaker<br>*Becher* | | | |
| Teapot<br>*Teekanne* | Teapot<br>*Teekanne* | | | |
| Kettle<br>*Kessel* | Mug<br>*Krug / Pinte* | | | |
| Drinking bowl<br>*Trinkschale* | Drinking bowl<br>*Trinkschale* | | Bowl<br>*Schale* | |
| Puzzle jug<br>*Vexierkrug* | Drinking jug<br>*Trichterhalskrug* | | | |
| | Tea-bowl<br>*Trinkschale* | Tea-bowl<br>*Trinkschale* | Tea-bowl<br>*Trinkschale* | Tea-bowl<br>*Trinkschale* |
| | Tankard<br>*Humpen / Schnelle* | Tankard<br>*Humpen* | | |

## Kitchenware

| I.<br>Lead-glazed Earthenware | II.<br>Stoneware | III.<br>Tin-glazed Earthenware | IV.<br>Porcelain | V.<br>Creamware |
|---|---|---|---|---|
| **A. Food preparation** | | | | |
| Bowl<br>*Schale* | Bowl<br>*Schale* | | | |
| Colander<br>*Sieb* | Bottle<br>*Flasche* | | | |
| Chafing dish<br>*Komfor* | | | | |
| Jar<br>*Topf* | Jug<br>*Krug / Kanne* | | | |
| Pancheon<br>*Aufrahmschüssel* | | | | |
| **B. Cooking** | | | | |
| Cauldron<br>*Grapen* | | | | |
| Casserole<br>*Pastetentopf* | | | | |
| Pipkin<br>*Henkeltopf* | | | | |
| Tripod pipkin<br>*Grapen* | | | | |
| Frying pan<br>*Pfanne* | | | | |
| Skillet<br>*Dreifußpfanne* | | | | |
| Dripping pan<br>*Bräter* | | | | |
| **C. Storage & Transport** | | | | |
| Jar<br>Topf | Storage jar<br>*Vorratsgefäß (Baare)* | | | |
| Storage jar<br>*Vorratsgefäß* | Bottle<br>*Flasche* | Drug jar<br>*Albarello* | | |
| Jug<br>*Krug / Kanne* | Jug<br>*Krug / Kanne* | | | |
| Lid<br>*Deckel* | Lid<br>*Deckel* | | | |
| Basket<br>*Bügeltopf* | Flagon<br>*Pulle* | | | |
| Ointment pot<br>*Salbgefäß* | Ointment pot<br>*Salbgefäß* | Ointment pot<br>*Salbgefäß* | | |
| | Costrel<br>*Feldflasche* | | | |
| | Mineralwater bottle<br>*Mineralwasserflasche* | | | |

## Sanitary ware

| I. Lead-glazed Earthenware | II. Stonware | III. Tin-glazed Earthenware | IV. Porcelain | V. Creamware |
|---|---|---|---|---|

A. Toilet

| | | | | |
|---|---|---|---|---|
| Basin<br>*Waschschüssel*<br>Chamber pot<br>*Nachttopf* | Chamber pot<br>*Nachttopf* | | | Chamber pot<br>*Nachttopf* |

## Miscellaneous domestic wares

A. Lighting

| | | | | |
|---|---|---|---|---|
| Oil lamp<br>*Öllampe*<br>Candlestick<br>*Kerzenleuchter* | | | | |

B. Heating

| | | | | |
|---|---|---|---|---|
| Stove-tile<br>*Ofenkachel*<br>Brazier<br>*Gluttopf* | | Tile (hearth)<br>*Fliese* | | |

C. Others

| | | | | |
|---|---|---|---|---|
| Pilgrim horm<br>*Pilgerhorn*<br>Bird whistle<br>*Tonflöte (Vogel)* | Writing set<br>*Schreibzeug*<br>Jardiniere<br>*Blumenkugel*<br>Figurine (toy)<br>*Figürchen* | | | |

# 4. Neutron activation analysis: the characterisation and attribution of Lower Rhine earthenware c. 1400–1800

## 4.1 Introduction: a probabilistic sampling strategy

### *4.1.1 The manipulation of the database: the hypothesis-testing approach*

During the course of this research project just under 100 samples of lead-glazed earthenware and stove-tile were selected for chemical analysis from excavation contexts and museum collections in the Lower Rhineland (Table 4). The majority of samples came from the town of Duisburg, where access to material was automatic and regarded as an integral part of the ceramic research priorities. The Duisburg samples have been complemented by the addition of further consumer site material from Wesel and Oberhausen, also held by the Kultur- und Stadthistorisches Museum Duisburg. Kiln waste from Frechen, Cologne, Mayen, Langerwehe and Utrecht and consumer assemblages from Cologne, Viersen and Heide (Schleswig-Holstein) were also generously provided by their respective institutions and by individual excavators.

In order to expand the sample size necessary for comparative analysis on a regional scale, the respective values were integrated into the existing NAA database of post-medieval Lower Rhine earthenwares and stove-tiles held at the British Museum (Table 3; see Cowell 1988; 1989; 1990 for previous use of this data).

It must be stressed, however, that this programme of analysis was necessarily limited in scope due to the limitations of specialist laboratory time and of financial resources. The analysis presented here is intended as a pilot stage to further problem-orientated work on post-medieval Lower Rhine ceramics. The analysis provides an overview of possible compositional relationships and may be seen as a pointer to current questions and priorities for future strategical sampling.

The samples were selected with the following objectives in mind:

i. Verification of the Ware-type series
ii. Attribution of marketed vessels to known source, with the aim of identifying regional variations in pottery distribution
iii. Assessment of fabric variability within recognised Ware-types, in order to clarify whether they came from one or more sources of manufacture
iv. Asessment of fabric similarity between Ware-types, in order to clarify whether they came from the same source of manufacture (e. g. stove-tiles and vessels in similar fabrics)
v. Assessment of chronological changes in fabric composition, in order to assess the possibility of different manufacturing sources represented at given periods.

These objectives necessitated the formulation of a problem-orientated approach to the manipulation of the NAA database. The strategy, presented as a series of principal components plots aimed at testing specific hypotheses, was preferred to simply presenting the data and looking for structures and patterns that emerge from it. With such a large number of samples covering such an extensive chronological timespan, the resulting picture would have appeared muddled and distorted. On the other hand, the hypothesis-testing approach (Lemoine *et al.* 1982; Leese *et al.* 1986) is able to test our Ware-type definitions and, moreover, to examine our a priori assumptions (e. g. that all Frechen-type whitewares share the same compositional fingerprint over a period of 100– 200 years). Keeping to this strategy, the data was divided into five separate subsets for analysis, each subset representing those samples thought most likely to share similar compositional traits. By this means a priori probabilities were built into the definition of the groups. The subsets were also defined according to chosen chronological periods (i. e. by century to ensure contemporaneity of the group or by several centuries to monitior chronological trends). The subsets selected for analysis were defined as follows:

i. Lead-glazed earthenware, c.1400–1500 (Diag. 2)
ii. Stove-tiles c. 1400-1600 (Diag. 3)
iii. Lead-glazed earthenware, c. 1500–1700 (Diag. 4)
iv. Lead-glazed earthenware, c. 1500–1700 (Diag. 5) (Expanded plot)
v. Lead-glazed earthenware, c. 1700–1800 (Diag. 6)

## 4.2 Discussion of the analytical strategy

### *4.2.1 Introduction*

Sample numbers given in Table 3 correspond to those in the principal components plots (Diagrams 2–6). A concordance of sample numbers and their respective Ware-type codes is provided in Table 4. The principal components plots are interpreted below, and their significance for the definition of ceramic production and distribution in the region is discussed in Section 5.

### *4.2.2 Lead-glazed earthenware c. 1400–1500 (Diag. 2)*

Samples of the two principal Ware-types in this category were subjected to neutron activation analysis, namely Rhenish Whiteware Ia.3 (No. 95) and Redware Ia.8 (No. 147). The precise source of both types was unknown. Whiteware wasters from Langerwehe (Nos. 90–94) and redware samples from Utrecht (Nos. 148–152; see Bruijn 1979) were sampled for possible relationships. No other 15th-century whiteware or redware wasters were available for sampling in the region. Unfortunately it was not possible to sample the 15th-century greyware kiln waste from Xanten held by the Rheinisches Landesmuseum in Bonn (Wegner 1981). It is hoped to analyse this in relation to Ware-types Ia.6 and Ia.7 at some point in the future.

To increase the size of the analytical sample and to improve the potential for compositional matching, a series of 15th-century stove-tile values were incorporated into the cluster analysis. Visually the fabrics of the whiteware tiles Ia.12 and the redware tiles Ia.11 are indistinguishable from their 15th-century vessel counterparts; and it may be assumed that both vessels and tiles were made at the same production centres, or at least that potters and tilers had access to the same clay sources. Therefore, whiteware tile wasters from Cologne (Nos. 41–42; Unger ed. 1988, Cat. 38–69) and Mayen, outside Koblenz (Nos. 82–86; Redknap 1988, Fig.12) were incorporated into the analysis; along with redware and whiteware stove-tiles found in Duisburg (Ia.12: Nos. 69–73; & Ia.11: Nos. 68–70) and Oberhausen (Ia.11: No. 81).

The analysis placed the samples into three principal groupings (Diag. 2). The Langerwehe kiln wasters appeared unrelated to any of the other clusters, thereby eliminating the site as a potential source of whitewares found on excavations along the Rhine. However, the majority of the remaining whitewares formed a discernible group, comprising the whiteware vessel-type (Ia.3) and stove-tiles (Ia.12) from Duisburg, the Mayen kiln wasters (Ia.12) and one of the Cologne whiteware tiles (Ia.12). The cluster points, as expected, to a whiteware industry along the Rhine, centred on Cologne and perhaps extending up-river towards the Koblenz-Mayen area (see Section 5.2.1). It is highly likely that the industry was responsible for both whiteware vessel and stove-tile production during the 15th century, or at least that one clay source was exploited for the manufacture of both products.

The Duisburg redware sample (Ia.8; No. 147) is located in close proximity to the Utrecht kiln wasters on the plot. However, the cluster appears somewhat diffuse, and it would be unwise at this stage to suggest any significant compositional relationship. Further sampling of the Ware-type Ia.8 is clearly necessary to determine a local or distant source for this material.

### *4.2.3. Stove-tiles c. 1400–1600 (Diag. 3)*

In view of the considerable problems involved in the stylistic attribution of post-medieval stove-tiles manufactured in the region (Sections 1.1.4; 2.3.1), all four principal stove-tile Ware-types covering the 15th and 16th centuries were sampled for NAA in order to define their respective chemical compositions and possible interrelationships, and to establish whether there was any continuity of production on individual sites over this period. The analysis comprised the redware tiles Ia.11 and Ib.7, and their whiteware counterparts Ware-types Ia.12 and Ib.8.

The values of whiteware kiln wasters from Cologne (Nos. 41–45), Mayen (Nos. 82–86) and Frechen (No. 158) were added to the analysis to complement the spectra of whiteware tiles from Duisburg (Nos. 71–73). No redware tiles from kiln sites could be incorporated into the analysis, although stylistically comparative tiles from Hesse (Nos. 13–16, from the British Museum collections) were added to complement the range of redware samples from Duisburg (Nos. 60–66, 68–70, 80–81) and Oberhausen (No. 81).

Two discrete clusters are evident on the principal components plot (Diag. 3). Firstly, the whiteware tiles from Duisburg appear to cluster with the whiteware wasters from Mayen and to a lesser extent with the Cologne kiln finds, again confirming the Cologne-Koblenz region as the principal source of whiteware tile and vessel production during the 15th and 16th centuries. Not all the whiteware tiles from Duisburg, however, were associated with this group (e. g. No. 69). Such outliers only serve to reinforce the possibility of several alternative production centres for whiteware stove-tiles. The plot also serves to emphasise the fact that the Cologne and Frechen whiteware industries were mutually exclusive, and did not share the same clay sources. This aspect requires further investigation, however, as only one sample from Frechen was available for analysis (No. 158).

The other clearly identifiable grouping consists almost entirely of the redware stove-tiles (Ia.11 & Ib.7) from Duisburg. The nature of the cluster seems to suggest that the chemical composition of redware stove-tiles found in the town remains fairly constant from the 15th to 16th centuries, indicating the continuity of the redware industry in one location, or at least the continuity of clay supplies from one source. Outliers to this grouping include the 16th-century redware tiles from Hesse.

It is also noticeable that the major redware cluster

includes two tiles from Duisburg (Nos. 74 & 75) which on visual grounds were thought to be made of a whiteware fabric (Ib.8). Their location in the cluster only serves to reinforce the dangers of basing fabric definition on visual grounds alone. By and large, however, the visual characterisation of the wares selected here was confirmed by the neutron activation analysis.

### *4.2.4 Lead-glazed earthenware c. 1500–1700 (Diags. 4–5)*

Diagrams 4 and 5 show the relative distribution of samples of 16th and 17th-century lead-glazed earthenwares from the Lower Rhineland after being subjected to neutron activation analysis. Elements of both the redwares (Ib.1 and Ic.1) and the whitewares (Ib.3 and Ic.1) display a visually definable continuity of fabric composition over this period.

The material selected for analysis comprised a range of redwares and whitewares from the consumer sites in Duisburg (Nos. 128, 135–141,146,153), Wesel (No. 107), Cologne (Nos. 96–101, 108–9) and from field-survey in in the Lower Rhine hinterland (Nos. 106–6). To increase the size of the analytical sample the 16th-century redware stove-tiles from Duisburg (Ware-type Ib.7) were also added (Nos. 60–66,74–5, 80). The group also includes a sample of 16th-century lead-glazed earthenware from Heide, Schleswig-Holstein (No. 121; Ware-type Ib.1), which is similar in fabric and glaze to the Rhenish wares (Arnold 1986; see Section 5.2.3). Finally, a series of 16th-17th-century wasters from Frechen (Jürgens & Kleine 1988) were incorporated to assist in the attribution of the green-glazed whitewares (Nos. 154–159; Ware-type Ic.3).

Unfortunately it was not possible to sample any of the 16th and 17th-century slipwares found in Duisburg or Wesel during the course of the project (Ware-types Ib.5 and Ic.4 respectively). They will form the basis of a supplementary study incorporating this data in due course. Their compositional relationship to the contemporary redwares (Ware-types Ib.1 and Ic.1) is a major question for future research (Section 5.2.4).

The principal components plot for this analytical group (Diag. 4) has been deliberately enlarged to separate the clusters and aid visual interpretation. The clusters have been redefined at a larger scale in Diagram 5 along with their sample numbers. Both plots show two broad groupings of samples, although a fair degree of overlap is immediately discernible. The smaller of the two includes the Frechen whitewares of the 17th century in the lower half of the plot. It also incorporates two samples of 16th-century whiteware (Nos. 160–161). Their position in the cluster may point to a Frechen source for some of the 16th-century green-glazed whitewares found in Duisburg and also poses the possibility of an earlier phase of earthenware production at the site than has hitherto been suspected from recent excavations on the kiln sites (Jürgens & Kleine 1988).

The larger cluster above is characterised by a predominant number of redware samples. The Duisburg redware stove-tiles are clearly identifiable as a concentrated cluster, while the grouping on the right-hand side of the plot comprises a range of redware and whiteware types. Chief among the latter are a group of 16th-century samples from the Cologne Apostelnstraße site (Appendix 3, Context 73) which includes Ware-types Ib.1 (redware) and Ib.3 (whiteware). Their clustering suggests that both Ware-types shared a similar chemical composition and possibly the same clay source. Moreover, the presence of whitewares in this group reinforces the suggestion that they were produced in more than one production centre in the region. The clustering of redware and whiteware has again highlighted the problems of defining Ware-types on the grounds of fabric colour as a primary attribute.

The widespread distribution of 16th and 17th-century redwares in the plot indicates the possibility of more than one source for this group, although the redware stove-tile cluster may be related compositionally. Future analysis will include sampling the recently-excavated wasters of 16th-century redware (Ib.1) from the Cologne Severinstraße (Neu 1990).

### *4.2.5 Lead-glazed earthenware c. 1700–1800 (Diag. 6)*

With the density of rural kiln sites producing lead-glazed earthenware and slipware in the Lower Rhineland during the 18th century (Scholten-Neess & Jüttner 1971), it has been impracticable to attribute products found on consumer sites in the region to their precise source on the basis of stylistic attributes alone. Production centres, such as Issum (Scholten-Neess & Jüttner 1971, Cat. 328) and Kervenheim (Frankewitz & Köster 1982; Frankewitz 1988) produced slipwares that are decorated with identical motifs and designs. Judging by this pilot study, a combined stylistic and scientific approach clearly holds the most potential for characterisation in the future. In this way, vessels, which on the basis of their matching slip decoration are attributed to the same source, could be re-examined and their common origin confirmed or disproved.

Diagram 6 shows only a relatively small number of values intended to illustrate the potential of isolating clusters of 18th-century wares. Of particular interest are the compositional relationships between slipwares and plain earthenwares found in Duisburg (Id.1, Id.3 and Id.12; Nos. 88–9, 122–6) and their similarity to material from other sites. The analysis also includes samples from field-survey in Kreis Viersen (Id. 1; Nos.

164–5), and, for comparative purposes, a sample of Middle Rhine slipware from Bonn (Id.12; No. 87). Of principal interest are the samples of 18th-century kiln waste from the slipware centre of Issum (Id.1; Nos. 129–34) donated by the Museum Burg-Linn, Krefeld (Scholten-Neess & Jüttner 1971, note 223).

With such a small sample it is always difficult to isolate clearly recognisable trends in the data, yet a number of important points emerge here. Firstly, wares attributed to the Middle Rhineland on stylistic grounds (Id.12) may well have a variety of sources, as the Duisburg and Bonn examples are mutually exclusive on the plot (Nos. 88 and 87 respectively). Secondly, the Duisburg samples are the closest in compositional terms to the kiln waste from Issum. More sampling is needed, however, before any firm relationship can be established. Finally, the sample of plain earthenware from Duisburg (No. 89) bears no discernible compositional similarity to that of the slipwares. A future research programme of analysis might, therefore, be directed to the question as to whether production had specialised into plain coarseware or decorated slipware manufacture at Lower Rhine production sites during the 18th century.

### *4.2.6 Significance of the analysis and implications for future research*

The establishment of a database of post-medieval ceramic compositions from the Lower Rhineland has proved pivotal to the study of pottery production and distribution in the region. Firstly, it has confirmed the legitimacy of the classificatory scheme developed to characterise the Lower Rhine ceramic assemblages. Furthermore, the analyses have substantially refined our knowledge of where individual wares were produced, and provided us with a vastly improved insight into the distribution of ceramics both within the region and outside.

For the first time in Continental post-medieval ceramic studies an attempt has been made to list and characterise all pottery made in and imported into a particular geographical region. The neutron activation programme has given the resultant type-series an added weight and significance. Wares which have been distinguished on purely visual grounds (by fabric or stylistic analysis) have now been confirmed, by virtue of their trace-elemental composition, as originating from a separate clay source to Ware-types of a similar appearance. The inclusion of waster material from five earthenware production sites (Table 2) has enabled a substantial proportion of the Wares recorded by this survey to be ascribed to their respective source.

Nevertheless, the programme of analysis has also demonstrated the complex development of earthenware production in the Lower Rhineland during the post-medieval period. The variation in trace-elemental composition identified within several of the major Ware-types (e. g. Ib.1; Ib.3; Section 4.2.4) suggests that these wares originate from a number of separate locations. Future sampling will concentrate on attempting to distinguish between these sources and clarify whether they represent geographically distant production sites or separate workshops within the same industries. In order to understand the relationship between local production and distribution more fully, it is at this micro-level that the analysis must now be directed. This approach is aimed at complementing the sampling of wasters from individual workshops within the individual Rhenish stoneware industries (Gaimster & Hook 1995).

The success of this research design depends ultimately on the sampling of material from production sites in the region. So far the vast majority of pottery samples have come from consumer assemblages. Despite the substantial archival record which testifies to their existence (J. Hähnel 1988, 17), few sites have been physically located. Future fieldwork will no doubt help to redress this imbalance and provide a larger quota of kiln-site samples for the NAA programme. To this end, local museums and archaeological bodies in conjunction with the Rheinisches Landesmuseum, Bonn, must be persuaded to coordinate a problem-orientated programme of survey and sampling across the region. Such a programme will reap dividends in helping to supplement and refine this preliminary type-series of post-medieval pottery and, in doing so, substantially reduce future post-excavation and research costs on ceramic assemblages found in the region.

For the international archaeological community, the database is of considerable significance, providing for the first time a scientific basis for the identification of a wide range of Rhenish earthenware pottery and stove-tiles exported to the neighbouring Low Countries, Britain and to Scandinavia (Section 1.2.7). The British Museum database will enable finds of exported wares to be correctly attributed to their original source. The supply of samples from excavations outside the Rhineland must be actively encouraged if the mechanics of the trade in Rhenish pottery during the post-medieval period are to be more fully understood.

## Table 3 Neutron Activation Analyses
## All ppm except Fe, K in %

| No. | Site | Reg/Context | Ce | Tb | Th | Hf | Cs | Sc | Fe | Eu | La | K | Yb | Lu | Ba | Rb |
|---|---|---|---|---|---|---|---|---|---|---|---|---|---|---|---|---|
| 1 | | MLA B280 | 54.4 | .57 | 10.4 | 7.0 | 7.34 | 15.4 | 3.81 | .96 | 29.2 | 1.9 | 1.9 | .30 | 335 | 134 |
| 2 | Hampton Court? | MLA B278 | 108. | .76 | 12.7 | 10.2 | 5.48 | 12.8 | 1.24 | 1.01 | 68.0 | 1.8 | 3.0 | .50 | 291 | 100 |
| 3 | Cove kiln | A1980.8 (1) | 142. | .99 | 12.5 | 10.1 | 5.55 | 13.1 | 2.48 | 1.65 | 80.3 | 1.8 | 2.9 | .47 | 286 | 110 |
| 4 | Cove kiln | A1980.8 (2) | 141. | .90 | 13.2 | 9.5 | 5.70 | 13.5 | 2.56 | 1.50 | 85.8 | 1.8 | 2.9 | .51 | 276 | 114 |
| 5 | Cove kiln | A1980.8 (3) | 139. | .74 | 13.8 | 10.4 | 5. 51 | 13.7 | 1.34 | 1.09 | 84.3 | 1.7 | 2.9 | .49 | 276 | 104 |
| 6 | Cove kiln | A1980.8 (4) | 149. | .71 | 14.3 | 10.1 | 5.98 | 16.5 | 1.53 | 1.17 | 89.7 | 2.0 | 2.9 | .48 | 371 | 116 |
| 7 | Cove kiln | A1980.8 (5) | 133. | .74 | 13.4 | 10.5 | 5.15 | 13.8 | 1.31 | 1.06 | 80.2 | 1.7 | 3.0 | .52 | 301 | 104 |
| 8 | Cove kiln | A1980.8 (6) | 133. | .97 | 15.4 | 6.7 | 7.73 | 16.7 | 1.93 | 1.77 | 73.2 | 2.0 | 3.0 | .52 | 344 | 139 |
| 9 | Cove kiln | A1980.8 (7) | 108. | .66 | 13.6 | 8.3 | 7.87 | 16.4 | 1.84 | 1.10 | 66.5 | 2.2 | 3.0 | .47 | 348 | 140 |
| 10 | Cove kiln | A1980.8 (8) | 99.0 | .68 | 12.1 | 10.7 | 5.38 | 12.2 | 1.29 | .91 | 62.4 | 1.7 | 2.8 | .46 | 319 | 100 |
| 11 | London, Thames | MLA B233 | 65.6 | .68 | 12.6 | 7.4 | 6.29 | 14.2 | 1.50 | .94 | 38.3 | 1.7 | 2.7 | .46 | 322 | 107 |
| 12 | City, Aldersgate | MLA 0A10268 | 69.4 | .65 | 13.4 | 7.1 | 7.09 | 14.8 | 1.83 | .96 | 41.8 | 1.7 | 2.6 | .43 | 316 | 107 |
| 13 | Hessen | MLA 0A9378 | 90.3 | 1.15 | 12.9 | 7.0 | 7.35 | 17.4 | 4.78 | 1.99 | 44.6 | 2.8 | 3.3 | .53 | 449 | 145 |
| 14 | | MLA 0A9378 | 71.0 | .69 | 9.8 | 8.4 | 6.57 | 13.5 | 3.36 | 1.22 | 35.0 | 2.0 | 2.4 | .41 | 315 | 112 |
| 15 | | MLA 0A9377 | 95.7 | .66 | 11.1 | 9.3 | 5.65 | 12.2 | 1.36 | .93 | 60.1 | 1.8 | 2.5 | .44 | 311 | 102 |
| 16 | Hessen | MLA 96,2-1,81 | 114. | 1.15 | 12.0 | 5.6 | 9.11 | 17.1 | 4.66 | 1.88 | 45.9 | 2.4 | 3.1 | .51 | 324 | 140 |
| 17 | City, Moorgate St | MLA B281 | 71.1 | .75 | 11.0 | 8.3 | 4.70 | 11.7 | 1.24 | 1.09 | 40.5 | 1.6 | 2.8 | .47 | 281 | 83. |
| 18 | Cove kiln | A1980.8 (9) | 75.4 | .50 | 9.9 | 8.3 | 5.43 | 11.8 | 1.25 | .78 | 48.4 | 1.6 | 2.1 | .37 | 284 | 104 |
| 19 | Cove kiln | A1980.8 (10) | 94.0 | .57 | 12.8 | 10.3 | 5.75 | 12.1 | 1.44 | .92 | 59.4 | 1.9 | 2.5 | .43 | 332 | 102 |
| 20 | MOL Tile James I | MOL enreg | 128. | .63 | 12.1 | 8.0 | 6.08 | 13.8 | 1.40 | 1.27 | 76.2 | 1.9 | 2.5 | .36 | 330 | 113 |
| 21 | London, Royal Mint | MOL 3964, 1928 | 67.9 | .81 | 10.3 | 10.1 | 8.54 | 10.8 | .76 | 1.11 | 34.6 | 1.3 | 3.2 | .52 | 246 | 94. |
| 22 | London, Royal Mint | MOL 3964, 1928 | 74.4 | .82 | 11.7 | 9.8 | 9.76 | 12.8 | 1.93 | 1.19 | 36.8 | 1.7 | 3.4 | .54 | 263 | 127 |
| 23 | Broadarrow Tower | MOL 80, 116 | 60.3 | .67 | 11.7 | 10.2 | 7.11 | 16.1 | 4.52 | 1.16 | 28.7 | 2.5 | 2.5 | .41 | 358 | 124 |
| 24 | Gorhambury Park Ho | HBMC(E) | 73.8 | .92 | 9.2 | 8.1 | 6.21 | 12.7 | 3.56 | 1.47 | 60.4 | 1.8 | 2.6 | .42 | 358 | 101 |
| 25 | Gorhambury Park Ho | HBMC(E) | 103. | .68 | 12.2 | 9.3 | 5.27 | 12.3 | 1.46 | 1.00 | 57.4 | 1.7 | 2.5 | .40 | 346 | 96. |
| 26 | Colchester,Maldon St | MRC 71 (91) | 67.3 | .78 | 11.6 | 6.8 | 8.73 | 16.3 | 4.08 | 1.28 | 35.5 | 1.9 | 2.5 | .42 | 346 | 136 |
| 27 | Colchester,Maldon St | MRC 71 (91) | 68.1 | .66 | 13.4 | 7.9 | 6.57 | 14.2 | 1.68 | .93 | 38.4 | 1.9 | 2.7 | .43 | 480 | 96. |
| 28 | Colchester,Crouch St | CSC 71 (1) | 66.9 | .69 | 13.5 | 7.8 | 7.41 | 15.1 | 1.53 | .88 | 38.5 | 1.9 | 2.6 | .41 | 347 | 125 |
| 29 | London, Whitefriars | HBMC(E) (1) | 106. | .75 | 11.9 | 10.0 | 6.23 | 14.0 | 2.36 | 1.21 | 38.2 | 1.6 | 2.7 | .43 | 343 | 103 |
| 30 | London, Whitefriars | HBMC(E) (2) | 78.4 | .81 | 10.6 | 6.6 | 7.54 | 15.1 | 4.17 | 1.37 | 31.4 | 2.2 | 2.3 | .38 | 302 | 127 |
| 31 | London, Whitefriars | HBMC(E) (3) | 78.5 | .80 | 10.6 | 6.6 | 7.79 | 15.7 | 4.29 | 1.49 | 33.0 | 2.1 | 2.4 | .37 | 283 | 119 |
| 32 | London, Whitefriars | HBMC(E) (4) | 81.7 | .83 | 11.4 | 7.5 | 7.69 | 16.4 | 4.49 | 1.47 | 33.0 | 2.1 | 2.4 | .41 | 345 | 123 |
| 33 | London, Whitefrlars | HBMC(E) (5) | 59.0 | .71 | 10.0 | 6.5 | 7.01 | 14.4 | 4.05 | 1.23 | 29.6 | 2.3 | 2.2 | .40 | 291 | 122 |
| 34 | Camber Castle | HBMC(E) (1) | 89.9 | 1.08 | 13.3 | 6.4 | 12.5 | 16.8 | 1.43 | 1.70 | 43.2 | 1.6 | 3.0 | .47 | 362 | 120 |
| 35 | Camber Castle | HBMC(E) (2) | 91.4 | 1.09 | 13.3 | 7.3 | 12.4 | 17.5 | 1.54 | 1.77 | 43.5 | 1.9 | 3.0 | .48 | 390 | 135 |
| 36 | Camber Castle | HBMC(E) (3) | 93.0 | 1.03 | 13.0 | 7.1 | 12.2 | 16.3 | 1.41 | 1.58 | 41.6 | 1.6 | 3.1 | .47 | 394 | 115 |
| 37 | Camber Castle | HBMC(E) (4) | 84.6 | .96 | 12.9 | 6.4 | 11.7 | 16.2 | 1.40 | 1.53 | 40.4 | 1.8 | 2.9 | .47 | 374 | 122 |
| 38 | Camber Castle | HBMC(E) (5) | 178. | 1.48 | 13.4 | 7.8 | 6.46 | 14.9 | 1.67 | 2.88 | 78.7 | 2.9 | 3.1 | .46 | 356 | 121 |
| 39 | Camber Castle | HBMC(E) (6) | 89.3 | 1.12 | 13.5 | 7.3 | 13.8 | 17.3 | 1.48 | 1.69 | 41.9 | 1.3 | 2.9 | .42 | 376 | 142 |
| 40 | Fountains Abbey | HBMC(E) | 96.3 | 1.27 | 16.2 | 11.8 | 10.3 | 16.8 | .89 | 1.78 | 42.1 | 1.9 | 3.8 | .61 | 523 | 109 |
| 41 | Cologne kiln | KS 200 (1) | 112. | 1.13 | 16.1 | 6.5 | 17.5 | 20.6 | 1.25 | 1.95 | 50.1 | 2.5 | 3.2 | .52 | 359 | 159 |
| 42 | Cologne kiln | KS 200 (2) | 111. | 1.01 | 13.1 | 17.8 | 14.0 | 11.0 | .85 | 1.61 | 56.0 | | 3.6 | .58 | 321 | 37. |
| 43 | Cologne kiln | KS 200 (3) | 81.7 | .66 | 14.7 | 8.7 | 12.3 | 11.8 | .80 | 1.09 | 42.5 | | 2.4 | .41 | 261 | 101 |
| 44 | Cologne kiln | KS 200 (4) | 164. | 1.43 | 18.9 | 8.0 | 11.1 | 15.5 | 1.32 | 2.83 | 73.3 | 2.3 | 3.3 | .50 | 614 | 166 |
| 45 | Cologne kiln | KS 200 (5) | 85.7 | .72 | 14.9 | 8.5 | 11.6 | 11.7 | .98 | 1.10 | 42.4 | 1.7 | 2.5 | .40 | 309 | 105 |
| 46 | Queenhithe, Thames | MOL 87.106 | 36.0 | | 8.9 | 4.9 | 4.81 | 13.3 | 2.24 | .62 | 20.7 | 1.4 | 1.5 | .25 | 308 | 87. |
| 47 | Queenhithe, Thames | MOL 87.106 | 56.9 | .66 | 9.2 | 7.9 | 7.18 | 14.4 | 3.59 | 1.08 | 27.6 | 2.1 | 1.9 | .32 | 353 | 130 |
| 48 | | MOL 7132 | 128. | .87 | 12.2 | 8.5 | 6.59 | 14.1 | 1.45 | 1.22 | 65.2 | 1.9 | 2.5 | .44 | 308 | 135 |
| 49 | | MOL 7132 | 51.2 | .56 | 9.3 | 7.2 | 5.47 | 12.2 | 2.05 | .88 | 28.3 | 1.9 | 2.1 | .34 | 266 | 105 |
| 50 | Arundel Ho, Strand | MOL unreg | 149. | .95 | 12.5 | 10.0 | 6.45 | 14.5 | 1.79 | 1.73 | 73.2 | 1.8 | 2.9 | .45 | 314 | 116 |
| 51 | Arundel Ho, Strand | MOL unreg | 90.4 | 1.19 | 13.6 | 6.7 | 9.06 | 19.5 | 5.12 | 2.10 | 44.0 | 3.1 | 3.1 | .42 | 413 | 228 |
| 52 | City, Trig Lane | MOL 3021 | 60.2 | .73 | 10.0 | 6.5 | 6.15 | 14.2 | 3.38 | 1.30 | 30.6 | 1.9 | 2.2 | .37 | 305 | 108 |
| 53 | City, Trig Lane | MOL 3021 | 90.8 | .82 | 17.0 | 10.5 | 9.16 | 20.5 | 2.67 | 1.14 | 53.8 | | 3.2 | .50 | 413 | 130 |
| 54 | Cove kiln | | 89.7 | .73 | 12.7 | 10.2 | 6.39 | 14.0 | 1.43 | .98 | 54.1 | 1.9 | 2.7 | .46 | 382 | 109 |

Table 3 (cont.)

| No. | Site | Reg/Context | Ce | Tb | Th | Hf | Cs | Sc | Fe | Eu | La | K | Yb | Lu | Ba | Rb |
|---|---|---|---|---|---|---|---|---|---|---|---|---|---|---|---|---|
| 55 | Cove kiln | | 115. | .78 | 13.6 | 10.8 | 5.73 | 13.8 | 1.89 | 1.08 | 67.4 | 1.8 | 2.9 | .50 | 297 | 124 |
| 56 | Cove kiln | | 122. | .90 | 15.3 | 5.6 | 9.68 | 19.8 | 2.51 | 1.65 | 62.5 | 1.9 | 3.0 | .49 | 336 | 134 |
| 57 | Cove kiln | | 128. | 1.04 | 17.0 | 6.8 | 10.8 | 21.2 | 2.66 | 1.82 | 66.5 | 2.1 | 3.0 | .50 | 362 | 149 |
| 58 | Cove kiln | | 167. | 1.23 | 12.8 | 9.0 | 6.67 | 14.7 | 3.16 | 2.24 | 91.7 | 1.9 | 3.3 | .52 | 293 | 129 |
| 59 | Cove kiln | | 226. | 1.49 | 14.1 | 9.7 | 7.17 | 17.3 | 3.69 | 2.80 | 112. | 2.2 | 3.4 | .51 | 323 | 145 |
| 60 | Duisburg Kuhstr. | Lfd Nr43 87:2/2 | 74.5 | .74 | 12.4 | 7.2 | 9.35 | 13.1 | 2.94 | 1.28 | 85.5 | 2.0 | 2.1 | .33 | 353 | 156 |
| 61 | Duisburg Kuhstr. | Lfd Nr43 87:2/2 | 96.6 | .92 | 15.0 | 6.9 | 12.0 | 15.7 | 3.20 | 1.74 | 46.5 | 2.5 | 2.5 | .42 | 404 | 171 |
| 62 | Duisburg Kuhstr. | Lfd Nr43 87:2/2 | 98.3 | .94 | 15.0 | 7.0 | 12.0 | 15.5 | 8.29 | 1.80 | 45.5 | 2.4 | 2.7 | .41 | 401 | 186 |
| 63 | Duisburg Kuhstr. | Lfd Nr12 87:2/2 | 96.8 | .92 | 14.6 | 6.6 | 11.9 | 15.4 | 3.23 | 1.79 | 44.8 | 2.4 | 2.8 | .42 | 447 | 157 |
| 64 | Duisburg Kuhstr. | Lfd Nr12 87:2/2 | 96.6 | .86 | 13.9 | 6.9 | 8.82 | 13.4 | 1.50 | 1.68 | 46.3 | 2.3 | 2.3 | .35 | 463 | 157 |
| 65 | Duisburg Kuhstr. | Lfd Nr12 87:2/2 | 85.3 | .73 | 12.6 | 6.6 | 8.51 | 12.1 | 8.36 | 1.47 | 43.0 | 1.9 | 2.3 | .40 | 367 | 142 |
| 66 | Duisburg Kuhstr. | Lfd Nr12 87:2/2 | 99.3 | .96 | 15.7 | 7.0 | 11.9 | 15.5 | 3.27 | 1.81 | 47.0 | 2.5 | 2.6 | .43 | 523 | 184 |
| 67 | Duisburg Niederstr. | 88/FI. 19 | 105. | 1.10 | 14.1 | 9.8 | 6.34 | 13.3 | 2.99 | 1.99 | 50.0 | 1.5 | 3.0 | .48 | 481 | 140 |
| 68 | Duisburg Niederstr. | 88/FI. 19 | 98.8 | .88 | 14.3 | 6.5 | 9.37 | 13.8 | 8.21 | 1.79 | 46.7 | 2.1 | 2.2 | .37 | 426 | 156 |
| 69 | Duisburg Innenhafen | Inv Nr 84:7/34 | 198. | 1.87 | 29.0 | 22.6 | 27.8 | 26.8 | 4.41 | 3.31 | 52.3 | 1.0 | 3.7 | .62 | 390 | 219 |
| 70 | Duisburg Niederstr. | 88/FI. 19 | 90.2 | .92 | 13.7 | 8.1 | 7.99 | 14.4 | 2.22 | 1.67 | 44.1 | 2.7 | 2.4 | .41 | 413 | 129 |
| 71 | Duisburg Innenhafen | Inv Nr 84:7/34 | 98.3 | .92 | 13.8 | 14.4 | 22.8 | 12.5 | 1.26 | 1.52 | 53.3 | .9 | 3.1 | .51 | 482 | 64. |
| 72 | Duisburg Minoriten | 84: 52 | 112. | .99 | 14.6 | 15.1 | 18.0 | 12.5 | 1.16 | 1.68 | 61.6 | .5 | 3.4 | .59 | 426 | 53. |
| 73 | Duisburg Minoriten | 84: 52 | 114. | 1.12 | 15.0 | 19.6 | 15.4 | 12.1 | 1.08 | 1.80 | 65.3 | .6 | 4.0 | .66 | 386 | 36. |
| 74 | Duisburg Ruhrort | 77: 26 | 98.8 | .82 | 14.6 | 6.7 | 11.0 | 14.4 | 1.73 | 1.65 | 49.4 | 1.8 | 2.2 | .37 | 440 | 150 |
| 75 | Duisburg Ruhrort | 77: 26 | 98.4 | .86 | 15.3 | 8.3 | 10.8 | 14.5 | 1.58 | 1.72 | 48.6 | 2.2 | 2.2 | .37 | 387 | 144 |
| 76 | | BM OA7396 | 133. | .98 | 13.6 | 7.5 | 7.52 | 15.7 | 1.61 | 1.70 | 76.6 | 1.9 | 3.0 | .46 | 363 | 118 |
| 77 | | BW OA7397 | 69.2 | .77 | 12.4 | 10.7 | 5.02 | 12.3 | 1.35 | 1.13 | 33.4 | 2.4 | 2.7 | .44 | 354 | 119 |
| 78 | London, Fenchurch S | MOL 11556 | 65.5 | .56 | 10.5 | 7.8 | 7.56 | 13.4 | 1.38 | .79 | 43.9 | 2.0 | 2.3 | .39 | 376 | 120 |
| 79 | Dover Priory | Ant. C12/161 | 61.7 | .73 | 11.7 | 8.6 | 7.11 | 12.4 | 3.37 | 1.15 | 29.6 | 2.1 | 2.6 | .41 | 384 | 122 |
| 80 | Duisb. Schwanenstr. | 86: 6/29-31 | 84.9 | .87 | 14.2 | 6.8 | 9.83 | 14.4 | 3.19 | 1.51 | 44.3 | 2.4 | 2.7 | .41 | 443 | 162 |
| 81 | Oberhausen Holten | 1977-374 | 43.9 | .50 | 9.5 | 8.0 | 9.85 | 10.9 | 3.23 | .75 | 23.1 | 2.0 | 2.0 | .33 | 291 | 148 |
| 82 | Mayen Siegfriedstr. | 12 | 102. | .95 | 17.5 | 10.8 | 9.42 | 15.8 | 1.42 | 1.64 | 52.6 | 1.5 | 3.3 | .53 | 316 | 131 |
| 83 | Mayen Siegfriedstr. | 13 | 93.9 | .84 | 12.0 | 15.9 | 12.9 | 9.1 | .82 | 1.35 | 52.1 | .9 | 2.8 | .47 | 370 | 35. |
| 84 | Mayen Siegfriedstr. | 14 | 120. | .96 | 15.9 | 8.4 | 11.8 | 14.4 | 1.75 | 1.69 | 62.9 | 1.9 | 3.0 | .50 | 420 | 137 |
| 85 | Mayen Siegfriedstr. | 1732 | 102. | .80 | 12.9 | 13.7 | 20.2 | 11.4 | .95 | 1.51 | 59.0 | .7 | 2.8 | .44 | 349 | 51. |
| 86 | Mayen Siegfriedstr. | 2326 | 111. | 1.03 | 11.4 | 18.4 | 9.73 | 10.4 | .80 | 1.54 | 59.5 | .5 | 4.2 | .69 | 275 | 20. |
| 87 | Bonn-Boeserlagerhof | 83.590-6 | 129. | 1.06 | 15.6 | 9.6 | 21.0 | 17.2 | 1.34 | 1.85 | 69.8 | 1.5 | 3.5 | .51 | 303 | 132 |
| 88 | Duisburg A.M. | | 94.0 | .88 | 14.5 | 10.0 | 20.5 | 29.4 | 1.89 | 1.85 | 56.4 | 1.1 | 2.6 | .40 | 301 | 91. |
| 89 | Duisburg A.M. | 83: 31/3 | 90.5 | .91 | 15.1 | 6.4 | 16.7 | 13.8 | 1.64 | 1.68 | 50.8 | 2.5 | 2.6 | .42 | 558 | 163 |
| 90 | Langerwehe kiln | | 73.2 | .83 | 13.6 | 11.5 | 18.7 | 11.1 | .75 | 1.07 | 40.1 | 1.2 | 3.6 | .58 | 288 | 98. |
| 91 | Langerwehe kiln | | 77.0 | .83 | 15.5 | 11.2 | 19.2 | 12.8 | 1.02 | 1.04 | 41.7 | 1.3 | 3.9 | .65 | 274 | 117 |
| 92 | Langerwehe kiln | | 65.6 | .78 | 14.0 | 13.9 | 17.1 | 10.7 | .79 | .96 | 37.2 | 1.2 | 3.6 | .58 | 220 | 92. |
| 93 | Langerwehe kiln | | 75.4 | .82 | 15.8 | 10.5 | 23.1 | 13.8 | 1.07 | 1.11 | 43.1 | 1.5 | 3.4 | .56 | 315 | 131 |
| 94 | Langerwehe kiln | | 89.5 | .90 | 18.0 | 9.4 | 22.6 | 15.6 | 1.12 | 1.31 | 51.6 | 1.8 | 3.5 | .55 | 501 | 166 |
| 95 | Duisburg Minoriten | 84: 52/29 | 108. | 1.03 | 16.6 | 11.4 | 17.8 | 11.8 | .81 | 1.61 | 48.4 | 1.5 | 3.3 | .51 | 314 | 85. |
| 96 | Cologne Apostelnstr. | 1980, 78/ 9 | 112. | 1.13 | 14.5 | 9.0 | 8.22 | 13.4 | 2.03 | 2.00 | 54.9. | 1.6 | 3.2 | .48 | 373 | 130 |
| 97 | Cologne Apostelnstr. | 1980, 78/ 9 | 122. | 1.38 | 14.9 | 11.5 | 7.65 | 14.4 | 2.20 | 2.47 | 53.0 | 1.3 | 3.4 | .55 | 403 | 126 |
| 98 | Cologne Apostelnstr. | 1980, 78/ 9 | 116. | .99 | 15.3 | 6.5 | 10.2 | 13.3 | 2.53 | 2.01 | 50.2 | 1.9 | 2.3 | .37 | 493 | 166 |
| 99 | Cologne Apostelnstr. | 1980, 78/ 9 | 107. | .93 | 14.8 | 6.8 | 8.41 | 13.7 | 2.53 | 1.71 | 56.0 | 1.8 | 2.5 | .42 | 533 | 136 |
| 100 | Cologne Apostelnstr. | 1980, 78/ 9 | 89.5 | .85 | 12.8 | 6.5 | 7.57 | 12.5 | 2.36 | 1.54 | 55.9 | 1.9 | 2.8 | .47 | 491 | 117 |
| 101 | Cologne Apostelnstr. | 1980, 78/ 9 | 120. | 1.08 | 18.0 | 9.7 | 9.91 | 17.0 | 3.07 | 2.01 | 56.5 | 1.7 | 2.7 | .45 | 645 | 171 |
| 102 | Norwich | 149N 513 | 106. | 1.64 | 15.0 | 7.7 | 9.01 | 16.7 | 5.15 | 2.78 | 55.3 | 2.3 | 4.1 | .70 | 506 | 162 |
| 103 | Norwich | 149N 1005 | 93.8 | 1.31 | 13.6 | 12.2 | 10.0 | 14.1 | 3.17 | 2.14 | 38.9 | 1.9 | 3.5 | .61 | 485 | 129 |
| 104 | Norwich | 416N u/s | 76.6 | 1.17 | 11.1 | 8.0 | 7.41 | 12.3 | 4.24 | 1.99 | 38.7 | 1.9 | 3.3 | .57 | 452 | 117 |
| 105 | Kreis Viersen | | 124. | 1.21 | 18.3 | 9.2 | 9.30 | 17.3 | 1.51 | 2.21 | 57.4 | 1.7 | 3.0 | .48 | 471 | 142 |
| 106 | Kreis Viersen | | 103. | 1.35 | 18.5 | 8.2 | 14.9 | 17.9 | 3.00 | 1.86 | 49.2 | 2.4 | 3.7 | .59 | 417 | 186 |
| 107 | Wesel Ziegelshacht | RLMB | 112. | 1.18 | 15.2 | 9.4 | 7.16 | 13.5 | 1.86 | 2.16 | 52.4 | 1.7 | 3.1 | .47 | 430 | 130 |
| 108 | Cologne Apostelnstr. | 1980, 78/ 9 | 110 | 1.08 | 15.7 | 10.0 | 7.44 | 15.7 | 3.59 | 2.01 | 51.9 | 1.4 | 2.9 | .46 | 386 | 128 |

## Table 3 (cont.)

| No. | Site | Reg/Context | Ce | Tb | Th | Hf | Cs | Sc | Fe | Eu | La | K | Yb | Lu | Ba | Rb |
|---|---|---|---|---|---|---|---|---|---|---|---|---|---|---|---|---|
| 109 | Cologne Apostelnstr. | 1980, 78/ 9 | 119. | 1.10 | 16.0 | 8.6 | 9.17 | 14.4 | 2.20 | 2.17 | 58.3 | 1.8 | 3.0 | .47 | 453 | 141 |
| 110 | Sheffield Manor | 226 | 51.3 | .59 | 11.7 | 6.1 | 5.37 | 14.2 | 1.57 | .72 | 24.9 | .3 | .3 | .33 | 264 | 83. |
| 111 | Sheffield Manor | 197 | 52.1 | .53 | 10.9 | 6.5 | 5.50 | 12.7 | 1.60 | .72 | 32.0 | 1.5 | 2.0 | .33 | 319 | 95. |
| 112 | Sheffield Manor | 224 | 51.7 | .52 | 10.8 | 6.7 | 5.22 | 12.7 | 1.59 | .68 | 31.1 | 1.4 | 2.1 | .34 | 278 | 83. |
| 113 | Sheffield Manor | 742 | 54.3 | .52 | 10.7 | 6.1 | 5.94 | 12.9 | 1.5.8 | .73 | 33.9 | 1.5 | 2.1 | .35 | 270 | 96. |
| 114 | London, Royal Mint | 1842 | 76.3 | .83 | 12.7 | 9.5 | 10.2 | 13.3 | 1.75 | 1.27 | 38.3 | 1.7 | 3.1 | .48 | 272 | 121 |
| 115 | London, Royal Mint | 1723 | 71.8 | .85 | 10.9 | 9.8 | 9.29 | 11.4 | .74 | 1.17 | 35.6 | 1.3 | 3.2 | .52 | 268 | 99. |
| 116 | London, Royal Mint | 4114 | 74.9 | .80 | 12.0 | 10.0 | 10.2 | 12.9 | 2.54 | 1.26 | 36.7 | 1.9 | 2.8 | .45 | 307 | 123 |
| 117 | London, Royal Mint | 4181 | 74.9 | .85 | 12.0 | 9.6 | 9.94 | 13.3 | 1.80 | 1.23 | 37.4 | 1.6 | 2.9 | .49 | 255 | 132 |
| 118 | London, Royal Mint | 1761 | 74.5 | .89 | 11.8 | 9.1 | 9.89 | 13.0 | 1.78 | 1.22 | 87.2 | 1.7 | 3.3 | .54 | 251 | 125 |
| 119 | London, Royal Mint | 1940 | 52.7 | .70 | 8.8 | 8.3 | 2.86 | 9.1 | 2.29 | 1.03 | 27.6 | 1.0 | 2.2 | .36 | 218 | 54. |
| 120 | London, Royal Mint | 1821 | 58.5 | .72 | 9.9 | 8.0 | 3.46 | 9.6 | 2.35 | 1.04 | 28.7 | 1.3 | 2.2 | .37 | 231 | 77. |
| 121 | Heide | H194B(1987) | 79.5 | .77 | 15.8 | 9.3 | 14.2 | 15.9 | 1.28 | 1.27 | 45.6 | 1.5 | 2.1 | .32 | 420 | 12.8 |
| 122 | Duisburg 18C slip | 83: 31 | 69.8 | .85 | 12.9 | 6.7 | 10.2 | 11.9 | 4.03 | 1.29 | 35.1 | 2.1 | 4.4 | .53 | 456 | 129 |
| 123 | Duisburg 18C slip | 83: 31 | 68.6 | .88 | 11.9 | 7.4 | 9.41 | 10.0 | 3.93 | 1.29 | 34.5 | 2.2 | 40. | .62 | 438 | 130 |
| 124 | Duisburg 18C slip | 83: 31 | 85.8 | 1.00 | 14.9 | 8.8 | 11.0 | 12.5 | 3.48 | 1.54 | 46.2 | 2.4 | 49. | .42 | 464 | 143 |
| 125 | Duisburg 18C slip | 83: 31 | 66.6 | .79 | 11.8 | 10.2 | 9.79 | 12.9 | 4.25 | 1.20 | 32.9 | 2.3 | 39. | .80 | 268 | 141 |
| 126 | Duisburg 18C slip | 83: 31 | 72.7 | .79 | 15.6 | 8.4 | 11.2 | 13.0 | 4.68 | 1.16 | 37.9 | 2.5 | 41. | .61 | 433 | 152 |
| 127 | Duisburg 17C Pb | 86: 2 | 62.3 | .60 | 12.1 | 6.2 | 12.5 | 13.9 | 3.54 | 1.12 | 32.3 | 2.5 | 30. | .73 | 310 | 167 |
| 128 | Duisburg 17C Pb | 86: 2 | 80.2 | .91 | 13.8 | 11.4 | 10.1 | 12.2 | 1.46 | 1.36 | 41.0 | 1.6 | 49. |  | 283 | 105 |
| 129 | Issum kiln | 1 | 61.6 | .59 | 11.7 | 7.8 | 10.9 | 10.5 | 2.76 | .90 | 32.1 | 2.3 | 32. | .65 | 397 | 139 |
| 130 | Issum kiln | 2 | 67.6 | .69 | 13.7 | 8.0 | 11.3 | 10.7 | 2.98 | 1.06 | 35.4 | 2.4 | 36. | .72 | 416 | 150 |
| 131 | Issum kiln | 3 | 69.2 | .75 | 14.5 | 6.6 | 11.3 | 13.0 | 4.60 | 1.24 | 37.3 | 2.5 | 37. | .29 | 483 | 147 |
| 132 | Issum kiln | 4 | 64.1 | .64 | 12.6 | 9.0 | 10.5 | 10.2 | 2.66 | .93 |  |  |  |  | 434 | 140 |
| 133 | Issum kiln | 5 | 80.6 | .94 | 15.0 | 8.4 | 13.2 | 13.8 | 4.15 | 1.42 |  |  |  |  | 472 | 161 |
| 134 | Issum kiln | 6 | 75.6 | .83 | 15.7 | 7.8 | 11.7 | 12.5 | 3.86 | 1.34 | 37.1 | 3.0 | 33. | .59 | 389 | 147 |
| 135 | Duisburg 16C Pb-gl | 85: 135 | 117. | .97 | 14.2 | 7.5 | 9.06 | 13.7 | 2.25 | 1.81 | 56.3 | 1.9 | 40. | .70 | 352 | 139 |
| 136 | Duisburg 16C Pb-gl | 85: 135 | 92.7 | .85 | 14.2 | 8.2 | 9.93 | 14.3 | 1.29 | 1.58 | 48.5 | 1.6 | 34, |  | 331 | 114 |
| 137 | Duisburg 16C Pb-gl | 85: 135 | 95.6 | .89 | 14.9 | 7.5 | 11.9 | 15.3 | 2.80 | 1.65 | 48.4 | 2.3 | 38. |  | 487 | 159 |
| 138 | Duisburg 16C Pb-gl | 85: 135 | 75.0 | 1.00 | 13.9 | 6.8 | 11.8 | 13.9 | 3.62 | 1.51 | 37.6 | 2.0 | 42. | .63 | 358 | 153 |
| 139 | Duisburg 16C Pb-gl | 85: 135 | 97.6 | .90 | 14.2 | 6.2 | 11.3 | 15.3 | 2.22 | 1.72 | 49.2 | 2.1 | 33. | .64 | 423 | 146 |
| 140 | Duisburg 16C Pb-gl | 85: 135 | 90.6 | .85 | 15.5 | 12.3 | 11.0 | 11.8 | 1.35 | 1.27 | 45.4 | 1.7 | 4.1 | .61 | 382 | 106 |
| 141 | Duisburg 16C Pb-gl | 85: 135 | 146. | 1.29 | 18.9 | 7.9 | 11.6 | 18.7 | 2.23 | 2.58 | 71.8 | 2.1 | 5.7 | .64 | 502 | 159 |
| 142 | Duisburg 18C Sn-gl | 83: 31 | 75.9 | .89 | 13.0 | 5.4 | 9.01 | 14.3 | 3.71 | 1.52 | 38.6 | 1.4 | 42. | .44 | 342 | 78. |
| 143 | Duisburg 18C Sn-gl | 83: 31 | 52.2 | .62 | 8.4 | 3.2 | 15.0 | 10.0 | 2.61 | 1.01 | 25.5 | 1.9 | 28. | .36 | 262 | 130 |
| 144 | Duisburg 18C Sn-gl | 83: 31 | 54.1 | .63 | 8.2 | 3.0 | 4.20 | 9.0 | 2.37 | 1.02 | 28.4 | .8 | 24. | .35 | 171 | 42. |
| 145 | Duisburg 18C Sn-gl | 83: 31 | 59.8 | .69 | 9.9 | 4.2 | 3.74 | 11.4 | 3.12 | 1.15 | 29.5 | 1.3 | 30. | .24 | 346 | 59. |
| 146 | Duisburg 17C Pb-gl | 86: 2 | 52.7 | .62 | 10.0 | 7.5 | 9.54 | 11.9 | 3.32 | 1.02 | 26.3 | 1.8 | 33. | .72 | 297 | 131 |
| 147 | Duisb. Schwanenstr. | 85: 135 | 69.4 | .69 | 11.8 | 6.6 | 11.4 | 14.7 | 3.72 | 1.20 | 32.3 | 2.3 | 4.2 | .58 | 341 | 155 |
| 148 | Utrecht | BM 1978, 5-4, 7 | 92.7 | 1.24 | 15.5 | 6.4 | 15.4 | 15.9 | 4.19 | 1.96 | 43.3 | 2.2 | 50. | .66 | 475 | 153 |
| 149 | Utrecht | BM 1978, 5-4, 8 | 82.8 | 1.08 | 15.3 | 7.0 | 15.2 | 14.8 | 3.61 | 1.73 | 39,8 | 2.1 | 46. | .66 | 534 | 163 |
| 150 | Utrecht | BM 1978, 5-4, 10 | 80.5 | 1.05 | 14.5 | 6.1 | 14.4 | 14.5 | 3.40 | 1.65 | 39.5 | 2.2 | 43, | .63 | 551 | 146 |
| 151 | Utrecht | BW 1978, 5-4, 9 | 72.5 | 1.05 | 13.6 | 6.1 | 13.0 | 13.4 | 3.25 | 1.65 | 36.8 | 2.0 | 41. | .53 | 430 | 140 |
| 152 | Utrecht | BW 1978, 5-4, 11 | 85.5 | 1.13 | 15.5 | 6.9 | 15.7 | 15.2 | 3.53 | 1.69 |  |  |  |  | 529 | 154 |
| 153 | Duisburg 17C Pb-gl | 86: 2 | 64.0 | .77 | 11.5 | 7.2 | 11.9 | 14.7 | 3.18 | 1.21 |  |  |  |  | 249 | 159 |
| 154 | Frechen kiln | 59/5/17 | 79.7 | .72 | 14.0 | 9.4 | 11.1 | 10.3 | .90 | 1.09 | 38.7 | 1.2 | 2.6 | .41 | 302 | 91. |
| 155 | Frechen kiln | 59/6 | 131. | 1.07 | 18.5 | 10.6 | 15.0 | 14.3 | .84 | 1.77 | 61.2 | 1.3 | 3.2 | .51 | 364 | 119 |
| 156 | Frechen kiln | 3 | 72.7 | .74 | 14.0 | 10.6 | 9.54 | 11.0 | .78 | 1.02 | 37.1 | 1.1 | 2.8 | .46 | 227 | 84. |
| 157 | Frechen kiln | 4 | 90.3 | .79 | 16.6 | 10.5 | 12.7 | 12.2 | .64 | 1.22 | 46.1 | 1.2 | 3.1 | .49 | 257 | 100 |
| 158 | Frechen kiln | 5 | 115. | 1.06 | 16.2 | 15.7 | 7.56 | 14.3 | 1.86 | 1.90 | 56.7 | 1.7 | 2.8 | .43 | 11$ | 145 |
| 159 | Frechen 6 | 6 | 79.3 | .80 | 14.0 | 11.1 | 10.9 | 11.5 | 1.66 | 1.17 | 37.0 | 1.5 | 2.7 | .44 | 315 | 105 |
| 160 | Duisburg | 88/1.8 | 54.8 | .75 | 14.3 | 12.9 | 10.9 | 11.7 | .88 | 1.01 | 26.4 | .9 | 2.4 | .41 | 203 | 53. |
| 161 | Duisburg | 88/1.8 | 77.8 | .71 | 14.2 | 7.4 | 12.6 | 11.9 | .83 | 1.04 | 42.1 | 1.5 | 2.5 | .40 | 305 | 114 |
| 162 | Duisburg | 88/1.8 | 105. | .96 | 15.5 | 16.3 | 9.92 | 14.6 | 1.08 | 1.80 | 51.5 | 1.8 | 2.3 | .37 | 17$ | 150 |
| 163 | Duisburg | 88/1.8 | 101. | 1.00 | 15.2 | 7.1 | 10.3 | 14.8 | 1.11 | 1.82 | 50.8 | 1.8 | 2.4 | .38 | 504 | 152 |
| 164 | Kreis Viersen |  | 96.3 | 1.03 | 14.6 | 10.0 | 8.06 | 14.0 | 2.41 | 1.77 | 44.7 | 1.7 | 3.0 | .47 | 448 | 127 |
| 165 | Kreis Viersen |  | 109. | 1.61 | 17.2 | 6.4 | 14.7 | 17.7 | 2.62 | 2.54 | 47.7 | 2.5 | 4.1 | .64 | 504 | 184 |

Table 4: Concordance of sample numbers in Table 3 and Diagrams 2–6

(K= Kiln site)

| sample | ware-type | sample | ware-type | sample | ware-type | sample | ware-type |
|---|---|---|---|---|---|---|---|
| 13 | Ib.7 | 80 | Ib.7 | 90 | Ia.3 (k) | 127 | Ic.1 |
| 14 | Ib.7 | | | 91 | Ia.3 (k) | 128 | Ic.1 |
| 15 | Ib.7 | 81 | Ia.11 | 92 | Ia.3 (k) | | |
| 16 | Ib.7 | | | 93 | Ia.3 (k) | 129 | Id.1 (k) |
| | | 82 | Ia.12 (k) | 94 | Ia.3 (k) | 130 | Id.1 (k) |
| 41 | Ia.12 (k) | 83 | Ia.12 (k) | | | 131 | Id.1 (k) |
| 42 | Ia.12 (k) | 84 | Ia.12 (k) | 95 | Ia.3 | 132 | Id.1 (k) |
| 43 | Ib.8 (k) | 85 | Ia.12 (k) | | | 133 | Id.1 (k) |
| 44 | Ib.8 (k) | 86 | Ia.12 (k) | 96 | Ib.1 | 134 | Id.1 (k) |
| 45 | Ib.8 (k) | | | 97 | Ib.1 | | |
| | | 87 | Id.12 | 98 | Ib.1 | 135 | Ib.1 |
| 60 | Ib.7 | | | 99 | Ib.1 | 136 | Ib.1 |
| 61 | Ib.7 | 88 | Id.12 | 100 | Ib.1 | 137 | Ib.1 |
| 62 | Ib.7 | 89 | Id.3 | 101 | Ib.1 | 138 | Ib.1 |
| 63 | Ib.7 | | | | | 139 | Ib.1 |
| 64 | Ib.7 | | | 105 | Ib.1 | 140 | Ib.1 |
| 65 | Ib.7 | | | 106 | Ib.1 | 141 | Ib.1 |
| 66 | Ib.7 | 142 | III.5 | | | 153 | Ic.1 |
| | | 143 | III.6 (k) | 107 | Ib.3 | | |
| 67 | Ib.3 | 144 | III.3 | | | 154 | Ic.3 (k) |
| 68 | Ia.11 | 145 | III.3 | 108 | Ib.3 | 155 | Ic.3 (k) |
| 70 | Ia.11 | | | 109 | Ib.3 | 156 | Ic.3 (k) |
| | | 146 | Ic.1 | | | 157 | Ic.3 (k) |
| 69 | Ia.12 | | | 121 | Ib.1 | 158 | Ib.8 (k) |
| 71 | Ia.12 | 147 | Ia.8 | | | 159 | Ic.3 (k) |
| 72 | Ia.12 | | | 122 | Id.1 | | |
| 73 | Ia.12 | 148 | Ia.8 (k) | 123 | Id.1 | 160 | Ib.3 |
| | | 149 | Ia.8 | 124 | Id.1 | 161 | Ib.3 |
| 74 | Ib.8 | 150 | Ia.8 | 125 | Id.1 | 162 | Ib.3 |
| 75 | Ib.8 | 151 | Ia.8 | 126 | Id.1 | 163 | Ib.3 |
| | | 152 | Ia.8 | | | | |
| | | | | | | 164 | Id.1 |
| | | | | | | 165 | Id.1 |

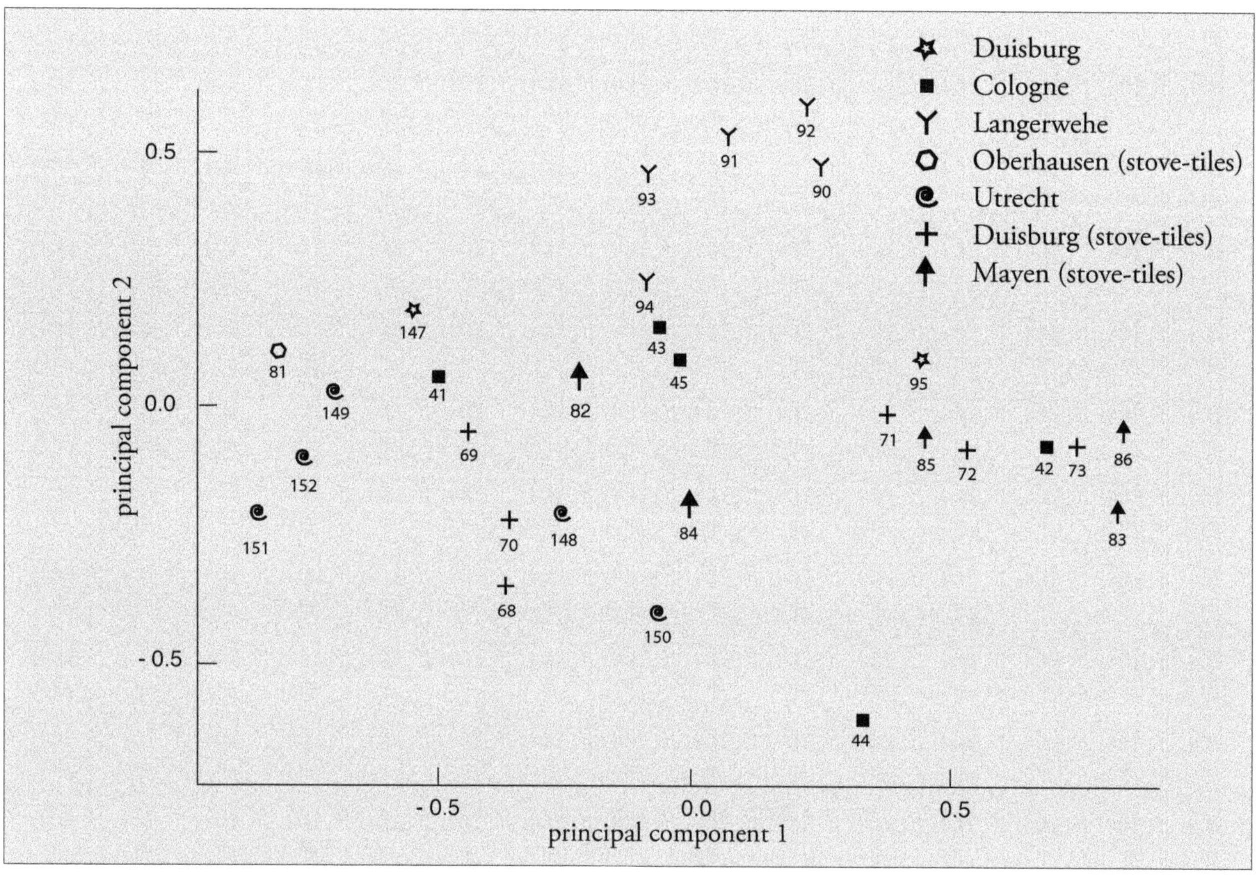


*Diagram 2 Earthenware pottery. Principal components plot: lead-glazed earthenware c. 1400–1500*

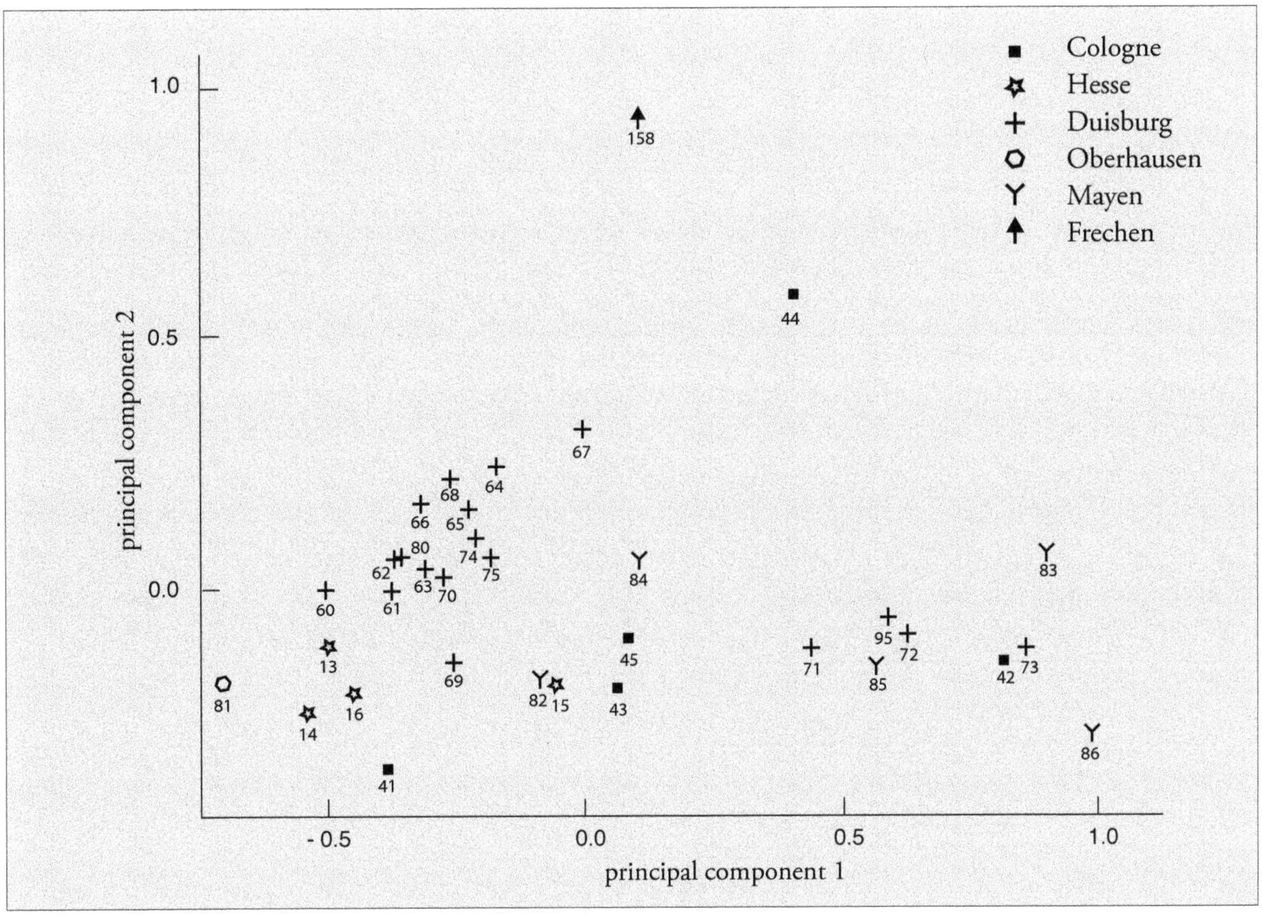


*Diagram 3* *Principal components plot: stove-tiles c. 1400-1500*

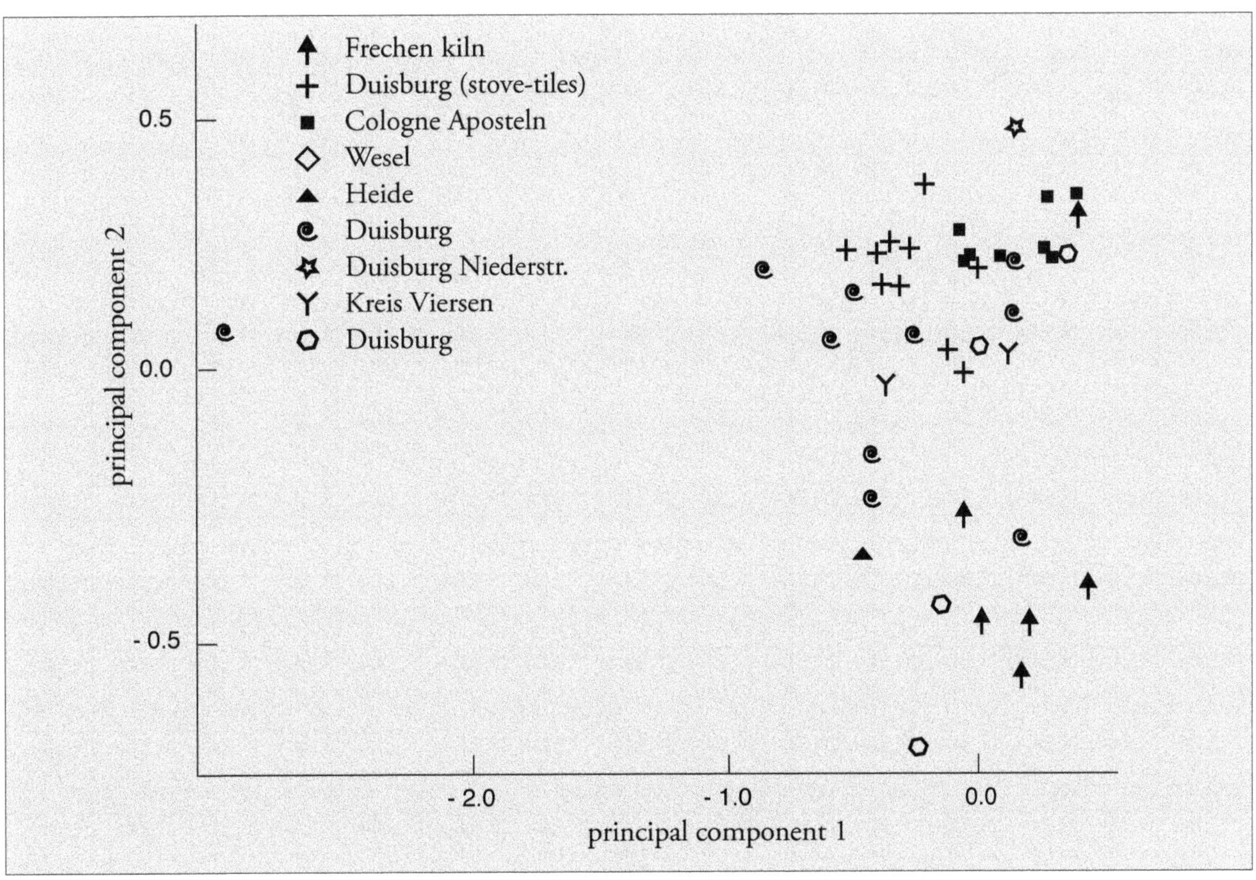


*Diagram 4* *Principal components plot: lead-glazed earthenware c. 1500-1700*

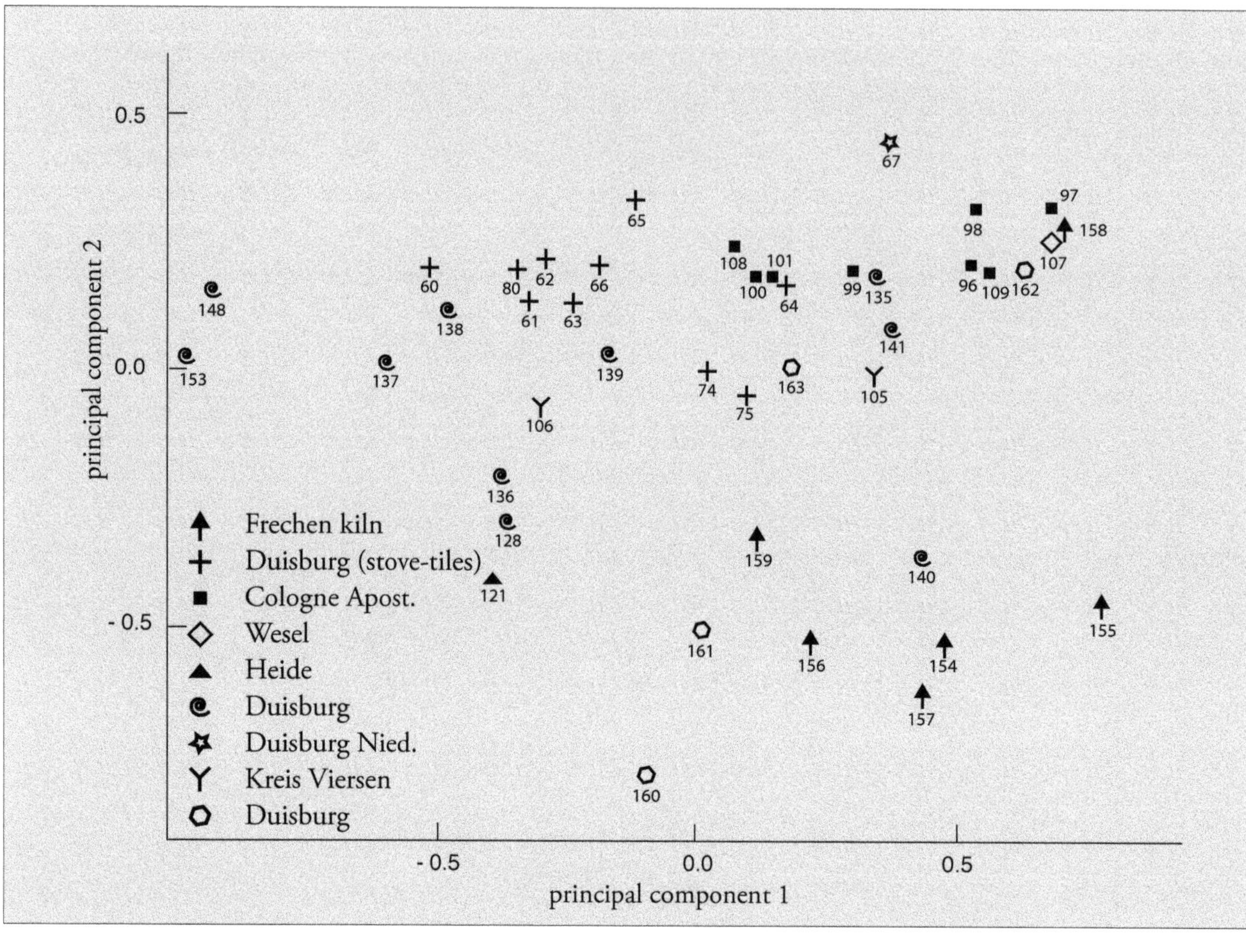


*Diagram 5* *Principal components plot: lead-glazed earthenware c. 1500–1700 (expanded version)*

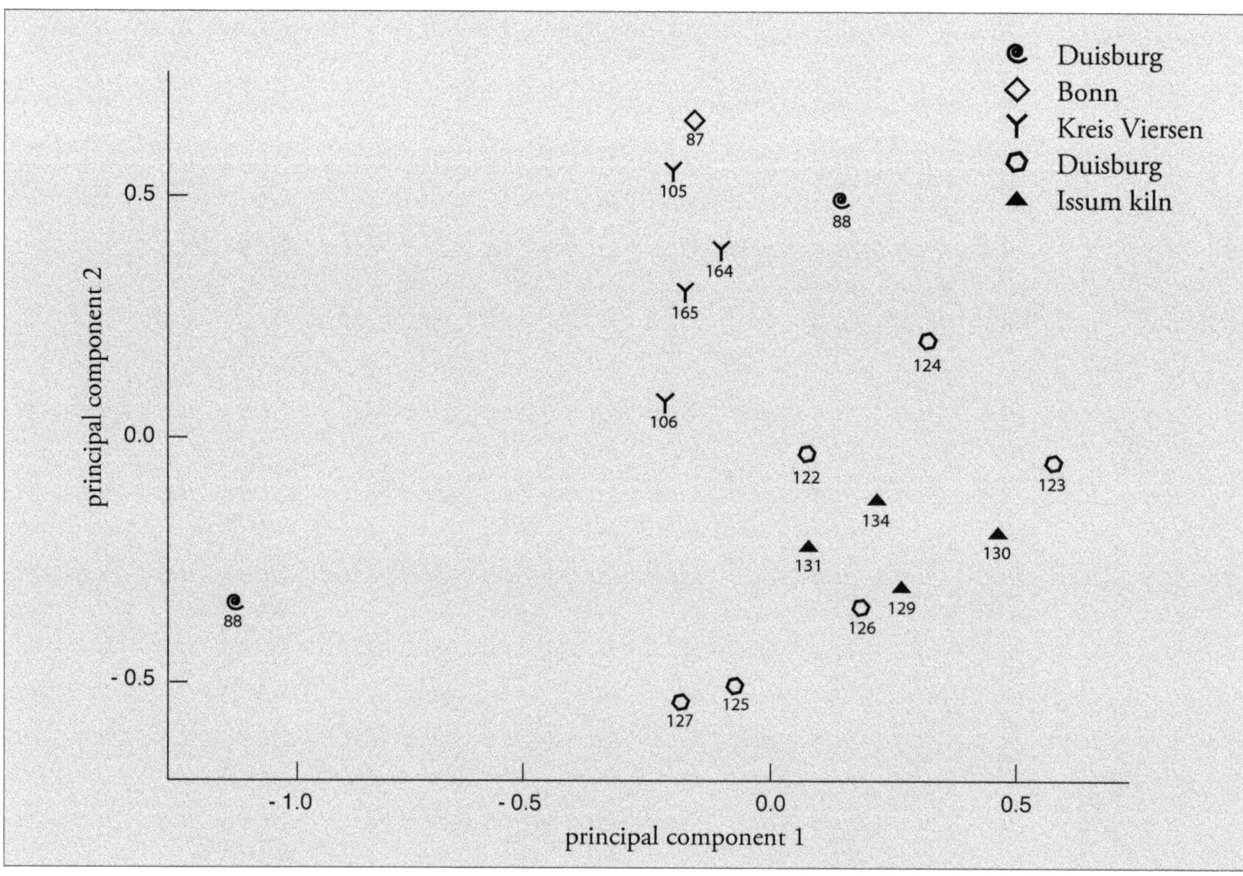


*Diagram 6* *Principal components plot: lead-glazed earthenware c. 1700–1800*

# 5. Post-medieval ceramic "traditions" in the Lower Rhineland c. 1400–1800

## 5.1 Introduction

### *5.1.1 Defining regional ceramic "traditions"*

It is intended to summarise in this Section the principal trends in regional ceramic production and distribution during the period c. 1400 to 1800. Sections 6 and 7 will deal with the relative composition of archaeological consumer assemblages on an intra-site and inter-site level respectively, and examine their implications for social, economic and functional analysis.

Once the initial classification of individual Ware-types has taken place (Section 3) and the problems of characterisation have been clarified, the respective Wares can be amalgamated into ceramic "Traditions" for discussion of their general typochronology. Traditions (cf. Moorhouse 1983a, 84) comprise Ware-types which share a set of common fabric, form or decorative characteristics identified with a given geographical region and timespan (e. g. Lower Rhine Slipware: Ware-types Ib.5, Ic.4, Id.1–2). Based on the ceramic sequence recovered from Duisburg and a number of other sites, the purpose of this section is to chart the development of the idividual ceramic traditions in the region and examine their typological, stylistic and technical relationships from the late Middle Ages to early modern period.

To aid the discussion here, a series of illustrations have been prepared. Diagrams 8a–8g summarise the principal forms and decorative types of each major Ware-category (I–V) found in the Lower Rhineland. They are followed by a series of maps (3–6) which contain schematic reconstructions of the relative distances and respective routes travelled by pottery made in and imported into the region. The section will also examine the sequences of Rhenish post-medieval ceramics excavated in the Low Countries and neighbouring regions of Germany, and the extent to which they compare to the Lower Rhine situation. The locations of the principal consumer assemblages found in The Netherlands and Belgium are shown in Map 3.

The regional ceramic traditions identified from excavations in the Lower Rhineland are composed of both indigenous wares and imported products. They will be discussed in the following sequence:

| | |
|---|---|
| 5.2 | Lead-glazed earthenwares |
| 5.2.1 | Whiteware |
| 5.2.2 | Greyware |
| 5.2.3 | Redware |
| 5.2.4 | Polychrome earthenware & slipware |
| 5.2.5 | Regional imports |
| 5.2.6 | Stove-tiles |
| 5.3 | Rhenish stonewares |
| 5.3.1 | Siegburg |
| 5.3.2 | Langerwehe |
| 5.3.3 | Raeren |
| 5.3.4 | Cologne |
| 5.3.5 | Frechen |
| 5.3.6 | Westerwald |
| 5.4 | Tin-glazed earthenwares |
| 5.4.1 | NL maiolica |
| 5.4.2 | NL faience |
| 5.4.3 | Rhenish faience |
| 5.5 | Porcelain |
| 5.5.1 | Oriental porcelain |
| 5.5.2 | German porcelain |
| 5.6 | English finewares |
| 5.6.1 | Staffs. creamware |
| 5.6.2 | earthenware |
| 5.6.3 | stoneware |

## 5.2 Lead-glazed earthenwares

### *5.2.1 Whiteware*

i. 15th century (Ia.2-5)

Alongside stoneware production a wide range of white-firing earthenwares were manufactured at several of the Rhenish stoneware centres from the 14th century onwards (Hurst *et al.* 1986, 227). The spectrum of forms produced suggest that they were intended to fulfil quite separate functions to their stoneware counterparts. The consumer site evidence confirms the emergence of a specialist whiteware industry, composed of a number of dispersed workshops, operating between the Maas and the Lower Rhineland during the 14th to 15th centuries. Typologically the industry continues with the inventory of forms made at the Andennes workshops on the Maas during their last phase of production after the second half of the 14th century (Borremans & Warginaire 1966).

Whitewares, attributed on glaze and typological grounds to Langerwehe (Ia.2), are present in small quantities in Duisburg contexts of the first half of the 15th century (Context 38). Typical forms include small pipkins and jugs (Fig. 52, Nos. 10–11). Larger groups of Langerwehe whiteware have been recognised at

Neuss (Contexts 69 & 70), including beakers, money boxes and pilgrim horns. Similar specialised products are known from consumer sites in the Netherlands (Hurst *et al.* 1986, 228). Recent excavations on the site of a whiteware kiln dump at Langerwehe Uhlhaus (pers. comm. W. Giertz) will help to clarify the range of vessel forms and decorative types being produced at the beginning of the 15th century.

Publication of the discovery will increase the recognition of Langerwehe whiteware in the region and outside.

Like their stoneware counterparts, white-firing earthenwares from Langerwehe were traded along the Rhine to the Netherlands, and were perhaps not intended for local consumption (Hurst 1988, 337). More quantified groups from Belgium are necessary before the westward distribution by land can be adequately assessed.

One explanation for the scarcity of Langerwehe whitewares in the Lower Rhineland during the 15th century might be provided by the compensatory frequency of green and transparent (yellow)-glazed whitewares from an entirely separate source (Ware-type Ia.3; Gaimster 1988a, 153). The mutual exclusivity of their clay compositions has been confirmed by neutron activation analysis (4.2.2; Diag. 2). The supply of fine white earthenware tripod pipkins, dripping pans (Fig. 48, No. 1) and deep bowls to the Lower Rhine towns of Duisburg and Neuss dates from the beginning to the third quarter of the 15th century (e. g. Contexts 38 and 69/70 respectively). To date no examples of this ware have been reported outside the Lower Rhine region. The Netherlands had its own source of whiteware pottery at this time, based at Utrecht (Hurst *et al.* 1986, Cat. 180).

The density of casual finds of this Ware-type in Cologne (Appendix 5, Nos. 1–3,7–8,29) points to a local source of manufacture. It is significant that the fabric is visually indistinguishable from the contemporary whiteware stove-tiles found on kiln dumps in the city (Unger ed. 1988, Cat. 7–69). Access to relatively rare white-firing clays from the nearby Siegburg or Westerwald area was facilitated by riverine connections (Unger ed. 1988, 31), in contrast to the potteries further downstream in the Lower Rhine hinterland which would not have been able to afford the heavier transportation costs. The possibility of a Cologne source has been confirmed by neutron activation analysis (Section 4.2.2), although further sampling is necessary before full confirmation of provenance can be established.

So far the archaeological and preliminary scientific evidence points to a small-scale whiteware industry along the Rhine pivoting on the Cologne-Koblenz region. The area is known for whiteware stove-tile production at this time (Unger ed. 1988; Mielke 1977; Redknap 1988), and it is not inconceivable that tilers were producing ceramic kitchenwares in the same clay as a profitable sideline (as they are documented as doing so during the 16th century; see Section 1.1.3). Further chemical analysis will be directed towards investigating this relationship.

The Duisburg excavations have also produced a further series of whiteware fabrics from 15th-century contexts. Coarse green-glazed tripod pipkins or jars are characterised also by their distinctive rouletted decoration around the upper body (Ware-type Ia.5). Their distribution is concentrated in the Lower Rhineland, with parallel finds known from the Castle of Bloemersheim, Kreis Wesel (Context 94), and Neuss (Context 85).

Finally, in contrast to the kitchen-orientated whitewares, the later 15th-century horizons in Duisburg have produced a complementary range of cups, porringers and bowls with interior glaze in hard-fired whiteware (Ware-type Ia.4; Gaimster 1988a, Fig. 2.). They all have flat, turned bases, and were clearly intended as fine tableware products to compete with the contemporary stonewares (e. g. Context 7; Fig. 11, No. 5). Their distribution and frequency are limited, however, and it appears that the production of white-firing earthenwares was only economically viable if concentrated on the less competitive kitchenware market. Graph 11 shows that 72 % of all 15th-century whitewares recorded during the survey are represented by the principal cooking forms: tripod pipkins (various sizes), colanders and dripping-pans (Diags. 8a–b).

Their fine white fabrics and bright interior glazing must have made them both attractive, functional and probably more desirable vessels than their redware or greyware counterparts in the utilitarian pottery market. Recent research on the emergence of the fine whiteware industry in Southern England during the late 15th to early 16th centuries (Holling 1971; Orton 1982a) has shown that the difficulties in whiteware manufacture (there being little margin of error between the temperature at which the glaze will flux and that at which the clay will melt) were tolerated for the sake of having a preferred product. Combined with the relative scarcity of clay deposits and with the high rate of kiln wastage (evident at Langerwehe, pers. comm. W. Giertz), the whitewares probably carried a marginally higher price tag.

ii. 16th to 17th Centuries (Ib.3, Ic.3)

By the end of the 15th century a number of fine green-glazed whiteware cups and porringers (Ware-type Ib.3) appear in the Duisburg sequence (Contexts 32 & 38; Diag. 8b bottom line). Optically, the fabric is virtually indistinguishable from the earlier 15th-century whitewares (Ia.3), although more samples are required for NAA before the continuity of production can be confirmed. By the beginning of the 16th century they are more frequent and the variety of flatware shapes has expanded to include plates, two-handled porringers and finely-turned cups in both yellow and green glaze (Diag. 8c, top line). These early 16th-century whitewares are represented by tablewares alone; kitchenwares in white-firing clay seem to disappear entirely at this time. The production of whiteware for table use at the beginning of the 16th century emphasises its relative exclusivity in comparison to contemporary redwares, which were essentially multi-purpose.

Deep bowls (Appendix 5, No. 4) and specialised forms, such as "ring"beakers or bottles (Appendix 5, Nos. 10–12) have been found in Cologne, and it may be assumed that they were products of the emerging whiteware industry in the locality. The industry gathers momentum during the course of the 16th century, and is responsible for the manufacture of a new range of dishes, plates and bowls decorated with spiral concentric bands of combed decoration under the glaze. Examples have been found in contexts dating to the first half of the 16th century in Duisburg (e. g. Context 30; Fig. 45, No. 14) and are prevalent on sites in Cologne (e. g. Context 73; Appendix 5, Nos. 22–4). The decorative technique is part of a regional fashion for incised ornament on red and white earthenware during the 16th to 17th centuries (Section 5.2.3; Gaimster 1988a; 1991, 54).

The distribution of Rhenish whiteware in the 16th century is not limited, however, to the home market. Excavations in the Low Countries and Britain have identified a limited export market for these finewares. Dishes with combed wavy decoration on the flange are known from Deventer (Clevis & Kottman 1989, Cat. 11–71), Kessel Castle, near Venlo (Clevis & Thijssen 1989, Cat. 246) and Newcastle-upon-Tyne (Ellison 1981, Fig. 29, No. 312). A porringer has also been found in Norwich (Jennings 1981, Cat. 1017).

Unfortunately sealed groups of pottery dating from the second half of the 16th century are rare in the Lower Rhine region, and it has not been possible to chart the development of the whiteware tradition with any degree of certainty at this time. However, the Duisburg excavations have produced a number of large latrine assemblages dating from the period c. 1580/1600 to 1670 containing a wide spectrum of whitewares (Contexts 4, 8, 16, 17). These finds have now been attributed to Frechen, outside Cologne, on the basis of their distinctive typology and decorative treatment (Gaimster 1988a, 159, 1991).

The demise of the stoneware and earthenware industries in Cologne after 1550 is well documented (Brill 1969; Göbels 1985, 112–9). Both industries shrank in favour of the existing pottery communities in neighbouring town of Frechen to the West between c. 1550 and 1570. Excavations over the past decade in the centre of the town (Jürgens & Kleine 1988; Kleine 1989) have revealed a series of kilns producing green and yellow-glazed whitewares. Situated on outcrops of white-firing clays, the workshops were capable of making these wares a staple product alongside the massproduced stonewares. Both wares were made to fulfil separate functional roles in the regional and international pottery markets.

The Frechen-type whitewares (Ware-type Ic.3) are characterised by a more refined, almost pipe-clay fabric, finished in a bright green or transparent (yellow) glaze. Flatwares tend to be green-glazed on the interior, while hollow wares, such as pipkins, have green glaze on the exterior and transparent glaze on the interior surfaces. The combed spiral and wavy decoration of the earlier 16th-century whitewares continues in the early part of the century on the dishes and bowls (Diag. 8d). Characteristic of the dishes are the pinched rim (Diag. 8d), which is also a feature of contemporary redware dishes, and the pedestal footring, indicative perhaps of a functional specialisation, namely the serving of food. The form is reminiscent of 17th-century faience dishes from Holland (e. g. Fig. 28, No. 5). The full range of forms produced by the industry include flat tablewares, such as plates, dishes and porringers, and vessels for food preparation, such as tripod pipkins and colanders (Gaimster 1991, Fig. 4).

The statistical analysis from Duisburg indicates that 69 % of 16th and 17th-century whiteware made in the region is represented by tripod pipkin cooking pots of varying size and sub-type (hollow or strap handle). Dishes and porringers for the table only make up 23 % of the total form count, although this is a much higher ratio of table to kitchen forms than the contemporary redwares (Graphs 15, 16). Specialised forms included tripod colanders (4 %) and ointment pots (3 %). The tradition is characterised not by a wide range of different form-types, but by a small number of basic shapes in varying sizes and with minor typological modifications.

Frechen produced whitewares for the international as well as the home market. They were shipped downstream via Cologne to the Low Countries and to Britain, as recent archaeological discoveries have illustrated. Frechen whitewares have been found at Newcastle-upon-Tyne (Ellison 1981, Fig. 28, 261–2; Gaimster 1988c, note 55), London (unpublished[1]), Amsterdam (unpublished[2]), Nijmegen (Thijssen 1981,

---

[1] Dish with interior combed concentric bands and overall green glaze (Ware-type Ic.3), found City of London (Museum of London 18, 837).

[2] Range of vessel types excavated at site of Trippenhuis, Kloveniersburgwal 20, Amsterdam (Amsterdams Historisch Museum, Dienst openbare Werken).

Cat. 47, 88–9; 1989, Cat. 3–4; 1991 ed., Cat. 160–3; Maastricht (Clevis 1980, Fig. 29.9), Deventer (Clevis & Kottman 1989, Cat. 11–167), and Maaseik (Heymans ed. 1989, Cat. 2.106) among other findspots.

Besides Duisburg, the Frechen products have been found on town excavations throughout the Lower Rhine region, notably at Wesel (Contexts 74, 76), Neuss (71, 72a, 72b), Düsseldorf (Context 67), Aachen (Context 89), Cologne (Appendix 5, Nos. 36–37) and Bonn (Context 87b). The importance of Cologne as the nodal point in the distribution of Frechen wares is reflected in the frequent references to "greune zu Frechen gebackene Duppen" (1635) in the Cologne civic archives (Göbels 1985, 276), and the prominent depiction of Frechen wares in an engraving of the Cologne Alter Markt by Johann Toussyn, dated 1660 (detail on titlepage).

Neutron activation analysis of waster samples has confirmed the homogeneity of the chemical composition of the clays used at the Frechen industry (Section 4.2.4; Diag. 4–5). The position of two samples of earlier 16th-century whiteware (Ware-type Ib.3) within the Frechen cluster may point to an earlier phase of production in the town, and at a possible alternative source to Cologne for this particular class of ware. Further sampling of 16th and 17th-century whitewares is necessary before a clearer picture of the spread of production sites can emerge. The evidence so far, both stylistic and scientific, emphasises the continuity of white earthenware production in the Cologne-Frechen region from the 16th to 17th centuries. The displacement of potting from Cologne to Frechen during the second half of the 16th century does not seem to have affected the regional supply of whiteware pots. Indeed, the market share of green-glazed whitewares increased dramatically in Duisburg during the second half of the century (Graphs 4–5).

iii. 18th century (Id.3)

Until the final quarter of the 17th-century green-glazed Frechen whitewares continued to form a substantial part of the Duisburg ceramic sequence. Thereafter they disappear and are replaced by a limited range of slipware vessels, notably dishes, plates and chamber pots (Ware-type Id.3; see Diag. 8f-g). Their market share was drastically reduced in the face of the overwhelming dominance of the local Lower Rhine slipwares.

Slipwares made at Frechen for the commemorative or display market are well known in the literature (Scholten-Neess & Jüttner 1971, 78–82), and emphasise the increasingly specialised nature of the industry during the 18th century. The occasional use of a red interior slip on the flatwares (Jürgens & Kleine 1988, Pl. 11) suggests perhaps the intention to compete with the red earthenwares of the Lower Rhine hinterland.

### *5.2.2 Greyware*

i. 15th to 16th Centuries (Ia.6–7, Ib.9)

As in the Low Countries (H.L. Janssen 1983b), the production of unglazed, reduced grey earthenware has enjoyed a long tradition in the Lower Rhineland. Greywares can be traced back at least as far as the 12th century (Stephan 1982, 99–103, Fig. 29). Greyware globular cooking pots and ladles were made in enough quantities at Paffrath (Lung 1956) and other sites, such as Xanten (Hinz 1971), to suggest a sizeable home market and export trade during the 12th century, which is confirmed by British finds (Vince 1985, Fig. 2). Evidence for the continuation of this potting tradition has come from waster heaps at Elmpt and Bruggen (Rech 1982), which date from the 11th/12th to late 14th centuries. The globular cooking pot, globular skillet, tripod pipkin, large bowl and various jug forms were the most common vessel-types recovered. These greyware types are common in the 12th-century levels at Duisburg (Krause 1988, Fig. 7), and continue uninterrupted into the 14th/15th centuries.

Evidence for their typological development has been provided by the excavation of a kiln in Xanten producing greywares during the 13th and late 14th centuries (Wegner 1981). The principal products of the workshop were represented by the globular cooking pot forms and by a range of wide-mouthed bowls with pulled lips and rudimentary frilled bases (Wegner 1981, Figs. 5, 6).

Excavations at the Minoritenkloster site in the Duisburg Altstadt (Context 36) produced a mixed assemblage of wares dating from the mid-14th to mid-15th centuries. It contained a small number of grey earthenware dishes or bowls (Fig. 48, Nos. 6–9) similar in profile to the Xanten types. Virtually all the subsequent early 15th-century contexts in the town have contained greyware pottery (e. g. Contexts 1,2,3,7,15,37,38). Principal forms include deep, wide-mouthed bowls with pulled lips (64 %), large globular and biconical jars (14 %), chamber pots (2 %), tripod pipkins (14 %) and colanders (2 %) (Gaimster 1988a, Fig. 3; Diag. 8a; Graph 12). With the exception of the tripod vessels, the bases are normally frilled, in contrast to the contemporary Low Countries products, which are characterised by pinched feet under the base (H. L. Janssen 1983b). A finer fabric was used for the production of small jugs (2 %) (Diag. 8a).

In sum, the industry specialised in the manufacture of coarse kitchen, storage and sanitary ware: a pattern repeated in the Low Countries (H.L. Janssen 1983b, 134–7). The improved imperviousness caused by the reduction atmosphere in the kiln would have made the wares ideally suited to these functions. Missing, finally, in the Rhenish inventory of greyware forms are any medium or large jugs commonly found on the Dutch or Flemish sites (e. g. Nijmegen: Thijssen ed. 1991, Cat. 72). Here again, it is probable that the Rhenish stoneware industry was too strong for any competition in the ceramic tableware market. The predominance of the deep bowl forms with the pulled lip (Diag. 8a; Gaimster 1988a, Fig. 3, No. 6) may allude to the development of a specialised greyware product for the regional earthenware market. According to Lehnemann (1978, 85–90), such vessels were traditionally used in a variety of dairy processes in North West Germany from the Middle Ages.

Chronologically the greywares continue in Duisburg (Context 1) and Neuss (Context 69, 85) in significant quantities until the third quarter of the 15th century. The lifespan of the greywares found in Duisburg is consistent with the Dutch picture (e. g. at Spangen Castle (Renaud 1952)) and at the nunnery at Mariendael (Renaud 1959a). However, greywares (Ware-type Ib.9) have been found in late 16th-century contexts in Wesel (Context 74) and in Bocholt on the Dutch border (Context 90). The evidence points to the small-scale survival of a marginal greyware industry in the region into the late 16th century. The observed pattern is not entirely without precedent in northern Germany as greywares continued in production in the Nordoldenburger Geest region (Zoller 1980, 15, Gruppe B), and at the Hagen kiln site, near Osnabrück, into the early 17th century (Gerdsen & Rotterdam 1986). Slowly their niche in the market was eroded and finally taken over by the glazed redwares.

In terms of regional marketing, the distribution pattern for Rhenish greywares seems to be widespread in both town and country during the 15th and early 16th centuries. A large group found in latrine contexts at the Castle of Brüggen, Kreis Viersen (Context 95; Rech 1979), indicates that the industry supplied high-status seignorial residences as well as the local town population. Despite the survival of sealed assemblages of greyware in Duisburg and Neuss, it is significant that, after so long, little regional greyware has been found in Cologne. Only a large bowl is known from the Cologne Elmstraße with incised zig-zag decoration on the rim (Appendix 5, No. 13). In view of the predominantly Lower Rhine distribution, it may be assumed that the source of greyware production was centred on the hinterland of the region itself (Map 3), although waster finds of the 15th century are still unknown. Future neutron activation analysis will examine the compositional relationship between greywares, redwares and and whitewares found in the region. Research at Andenne immediately to the West has shown that one clay source could have been responsible for the production of all three ware types (Borremans & Wargginaire 1966).

### *5.2.3 Redware*

#### i. 15th century (Ia.8–9)

The Duisburg sequence indicates that red earthenwares with interior coloured glazes (Ware-types Ia.8 and Ia.9) were available to the customer in the Lower Rhine by the middle of the 15th century, gradually displacing the unglazed greywares from their market niche (Graphs 1 & 2). The chronology of their introduction in the region coincides roughly with parallel developments in the South Netherlands, where, for example, in Utrecht greywares were finally ousted by new redware products by c. 1450 (H. L. Janssen 1983b, note 43). Redware production at the Utrecht II and Amersfort kilns (Bruijn 1979) dates from c. 1400–25 and 1450–75 respectively. The gradual ascendancy of redwares over greywares is also parallelled in northern Germany at this time (Zoller 1980, 54–57); although, as in the Lower Rhineland, the new products retained the general typological characteristics of their predecessors.

It is likely that the potters producing greywares during the earlier half of the century switched to redware production in line with consumer demands (cf. Blake 1980), for both the same clay and the same kiln could be used. Only the final stage of the production process, involving firing the vessels in a reducing or oxidising atmosphere, decided the final colouration. To reduce the porosity level for red earthenwares, it was necessary to introduce a lead glaze, which was both more effective than simple reduction techniques, but also more expensive on account of the lead required. The glazing would, therefore, have introduced a price differential. According to H. L. Janssen (1983b, 137), the success of lead-glazed redwares in the Low Countries was based not on the development of new forms , but on the improved efficiency of the earthenware body to perform a wide variety of tasks in the kitchen and dining environment. Glazing on the Lower Rhine wares varies from black-brown (iron-rich), transparent (with iron flecks) to dark olive-green (copper-rich) in colour. The uniformity of glazing colours suggests a selection deliberately chosen to appeal to the consumer.

The typological range of redwares found in the Lower Rhineland is more limited than that found in the Netherlands at this time (Bruijn 1979), and possibly hints at a more conservative consumer market or perhaps more likely at the stranglehold exerted by the Rhenish stonewares on the supply of tableware to the region. However, the impression may be altered by the discovery of a production site assemblage. The principal forms recovered in Duisburg to date include tripod pipkins (45 %), flat-based pipkins and chamber pots (22 %), bowls with pulled lips and frilled bases (16 %), dripping pans (5 %) and tripod skillets (5 %).

Small bowl-salts and jugs appear to have been specialist products (7 %), while only one jar with a basket handle has been identified to date (Fig. 44, No. 4; see also Gaimster 1988a, Fig. 4; Diag. 8b for a general summary of principal formtypes). Again, jugs (2 %) do not feature strongly in the Lower Rhine redware inventory, probably as a result of the stoneware domination in this paricular field (68 % of 15th-century Siegburg stoneware founds in Duisburg are jug forms).

Functionally, like the greywares, the majority of redwares were destined for kitchen or sanitary use, although specialist products, such as salts, were clearly earmarked for the tableware market. The primary indicator of functional variation among the range of bowls, tripod pipkins and other kitchenwares is their relative size: the variations in dimensions reflective of diversification of use. The pulled lip which characterise the deep bowl forms (Diag. 8b; Gaimster 1988a, Fig. 4, Nos. 6–7) of both the 15th-century redwares and the greywares is suggestive of specialist dairy use (Lehnemann 1978, 85–90).

Dutch-style pulled feet do not feature in the Lower Rhine spectrum of 15th-century redware or greyware forms. Bases of chamber pots, bowls and the taller pipkin or chamber pot forms are all flat, usually with some rudimentary frilling. The profiles repeat those of their greyware counterparts almost exactly, and add weight to the supposition that the same production sites were responsible for the manufacture of both wares, at least initially during the middle of the 15th century. The hypothesis will be tested during the next phase of chemical analysis on Lower Rhine post-medieval ceramics.

The one innovation in the production of red earthenware in the Lower Rhineland was the introduction of slip decoration. So far only a small number of chamber pots from Duisburg have produced evidence of this type of ornament (Diag. 8b; Fig. 11, No. 1). The arcaded trailed patterns with dots recall contemporary Netherlands redwares (Ruempol & Garthoff-Zwaan 1988), notably from the Utrecht II kiln (Bruijn 1979, Fig. 49). The introduction of slip decoration, if only sparse, re-emphasises the strong influence of the Netherlands in the evolution of an independent redware tradition in the Lower Rhineland.

Neutron activation analysis of the 15th-century redwares from Duisburg failed to provide an indication of source (4.2.2: Diag. 2); although the dispersed nature of the Lower Rhine redware and Utrecht kiln cluster has excluded the possibility that redwares were imported upstream from the Netherlands. Further consumer site asemblages are required in the Lower Rhine region in order to define the geographical distribution of redwares during the 15th century. So far only Duisburg, along with Neuss (Contexts 70, 85) and Schloss Bloemersheim (Context 94), has produced quantifiable assemblages. The archaeological evidence, meagre though it is, points to a source or series of production sites nearby in the Lower Rhine hinterland (Map 3), where alluvial, ferrous, red-firing clays were easily accessible (Scholten-Neess & Jüttner 1971, 17–21). It is significant that no redware vessels are known from Cologne at this time (the area of fine white-firing clays).

ii. 16th to 17th Centuries (Ib.1, Ib.2, Ic.1, Ic.2)

According to the Duisburg sequence (e. g. Contexts 30, 41, 42), the 15th-century redware types (Ware-types Ia.8, Ia.9) were replaced at the turn of the century by an innovative range of glazed red earthenwares (Ware-types Ib.1-2). The frequency of quartz sand inclusions and fabric colour is very variable, ranging from buff to pinkish orange. The discrepancies may point to a variety of geographical sources for the Ware, as the neutron activation analysis suggests (Section 4.2.4; Diags. 4–5).

The range of glazing effects is also varied, ranging from transparent (iron-speckled), dark green (copper-rich) to black-brown (iron-rich) in colour. The variety was probably intended to increase the marketability of the wares, and is not indicative of production source in its own right.

The principal forms cover the full range of functional categories: tablewares, kitchen wares, sanitary wares and vessels for storage. The principal tablewares comprise dishes (often with combed under-glaze decoration (Ib.2)), cups and porringers (Diag. 8c; Gaimster 1988a, Fig. 5). The introduction of red earthenware tablewares around c. 1500 is parallelled in whiteware from the Cologne-Frechen region (see above Section 5.2.1). The development represents a "revolution" (*cf.* Dawson 1979; Orton 1982) in regional ceramic manufacturing and consumption (See Section 8.3.2), as so little earthenware had been made for table use before. Tablewares made up 23 % of red earthenware forms in Duisburg during the 16th century (Graph 15).

It is at this time that the Rhenish lead-glazed earthenware dishes develop their charactertistic angular profile which continued well into the 17th century. The typical offset flange indicates the use of a template to create the profile. The uniformity of individual profiles in both flatware and hollow-ware points to a conformity of regional production irrespective of specific source. In other words a "brand image" for post-medieval Rhenish earthenware was established, as immediately recognisable as the regional stoneware products or the contemporary earthenwares in the Netherlands.

The introduction of earthenware dishes to the region also provided an opportunity for ceramic ornament. Like the whitewares, the redware dishes (Ib.2) are mostly decorated with combed wavy bands around the flange or centre of the vessel (Diag. 8c; Gaimster

1988a, Fig. 5, No. 1).The decoration was incised into the leather-hard body of the vessel before glazing and firing. The pie-crust rim on several Duisburg dishes (e. g. Fig. 36, No. 11) is also reminiscent of the Frechen-type whitewares. Several of the dishes have suspension holes suggesting the wares might have been made as much for display as for table use (Gaimster 1991, 54), although the precise implications of suspension holes in post-medieval earthenware remains the focus of debate (Burhenne *et al.* 1991, 27).

The majority of redware forms (65 % overall) were intended for kitchen use: with tripod pipkins with strap or hollow handles and lids predominant (42 %); and flat-based pipkins, deep bowls or dairy pancheons with pouring lips, casseroles, cauldrons, and skillets making up the remainder of forms (25 %). Redware is more ideally suited for cooking and preparing food as it is capable of withstanding the constant pressures of heating and cooling more effectively than the whiteware body (Orton 1982, 82). Storage vessels, including large tripod jars (Fig. 53, No. 2) and sanitary wares make up the rest of the typological spectrum (11 %). Several of these cooking forms also represent innovations in the Lower Rhine post-medieval earthenware tradition, principally the large cauldrons and casseroles, for which there is no evidence for their use in the region before this period.

The typological range is broadly consistent with comtemporary developments in the Low Countries (e. g. Deventer: Clevis & Kottman 1989, 96–103) and northern Germany (e. g. the Oldenburg Geest area: Zoller 1980), although the overall picture here is not as comprehensive. An extensive range of vessels in this Ware-type has been excavated in Cologne. The Apostelnstraße assemblage (Context 73) contained a large quantity of redware (Ib.1–2) and whiteware (Ib.3) dating, on the basis of the Cologne stoneware present in the group, to the second quarter of the 16th century. Additional redware forms included squat jars and sugarmoulds. Dishes of every size were predominant. The recent excavation of a 16th-century earthenware kiln site in the Severinstraße (Neu 1990) will provide valuable attributional evidence for the redwares of this date found in the city (Appendix 5). It is hoped to sample wasters from this site for neutron activation in the near future.

The regional distribution of redware was extensive during the 16th century with excavations in Duisburg, Düsseldorf (Context 66), Neuss (Context 72b) and Wesel (Contexts 74, 75, 77, 78, 79, 80) all producing substantial assemblages. A varied collection of fragments in this ware-type is known from Frankfurt am Main (Döry 1978, Cat. 348–353), although the excavator suggests that they could have come from a more local source. To date no kilns outside Cologne are known, but it is clear from the range of fabric variations and the chemical analysis of a small sample of wares (Section 4.2.4) that production was probably spread over a wide geographical area. Documentary evidence from Duisburg suggests a local source for earthenware from the beginning of the 16th century (Scholten-Neess 1979). The award of town citizenship to local Duppenbäcker (earthenware potters as opposed to the Kannenbäcker or stoneware potters) is recorded in 1510 and 1519.

The scale of the industry is illustrated by the frequency of finds of Rhenish redware in the Low Countries and Britain, notably at Deventer (Clevis & Kottman 1989, 129–133); 's-Hertogenbosch (H.L. Janssen 1983a, Fig. 32); Kessel Castle, near Venlo (Clevis & Kottman 1989, Cat. 228); Nijmegen (Thijssen ed. 1991, Cat. 166, 174); Bruges (Hillewaert & Verhaeghe 1991, Fig. 176, Nos. 5–6) and Newcastle-upon-Tyne (Ellison 1981, Cat. 306–12). In many cases it is difficult to differentiate between the white-firing earthenware (Ware-type Ib.3) and the light orange to pinkish fabrics (Ware-type Ib.1). In the above cases all the wares have been classified as "whitewares", although enormous variation in fabric colour is evident from the reports. Neutron activation analysis conducted during the course of this survey has demonstrated that some of the regional 16th century redwares and whitewares share similar, if not identical, compositional traits, and are likely to have come from the same source in many cases (Section 4.2.4; Diags. 4–5). The clustering of redware and whiteware samples during analysis emphasises the dangers of ware definition based on fabric colour as the principal attribute.

The continuity of red earthenware production in the Lower Rhineland into the following century (Ware-type Ic.1) has been confirmed by the recovery of large assemblages of ceramics in Duisburg and Wesel dating from the beginning to the third quarter of 17th century (e. g. Contexts 4,8,14,16,17,20 for the Duisburg finds). The typological spectrum continues unchanged except for a number of minor additions (Diag. 8d; Gaimster 1989, Fig. 9).

New forms include deep multi-purpose bowls, tripod colanders, handled storage jars, pedestal salts and cups/porringers with straight upper profiles. In terms of functional types, the 17th-century redwares continue to be dominated by kitchen wares, including tripod pipkins (43 %), bowls for food preparation (26 %) and skillets, cauldrons and flat-based pipkins (10 %). Combed dishes (Ic.2), porringers, salts and jugs make up only 14 % of the entire inventory of vessel shapes. It is surprising, however, that chamber pots make up only 2 % of 17th-century redware forms found in Duisburg. The low priority for sanitary ware is possibly explained by the growing popularity of stoneware for this purpose

during the course of the century (Graph 20).
In terms of fabric, the Ware-type Ic.1–2 displays a more homogenous orange to red-brown colour and a more uniform frequency of quartz sand inclusions. Nevertheless, when subjected to chemical analysis, the Waretype samples displayed a discernible lack of conformity. Further testing of material from regional consumer sites is required before it can be established whether one or more production centres were in existence. Documentary references to earthenware potters just outside Duisburg in 1618 (Scholten-Neess 1979) serve to emphasise the continuity of production in the area from the 16th century.
To date no exports of Lower Rhine redwares of the 17th century have been recognised on excavations in the Low Countries or in Britain. This is hardly surprising in view of the strength of the indigenous redware industries. Only the fine whitewares from Frechen could make an impact on the international pottery market at this time.

iii. 18th century (Id.4, 5, 6, 7, 8)

Until recent excavations in Duisburg and at the farmhouse site of Haus Gelinde (Context 93) little was known of plain undecorated earthenware production (Id.1) in the Lower Rhineland. Research had concentrated almost entirely on the decorated slipwares made in the region (Section 1.1.3). The Duisburg sequence and hinterland sites (e. g. Krefeld-Linn, Contexts 60, 61) have now provided a detailed picture of the range of forms produced for the utilitarian pottery market from the end of the 17th to the beginning of the 19th centuries.
The 18th-century horizons in the region reinforce the impression that the redware industry continued uninterrupted from the previous century. The same basic range of forms was available, but was supplemented by a wide variety of specialised forms, designed to fulfil specific tasks (Hackspiel 1988). The increased specialisation evident in the local plain earthenware industry is characteristic of wider European trends. A detailed picture of relative form proportions are provided by the analysis of both the Duisburg sequence and sealed 18th-century groups in Krefeld-Linn (Graphs 22 and 28/29 respectively). Of interest here is the increasing dominance of the multi-purpose deep bowl form (Diag. 8f, bottom line).
While the spectrum of basic forms had not changed dramatically, it is noticeable that a far greater selection of glaze effects were available: green-glazes (Id.8) and black iron-rich glazes (Id.6–7) to name but a selection. Whether these different glaze effects represent separate geographical sources for the products will be a question for future chemical analysis (Section 4.2.5).

### *5.2.4 Polychrome earthenware and Slipware*

i. 16th century (polychrome earthenwares Ib.1i, Ib.3i)

In line with pan-European developments in decorated pottery production inspired by the Renaissance (Stephan 1987b), the Rhineland became the source of a polychrome lead-glazed earthenware industry during the 16th century, albeit on a relatively limited scale. Von Falke (1898a) first recognised its emergence at the end of the 19th century when a number of spectacular casual finds came to light in the city of Cologne (see Section 1.1.3). Recent research by Unger (1988 ed., 20–21) suggests that the vessels were made as a sideline by the local stove-tile and stoneware manufacturers who had access to the same glazes and relief-mould technology.
A small range of highly ornamented drinking jugs, beakers and specialist products such as bird whistles are known from Cologne (Reineking-von Bock 1966, Cat. 219–221; Appendix 5, Nos. 15–18), although with successive museum restorations, the precise nature of their decoration and individual profiles urgently requires re-examination. The wares are treated with a variety of different glaze colours ranging from copper green to cobalt blue, or are decorated with overall clay pellet "encrustation". Applied relief decoration, typical of contemporary local stoneware, is the other principal Ware-type characteristic. Fabrics types, such as the 16th-century plain earthenwares, range from fine whiteware (Ib.3i) to pinkish-buff redware (Ib.1i).
As we have seen (Section 1.1.3), individual examples of this class of pottery enjoyed a widespread distribution in the Netherlands (Hurst *et al.* 1986, Cat. 346–50, 354, 358, 361–62); and isolated finds are known from Britain (unpublished[3]). The international distribution pattern contrasts with the Lower Rhine situation, where, to date, the one polychrome bird whistle found in Neuss (Hupka 1988, Pl. 7b) remains the only find outside Cologne. The combined evidence points to the relative exclusivity of the polychrome-glazed Rhenish earthenwares. Clearly production was small-scale as the stoneware industry had cornered the mass-market for ornamental tableware at this time; and vessels may only have been made intermittently, for individual commission (Unger ed. 1988, Figs. 3–5; Dubbe 1960) or for annual festivals and fairs as decorative novelty items.

[3] Bear jug lid with overall green glaze over encrusted decoration, found City of London (British Museum MLA 1856, 7–1,1597); polychrome bird-whistle, found City of London (British Museum MLA 1915, 12–8, 200).

Whatever their true market share, the polychrome-glazed wares are illustrative of the development of an increasing demand for highly decorated drinking wares: a trend parallelled across north-West Europe from the beginning of the 16th century (Stephan 1987b). These demands were swiftly satisfied to the virtual exclusion of all other decorative wares by the regional stoneware industries, which introduced relief-moulded decoration in the latest Renaissance styles.

ii. 16th to 17th-century slip-decorated earthenware (Ib.4, Ib.5)

Until excavations began in the centre of Duisburg at the beginning of the 1980s, archaeological evidence for the production of slip-decorated leadglazed earthenware was unknown in the the region before the middle of the 17th century. This paucity of knowledge owed itself in part to the lack of investigation and also to the non-survival of vessels from the early post-medieval period (Stephan 1987b, 120). Until recently the dated 1664 dish from Issum (Scholten-Neess & Jüttner 1971, Cat. 314) provided the only documentary or physical evidence of decorative slipware production at this time. Until the Duisburg excavations, the lack of any evidence for an indigenous slipware industry on a par with the well established production in the neighbouring Netherlands and the Hesse region was attributed to the dominance of the regional stoneware industry and the influx of maiolica wares from the Netherlands (Stephan 1987b). The archaeological evidence from Duisburg and other sites, however, points to a significant Lower Rhenish tradition for slipware production stretching back to the end of the 16th century, fulfilling a specific functional and social niche in the regional pottery market (Gaimster 1988a; 1991).

In the Low Countries trailed slip-decoration was firmly established as part of the regional earthenware tradition by 1550 at the latest (Hurst *et al.* 1986, 154). The techniques and motifs originated from the rudimentary slip-decorated redwares of the 15th century (e. g. from Utrecht: Bruijn 1979) and the Dutch sgraffito wares of the period c. 1500–1550 (Renaud 1959b; 1989). These developments culminated in the dominance of the North Holland slipware industry which operated from the middle of the 16th to the end of the 17th centuries distributing its wares throughout the Low Countries and even across the Channel to Britain. Examples of North Holland Slipware are known from both Duisburg and Wesel in the Lower Rhine region (Section 5.2.6).

The growth of slip-decorated earthenwares in the Netherlands was part of a general pan-European trend towards increasing sophistication in ceramic tableware design during the early Renaissance period (Stephan 1987b). An artistic high-point was reached by the slip-ware workshops of the Werra region of Hesse, which operated during the late 16th and first quarter of the 17th centuries. Production was on such a scale that a sizeable export trade was conducted along both rivers via the north German ports (Stephan 1991, Fig.1). The wares are characterised by intricate sgraffito and trailed slip decoration; and it has been suggested by Stephan (1987b, 110–13) that they were directly responsible for the spread of the ornate slipware tradition to the West and the area North of the river Main. Nevertheless, archaeological confirmation of the Werra or Weser industries acting as catalysts for the production of slip-ware in the Lower Rhineland remains scanty. To date only a handful of Werra wares have been excavated in Duisburg and Wesel (see Section 5.2.6).

Technologically and stylistically the more rudimentary Lower Rhine slipwares of the period c. 1580 to 1650 have far more in common with contemporaneous products of North Holland (Hurst *et al.* 1986, Cat. 231–168), northern France (Lille 1986, Cat. 1–27), northern Germany (e. g. Arnold 1984) and southern Scandinavia (Stephan 1987b, 123–143, 187–194).

The combined evidence suggests that slipware production in the Lower Rhineland developed independently out of a well-established indigenous tradition for decorated earthenwares represented by the comb-decorated wares (Ib.2, Ic.2) and polychrome glazed wares (Ib.1i, Ib.3i) dating from the early 16th century. The stimulus to develop a further specialised range of tableware probably came from the neighbouring Low Countries, which, via the Rhine, was the principal trading link with the Lower Rhine region. This relationship may point to an indirect link between the Lower Rhine and the Werra region, however, as the case for the strong influence of the Werra wares on the North Holland slipware industry is well established (Stephan 1991).

Excavations between 1985 and 1989 in the Duisburg Schwanenstraße and Niederstraße have produced a series of sealed contexts containing regional slipwares (Ware-types Ib.5, Ic.4) dating to the period c. 1580 to 1650 (Contexts 4, 8, 14, 16, 17, 20). The wares are characterised by a hard orange-red to dark buff fabric, interior trailed slip and green painted decoration and transparent (often iron-speckled) lead glaze. During the excavations the earliest dated vessel of Lower Rhine slipware (1639) was recovered (Fig. 35, No. 2), but the find does not necessarily date the beginning of slipware manufacture in the region. The stratigraphical sequence identified at Duisburg confirms that slipwares were in demand in the Lower Rhine region from c. 1580 onwards. The observed chronology is consistent with the situation in the Netherlands where similar slipwares bear dates as early as 1573 (Hurst *et al.* 1986, 154).

The form spectrum during this period was relatively limited, with dishes and porringers predominating

(Graph 18; Gaimster 1991, Figs. 1–3). Slipdecorated tripod pipkins do not appear in the Duisburg sequence until the final quarter of the 17th century. Slipwares of the late 16th to mid 17th centuries were manufactured primarily for the tableware market, probably as a slightly cheaper alternative to the imported tin-glazed earthenwares from the Netherlands. The added costs of decoration would, nevertheless, have made it more expensive than the undecorated earthenwares (see Diag. 7).

The uniform angular profile of the flatwares repeats that of the contemporary plain red earthenware dishes (Ware-types Ib.1–2, Ic.1–2). Their flange angles and flat turned bases (e. g. Figs. 32, No. 1; 35, No. 1) are quite unlike their Netherlands counterparts, but conform to the Lower Rhenish earthenware typology of the late 16th to mid-17th centuries (Diag. 8c-d; see Section 5.2.4). The typological conformity adds weight to the argument that the same workshops were responsible for the two categories of ware. The hypothesis remains to be tested by chemical analysis.

Dishes with pie-crust rims (Diag. 8c) also belong to this phase of production and recall a widespread North German potting tradition (Hurst *et al.* 1986, Cat. 391). Dishes with pedestal footrings (Diag. 8c; Gaimster 1991, Fig. 3, No. 3), possibly used as pancake dishes (Lehnemann 1978, Cat. 7.1.7), are also known in Frechen-type whiteware (Diag. 8d). During the second half of the 17th century the flatware profile changes: deeper double-handled dishes are introduced (Diag. 8e; Gaimster 1991, Fig. 3, Nos. 4,6; Schiller 1991, Cat. 33 dated 1667) along with flangeless dishes (Diag. 8e; Gaimster 1991, Fig. 3, No. 2), providing a link with the 18th-century products. The porringers also display a remarkable degree of similarity in profile to the contemporary whiteware types from Frechen (Diag. 8d; Gaimster 1991, 3 No. 1).

The central slip motifs range from simple botanical designs in trailed white (yellow) slip with leaves picked out in green, to geometric patterns such as stars and chequers, and to birds such as cockerels, so reminiscent of the North Holland designs (Hurst *et al.* 1975, Fig. 5, No. 29). As in the Netherlands, it is clear that some of the motifs are influenced by contemporary maiolica wares, especially the chequer-pattern (Korf 1981, Cat. 283–317). The slip trailing is simple, and technologically far inferior to the sophisticated Werra wares.

To date no examples of Lower Rhine Slipware of the 16th and 17th centuries have been identified on excavations immediately outside the core area of production. The localised distribution pattern contradicts the 18th-century picture almost entirely, in which the region's slipware enjoyed an appreciable international market share (see part iii. below). In addition to the Duisburg finds, vessels have been identified in Düsseldorf (Context 66; Schiller 1991, Cat. 20, 23), Neuss (Context 72b; Schiller 1991, Cat. 75), Oberhausen-Holten (Context 62) and in a series of pit groups at Wesel dating to the period c. 1580 to 1620 (Contexts 74, 75, 76, 78; Müller 1988). The dishes and porringers recovered from Wesel are of particular interest as their slip motifs bear the closest similarity to the Netherlands wares (Müller 1988, Figs. 1 & 2). The possibility that the monochrome slip patterns may be of chronological significance remains a question for further investigation.

Finally, rescue work at the castle site of Burg Uda, near Grefrath (Siepen-Koepke 1990), has produced a small assemblage of slipware from a destruction horizon dating to the Thirty Years War (1614–48). Full analysis of the discoveries will provide much-needed evidence for the early typochronology of slipwares in the region. Significantly, the distribution of Lower Rhine slipware of this period does not yet extend to Cologne, Neuss being the southernmost findspot.

So far no kiln site responsible for producing early slipwares has been identified in the Lower Rhineland, and the question of their precise source(s) remains a priority for future scientific analysis. The typlogical and stylistic variation visible in the Duisburg and Wesel assemblages suggests that more than one source was in operation in the region. In view of the similarities in vessel profile and glazing techniques, it is a strong possibility that both the plain earthenwares (Ib.1–2, Ic.1–2) and the slipwares (Ib.5, Ic.4) were made at the same workshops, although this hypothesis remains to be tested by chemical analysis.

iii. 18th century (Id.1, Id.2)

Excavations in Duisburg (particularly Contexts 6, 9–13, 18, 19, 44, 45), Krefeld-Linn (Contexts 60–61) and at the farmhouse site of Haus Gelinde (Context 93) have revealed a detailed picture of slipware production in the Lower Rhineland during the 18th century. The archaeological evidence suggests that production continued uninterrupted from the previous century. Moreover, the frequency of finds combined with the surviving documentary evidence suggests a massive expansion in production, with a more widespread distribution of slipware workshops. The documentary record alone has identified 19 major kiln centres operating from the end of the 17th century between Raeren-Berlotte in the South-West of the region to Till-Moyland in the North (Scholten-Neess and Jüttner 1971; Map 1).

The form inventory for Lower Rhine Slipware found in 18th-century contexts in Duisburg (Graph 23) comprises dishes (42 %), plates (27 %), porringers/cups (15 %), and tripod pipkins and chamber pots (19 %). The two sealed assemblages of domestic pottery found at Krefeld-Linn have provided a more detailed picture of how this composition changes through time on one site (Graphs 26–27). Again dishes and plates for table use emerge as the primary forms. Size differentials provide the only clues to respective function. According to regional folk tradition, the larger dishes were intended for communal eating, the smaller plates for individual place settings (Lehnemann 1978). The predominance of the former types emphasises the communal eating habits prevalent in Lower Rhine society during the 18th and 19th centuries. The picture does not differ markedly between urban and rural sites.

The dated dish of 1664 from Issum (Scholten-Neess & Jüttner 1971, Cat. 314) provides an early datum-point for the introduction of sgraffito decoration on Lower Rhine slipware. The technique, which is characterised by the scratching through of a layer of slip to expose the contrasting fabric colour beneath, was employed from the third quarter of the 17th century to the middle of the 18th century (Ware-type Id.2). The method was used principally to define the outlines of figures (Diag. 8f top line; Fig.17, No. 1), zoomorphic, botanical or geometrical motifs.

The cellar assemblage dated to c. 1700–1740 from Krefeld-Linn (Context 60) contains a wide spectrum of sgraffito-decorated dishes, including rouletted examples. It is significant that few sgraffito wares were found in the second Krefeld-Linn assemblage dating to c. 1740–84 (Context 61). The quantified evidence from Duisburg confirms the impression that the technique had become less popular by the middle of the 18th century (Contexts 12, 13).

It may be assumed that the workshops responsible for the decorative display wares (Scholten-Neess & Jüttner 1971) were also involved in the production of more utilitarian vessels for the domestic market, the massproduced wares providing a steady income. Nevertheless, the stylistic gap between the documentary commemorative dishes and the wares made for everyday use is so immense that no atributional conclusions may be drawn about the majority of archaeological finds.

The spectrum of trailed white slip motifs continues the traditions of the previous century: birds, flowers, geometric patterns and concentric or spiral slip decoration, often overpainted in green. A new innovation is the feathering and marbling techniques evident on plates (Diag. 8f). The slip colours, white (yellow) and green, are supplemented also by brown and orange.

The two kiln assemblages from Issum (Scholten-Neess & Jüttner 1971, Cat. 323–324; Hurst *et al.* 1986, Cat. 393–395) and Kervenheim (Frankewitz & Köster 1982; Frankewitz 1988) have substantially improved our knowledge of the range of slipware types being produced by an individual workshop at any one time. However, the fact that the bird, flower, spiral and blobbed motifs at both kiln sites are virtually identical has limited the potential of stylistic analysis as an attributional aid. A systematic sampling programme of both production and consumer sites for neutron activation analysis holds the key to the problems of sourcing slipwares of this period (Section 4.2.5.–6).

The success of the Lower Rhine slipware industry at this time is reflected in the international distribution of its wares. Groups from Amsterdam (Baart 1988) and Nijmegen (Thijssen *et al.* 1984) point to a systematic commercial trade, whereas the British coastal distribution is more likely to reflect personal contacts or the popularity of Lower Rhine Slipware among the crews of Dutch coastal traders (Gaimster 1988c).

### *5.2.5 Regional imports*

Comparatively few earthenware products from outside the region have been recovered from archaeological contexts in the Lower Rhineland. The exception to the rule are the English finewares which were imported in bulk during the 18th century, and which will be dealt with separately here (Section 5.7).

The only earthenware "imports" identified in the region's 15th-century assemblages are a series of tall biconical jars, attributed on the basis of their form and heavy external rilling to the region of Franconia, to the south-east of the river Main (Ware-type Ia.10). The jars (e. g. Context 38; Fig. 51, No. 11) are characterised by their unglazed, buff to orange-red fabric. Excavations in Nuremberg (Brandl 1984b) and Regensburg (Endres & Loers 1981) have assigned the type to the period c. 1400 to 1500, which is entirely consistent with their position in the Lower Rhine sequence. The presence of Franconian earthenware in the region marks the first recorded instance of a ceramic trading link with the area to the south of Cologne. As with the later imports from the Middle and Upper Rhineland, Frankfurt probably acted as a nodal point in the inter-regional distribution network (Frankfurt 1991, Cat. 1.3.25). Nevertheless, the relatively small quantity of this Ware-type found so far in the Lower Rhine is not consistent with a recognisable commercial trade.

A small number of red earthenwares from The Netherlands with internal slip have been found in 16th-century contexts in the region (Ware-type Ib.6). The forms and slip motifs recall similar types recorded in Groningen with pulled feet and simple blobs and dashes of white (yellow) slip around the rim (van Gangelen & Lenting 1986). Finds of this Ware-type at Tilburg Castle suggest a more likely southern Dutch source for these imports (Stoepker 1986, Fig. 68). The wares are best represented in the Lower Rhineland by the Duisburg finds (Context 16; Fig. 32, No. 5) dating by context to the period c. 1580–1650.

The Dutch slipwares, which lend force to the argument that the Netherlands may have provided the stimulus for slipware production in the Lower Rhineland, were followed at the beginning of the 17th century by imports of high-quality slipware from the Werra region of Hesse (Ware-type Ic.5; Stephan 1981; 1987b). Dishes with intricate polychrome sgraffito designs are known from Duisburg (Context 20; Fig. 42, Nos. 7 (dated 1612) & 8) and Wesel (Context 78; Müller 1988, Fig. 2, Nos. 3,5). Stephan (1991, 83) suggests that the wares penetrated the Lower Rhine by river from The Netherlands, following their transportation along the North Sea coast from the mouth of the river Werra at Bremen. This would explain the sudden fall-off in Werra wares to the south of Duisburg and the absence of Werra or Weser wares in Düsseldorf or Cologne, to which the pottery would have had to travel overland.
The final discernible class of earthenware imports which feature consistently in the Lower Rhine 18th-century assemblages is a group of slipware dishes and plates from the Middle Rhine and Main area (Ware-type Id.12). The wares display a wide variety of slip decoration, of which the most distinctive is an overall internal red slip under trailed white, orange and brown slip motifs (Döry 1978, Fig. 15). Despite the diversity of designs, the form profiles are consistent, and differ markedly from their Lower Rhine counterparts. The most representative assemblages have been found in Duisburg (Context 45) and Krefeld-Linn (Contexts 60, 61; Fig. 65, Nos. 7–10). The chronology of the latter groups indicate that the wares enjoyed an extended lifespan covering the entire 18th century. Their presence in the Lower Rhineland may be explained by the riverine connection between the Main and the Rhine, the main artery of trade between central Germany and the North Sea (Frankfurt 1991, 33–35).
Statistically the regional earthenware imports make up only a minute proportion of the overall pottery supply in the Lower Rhineland during the post-medieval period. Their archaeological survival is unlikely to represent a commercial trade in ceramics per se.

### *5.2.6 Stove-tiles*

i. 15th century (Ia.11, Ia.12)

Stove-tiles found in 15th-century contexts in the Lower Rhineland fall into one of either two categories: those made in redware (Ware-type Ia.11), and those tiles made from a white-firing clay (Ware-type Ia.12). Despite the fabric variation of the tiles, their typology is uniform, with the half-cylinder niche form the primary shape (Franz 1981, Fig. 13).
The niche-tile was developed during the 14th century in northern and central Europe as stove construction increased in sophistication (Gaimster *et al.* 1990, 8). The niche form was introduced to optimise heat radiation in the free-standing upper section of the stove. Surface treatment of the tiles consisted of an overall monochrome lead glaze (copper-green or transparent yellow).
Niche-tiles from the Castle of Tannenberg, Hesse, destroyed in 1399 (Hefner-Alteneck & Wolf 1850), incorporate some of the typical decorative features of the Gothic architectural tradition: tacery openings, overhanging baldachin canopies, crenellated crests and relief-moulded beasts and foliage set into the spandrels. The design was adopted by stove-tile workshops across transalpine Europe, with Cologne the principal niche-tile producer in the Rhineland north of the Main. Here a wide range of relief-decorated niche-tiles were produced (Unger ed. 1988).
Excavations and casual finds from the city have given us a detailed picture of the variety of ornamental designs employed by the local industry from the end of the 14th to the end of the 15th centuries (Unger ed. 1988, Cat. 7–60). The most popular canopy and spandrel designs were the spoked wheel (Mainzer Rad), heraldic shield, the oak leaf and the zoomorphic or anthromoporphic figure. The fabric of the Cologne stove-tiles is a consistent off-white to pinkish white colour with prominent quartz sand inclusions (Ware-type Ia.12), not unlike the whiteware vessels produced in the same area (Ware-type Ia.3). Preliminary chemical analysis points to a possible compositional relationship between the two, but this must be confirmed by further sampling (Section 4.2.2).
The whiteware stove-tile industry during the 15th century stretched from Cologne southwards along the Rhine to Mayen, outside Koblenz. The spectrum of relief-decorated deigns from Mayen is remarkably similar (Mielke 1977; Redknap 1987, 573–579), and stylistic differentation between the two sources is virtually impossible. The regional tradition of stove-tile forms and ornament is also marked in the tile finds from Frankfurt-am-Main, which acted as the market place for products from the entire Middle Rhine area (Laffer 1903; Döry 1978, Cat. 231–235). An outlier of the Rhenish whiteware tile industry has also been identified at Raeren, where wasters were recovered from the Eynatten kiln site dating to c. 1500 (Mayer 1977, Fig. 21). Green-glazed whiteware stove-tiles of this period are also known from Frechen (unpublished; see Section 4.2.2). The emerging distributional pattern reveals a consistent link between the location of whiteware stove-tile and stoneware production. They invariably coincided, and shared the same decorative vocabulary (Gaimster *et al.* 1990, 32).
Stove-tiles of the 15th century are also known in a "redware" fabric (Ware-type Ia.11), and probably

represent production sources in the Lower Rhine hinterland where red-firing clays are prevalent. The fabric colour ranges from a light pinkish buff colour to bright orange, in some cases with only a marginally more ferrous component than the whiteware tiles. The mutually exclusive chemical compositions of the redware and whiteware stove-tile groups have been confirmed by the neutron activation analysis (Diag. 2, Section 4.2.3). The redware stove-tiles are less frequent at this time, and probably represent a much smaller output of production, perhaps as a specialised sideline of the local red earthenware potters. Whiteware tiles were more suited to green and transparent (yellow) glazing than the redware fabrics, which tended to make the glaze very dark unless a white slip was applied before glazing. No kiln sites producing redware stove-tiles are known at the present time.

Stylistic uniformity in the ornament of both whiteware and redware stovetiles in the region may be explained by the widespread trade in relief moulds between production centres (Mielke 1981a; Gaimster 1989). The cutting of moulds for stove-tiles was a specialised craft, and not within the capabilities of every workshop. Both positive and negative moulds were exchanged over long distances, complicating the process of attributing individual tiles to their original source of production. Stove-tile moulds in the Rhenish style of the 16th century have been excavated as far away as northern Germany and Scandinavia (Section 1.1.4; Gaimster 1989). In view of the difficulties of stylistic differentation between production sources and with fabric colour offering only a general guide, representative samples of redware and whiteware fragments found in Duisburg were submitted for neutron activation analysis along with a selection of wasters from production sites in Cologne, Mayen and Frechen (Section 4.2.3). The overall impression is of a range of sources for both whiteware and redware stove-tiles of 15th century date found in the region.

Niche-tiles of the 15th century have been recovered from a number of contexts in the Duisburg Altstadt. The Duisburg Innenhafen site has produced the earliest dated assemblage of c.1400–1475 (Context 38), containing several green and yellow-glazed whiteware examples (Ia.12). The spandrels are decorated with oak-leaf designs of Cologne type (Unger ed. 1988, Cat. 22–23). Although a whiteware fabric, and similar in decoration to the Cologne types, neutron activation analysis failed to match these tiles with the Cologne waster samples (Diag. 2; Section 4.2.3). The analysis may point to a greater number of whiteware production sources than presently known. The type of relief ornament was found on niche-tiles excavated at Burg Tannenberg (destroyed in 1399) and enjoyed a relatively long lifespan running from the middle of the 14th to beginning of the 15th century. The dating of the Duisburg context is not indicative of their production date but reflects the charactertistic timelag between production, lifespan and final deposition common to other stove-tile finds (cf. Gaimster 1989; Gaimster *et al.* 1990).

In 1988 a pit group in the Duisburg Niederstraße dating to the period c. 1450 to 1550 (Context 30; Ruppel 1989) produced the other main assemblage of decorated niche-tiles from the town. Out of a total of 16 individual tiles, 13 were in red earthenware (Waretype Ia.11), fired mainly in the light buff-coloured fabric variety (see above). Glaze colouring was limited to copper green, with only one transparent (yellow)-glazed fragment found.

The uniformity of decorative treatment, of both glaze and relief ornament, emphasises the contemporaneity of the redware and whiteware tiles and the use of the same relief moulds, despite their mutually exclusive production sources. The decorative and typological conformity of the group also suggest that the tiles were once part of a single stove construction which was systematically dismantled and dumped in the pit at the same time. The extended chronology of the assemblage as a whole (up to c. 1550) may indicate that the stove enjoyed a lifespan of up to 50 years before final dismantling. That said, the production of niche-tiles in the late Gothic style continued until the end of the first quarter of the 16th century (Unger ed. 1988; Mielke 1989; Gaimster *et al.* 1990). Imported stove-tiles of this type are also known from monastic Dissolution contexts (1536–40) in Britain (Gaimster 1988d).

The canopy sections of the Niederstraße tiles are decorated in relief using the same or very similar moulds with facing fabulous beasts supporting either side of the central tracery opening which is surmounted by an acorn finial. The relief design on one of the tiles has been supplemented with the addition of a horizontal scroll extended between the two facing beasts. The general decorative composition of this tile group is typical of early 16th-century stove-tiles from Cologne (Unger ed. 1988, Cat. 38–48) and the Middle Rhine region (Mielke 1977, Cat. 45–50). Although employing the same range of moulds, the fabric colour and chemical composition of the redware tiles probably point to a separate source from the Cologne-Koblenz region, possibly within the Lower Rhine hinterland itself (Section 4.2.3).

The final phase of the regional manufacture of stove-tiles in the late Gothic architectural tradition is illustrated by an almost complete nichetile from the upper fill of a building adjoining the Aachener Turm bastion on the Duisburg town wall (Context 24). The whiteware tile (Waretype Ia.12) is decorated in overall green glaze and ornate moulded relief on both the interior of the niche and on the overhanging baldachin. The latter is pressed with an intricate floral design paralleled on a number of fragments found in the city of Cologne (Unger ed. 1988, Cat. 52–53) which have been dated stylistically to the period around 1500. Unfortunately the Duisburg context is too disturbed to be of any assistance in the refined dating of this class of decorative niche-tile.

The distribution of stove-tiles made in the regional tradition was extensive during the 15th century, with finds stretching from Grefrath in the North (Mielke 1989, Fig. 1, No. 1) to Frankfurt-am-Main in the South (Döry 1978, Cat. 235). Quantifiable groups of stove-tiles of this date have been identified in recent years from Neuss (e. g. Context 70) and Bonn (Gaimster *et al.* 1990, Pl. 8–9). In Neuss a number of green-glazed whiteware tiles and stove components (Ware-type Ia.12) in the late Gothic decorative tradition are known (Hupka 1986, Figs. 6–7). Their ornate floral relief decoration and form details are parallelled by the Bonn finds, a small group of whiteware niche-tiles from Wesel (Context 81b) and by exports of Rhenish stove-tiles excavated in London (Gaimster 1988 f, Figs. 15–17; Gaimster *et al.* 1990) and the Netherlands (Dubbe 1980, Fig. 3; 1987). The decorative and typological repertoire displayed by this group is paralleled on waster finds from Cologne (Unger ed. 1988, Cat. 55–61; Gaimster *et al.* 1990, Pl. 4–7).

The overall impression given by the 15th-century distribution pattern is of the prolific output of the Cologne industry at this time and its domination of the regional lead-glazed stove-tile market. More quantified data from sites in the Lower Rhine hinterland is necessary for confirmation of this observation. At present, with the exception of the Duisburg finds, it is difficult to monitor the fall-off in distribution downstream from Cologne. Isolated finds of redware stove-tiles of 15th-century date along the Lower Rhine serve to emphasise the importance of the competing local industries (e. g. Oberhausen-Holten: Context 62).

ii. 16th century (Ib.7, Ib.8)

The distribution of stove-tiles during the 16th century is characterised by an increased frequency of finds, which demonstrates the growing demand for ceramic stoves as a means of interior heating over this period. The discovery in the Lower Rhineland of stove-tiles manufactured outside the region is indicative of a booming inter-regional market in these specialised products (Mielke 1983).

By the second quarter of the 16th century the influence of the Northern Renaissance is reflected in the new range of products produced by the Cologne stove-tile industry. Kiln wasters from the Karthäuserkirche and Streitzeuggasse in the city display the full spectrum of newly-introduced Renaissance polychrome relief ornament (Unger ed. 1988, Cat. 70–79; Unger 1991). The change in decorative vocabulary, in keeping with trends in the architectural sphere, can also be identified in the extended range of wares produced by the Cologne stoneware industry (Hurst *et al.* Cat. 328–9).

Relief ornament on the Cologne products is typified by a variety of biblical and mythological scenes, and allegorical figures framed by a Renaissance-style arcade on neo-classical pilasters. Sophisticated polychrome painting and slip techniques were developed by this time, with green (copper), blue (cobalt), yellow (transparent lead glaze), brown (iron) and white (possibly with tin added to the lead glaze) making up the general colour scheme. The relief surface was also often covered in a fine layer of white slip in order to take the negative mould more accurately and to enhance the colours under the glaze. An alternative (and probably less expensive) surface treatment was to employ a monochrome (green) glaze or to coat the relief side of the tile in a graphite-black wash (see find from Düsseldorf below).

It is also at this time that the form of the stove-tiles changed fundamentally. By the second quarter of the 16th-century niche-tiles were slowly replaced by panel-tiles characterised by a vertical panel across the niche-opening, thereby creating a greater area for relief ornament, more in keeping with Renaissance architectural schemes.

The production of stove-tiles in redware (Ware-type Ib.7) and whiteware (Ib.8) fabrics continued uninterrupted in the region, as the consumer site evidence clearly shows. The question of individual attribution, however, is further complicated by the expanded range of decorative types and colour combinations displayed by the finds. With improved communications, the interchange of tiles and their moulds between production centres was particularly common during the 16th century (Mielke 1983), even across considerably long distances. Negative moulds of Rhenish type have been excavated in Lübeck, northern Germany, and Lund, southern Sweden (Gaimster 1989).

The use of Cologne-type moulds being used to manufacture tiles in a redfiring fabric (a separate source?) is illustrated by a panel-tile corner fragment from the Duisburg Schwanenstraße (Unger ed. 1988, Cat. 80–81 for mould-type). By way of comparison, many of the Cologne-type stove-tiles of 16th-century date imported into London range from bright orange to light buff in fabric (Gaimster 1988d). Only a combination of stylistic or chemical analysis can be relied upon to differentiate between finds on consumer sites (see Gaimster *et al.* 1990 on the problems of attributing the British imports).

To date, the main urban excavations in the region have

produced a varied range of stove-tiles dating to the 16th century. In Duisburg the most coherent group comes from a latrine in the Niederstraße (Context 20), which includes three green-glazed whiteware panel and frieze- tiles (Ib.8) with ornamental relief decoration, incorporating elements of the Cologne mould-types. The first depicts a draped figure with the scrolled inscription IVDAS. The form of the figure suggests that the tile could have been made in the same Cologne workshop which produced the Planets Series (Unger ed. Cat. 94–96). The corner relief of the second tile fragment is also repeated on tiles of this Series (ibid., Cat. 95, 97), several of which are dated 1566. The third example is a frieze tile from the lower or central portion of the tile-stove (Gaimster *et al.* 1990, Fig. 7, No. 10). Such tiles are known from the second quarter of the 16th century in Cologne (Unger ed. 1988, Cat. 170). Although stylistically, and on the basis of their uniform white fabric, the three tiles could be attributed to Cologne, only chemical analysis can confirm this assumption. Whatever their source, the assemblage is typical of the range of mid-16th-century tile types found in the city. No tiles of a demonstrably later date have yet been found.

Outside Duisburg, the largest urban assemblages of 16th-century stovetiles have been found in Wesel and Düsseldorf. At the former site one assemblage included a number of Cologne-type polychrome fragments in whiteware (Ib.8; Context 76), and another a series of green-glazed tiles in a buff-red fabric (Ib.7) from a brick-lined latrine deposit dated by coin evidence to c.1550–1625 (Context 78). Several of these fragments bear the signature of the mould-cutter HANS BERMAN who is documented as working in Hesse during the third quarter of the 16th century (Mielke 1981). Several of his moulds bear the dates 1558 and 1562. One of the Wesel tiles depicts Christ on the Sea of Galilee in the Life of Christ Series (Mielke 1981b, Cat. 12–17). The known distribution of the Berman stove-tiles is concentrated in the Hesse region with Frankfurt-am-Main acting as the nodal point of the stove-tile market (Mielke 1981), although examples have also been found in Scandinavia, northern Germany, the Baltic region and in Switzerland (Franz-Berdau 1959, note 11). The distribution of the moulds was also widespread as finds in Speyer, the middle Rhineland, and the discovery of a positive ceramic mould in a Lübeck rubbish pit testifies (Hasse 1969, Cat. 340; Arnold *et al.* 1990, Fig. 39). It is hard to say, therefore, without sampling for chemical analysis, whether this find represents an import or a locally-produced tile. No such tiles are known to have been produced using this mould-type at Cologne. Whatever the precise source of the tiles, the assemblage bears testimony to the frequent long distances over which stove-tiles or their moulds were traded during the 16th century. Further tiles in the Hans Berman Life of Christ Series have recently come from excavations on the Castle of Brake on the Lippe (Luley 1990; Fig. p. 324).

In 1989 an assemblage of graphite-painted panel-tiles was excavated at the Rheinort site, Düsseldorf (Context 68; Beckers & Siegmund 1990, 32–38). The group, probably representative of a single stove, included armorial, allegorical and figurative designs, incuding individual tiles from the well-documented Ages of Man Series (dated 1566; Unger ed. 1988, Cat. 122–124; Gaimster 1989), usually associated with Cologne production of the period c. 1550–75 (Unger ed. 1988, Cat. 122–24). Further chemical research must be conducted before assigning this assemblage to a source, as the pinkish-white tiles (Ib.8) are difficult to identify on fabric colour alone (see above).

Despite the improving rate of stove-tile recognition and recovery in the region, the problems of attributing the material to its respective source remain immense (Stephan 1990). As we have seen, the use of stylistic analysis for ascribing provenance has proved problematic on account of the widespread movement of stove-tile moulds between production centres. Chemical techniques, such as neutron activation analysis, used in tandem with stylistic classification, offers the greatest hope for precise source identification (Section 4.2.3).

Finally, it is significant that no stove-tiles have been found in contexts dating any later than the final quarter of the 16th century in the Lower Rhine region. Clearly the demise of Cologne as a major production centre for stove-tiles after c. 1600 played a significant role in the fall-off in stove-tile finds (Unger ed. 1988). A further explanation lies in the changing nature of interior heating in the region. By this time, as in the Netherlands, ceramic stoves were no longer in fashion, and had been replaced by the kitchen hearth as the main source of heat and cooking activity. The growing importance of the domestic hearth is reflected in the finds of Dutch tin-glazed wall-tiles in 17th-century contexts in Duisburg (Context 8). Unlike other areas of North-West Germany (Mielke 1981; Arnold *et al.* 1990), tin-glazed stoves did not become fashionable in the Lower Rhine region during the late 17th and 18th-centuries, as the complete absence of archaeological finds demonstrates. Nevertheless, the precise nature of the decline in tiled stoves for urban domestic heating in the region is a complex one and urgently requires further examination.

## 5.3 Rhenish stonewares

### *5.3.1 Siegburg (Ia.1, II.1–4)*

Siegburg is situated on the river Sieg, a tributary of the Rhine, 12 km east of Bonn (Map 2). Between the 13th century and its destruction in 1632 during the Thirty Years War, a major industry developed, exporting its products along the Rhine to the Low Countries and beyond. The industry supplied up to 50 % of the overall ceramic assemblage on some sites (Hurst *et al.* 1986, 176).

The success of the industry resulted from the development of a fullyfused stoneware body during the first half of the 14th century (H. L. Janssen 1983b, 173–5; Stephan 1988, 107–8). With the much reduced porosity level, the innovation led to the introduction of a new range of drinking and decanting forms, including the cylindrical jug (*Jacobakanne*) and "beer mug" types (ibid., Fig. 9.24; 1988). Coin-hoard vessels in this class found in the Netherlands demonstrate their continuing production with only minor modifications until the middle of the 15th century (Sarfatij 1979, Cat. 15).

From the beginning of the 15th century the spectrum of forms made by the Siegburg potters had expanded significantly to include funnel-necked beakers and jugs (*Trichterhalsbecher/-krüge*), biconic jug forms, globular costrels and a variety of beaker shapes (Hurst *et al.* 1986, Pl. 30, Cat. 260 and 258 and Pl. 30 respectively). Surface treatment at this time comprised a rudimentary ash glaze, spread in patches over the body (Ware-type II.2; E. Hähnel ed. 1987, 31). The Rhenish and Low Countries chronology is backed up by the contexts of the British finds (Gaimster 1987a, Fig. 1).

The composition of the early 15th-century assemblage at the Duisburg Minoritenkloster site (Context 36; Fig. 48) confirms the spectrum of stoneware shapes produced for the home market. Here over half the site assemblage was provided by the Siegburg industry (56 %). The sheer quantity of stoneware from one source and the uniform nature of the assemblage suggest that the deposit may represent the remains of a bulk order of drinking and pouring vessels for monastic use.

Siegburg was also responsible for the manufacture of an additional waretype from the end of the 14th century, namely a hard yellow earthenware body which was usually covered in a dark purple wash (Ware-type Ia.1). This "weiche Ware" (Beckmann 1975, Period IV), was used for a variety of jug and bottle forms, handled jars along with a series of bowls of different dimensions (E. Hähnel ed. 1987, Cat. 123–128). Hardness and porosity analysis by Strunk-Lichtenberg (1975, 349) suggests that the ware was developed for specific functional reasons, primarily for kitchen use, as its ability to withstand frequent changes of temperature and its usefulness in keeping liquids cool were an advantage over the contemporaneous stoneware bodies. The purple wash was added to lower its porosity on the outer surface. This surface finish was also applied to fully-fused stoneware (Ware-type II.1), although its purpose could only have been cosmetic in this case.

The regional typology of Siegburg wares, as reflected in the Duisburg sequence (Contexts 3, 7, 21, 38), developed further during the course of the 15th century, when a modified spectrum of jugs, beakers and drinking cups became available (Diag. 8b). The range of products is repeated at Neuss (Contexts 69, 70, 85), where both ash-glazed bodies and wares with a purple-wash were found together. Proportionally, the typological repertoire of 15th-century Siegburg stoneware found in Duisburg (Graph 14) is dominated by the multipurpose jug forms (53 %), followed by the specialised drinking wares (mugs, cups, beakers and drinking jugs at 36 %). Costrels for liquid transportation make up 10 % of the form spectrum.

The first half of the 15th century also marked the introduction of applied ornament on Siegburg stoneware. Small oval or roundel medallions and prunts were the most popular forms of applied relief decoration (Radomersky 1968).

As in the neighbouring Netherlands, the Siegburg industry dominated the regional stoneware market during the 15th century (Hurst 1988, 336). Its position so close to the Rhine facilitated the distribution of its wares to the virtual exclusion of the more distant competing workshops at Langerwehe and Raeren. No Langerwehe stoneware of this date has yet been excavated in Duisburg, and only a handful of Raeren mugs have come to light so far (Fig. 46, No. 2).

This domination continued into the 16th century in the Lower Rhine hinterland, as statistical analyses in Duisburg show (Graph 3), with only the more specialised Langerwehe, Raeren and Cologne products making a relatively low-key impact (10 %). The few available 16th-century assemblages from the region contain a selection of Siegburg products, namely bellied jugs with distinctive neck cordons, flagons with narrow necks, along with funnel-necked beakers and drinking jugs, straight-sided tankards (*Schnellen*), globular costrels and chamber pots (Diag. 8c; Graph 19). The jug and flagon forms make up 62 % of the stoneware present. It was during the 16th century that Siegburg reached its artistic peak, with the introduction of a complex decorative repertoire including incised motifs (Fig. 42, No. 1) and applied relief-moulded panels and medallions (Fig. 63, Nos. 1–2). The designs reflect the emergence of a popular Northern Renaissance style in ceramic ornament, with biblical, allegorical and floral motifs the most common. Cobalt-blue painting was also introduced to highlight the applied reliefs. The designs are well represented in the Duisburg assemblages (e. g. Context 20; Fig. 42, Nos. 1–4). Advances in firing techniques enabled the potters to achieve maximum control in applying an even salt-glazed finish to the surface of the wares (Ware-type II.3).

A datum-point for the bellied jugs, beakers and tankards has been provided by the finds from Kessel Castle, the Netherlands, destroyed by the Spanish in 1579 (Clevis & Thijssen 1989). A further terminal date for many of these wares has been supplied by the recovery of wasters from the workshop of the Knütgen family in the Siegburg Aulgasse sealed by a destruction horizon of 1588 (Ruppel 1991b). It is significant that cobalt-blue painted decoration had been introduced to the workshop before it was destroyed, as several waster sherds testify.

The final class of Siegburg stonewares characteristic of Lower Rhine consumer sites is represented by the Duisburg sequence of unglazed incised beakers and small tankards dating to the end of the 16th to the beginning of the 17th centuries (Diag. 8c, bottom line; 8d top). The range of unglazed wares from Duisburg (Ware-type II.4) has been supplemented recently by the recovery of a pit group from the centre of Wesel (Context 74 dating to c.1580 to 1620) containing unglazed tankards, beakers, jugs and a dated flagon (1577). Several medallion fragments were painted with cobalt-blue before glazing.

In terms of its functional role, the Siegburg stonewares successfully fullfilled a multitude of domestic demands over several centuries. Drinking jugs, beakers and tankards were used at the table; large jugs, flagons and costrels were used for decanting and transportation; and chamber pots were employed in the sanitary sphere. The industry's functional versatility and sheer scale of output is reflected in its virtual domination of the Lower Rhine stoneware market until its final destruction in the 17th century, when the Westerwald industries to the South took over its former market share (Section 5.3.6).

### *5.3.2 Langerwehe (II.5)*

The stock products of the Langerwehe industry, situated on the northern border of the Eifel (see Map 2), are poorly represented in the consumer assemblages of medieval and later date along the Rhine. It seems that they mainly travelled west along the Imperial road towards the Maas and thence to the Low Countries and Britain (Hurst *et al.* 1986, 184). The industry, much reduced by the middle of the 16th century, began to produce a specialised range of large storage jars and jugs in a coarse grey salt-glazed stoneware (Baaren: Ware-type II.5). The vessels are decorated with applied armorial medallions and occasionally with bearded face-masks applied to the neck (Ohm *et al.* 1971, Figs. 14, 15).

Examples of the Langerwehe storage vessels have been found in sealed late 18th-century contexts in Duisburg (Context 13; Fig. 25, No. 1) and Krefeld-Linn (Context 61; Fig. 72, Nos. 8, 11). The dating of the groups emphasise the continuity of the form into the late post-medieval period. Clearly the specialised nature of the product range enabled the Langerwehe potters to compete in the Lower Rhine ceramic market, offering a product that was difficult to reproduce profitably on the same scale elsewhere.

### *5.3.3 Raeren (II.6)*

Like the Langerwehe stonewares, the products made at Raeren, 10 km south-west of Aachen, are poorly represented in the consumer assemblages of pottery along the Rhine. This is perhaps surprising in view of the massive scale of production at the centre from the middle of the 15th to beginning of the 17th centuries and of the ubiquity of Raeren wares on sites in the Low Countries and Britain (Gaimster 1987a, Fig. 3; Hurst 1988, 339). Again it appears that the wares travelled by road to the Maas before shipping to the Channel coast. The wide-ranging assemblage from the Dutch coastal port of Bergen-op-Zoom, associated with the stoneware merchants Jan-Peterss and Cornelis-de-Kannemann, illustrates the range of forms being traded at this time (Vandenbulke & Groeneweg 1988, Figs. 5–12).

The Raeren stonewares are best represented in 15th to early 16thcentury contexts in the region, with mug and funnel-necked jug types present on excavations in Duisburg (Context 15; Fig. 46, No. 2), Neuss (Contexts 70, 72b) and Wesel (Context 77). Full quantification of the Neuss assemblages is required, however, to refine this somewhat interim picture.

Significantly no examples of the later 16th-century output of highly decorative wares with applied relief ornament have so far come to light archaeologically in the region (von Falke 1908 vol. 2, Figs. 153–206). Nor for that matter have any of the plainer utilitarian wares of the later period of Raeren production (second half of 16th century) been identified with any certainty along the Lower Rhine.

### *5.3.4 Cologne (II.7)*

The Siegburg monopoly of the Lower Rhine pottery market during the first half of the 16th century is again reflected in the relative paucity of Cologne products on consumer sites in the region. Only isolated examples have been found outside Cologne itself, notably in Duisburg (Context 27, Fig. 44, No. 9; Context 30, Fig. 45, No. 9; Context 35, Fig. 46, o. 13).

Decorative types are limited to the sprigged rose

and oak-leaf jugs and mugs, dating to the period c. 1500–1525 (Gaimster 1987a, Fig. 5, Nos. 3, 4; Hurst 1988, 338–9). Perhaps the relative scarcity of Cologne stonewares in the region, in contrast to the Siegburg products, reflects simply the relative scale of production at the two sites.

Alternatively, much of the Cologne production could have been intended for the export market, and therefore bypassed the Lower Rhenish towns altogether. It is significant that Cologne stoneware, although not as frequent as the contemporary Raeren wares, is represented widely on British and Low Countries sites (Gaimster 1987a; Clevis & Kottman 1989, Cat. 11–3 to 11–5 for examples from Deventer; Vandenbulcke & Groeneweg 1988, Figs. 3–4 for range of types found in coastal port of Bergen-op-Zoom). Several surviving jugs of the same decorative type, bearing the arms of Amsterdam, may represent a specific foreign order (Hurst *et al.* 1986, Pl. 39).

### *5.3.5 Frechen (II.8)*

The stoneware potting community at Frechen, 10 km south-west of Cologne, is documented as being in operation by the 1540s (Göbels, 1981). Their plain brown stoneware jugs and *Bartmänner* were widely distributed throughout the Low Countries and Britain where they replaced the Raeren mug and jug types from c. 1550 (Gaimster 1987a; Hurst 1988, 340). They were able to maintain their monopoly of the export trade in Bartmann jugs and bottles until the emergence of the glass bottle industry during the 18th century.

The Siegburg stranglehold on the Lower Rhenish stoneware market is evident until the period immediately after c. 1600. Until then, even bottle forms were supplied by the Siegburg industry (Fig. 56, Nos. 20–22). Thereafter Frechen wares gradually began to make an impression in the consumer assemblages. So far no plain tankard-types of the second half of the 16th century, so prevalent in Britain (Hurst *et al.* 1986, Cat. 332), have been found. In Duisburg, for instance, the 17th-century spectrum of forms is represented by simple undecorated bottles (Fig. 15, Nos. 14–15), large plain jugs (Fig. 15, No. 13), handled jars (Fig. 15, No. 17; Fig. 26, No. 2) and chamber pots (Fig. 26, No. 9). The characteristic Bartmann bottles, so typical of shipwreck finds (see Appendix 6), are also represented (Fig. 31, No. 5).

Despite the variety of forms, the Frechen products enjoyed only a minor market share in the Rhenish pottery trade during the 17th century (Graphs 4, 5). The disparity may be accounted in part by the emerging supremacy of the Westerwald industries after c. 1600. It is also significant that much of the 17th-century bottle production at Frechen was commissioned for the international trade by stoneware dealers based in Dordrecht on the Dutch coast and in London (van Loo 1986; Haselgrove 1989; 1990).

### *5.3.6 Westerwald (II.9, II.10, II.11)*

With the migration of potters from Raeren and Siegburg at the end of the 16th century to the Westerwald region on the east bank of the Rhine opposite Koblenz (von Falke 1908, II, 65–116), a new source was established for the production of blue and grey salt-glazed stoneware. Stylistically and typologically the products of the new workshops are indistinguishable from the contemporaneous cobalt-blue decorated wares from Raeren (e. g. Hurst *et al.* 1986, Pl. 45) and the end-phase of production at Siegburg. The emigrant potters took their relief moulds with them to the new production sites, and many of the early forms and decorative motifs were designed to replicate the former Raeren and Siegburg products. In view of the problems of characterisation, highlighted by the lack of any kiln excavations in the area, the grey-blue wares have been grouped together for the purposes of this survey under the heading “Westerwald-type” (Ware-type II.9).

The chamber pot found at Duisburg (Context 17; Fig. 36, No. 5), decorated with a medallion incorporating the date 1581 and the monogram IE of the Raeren potter Jan Emens (von Falke 1908, II, 77), was most probably made in the Westerwald region (E. Klinge & E. Hähnel pers. comm.), and represents the earliest phase of stoneware imports from this area into the Lower Rhineland. The Schwanenstraße contexts in Duisburg provide a representative overview of Westerwald-type wares found on Lower Rhine consumer sites (Contexts 4, 8, 12, 14, 17). The spectrum of forms spans the late 16th to mid-17th centuries and includes baluster jugs (Fig. 26, No. 4), flagons (Fig. 15, No. 16), and chamber pots (Fig. 36, Nos. 5, 10). In terms of new decorative styles, the impact of the prevailing Baroque fashion is most evident on a tankard applied with repeating cherub heads (Fig. 4, No. 4). A virtually identical range of forms continues during the second half of the 17th century (Diag. 8e). The Westerwald products outnumber the Frechen wares by a ratio of two to one at this time (Graph 5).

The increasing specialisation of the regional ceramic market during the 18th century is reflected in the development of an extended range of stoneware forms at the Westerwald workshops. The new forms are identifiable on the urban and rural consumer sites of the region. Tankards, jugs and chamber pots continue with little modification, but the spectrum of forms is supplemented by terrines (Fig. 61, No. 5), porringers (Fig. 58, No. 11), storage jars (Fig. 58, No. 7), large flagons (Fig. 61, No. 6) and general household utensils such as writing sets (Fig. 61, No. 2). Plates in stoneware (a relatively late innovation designed to compete with the press-moulded wares arriving from England; see Section 5.7) are also represented in the pottery from the farmhouse site at Haus Gelinde, near Rheinberg (Context 93; Hackspiel 1982, Cat. Sz.10). The 18th century also witnesses a gradual replacement of applied ornament by overall or zonal incised and stamped decoration. Motifs are primarily geometric and floral.

The first half of the 18th century also sees the development of a range of delicate teawares with concentrated incised decoration (Ware-type II.10). The forms comprise tea bowls and saucers in the current Chinese porcelain style (Fig. 23, No. 5; Fig. 65, Nos. 4–5). Teapots were also produced (Reineking-von Bock 1986, Cat. 668–9), but have not yet been recovered from excavations in the region.

The final major specialist class of stoneware produced by the Westerwald industry is the mineralwater bottle (Ware-type II.11), represented in virtually every mixed 18th-century context sampled by the survey. The characteristic bottle form, recognisable in Dutch still- life paintings dating from the second half of the 17th century (Appendix 7, Cat. III.38), continued until the beginning of the 19th century when it was replaced by machine-made cylindrical versions (Brinkmann 1982; Nienhaus 1989a). The bottles bear the stamp of the spa where they were filled. Like the Langerwehe storage-jar producers of the 16th to 18th centuries, a number of Westerwald workshops specialised in the manufacture of mineralwater bottles to the exclusion of all other wares.

## 5.4 Tin-glazed earthenware

### *5.4.1 North Netherlands maiolica (III.1)*

Maiolica is a generic term given to European decorative tinglazed earthenware pottery of the 16th to 17th centuries. The technique involves applying a tin-opacified lead glaze to the surface of a biscuit body to provide a uniform white surface for painted decoration. After painting the ware was dipped in or sprinkled with a clear lead glaze before a second firing (Wilson 1987, 12–14). The production of maiolica on the Continent spread during the late 15th and early 16th centuries with the migration of potters from Italy across the Alps to northern Europe. Italian potters are known from documentary evidence to have been working at Antwerp in the South Netherlands from at least 1508 (Rackham 1926).

The Spanish persecutions of the second half of the 16th century forced potters from Antwerp and possibly Bruges to make their way to the North as part of the general shift in manufacturing and trade to Amsterdam. The earliest documented kilns were at Haarlem and Amsterdam (van Dam 1982). The North Netherlands flatwares are characterised by the application of tin glaze on the interior side and a (cheaper) lead glaze on the reverse (as opposed to the later "faience" wares which have tin glaze on both sides). Products of 16thcentury date are identifiable by their Mediterranean-style polychrome painted decoration, which was superseded by the fashion for Far Eastern blue and white designs resulting from the initiation of trading contacts with China after 1600 (Lunsingh-Scheurleer 1973). Maiolica production continued in the northern Netherlands, primarily at Rotterdam and Delft (Korf 1981), until the middle of the 17th century when it came into local competition with the more thinly potted and whiter faience wares (van Dam 1982).

As in the Low Countries (Renaud 1959c), finds of Netherlandish maiolica are rare in consumer contexts of the period before 1600 in the Lower Rhineland. To date, no examples of early maiolica from the southern Netherlands (Antwerp/Bruges) are known from the region (Rackham 1926; Hurst *et al.* 1986, 117–119). Their absence reinforces the impression that the primary route for maiolica imported into the region was the Rhine itself, along which it was traded from present-day Holland during the first half of the 17th century. The overall picture from the Netherlands and the Lower Rhineland suggests that the northern Netherlands industry was far larger and more geared for the inland export market than its Flanders counterpart.

From a negative point of view it is also significant that no items of Italian maiolica of the 15th to 16th centuries have so far been excavated in the Lower Rhineland, in contrast to their relative frequency in the Low Countries (Baart 1991) and across the Channel in Britain (Hurst 1991). Likewise post-medieval tin-glazed lustrewares from Spain are also absent from consumer assemblages in the region, a situation which again conflicts with their distribution in the Low Countries (Hurst and Neal 1982) and along the North German coast (Hurst 1978, Fig. 52, No. 5). Such exotica clearly did not penetrate upstream to the Lower Rhenish towns, but enjoyed a more localised distribution centred on their initial port of entry in the Low Countries. To the South, polychrome Isnik wares from Anatolia, Turkey, have been found in Fankfurt-am-Main (Döry 1978, Cat. 390–392), but the lack of such luxury wares in the Lower Rhineland suggests that they were traded no further.

In Duisburg the earliest North Netherlands maiolica (Ware-type III.1) appears in contexts dating to the period just before 1600 (Contexts 4, 8, 14). Dishes and plates predominate (Graph 21), with some porringers and drug jars represented. Dutch maiolica floor and hearth tiles were also evidently in demand as specialised products in the region (Fig. 6, Nos. 5–7; Fig. 27, Nos. 4–5). The decorative repertoire is limited to a number of principal common designs: the pomegranate and bunch of grapes motif (Fig. 5, No. 1), the running putto (Fig. 5, No. 2), the bird-on-the-rock (Fig. 5, No. 3) and the chequer-board motif (Fig. 58, No. 1).

The most common border motif by the second quarter of the 17th century was the Chinese-style Wan-Li panelled ornament (Fig. 27, No. 1) imitating contemporary Chinese blue and white porcelain imports (Lunsingh-Scheurleer 1973; see Section 5.5). The bird-on-the-rock-motif was also borrowed directly from Chinese blue and white porcelain of the Wan-Li period (1573–1619). The dishes incorporating both the border ornament and the central designs of Wan-Li-type porcelain (Figs. 5, No. 3 & Fig. 13, No. 5) were intended as replicas of the fashionable Chinese imported wares. Wares painted with fruit and running *putti* were also based on contemporary Italian maiolica designs. The *putti* motif, for instance, was a common motif on wares made in Faenza during the period c. 1575-1625 (Hurst *et al.* 1986, Cat. 14). As several commentators have pointed out, tin-glazed wares may be regarded as particularly sensitive measures of ceramic fashion (Blake 1980; Orton 1985).

Although all casual finds, a comparable range of wares has been excavated in Cologne (Tietzel 1980, Cat. 1–12). Dishes decorated with the chequer-board motif appear to have been staple exports. Again based on Italian (Montelupo) precursors (Hurst *et al.* 1986, Cat. 2), they are most likely in turn to have been a direct influence on slipware potters in the Lower Rhineland who replicated the chequerboard motif in their own medium (e. g. Fig. 12, No. 4).

Frankfurt-am-Main remains the southernmost findspot for Dutch maiolica of the first half of the 17th century (Döry 1978, Cat. 376–378), although its frequency declined with the rise of the local faience industry after c. 1660. In the Lower Rhine hinterland, finds have been made in Düsseldorf (Context 66), Neuss (Contexts 72b, 86) and Wesel (Contexts 74, 76, 78, 80), the latter contexts dating to the period c. 1580–1620.

Further excavations of urban centres will doubtless produce more finds of Netherlands maiolica and help refine the chronology of their introduction into the region, their longevity of use and our understanding of their social distribution (Section 7.1). In the absence of a native tin-glazed pottery industry at this time, the imported Netherlands products enjoyed an exaggerated prestige as decorative tableware, performing quite separate functions from the contemporaneous stonewares (Section 5.3). However, the precise nature of their stylistic influence on early Lower Rhine Slipware remains a crucial area for further investigation (Gaimster 1991).

### *5.4.2 Netherlands faience (III.2, III.3, III.4)*

During the late 1620s to 1630s a number of experimental wares were produced in the northern Netherlands (probably in Delft) characterised by the application of tin glaze on both sides of the body. By 1650–60 the production of the "faience" wares had become standard practice, stimulated by the cessation of the Dutch East India Company trade in Chinese porcelain (van Dam 1982, 27). Only the Friesland region continued to manufacture the maiolica-type glazed bodies, albeit in the current decorative styles (Ware-type III.4; Tichelaar 1982). The continuing widespread popularity of the wares made in Friesland is testified by their appearance in the Lower Rhineland (e. g. Contexts 10, 93).

The wares produced from the mid-17th century in the northern Netherlands were extremely varied and are well represented in the Lower Rhine ceramic assemblages. Both plain white (Waretype III.2) and painted faience (Ware-type III.3) were exported up the Rhine to the Lower Rhenish towns. They appear together from c.1640 in Duisburg (Contexts 4, 14) and Wesel (Contexts 74, 80).

The monochrome white faience forms (Ware-type III.2; Diag. 8e) include plain dishes, salts, tankards and lobed dishes based on contemporary silver shapes (Bouvy 1965). The production of white faience continued uninterrupted in centres such as Delft until c. 1725, a timespan which coincides with the chronology of the Duisburg finds (Contexts 6, 10). According to the latest survey of these wares by Baart *et al.* (1990), white faience was a relatively costly commodity between c. 1660 and 1675, and was mostly purchased for display, as many 17th-century depictions of domestic interiors show (Appendix 7; I.C.8). Thereafter it became a staple table- and kitchenware item available to a broader social spectrum of consumers as its archaeological frequency demonstrates.

Blue-painted wares display a richly-diverse range of decorative styles: floral, armorial, oriental and purely geometric. The Netherlands products were exported along the Rhine in sigificant quantities until the onset of indigenous faience production in North West Germany at end of the 18th century (Section 5.3). In the cellar group from Krefeld-Linn dated to c. 1740–1784 (Context 61) Dutch faience still makes up 23 % of the total assemblage.

So far none of the armorial plates or dishes have been attributed directly to Rhenish or German families. The form and style of heraldic decoration on many of the wares point to commissions for Dutch and German clients. The wares may then have been traded further as surplus stock or as individual gifts. Late 17th-century plates with Dutch inscriptions surrounded by swags and arabesques (e. g. Fig. 18, No. 4) occur quite commonly in the Lower Rhine area. Linguistically there was little difference between Dutch and the Lower Rhine dialect at this time. Traditional Dutch motifs, such as the bowl of fruit and the flat landscape scene (Fig. 6, Nos. 3 & 4 respectively), were just as popular in the Lower Rhineland as they were in the Netherlands. Moreover, the overall range and frequency of Netherlands faience on consumer sites in both the Netherlands (e. g. Deventer: Clevis & Kottman 1989, 117–127, Amsterdam: Baart *et al.* 1986, Fig. 13) and the Lower Rhineland are almost identical. The inter-regional distribution highlights the cultural unity of the two neighbouring territories during the postmedieval period.

With the overthrow of the Ming dynasty in China in 1644 and the accession of the Ch'ing emperors, the vogue for Chinese porcelain reached its greatest height in Europe. The Chinese porcelain industry flourished particularly under the Emperor K'ang-hsi (1661–1722) and his two successors, and its wares were sold by the Dutch East India Company throughout Europe. With the K'ang-hsi style a wealth of new motifs were introduced to faience decoration, previously dominated by the influence of Wan-Li porcelain. It can be seen, for example in the delicate representation of human figures, in the depiction of different flora and fauna, and in the frequency of Chinese landscape motifs (Diag. 8f). The influence of Chinese floral patterns, for instance, is apparent on the range of flatwares displaying the marks of the Delft De Paauw factory (1705–25) from Duisburg Contexts 10 and 18 (Fig. 18, Nos. 6–8; 39, Nos. 5–7). The influence of Chinoiserie on the Dutch faience imported into the Lower Rhineland continued until the final quarter of the 18th century (Context 61; Fig. 71, Nos. 2–14).

By the beginning of the 18th century (Graphs 25 & 32) the range of tin-glazed wares imported into the region consisted principally (up to 90 %) of flat tablewares (dishes and plates) and teawares (tea-bowls, saucers). With virtually no other forms known, a similar ratio of tablewares to teawares is evident in the later 18th-century groups (Graph 33, 47 % to 53 % respectively). The development of teaware forms coincided with the introduction of hot beverage drinking on the Continent from the end of the 17th century (Th. H. Lunsingh-Scheurleer 1976; Ball 1990). Typologically and decoratively the faience teawares replicated the contemporary blue and white porcelain imports from China (Diags. 8f-g).

Finally, despite the close stylistic similarities, no diagnostic examples of faience from the Frankfurt region have so far been identified in the Lower Rhineland. Workshops were established in Hanau and Frankfurt-am-Main in the 1660s, although on a much smaller scale than Delft (Bauer 1989). The Frankfurt output during the 17th century is still largely unknown, with archaeological evidence of production limited to the 18th century (Döry 1984). However, it is now clear that a large proportion of wares traditionally attributed to Frankfurt and Hanau were in fact made in Delft (van Dam 1982; Scholten 1989). The combined evidence suggests that the Middle Rhine products enjoyed only a limited localised distribution, and were not traded downstream where the faience market was already dominated by the Delft industries.

### *5.4.3 Rhenish faience (III.5, III.6)*

Lehnemann (1982) has drawn attention to the little-known workshops operating between the Rhine and the Weser during the mid to late 18th century. One of the most long-lived was the workshop established by Johann Gottfried Becker between 1764 and 1787 in Duisburg. Becker had previously managed the works at Telgte in neighbouring Westphalia between 1763 and 1764 (Lehnemann 1976). The faience teawares (Ware-type III.5) from Duisburg are visually similar to marked wares excavated at Telgte (*idem.*, Fig. 6). It is possible that Becker was manufacturing identical wares at both locations.

It is hoped to assess this question further now that wasters (Ware-type III.6) from Becker's faience manufactory have come to light during the Duisburg excavations of the past decade (Gaimster 1988a, Fig. 11, No. 1; Ruppel 1988). As with the Telgte finds, the glaze colour is characteristically off-white in contrast to the contemporary Delft products which have a light-bluish tinge. These recent finds are currently being sampled for neutron activation analysis at the British Museum in order to establish a possible production link with Ware-type III.5.

## 5.5 Porcelain

### *5.5.1 Oriental porcelain (IV.1, IV.2, IV.3)*

In 1602, the same year the Dutch East India Company was founded, the Dutch captured the Potuguese carrack the San Jago, and its cargo of Chinese porcelain was sold by auction at Middleburg. This was the first major landing of Chinese porcelain in the Low Countries and was followed by a succession of further sales. The combined booty of the 1602 and 1604 auctions comprised over a quarter of a million pieces of blue and white porcelain (Harrison 1981). The trade rapidly increased with large quantities of porcelain flooding the Dutch markets between 1600 and 1640.

This Carrack porcelain or *Kraak* porcelain (Ware-type IV.1) was made for export during the reign of the emperor Wan-Li (1573–1619). It is characterised by flat shapes with a thin body and a slightly foliated rim with blue-painted panel designs. The rim panels and central medallions are painted with a wide range of flowers, insects and religious symbols. The chronology of the Ware-type has been refined extensively in recent years with the discovery of dated wrecks of the Dutch East India Company such as the *Witte Leeuw* which sank off St. Helena on a return voyage to Europe in 1613 (Appendix 6, B.2; van der Pijl-Ketel ed. 1982). The frequent depiction of *Kraak* porcelain in Dutch Still Life paintings of the 17th century suggests they were purchased as much for display as for table use (Appendix 7, I.C).

Despite the documentary record of huge sales, the distribution of *Kraak* porcelain on archaeological sites in both the Netherlands and the Lower Rhineland remains limited. The observed scarcity may well be related to the relatively high cost and social prestige associated with these wares. To date only excavations in Duisburg (Context 4) and Wesel (Context 75) have produced vessels in the Lower Rhine region. The two Duisburg dishes (Fig. 13, Nos. 1–2) correspond in both form and ornament to the wares recovered from the *Witte Leeuw* (e. g. van der Pijl-Ketel ed. 1982, Group 1.1). As with the Netherlands maiolica, the trade in Oriental porcelain was conducted upstream along the Rhine from the Netherlands.

Oriental porcelain does not appear in the regional ceramic assemblages again until the end of the 17th century (e. g. Context 42). The picture is duplicated by the archaeological evidence in the Low Countries (Hurst 1965) and in Britain (Pearce 1981), where export wares attributed to the reign of the second Ch'ing emperor, K'ang Hsi (1662–1722), mark the renewal of the porcelain trade after the slump in activity caused by the fall of the Ming dynasty in 1644.

The blue-painted and overglaze polychrome wares of the late 17th to late 18th centuries found in the Lower Rhineland (Ware-types IV.2 and IV.3) consist almost entirely of teawares (tea-bowls, saucers, bowls). Wares with the *cafe au lait* external glaze (Ware-type IV.3) were probably intended for the consumption of coffee (Sheaf & Kilburn 1988, 144–47). The decorative repertoire includes "willow pattern" landscapes, garden scenes with peonies, floral designs and figures; all of which were imitated by the Dutch faience painters. A wide spectrum of comparable wares from the wreck of the Dutch East Indiaman the *Geldermalsen*, which sunk in the South China Sea in 1752 (Apendix 6, B.7), suggests that the highpoint of Chinese porcelain imported into the Lower Rhineland occured during the mid 18th century. The typochronological picture is duplicated at Amsterdam (Baart *et al.* 1986, Fig. 9), where plate and dish forms also survive. The sheer scale of the Dutch market for Chinese porcelain is illustrated by the fact that one dealer, Jan Beukelaar, frequently bought more than 100,000 pieces at individual Zeeland auctions (Jörg 1982, 132). Moreover, the salvaged *Geldermalsen* cargo alone totalled over 22,000 pieces (Sheaf & Kilburn 1988, Appendix A).

Chinese porcelain continued to be imported until the final quarter of the 18th century (e. g. Context 61). It is at this time that the indigenous German porcelain products begin to make an impact in the archaeological record (Ware-type IV.4) , although this was slight in the face of the overwhelming dominance of the Chinese wares. Finally, it is of note that no sherds of Oriental porcelain found in the region have been diagnostically attributed to Japan, although archaeological finds are known from the British Isles (Sweetman 1981, Fig. 87).

### *5.5.2 German porcelain (IV.4)*

Lower Rhine contexts of the last quarter of the 18th century (e. g. Context 13) include examples of off-white blue-painted porcelain teawares attributed to the German porcelain factories. They are characterised by their stylised floral *Strohblumenmuster* decoration (Fig. 25, No. 12), which originated in Meissen during the 1750s, the first and premier porcelain centre in Germany (Hamburg 1989a, Cat. 117–21). The design was adopted by a large number of other factories across Germany by the 1780s (Röntgen 1989), thus making the precise attribution of the Duisburg and Lower Rhine finds problematic. The design was also adopted by the Royal Danish Porcelain factory in Copenhagen during the 1770s, which has continued its production to the present day. Like the original Meissen models, the derivative wares are also often ribbed vertically and include cups with handles in contrast to the contemporary Chinese porcelain tea-bowls which have no handle (Fig. 25, No. 13).

Recent discoveries of marked Meissen wares in Lübeck (Falk 1983, Fig. 9, No. 4) attest to the wide distribution of its wares throughout Germany during the late 18th century. The Lower Rhine finds are unmarked, however, and are therefore more likely to derive from a factory other than Meissen. Whatever the source, it probably came a long-distance since porcelain was not made in the Rhineland until the mid 19th century at Poppelsdorf, outside Bonn (Weisser 1980).

## 5.6 English finewares

### *5.6.1 Staffordshire creamware (V.1)*

At the beginning of the 18th century the fine tableware and teaware market in Europe was dominated by the imported porcelains from the Far East. But by 1750 Staffordshire creamware, a light fine earthenware body adaptable to a variety of moulded, painted or transfer-printed decoration, was visible on the tables of the middle-classes across the Continent, as many contemporaries attested (Halfpenny 1986). Both the documentary and archaeological evidence confirm the commercial success of "the English Ware" on an international scale.

Such was the success of Josiah Wedgwood at marketing his creamware abroad that he had in the words of Faujas de Saint Fond, "created a commerce so active and so universal, that in travelling from Paris to St. Petersburg, from Amsterdam to the farthest point of Sweden, from Dunkirk to the southern extremity of France, one is served at every inn from English earthenware ..." (McKendrick 1982, 137).

The wares were deliberately marketed at the lower middle classes as a somewhat cheaper alternative to fine porcelain (McKendrick 1983, 131; Barker 1990, 13). The ever-increasing demand for Wedgwood's products necessitated the opening of warehouses in Amsterdam, Paris and Dublin, and the hiring of foreign agents. It was the warehouse in Amsterdam which supplied the Lower Rhine hinterland with Staffordshire finewares after c. 1770 (McKendrick 1982, 132). The ports of Rotterdam and The Hague were the two further ports of entry for English pottery destined for the Rhenish market (Treue 1973).

Products reaching the Lower Rhine towns and rural sites during the second half of the 18th century comprise a wide range of functional types including teawares, flat tablewares and sanitary wares (Diag. 8g). The creamwares are predominantly plain with occasional sprigged or moulded relief decoration. Little painted ware was recovered and no coloured glaze ware. The vessels are all unmarked, and despite the evidence that Wedgwood dominated the export market, it would not be impossible that wares from other factories in the close vicinity or in South Yorkshire were responsible for some of the Lower Rhine finds (over 100 potworks were producing cream-coloured earthenware in North Staffordshire alone (Halfpenny 1986)). By the end of the 18th century a number of factories were set up on the Continent to reproduce "the English Ware". One such establishment at Septfontaines, Luxemburg, founded in 1767 (Thomas 1977, Cat. 19–26), was responsible for a wide range of moulded wares derived from Saffordshire patterns. Although the most proximate factory to the Rhineland, no wares from this site have been diagnostically identified in the region.

Staffordshire creamwares began to appear in the domestic households of the region by the middle of the 18th century, and occasionally dominate the entire fineware component of an excavated assemblage (Context 44). The picture is repeated in the Low Countries, where excavations have revealed the intensity of the export market in English finewares. In one Nijmegen pit-group for instance, English earthenwares and creamwares make up 42 % of the total ceramic assemblage (by minimal vessel count (Thijssen *et al.* 1984)). A similarly extensive variety of creamware exports are known from Maaseik (Heymans ed. 1989, Cat. 6.138–145), Amsterdam (Thijssen 1985; Baart *et al.* 1986, Fig. 11), and Bruges (unpublished[4]). The North German demand for English fineware exports has been revealed at Lübeck (Falk 1988).

### *5.6.2 Staffordshire Earthenware (Id. 9–11)*

As sidelines to the international trade in Staffordshire creamwares a number of other finewares from the same production area were traded via the Dutch ports to the Lower Rhine region, namely Jackfield-type blackware (Id.9), Astburytype red earthenware (Id.10) and Agate ware (Id.11). Functionally, the individual vessels found belong to tea or coffee services: teapots, milk jugs, sugar bowls, cups and saucers. This range of wares appears in contexts dating to the second half of the 18th century (e. g. Duisburg Contexts 13 & 44).

The typological range of the Staffordshire earthenwares sent for export is again duplicated on post-medieval sites in the Low Countries (e. g. Thijssen *et al.* 1984, 14; Baart *et al.* 1986, Fig. 11). Like their creamware counterparts, the earthenwares filled a market niche created by the gradual decline in Oriental porcelain imports. The local Lower Rhine potters also produced

---

[4] Bruges Wollestraat excavations 1989.

refined earthenware bodies (e. g. Ware-type Id.7), but could not compete with the quality of the English imports. Attempts to manufacture teawares in plain red earthenware (Ware-type Id.4) were made (Hackspiel 1988, Cat. 42, 113), but appear clumsy alongside the fashionable imported wares with their rococo and neo-classical sprigged decoration.

### *5.6.3 Staffordshire Stoneware (II.12–14)*

An extensive range of stoneware bodies was also made in North Staffordshire during the 18th century, the most important of which have also been excavated in the Lower Rhineland, namely plain salt-glazed stoneware (II.12), Black Basalt ware (II.13) and Red Stoneware (II.14). The latter two wares are limited to finds of teapot fragments (Diag. 8g bottom), whereas the former is represented by a broad spectrum of flat tablewares, teawares and sanitary wares. Their typological range is closely related to that of the contemporary creamware products. Made with flint and ball-clays from Devon and Dorset, the resulting off-white body was intended to imitate Oriental porcelain.

Due to its weight, stoneware was a difficult medium for flatware production. It was only in the later 18th century that the Westerwald industries began to produce plates (Reineking-vonBock 1986, Cat. 679–702). But with the introduction of pressmoulding technology, the Staffordshire potteries were able to mass-produce an extremely durable range of stoneware plates and other flatwares. Their versatility and robustness made them ideally suited to the Continental export market.

Archaeological finds of Staffordshire Red Stoneware and Black Basalt ware are extremely rare on the Continent, with the Duisburg and Wesel discoveries the only material identified so far in the Rhineland (Contexts 45b and 80 respectively). A Red Stoneware teapot has recently been found in Nijmegen (Thijssen ed. 1991, Cat. 70). Plain salt-glazed stonewares, however, are more frequent finds, as fragments from the town testify (Thijsssen *et al.* 1984, 14).

The Black Basalt teapot from Duisburg (Fig. 58, No. 13) is one of the few documentary pieces of Staffordshire pottery so far excavated in Germany (Gaimster 1987b). It is stamped with the mark BIRCH on the underside of the base, and comes from the factory of Edmund John Birch of Hanley (working c. 1790–1810). The discovery emphasises the fact that Wedgwood was not alone in exporting fine tableware and teaware to the Continent during the 18th century.

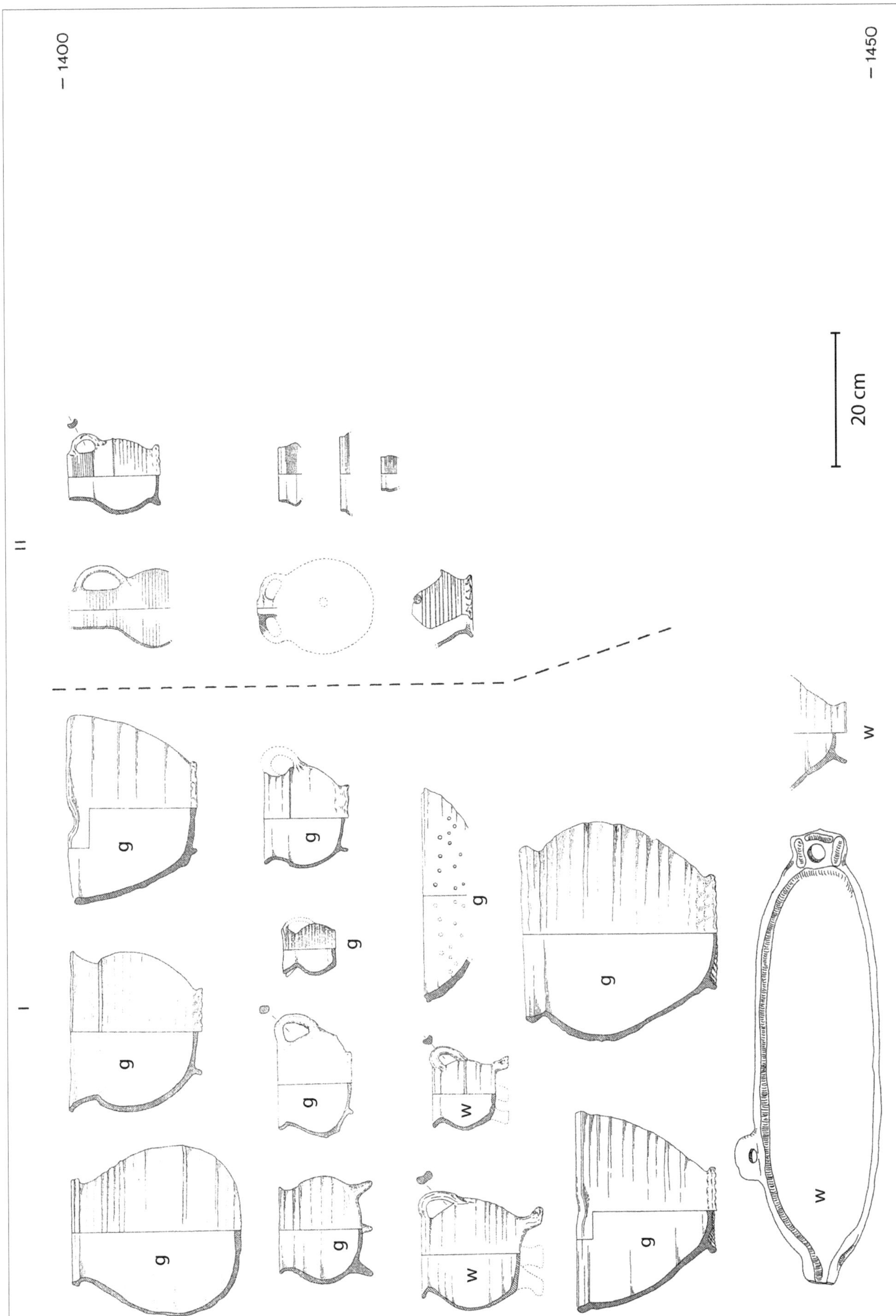


*Diagram 8a* *Summary of principal forms c. 1400-1450; g = Greyware; w = Whiteware; r = Redware; I = earthenware; II = stoneware*

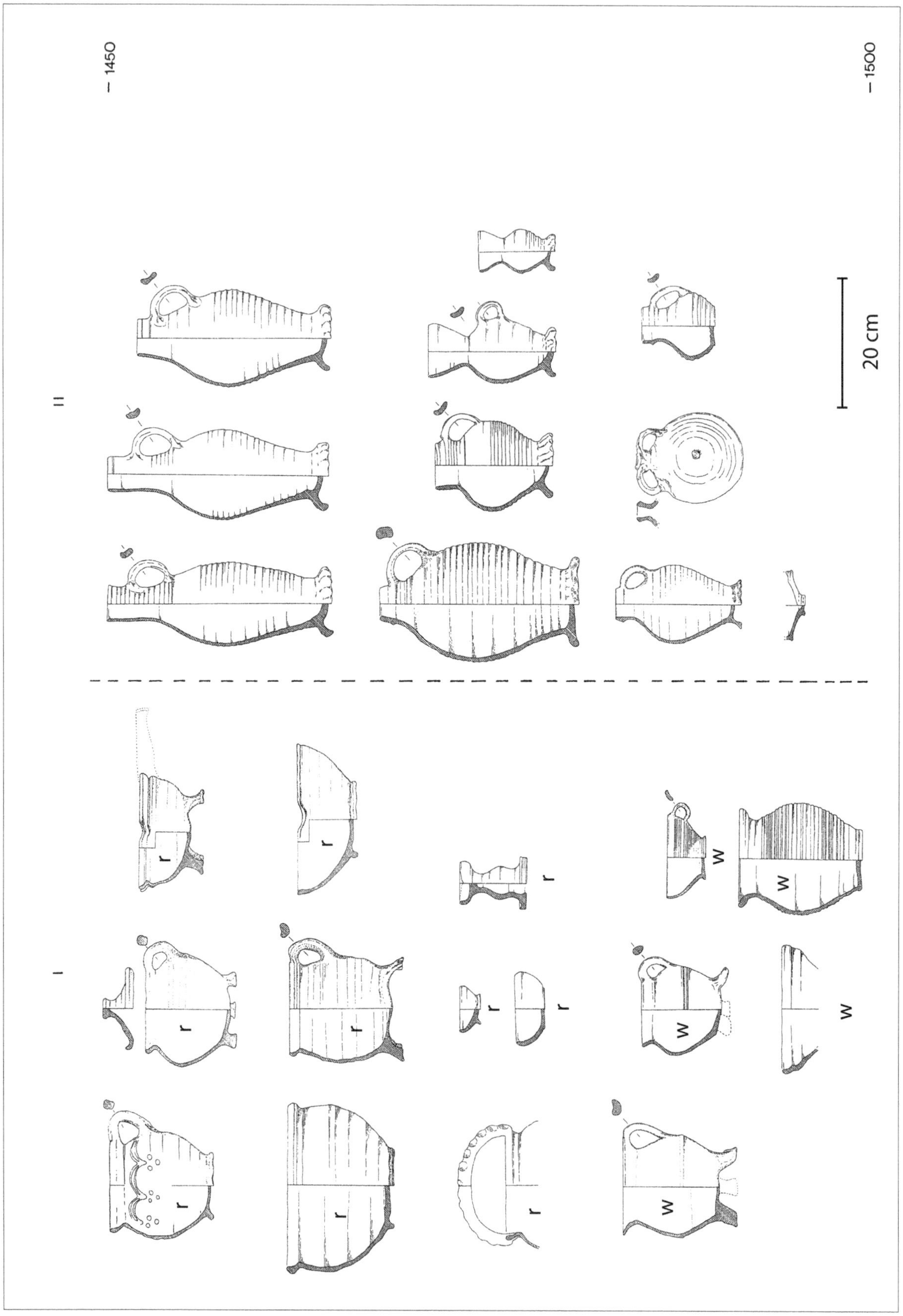


*Diagram 8 b* *Summary of principal forms c. 1450–1500; w = Whiteware; r = Redware; I = earthenware; II = stoneware*

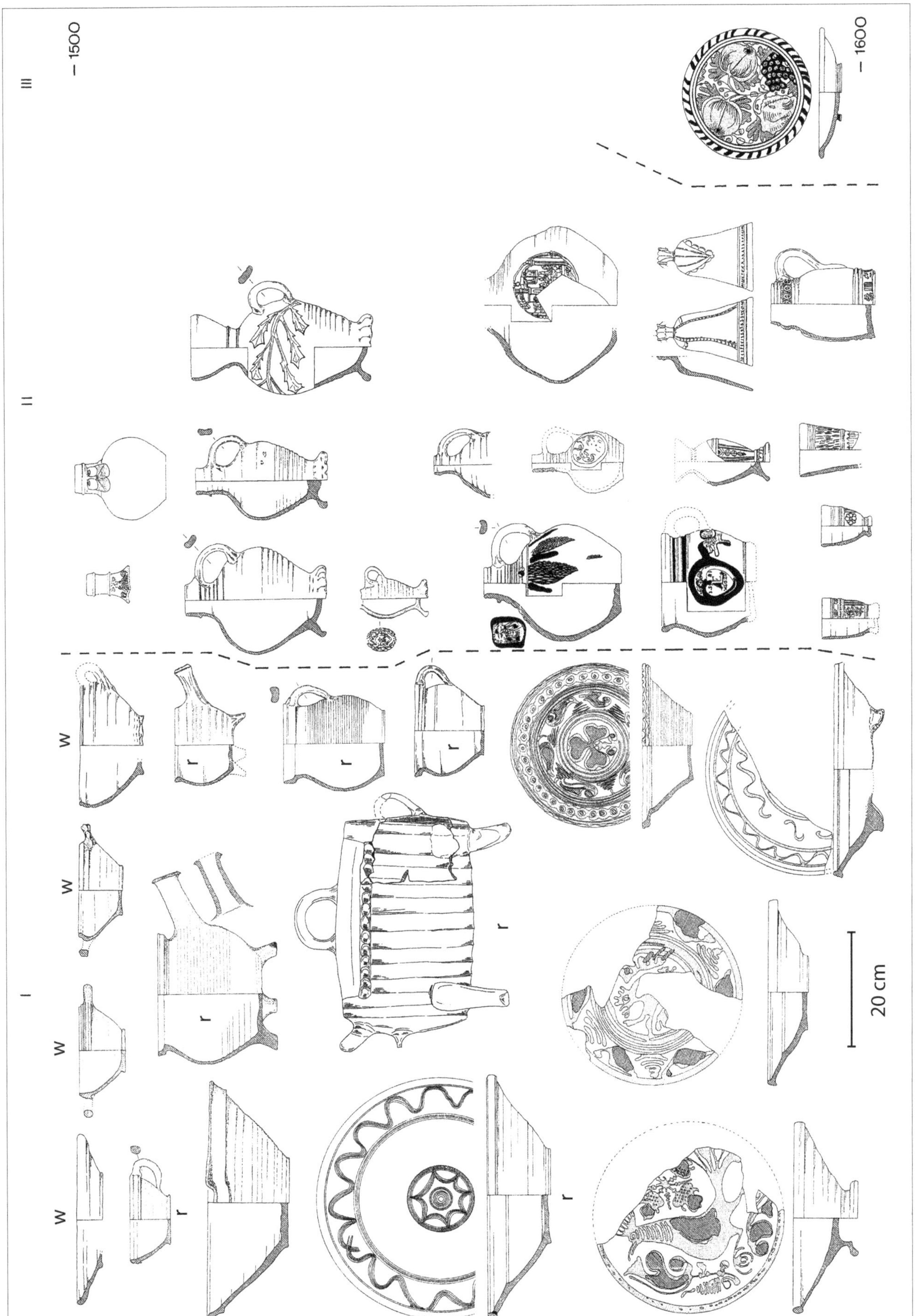


*Diagram 8 c* *Summary of principal forms c. 1500–1600; w = Whiteware; r = Redware; I = earthenware; II = stoneware; III = maiolica and faience*

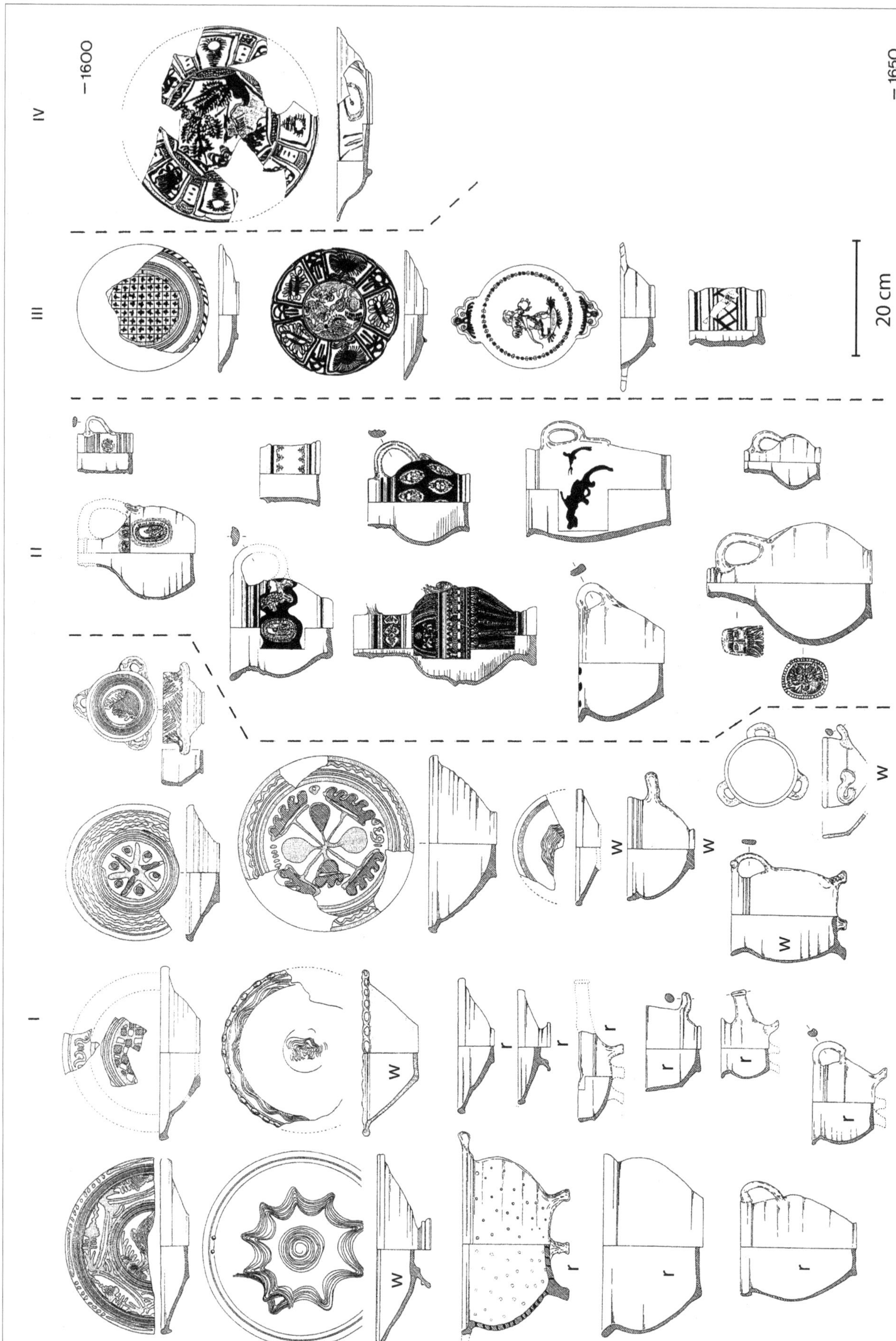


*Diagram 8 d* *Summary of principal forms c. 1600–1650; w = Whiteware; r = Redware; I = earthenware; II = stoneware; III = maiolica and faience; IV = porcelain*

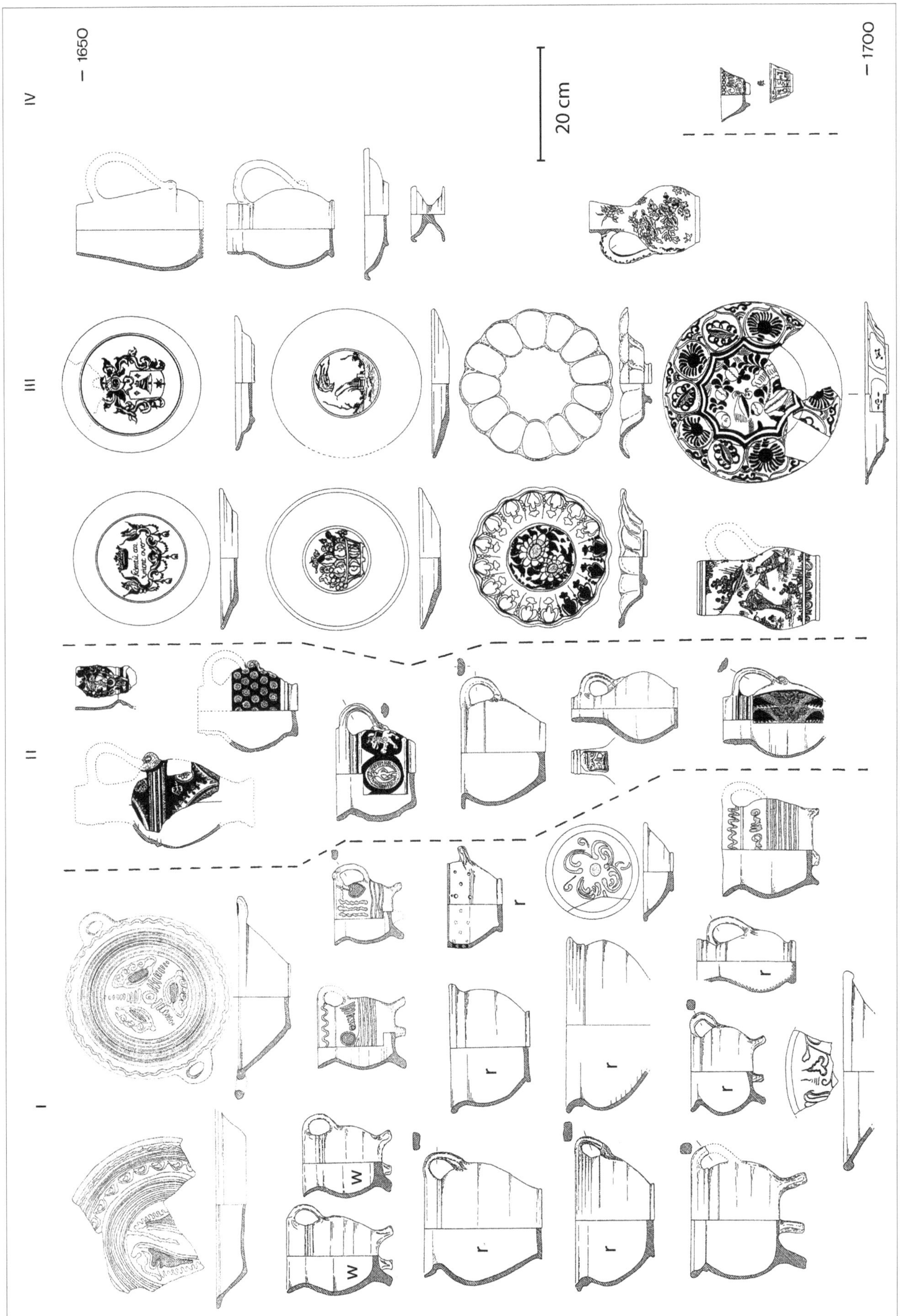


*Diagram 8 e* *Summary of principal forms c. 1650–1700; w = Whiteware; r = Redware; I = earthenware; II = stoneware; III = maiolica and faience; IV = porcelain*

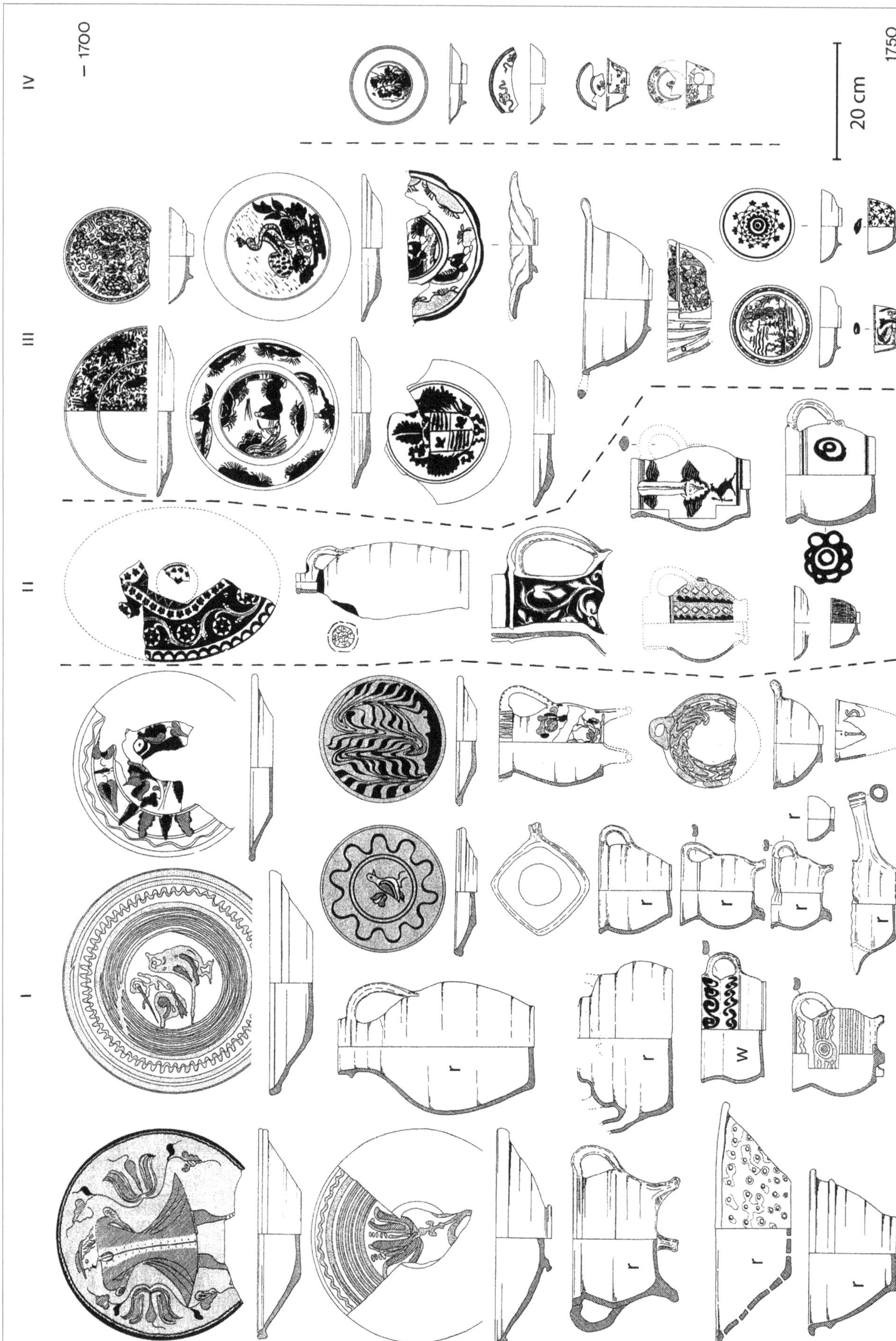


*Diagram 8 f* *Summary of principal forms c. 1700–1750; w = Whiteware; r = Redware; I = earthenware; II = stoneware; III = maiolica and faience; IV = porcelain*

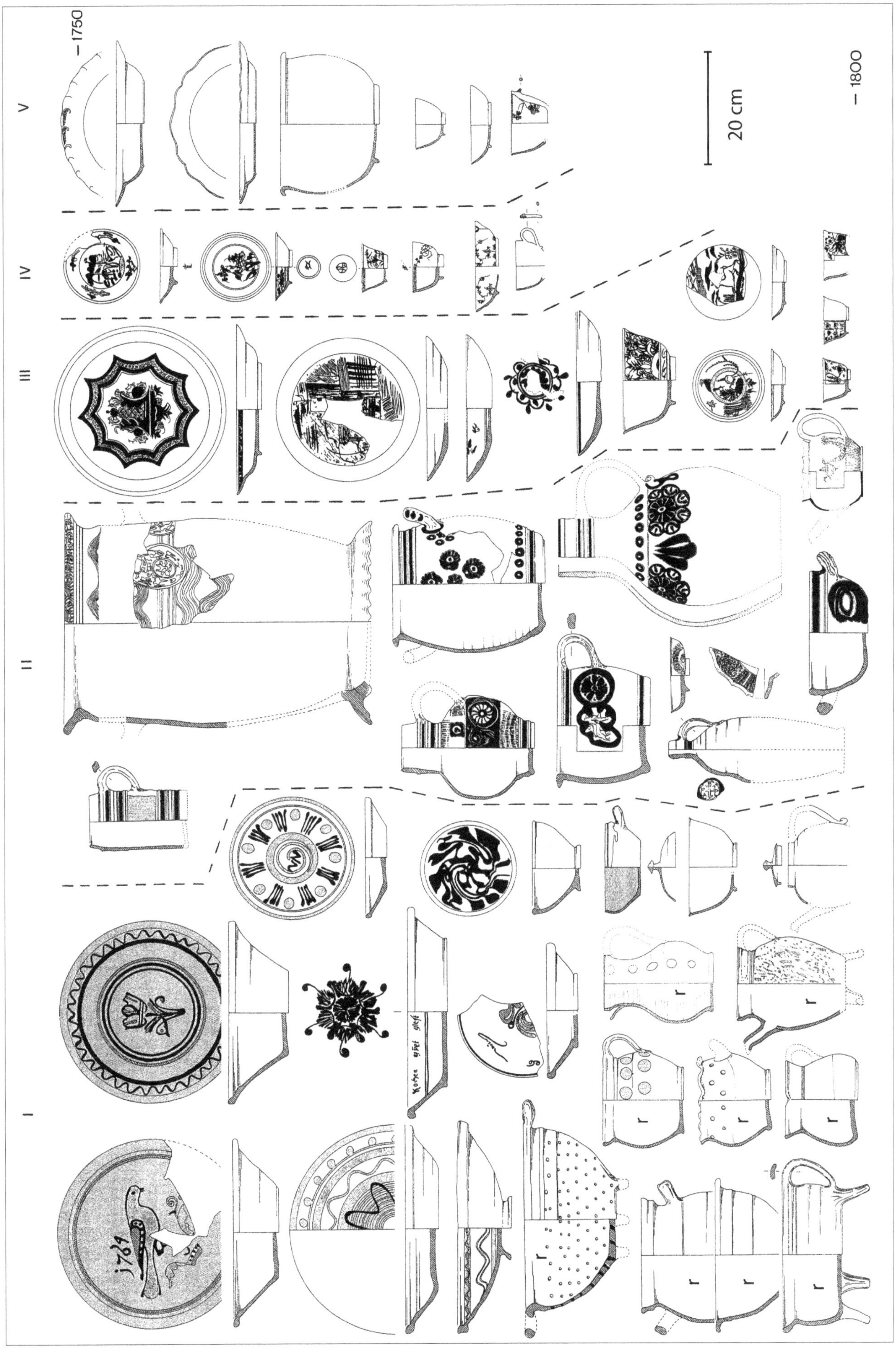


*Diagram 8 g* *Summary of principal forms c. 1750–1800; r = Redware; I = earthenware; II = stoneware; III = maiolica and faience; IV = porcelain; V = creamware*

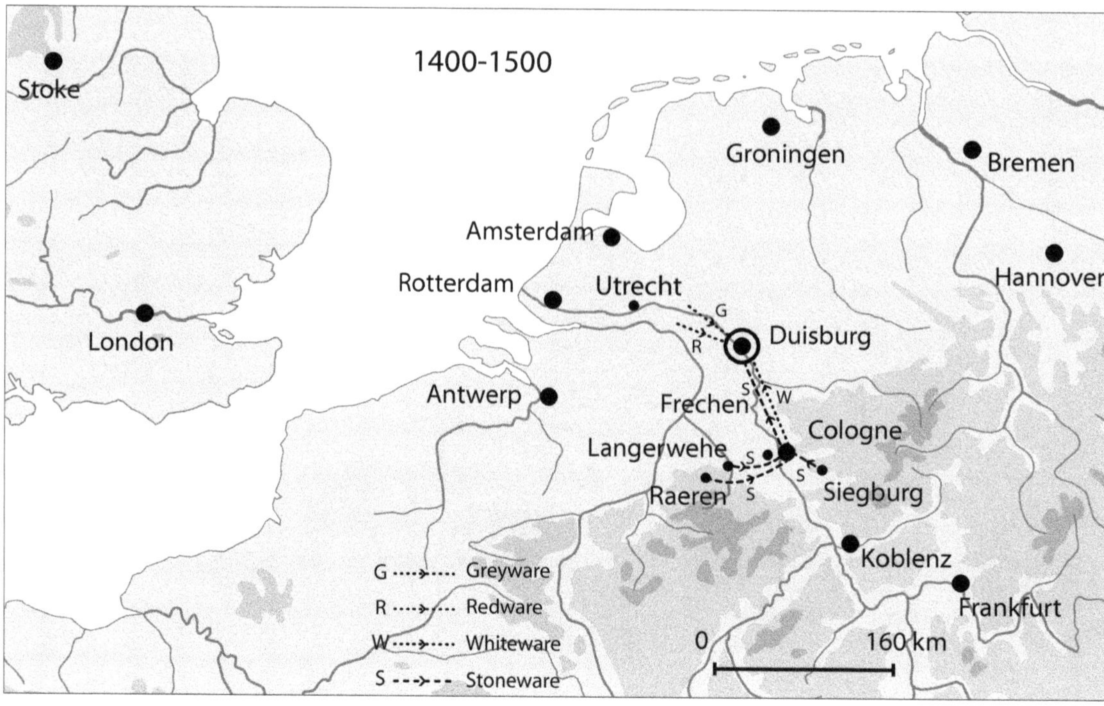


*Map 3 Sources and relative distancs of the pottery supply to Duisburg c. 1400–1500*

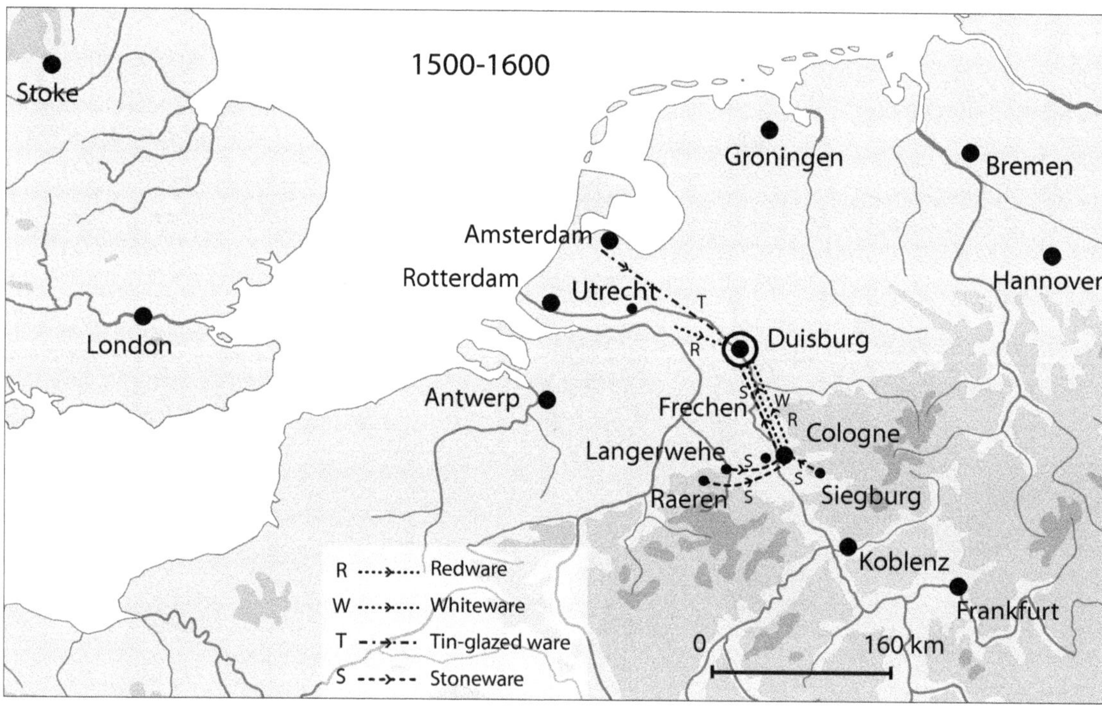


*Map 4 Sources and relative distances of the pottery supply to Duisburg c. 1500–1600*

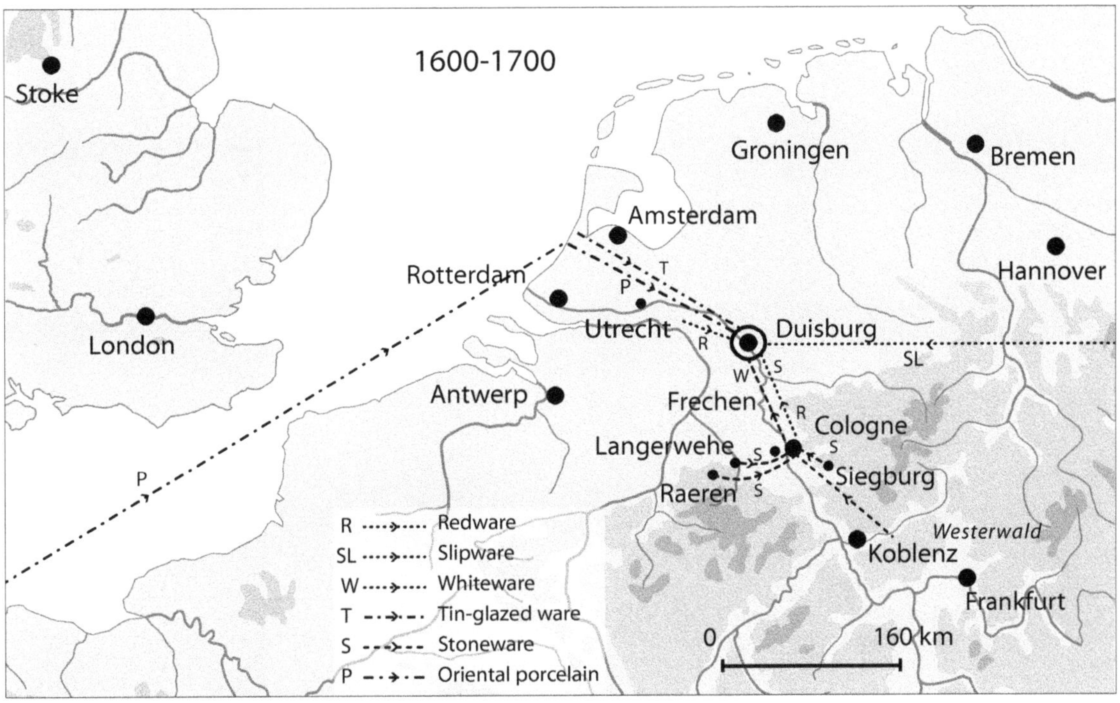


*Map 5 Sources and relative distances of the pottery supply to Duisburg c. 1600–1700*

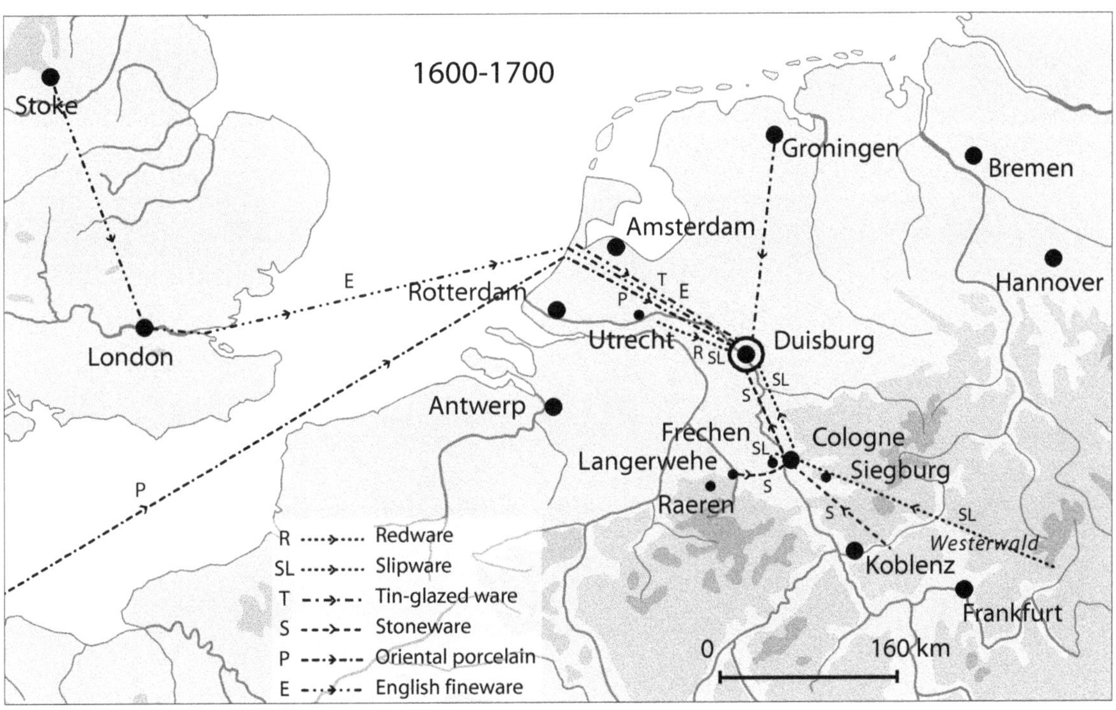


*Map 6 Sources and relative distances of the pottery supply to Duisburg c. 1700–1800*

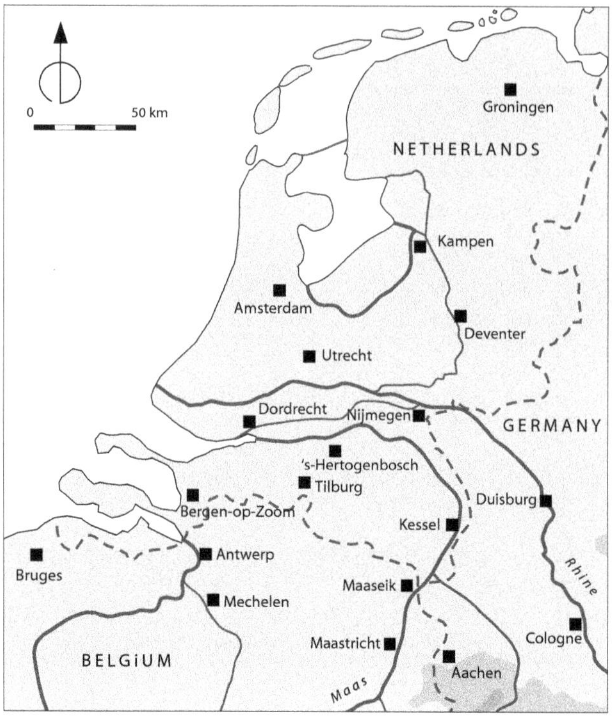


*Map 7 Location of principal assemblages of Rhenish post-medieval pottery in The Netherlands and Belgium*

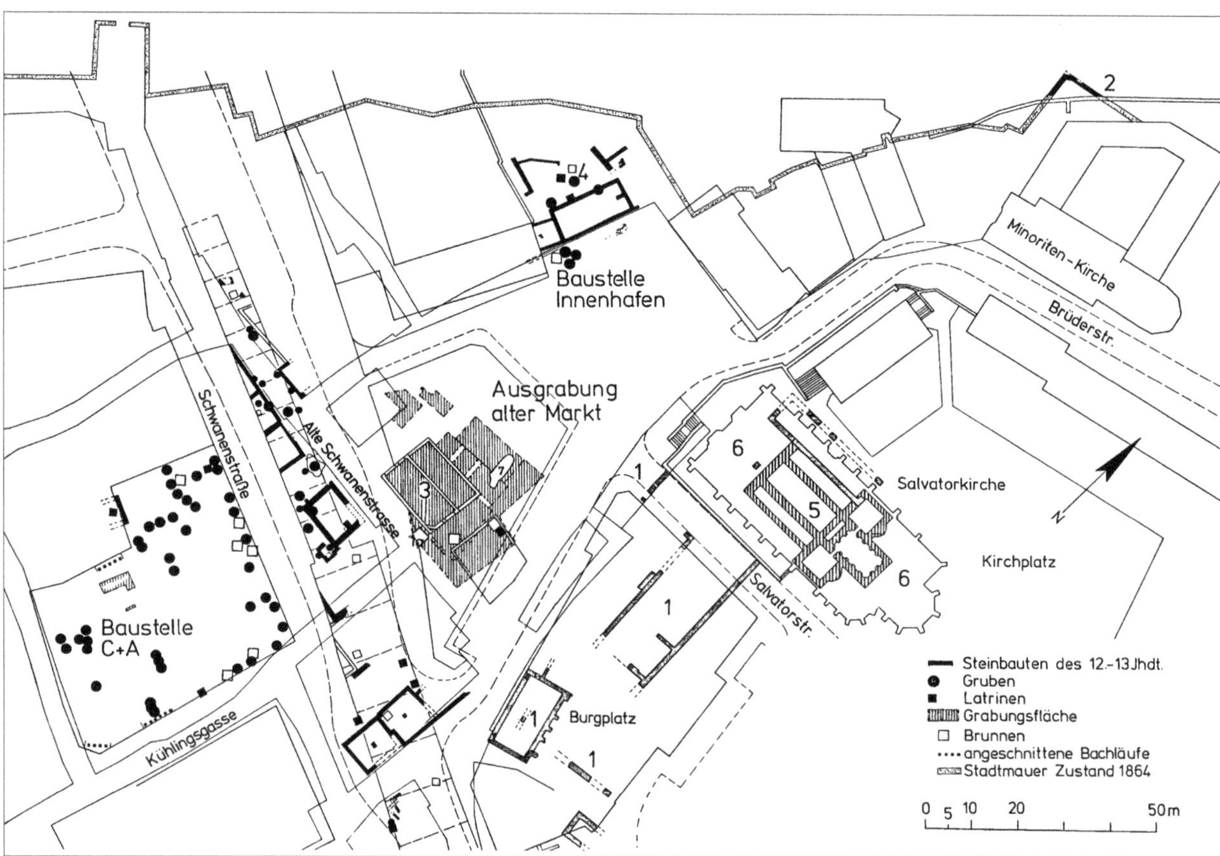


*Plan 3 Location of Duisburg Alter Markt and Schwanenstraße sites (up to July 1986)*
*1 – remains of Carolingian palace site, 2 – rescue excavation of the Minorites' friary, 3 – medieval market hall, 4 – stone residential building of the 12th century, 5 – Church of St Saviour, Staufen period, 6 – Church of St Saviour, late Gothic extension*

# 6. Intra-site analysis: a selection of ceramic assemblages from the town of Duisburg

## 6.1 Introduction

### *6.1.1 Intra-site analysis*

Before progressing to discuss regional patterns of ceramic consumption (Section 7), it is appropriate to consider the evidence recovered from individual archaeological contexts recorded during the course of the project. The aim of Sections 6 and 7 is to evaluate the variability in interpretation available from the pottery analysed at the micro- and at the macro-level. The relative proportions of ceramics excavated in a selection of Duisburg contexts are discussed here in the light of contemporaneous regional trends.

The importance of an intra-site approach to the socio-economic interpretation of artefactual assemblages has recently been demonstrated in the town of Lübeck (Falk 1987b), where an integrated policy of examining the relative composition of individual ceramic groups in relation to their respective socio-topographical contexts has been pursued. Unfortunately, it was not possible during the course of this survey to assimilate the available archival information for Duisburg, although this is planned for the future (see Section 8.3.5). For the purposes of this survey, interpretation of each assemblage and its socio-economic status has been based on the archaeological evidence alone.

This evaluation has been conducted on a selective basis, focusing on those Duisburg sites with quantitatively reliable sequences and individual groups. Each of the assemblages have been dated internally on the basis of their respective ceramic composition (see Section 2.2.2).

The following assemblages from the Schwanenstraße excavations, conducted during 1985–6 (Plan 3), have been selected for individual discussion. Their respective quantitative compositions can be consulted in Appendix 2. All groups have been systematically illustrated (see Appendix 8 for a concordance of figure numbers and Ware-type codes).

Duisburg Schwanenstraße

- 85:135/5a-d (Contexts 3– 6)
- 85:135/15a-g (Contexts 7–13)
- 85:135/3 (Context 14)
- 86:4a-b (Contexts 15, 16, 31, 33)
- 86:2 (Context 17, 34)

## 6.2 The Duisburg groups

### *6.2.1 Schwanenstraße 85:135/5a-d (Contexts 3-6; Figs. 3-10)*

The site, located between tenement houses, comprises a circular bricklined latrine containing a series of four overlying rubbish fills. The fills, containing a combined total of 149 vessels, date to the period c.1425–1750. Due to an episode of waste clearance during the 16th century, this phase is not represented in the sequence. The bottom fill (85:135/5a; Context 3) contained only 8 vessels dating to the period c. 1425–1475 (Fig. 3), of which 6 were Siegburg stoneware forms.

The overlying level (85:135/5b; Context 4) produced pottery dating to the period c. 1600–1670. In all 74 vessels were represented in the assemblage. Proportionally the largest component of the group were the local plain red earthenwares (Ware-type Ic.1 at 46 %), which comprised a comprehensive range of utilitarian kitchenware forms (Fig. 7). The Frechen whiteware industry (Ware-type Ic.3) supplied 24 % of the total number of ceramics recovered from the fill, of which 14 out of 17 vessels were tripod pipkins. Both the Siegburg and Westerwald workshops supplied stoneware to fulfil the diversity of drinking and decanting needs (7 %; Fig. 4, Nos. 1–5).

Of primary significance is the appearance of slip-decorated earthenware in the group (Ware-type Ib.5). Albeit a comparatively small sample (only 2 dishes at 3 % of the total), they form an important complement to the far larger group of imported Dutch maiolica (11 %). Both sets of wares date stylistically to the first quarter of the 17th century. Collectively the slipware, stoneware and the maiolica form the majority of the tablewares in the assemblage (21 % of the total). By the end of the accumulation of the fill, Dutch faience dishes had replaced the earlier maiolica types (Fig. 6, Nos. 1–4). A Frechen green-glazed dish (Ware-type Ic. 3) with incised and rouletted decoration may also have been used in a dining context (Fig. 4, No. 6). The qualitative composition of the group is marked in relation to other contexts of the same period. Few others contain such high ratios of decorative tableware and imported pottery. If the degree of ceramic ornamentation, distance from source and relative scarcity of particular wares are to be regarded as criteria for defining status (Section 8.3.3), this assemblage must rank relatively highly.

The general compositional pattern is repeated in the

two subsequent fills (85:135/5c-d). In the earlier phase dating to c. 1670–1700 (85:135/5c; Context 5) plain white and decorated faience from the Netherlands accounts for 52 % of the entire fill. Combined with the Lower Rhine Slipware (Ware-type Ic.4) and the Westerwald stoneware, the tableware component amounts to over 70 % of the total. The two maiolica dishes represented in the group (not drawn) are residual, and likely to have been socially curated for a relatively long period prior to final deposition (see Section 8.3.4). Full-scale maiolica production had ended by the middle of the century in Holland (van Dam 1982).

The tableware ratio in the upper level of the latrine dating to c. 1700–1750 (85:135/5d; Context 6) is represented by Lower Rhine Slipware dishes and porringers, Westerwald stoneware drinking forms, plain and painted Dutch faience and a small number of Chinese porcelain teawares (a combined total of 49 % of the entire assemblage). This percentage is roughly similar to the Krefeld situation (56 %: Context 60), although the proportion of faience is far lower in the countryside during this phase (6 %: see Graph 6). Moreover, Oriental porcelain is entirely absent at Krefeld during this phase. The discrepancy may possbily be explained by the larger proportion of local slipware consumed in the rural market for table use (37 %). The evidence from this context confirms the essentially urban pattern of ceramic tableware consumption during the first half of the 18th century, which is characterised by a greater reliance on imported Dutch tin-glazed pottery and porcelain (Graph 6) than on locally-made earthenware.

### *6.2.2 Schwanenstraße 85:135/15a-g (Contexts 7–13: Figs. 11–25)*

The site, like 85:135/5, consists of a circular brick-lined latrine located between houses on the Schwanenstraße. Excavation of the shaft revealed a series of fills (Contexts 7–13) containing in total a minimum number of 342 vessels dating to the period c. 1425–1800.

The latrine has produced the longest urban sequence of medieval to post-medieval pottery yet excavated in the Lower Rhine region. As with the other Schwanenstraße sites, no 16th-century material has been preserved in situ.

The deepest fill (85:135/15a; Context 7), dating to c. 1425–1475, contained 12 vessels representing 6 different Ware-types. Lead-glazed red earthenware (Ware-type Ia.8) accounted for half the group, fulfilling the majority of sanitary and cooking needs Lead-glazed whitewares (Ia.34) and unglazed greywares (Ia.6–7) were also represented. The dominance of redware over greyware and the presence of whiteware tableware and cooking forms within the group alludes to the relatively high status of the group as a whole (Sections 5.2; 8.3.2–3). The impression is reinforced by the recovery of a redware chamber pot with white slip decoration (Fig. 11, No. 1), so far unique in the Lower Rhine 15th-century pottery assemblages, and by the presence of glass tableware in the fill . The overall composition of the group gives the impression that glass was preferred here to stoneware for drinking needs, although it is just as likely that glass and stoneware were used together in combination at the table as several contemporary pictorial sources show (e. g. Dieric Bout's "Christ in the House of the Pharasee Simon": Appendix 7, I.A.2).

The overlying fill (85:135/15b; Context 8) contained material dating from the beginning to the mid-17th century. Statistically dominant were the plain red earthenwares (64 % of the total), principally intended for kitchen use, followed by the Frechen green-glazed whitewares (20 %). Of both Ware-types the tripod pipkin was the most frequent form. Representing the tableware component in the assemblage, local slipware dishes and porringers accounted for 4 % of the total pottery found (Fig. 12, Nos. 27). At 8 % of the total vessel count these were complemented by an extensive range of imported Dutch maiolica and two dishes of Chinese *Kraak* porcelain (Fig. 13, Nos. 3–6 and 1–2 respectively). The fact that the chequer-board motif appears on both maiolica and slipware dishes in the same archaeological context underlines how closely imported maiolica motifs were followed in local slipware at this time (Fig. 13, No. 6 & Fig. 12, No. 4 respectively). Finally, plain and incised dishes and porringers in redware (Ware-type Ic.2) and green-glazed Frechen whiteware accounted for the remainder of the decorated tableware (Fig. 15, Nos. 1–4, 10; Fig. 14, Nos. 1–3 resepectively).

The stoneware amounted to little more than 3 % of the entire assemblage. No drinking vessels were recovered, and it must be assumed that those needs were met by the extensive collection of glass recovered (pers. comm. P. Müller).

Looking at its overall character, the assemblage would appear to represent one single or relatively short period of deposition. This impression is supported by the low fragmentation ratio (see Section 2.2.1). The fill possibly represents the remains of a single household making a wholesale clear-out of its domestic pottery, both from the kitchen and from the dining room. Stylistically the wares date to the duration of the first half of the 17th century, although some items had probably enjoyed a lengthy lifespan (up to 50 years) by the time of deposition. In this regard, the Chinese export porcelain dishes (Fig. 13, Nos. 1–2) and the polychrome maiolica dish painted with fruit (Fig. 13, No. 3) were probably manufactured during the first decade of the 17th century (pers. comm. J. D. van Dam). The Westerwald flagon applied with a dated portrait medallion of 1633 (Fig.

15, No. 16) was also in use for several decades before being discarded if the assumed dating of the deposition episode is correct (c. 1650 based on the presence of a faience plate: Fig. 14, No. 11). The observed curation of many of the wares in this assemblage (see Section 8.3.4) confirms the undoubted social prestige of the group as a whole. The comparatively high ratios of imported porcelain, maiolica, faience, native slipware and incised earthenware (13,5 % overall) confirm this impression. The frequent depiction of Chinese *Kraak* porcelain in contemporary Dutch still-life paintings (see Appendix 7, Section III) provides a further evidence of their widespread desirability and their function as display items emblematic of material wealth.

The two subsequent fills of the latrine cover the period c. 1675–1725 (85:135/15c-d; Contexts 9, 10). They contain a wide selection of local slipware and plain red earthenware together with imported tin-glazed pottery from the Netherlands (50 % and 25 % of the total respectively). Perhaps another candidate for social curation, Figure 18, No. 1 depicts an armorial maiolica dish which probably pre-dates the deposition of the fill by at least 25 years (pers. comm. J. D. van Dam). The presence of faience and porcelain tea-wares and coffee utensils also documents the introduction of the fashion for hot beverage consumption amongst the region's urban middle-classes at this time (see Section 8.3.2).

The following 50 years in the sequence (c. 1725–1775) are represented by two overlying fills (85:135/15e-f; Contexts 11, 12), which contain a preponderance of locally-made slipware and plain earthenware (Figs. 20–24). This bias contrasts markedly with the previous phase on the site, which is characterised by the relatively high ratio of decorated tin-glazed earthenware; but is consistent with the overall regional trend (Section 7.2.6). It is possible that the decline in imported finewares reflects the declining purchasing power of the household using the latrine. Whatever the true explanation, the fall-off in faience demand in evidence here was compensated by an extended range of slipware products, including plates and small drinking cups (Fig. 21, Nos. 3–5; Fig. 22, No. 11 respectively). Specialised sanitary needs were met by the Westerwald stoneware industry (Figs. 23, No. 4; 24, No. 4).

The upper fill of the latrine (85:135/15g; Context 13) contained material dating to the period c. 1775–1800 (Fig. 25). Here a much greater selection of ceramic Ware-types was in use, reflecting the impact of the Staffordshire industries on the region after c. 1750. Staffordshire red earthenware and creamwares are represented (9 %) along with Chinese export porcelain and native German porcelain (17 %). Apart from a large stoneware storage jar from Langerwehe and a jardiniere fragment from the Westerwald (Fig. 25, Nos. 1–2), the majority of vessel forms identified in this group were used in the consumption of hot beverages. Even the local slipware workshops were endeavouring to compete in the fine tableware market by the end of the century (Fig. 25, Nos. 18–19). The contents of the fill suggest that the household(s) associated with the latrine were in touch with both regional and international ceramic trends at this time.

### *6.2.3 Schwanenstraße 85:135/3 (Context 14: Figs 26–30)*

The assemblage of pottery discussed here was excavated from a rubbish pit at the South end of the Schwanenstraße during 1985 (Plan 3). Excavation revealed only one primary fill, suggesting a single dump or at least a relatively short episode of artefactual deposition. The low fragmentation ratio of the pottery confirms this initial impression, and also suggests that the ceramics were deposited soon after they were considered superfluous or immediately after breakage. In all a minimum of 61 vessels were recovered, dating from c. 1600– 1675.

Statistically the plain redwares (Ware-type Ic.3; Fig. 30) dominate the assemblage (44 %). This high percentage of utilitarian pottery is typical of all 17th-century groups found in the town, and is not necessarily indicative of low status; rather, the ratios serve to illustrate the reliance, of both rich and poor households, on locally-made earthenwares for kitchen and sanitary use. Also included in the assemblage of redwares were a number of large dishes designed for table use (Fig. 30, No. 14). Their size (diam. 36 cm) suggests that they were either used for the serving of food or in its communal consumption. The Frechen workshops were also responsible for a series of dishes with incised wavy decoration and pedestal footrings in green-glazed whiteware (Ware-type Ic.3), which were likewise intended for the serving of food items (see Section 5.2.1). Two such dishes are present here (Fig. 29, Nos. 1 & 2), along with two tripod pipkins and a porringer (Fig. 29, Nos. 3 and 4 respectively). Finally, with regard to lead-glazed earthenware, the group is characterised by the scarcity of slipware (only 4 % overall). A small porringer with concentric slip decoration constitutes the only tableware form (Fig. 30, No. 13).

The lack of decorative slipware in this assemblage may possibly be explained by the relatively high ratios of tin-glazed earthenware imported from the Netherlands (22 % overall). Chronologically the wares span the full duration of the assemblage, starting at c. 1600 with the maiolicas (Fig. 27), which were in turn superseded around 1640–50 by decorated (Fig. 28, Nos. 1–4) and plain white faience (Fig. 28, Nos. 5–6). The armorial dishes in blue-painted faience (Fig. 28, Nos. 1 & 2) were perhaps once part of a table service, and may also have functioned as mural display pieces as contemporary

pictorial sources indicate (e. g. Appendix 7, I.A.C.). The dishes reinforce the impression of social status and material emulation characterising this assemblage as a whole (cf. van Dam 1982, Fig. 7). Moreover, the presence of several maiolica wall tiles from the Netherlands, dating to the period c. 1600–25 (van Dam 1988, Figs. 27,35), provide evidence for social emulation in the sphere of domestic interior decoration. To date, such tiles are rare finds on Lower Rhine excavations.
Salt-glazed stoneware accounted for 22 % of the total assemblage, fulfilling the majority of storage and sanitary needs in this particular case. With exception of a late Siegburg incised beaker (Fig. 26, No. 1), drinking wares are scarce in the group. This may be explained by the comparatively large number of drinking glass found (not illustrated). Nevertheless, stoneware was used for decanting purposes at the table as the presence of three Westerwald-type jugs indicates (Fig. 26, Nos. 3–5). The latter piece illustrates the introduction of the latest Baroque styles into stoneware ornament during the mid-17th century. The squat drug jar (Fig. 26, No. 7) and feeding bottle (Fig. 26, No. 8) represent rare forms in Rhenish stoneware, and mark this assemblage as a qualitatively exceptional one.
Unlike some of the other early to mid-17th-century contexts excavated in the town (and the region), this group is characterised by its low quota of local slipware and lack of Chinese export porcelain. These absences and the overall composition of the group hint at underlying social dynamics. For instance, the bias towards imported tin-glazed pottery for table use in place of local slipware suggests a relatively high purchasing power, especially as slipware, according to Orton's (1985) hierarchy of ceramic technologies, may have been the cheaper option at this time (Section 8.2.4; Diag. 7). The relative composition of Context 14 provides important comparative evidence for the socio-economic analysis of the two following groups of broadly contemporary date (86:4b and 86:2).

### *6.2.4 Schwanenstraße 86:4a & b (Contexts 15, 16, 31, 33: Figs. 31–34, 46)*

During 1986 further rescue excavations on the Duisburg Schwanenstraße revealed a brick-lined latrine complex containing two main fills (86:4a and b). The material found in the lower level (86:4a; Context 15) covers a 75year timespan (c. 1425–1500). Its small size and diverse composition suggests that it may have been disturbed several times. Yet again very little 16th-century pottery was found in this particular Schwanenstraße context. The overlying stratum (86:4b; Contexts 16, 31, 33) contains pottery dating from c. 1585–1650, although the vast majority of the wares date from the 17th century proper. The earlier datable pieces were perhaps in circulation for a considerable time prior to final deposition. The generally low fragmentation of the group as a whole suggests that the upper fill of the latrine was deposited during a relatively short timespan.
The upper fill of the latrine (86:4b; Contexts 16, 31, 33) contained a minimum vessel count of 108, of which over half (58 %) comprised plain red earthenware: a quota consistent with the majority of other 17th-century assemblages from Duisburg. The group represents perhaps the most comprehensive range of locally-made kitchenwares for the period (Figs. 33–34): tripod pipkins, colanders and cauldrons, skillets, and multipurpose bowl forms. Green-glazed whitewares from Frechen (18 %) are represented almost entirely by kitchenware forms. The assemblage is also characterised by an extensive selection of slipware table forms: dishes and porringers (Fig. 32, Nos. 1–6). The virtual absence of any maiolica or faience (4 %) suggests that slipware fulfilled the primary table functions in this particular household or community. Their low representation in favour of local slipware possibly points towards a slightly lower purchasing ability than say the the household associated with Context 14 above.
Two white faience tankards (Ware-type III.2; Fig. 33, Nos. 10–11) combined with beakers and jugs from Siegburg and the Westerwald to form the small drinking and decanting component of the group. Two late 16th-century drinking forms from Siegburg, as in Context 14, may have been in circulation for an extensive period of time before being discarded along with the rest of the stoneware group which dates in the main to the period c. 1650. Typologically comparable beakers and jug handles to those illustrated (Fig. 31, No. 8) were also found in the 1588 destruction horizon at a Siegburg production site (Ruppel 1991a, Fig. 5). Post-excavation sorting of this assemblage is not yet advanced enough to comment on the glass finds.

### *6.2.5 Schwanenstraße 86:2 (Contexts 17, 34; Figs. 35–37, 46)*

The final pottery assemblage to be discussed here came from a bricklined latrine excavated in the Duisburg Schwanenstraße during 1986. Only one main domestic rubbish fill was identified, its homogeneity suggesting one short phase of deposition for the pottery found. In all a minimum of 77 individual vessels was recovered, the vast majority of which date to the period c. 1600–1640, although a number of stonewares bear late 16th-century dates.
Virtually three-quarters of the assemblage (73 %) is composed of plain red earthenware (Ware-type Ic.1), the typology of which is dominated by kitchenware and sanitary forms (Fig. 37). Exceptions to this rule

include a number of medium-sized dishes (Fig. 36, Nos. 11–15) and a rare pedestal salt (Fig. 46, No. 11). The principal tablewares in this case were supplied by the local slipware industry (7.5 %), providing both dishes and porringers (Fig. 35). A large dish with incised decoration (diam. 32 cm) in the local 16th-century redware fabric (Ware-type Ib.2; Fig. 36, No. 11) may have been in use for several decades before discarding along with the rest of the assemblage.

Similarly, elements of the stoneware assemblage (15 % overall) suggest that they may have been in circulation for up to 40–50 years before final deposition. A large jug from Siegburg applied with a dated medallion of 1598 (Fig. 36, No. 2) and a Westerwald-type chamber pot bearing a medallion with the date 1581 (Fig. 36, No. 10) both have a significantly earlier manufacturing date than the rest of the assemblage. The group represents one of the largest and most varied of the stratified early to mid-17th-century stoneware assemblages from the town, including wares from Siegburg, Frechen, Raeren and the Westerwald. Stoneware fulfilled a number of separate functions in this context, namely drinking, decanting, transportation and sanitary needs.

As with Context 16, the assemblage is characterised by an emphasis on slipware as the primary decorative tableware. In this case the group was completely devoid of tin-glazed pottery. The composition of the assemblage as a whole suggests that the household or community associated with this latrine enjoyed marginally less purchasing ability than those able to afford imported tin-glazed pottery or porcelain at this time (e. g. Contexts 8, 14). An alternative scenario would conclude that the "missing artefacts" played a major role in this context (see Section 8.2). For instance, pewter may have comprised the primary tableware material, and slipware possibly performed only a subsidiary function. Moreover, until the post-excavation sorting of this assemblage is complete, it is difficult to gauge the importance of the glass finds. Irrespective of these factors, it is still difficult to explain the total absence of tin-glazed pottery from this context, particularly in view of the regional trends in ceramic consumption (Section 7.2.4).

# 7. Inter- and multi-site analysis: the composition of ceramic assemblages in the Lower Rhine region

## 7.1 Introduction

### *7.1.1 A quantitative study of the regional pottery supply*

A total of 95 assemblages of post-medieval pottery was recorded during the course of this survey from a wide range of archaeological sites in the Lower Rhine region (Appendices 2–4). Of this total only 38 contexts were considered sufficiently reliable for full statistical analysis (Section 2.2.4). Of this number 15 Duisburg contexts were selected for detailed discussion (see Section 6). In keeping with the problem-orientated nature of the survey, the aim of the following analysis is to provide an overall picture of quantitative trends on a multi-context basis both within the town of Duisburg and across the region as a whole, thereby achieving a geographically more representative insight into regional ceramic consumption than any one site or context can provide.

The model for this macro-level or aggregate approach is the City of London where individual assemblages have been treated as originating from one vast archaeological site (Rhodes 1977; Orton 1977; 1979). Ceramic trends are judged on an aggregate basis with individual assemblages of the same date quantified together to give a thematic overview of the City's pottery supply through time. An example of the approach is provided by Vince's review of the London Saxon and medieval pottery sequence (Vince 1985) and by the Museum of London pottery fasicule series (review Jones 1989). In Humberside, Britain (Hayfield 1988), this approach has proved an effective means of studying medieval ceramics on a regional inter- and multi-site basis.

For the purpose of this overview of regional ceramic trends, a series of pie-charts and bar-charts have been prepared (Graphs 1–33 and 34–36 respectively), which provides a multi-context summary of the relative frequency of Ware-types, forms and functional ceramic-types from excavations across the Lower Rhineland. The analysis is presented by phase covering the period c. 1400–1800 with, for example, a series of contexts from the town of Duisburg collectively representing one ceramic phase. In order to increase the potential sample size, the ratio of individual forms within each major Ware-type (Graphs 11–33) has been based on an aggregate of all vessels of the same Ware found in the town of Duisburg. The Wesel and Krefeld-Linn groups are presented separately in order to provide a quantitative and distributional yardstick for the Duisburg evidence.

To assess the significance of the Lower Rhine ceramic situation, reference will also be made to quantitative trends identified in the neighbouring Low Countries (see Map 7 for the location of principal consumer sites) and parts of North West Germany. Socio-economic and functional interpretation of the ceramic trends presented here will be amplified in Section 8.3.

## 7.2 Ceramic group composition by phase

### *7.2.1 Phase c. 1400–1450*

Four individual pottery groups from Duisburg dating to the early 15th century were considered worthy of quantification (Contexts 3, 7, 15, 38). No assemblages of this date outside Duisburg were available for statistical quantification. Collectively the Duisburg groups can be summarised in terms of Ware-type composition by Graph 1. Siegburg stoneware (II.1, II.2) forms the largest single component of the groups (32 %), accounting for the vast majority of drinking and decanting forms for the table (Graphs 14 & 34a). Local greywares (Ia.6–7), redwares (Ia.8) and white-firing earthenwares from the Cologne area and less so from Langerwehe (Ia.2–5) make up the remainder of the assemblages (Graph 1, 63 %), and provide the bulk of the kitchen, cellar and sanitary ware (Graphs 12, 13, 11 respectively). The few vessels of Franconian whiteware (Ia.10) provide the only evidence for long-distance ceramic supply at this time (under 5 %). In one instance, at the Minoritenkloster site (Context 36), Siegburg provided almost 70 % of the total number of ceramics found (by Estimated Vessel Equivalent), inclusive of both earthenware (Ia.1) and stoneware (II.2), the latter making 53 % of the assemblage alone. No other source of stoneware was identified on the site.

Graphs 11 and 13 demonstrate that whitewares and redwares provide the majority of cooking vessels at this time (tripod pipkins, pipkins, dripping pans and skillets making up 68 % and 66 % of their respective functional range). Greywares (Graph 12) are mainly represented by large bowls and colanders associated with food preparation (66 %), while tripod pipkins make up only 14 % of this ware-type. Redwares and greywares provide the only chamber pots found (11 % and 2 % respectively).

Siegburg emerges as the source of virtually all stoneware found in Duisburg during the first half of the 15th century with the exception of a very limited number of Raeren drinking vessels (II.6). The same picture is repeated in the Dutch towns along the Rhine, where Siegburg, as opposed to Langerwehe, dominates the stoneware supply ('s-Hertogenbosch: H. L. Janssen 1983a, 207–209; Deventer: Clevis & Kottman 1989, 23). A similar ratio of stoneware to grey and red earthenware has also been identified in The Netherlands, with Siegburg products forming the largest component of excavated groups. At Nijmegen, for instance, Siegburg supplied 43 % of all pottery found in the 1425–1550 horizons (Thijssen ed. 1991, 30). To date, only isolated finds of 15th-century Rhenish whiteware have been identified in the Low Countries, most of it coming from Langerwehe (e. g. Hurst *et al.* 1986, Cat. 344).

Despite the lack of exotic imports at this time, it is significant that the Lower Rhineland, with its access to a greater number of clay sources used for the production of grey, red and white-firing earthenwares, besides the clays suitable for stoneware production, enjoyed a more diverse range of native ceramic products during the early part of the 15th century than did its neighbouring regions.

### *7.2.2 Phase c. 1450–1500*

Four Duisburg contexts were dated to the second half of the 15th century (Contexts 1, 2, 22, 37). Their relative composition is characterised by the same range of Ware-types as the previous half century, only in slightly different proportions (Graph 2). The greyware (Ia.6–7) component is virtually identical (21 %), but the proportion of redware (Ia.8) doubled to 40 %. The supply of lead-glazed red earthenware to the town increased at the expense of the whiteware (Ia.3) and the Siegburg stonewares which both decreased by 10 %. The general decline of unglazed greyware in favour of oxidised, red-firing, lead-glazed earthenwares during the course of the 15th century is also a significant feature of ceramic sequences across the Netherlands (H. L. Janssen 1983b, 136). The quantitative evidence from Deventer, for instance (Clevis & Kottman 1989, 53), shows a significant increase in the proportion of red earthenware found in the town (an increase from 20 % to 50 % over 50 years), with the greyware component remaining constant at around 10 %. The inter-regional pattern shows that unglazed greywares were sidelined to storage and food-preparatory functions, while the redwares increasingly dominated the cooking activities (Graphs 12 and 13 respectively). Their lead-glazed bodies clearly ensured their success as robust, non-porous utensils designed to perform a multitude of domestic tasks.

By 1500 the more refined redwares and whitewares characteristic of the 16th-century pottery groups in the region (Ware-types Ib.1 and Ib.3 respectively) begin to appear in the Duisburg sequence, but form only a minor component of the regional earthenware market (Contexts 22 & 37). Siegburg remains the dominant supplier of stoneware to the region with only a limited number of Raeren-type mugs and jugs identified to date. The Siegburg wares are represented by jug forms (53 %), drinking-jugs, mugs, cups and beakers (36 %), and costrels (10 %). Pouring and drinking wares were clearly the main emphasis of the Siegburg industry. The Siegburg monopoly of the regional stoneware market continued similarly in the Netherlands throughout the 15th century, although mugs from Raeren also began to make an impression at this time (e. g. 's-Hertogenbosch: H. L. Janssen 1983a, Fig. 18; Nijmegen: Thijssen ed. 1991, Cat. 57, 62).

The functional composition of the later 15th-century assemblages from Duisburg largely continues the pattern established at the beginning of the century (Graph 34b). Kitchen wares continue to account for the majority of forms (58 %), while the proportion of storage and transport vessels increases from 7 % to 15 %. The tableware component of the groups (22 %) was augmented by the additon of a number of new forms in redware (Ia.8) and white earthenware (Ia.3), including bowl-salts and small porringers respectively (Diag. 8b).

### *7.2.3 Phase c. 1500–1580*

Only two 16th-century contexts from Duisburg were considered suitable for systematic quantification (Contexts 30, 41), although the aggregate minimal vessel count totalled 158 (Graph 3). Immediately apparent is the continuing decline in the importance of the Siegburg stoneware industry (16 %) in favour of the emerging workshops producing ornate relief-moulded stonewares at Cologne and, after c. 1550, at Frechen (5 %). Large storage jars from Langerwehe (II.5) and a variety of forms from Raeren (II.6) provide the remainder of the stoneware component in the two assemblages (10 %).

By 1500 greywares (Ia.6–7) completely disappeared from the Duisburg sequence, but continued in isolated pockets on the periphery of the region (i. e. Ware-type Ib.9 at Wesel and Bocholt: Contexts 78 & 90 respectively). The extended spectrum of local redware forms (Ib.1) dominated the assemblages with 47 % of the total vessel count. The development of an innovative range of new shapes (Graph 15; Diag. 8c), such as dishes, cauldrons, casseroles, and porringers among others, ensured the continuing demand for lead-glazed red earthenware for the duration of the 16th century. Cooking wares such as flat-based and tripod pipkins continued to dominate the excavated groups (40 %). The redwares also accounted for the majority of chamber pots produced at this time (9 % of the total redwares found as opposed to 2 % of the stoneware forms; see Graphs 15 & 19). Surprisingly the market share enjoyed by greenglazed whitewares from the Cologne area was comparatively minor (1 %). The scarcity of whitewares from the period c. 1500 to 1580 may perhaps be related to their relative cost and associated difficulties of manufacture (Section 5.2.1). Nevertheless, further quantifiable groups are urgently needed for this period so that a more representative picture of the relative importance of white-firing earthenwares in the region can be drawn.

The stoneware component in Duisburg (Graph 19) was still dominated by the various jug forms (57 %) and drinking wares (tankards, drinking-jugs and beakers at 24 % of all stonewares found). Functionally, the two groups reviewed here appear to have a similar composition as the previous half century (Graph 34c): with kitchen wares the most frequent functional category (62 %).

The functional versatility of the redware range ensured its predominance not only in the Lower Rhineland but in the neighbouring Netherlands and in other areas of North West Germany. At Deventer it maintained a 55 % share of the local pottery market throughout the 16th and 17th centuries (Clevis & Kottman 1989, 53). A comparable proportional scenario has been recorded in the towns of Höxter and Göttingen along the Weser (Stephan 1980b, Fig. 16).

### *7.2.4 Phase c. 1580–1650*

Within the town of Duisburg six major contexts covering the first half of the 17th century were eligible for statistical analysis (4, 8, 14, 16, 17, 20), forming an aggregate vessel count of 484. In three out of six cases the individual sequence began around 1580. Outside Duisburg a chronologically comparable sequence was provided by a series of latrine and pit groups in Wesel comprising an aggregate vessel count of 222 and dating to the period c. 1580–1620 (Contexts 74–76, 78–79). Collectively the Duisburg and Wesel assemblages represent a period of maximum development and change in both local production and consumer demand, with the introduction of a range of highly decorated tablewares made both within and imported from outside the region.

Lead-glazed red earthenware (Ware-types Ib.1, Ic.1) continued to dominate the Duisburg groups (60 % of all pottery found). This figure also includes the earliest flatwares with incised decoration at 1 % of the total (Ib.2, Ic.2). These statistics (Graph 4) illustrate the increasing output of the Lower Rhine earthenware industry at this time, which improved its market share in Duisburg by over 10 % from the previous half-century (Graph 3). This increase would appear to have occured during the second quarter of the 17th century, as the evidence from Wesel suggests (45 % of the total between c. 1580–1620: Graph 10). The dominance of red earthenwares on an inter-regional scale during the 16th and 17th centuries is confirmed by the evidence from Deventer, The Netherlands, where they accounted for over 50 % of the entire pottery found (Clevis & Kottman 1989, 53).

Proportionally the frequency of individual redware forms changed little between the 16th and 17th centuries (Graphs 15, 16). The one significant feature was the growing importance of the multi-purpose bowl form (from 7 % to 26 %). Figure 37, 16–22 show the variety of rim shapes common during the period 1580–1640. The tripod pipkin remained the predominant form made by the redware industry (over 40 %).

The post-c. 1580 groups from Duisburg are characterised by some of the earliest examples of local slip-decorated red earthenware to be found in the region (Ware-type Ib.5; Diag. 8c bottom). Slipware dishes and porringers accounted for only 5 % of the entire pottery sequence during the first half of the 17th century. They also comprised 9 % of the aggregate vessel count in Wesel during the period c. 1580–1620 (Graph 10). Their relative scarcity suggests that either the production of decorative slipware was minimal in the Lower Rhineland at this time or that these wares enjoyed a markedly higher retail value and social premium than their undecorated counterparts (Gaimster 1991). In terms of their exclusivity, the early slipwares from the Lower Rhine enjoyed a similar market share to tin-glazed maiolica and faience (Ware-type III.1–3) imported from the northern Netherlands (8 % in Duisburg; 9 % in Wesel: Graphs 4 & 10 respectively).

The other principal supplier of lead-glazed earthenware to the Lower Rhine towns was the Frechen industry, from which green-glazed whitewares (Ib.3, Ic.3) accounted for 16 % of the ceramic total in Duisburg alone (Graph 4). At Nijmegen Frechen-type whitewares comprised over 25 % of the total pottery found in the phase dating to the period c. 1600–1640 (Thijssen ed. 1991, 30). The range of whiteware forms expanded considerably during the early 17th century, constituting a far wider range than before of dish and porringer forms, tripod pipkins, colanders and ointment pots (Graph 17). Tripod pipkins came in a variety of dimensions and shapes, and comprised 69 % of the entire whiteware supply.

The proportional share enjoyed by the Rhenish stoneware industries receded quite dramatically from the beginning of the 17th century at Duisburg (from 26 % to 9 %: Graphs 3 & 4 respectively), although the Wesel sequence shows a quite opposite trend (27 % in total:

Graph 10). One thing is quite clear, however: the traded Siegburg wares were no longer represented solely by the mass-produced undecorated jugs and beakers as in the 15th and early 16th centuries. By 1600 a series of highly ornamented salt-glazed vessel-types had been introduced, including flagons, tankards, inverted beakers and unglazed beakers with incised decoration (Diag. 8c bottom). After 1600 the overall ratio of Siegburg stoneware found in Duisburg shrank to negligable proportions (2 %). The decline in Siegburg's monopoly of the regional pottery market is also documented at Nijmegen where it supplied only 2 % of all pottery dating to the phase c. 1600–1640 (Thijssen ed. 1991, 21–23). Collectively other sources were responsible for a further 10 % in the town (*ibid.*). This trend may perhaps be explained by the gradual transition of Siegburg from a mass-market producer to a supplier of decorated wares for the luxury market. Final analysis of the relative proportions of undecorated to decorated wasters from the recently excavated late 16th century Knütgen workshop at Siegburg (Ruppel 1991a; 1991b) will help to clarify this change in the future.

During the early 17th-century potters from Raeren and Siegburg migrated to the Westerwald region below Koblenz and began to produce stonewares using the same decorative techniques, and frequently the same applied moulds (von Falke II 1908, 65–72). The impact of the Westerwald industry (Ware-type II.9) can be seen in both the Duisburg and Wesel sequences of the early 17th century, where they, along with storage jars from Langerwehe (II.5) and jugs, bottles and chamber pots from Frechen (II.8), account for 7 % and 13 % respectively of the entire ceramics recovered (Graphs 4 & 10). At the latter site they represent 50 % of all stonewares found. Typologically the Westerwald products are represented by chamber pots, tankards, and flagons during this early 17th-century period (Diag. 8d; Graph 20).

This phase of ceramic consumption in the Lower Rhineland is marked for the first time by the supply of a series of highly decorated tablewares imported from outside the region. By 1580–1600 the earliest tin-glazed earthenwares appear in the Duisburg and Wesel sequences. Polychrome maiolica dishes and porringers from the northern Netherlands (III.1) account for 8 % of the total vessel count at Duisburg and 9 % at Wesel during the first half of the 17th century (Graphs 4 & 10). Isolated examples of early Dutch faience (III.2–3), which appear by 1640, are included in this figure. Both the Duisburg and Wesel groups also include examples of early 17th-century blue- and-white Chinese export porcelain or Kraak porcelain (IV.1). The undeniable social status attributed to Chinese porcelain during the early 17th century is emphasised by its relative scarcity in the archaeological record, accounting for less than 1 % of the pottery recovered. Occasional sherds of slipware from the Werra region to the East of the Rhine represent the only other long-distance import at this time (under 1 %).

In terms of the relative proportions of functional types recovered from this phase, the picture at Wesel and Duisburg is strikingly similar (Graph 35, a & b respectively). Vessels for cooking and food preparation were the most common (61 % at Wesel; 65 % at Duisburg), and accounted for most of the lead-glazed earthenware pottery. Tablewares provided 31 % of the total vessel count at Wesel, and 29 % at Duisburg. Sanitary, storage and other wares contributed less than 8 % of the total at both sites. The statistics represent a marginal but significant rise in the ratio of ceramic tableware to kitchenware on Lower Rhine sites during the first half of the 17th century. The trend is likely to be linked to the introduction of a new and varied range of decorative ceramics, namely slipware produced in the region, tin-glazed pottery from the neighbouring Netherlands and Chinese blue-and-white porcelain imported via The Channel ports. The trend is even more marked on individual sites, such as Duisburg Context 14, where tin-glazed pottery (Ware-types III.1-3) accounts for nearly one quarter of the entire site assemblage.

### *7.2.5 Phase c. 1650–1700*

Only two Duisburg contexts dating to the second half of the 17th century were sufficiently intact to allow quantitative analysis (Contexts 5 & 43). Together they amounted to an aggregate vessel count of only 31. The sample is too small to enable detailed interpretation to be attempted, although some general points will be outlined here. Unfortunately, no quantifiable groups of the same date were available for comparison from the Lower Rhine hinterland.

Graph 5 shows the relative proportions of Ware-types from this phase. Immediately striking is the increase in the ratio of tin-glazed earthenware to other wares (61 % of the aggregate total of ceramics found). The changeover from workshop to factory production in the Netherlands after c. 1660 (van Dam 1982, 80) was primarily responsible for the increase in wares made for the export market. By this time production of tin-glazed maiolica was in fast decline (*idem*, 38–40), and was replaced by the manufacture of faience wares, in both monochrome (Ware-type III.2) and painted varieties (III.3) (see Section 5.4.2). The latter category of wares account for the vast majority of plates, dishes, tankards and jugs found on the Duisburg sites at this time (Diag. 8e). This picture must be calibrated, however, by the study of further groups of this date, as the trends identified here from only a very small sample may be biased by site-specific depositional or social factors.

The starkest contrast between the early and later 17th-century pottery groups is illustrated by the virtual lack of redware (3 %), although the proportion of slipware increased significantly on the previous half century (up to 13 % from 5 %). The demand for fine green-glazed whiteware from Frechen was maintained at around 13 % of the combined total vessel count. The ratio of stoneware to the lead-glazed earthenware types remained virtually unchanged (Graphs 4 & 5).
Even with such a small sample of quantifiable material, it is not without significance that the ratio of tableware to wares used in the kitchen increased once again from the previous phase (from 5 % to 25 %: Graph 35c). This quantitative relationship is confirmed when looking at the individual sites themselves (e. g. section 6.2.1). In Duisburg Context 5 the faience wares are represented by entire services of tableware. The native slipware industry also achieved a higher share of the tableware market than during the previous half century. The increasing dominance of the Low Countries faience industries during the second half of the 17th century is also demonstrated by recent excavations in the centre of Bruges, Belgium (Hillewaert & Verhaeghe 1991), where these products served the vast majority of tableware needs. As in Duisburg, tablewares of all Ware-types formed the largest single functional component of the ceramic assemblages (*idem*, Fig. 187).

### *7.2.6 Phase c. 1700–1750*

Four contexts of the first half of the 18th century, comprising a combined vessel count of 181, were selected for quantification and combined analysis from Duisburg (Contexts 6, 10, 11, 18). The relative proportions of Ware-types are presented in Graph 6. For comparative purposes, the cellar assemblage from Krefeld-Linn (Context 60), dating to c. 1700–1740, was assessed (Graph 10) in order to to provide an insight into contemporary rural as opposed to urban consumer trends.
Plain redwares and slipwares account for 27 % and 24 % respectively of the ceramic sequence recorded in Duisburg. These figures conflict with the picture in the countryside where they contribute 34 % and 37 % to the overall total (Graph 10). The pattern points to a greater use of local slipware for the table in the countryside (dishes accounted for 76 % of slipwares found at Krefeld alone; see Graph 26), in contrast to a greater proportional consumption of imported faience (29 %) and other finewares, such as Chinese porcelain, for table use in the urban environment. Only nine sherds of faience from this phase were found at Krefeld. The decline of the green-glazed whiteware industry at Frechen is reflected in the diminishing proportions of the Ware at Duisburg (6 %) and in its absence at Krefeld-Linn.
The Westerwald region supplied 100 % of Duisburg's stoneware during the first half of the 18th century. Diagram 8f summarizes the principal forms supplied to the Lower Rhineland at this time. These include jugs, tankards, chamber pots, a new range of delicate teawares based on porcelain and faience forms (Ware-type II.10) and ornate tablewares, such as terrines. This diversification of production ensured the commercial success of the Westerwald industries on a regional basis. At Krefeld-Linn, however, although still the dominant stoneware supplier, the Westerwald (13 %) shared the market with specialized stoneware products such as large storage jars from Langerwehe and Bartmann-type jugs from Frechen (combined total of 6 %). The latter were probably over 50 years old by the time of their deposition.
Chinese porcelain reappears in the Duisburg sequence by 1700 (3 % of total vessel count), although the supply is limited to a highly specialized range of teawares. Together with the Dutch faience wares (29 % of total) they form over half of the regional teaware and tableware supply at this time; with slipware dishes, plates and porringers constituting the only alternative range of products for table use. During this phase the superior ratio of tableware to other functional types is maintained in both the urban and rural environments from the previous half century (Graph 36a).
The emerging picture from Duisburg and Krefeld-Linn may be calibrated on a regional basis by the quantification of the extensive 18th-century ceramic assemblage excavated at Haus Gelinde, outside Rheinberg (Context 93; Hackspiel 1982). Although a farm site, as opposed to a village house, the proportion of local redware and slipware is similar to the other rural assemblage at Krefeld-Linn (72 % of the total). In keeping with the Krefeld pattern, stoneware accounted for 4,5 % and faience 7,7 % of the pottery found on the site. Only in the towns, such as Duisburg, was a more diverse range of ceramics available, with a more even consumption of local red earthenware and slipware alongside „luxury" imported products, such as faience and porcelain. This essentially urban pattern is repeated in Amsterdam (Thijssen 1985, Table 1; Baart 1988, Fig. 7), where redwares and slipwares predominate followed by faience as the next major component of the pottery groups during the first half of the 18th century. This distinctive ratio of local red earthenware to imported and native faience occurs in early 18th-century British instances, such as Croswall, City of London (Vince & Egan 1981).

### *7.2.7 Phase c. 1750–1800*

Four major groups of pottery from Duisburg were dated to the second half of the 18th century in Duisburg

(Contexts 12, 13, 19, 44). The trends in urban ceramic consumption (Graph 7) were calibrated by analysis of the rural picture provided by the second sealed cellar complex from Krefeld-Linn, dating to the period c. 1740–1784 (Graph 9). The composition of both sets of data is characterised by a marked increase in the range of Ware-types available to the consumer after the middle of the 18th century. The most significant development was the importation of a series of innovative fineware bodies and forms from Staffordshire, England.

The local plain earthenware and slipware pottery continued to predominate in Duisburg as the single largest component of the contexts sampled (17 % and 25 % of the total respectively). 80 % of Lower Rhine slipware found in the quantifiable Duisburg contexts dating to the 18th century was produced for table use (Graph 23). Plain redware was manufactured almost entirely for the kitchen and cellar (Graph 22).

The market share in ceramic tableware held by the Dutch faience industry in the Lower Rhine during the early 18th century came into severe competition from the Staffordshire potteries in England, which started exporting plain creamwares (Ware-type V.1) and other fine earthenware bodies to the Continent by the middle of the century (Section5.6). Both Dutch faience and Staffordshire creamware comprise 15 % each of the entire vessel count at Duisburg. Collectively, fine Staffordshire teawares, such as Blackware (Id.9), Redware (Id.10) and Agate ware (Id.11), account for 5 % of the pottery recovered during this phase.

With the flooding of the European pottery market with Chinese export porcelain during the middle part of the 18th century (Section 5.5), it is hardly surprising that the frequency of Chinese porcelain increases significantly in the Duisburg groups (up from 3 % to 11 %). Across the Channel the impact of the Dutch porcelain auctions at this date (Sheaf & Kilburn 1988) is also demonstrated by the London sequence (Vince & Egan 1981), where Chinese porcelain constitutes a third of some domestic groups after c. 1740. The typological range of the wares found in the Lower Rhineland is limited, however, to teawares, which were in turn copied by the local Dutch faience producers (see Diag. 8g for a spectrum of export wares common during this phase). The quota of porcelain from Duisburg also contains the first examples of porcelain made at German factories (IV.5), although it is not represented in any quantity until the beginning of the 19th century (Gaimster 1986a).

The proportion of stoneware to other wares remained constant during the second half of the century (11 % of the total), with the Westerwald region supplying just over 50 % of the stoneware found in the town of Duisburg. Specialised storage jars from Langerwehe (Ware-type II.5) and jugs from Frechen (II.8) accounted for the majority of other stonewares supplied to the region at this time.

Although the local plain redware and slipware continued to dominate the composition of the second Krefeld-Linn cellar group (27 % and 24 % respectively), a slight increase in the variety of wares from outside the region is also evident. Faience teawares and tablewares from the Netherlands increased significantly from the previous half century (6 % to 29 %). In contrast to the urban groups from Duisburg, the English finewares hardly made an impact in this particular rural context (under 1 %), although they accounted for over 5 % of the total at Haus Gelinde. During the first half of the 18th-century porcelain was absent from Krefeld, but composed 6 % of the later assemblage relating to this phase (Graph 9). The innate conservatism of rural ceramic demand or possible lower purchasing power in the countryside is illustrated by the reliance on Dutch faience and Chinese porcelain to provide all teaware needs in contrast to Duisburg or Wesel where Staffordshire exports were clearly more frequent (e. g. Context 80). The Westerwald and the other major stoneware industries maintained their share of the rural pottery market during this phase (combined total of 18 %). The consistent proportion of stoneware on both urban and rural sites during the 18th century is the only example of parallel consumer trends in the region (Graphs 6–9).

The impact of the English fineware industries after the middle of the 18th century on the European pottery market can be seen in the neighbouring Netherlands. In Nijmegen (Thijssen 1985, Tables 2 & 3), for instance, English imports constitute up to 30 % of the minimum vessel count of selected contexts, provoking a dramatic drop in the quantity of native faience in use (under 9 %).

The growth in the supply of wares for general table use and specialised beverage drinking during the second half of the 18th century is reflected in the increase of tableware in proportion to other functional types in the Lower Rhine ceramic sequence (over 60 % at both Duisburg and Krefeld: Graph 36b). The increasing frequency of faience, porcelain and English finewares during the course of the century on consumer sites in the Lower Rhineland alludes to the large quantities of these wares released into the regional pottery market. However, as in the Netherlands (Baart 1988), their inherent social premium remained relatively high in comparison to locally-produced wares (see Section 8.3.3).

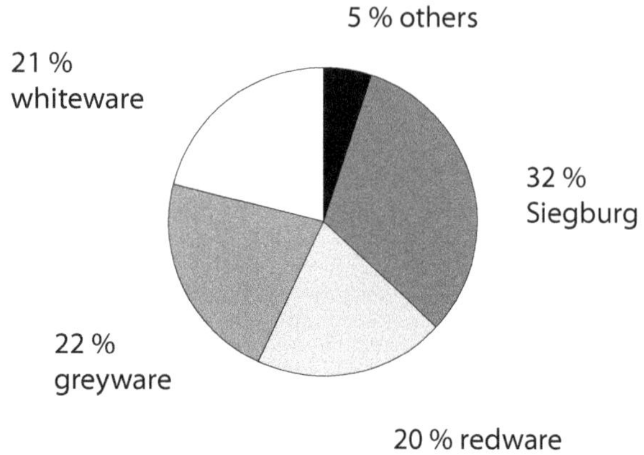


*1. Duisburg c. 1400–1450 (contexts 3, 7, 15, 38)*
*Pie chart showing relative frequency of fabrics*
*Min. vessels 76*
*Whiteware (Ia.2, Ia.3, Ia.4, Ia.5); greyware (Ia.6, Ia.7); redware (Ia.8); Siegburg (II.1, II.2); others (Ia,1, Ia.10, II.6).*

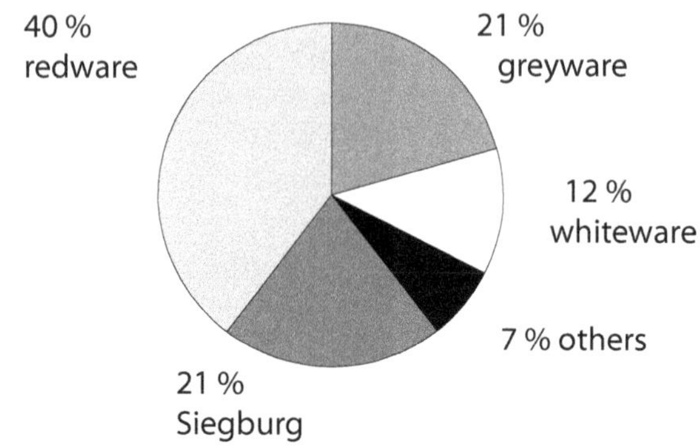


*2. Duisburg c 1450–1500 (contexts 1, 2, 22, 37)*
*Pie chart showing relative frequency of fabrics*
*Min. vessels 56*
*Whiteware (Ia.3, Ib.3); greyware (Ia.6, Ia.7); redware (Ia.8, Ib.1; Siegburg (II.1, II.2); others (II.5, II.6, intrusive wares).*

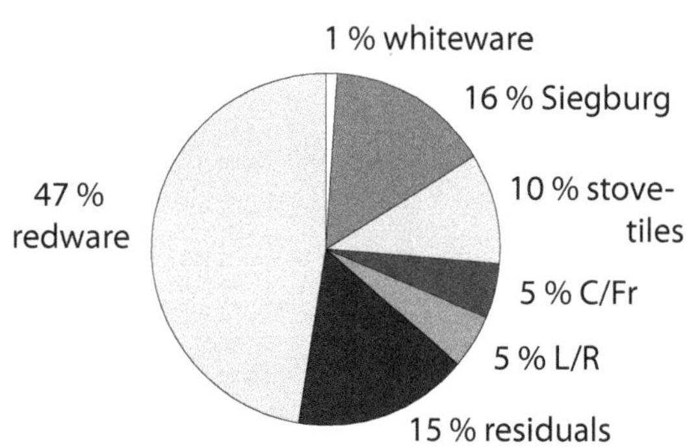


*3. Duisburg c. 1500–1580 (contexts 30, 41)*
*Pie chart showing relative frequency of fabrics*
*Min. vessels 158*
*Whiteware (Ib.3); redware (Ib.1); Siegburg (II.1, II.2, II.3); Langerwehe/Raeren stoneware (II.5, II.6), Cologne/Frechen stoneware (II.7, II.8); stove-tiles (Ia.11, Ia.12); resid. (Ia.7, Ia.8, Ia.9).*

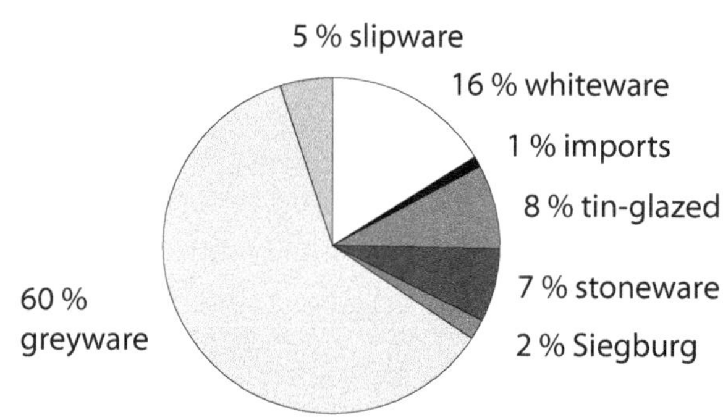


*4. Duisburg c. 1580–1650 (contexts 4, 8, 14, 16, 17, 20)*
*Pie chart showing relative frequency of fabrics Min. vessels 484*
*Whiteware (Ib.3, Ic.3); redware (Ib.1–2, Ic.1–2); slipware (Ib.5, Ic.4); Siegburg (II.3, II.4); stoneware (II.5, II.6, II.8, II.9); tin-glazed (III.1–3); imports (Ic.5, IV.1).*

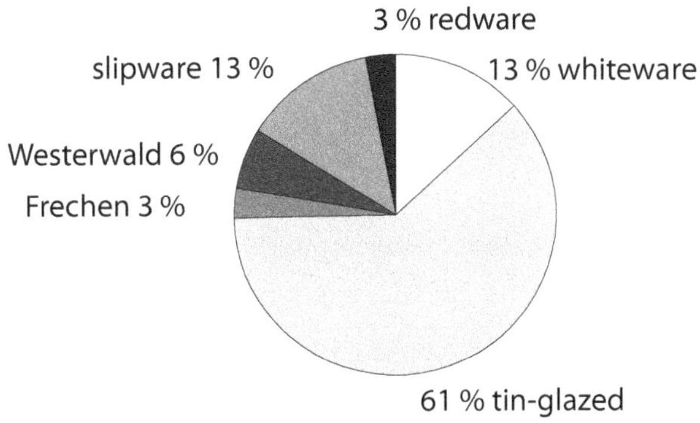


*5. Duisburg c. 1650–1700 (contexts 5, 43)*
*Pie chart showing relative frequency of fabrics*
*Min. vessels 31*
*Whiteware (Ic.3); redware (Ic.1); slipware (Ic.4); Westerwald stoneware (II.9), Frechen (II.8); tin-glazed (III.1, III.2, III.3).*

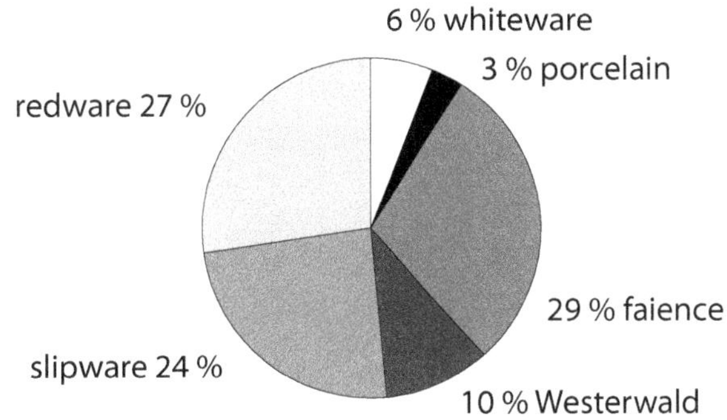


*6. Duisburg c. 1700–1750 (contexts 6, 10, 11, 18)*
*Pie chart showing relative frequency of fabrics*
*Min. vessels 181*
*Whiteware (Ic.3); redware (Id.4, Id.8); slipware (Ic.4, Id.1–2); Westerwald stoneware (II.9–10); faience (III.2–3); porcelain (IV.2–3)*

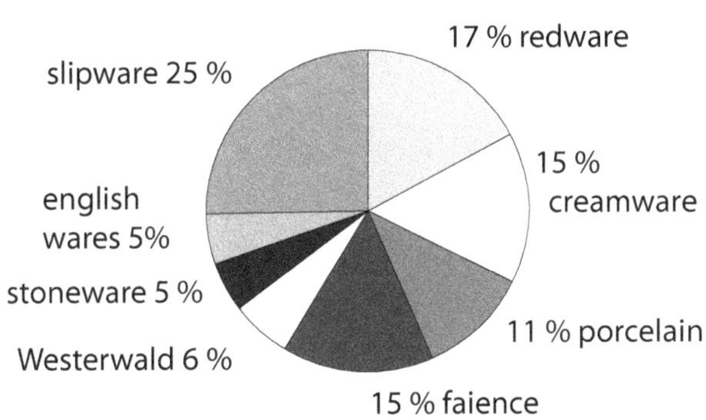


*7. Duisburg c. 1750–1800 (contexts 12, 13, 19, 44)*
*Pie chart showing relative frequency of fabrics*
*Min. vessels 110*
*Redware (Id.4); slipware (Id.1, Id.3); english wares (Id.9, Id.10, Id.11); Westerwald stoneware (II.9–10); stoneware (II.5, II.8, II.11); faience (III.3, III.5); porcelain (IV.2–4); creamware (V.1)*

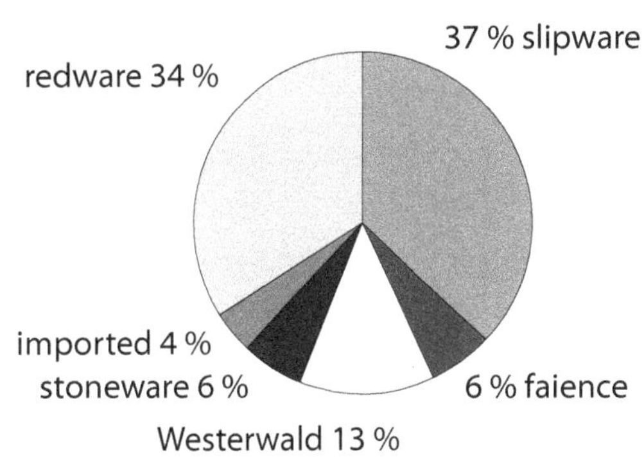


*8. Krefeld-Linn c. 1700–1740 (context 60)*
*Pie chart showing relative frequency of fabrics*
*Min. vessels 162*
*Slipware (Id.1, Id.2, Id.3); redware (Id.4, Id.5); imports (Id.12); stoneware (II.5, II.8, II.11); Westerwald stoneware (II.9, II.10); faience (III.1, III.3)*

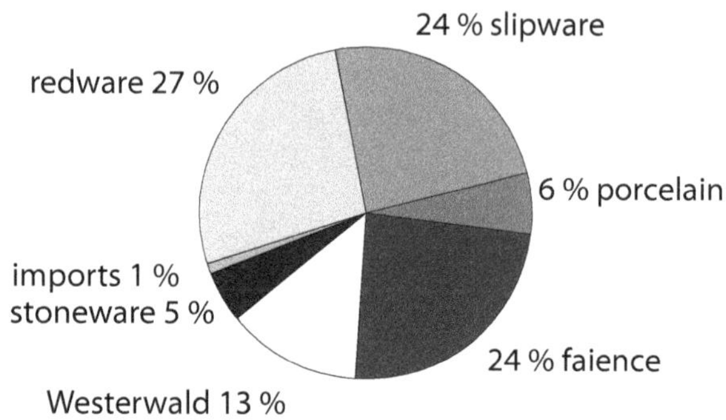


*9. Krefeld-Linn c. 1740–1784 (context 61)*
*Pie chart showing relative frequency of fabrics*
*Min. vessels 263*
*Slipware (Id.1, Id.2, Id.3); redware (Id.4, Id.5); imports (Id.12); stoneware (II.5, II.8, II.11); Westerwald stoneware (II.9, II.10); faience (III.1, III.3), porcelain (IV.2, IV.3); english wares (Id.10)*

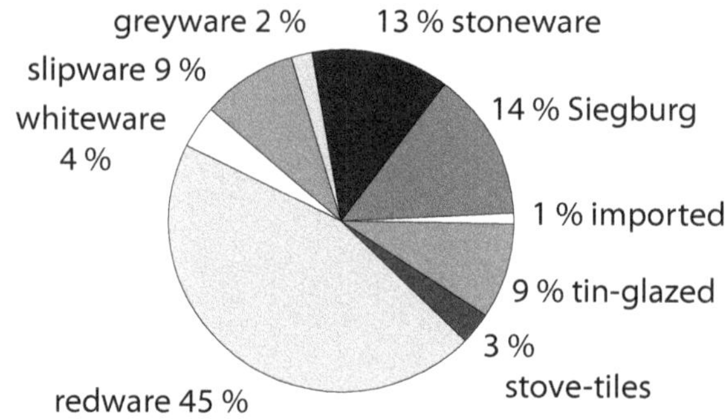


*10. Wesel c. 1580–1620 (contexts 74, 75, 76, 78, 79)*
*Pie chart showing relative frequency of fabrics*
*Min. vessels 222*
*Siegburg (II.1–II.4); stoneware (II.5, II.6, II.8–9); greyware (Ib.9); slipware (Ib.5, Ic.3); whiteware (Ib.3, Ic.3); redware (Ib.1–2, Ic.1–2); stove-tiles (Ib.8); tin-glazed (III.1–3); imports (Ic.5, IV.1).*

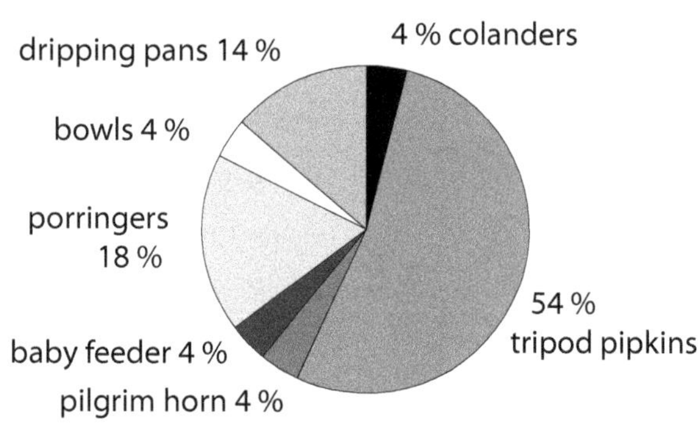


*11. Form*
*15th century whiteware from Duisburg*
*Pie chart showing relative frequency of whiteware forms from Duisburg c. 1400–1500*
*Total min. vessels 28*
*Fabrics Ia.2, Ia.3, Ia.4, Ia.5*

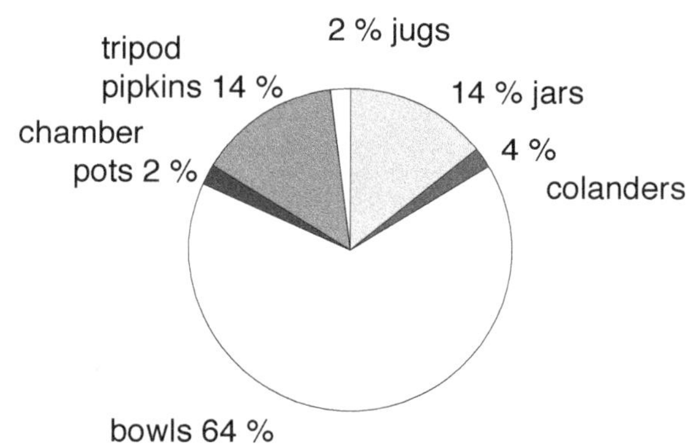


*12. Form*
*15th century greyware from Duisburg*
*Pie chart showing relative frequency of greyware forms from Duisburg c. 1400–1500*
*Total min. vessels 42*
*Fabrics Ia.6, Ia.7*

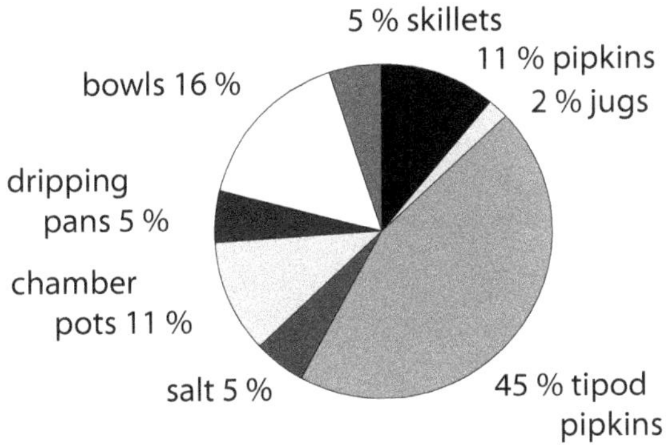


*13. Form*
*15th century redware from Duisburg*
*Pie chart showing relative frequency of redware forms from Duisburg c. 1400–1500*
*Total min. vessels 55*
*Fabrics Ia.8, Ia.9*

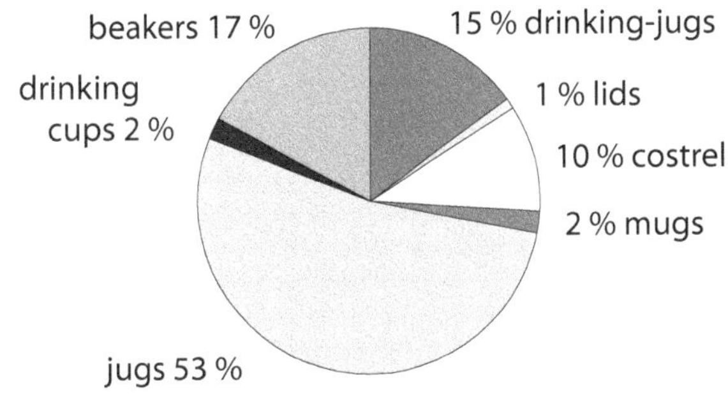


*14. Form*
*15th century Siegburg from Duisburg*
*Pie chart showing relative frequency of Siegburg stoneware forms from Duisburg c. 1400–1500*
*Total min. vessels 93*
*Fabrics Ia.1, II.1, II.2, II.3*

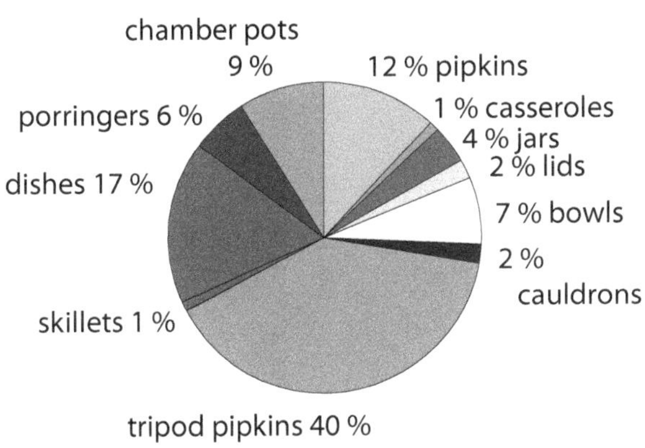


*15. Form*
*16th century plain redware from Duisburg*
*Pie chart showing relative frequency of plain redware forms from Duisburg c. 1500–1600*
*Total min. vessels 122*
*Fabrics Ib.1, Ib.2, Ib.4*

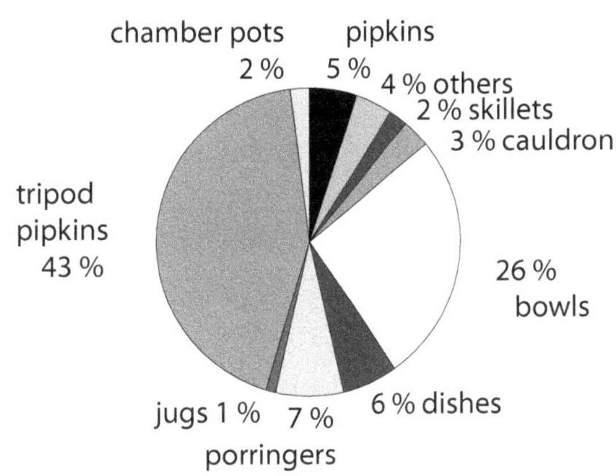


*16. Form*
*17th century plain redware from Duisburg*
*Pie chart showing relative frequency of plain redware forms from Duisburg c. 1600–1700*
*Total min. vessels 299*
*Fabrics Ic.1, Ic.2*

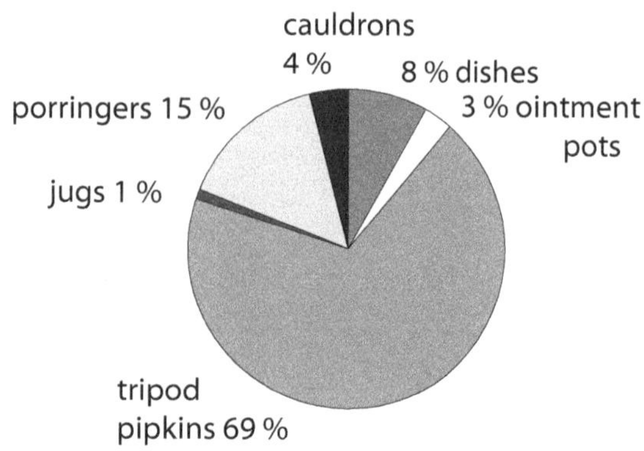


*17. Form*
*16–17th century whiteware from Duisburg*
*Pie chart showing relative frequency of whiteware forms from Duisburg c. 1500–1700*
*Total min. vessels 101*
*Fabrics Ib.3, Ic.3*

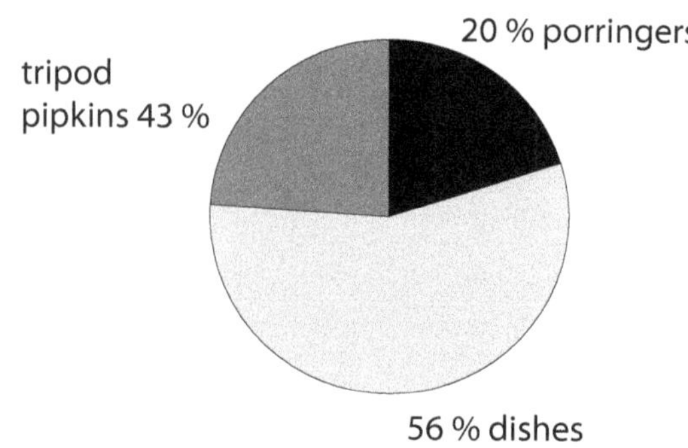


*18. Form*
*16–17th century slipware from Duisburg*
*Pie chart showing relative frequency of slipware forms from Duisburg c. 1500–1700*
*Total min. vessels 41*
*Fabrics Ib.5, Ib.6, Ic.4, Ic.5*

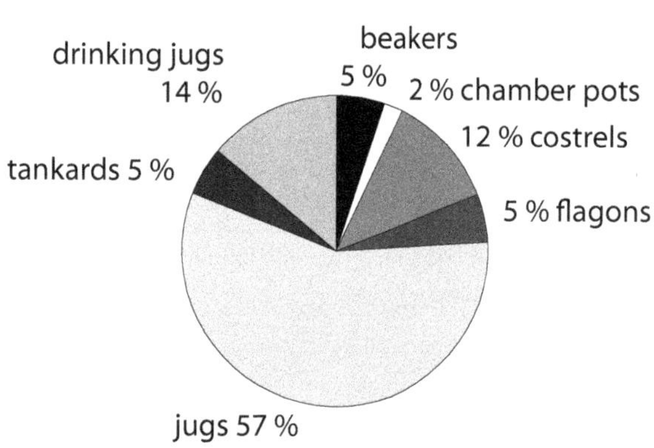


*19. Form*
*16th century stoneware from Duisburg*
*Pie chart showing relative frequency of stoneware forms from Duisburg c. 1500–1600*
*Total min. vessels 59*
*Fabrics II.1, II.2, II.3, II.4, II.5, II.6, II.7, II.8*

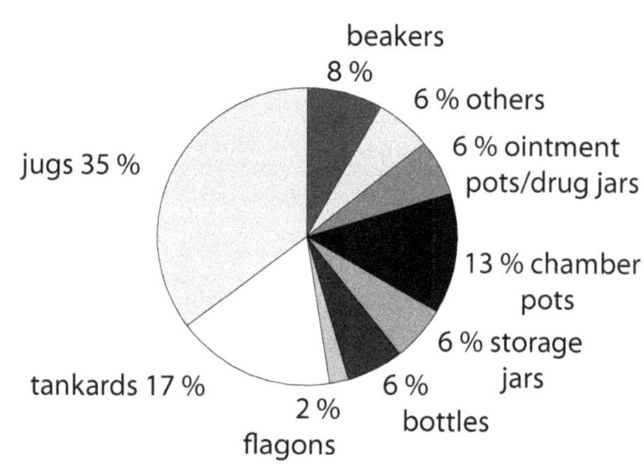


*20. Form*
*17th century stoneware from Duisburg*
*Pie chart showing relative frequency of stoneware forms from Duisburg c. 1600–1700*
*Total min. vessels 45*
*Fabrics II.3, II.4, II.5, II.6, II.8, II.9, II.11 (others: porringer, feeding bottle)*

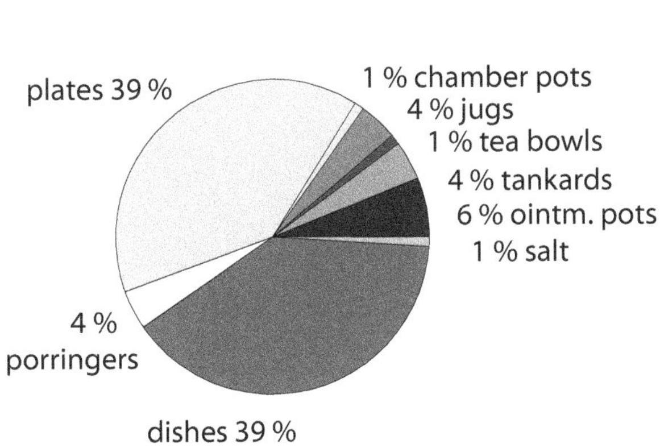


*21. Form*
*16–17th century tin-glazed pottery from Duisburg*
*Pie chart showing relative frequency of tin-glazed earthenware (NL maiolica) forms from Duisburg c. 1580–1650*
*Total min. vessels 75*
*Fabrics III.1, III.2, III.3*

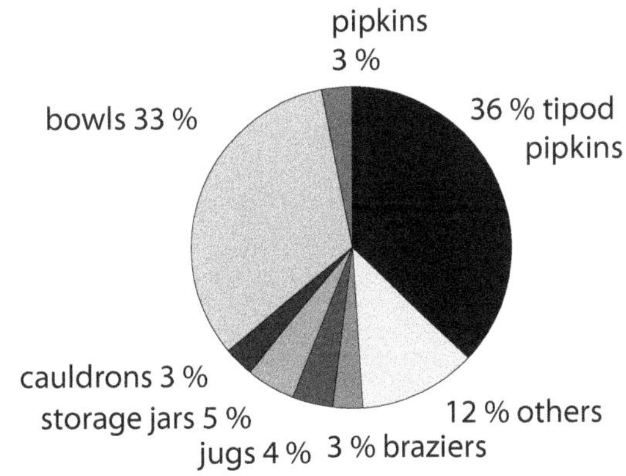


*22. Form*
*18th century plain redware from Duisburg*
*Pie chart showing relative frequency of plain redware forms from Duisburg c. 1700–1800*
*Total min. vessels 73*
*Fabrics Id.4, Id.5, Id.6, Id.7, Id.8 (others: lamp, cup, colander)*

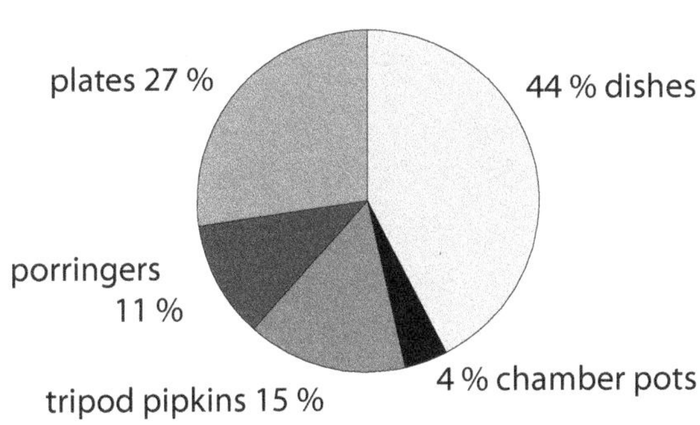


*23. Form*
*18th century slipware from Duisburg*
*Pie chart showing relative frequency of slipware forms from Duisburg c. 1700–1800*
*Total min. vessels 72*
*Fabrics Id.1, Id.2, Id.3, Id.12*

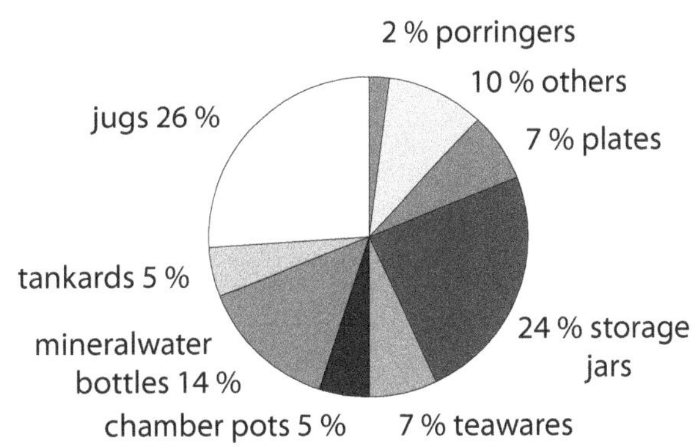


*24. Form*
*18th century stoneware from Duisburg*
*Pie chart showing relative frequency of stoneware forms from Duisburg c. 1700–1800*
*Total min. vessels 39*
*Fabrics II.5, II.8, II.9, II.10, II.11 (others: writing set, terrine)*

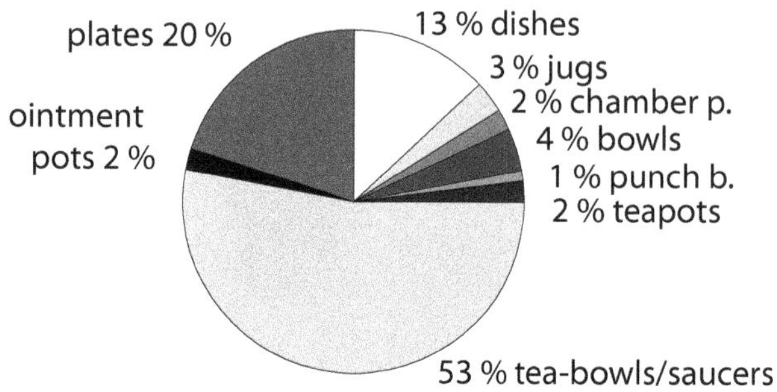


*25. Form*
*18th century finewares from Duisburg*
*Pie chart showing relative frequency of assorted fineware forms from Duisburg c. 1700–1800*
*Total min. vessels 127*
*Fabrics Id.9, Id.10, Id.11, III.2, III.3, III.4, IV.2, IV.3, IV.4, V.1*

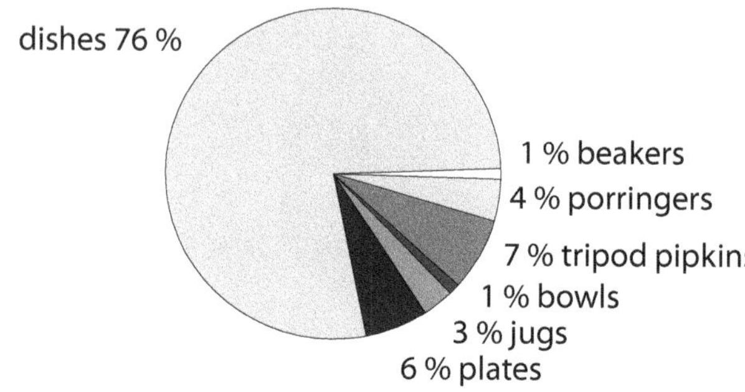


*26. Form*
*Krefeld-Linn slipware c. 1700–1740*
*Pie chart showing relative frequency of slipware forms from Krefeld-Linn c. 1700–1740*
*Total min. vessels 68*
*Fabrics Id.1, Id.2, Id.3, Id.12*

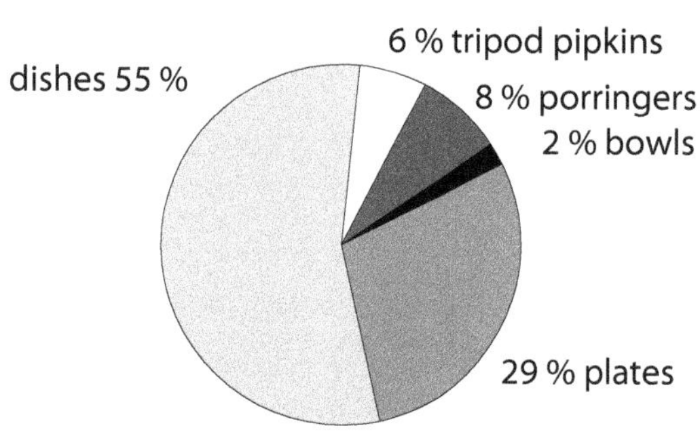


*27. Form*
*Krefeld-Linn slipware c. 1740–1784*
*Pie chart showing relative frequency of slipware forms from Krefeld-Linn c. 1740–1784*
*Total min. vessels 65*
*Fabrics Id.1, Id.2, Id.3, Id.12*

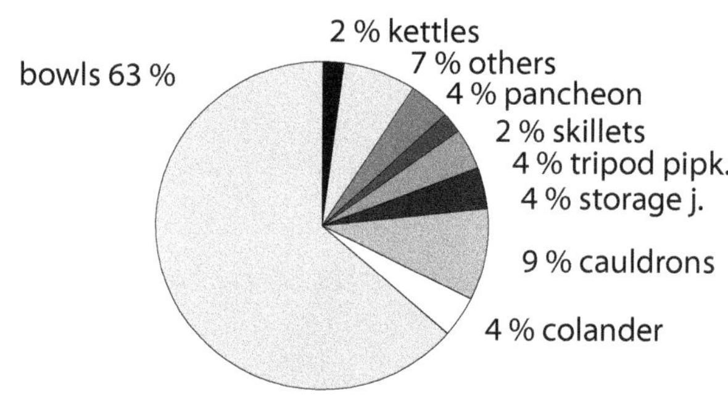


*28. Form*
*Krefeld-Linn plain redware c. 1700–1740*
*Pie chart showing relative frequency of plain redware forms from Krefeld-Linn c. 1700–1740*
*Total min. vessels 47*
*Fabrics Id.4, Id.5, Id.6, Id.7, Id.8 (others: brazier, basket, pipkin, jug)*

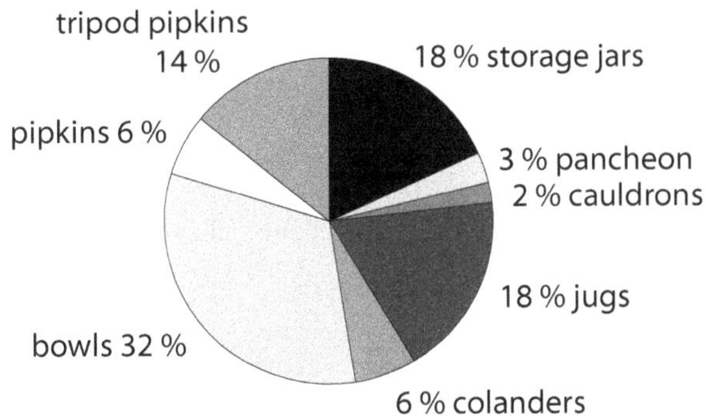


*29. Form*
*Krefeld-Linn plain redware c. 1740–1784*
*Pie chart showing relative frequency of plain redware forms from Krefeld-Linn c. 1740–1784*
*Total min. vessels 65*
*Fabrics Id.4, Id.5, Id.6, Id.7, Id.8*

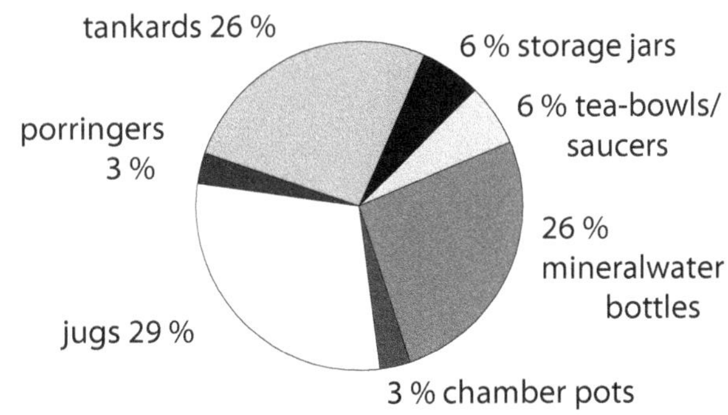


*30. Form*
*Krefeld-Linn stoneware c. 1700–1740*
*Pie chart showing relative frequency of stoneware forms from Krefeld-Linn c. 1700–1740*
*Total min. vessels 31*
*Fabrics II.5, II.8, II.9, II.10, II.11*

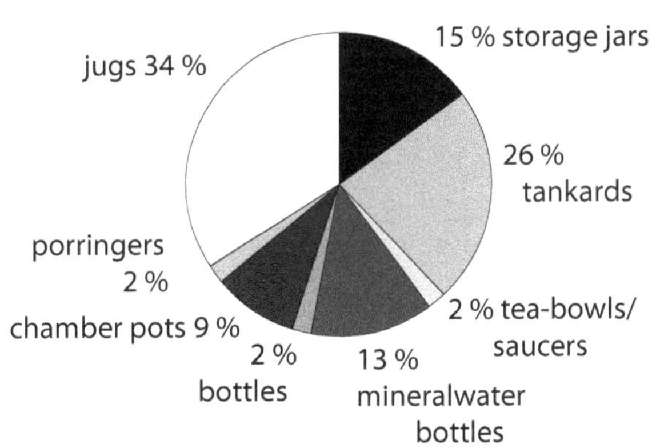


*31. Form*
*Krefeld-Linn stoneware c. 1740–1784*
*Pie chart showing relative frequency of stoneware forms from Krefeld-Linn c. 1740–1784*
*Total min. vessels 38*
*Fabrics II.5, II.8, II.9, II.10, II.11*

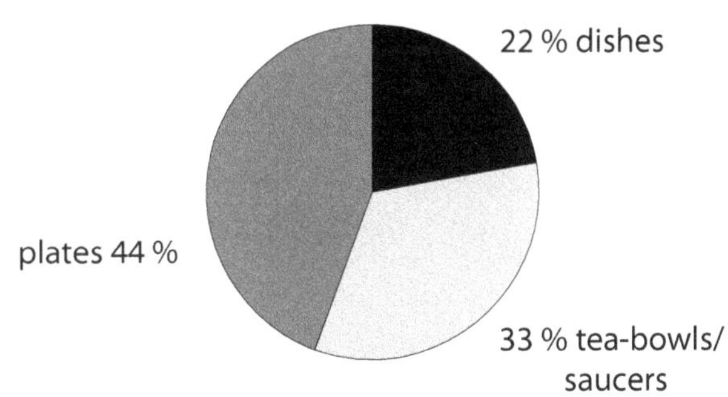


*32. Form*
*Krefeld-Linn faience c. 1700–1740*
*Pie chart showing relative frequency of faience forms from Krefeld-Linn c. 1700–1740*
*Total min. vessels 9*
*Fabrics III.1, III.2*

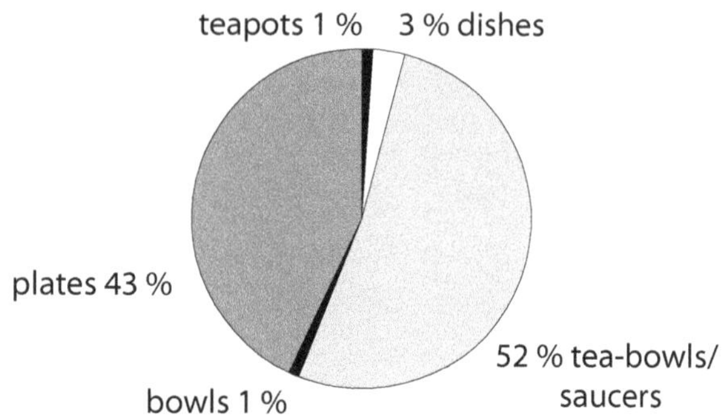


*33. Form*
*Krefeld-Linn stoneware c. 1740–1784*
*Pie chart showing relative frequency of assorted fineware forms from Krefeld-Linn c. 1740–1784*
*Total min. vessels 79*
*Fabrics Id.10, III.1, III.3, IV.2, IV.3*

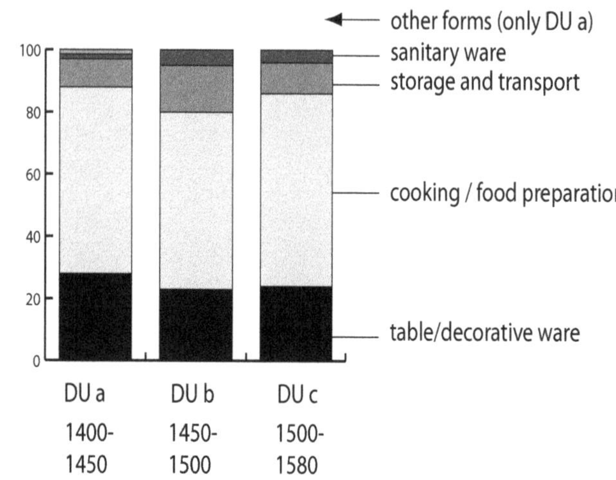


*34. Function*
*Stacked bar chart showing the relative proportion of functinal categories from three Duisburg phases, c. 1400–1450, c. 1450–1500, c. 1500–1580*
*DU a: Contexts 3, 7, 15, 38*
*Total min. vessels 79*
*DU b: Contexts 1, 2, 22, 37*
*Total min. vessels 65*
*DU c: Contexts 30, 41*
*Total min. vessels 91*

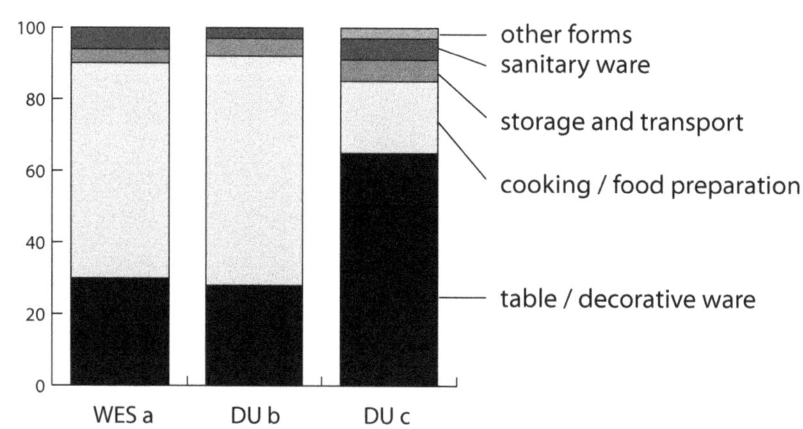


*35. Function*
*Stacked bar chart showing the relative proportion of functional categories from Wesel (c. 1580–1620) and Duisburg (c. 1580–1650) and c. 1650–1700)*

*WES a: c. 1580–1620; Wesel contexts 74, 75, 76, 78,79; total min. vessels 241*
*DU b: c. 1580–1650, Duisburg contests 4, 8, 14, 16, 17, 20, total min. vessels 484*
*DU c: c. 1650–1700, Duisburg contexts 5, 43, total min. vessels 40*

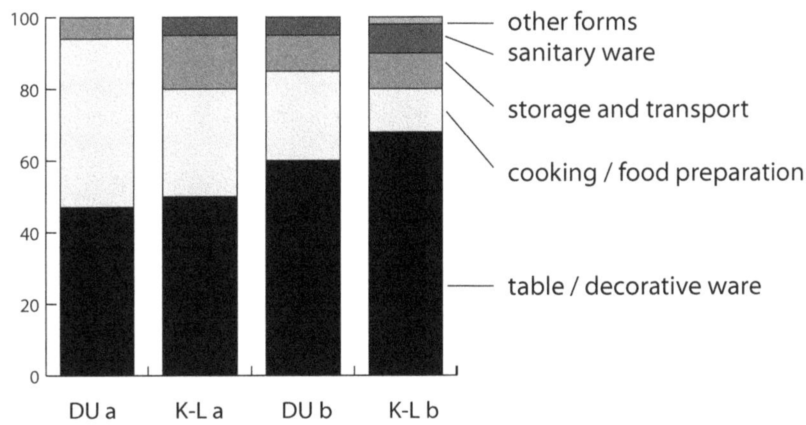


*36. Function*
*Stacked bar chart showing the relative proportion of functional categories from Duisburg (c. 1700–1750, c. 1750–1800) and Krefeld-Linn (c. 1700–1740, 1740–1784)*

*DU a: c. 1700–1750; Duisburg contexts 6, 10, 11, 18, total min. vessels 174*
*K-L a: c. 1700–1740; Krefeld-Linn context 60, total min. vessels 162*
*DU b: c. 1750–1800; Duisburg contexts 12, 13, 19, 44, total min. vessels 109*
*K-L b: c. 1740–1784; Krefeld-Linn context 61, total min. vessels 263*

# 8. Discussion: ceramic consumption in the Lower Rhineland c. 1400–1800

## 8.1 Introduction

### *8.1.1 The potential of pottery as a historical source*

From the very outset of this project, the primary aim of systematic classification and quantification of pottery assemblages from consumer sites in the region has been to gather the necessary data for the analysis of socio-economic trends in ceramic consumption. As has already been stated, these two fundamental archaeological procedures have been undertaken as means to an end rather than ends in themselves (Sections 1.2.5.–6.). By identifying the variable composition and distribution of ceramic groups in the region, it is hoped to gain an insight into the changing functional, economic and socio-behavioural role of pottery in Lower Rhine society over a 400-year timespan.

The wide spectrum of contexts sampled, although many only on a presence and absence basis, has enabled these questions to be applied to a series of sites of different economic and social status. The research strategy has been designed to test how pottery consumption on a range of urban, rural, monastic, peasant, burgher or seignural sites in one region varies through time. The approach follows some of the more recent theoretical discussions on the value of ceramic research in medieval and later archaeology: "*The basic questions would appear to be how and why [medieval] pottery was produced, used and lost and what was its role within the wider dynamic of society. In addition how far do answers to the above vary within time and place*" (Davey 1983, 92).

Traditionally, archaeological ceramic finds have been regarded as no more than a dating tool or, at best, a useful guide to trading activities. During the last 15 years this attitude has changed, with the potential of ceramics fully realised as a primary historical source for past social and economic activities (Moorhouse 1986; Davey 1988). By virtue of its omnipresence and utility in the post-medieval period (at all social levels), its relatively short lifespan, and its durability in the archaeological record, ceramics have proved to be the most sensitive and reliable indicator of socio-cultural trends (Le Patourel 1976; Deetz 1977; Blake 1980). This is equally true of the post-medieval period as it is of earlier epochs, as little documentary evidence relating to the domestic social environment survives. References to utilitarian ceramics in post-medieval probate inventories, household accounts and diaries are particularly scarce (Löbert 1980), even in the immediate pre-industrial period (Weatherill 1988, 206). In contrast, the ceramic record relates to virtually all aspects of everyday life in the past: "*As with all artefacts, ceramics are part of a living totality, and they must be understood in their functional and symbolic role*" (Deetz 1977, 50).

It is the purpose of this final section, therefore, to explore both the functional and socio-economic patterning in the composition of postmedieval ceramic assemblages excavated in the Lower Rhineland. Using the Lower Rhine evidence, it is intended to investigate Blake's (1980) model that patterns in ceramic production and distribution in the historic period are dependent on the changing nature of consumer demand through time and space. During the course of the discussion reference will be made to contemporary pictorial sources (Appendix 7) which provide a context for specific vessel use and social milieu (Löbert 1980).

The historical interpretation of post-medieval ceramics found in the Lower Rhineland will focus on the following key areas:

i. Organisation of the regional pottery supply, including the transportation and marketing of pottery to and within the region;
ii. Ceramic form, function and decoration as indicators of evolving material comfort, eating and living habits;
iii. Ceramics as an index of social emulation and changes in fashion;
iv. The social curation of ceramics in post-medieval society;
v. Future priorities for socio-economic analysis.

## 8.2 Organisation of the regional pottery supply

### *8.2.1 Introduction*

Before investigating the dynamics of ceramic demand in the Lower Rhineland, it is necessary to assess the changing nature and organisation of the supply network. Blake (1980, 5) has stated the principles of ceramic marketing: "*the assumption behind all distribution studies is that the consumers wanted and were able to buy the products. Purchasing power, price, value and even the necessity to have a minimum amount of people or demand for a good in a given area have been acknowledged but not explored*". The marketing of medieval and later pottery should therefore be studied in relation to contemporary settlement patterns and the relative frequency of wares found in relation to them.

Various writers have summarised the possible methods

by which a potter's wares might reach the customer (Moorhouse 1981; 1983b; Dyer 1982). In theory, at least, different methods of distribution should be identifiable in the archaeological record, although Vince (1981b) is pessimistic about the possibility of distinguishing between similar patterns derived from quite different methods of distribution. Certainly, if progress is to be made, it is necessary to establish a framework within which inferred methods of distribution can be compared with their anticipated characteristics in the archaeological record. The methods of distribution and mechanics of the regional pottery market which can be inferred from the pattern of archaeological evidence will be considered below.

Despite concentrating during the course of this survey on the Duisburg excavations, enough data has been collected from sites in the town's hinterland to allow a general overview of the regional distribution pattern during the post-medieval period. Maps 3–6 illustrate schematically the principal sources, direction and relative distances travelled by pottery found in the region. Essentially, this Section will consider the following aspects of the Lower Rhine pottery market:

i. Transport and distribution mechanisms;
ii. Modes of production in the Lower Rhineland;
iii. Competition for customers with typologically similar vessels made in different materials.

### *8.2.2 Transport and distribution mechanisms*

Since the Roman period the river Rhine has been acknowledged as the primary means of transport for material goods in the region: "*The Rhine was the most important artery of communication, which connected the goods of the region to the outside world*" (Walz 1984, 109).

It must be assumed that the transport of pottery by river was always cheaper and more efficient than by road. In the Lower Rhineland the major towns are situated either on or in close proximity to the Rhine or its many tributaries (Map 2), and were therefore well served by both local and long-distance barge traffic (Schnall 1989). This was controlled well into the 19th century by an intricate system of customs houses and tolls belonging to the regional political authorities (Walz 1984).

Wooden barges of clinker construction and propelled by sail, such as those excavated at Krefeld (Hamburg 1989b, Cat. 16.2–3), would have been used to ferry consignments of stoneware upstream from their sources in the Middle Rhine area during the post-medieval period. Barges, although by this time mechanised, were used for the transport of stoneware as late as the mid 20th century in the region (Baaden 1985, 1610).

The majority of stoneware production sites are also all situated in close proximity to the Rhine or a navigable tributary (e. g. Siegburg on the river Sieg). Their situation was chosen, therefore, as much for easy access as for the location of suitable clay resources. Both Langerwehe and Raeren are situated, in contrast, not on a riverine route, but close to the Imperial road linking Cologne to Bruges, via Aachen (Nottebrock 1926). The negligible quantities of stoneware from both industries on Lower Rhenish sites can be explained by their inconvenient location, from which pots would have had to travel a significant distance by road. As we have seen (Section 5.3) firstly Siegburg, followed by Cologne and Frechen and finally the Westerwald industries dominated the Lower Rhenish stoneware market: all utilising the same arterial riverine route for the distribution of their wares.

Thanks to Göbels's initial work (1971) on the Frechen archives, it is now known that the stoneware trade was not controlled by the potters themselves but by pottery dealers and merchants. Several of them are well documented, and are known to have commissioned decorative medallions bearing their own initials or merchant's marks (van Loo 1984; 1986; 1989). Much of the Rhine trade was controlled by dealers from The Netherlands, as the entire stockroom of one merchant excavated in Bergen-op-Zoom on the Dutch coast demonstrates (Vandenbulke & Groeneweg 1988). Equally powerful in the Rhenish pottery market were the Cologne merchants (Herborn *et al.* 1987), who exercised a monopoly of distribution along the Rhine from Andernach downstream to Düsseldorf during the 16th century.

Cologne, a premier Hanseatic city, acted as the nodal point of the regional pottery market during the medieval and later period (Göbels 1985 edition, 257–283). Maps 3–6 show Cologne's central position in the redistribution of ceramics from both stoneware and earthenware production sites. The engraving by Johann Toussyn showing pottery being sold at the Alter Markt in Cologne around 1660 demonstrates the importance of the city's market place for the regional ceramic trade. Frequent references in the city archives (e. g. 1635) to local merchants trading in stonewares and green-glazed whitewares from Frechen (*greune zu Frechen gebackene Duppen*) confirm Cologne's pre-eminence in the regional ceramic trade (Göbels 1985 edition, 276).

While it is almost certain that Cologne controlled the distribution of the majority of ceramics moving downstream towards the Lower Rhineland and beyond (Maps 3–6), it cannot be assumed that the city was responsible for the movement of pottery imported into the region from or via the Netherlands or from sources directly to the East. Although finds of both Dutch maiolica and Oriental porcelain are known from Cologne (Section 5.4.1; Appendix 5), the quantitative and distributional evidence suggests that there was a distinctive fall-off upstream along the Rhine, with towns such as Duisburg, Neuss and Wesel receiving most of the trade. Only future excavations in Cologne can help to confirm or discount this preliminary impression.

So far, little, if any, historical research has been conducted into the movement of tin-glazed pottery, Oriental porcelain or English fineware from or via the Low Countries upstream into the Rhenish hinterland. It can only be assumed at this stage that the same or a similar network of ceramic dealers, based either in Holland or in the Lower Rhine towns, operated here as in the stoneware or Rhenish earthenware trade. In the 18th century the Wedgwood warehouses at Amsterdam, Rotterdam and the Hague were responsible for the distribution of Staffordshire products into the Rhineland (McKendrick 1983, 132; Treue 1973).

The riverine route, although punctuated by markets strategically placed in the towns along its course, does not, however, explain the distribution of pottery in the rural hinterland of the Lower Rhine. Here road transport was the only means of dispersal of both locally-made and imported products. It is a long tradition in the Rhineland for pedlars to carry pots from source to the towns and villages, to weekly or daily markets and to seasonal fairs. Pedlars (*Hausierer*) carried both stoneware pots (Kerkhoff-Hader 1980, 214–222) and local earthenwares (Scholten-Neess & Jüttner 1971, 14–16) over long distances. The individual pedlar with his pack full of pots is illustrated in an engraving of c. 1589 by Franz Hogenberg showing the street cries of Cologne (illustrated in Göbels, 1985 edition, 279).

### *8.2.3 Modes of production in the Lower Rhineland*

Perhaps the most comprehensive attempt to look at the modes of pottery production is Peacock's for the Roman world (1982). It would not be appropriate to use this model uncritically but it does offer a useful framework in which to study the various modes and scales of production and distribution of wares made both within and those imported into the region from outside. The respective modes of production are reflected to an extent in the regional pottery supply-pattern. The model below has been adapted from Peacock (1982) to demonstrate the post-medieval situation in the Lower Rhineland. On a superficial level this adaption also draws attention to the the changes in the modes of production over time (stoneware, tin-glazed pottery and porcelain manufacture progress between modes).

| | Mode | Ware-type |
|---|---|---|
| 1. | Household industry: a secondary, part-time-activity. Little investment in equipment. Probably no proper wheel or kiln. | – |
| 2. | Individual workshop: similar to 1, but primary source of income. May still be part-time but more equipment used. Possible employment of assistants. Use of middlemen. | I, II |
| 3. | Nucleated workshop: as 2, but grouped together. Any other income is subsidiary. Standard range of high-quality products. Co-operation. Use of middlemen as principal means of distribution. | II, III |
| 4. | Manufactory: a group working in a single place or building. Division of labour. Use of machinery. >12 workers or more (to distinguish it from 3). | III, IV |
| 5. | Factory: Fully mechanised mass-production. | IV, V |

from Peacock 1982

The use of this scheme serves to illustrate the scales of say local earthenware to stoneware production and the relative distribution of finished products during the post-medieval period. Technologically and commercially, the Lower Rhine earthenware industry operated on mode 2 of the model, as both excavations and documentary research on 18th-century production sites have demonstrated (Sections 1.1.3 and 5.2.4). Their dense distribution in the Lower Rhine hinterland at this time ensured that plain utilitarian earthenware and decorative slipware were available throughout the region both to the local rural consumer and to the middle-distance urban market. Such operations were clearly not designed for the level of mass-production required for the export market, and this is reflected in the comparatively small numbers of vessels found immediately outside the region (Section 5.2.4).

Semi-professional and full-time stoneware potters in the Rhineland (modes 2 and 3) were fully geared for the mass-production and distribution of a standard range of wares for both the regional and international ceramic markets from the 15th to 17th centuries (Section 7.2.1–3). The exchange between workshops of moulds for applied ornament is consistent with the level of cooperation and commercial organisation necessary for this scale and mode of ceramic production. The reliance of the stove-tile workshops on independent mould-cutters (Section 5.2.6) also underlines the degree to which inter-artisanal cooperation was required at this level. Both industries also depended heavily on the intervention of middlemen to distribute and market their products.

The flooding of the Lower Rhine pottery market with

faience from The Netherlands during the second half of the 17th century may be explained by the transition from workshop (mode 3) to manufactory production (mode 4) after c. 1660 at centres such as Delft (Section 7.2.5). Similarly, the frequency of Oriental porcelain in mid- to late 18th-century contexts in the region (Section 7.2.7) may be partly attributed to the factory-scale of production at its source in China (mode 4) and by its mass-export to the West (Section 5.5.1). Finally, it was only through a changeover to fully mechanised production in the mid-18th century that the Staffordshire industries were able to mass-market the innovative ceramic bodies being developed at this time (Section 5.6). Factory-scale production enabled Wedgwood and his competitors to export their products to the Continent and market them at a lower cost than porcelain or metalware goods (Section 8.33).

Essentially, the modes of production briefly discussed here entail only permissive causes (*cf.* Goldthwaite 1989) for the pattern of ceramic consumption identified in the post-medieval Lower Rhineland. Section 8.3 will attempt to construct a more balanced picture of ceramic production and distribution in the region, incorporating arange of effective causes which help to explain the nature of consumer demand for the products themselves.

### *8.2.4 Competition for customers*

In seeking to find a market for their wares, potters and middlemen found themselves in competition not only with one another but with industries producing similar vessels in different materials such as metal or glass. As Blake has stated (1980, 5; see Section 1.2.8), the success of an individual ceramic product depended on its ability to compete economically, functionally and symbolically with the other media. Essentially, this depended on a complex set of factors, of which the most important were the tastes and purchasing power of the individual consumer (Section 8.3.3).

The problem with assessing the functional and social competition in the Lower Rhineland between vessels of different media is that, with the exception of glassware, only ceramics are represented in the archaeological record. The principal "missing artefacts" include silver, pewter, copper alloy and treen, which are known from probates and other sources to have formed collectively a substantial part of the household inventory (Yentsch 1990). This study is, therefore, restricted by its reliance on archaeologically retrievable goods and falls short of the "full range of behavioural patterning" (Smart Martin 1989, 1). Nevertheless, by considering the functional and social value of certain types of ceramics within a framework of the available sample, perhaps some more sophisticated statements about ceramics and their behaviour can be made.

Post-medieval treen and other domestic utensils are common on urban sites in North Germany (e. g. Lübeck: see Falk 1983; 1987c) and the Low Countries (e. g. Amsterdam: see Baart ed. 1977, Cat. 649–656), but are negligible on post-medieval sites in the Lower Rhine despite the profusion of waterlogged latrine, well and brick-lined pit contexts. Turned treen tablewares (bowls and dishes) have been found in the levels dating to the 12–13th centuries on the Duisburg *Alter Markt* site (Krause 1983, Fig. 49) but are absent thereafter. Their demise can only be linked to the growth of the Lower Rhine earthenware industry during the late 14th to 15th centuries (Sections 5.2.1–3.). The dramatic negative evidence suggests that potters in the Lower Rhineland could compete with the basement-end of the utilitarian goods market. Further research on this "missing artefact" is required, however, before such a conclusion can be justified fully.

Metal vessels are much more likely to have been in use in the Lower Rhine region in both domestic and display contexts. They are frequent entries in probate inventories in Germany (Löbert 1980, Table 1) and in the neighbouring Netherlands (ter Molen *et al.* eds 1986). In the latter region pewter was referred to as the "silverware of the common citizen" (Baart 1986), thereby emphasising its place in the economic hierarchy of material goods. Its popularity in the Netherlands has been confirmed by a recent study of its archaeological distribution (Wustenhoff 1989). Pewter jug forms are known from dredging operations in the Lower Rhine itself (Haedecke 1983, Fig. 56). From these and a range of other finds found in the region and in The Netherlands a thriving Lower Rhine pewter industry has been postulated for the late 14th to 16th centuries (*ibid.*, 57–59). To an extent, stoneware jugs, by virtue of their non-porous body and durability, may well have mitigated against the need for metal decanting, drinking and storage vessels, although in the more high-status households a combination of pewter and stoneware is much more likely (Appendix 7, Cat. I.A.11). To date, pewter finds of the 17th and 18th centuries are absent from the archaeological sequence in the Lower Rhine. As a next stage, probate inventories must be consulted to assess the relationship between this "missing artefact" and the domestic ceramic repertoire in the region (Smart Martin 1989).

Similarly, a wide spectrum of copper-alloy (bronze or brassware) utensils is missing from the post-medieval sequence in the Lower Rhineland. Metal kitchenware enjoyed a relatively long lifespan and was recycled rather than simply discarded at the end of it (Cherry 1987). Contemporary graphical sources of the 16th and 17th centuries clearly show the diversity of metal items in use in the kitchens of the urban middle classes (e. g.

Appendix 7, Cat. I.B.2): dripping pans, mortars, tripod cauldrons, pipkins, spits and jugs. In representations of well-to-do households, such as this, ceramics are entirely absent, although the scene may be intended as an ideal and not as an accurate reconstruction. Nevertheless, these sources, like probates, do at least emphasise the economic and social premium attached to metalware. In order to compete, potters began to imitate metal vessels at the end of the Middle Ages (Cherry 1987; Verhaeghe 1991), thereby providing an alternative range of specialised cooking vessels (tripod pipkins, tripod cauldrons, skillets, and dripping pans) at a lower price. Precisely these forms emerge in the Lower Rhine sequence during the 15th century in redware (Ia.8), whiteware (Ia.3) and greyware (Ia.6). Previously only globular greyware pots had been available for cooking purposes (e. g. Krause 1983, Fig. 38).

Glass is the most common non-ceramic commodity found on post-medieval sites in the Lower Rhineland, and therefore offers more scope for monitoring the relationship between ceramics and other media in the domestic environment. The archaeological evidence from the region accords with Dexel's model (1939, 77) that glass production in Germany experienced a boom during the 15th century. The glass assemblage from one of the main 15th-century latrine levels (Context 7) suggests that glass was a strong contender in the regional tableware market. In this particular context there were more glass than stoneware drinking vessels (a ratio of 6:2 vessels). Small squat beakers and tall drinking glasses characterise this group. The archaeological evidence accords with the contemporary graphical sources, in which stoneware vessels and glassware are shown together on the same dining table (e. g. Appendix 7, Cat. I.A.2; see Ricke 1987). During the 16th to 17th centuries in Duisburg the ratio of glass drinking ware to ceramic forms increased along with the range of forms available (e. g. Context 42; Context 43). The glass finds from the farmhouse site of Haus Gelinde (Context 93; Hackspiel 1987) represent the largest of any 18th-century assemblages to be published so far in the region, comprising 5,4 % of the entire artefactual assemblage. The introduction of glass bottle forms at this time provided yet another source of competition for the specialist stoneware products (*ibid.*, Cat. 56–57). Unfortunately, due to the constraints of time and resources, it has not yet been possible to process and quantify the associated glass assemblages from Duisburg or other major sites in the region. Most are still in the process of post-excavation sorting and restoration. It will be a priority of future work to complete this process and reassess the composition and socio-economic interpretation of the Lower Rhine ceramic assemblages in relation to the associated glass sequence. Whatever the reality of their relationship in terms of respective retail cost and social value, it is clear that the stoneware potters of the Rhineland received their most intensive competition in the tableware market from the contemporary glass industry. Future research will also be directed towards establishing the source of the Lower Rhine glass finds. To date, two possibilities have emerged: 1) the Netherlands (Baart 1984) and 2) the Middle Rhine/Franconia (Grimm ed. 1984).

Sections 6 and 7 have already summarised by phase the extent of competition between different ceramic industries to create and maintain a niche in the Lower Rhine pottery market. Success in this depended on producing the right product at the right price for the right market. Clearly a wide and often closely-linked set of technical, functional, economic and social considerations were involved in this process. Their interaction and implications for ceramic consumption will be discussed more fully in Sections 8.2.–3.

## 8.3 Ceramics as an index of consumer habit, taste and social emulation in the Lower Rhineland c. 1400–1800

### *8.3.1 Introduction*

It is now generally accepted that the excavated ceramic record can provide an insight into general and particular aspects of past economic and social life (Sections 1.2.8; 8.1.1). It is the purpose of this section to demonstrate the relationship between the relative composition of post-medieval ceramic assemblages in the Lower Rhineland and the development of material comfort and social competition across a variety of sites of differing functional status.

As Sections 5, 6 and 7 have shown, the quantity, quality and variety of the pottery supplied to the region increased steadily over the 400-year period. This pattern of innovation and diffusion (Orton 1985) has been observed both in the towns and the countryside, although at variable rates. However, the increasing availability and use of ceramics both in the functional and social sphere cannot be explained solely by a model of permissive causes such as those identified by Goldthwaite (1989), which comprise technological improvements, and advancements in the modes of production (Section 8.2.3). It is becoming increasingly clear that when dealing with a pre-industrial society we must divert our attention to the rather more complex effective causes of the socio-economic matrix. In other words the nature of the pottery supply was dictated by the consumer, his habits, values and aspirations (Blake 1980).

The following Sections will investigate how changes in culinary practice, dining habits and improvements in material comfort during the postmedieval period are reflected in the increased functional specialisation and decorative sophistication of ceramics. The discussion will also attempt to show how ceramics attained not only a widening functional importance but also a social meaning in their own right (Hodder 1982; Appadurai 1986), which, when identified, may help to extract socio-behavioural patterns contained within excavated assemblages (Falk 1987b).

By comparing the statistical variation displayed by ceramic groups, it is hoped to demonstrate social differentation in the consumption of ceramics. The analysis is designed to test some of the suggested criteria for the evaluation of the social status of pottery assemblages (e. g. Redman 1986; Falk & Hammel 1988). These include:

i. Scarcity as opposed to profusion of particular wares;
ii. Relative distance travelled by particular wares; ratio of imported to locally-made wares;
iii. Ratio of decorated pottery to undecorated types;
iv. Ratio of tableware to utilitarian pottery;
v. Relative time and cost involved in production.

The purpose of this section is also to evaluate the social differentation of ceramic assemblages in the light of the hierarchy of pottery types established by Blake (1980) and Orton (1985). This scheme has been adapted to illustrate the Lower Rhine situation (Diag. 7). It will be demonstrated how this model is inadequate as it assumes that particular ceramics had one social meaning that was shared across time, space and the social hierarchy. As Smart Martin (1989, 21) has demonstrated in the case of pewter, "*differing social groups may transform or recast meanings specific to the social and cultural position of the users*". The scheme can only be used to explain the value of pottery at the point when it enters the circulation matrix. The use of ceramics as an index of social emulation (*cf.* Weatherill 1988, 194–7), therefore, depends on the comparison of assemblages to each other and on the accuracy of the archaeological record to provide reliable chronological and quantitative information for each.

The following discussion will also deal with the problems of interpreting the nature of ceramic assemblages which are distorted by the presence of socially curated items. Finally, a number of suggestions are offered towards the future socio-economic analysis of post-medieval ceramic assemblages in the region. The merits of a more integrated multi-media and multi-disciplinary approach are considered.

### *8.3.2 The role of ceramics in the evolution of material comfort, culinary practice and dining habits*

i. 15th century

The growth of towns in northern Europe during the High Middle Ages and the concomitant improvements in domestic living standards have been well documented by studies of surviving probate inventories (e. g. Hasse 1979). The differences between rich and poor were much more obvious by the late 14th-century, culminating in the establishment of an urban mercantile elite with access to an ever-increasing variety of material goods (Mohrmann 1985), ranging from furniture to domestic utensils and wares for the kitchen, table and cellar. Hasse (1979) has documented an expansion in the range of metalware forms in use over the 13th to 14th-century period, each indicative of a specialised function. Urban secular life began to develop its own characteristics and rituals. Most importantly the increasing functional division of the household resulted in the physical compartmentalisation of the home (Schütte 1985). The urban ceramic inventory in the Lower Rhineland of the 15th century differs in typological composition from previous epochs, and reflects the increasing variety and specialisation of domestic roles emerging at this time.

With the internal division of the urban household came the adoption in northern Germany of ceramic stoves for the heating of discrete areas of the domestic living space (Kühnel 1985, 260–261). Ceramic stove-tiles first appear in the Lower Rhine archaeological sequence at the beginning of the 15th century (e. g. Duisburg Context 36). The evidence for the secular or urban use of ceramic stoves at this date (as opposed to monastic or seignurial use) is paralleled in other North West German cities, such as Göttingen (Schütte 1985, 554). The stove-tile industry at Cologne developed rapidly at this time (Unger 1988 ed.), meeting demand for tile-stove heating throughout the Lower Rhine area, and exporting stove-tiles down the Rhine to the Netherlands (Dubbe 1987) and across the Channel to England (Gaimster 1988d). The use of tiled stoves clearly indicates the development of a more sophisticated domestic heating system which could only be effective in well-constructed, draught-free living accommodation. Stove-tiles are common finds on castle or monastic sites at this period, and their discovery in towns suggests a democratisation of the tile-stove tradition and a high degree of urban material comfort.

Developments in the culinary and dining practices in northern Europe of the 15th century (Borst 1983) are also mirrored in the Lower Rhine ceramic inventory. The range of vessel forms involved in the preparation of food and its storage, the serving of food and beverages and in their consumption undergoes rapid development at this stage. This interpretation assumes that vessel typology relates directly to the contemporary eating habits or what has been termed the "foodways system" (Yentsch 1990, 27).

Contemporary graphical sources showing domestic interiors and dining scenes (Appendix 7; I.A.1–11), although depicting in many respects an ideal, document the relative importance of domestic metalware, treen, glass and pottery in use during the 15th century. Dining scenes, such as Dieric Bouts's painting of *Christ in the House of the Pharisee Simon* (Appendix 7; I.A.2), depict Rhenish stoneware drinking vessels in conjunction with glass and pewter flatwares. This seems to have been a common combination and emphasises the variety of different materials in use at the table.

Dining, by this stage, had become increasingly formalised with the development of place settings and the need for individual eating and drinking utensils (Kühnel 1985, 210–213). Not only is this evident in banqueting scenes of the nobility (e. g. Appendix 7; I.A.1) but among the urban artisan culture as Jan Mostaert's informal *Holy family at a Meal* (c. 1495–1500) illustrates (Appendix 7; I.A.4). The ritual of dining with all its paraphernalia was replicated, although on a more modest scale, by the urban middle classes during the 15th century (New York 1975; Mennell 1988). The stoneware depicted in these paintings fulfilled a variety of roles, namely in drinking and pouring liquids at the table, and in transporting and decanting wine or beer for table use (Appendix 7; I.A.1, I.A.11). The range of capacities of Siegburg stoneware excavated in Duisburg reflects the diversity of different functions demanded of it during the 15th century. These roles had been and were no doubt still performed by pewter or treen vessels, but the quantities of stoneware flooding onto the market at this time suggest that substantially more ceramic tableware and decanting vessels were needed to satisfy demand across the social spectrum. Virtually 90 % of Siegburg stoneware found in 15th century Duisburg contexts is composed of drinking-jugs, beakers, mugs and larger jugs (Graph 14). Finds of Siegburg stoneware are equally represented on high-staus sites of the 15th century in Lübeck as they are on poorer ones (Schütte 1985). Stoneware, by virtue of its versatility and durability, played an important role in fulfiling specialist needs at the table, in the kitchen or in the cellar.

Finally, developments in the local earthenware industry serve to illustrate the increasing demands of the culinary sphere and, for the first time, an element of consumer choice. Previously, during the 14th century, unglazed greywares (Ia.6) dominated the Lower Rhine earthenware market (Stephan 1982, Fig. 28). They continued in use until the third quarter of the 15th century in Duisburg (Section 5.2.2), and even later on the periphery of the region. Slowly they were replaced by red firing earthenwares which were characterised by the addition of an internal lead glaze (Ia.8), making them less porous than their grey-fired counterparts. However, typologically the redwares comprise only a marginally greater number of forms (Graphs 12 & 13), suggesting that their popularity was due primarily to their superior efficiency as liquid containers and also due to the variation in surface colour provided by the introduction of glaze. Whitewares from the Cologne area (Section 5.2.1) also formed a significant share of the regional earthenware market (Graphs 1 & 2). Their popularity may also be explained by the aesthetic factor: white pottery was ideally suited for the application of colourless and coppertoned lead glazes.

The 15th-century ceramic inventory is distinguishable from that of previous phases by the introduction of an innovative range of forms: namely tripod pipkins, skillets and chamber pots, each closely imitating well-established metalware types (*cf.* Hasse 1979). The horizontal cordon visible around the waist of tripod pipkins of Rhenish whiteware (Ia.3) replicates the seamline typical of their metal counterparts. The diversity of new types represents a substantial improvement on the range of culinary and other ceramic forms available in the Lower Rhineland during the 14th century (Stephan 1982, Fig. 28). The diversification reflects a higher degree of functional specialisation. The developments provide further evidence of improving living standards, and of the direct response of the ceramic industries to changing consumer demands in the kitchenware market. For the first time in the region potters were able to compete with metalware producers by manufacturing a range of cheaper alternatives. A similar scenario has been identified in neighbouring regions of North West Europe for this period (Verhaeghe 1991).

### ii. 16th –17th Centuries

From the beginning of the 16th century the typology of native glazed redware expanded dramatically to cater for the full range of domestic functional categories: tableware, kitchen ware, sanitary and storage wares (Section 5.2.3). The Ware-type (Ib.1 and Ic.1) accounted for 47 % of the total market share of pottery supplied to Duisburg over the period c. 1500–1580, with stoneware only accounting for 26 % (Graph Diag. 3). The proliferation in the variety of forms (Graph 15) reflects the increasingly specialised nature of culinary practice and domestic activities. Tripod pipkins, casseroles, cauldrons and skillets for were intended for cooking, pancheons for making dairy products, dishes and bowls for preparing and serving food, porringers for eating liquid foods, and storage jars for the cellar. Chamber pots were also produced. The diversity of 16th-century kitchen activities fulfilled by lead-glazed redware is realistically documented in the paintings of Joachim Beuckelaer (Appendix 7; Cat. I.B.8–9) and Pieter Aertsen (Appendix 7; Cat. I. B.7).

Stonewares from Siegburg, Cologne, Langerwehe and Raeren are represented in the Duisburg sequence by drinking, decanting and long-term storage vessels: precisely those roles not performed by earthenware for technical reasons. By 1500 these wares began to display applied, incised and stamped decoration in keeping with their visible tableware and socio-ritual role (Löbert 1980, 39–40). The repertoire of stoneware forms and ornament increased throughout the century (Diag. 8c), the latter incorporating fashionable design elements derived from the current northern Renaissance style (Lipperheide 1961). The increasing ornamentation of Rhenish stoneware and the introduction of a limited range of lead-glazed earthenware table-forms, including plates and porringers (Diag. 8c top) provide the physical evidence of the refinements in dining habits spreading down the social scale during the course of the 16th century, particulary among the urban population (Borst 1983).

The evidence, therefore, suggests that the Lower Rhine pottery market was divided essentially by opposing practical and social functions during the first three-quarters of the 16th century, with very little cross-over of ceramic Ware-types. Earthenware displayed little sign of ornament, apart from the variation in glaze colour depending on the amount of copper or iron added. What is significant, however, is a proportional increase in the market share of locally-made redware pottery in the region (Graph 3), which suggests a growth in the general demand for ceramics at the middle and lower end of the commodity market, in relation to other media, to fulfill an ever-widening utilitarian but still limited social role.

A dramatic change occurs in the composition of the Lower Rhine ceramic sequence at the end of the 16th century, with the introduction of decorated ceramic flatware for table use. Duisburg and Wesel contexts dating from c. 1590 contain both local slip-decorated red earthenware (Ib.5), incised red and white-firing earthenware (Ib.2; Ib.3) and imported tin-glazed earthenware (maiolica: III.1). Although preceded chronologically by the polychrome *Hafnerware* excavated in Cologne (Ib.1i), these vessels represent the first earthenwares in the Lower Rhine region to be employed for both a functional and decorative purpose at the table. The introduction of slipware production reflects the growing demand for more choice in decorative tableware which could complement stoneware and undercut the more highly priced metalware and maiolica vessels (Orton 1985, 30).

The timing and tempo of these developments can be paralleled across central and northern Europe at the end of the 16th century (Stephan 1987b). The initiation of full-scale slipware maufacture in the neighbouring Netherlands and the availability of ornate maiolica imports from the same area are the most likely factors to have stimulated earthenware potters in the Lower Rhine (Section 5.2.4). Stephan (1987b) suggests that these innovations reflect further refinements in dining habits related to the influence of prevailing Renaissance fashions.

During the first half of the 17th century the relative quantities of local slipware and Dutch maiolica in circulation in the Lower Rhineland increased steadily (Graph 4). The popularity of maiolica tableware during this period in northern Europe can be directly related to its ability to respond to rapid changes in taste with innovative decorative designs (Orton 1985). Its suitability for keeping one step ahead in the status stakes (Section 8.3.3) was a crucial feature of its success. In terms of expense, maiolica pottery was only superseded by the few imports of Chinese porcelain (IV.1), which filtered into the Lower Rhineland during the early part of the century. The evidence at this stage for the growth of systematic, long-distance trade in ceramics represents a fundamental shift from earlier epochs characterised by local pottery supply mechanisms. The development provides additional evidence for improved contact and communications between regions.

The period c. 1575–1625, therefore, witnessed a dramatic transformation in the composition of the ceramic assemblages excavated in the region. From a situation in the earlier 16th century when decorative earthenware was virtually absent, a comprehensive range of sophisticated earthenware was introduced for table use (slipware, maiolica and porcelain), each intended to satisfy a discrete niche of the consumer market. These developments came as a response to a changing emphasis in contemporary dining habits, characterised by the increasing desire for individual dishes and plates as opposed to large communal serving dishes or bowls (Kisbán 1986; Stephan 1987b).

This process developed during the second half of the 17th century with the introduction of entire services of tin-glazed plates, dishes and bowls (faience: III.2–3) for individual use. Their success is reflected in the Duisburg sequence of this period (Graph 5). Unfortunately, no rural sites in the region have been investigated to assess the timing of these changes in the countryside.

During the 16th and 17th centuries the quotas of local plain red (Ib.1, Ic.1) and white-firing earthenware (Ib.3, Ic.3) stayed constant, catering for the majority of culinary needs. The proportions of form-types in circulation also remained fairly stable (Graphs 15, 16, 17). Both industries produced plain dishes and porringers for the table as important sidelines to the main output of cooking wares. It may be assumed that they were intended to serve as low-cost dining utensils. Stoneware jugs and drinking forms also maintained their specialised niche in the Lower Rhine pottery market during this period (Graphs 4, 5, 10). Tin-glazed jugs and tankards are rare finds in the Lower Rhine and do not appear in the sequence until after the mid-17th century. The reliance on the native stoneware industry to supply virtually all jugs, bottles and tankards reflects not only the undoubted functional superiority of the products but also a perceivable conservatism among Lower Rhine consumers (Orton 1985, Fig. 4).

iii. 18th century

The beginning of the 18th-century is characterised by the increasing ratio of slip-decorated earthenware on the Lower Rhine pottery market (24 % in Duisburg: Graphs 5–6). Significant also is the fact that imported faience from the Netherlands accounted for just under a third of the pottery recovered from the town of Duisburg during this phase (29 %). The statistics illustrate the continued growth in the demand for decorated ceramic tableware stimulated by the the effects of increasing refinement in dining habits at both the upper and now lower end of the social scale. The evidence suggests that this was previously an entirely middle-class phenomenon.

The picture gained from an early 18th century cellar asemblage at the village of Krefeld-Linn (Context 60; Graph 8) differs from the urban one in that there was a marked disparity in favour of local slipware over faience (37 % to 6 %). The statistics suggest that the popular fashion for painted or plain white tin-glazed pottery had not penetrated into the Lower Rhine countryside by this stage. The breakdown in slipware forms recovered from Krefeld-Linn indicates that the local slipware producers could satisfy virtually all tableware needs (76 % dishes, 6 % plates, 4 % porringers; Graph 26). The reliance on slipware is also confirmed by the diversity of dish and plate diameter size (for spectrum see Fig. 64).

The development of hot beverage drinking as a popular social fashion from the beginning of the 18th century (Clair 1965, 134) can also be traced in the variety of fineware ceramics coming onto the market. Tea, coffee and chocolate consumption required a vast array of specialist equipment, including drinking cups or bowls, saucers, tea/coffee/chocolate pots, sugar bowls, milk jugs, slop bowls etc. The very wealthy could afford silver teapots and other items of prestige equipage, but porcelain from the East proved to be the most suited for drinking purposes. This practical need helped to stimulate the export of Chinese porcelain to the West. The quantities shipped to Europe throughout the century by the European East India Companies reflect the enormous demand for sets of Chinese teaware (Sheaf & Kilburn 1988). Middle class society aspired to tea, coffee and chocolate sets for their civilised entertaining. With imported Chinese porcelain being too exclusive for widespread use during the early 18th century (Graph 6; Section 8.3.3), the demand for teawares was met by the Dutch faience industry, which produced a range of drinking bowls and saucers based on porcelain prototypes (Diag. 8f). At the same time the stoneware potters of the Westerwald region began to produce a range of teawares based on porcelain forms (Ware-type II.10; Diag. 8f bottom). Stoneware, like porcelain, was ideally suited for the serving of hot beverages. The Westerwald products were probably intended to fulfil demand at the slightly lower end of this particular market.

This picture changed again during mid-18th century with the development in England of an innovative range of in ceramic bodies suited for the massproduction of teaweares and fine tablewares. By c. 1750 the Staffordshire industries had secured a significant share of the Continental ceramic market, shipping a wide variety of fine earthenwares, stonewares and the revolutionary creamware bodies across the Channel (Section 5.6). In Duisburg Dutch faience, Oriental porcelain and English exports acounted for 46 % of the pottery consumed during the second half of the 18th century (Graph 7). In the rural hinterland of the towns the archaeological record (i. e. Krefeld-Linn, Context 61) shows a marked increase in the quantity of Dutch faience in use along with the introduction of Chinese porcelain for the first time (combined share of 30 %: Graph 9). English finewares figure only marginally in the countryside at this time (less than 1 %).

The pattern of evidence suggests that the fashion for hot beverage consumption had lost its exclusive status by this stage. This is also confirmed by the social-historical record on the Continent (Kisbán 1986). The drop in tea, coffee and chocolate prices following the increase in imports meant that the custom of drinking hot beverages spread down the social scale, creating a new market for the respective ceramic industries to exploit.

The fashion for matching sevices of tableware was well established in the region by the end of our period of study. The cellar assemblage from Krefeld-Linn (Context 61) demonstrates the popularity of Dutch faience for this purpose (Fig. 70). The pattern is repeated in the urban sequence but with the addition of creamware, stoneware and fine earthenware products from England (Context 44 where Staffordshire imports account for 29 % of the assemblage; Fig. 59). The phase is also marked by the limited introduction of porcelain teawares made in Germany (IV.4) and of polychrome faience manufactured locally in the centre of Duisburg (III.56). Both developments were stimulated by foreign imports. Nonetheless, the native slipware producers

were still able to compete successfully at the lower end of the tableware market as the frequent finds of sets of slipware plates, dishes, bowls and porringers clearly shows (Graphs 7 & 9; see Diag. 8g).
The trends in 18th-century dining habits and popular fashion outlined above are emphasised again in Graph 36. Here the overall quantitative picture shows that there was a general proportional increase in the quantity of tableware in use over the period (from around 50 % between 1700–1750 to over 60 % at the end of the century). It is likely that social factors were responsible for this rise, and they will be explored in Section 8.3.3.

### *8.3.3 Ceramics as an index of changing fashions and social emulation*

#### i. 15th century

As we have already seen, the steady diversification of ceramic forms occurring during the 15th century reflects a gradual improvement in living standards and a higher degree of functional specialisation in the home. The imitation of metal vessel forms in earthenware suggests that the new products were aimed not at the top end of the social hierarchy but at the emerging urban Burgher classes prone, to a degree, to social emulation (Verhaeghe 1991). It is difficult, however, to assign a precise degree of social meaning to these items, especially as only a few are decorated (e. g. chamber pot: Fig. 11, No. 1). Nevertheless, the introduction of red and white-firing earthenware bodies accompanied by a variety of coloured glazes implies a marginally greater economic and social value than the rather old-fashioned unglazed greywares (see Diag. 7).
Stonewares, principally from Siegburg at this time, are present on the tables depicted in contemporary interior or dining scenes (Appendix I. A.). Their use in conjunction with metal and glass drinking and pouring vessels implies a certain status, but such a conclusion must be tempered by the sheer quantities of Siegburg products found in the region and in the neighbouring Low Countries, where they acount for up to 50 % of all ceramics found on some sites (H. L. Janssen 1988, 311). The ability of the Siegburg workshops to mass-produce wares for home and international export tends to mitigate against the attribution of status to these wares, although the relative proportions contained within individual assemblages hold the key to our interpretation here (Section 6).
One clear example of ceramics reflecting conspicuous consumption in society is provided by the adoption of the case of ceramic stoves for interior heating. Finds from Duisburg and other towns in the Lower Rhineland demonstrate how this tradition migrated down the social scale during the course of the 15th century: from seigniorial and monastic contexts to the middle-class urban sphere. That said, the presence of stove-tiles in towns at this stage is suggestive of a high degree of domestic sophistication and the desire to emulate the social standing of others. Only the wealthiest burghers would have been able to afford the high purchase and installation costs involved, not to mention the on-going fuel costs (Unger 1983a).

#### ii. 16th –17th century

The process of diversification in ceramic form-types continued during the 16th century in the Lower Rhineland, and is best illustrated by the introduction of new shapes in local redware and whiteware from the Cologne-Frechen area. Decoration was minimal at this stage, with only coloured glazing a discriminatory factor.
Green-glazed whiteware only accounts for 1 % of the total market share of pottery in Duisburg during the 16th century. Perhaps its scarcity implies a superior social value to redware; certainly it travelled a much longer distance to reach the Lower Rhineland, if this may be taken as a valid indicator of social status (Section 8.3.1). Its relative prestige in comparison to the other earthenware bodies may be explained by the higher production costs involved in its manufacture (Section 5.2.1). The possibility would introduce an additional dimension to the model of ceramic hierarchies postulated by Orton (1985; see Diag. 7).
Rhenish stoneware, characterised by its durability, was deemed less suitable during the 15th century for "symbolic manipulation" through the addition of ornament (Orton 1985). However, during the 16th century its suitability for plastic decoration began to be exploited. This development sprang from the prevailing influence of the Northern Renaissance style already established in architecture, metalwork, jewellery and in other media. The introduction of stamped and incised designs and of elaborate applied relief motifs dates from the second quarter of the 16th century at Cologne and Siegburg (Reineking-von Bock 1986). The applied relief panels, medallions and friezes contain a wide variety of heraldic motifs, and mythological, biblical and allegorical scenes taken from popular contemporary engravings such as those of the *Kleinmeister* artists (Lipperheide 1961) (e. g. a Siegburg flagon from Duisburg-Hamborn applied with a medallion containing a scene from the New Testament: Fig. 63, No. 1).
Thus Rhenish stoneware became a focus of the latest trends in decorative art styles in Germany, and increased in status accordingly. Its depiction in contemporary interior scenes and still-life paintings from the Netherlands (Appendix I.B & III) demonstrates the relatively high social premium attached to the decorated wares during the mid 16th to early 17th centuries. This

conclusion must be tempered again, however, by the evidence for the enormous output achieved by individual stoneware producers in the Rhineland. The 1588 fire which destroyed the Knütgen family workshop in Siegburg revealed an as yet unquantified mound of wasters, virtually all with applied relief ornament (Section 5.3.1). It is clear that decorated stoneware was by no means an exclusive commodity as imports to London and other British ports show (Gaimster 1987a). The re-use of moulds for the purpose of applied decoration (Section 5.3.1) suggests that the final product was aimed as much at the mass-market as the exclusive private commission. This social duality places stoneware at the centre of the post-medieval ceramic hierarchy (Diag. 7): above earthenware and slipware, but below tin-glazed earthenware which was potentially much more sensitive to prevailing style changes (see below).

The fashion for Renaissance-derived ornament is also evident in the decorative treatment of stove-tiles of the 16th century. Stove-tile design underwent a dramatic change after the second quarter of the 16th century, with the conversion from simple niche-tiles with minimal relief decoration to panel-tiles designed to maximise the opportunity for intricate moulded ornament and polychrome-glazed decoration (Unger ed. 1988, Cat. 70–142). Advances in stove technology led also to the proliferation of additional ceramic components, all providing extra scope for decorative treatment. The main motifs chosen by the mould-cutters repeated the repertoire employed by stoneware producers: allegorical figures and biblical scenes to name but a few. Many are directly attributable to *Kleinmeister* engravers such as H. S. Beham or Hans Holbein The Younger (*ibid.*). Fragments of stove-tiles produced by the local Cologne industry and imports from outside the region have been found in both Duisburg and Wesel (Section 5.2.6). They represent a high degree of domestic sophistication both in heating technology and in interior design trends. Their relative scarcity in the archaeological record emphasises their value as potential indicators of social differentiation between ceramic assemblages.

It is now generally accepted that the introduction of slip-decorated and incised earthenware in the Lower Rhineland at the very end of the 16th century represents a considerable upgrading in the social value of locally-made ceramics (Stephan 1987b). This is underlined in their apparent scarcity in Duisburg and Wesel during the period c. 1575 to 1625 (5 % and 9 % of all pottery found respectively: see Graphs 4 & 10). Nevertheless it cannot be argued that they enjoyed a greater degree of social status than imported maiolica from the Netherlands. At 8 % and 9 % of the aggregate assemblages at Duisburg and Wesel they also display a marked exclusivity. Indeed Dutch maiolica meets every one of the criteria for social ranking outlined in our model (Section 8.3.1): relative scarcity, an imported commodity, ornate decoration, relative expense in production and its role as tableware. Orton (1985, 28) attributes its suitability as a status possession to its suitability for rapid changes in design without the need for technical or technological change. With constant variation in style it was able to keep one jump ahead in the status stakes. Once again this interpretation is valid at the point when maiolica enters the Lower Rhine market around 1600 (Diag. 7).

The relative frequency of maiolica and slipware on post-medieval sites in the region reveals a wealth of potential information about social dynamics. It is significant that on several Duisburg sites maiolica and slipware finds are almost mutually exclusive. In Contexts 16 and 17, for instance, slipwares comprise the only decorative tableware found, whereas in Context 14 tin-glazed wares are predominant. It is possible that these sites represent extreme examples of social differentiation in the ceramic record: with those households with access to imported tin-glazed pottery to the exclusion of the lower ranking indigenous wares clearly distinct from those with only enough purchasing power to afford slipware (Section 7).

The question of displaying slipwares and maiolica in the domestic context during the 16th and 17th-centuries has come under scrutiny recently (Burhenne *et al.* eds 1991, 27–29). Suspension holes in the flanges of slipware, incised earthenware and maiolica dishes have long been regarded as evidence of domestic display (Gaimster 1991). However, this interpretation contrasts with the impression given by contemporary graphical sources from Holland (Burhenne *et al.* eds 1991, Fig. p. 28–29) which show ceramic dishes suspended with the open decorated side against the wall. This would certainly have reduced the risk of mould growth on the underside of earthenware vessels. The entire question deserves more attention, particularly as our understanding of what is meant by "display ware" is handicapped by a lack of recognised criteria. That said, contemporary graphical sources cleary show that the majority of ceramics illustrated in a display context were supported on shelves or sideboards, and were not necessarily hung on the wall (Appendix 7; I.C.).

A number of exotic ceramic imports made an appearance in the Lower Rhine sequence at the beginning of the 17th century, namely delicate sgraffito slipware from the Werra region of northern Germany (Ware-type Ic.5) and Oriental Kraak porcelain (IV.1). It is hard to say whether the few dishes of Werra ware found in Duisburg and Wesel represent a formal trade in ceramics between the two regions, or whether the finds are no more than testimonies to personal contacts. Their workmanship is of the highest order, and represents a far higher input of man-hours in production than the native Lower Rhine slipwares, which were hardly ever decorated with sgraffito at this time.

Undoubted was the social premium attached to imports of Oriental porcelain during the early 17th century. To date only a handful of *Kraak* porcelain dishes have been excavated in the Lower Rhineland. The fact that so much of Dutch maiolica production was geared to replicating the designs of *Kraak* porcelain emphasises its position as a status commodity in the European ceramics market. Its frequent inclusion in the sumptuous still-life paintings of the Dutch School (*Pronkstilleven*: see Appendix 7; III) suggests that it shared a similar social importance as precious metalware and other exotica. Despite the interpretative problems associated with the *Pronk* still-life paintings of the 17th century (Segal 1989), it is clear that Oriental porcelain was a symbol of material wealth and conspicuous consumption in contemporary Dutch society (Schama 1988, 160–1).

The assemblage of Oriental porcelain, Dutch maiolica and Lower Rhine slipware dating to c. 1600–1650 from a latrine level in Duisburg (Context 8) shows the complementary use of decorative tablewares of different prestige values during one phase. The discovery of the latrine group serves to emphasise that the attribution of social status to a particular assemblage must be based on the composition of the group as a whole and not on the presence and absence of specific wares.

The practice of applying decoration to stoneware continued into the 17th century in the Rhineland. By this stage, however, the decorative repertoire had changed out of all recognition, with the introduction of motifs in the latest fashions (e. g. cherub heads: Diag. 8d, centre). In line with Baroque taste the vast majority of stoneware produced by the early 17th century was grey in colour, embellished by under-glaze cobalt-blue painting. The changes in decorative treatment fulfil Orton's criteria (1985, 28) for status attribution, in that stoneware displayed the ability to sustain variation and differentiation. Its central position in the pottery hierarchy reflects its suitability for both the functional and symbolic spheres (Diag. 7). This inherent duality of use is demonstrated by the inclusion of Rhenish stoneware in contemporary Dutch paintings of bawdy tavern scenes and socially pretentious still-lives (Appendix 7; II.c & III).

The transition from maiolica to faience production after the middle of the 17th century resulted in an increase in the general availability of tin-glazed pottery both at home and over a longer distance (Sections 5.4.2; 7.2.5). Although available to a larger cross-section of the population, contemporary genre paintings from The Netherlands show that its social premium remained high. Faience is frequently represented in prominent positions in households of differing social status (Appendix 7; I.C.4–8). Jugs and tankards in painted faience (Diag. 8e) are rare in the Lower Rhine sequence and possibly represent status enhancing alternatives to the more common stoneware varieties.

iii. 18th century

As we have seen (Section 7.3.2.iii) the introduction of hot beverage consumption in North West Europe at the end of the 17th century resulted in the widespread demand for high-quality equipage. This need stimulated the mass-production of teawares in China and the prolific export trade controlled by the European East India Companies. The archaeological record shows that Chinese porcelain remained a relatively exclusive commodity for the duration of the first half of the 18th century. The range of specialised forms which came on to the market were accorded a high symbolic value due to their association with a prestige drink. Porcelain accounts for only 3 % of the ceramics found in Duisburg dating to this period (Graph 6). It is entirely absent in the countryside at this time (i.e. Context 60: Graph 8). Oriental porcelain only appears in any quantity after beginning of the second quarter of the 18th century in Amsterdam and Nijmegen (Thijssen 1985). Its presence is regarded as a criterion of social differentiation in Dutch urban culture at this time.

Once again the archaeological evidence demonstrates that a new commodity displays significantly more prestige value at the point at which it enters the market. Thereafter it suffers from the popularisation effect, moving from the elite tradition into the folk tradition (Yentsch 1990, 43–46). Thus Orton's model (1985) of porcelain as a status commodity only holds good for the early part of the 18th century (Diag. 7). By the middle of the century Chinese porcelain accounts for 11 % of the Duisburg pottery supply and 6 % at Krefeld-Linn (Graphs 7 & 9 respectively).

During the first half of the 18th-century Dutch faience supplied the majority of tea-table wares for the Lower Rhine market, although there was a marked bias in quantity and variety of town over country. It was only after 1750 that this tradition took root in the Lower Rhine hinterland (Graph 33). The timelag in the adoption of ceramic fashions is characteristic of urban sophistication and rural conservatism.

With the gradual popularisation of Chinese porcelain (a group representing an entire tea service was found among the Krefeld-Linn finds: Fig. 71, Nos. 15–23), new products were sought to reinstate material superiority between consumers. This objective was achieved by the Staffordshire industry in England which introduced a comprehensive range of teawares and tablewares in fine-bodied stoneware, creamware and a series of fine earthenware bodies to the Continental market (McKendrick 1982). Together they accounted for over 20 % of the Duisburg pottery supply between c. 1750 and 1800 (Graph 7). At Krefeld-Linn they formed less than 1 % of the entire assemblage for the same period (Graph 9). Porcelain made in Germany (Ware-type IV.4) also began to make an impact on the Lower Rhine ceramic sequence by the end of the 18th century. Its decorative repertoire was based on patterns previously made popular by the prestigeous Meissen factories (Hamburg 1989a).

The Krefeld-Linn flood groups (Contexts 60–61) provide crucial evidence about rural as opposed to urban ceramic consumption during the 18th century. They supply an accurate picture of the range of pottery in use at the time of the two catastrophe phases and not of the piecemeal accumulation of broken or discarded items. Research by Reichmann (1988) has revealed the name and occupation of the owner of the property in question. In the second half of the 18th century the house came into the possession of a local solicitor, Johan Küpers, who was also a legal consultant to the ducal civil service. The finds represent, therefore, the ceramic inventory of a man of the professional middle classes: an ideal context in which to examine our hierarchical model of pottery use (Diag. 7). The composition of Context 61 reflects the nature of a rather conservative consumer. Chinese porcelain and faience tea services appear in the sequence only after they have been popular in the region for some time. English finewares are virtually absent. The evidence also displays a continuing reliance on comparatively rudimentary local slipware for table use (Section 7.3.2). This pattern of regional ceramic consumption continues into the industrial period in the hinterland of the towns (Gaimster 1986a).

A further indication of the economic and social relationship between ceramics available to the Lower Rhine consumer has been provided by the publication of the retail value of plates of different wares sold in Amsterdam during the 18th century (Baart 1988):

| Ware | Groschen |
|---|---|
| Lower Rhine plain earthenware (Id. 4): | 1 |
| Local plain earthenware: | 1–2 |
| Maiolica (III.1): | 3 |
| English finewares (Id. 9-11; II.12–14; V.1): | 3 |
| White faience (III.2): | 3 |
| Painted faience (III.3): | 3–4 |
| Chinese porcelain (IV.2–3): | 8 |
| European porcelain (IV.4): | 40 |
| Pewter: | 10 |

If price may be equated to prestige-value, this breakdown confirms some of the patterning emerging from the Lower Rhine archaeological record. English finewares were not intended for the luxury end of the consumer market, but for the "Middle market" as a cheaper alternative to Oriental porcelain. Josiah Wedgwood's Continental marketing policy of the 1770s clearly demonstrates this shift (McKendrick 1982, 131). By 1785 the Staffordshire potteries were exporting 84 % of their produce abroad (*ibid.*, 136). It is the perfect example of the commercialisation of what was once a luxury product. The relatively high costs of native porcelain production are reflected in its retail price. They also explain the continued success of Chinese porcelain in the second half of the 18th century. The percentage of German porcelain in use in the Lower Rhineland is correspondingly small between c. 1775 and 1800 (e. g. 5 % of total in Context 13; see Section 6.2.2).

### *8.3.4 The social curation of ceramics in post-medieval society*

In addition to the combination of depositional and post-depositional factors which help determine the composition of a given archaeological assemblage (see Section 2.2.1.), several other important variables must be considered when analysing individual contexts or comparing groups on an inter-site basis. Of primary importance is the recognition of residual or socially-curated pottery types in an assemblage. Failure to do so may result in the skewing of pottery dating and the misinterpretation of social meaning.

According to Millett's model (1987, Fig. 4) of identifiable variables which influence the composition of pottery assemblages, the residual factor is of crucial importance. The situation involves the deposition of material from an earlier period in a chronologically later group. While the vast majority of residual material identified during the course of this survey has been caused by depositional processes (Moorhouse 1986, 113–5), a significant proportion is clearly the result of deliberate "curation" on the part of the owner or secondary use by a subsequent owner (Deetz 1977). In this case the "active life" of the individual vessel is artificially extended (Orton 1982b).

The presence of curated objects, when identified, can provide a valuable source of information regarding the functional and social interpretation of ceramic assemblages. Certain form-types enjoyed a relatively longer lifespan than others. For instance, storage jars are far less frequent in the archaeological record than cooking pots as they are not subjected to daily wear and tear in the same way (Löbert 1980, 30). Due to its relative social value, highly decorated tableware, such as maiolica plates, is also more likely to enjoy a longer active life than say slipware (Section 8.3.3).

The Lower Rhine ceramic assemblages contain a significant proportion of socially curated wares, artificially extending the date range of many of the groups. Stonewares, because of their durability, tend to have the longest active lives, especially those wares with applied relief decoration. In the case of the Duisburg Contexts 14, 15 and 16 stonewares of late 16th-century date have been found in levels deposited around the middle of the following century (Section 6). Similarly, tin-glazed wares, thanks to their colourful painted decoration, also enjoyed extensive lifespans as display items. Dutch maiolica has been found in contexts deposited up to 75 years after their initial date of manufacture (e. g. Contexts 10, 60: Section 6).

Recognition of the socially-derived residuality factor is a prerequisite of the interpretation of the Lower Rhine pottery groups, particularly when comparing the relative proportions of pottery and their significance on an inter-site basis. Future work is planned to investigate this factor more closely over a range of sites of differing socio-economic and functional status in the region.

### *8.3.5 Future priorities for socio-economic analysis*

Until more comparative data can be generated the conclusions presented here regarding the socio-economic interpretation of post-medieval ceramic assemblages in Duisburg and its hinterland must be taken as indicative of broad trends only. In order to refine this, a set of internationally-recognised criteria for the identification of social trends in excavated pottery must be established as a first priority. At present the socio-economic significance of medieval to later ceramic assemblages can only be assessed on a purely intuitive basis. In the meantime, in order to maximise our interpretation of the pottery recorded during this survey, the following

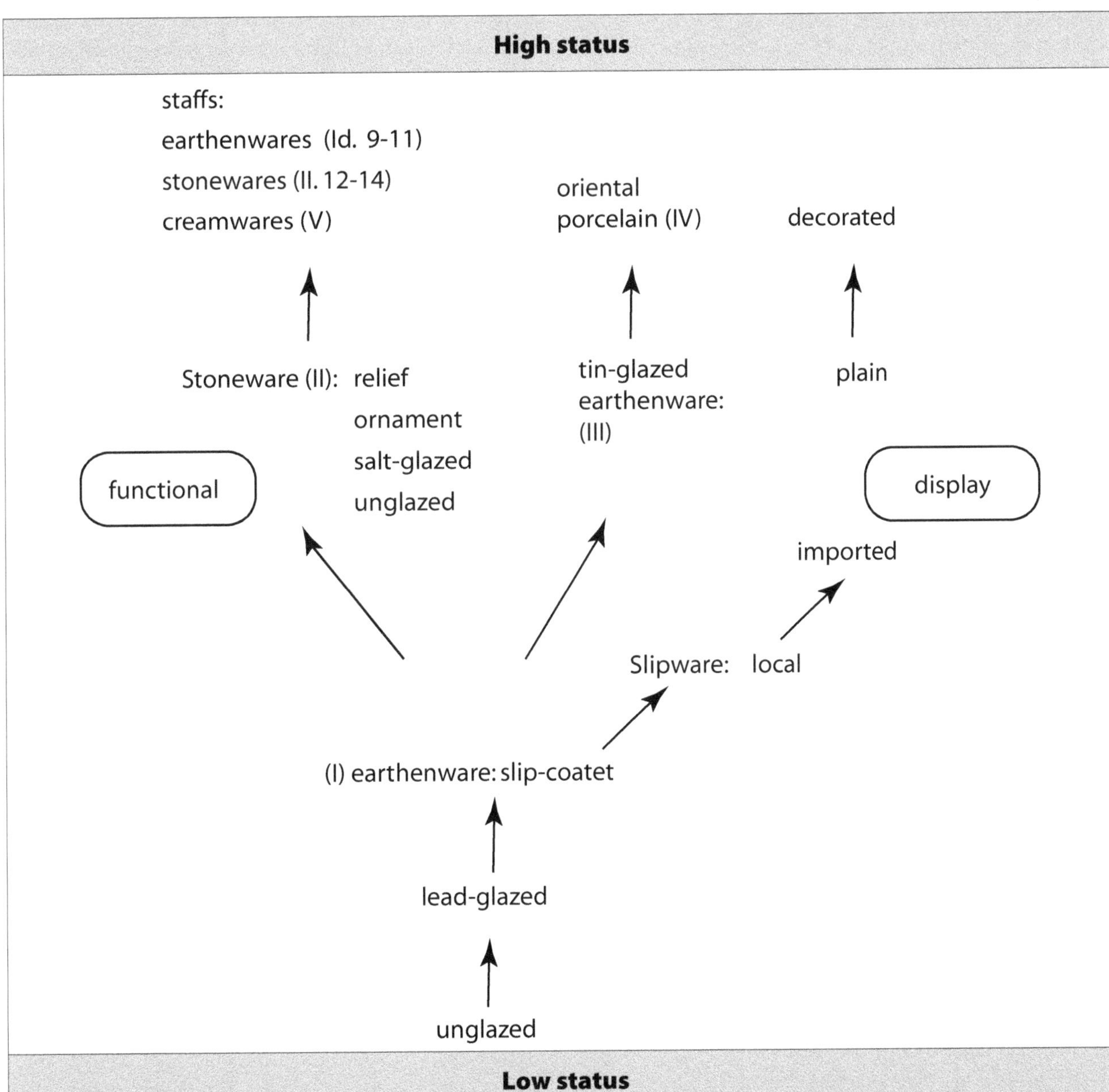


*Diagram 7 Hierarchy of potting technologies applied to the Lower Rhineland c. 1400-1800 (after Blake 1980; Orton 1985)*

research priorities have been identified:

i. Socio-topographical analysis

The ceramics recorded and discussed here have been studied in a vacuum. Their interpretation is limited by the lack of any historical context information. An urgent priority is to initiate a programme of micro-topgraphical research in the Lower Rhine towns in order to establish the identities and occupations of ownership which can then be related to the excavated artefactual groups. In Duisburg for instance, with such a wealth of cartographic control afforded by the Corputius map of 1566 (Plan 1), the programme would form a principal element of a more integrated multidisciplinary strategy for urban archaeology. The potential of using documentary sources in the study of urban topography has been justified by the success of projects carried out at Lübeck (Falk & Hammel 1980; Grassmann 1980), Göttingen (Löbert 1980), Nuremberg (Nuremberg 1984); Amsterdam (Baart 1984); Nijmegen (Clevis 1990), and in London (Keene 1983). Each programme of research has provided invaluable calibratory information about the nature of the associated archaeological assemblages, particularly about their respective socio-economic status.

Nevertheless, problems of linking discarded artefacts with individual households remain immense, especially when it is realised that latrines and wells in urban situations were very often used communally over considerable periods of time. Archival records in North German towns frequently only record the names of property owners and not their tenants. The difficulties of archaeological and socio-topographical linkage on the micro-scale have been ably demonstrated in Lübeck by Falk (1987b). Both the complexity of the historical record and the problem of being able to date pottery groups closely enough combine to blur the issue here. For Duisburg perhaps the most promising line of approach is to examine the socio-topographical structure at the macro-scale. Ongoing research by the Stadtarchiv Duisburg is aimed at establishing the broad social niveau of particular street or tenement units (Milz 2005). In the future, therefore, the archaeological sequences from well-to-do and less wealthy districts in the town may be compared to each other.

ii. Multi-media analysis

Any ceramic assemblage is only a limited selection of the actual utensils in use within a home (Section 8.2.4). It is a matter of the utmost urgency, therefore, that the analyses of the non-ceramic finds from the assemblages examined in this study are completed and their results integrated. Finds research in the town of Duisburg and in the region must be amalgamated to produce multi-media studies of individual contexts on a comparative basis.

In order to understand the complexity of material trends and their relationship to past foodways it is essential to integrate the study of ceramics with those of glass, metalware and treen, and of the various organic assemblages (botanical and faunal), each capable of dramatically refining the socio-economic interpretation of the ceramic record. In the case of the botanical remains from Duisburg, research is well advanced (Knörzer 1983; 1991; 1992), and will substantially improve our knowledge of the development of eating and dining habits during the post-medieval period. The survival of exotic seeds and nuts in waterlogged well and latrine environments may also shed light on the expansion of international trade and the social status of individual sites. Similarly, recent archaeozoological studies of post-medieval faunal assemblages in Amsterdam have demonstrated the potential of examining animal bones as a means of differing between wealthy and poor households within towns (Ijzereef 1989). Given the difficulties in studying pottery in isolation, it is probably only by integrating the ceramic analyses with those of other disciplines that a more coherent and representative picture will emerge of socio-economic trends at the micro-scale.

iii. Town and country

Finally, the potentially rewarding comparison of urban and rural sites must be expanded if a truly regional overview of ceramic consumption is to be reached in the Lower Rhineland. To date only three 18th-century rural sites excavated in the Lower Rhine hinterland have provided quantified data. This quota must be improved if we are to gain a more representative picture of regional as opposed to site-specific ceramic trends over time and space. Analysis of the Krefeld-Linn cellar assemblages (Contexts 60–61) and that from the farmhouse at Haus Gelinde, Rheinberg (Context 93), have demonstrated the value of calibrating the variable momentum of changing ceramic fashions on rural as well as urban sites in the region.

## Bibliography


ALLAN, J. P. 1984. *Medieval and Post-Medieval Finds from Exeter, 1971–1980*, Exeter Archaeological Reports 3, Exeter

ANDERSEN, A. B. 1974. A Dutch Galliot which struck a rock in 1677, *International Journal of Nautical Archaeology*, 3:1, 91–100

Antwerp, 1978. *Museum Mayer van den Bergh, Catalogue I*, Museum Mayer van den Bergh, Antwerp

Antwerp, 1982. *Van Nederzetting tot Metropol. Archeologisch-Historisch Onderzoek in de Antwerpse Binnenstad*, Stad Antwerpen Oudheidskundige Musea, Antwerp

APPADURAI, A. 1986. Introduction: commodities and the politics of value, in A. APPADURAI ed. *The Social Life of Things: commodities in cultural perspective*, Cambridge, 3–63

ARNOLD, V. 1984. Der Schatz im Brunnen. Heider Töpferware von 1620, *Dithmarschen* N. F., 1984, 53–57

ARNOLD, V. 1986. Die Niederbrennung Heides am 13.6.1559 im Spiegel neuer Bodenfunde, *Dithmarschen* N. F., 1986, Heft 1, (March 1986), 1–9

ARNOLD, V., WESTPHALEN, Th. & ZUBECK, P. 1990. *Kachelöfen in Schleswig-Holstein. Irdenware – Gusseisen – Fayence*, Kleine Schleswig-Holstein-Bücher 40, Heide

ASPINALL, A. 1977. Neutron activation analysis of Medieval ceramics, *Medieval Ceramics*, 1, 5–16

Ausstellungskatalog Frechen 1995. Stadt Frechen (eds), *Ausgegraben. Keramik aus Frechen vom Mittelalter bis zum 19. Jahrhundert.* Begleitbuch zur gleichnamigen Ausstellung im Keramikmuseum Frechen, Frechen

BAADEN, F. 1985. *Ransbach-Baumbach in alten Ansichten*, Ransbach-Baumbach

BAART, J. M. ed. 1977. *Opgravingen in Amsterdam: 20 jaar Stadskernonderzoek*, Amsterdam

BAART, J. M. 1984. Der Gebrauch von Glas in Amsterdam im 17. Jahrhundert, in C. GRIMM ed. 1984, 34–47

BAART, J. M. 1986. Materiele cultur in de late 16de eeuw: het milieu van een aasweduwe, in TER MOLEN *et al.* eds 1986, 93–103

BAART, J. M. 1988. Niederrheinische Keramik des 18. Jahrhunderts in den Niederlanden, in J. NAUMANN ed. 1988, 159–165

BAART, J. M. 1991. Italian pottery from the Netherlands and Belgium, in T. WILSON ed. 1991, 232–240

BAART, J. M., KROOK, W., & LAGERWEIJ, A. C. 1986. Opgravingen aan de Oostenburger Middenstraat, in J. B. KIST *et al.* eds, *Van VOC tot Werkspoor, het Amsterdamse Industrieterrein Oostenburg*, Utrecht, 83–151

BAART, J. M., KROOK, W. & LAGERWEIJ, A. C. 1990. Italiaanse en Nederlandse witte faience (1600–1700), *Mededelingenblad nederlandse vereniging van vrienden van de ceramiek*, 138, No. 2

BALL, D. U. 1990. Zur Kulturgeschichte des Kaffees, *Weltkunst*, 60, No. 6 (March 1990), 845–847

BARFIELD, C. H., WENTSCHER, J. & WILD, J. P. 1963. Die Ausgrabungen unter dem Universitätsgebäude Bonn im März 1962, *Bonner Jahrbücher*, 163, 342–367

BARKER, D. 1984. 18th and 19th-century ceramics excavated at the Foley pottery, Fenton, Stoke-on-Trent, *Staffordshire Archaeological Studies*, 1, 63–86

BARKER, D. 1990. *William Greatbatch: a Staffordshire Potter*, London

BARKER, D. & HALFPENNY, P. A. 1990. *Unearthing Staffordshire. Towards a New Understanding of 18th-century Ceramics*, City of Stoke-on-Trent Museum & Art Gallery, Stoke-on-Trent

BARTELS, M. 1982. *Aus Erde werden Schüsseln gemacht. Volksleben und Brauchtum auf niederrheinischer bleiglasierter Irdenware*, Niederrheinisches Museum der Stadt Duisburg, Duisburg

BARTELS, M. 1988. Bildmotive und Motivwandergruppen auf ritzverzierter Irdenware, in J. NAUMANN ed. 1988, 269–372

BARTELS, M. 1999. *Steden in Scherven/Cities in Sherds.* Vondsten uit beerputten in Deventer, Dordrecht, Nijmegen en Tiel 1250-1900, Zwolle

Bartmann, H. 1914. Niederrheinische Bauerntöpferei, *Der Niederrhein*, Düsseldorf, 177 ff.

Bauche R.-D. 1997. Die Keramik des 12. Jahrhunderts zwischen Köln und Aachen. *Archäologische Berichte* 9, Bonn

Bauer, I., Endres, W., Kerkhoff-Hader, B., Koch, R. & Stephan, H.-G. 1987. *Leitfaden zur Keramikbeschreibung (Mittelalter – Neuzeit). Terminologie – Typologie – Technologie*, Katalog der Prähistorischen Staatssammlung, Beiheft 2, München

Bauer, M. 1989. *Frankfurter Fayencen aus der Zeit des Barock*, Museum für Kunsthandwerk, Frankfurt am Main

Bax, A. & Martin, C. 1974. De Leifde: A Dutch East Indiaman lost on the Out Skerries, Shetland, in 1711, *International Journal of Nautical Archaeology*, 3:1, 81–90

Beckers, P. & Siegmund, F. eds 1990. *Bevor der Bagger kam. Ausgrabungen am Rheinort 1989*, Stadtmuseum, Düsseldorf

Beckmann, B. 1974. The main types of the first four production periods of Siegburg pottery, in V. I. Evison, H. Hodge & J. C. Hurst eds *Medieval Pottery from Excavations*, London, 183–200

Beckmann, B. 1975. *Der Scherbenhügel in der Siegburger Aulgasse, 1. Die Formen der Keramik von ihren Anfängen bis zum Beginn der sogenannten Blütezeit (Perioden 1 bis 4)*, Rheinische Ausgrabungen, 16, Bonn

Bergström, I. 1956. *Dutch Still-Life Painting in the Seventeenth Century*, London

Berlin 1978. *Catalogue of Paintings. 13th–18th century*, S. M. P. K. Gemäldegalerie, Berlin

Billberg, I. 1987. *Från trattbägare till fajans*, Malmö Museer, Malmö

Bimson, M. 1964. The relative distribution of pottery types in an eighteenth century deposit, *Transactions of the English Ceramic Circle* 5, Pt. 5, 92–293

Blake, H. 1980. Technology, supply or demand? *Medieval Ceramics* 4, 3–12

Blake, H. & Davey, P. 1983. *Guidelines for the Processing and Publication of Medieval Pottery from Excavations*, Directorate of Ancient Monuments & Historic Buildings, Occasional Paper No. 5, London

Blomqvist, R. 1936. *Kakel och kakeltillverkning i Lund under dansk tid*, Kulturens årsbok 1936, Lund

Bocholt 1987. *Entdeckte Spuren. Archäologische Funde aus dem Bocholter Alltag vom Mittelalter zur Neuzeit*, Unser Bocholt. Zeitschrift für Kultur und Heimatpflege, 38, Heft 2/3

Bonn 1936. *Rheinisches Landesmuseum, Guidebook*, Rheinisches Landesmuseum, Bonn

Bonn 1986. *Vorschläge zur systematischen Beschreibung von Keramik*. Führer des Rheinischen Landesmuseums Bonn, 124, Bonn

Borremans, R. & Warginaise, R. 1966. *La Ceramique d'Andenne. Recherches de 1956–1965*, Rotterdam

Borst, O. 1983. *Alltagsleben im Mittelalter*, Frankfurt am Main

Bosing, W. 1987. *Hieronymus Bosch c. 1450–1516. Between Heaven and Hell*, Cologne

Bousquet, G. *et al.* 1990. The discovery of an English East Indiaman at Bassis de India, a French atoll in the Indian Ocean: the Sussex (1738), *International Journal of Nautical Archaeology*, 19.1, 81–85

Bouvy, D. P. R. A. 1965. Een zilveren Lavaboblad in het aartsbisschoppelijk Museum, in P. Bloch & J. Hoster ed. *Miscellanea Pro Arte*, Düsseldorf, 291–294

Brandl, R. 1984a. *Essen und Trinken im spät-mittelalterlichen Nürnberg*, in Nuremberg 1984, 11–31

Brandl, R. 1984b. Keramik, in Nuremberg 1984, 67–105 & 158–201

Braunschweig 1985. *Stadt im Wandel. Kunst und Kultur des Bürgertums in Nordwestdeutschland 1150–1650*, Braunschweigisches Landesmuseum, Braunschweig

Bremen 1982. *Aus dem Alltag der mittelalterlichen Stadt*, Hefte des Focke Museums, Bremer Landesmuseum für Kunst und Kulturgeschichte (Focke-Museum)

Brill, F. 1969. Die Töpferei in der Streitzeuggasse zu Köln, *Aus Kölnischer und Rheinischer Geschichte*, Cologne, 255–274

BRINKMANN, B. 1982. Zur Datierung von Mineralwasserflaschen aus Steinzeug, *Keramos* 98 (October 1982), 7–36

BRONGERS, J. A. & WIJNMANN, H. F. 1968. Chronological classification of roemers with the help of 17th-century paintings in the Low Countries, *Rotterdam Papers* 1, Rotterdam, 15–24

BROWN, D. 1985. Looking at cross-fits, *Medieval Ceramics* 9, 35–42

BRUIJN, A. 1979. *Pottersvuren langs te vecht. Aardewerk rond 1400 uit Utrecht*, Rotterdam Papers 3, Rotterdam

BURHENNE, V., GAIMSTER, D. R. M., STEPHAN, H.-G. & SCHILLING, L. 1991. *Frühe dekorierte Irdenware. Malhorndekor und Kammstrichverzierung vom Niederrhein und aus dem Köln-Frechener Raum*, Führer und Schriften des Rheinischen Freilichtmuseums – Landesmuseum für Volkskunde 43, Cologne

CASTENS, A., KRAUSE, G. 1992, Archäologisch-historische Literatur zur Duisburger Altstadt, in: KRAUSE, G.(ed.), *Stadtarchäologie in Duisburg 1980-1990*, (Duisburger Forschungen 38), 538–545

CELORIA, F. 1980. An examination of terminologies for pottery classification in archaeology, *Science and Archaeology* 22, 35–54

CHAPELOT, J., GALINIÉ, H. & PILET-LEMIÈRE, J. 1987. *La céramique (Ve–XIXe s.). Fabrication – commercialisation – utilisation*, Société d'Archéologie Médiévale, Caen

CHATELET, A. 1988. *Early Dutch Painting. Painting in the Northern Netherlands in the fifteenth Century*, Lausanne

CHERRY, J. 1986. The national reference collection of Medieval pottery, *Medieval Ceramics* 10, 125–130

CHERRY, J. 1987. Cauldrons and skillets: metal and pottery in cooking, in B. VYNER & S. WRATHMALL eds 1987, 145–160

CHERRY, J. F., GAMBLE, C. & SHENNAN, S. eds 1978. *Sampling in Contemporary British Archaeology*, *British Archaeological Reports*, British Series 50, Oxford

CLAIR, C. 1965. *Kitchen and Table*, New York

CLARK, A. 1979. German wares, in C. GASKELL BROWN ed. *Castle Street: the Pottery*, Plymouth Museum Archaeological Series 1, Plymouth, 32–41,

CLARKE, H. 1988. Review of J. G. HURST *et al.* 1986, *Antiquaries Journal*, 68, Pt. II, 365–366

Cleves 1984. *Land im Mittelpunkt der Mächte. Die Herzogtümer Jülich-Kleve-Berg*, Städtisches Museum Haus Koekkoek, Cleves

CLEVIS, H. 1981. Maastricht, in J. H. F. BLOEMERS & W. J. H. WILLEMS eds, Archeologische kroniek van Limburg over de jaren 1977–1979, *Publications de la Société Historique et Archéologique dans le Limbourg*, 116–117, 1980–1981, 62–71

CLEVIS, H. 1990. *Nijmegen: Investigations into the Historical Topography and Development of the Lower Town between 1300 and 1500*, Amersfoort

CLEVIS, H. & KOTTMANN, J. 1989. *Weggegooid en teruggevonden. Aardewerk en glas uit Deventer vondstkomplexen 1375–1750*, Stichting Archeologie Ijssel/Vechtstreek, Kampen

CLEVIS, H. & SARFATIJ, H. 1982. Borden uit een Dordtse Beerput (ca. 1600), *Rotterdam Papers*, 4, Rotterdam, 23–24

CLEVIS, H. & THIJSSEN J. 1989. Kessel, huisvuil uit een Kasteel, *Mededelingenblad Nederlandse Vereniging van Vrienden van de Ceramiek*, 136, No. 4, 4–33

CLEVIS H. & THIJSSEN J. 1994 (eds), Assembled Articles 1. Symposium on Medieval and Post-Medieval Ceramics, Nijmegen 2–3 September 1993, Nijmegen

Cologne 1987. *Wallraf-Richartz Museum Köln, Guidebook*, Munich

COWELL, M. 1988. A provenance study of English armorial stove-tiles, in D. R. M. GAIMSTER 1988f., 338–340

COWELL, M. 1989. Report on the analysis of a post-medieval stove-tile from Dover and three comparative pieces, in D. R. M. GAIMSTER 1989, 302–303

COWELL, M. 1990. Report on the analysis of nine early post-medieval stove-tile fragments from St. Mary Graces, in D. GAIMSTER et al. 1990, 40–45

CREUTZ, M. 1924. *Deutsche Volkskunst 3. Die Rheinlande*, Munich

Cunningham, C. M. 1985. A typology for post-Roman pottery in Essex, in C. M. Cunningham & P. J. Drury, *Post-Medieval sites and their pottery: Moulsham Street, Chelmsford*, Council for British Archaeology Research Report 54, 1–16

Curtis, J. B. 1985. Transition Ware made plain: a wreck from the South China Sea, *Oriental Art* 31, No. 2 (Summer 1985), 161–173

Davey, P. 1983. A future for medieval pottery studies?, *Medieval Ceramics* 7, 89–94

Davey, P. 1987. Review of Corpus van middeleeuws aardewerk uit gesloten vondstkomplexen in Nederland en Vlaaderen (1985–1987), *Medieval Ceramics* 11, 78–80

Davey, P. 1988. Theory and practice in medieval ceramic studies. *Medieval Ceramics* 12, 3–13

Davey, P. & Hodges, R. 1983. Ceramics and trade: a critique of the archaeological evidence, in P. Davey & R. Hodges eds 1983, 1–14

Davey, P. & Hodges, R. eds *Ceramics and Trade. The production and distribution of later medieval pottery in north-west Europe*, University of Sheffield

Dawson, G. J. 1979. Excavations at Guy's Hospital 1967, *Research Volume of the Surrey Archaeological Society* 7, 27–65

Deetz, J. 1977. *In Small Things Forgotten: The Archaeology of Early American Life*, New York

de Jonge, C. H. 1970. *Delft Ceramics*, London

Deneken, F. 1914. *Die Sammlung niederrheinischer Tonarbeiten im Kaiser-Wilhelm-Museum*, Krefeld

De Ridder-Blenska, G., Mayer, O. E. & Papeleux, J. 1977. Spätmittelalterliche Töpferöfen aus Hauset und Raeren, *Vereinigung für Kultur, Heimatkunde und Geschichte im Göhtal*, 2, 1–32

Despriet, Ph., Goddeeris, T., Beekmans, L. 1999. *Kortrijk 1382. De muntschat uit het Begijnenhof.* Archeologische en Hist. Monogr. van Zuid-West-Vlaanderen 19, Kortrijk

De Witte, H. ed. 1988. *Brugge Onder-Zocht. Tien jaar stadsarcheologisch onderzoek*, Archeo-Brugge 1, Bruges

De Witte, H. ed. 1991. *De Brugse Burg. Van grafelijke versterking tot moderne stadskern*, Archeo-Brugge, 2, Bruges

Dexel, W. 1939. *Deutsches Handwerksgut. Eine Kultur- und Formgeschichte der Hausgeräte*, Berlin

Dexel, T. 1980. *Gebrauchsgerättypen. Das Gebrauchsgerät Mitteleuropas von der römischen Zeit bis ins 19. Jahrhundert* 1, Braunschweig

Dierkes, H., Jakobi, W. 1998. A city at war with its past. Museum rescue archaeology in Duisburg, Lower Rhineland, in *Rescue News*, The British Archaeological Trust, Nr. 75

Dilly, G. & Hurtrelle, J. 1987. La céramique vernissée decorée à la Corne du "Bout de la Garenne", 1ère Partie, *Dossiers Archéologiques Historique et Culturels du Nord et du Pas-de-Calais, Supplement Archéologique* 2, Berck-sur-Mer, 51–60

Dilly, G., Hurtrelle, J. & Jacques, A. 1986. Arras et les ateliers artesiens, in *Terres vernissées, XVIIe–XIXe siècle, dans les Musées du Nord – Pas-de-Calais*, Association des Conservateurs de la Région Nord – Pas-de-Calais, Lille, 33–55

Döry, Baron L. 1978. *Keramika. Frankfurt als Herstellungsort und Markt für keramische Erzeugnisse im 16. und 17. Jahrhundert*, Kleine Schriften des Historischen Museums Frankfurt a. M., 9, Frankfurt

Döry, Baron L. 1988. Grabungserfahrungen in Frankfurt a. Main und Umgebung – zur Geschichte der Keramik im 16.–19. Jahrhundert, in W. Endres & W. Loibl eds, *Beiträge zur handwerklichen Fränkischen Keramik*, Arbeitskreis für Keramikforschung, 22, Spessartmuseum, Lohr am Main, 13–23

Dresden 1983. *Das Stilleben und sein Gegenstand*, Dresden

D. U. A. (Dept. of Urban Archaeology, Museum of London) 1984. *Pottery Archive. User's Handbook*

Dubbe, B. 1960. Die ehemalige St. Anthonius-Zunft in Vollenhove, *Keramos*, 9 (July 1960), 3–10

Dubbe, B. 1963. De kacheloven in Nederland, *Mededelingenblad Nederlandse Vereniging van Vrienden van de Ceramiek* 32 (September 1963), 1–31

Dubbe, B. 1966. *De kacheloven in onze gewesten*, Lochem

Dubbe, B. 1980. Import van kacheltegels in de zestiend eeuw, *Antiek* 14, No. 8 (March 1980), 519–522

Dubbe, B. 1987. Een vondst van gotische kacheltegels in de Deventer binnenstad, *Antiek* 21, No. 6 (January 1987), 329–336

Duisburg 1983. *Duisburg im Mittelalter*. Begleitschrift zur Ausstellung, Stadtarchiv und Niederrheinisches Museum der Stadt Duisburg, Duisburg

Duisburg 1986. *Volkstümliche Keramik vom Niederrhein. Töpferware des 8. bis 20. Jahrhunderts*, Niederrheinisches Museum der Stadt Duisburg, Duisburg

Düsseldorf 1967. *Keramik des Niederrheins aus Gegenwart und Vergangenheit*, Hetjens-Museum, Düsseldorf

Düsseldorf 1988. *Funde aus der Altstadtgrabung*, Hetjens-Museum, Düsseldorf

Dyer, C. 1982. The social and economic changes of the later Middle Ages and the pottery of the period, *Medieval Ceramics* 6, 33–42

Egloff, B. J. 1973. A method for counting rim sherds, *American Antiquity* 38, 351–353

Ellison, M. 1981. The Pottery, in B. Harbottle & M. Ellison, An excavation in the Castle Ditch, Newcastle-upon-Tyne, 1974–1976, *Archaeologia Aeliana*, 5th Series 9, 75–250

Endres, W. 1989a. Bericht vom Internationalen Hafnerei-Symposium in Düsseldorf, *Keramos* 123 (January 1989), 86–87

Endres, W. 1989b. Review of *Keramik vom Niederrhein* (ed. J. Naumamn), *Zeitschrift für Archäologie des Mittelalters* 16/17, 1988/1989, 220–223

Endres, W. & Loers, V. 1981. *Spätmittelalterliche Keramik aus Regensburg: Neufunde in Prebrunn*, Regensburg

Erdmann, W., Kühn, H.-J., Lüdtke, H., Ring, E. & Wessel, W. 1984. Rahmenterminologie zur mittelalterlichen Keramik in Norddeutschland, *Archäologisches Korrespondenzblatt* 14, Heft 4, 417–436

Erichson-Firle, U. & Vey, H. 1973. *Katalog der deutschen Gemälde von 1550 bis 1800 im Wallraf-Richartz-Museum*, Kataloge des Wallraf-Richartz-Museums, 10, Cologne

Evans, D. H. 1985. The Pottery, in D. H. Evans & A. Carter, Excavations on 31–51 Pottergate, in M. Atkin, A. Carter & D. H. Evans eds *Excavations in Norwich 1971–1978*, II, East Anglian Archaeology, Report 26, 27–49

Evans, D. H. 1987. Reflections on the study of imported ceramics, in B. Vyner & S. Wrathmell eds 1987, 199–224

Falk, A. 1980. Archäologische Erkentnisse zu Wirtschafts- und Alltagsleben, Archäologie in Lübeck, *Hefte zur Kunst und Kulturgeschichte der Hansestadt Lübeck*, 3, 94–97

Falk, A. 1983. Holzgeräte des Mittelalters und der Neuzeit aus Lübeck, *Zeitschrift für Archäologie des Mittelalters*, 11, 31–48

Falk, A. 1987a. Archäologische Funde und Befunde des späten Mittelalters u. der frühen Neuzeit aus Lübeck, Materialvorlage und erste Auswertungsergebnisse der Fundstellen Schüsselbuden 16/Fischstraße 1–3 und Holstenstraße 6, *Lübecker Schriften für Archäologie und Kulturgeschichte* 10, 9–84

Falk, A. 1987b. Materielle Kultur und soziale Struktur. Erfahrungen und Ergebnisse Archäologisch-historischer Arbeiten in Lübeck, *Zeitschrift des Vereins für Lübeckische Geschichte und Altertumskunde* 67, 9–30

Falk, A. 1987c. Holzgefäße und Geräte aus der Lübecker Innenstadt, *Lübecker Schriften für Archäologie und Kulturgeschichte* 17, 162–164

Falk, A. 1988. Keramikfunde aus der Lübecker Innenstadt, *Lübecker Schriften für Archäologie und Kulturgeschichte* (25 Jahre Archäologie in Lübeck) 17, 158–161

Falk, A. & Hammel, R. 1988, Archäologisch-historische Untersuchungen zur Sozial und Wirtschaftsgeschichte, *Lübecker Schriften für Archäologie und Kulturgeschickte 17* (25 Jahre Archäologie in Lübeck), 68–69

Falk, A., Gläser, M., & Moeck-Schlömer, C. 1989. *Wasserversorgung und Abfallbeseitigung in den Hansestädten*, in Hamburg 1989b, 409–413

Farke, H. 1992, Faser- und Gewebereste aus Grabungen in der Stadt Duisburg, in Krause, G. ed., *Stadtarchäologie in Duisburg 1980–1990* (Duisburger Forschungen 38), 316–329

FLETCHER, W. & HEYWORTH, M. 1987. The quantification of vessel fragments, in C. F. GAFFREY & V. L. GAFFREY eds *Pragmatic Archaeology. Theory in Crisis*, British Archaelogical Reports, British Series 167, 35–46

FLINK, K. 1984. Die klevischen Herzöge und ihre Städte (1394–1592), in Cleves 1984, 75–95

FOSTER, W. A. & HIGGS, K. B. 1973. The Kennemerland, 1971. An Interim Report, *International Journal of Nautical Archaeology* 2:2, 291–300

FOX, R. & BARTON, K. 1986. Excavations at Oyster Street, Portsmouth, Hants., 1968–71, *Post-Medieval Archaeology*, 20, 31–256

FRANCKE, U. 1999. *Kannenbäcker in Altenrath.* Eine Töpferwerkstatt des Frühbarocks in Troisdorf-Altenrath, Siegburg

FRANKEWITZ, S. 1988. Kervenheim – Zur Datierung der Produkte einer niederrheinischen Töpferei des 18. Jahrhunderts, in J. NAUMANN ed. 1988, 141–152

FRANKEWITZ, S. & KÖSTER, G. P. 1982. Die Töpferei Kervenheim, *Rheinisches Jahrbuch für Volkskunde*, 24, 221–235

Frankfurt 1991. *Brücke zwischen den Völkern. Zur Geschichte der Frankfurter Messe* 3, Historisches Museum, Frankfurt am Main

FRANZ-BERDAU, R. 1959. Die Anfänge der Zierkachel, *Keramos*, 3 (January 1959), 3–14

FRANZ, R. 1981. *Der Kachelofen,* Forschungen und Berichte des Kunsthistorischen Instituts der Universität Graz, 1, Graz

FRANZEN, J. & PÄFFGEN, B. 1989. Untersuchungen im Nordwestbereich des Aachener Domhofs, in *Archäologie im Rheinland 1988*, Rheinisches Amt für Bodendenkmalpflege, Cologne, 98–101

FRECKMANN, K. ed. 1983. *Rheinisches Töpferhandwerk. Eifel. Mosel. Hunsrück. Nahe. Rheinhessen*, Schriftenreihe des Freilichtsmuseums Sobernheim, 2

FRIEDLÄNDER, M. J. 1949. *Memling*, Amsterdam

FRIEDLÄNDER, M. J. 1956. *Early Netherlands Painting from van Eyck to Brueghel*, London

FRIEDRICH, R. 1997. Die Keramik aus dem mittelalterlichen Stadtgraben von Jülich. *Bonner Jahrbücher* 197, 1997, 191–228.

FRIEDRICH, R. 1998. *Mittelalterliche Keramik aus rheinischen Motten.* Rheinische Ausgrabungen 44, Köln/Bonn

GABBERT, G. 1977. *Chinesisches Porzellan*, Museum für Kunsthandwerk, Frankfurt a. Main

GAIMSTER, D. R. M. 1984. *A Problem-orientated fieldwalking survey in the Xanten region of the Lower Rhineland*, B. A. Diss., University of Durham

GAIMSTER, D. R. M. 1986a. Preliminary observations on the post-medieval pottery from the *Alter Markt* site, Duisburg, W. Germany, *Post-Medieval Archaeology* 20, 19–30

GAIMSTER, D. R. M. 1986b. Die neuzeitliche Keramik (ca. 1550–1900) am Unteren Niederrhein nach den Funden aus Duisburg, in Duisburg 1986, 29–44

GAIMSTER, D. R. M. 1987a. The supply of Rhenish stoneware to London, 1350–1600, *The London Archaeologist*, 5, 13 (Winter 1987), 339–347

GAIMSTER, D. R. M. 1987b. A Black Basalt teapot from Duisburg, W. Germany, *The Northern Ceramic Society Newsletter*, 67 (September 1987), 23–24

GAIMSTER, D. R. M. 1988a. Pottery production in the Lower Rhineland: the Duisburg sequence ca. 1400–1800, in D. R. M. GAIMSTER *et al.* eds 1988, 151–171

GAIMSTER, D. R. M. 1988b. Keramikproduktion vom Niederrhein: die Duisburger Abfolge von ca. 1400–1800, in J. NAUMANN ed. 1988, 55–74

GAIMSTER, D. R. M. 1988c. Lower Rhine Slipware found in Britain, in J. NAUMANN ed. 1988, 167–178

GAIMSTER, D. R. M. 1988d. A Survey of Cologne-type stove-tiles found in Britain, in I. UNGER ed. 1988, 44–54

GAIMSTER, D. R. M. 1988e. Review of Bonn 1986 & I. Bauer *et al.*, 1986 in *Medieval Ceramics*, 12, 78–80

GAIMSTER, D. R. M. 1988f. Post-medieval stove-tiles bearing the Royal arms: evidence for their manufacture and use in southern Britain, *Archaeological Journal* 145, 314–343

GAIMSTER, D. R. M. 1989. An imported Renaissance stove-tile from Dover in the collections of the Society of Antiquaries, *Antiquaries Journal* 69ii, 298–303

GAIMSTER, D. R. M. 1990a. "Renaissance" Rhenish stoneware, in M. JONES ed. 1990, Catalogue 222

GAIMSTER, D. R. M. 1990b. *An analytical study of post-medieval pottery and tiles from the Rhineland*, Lecture to congress of Nordwestdeutscher Verband für Altertumsforschung e. V., Duisburg 1990

GAIMSTER, D. R. M. 1991a. The Development of decorated earthenware in the Lower Rhineland c.1550–1675: recent finds from Duisburg, in U. BURHENNE *et al.* 1991, 45–60

GAIMSTER, D. R. M. 1992a. Frühneuzeitliche Keramik am Niederrhein in: KRAUSE, G.(ed.), *Stadtarchäologie in Duisburg 1980-1990*, Duisburger Forschungen 38, 330–353

GAIMSTER, D. R. M. 1992b. Renaissance stoneware from the Rhineland: continuing problems of authentication, in M. JONES ed. *Why fakes matter. Essays on the problems of Authenticity (1992)*, 108–116, British Museum, London

GAIMSTER, D. R. M. 1997a. Rhenish stonewares from shipwrecks: the study of ceramic function and lifespan. In: M. Redknap (ed.), *Artefacts from Wrecks.* Dated Assemblages from the Late Middle Ages to the Industrial Revolution. Oxbow Monogr. 84, Oxford 1997, 121–128

GAIMSTER, D. R. M. 1997b. *German Stoneware 1200-1900.* Archaeology and cultural history, British Museum, London

GAIMSTER, D. R. M., GOFFIN, R. & BLACKMORE, L. 1990. The Continental stove-tile fragments from St. Mary Graces, London, in their British and European context, *Post-Medieval Archaeology* 24, 1–49

GAIMSTER, D. R. M., REDKNAP, M. & WEGNER, H.-H. eds 1988. *Zur Keramik des Mittelalters und der beginnenden Neuzeit im Rheinland. Medieval and later pottery from the Rhineland and its markets*, British Archaeological Reports International Series, 440, Oxford

GAIMSTER, D. R. M. & HOOK, D. R. 1995 Post-medieval stoneware manufacture and trade in the Rhineland and soutehern Britain: a programme of Neutron Activation Analysis at the British Museum; in D. R. HOOK & D R. M. GAIMSTER eds, *Trade and discovery. The scientific study of artefacts from post medieval Europe and beyond.* British Museum Occasional Paper 109 (1995), 69–77

GERDSEN, H. & ROTTMAN, R. 1986. Die Töpferei Alte Tiemann in Natrup-Hagen, Landkreis Osnabrück, *Archäologisches Korrespondenzblatt* 16, 473–480

GERLACH, R., RADTKE, U., SAUER, K.-H.1992. Historische Bodenbelastungen in Duisburg, in KRAUSE, G. ed., *Stadtarchäologie in Duisburg 1980–1990*, Duisburger Forschungen 38, 365–379

Ghent 1986. *Joachim Beuckelaer. Het markt- en keukenstuk in den Niederlanden 1550–1650*, Museum voor Schone Kunsten, Ghent

GIERTZ, W. 1988. Ein Majolicateller des 17. Jahrhunderts aus dem Neusser Klarissenkloster, *Neusser Jahrbuch für Kunst, Kulturgeschichte und Heimatkunde* 1988, 52–53

GLANVILLE, P. 1990. An Elizabethan silver-mounted stoneware pot and agate cup, in M. JONES ed. 1990, Catalogue 204–205

Glasgow 1961. *Dutch & Flemish, Netherlandish & German Paintings*, Glasgow Art Gallery & Museum, Glasgow

GÖBELS, K. 1971. *Rheinisches Töpferhandwerk gezeigt am Beispiel der Frechener Kannen-, Duppen- und Pfeifenbäcker*, Cologne (2nd edition 1985)

GOLDTHWAITE, R. A. 1989. The economic and social world of Italian Renaissance maiolica, *Renaissance Quaterly* 42, 1 (Spring 1989), 1–32

GRANT, M. H. 1967. *The Makers of Black Basaltes*, London

GRASSMANN, A. 1980. Quellenwert und Aussagemöglichkeiten von Lübecker Archivalien zu den Fragen von Haus und Grundbesitz und Hausbewohnern vor dem Hintergrund der Wirtschafts- und Sozialstrukur, *Lübecker Schriften für Archäologie und Kulturgeschichte* 4, 27–30

Green, J. N. 1977. *The VOC Jacht Vergulde Draeck wrecked in Western Australia 1656*, 1, *British Archaeological Reports* Supplement Series 36, Oxford

Grefrath 1978. *Bauerntöpferei vom Niederrhein 17. bis 20. Jahrhundert*, Schriften des Museumsvereins Dorenburg e. V. 22, Niederrheinisches Freilichtmuseum, Grefrath

Grimm, C. 1984. Stilleben als Quelle für Glasbesitz und Glasgebrauch, in C. Grimm ed. 1984, 294–309

Grimm, C. ed. 1984. *Glück und Glas. Zur Kulturgeschichte des Spessartglases*. Veröffentlichungen zur Bayerischen Geschichte und Kultur 2, Munich

Grimm, C. 1988. *Stilleben. Die niederländischen und deutschen Meister*, Stuttgart, Zürich

Grossmann, F. 1973. *Pieter Brueghel: Complete Edition of the Paintings*, London

Gunson, N. 1982. Black Basalt, in T. A. Lockett & P. A. Halfpenny eds 1982, 53–78

Hackspiel, W. 1982. Zum Haushaltsgeschirr im 18. und 19. Jahrhundert, Archäologie eines Bauernhofes, *Romerike Berge* 32, 2 (May 1982), 10–68

Hackspiel, W. 1987. Neuzeitliche Gläser aus dem Fundkomplex von Haus Gelinde, in *Beiträge zur Archäologie des Rheinlandes*, Rheinische Ausgrabungen 27, Cologne, 437–453

Hackspiel, W. 1988. *Formen der Gebrauchsirdenware vom Niederrhein im 18. und 19. Jahrhundert*, Hetjens-Museum, Düsseldorf

Hackspiel, W. 1993. *Der Scherbenkomplex von Haus Gelinde. Gebrauchsgeschirr des 18. und 19. Jahrhunderts.* Kunst und Altertum am Rhein Nr. 139, Landschaftsverband Cologne/Bonn.

Haedecke, H.-H. 1983. *Zinn*, Munich (3rd edition)

Hagen, J. 1937. Rheinische Münzschatzgefäße aus Mittelalter und Neuzeit, *Bonner Jahrbücher* 142, 177–182

The Hague 1984. *Dutch Painting of the Golden Age*, Mauritshuis, Royal Picture Gallery, The Hague

Hahn, K.-D. 1980. Fundmaterialien, Archäologische Arbeitsmethode und vorläufige Ergebnisse, *Lübecker Schriften für Archäologie und Kulturgeschichte* 4, 17–25

Hähnel, J. ed. 1987. *Siegburger Steinzeug* 1. Führer und Schriften des Rheinischen Freilichtsmuseums und Landesmuseums für Volkskunde in Kommern 31, Cologne

Hähnel, J. 1988. Töpferorte am Niederrhein, in J. Naumann ed. 1988, 15–26

Hähnel, J. 1992. *Siegburger Steinzeug* 2. Führer und Schriften des Rheinischen Freilichtmuseums und Landesmuseums für Volkskunde in Kommern 38, Cologne

Halfpenny, P. A. 1986. Early creamware to 1770, in T. A. Lockett & P. A. Halfpenny eds 1986, 14–19

Hamburg 1989a. *Meissener Blaumalerei aus drei Jahrhunderten*, Museum für Kunst und Gewerbe, Hamburg

Hamburg 1989b. *Die Hanse. Lebenswirklichkeit und Mythos*, Museum für Hamburgische Geschichte, Hamburg

Harrison, B. 1981. *Kraakporselein. een introduktie met 12 voorbleeden*, Gemeentelijk Museum Het Princessehof, Leeuwarden

Harrison, B. 1984. Die Sammlung Captain Hatcher – Chinesisches Porzellan von etwa 1645, *Keramos* 106 (October 1984), 3–12

Haselgrove, D. 1989. Steps towards English stoneware manufacture in the 17th century, *The London Archaeologist* 6, No. 5 (Winter 1989), 132–138

Hasse, M. 1969. *St.- Annen-Museum Lübeck. Bilder und Hausgerät*, Lübeck

Hasse, M. 1979. Neues Hausgerät, neue Häuser, neue Kleider. Eine Betrachtung der städtischen Kultur im 13. und 14. Jahrhundert sowie ein Katalog der metallenen Hausgeräte, *Zeitschrift für Archäologie des Mittelalters* 7, 7–83

Hastenrath, W. 1988. *Töpferware und anderes Haushaltsgerät im Sprachgebrauch des Niederrheins am Beispiel der südniederfränkischen Mundart*, Rheindalen

Hauser, G. 1990. Alltagsgeschirr des 14. Jahrhunderts in Köln, in S. Wirth ed. 1990, 23–36

Hausmann, T. 1973. Review of E. Klinge 1972, in *Keramos*, 61 (July 1973), 65–68

Hayfield, C. 1988. The popularity of medieval vessel forms in Humberside, *Medieval Ceramics*, 12, 57–68

Heege, A. 1995. Die Keramik des frühen und hohen Mittelalters aus dem Rheinland. Stand der Forschung – Typologie, Chronologie, Warenarten, Bonn

Heege, A. 1997. *Hambach 500. Villa rustica und früh- bis hochmittelalterliche Siedlung Wüstweiler* (Gemeinde Niederzier), Kreis Düren. Mit einem Beitrag von K.-H. Knörzer. Rheinische Ausgrabungen 41, Köln/Bonn

Hefner-Alteneck, J. H. & Wolf, J.W. 1850. *Die Burg Tannenberg und ihre Ausgrabungen*, Frankfurt am Main

Heide, H. 1975. Zur Tonaufbereitungs- und Brenntechnik anhand von Dünnschliffen, in B. Beckmann 1975, 340–345

Heinrich, A. 1992. Fischknochen aus mittelalterlichen Siedlungsreste in Duisburg, in Krause, G. ed. *Stadtarchäologie in Duisburg 1980–1990*, Duisburger Forschungen 38, 295–305

Hellebrandt, H., Mayer, O. E. & Hugot, L. 1977. *Steinzeug aus dem Raerener und Aachener Raum*, Aachener Beiträge für Baugeschichte und Heimatkunst 4, Aachen (2nd edition)

Hellenkemper, H. 1990. Archäologische Forschungen in Köln seit 1980, in H. Hellenkemper *et al.* eds 1990, 75–88

Hellenkemper, H., Horn, H.-G., Koschik, H. & Trier, B. eds 1990. *Archäologie in Nordrhein-Westfalen. Geschichte im Herzen Europas*, Schriften zur Bodendenkmalpflege in Nordrhein-Westfalen 1, Römisch-Germanisches Museum der Stadt Köln, Cologne

Herborn, W., Klinger, S., & Schainberg, H. 1987. Studien zur Siegburger Töpferei, in E. Hähnel ed. 1987, 69–103

Heymans, H. ed. 1989. *Van Put naar Kluis. Historisch, bouwhistorisch en archeologisch onderzoek van "Den Prince van Luyck" en "De Stadt Amsterdam" te Maaseik*, Museactron, Maaseik

Hillewaert, B. 1988. Laat-middeleeuwse importceramiek te Brugge, in H. De Witte ed. 1988, 123–140

Hillewaert, B. & Verhaeghe, F. 1991. Een afvalput uit de 16de–18de eeuw, in H. De Witte ed. 1991, 207–251

Hillewaert, B. 1993. Imported Pottery in the Bruges Area. Medieval Ceramics 17, 1993, 61–68

Hillewaert, B. 1995. Daar men potten vercoept... Een laat-middeleeuwse handelaar in aardewerk te Brugge. In: H. Clevis (ed.), Assembled Articles 2. Symposium on Medieval and Post-Medieval Ceramics, Antwerpen 25 and 26 January 1995, Zwolle 15-23

Hinz, H. 1971. Ein mittelalterlicher Töpferofen in Xanten, Kr. Moers, in *Beiträge zur Archäologie des Mittelalters*, 2, Rheinische Ausgrabungen 9, 237–241

Hodder, I. 1982. *Symbols in Action*, Cambridge

Hodder, I. 1986. *Reading the Past. Current Approaches to Interpretation in Archaeology*, Cambridge

Hofius, H. 1978. Archäologische Befunde am Kastellplatz in Duisburg-Ruhrort, *Duisburger Journal* 12, 9–11

Hofius, K. 1982. Archäologische Untersuchungen am Haus Hagen in Duisburg-Meiderich, *Duisburger Forschungen* 31, Duisburg, 137–147

Holling, F. W. 1971. A preliminary note on the pottery industry of the Hampshire-Surrey borders, *Surrey Archaeological Collections*, 68, 57–88

Hook, D. R. 1997. Provenancing Rhenish Stoneware using Neutron Activation Analysis, in D. R. M. Gaimster (1997), 344–353.

Howard, D. S. 1984. *New York and the China Trade*, N. Y. Historical Society, New York

Hughes, M. J. 1991. NAA of Italian maiolica, in T. Wilson ed. 1991, 293–298

Hughes, M. J., Cowell, M. R. & Hook, D. R. 1991. Neutron activation analysis procedures at the British Museum research Laboratory, in M. J. Hughes, M. R. Cowell & D. R. Hook eds, *Neutron activation and plasma emission spectrometric analysis in archaeology: techniques and applications*, British Museum Occasional Paper, 82, 29–45

HUGOT, L. 1977. Aachener Steinzeug, in H. HELLEBRANDT et al. 1977, 225–262

HUPKA, D. 1986. Ofenkacheln aus Neusser Bodenfunden, *Neusser Jahrbuch für Kunst, Kulturgeschichte und Heimatkunde, 1986*, 29–33

HUPKA, D. 1988a. Die Bodenfunde bleiglasierter Irdenware aus Neuss, in J. NAUMANN ed. 1988, 89–99

HUPKA, D. 1988b. Drei Fundkomplexe mit niederrheinischer Irdenware aus Dormagen, Nievenheim und Stürzelberg, Kreis Neuss, *Blätter zur Geschichte von Zons und Stürzelberg*, 4, 4–14

HUPKA, D. 1989. Neue Neusser Bodenfunde. Zur bleiglasierten Irdenware des 13.–18. Jahrhunderts, in J. NAUMANN ed. 1989, 20–23

HURST, J. G. 1965. Post-medieval imported pottery, *Post-Medieval Ceramic Research Group Broadsheet* 2 (January 1965), 5–12

HURST, J. G. 1978. Medieval and post-medieval imports of pottery in Lübeck, *Lübecker Schriften für Archäologie und Kulturgeschichte*, 1, 113–117

HURST, J. G. 1979. Imported pottery, in D. ANDREW & G. MILNE eds, *Wharram: a study of settlement on the Yorkshire Wolds*, 1, Society for Medieval Archaeology, Monograph Series 8, London, 94–95

HURST, J. G. 1988. Problems of Middle-Rhenish stoneware in Britain, in D. R. M. GAIMSTER *et al.* eds 1988, 335–372

HURST, J. G. 1991. Italian pottery imported into Britain and Ireland, in T. WILSON ed. 1991, 212–231

HURST, J. G. & NEAL, D. S. 1982. Late medieval Iberian pottery imported into the Low countries, *Rotterdam Papers* 4, Rotterdam, 83–110

HURST, J. G., NEAL, D. S. & VAN BEUNINGEN, H. J. F. 1975. North Holland Slipware, *Rotterdam Papers*, 2, Rotterdam, 47–65

HURST, J. G., NEAL, D. S. & VAN BEUNINGEN, H. J. E. 1986. *Pottery Produced and Traded to north-west Europe 1350–1650*, Rotterdam Papers 6, Rotterdam

IJZEREEF, F. G. 1989. Social differentation from animal bone studies, in D. SERJEANTSON & T. WALDRON eds 1989, *Diet and Crafts in Towns. The evidence of animal remains from the Roman to the Post-Medieval period*, British Archaeological Reports, British Series 199, 41–53

JANSSEN, H. L. 1983a. Het middeleeuwse aardewerk: ca. 1200 – ca.1550, in H. L. JANSSEN ed., *Van Bos tot Stad. Opgravingen in s'-Hertogenbosch*, Dienst van Gemeentewerken, s'-Hertogenbosch, 182–222

JANSSEN, H. L. 1983b. Later medieval pottery production in the Netherlands, in P. DAVEY & R. HODGES eds 1983, 121–185

JANSSEN, H. L. 1988. The dating and typology of the earliest Siegburg stoneware in the Netherlands, in D. R. M. GAIMSTER et al. eds 1988, 311–333

JANSSEN, W. 1973. Note in Jahresbericht 1971, *Bonner Jahrbücher* 173, 422–455

JANSSEN, W. & JANSSEN, B. 1973. Stand und Aufgaben der Archäologie des Mittelalters im Rheinland. Mit einer Bibliographie 1945–1972, *Zeitschrift für Archäologie des Mittelalters* 1, 141–195

JENNINGS, S. 1981. *Eighteen Centuries of pottery from Norwich*, East Anglian Archaeology 13, Norwich

JONES, M. ed. 1990. *Fake? The Art of Deception*, British Museum, London

JONES, P. 1989. Review of J. PEARCE & A. VINCE, A Dated Type-series of London Medieval Pottery Part 4: Surrey Whitewares, Museum of London & L. A. M. A. S. (1988), *Medieval Ceramics*, 13, 53–55

JOPE, E. M. 1962. The regional cultures of medieval Britain, in I. FOSTER & L. ALCOCK eds, *Culture & Environment*, London, 327–350

JÖRG, C. J. A. 1982. *Porcelain and the Dutch China Trade*, The Hague

JÖRG, C. J. A. 1986. *The Geldermalsen. History and Porcelain*, Groningen

JÖRG, C. J. A. 1990. Kraakporselein, *Antiek* 25, No. 2 (August/September 1990), 53–63

JÜRGENS, A. 1988. Langerwehe – Brühl – Frechen. Neue Grabungen und Erkenntnisse in rheinischen Töpfereizentren, in D. R. M. GAIMSTER et al. eds 1988, 125–150

Jürgens, A. & Bös, B. 1983. Spätmittelalterliche und frühneuzeitliche Töpferöfen in Langerwehe, Kr. Düren, und Frechen, Erftkreis, in *Ausgrabungen in Rheinland '81/82*, Führer des Rheinischen Landesmuseums Bonn, 112, 201–207

Jürgens, A. & Kleine, D. 1988. Werkstattfunde aus Frechen. Brennofen und Irdenware, in J. Naumann ed. 1988, 101–116

Kalmar 1990. *Kronan, Kalmar Läns Museum guide*, 1990

Keene, D. 1983. The use of documentary sources in studying the topography and archaeology of medieval London, *Lübecker Schriften für Archäologie und Kulturgeschichte* 7, 77–84

Kerkhoff-Hader, B. 1980. *Lebens- und Arbeitsformen der Töpfer in der Südwesteifel. Ein Beitrag zur Steinzeugforschung im Rheinland*, Rheinisches Archiv 110, Bonn

Kesselring-Poth, L. 1989. Bemalte Irdenware des 18. Jahrhunderts aus dem Bonner Kapuzinerkloster, in J. Naumann ed. 1989, 35–37

Kessler, G. 2002. *Zur Geschichte des Rheinisch-Westerwäldischen Steinzeugs der Renaissance und des Barock.* Die Werkstätten, Forscher und Sammler, Höhr-Grenzhausen

Kevelaer 1970. *Bauerntöpferei am Niederrhein, 17.–19. Jahrhundert*, Museum für Niederrheinische Volkskunde, Kevelaer

Kisbán, E. 1986. Food habits in change: the example of Europe, in A. Fenton & E. Kisbán eds *Food in change. Eating habits from the Middle Ages to the Present Day*, Edinburgh, 2–10

Klein, A. 1957. *Rheinisches Steinzeug des 15. bis 18. Jahrhunderts*, Wohnkunst und Hausrat – Einst und Jetzt 9, Darmstadt

Kleine, D. 1982. Ofenfunde in Frechen, *Keramos*, 98 (October 1982), 37–44

Kleine, D. 1989. Werkstattfunde aus Frechen – Irdenware, in J. Naumann ed. 1989, 30–34

Klinge, E. 1972. *Siegburger Steinzeug*, Hetjens-Museum, Düsseldorf

Klinge, E. 1979. *Deutsches Steinzeug der Renaissance- und Barockzeit*, Hetjens-Museum, Düsseldorf

Klinge, M. 1982. *Adriaen Brouwer – David Teniers the Younger. A loan exhibition of paintings*, New York, Maastricht

Klinge 1996. *Duits steengoed – German stoneware.* Rijksmuseum Amsterdam, Aspecten van de verzameling Beeldhouwkunst en Kunstnijverheid 7, Amsterdam

Knörzer, K.-H. 1983. Mittelalterliche Pflanzenfunde unter dem Alten Markt in Duisburg, in Duisburg 1983, 78–87

Knörzer, K.- H. 1991. Koproanalyse. Ein neuer Beitrag zur Geschichte der Ernährung, in: Renfrew, J. N. ed., *New light on early farming*, Edinburgh 39-50.

Knörzer, K.-H. 1992. Vorbericht über paläo-ethnobotanische Untersuchungen in Duisburg, in Krause, G. ed. *Stadtarchäologie in Duisburg 1980–1990*, Duisburger Forschungen 38, 1992, 223–236.

Koetschau, K. 1923. *Rheinisches Steinzeug*, Munich

Kohnemann, M. 1982. *Auflagen auf Raerener Steinzeug: Ein Bildwerk*, Raeren

Kommern 1968. *Volkskunst im Rheinland*, Führer und Schriften des Rheinisches Freilichtmuseums Kommern, 4, Kommern

Korf, D. 1971. *Antwerps plateel*, Mededelingenblad nederlandse vereniging vrienden van de ceramiek, 62/63, Nos. 1–2

Korf, D. 1981. *Nederlandse Majolica*, Bussum

Korte-Böger, A. ed. 1991. *Eine Siegburger Töpferwerkstatt der Familie Knütgen. Neue archäologische und historische Forschungen zur Unteren Aulgasse*, Kunst und Altertum am Rhein 133, Cologne

Koschik, H. 1990. Bodendenkmalpflege im Rheinland, in H. Hellenkemper et al. eds 1990, 44–57

Krause, G. 1983. Archäologische Zeugnisse zum mittelalterlichen Duisburg, in *Duisburg* 1983, 23–77

Krause, G. 1986. Übersicht über die mittelalterliche Keramik am Unteren Niederrhein (ca. 800–1500) nach den Funden aus Duisburg, in *Duisburg* 1986, 7–28

KRAUSE, G. 1987. Ausgrabungen und Fundbergungen in der Duisburger Altstadt 1985/1986, in *Ausgrabungen im Rheinland '85/86*, Rheinisches Amt für Bodendenkmalpflege, Bonn, 176–183

KRAUSE, G. 1988. Keramikproduktion am Niederrhein. Die Duisburger Abfolge von ca. 5.–14. Jahrhundert, in J. NAUMANN ed. 1988, 37–54

KRAUSE, G. 1989. Eine Schichtenabfolge vom 5. bis ins 20. Jahrhundert auf dem Alten Markt in Duisburg, in *Archäologie im Rheinland 1988*, Rheinisches Amt für Bodendenkmalpflege, Bonn, 93–95

KRAUSE, G. 1990a. Stadtarchäologie in Duisburg, in H. HELLENKEMPER et al. eds 1990, 294–303

KRAUSE, G. 1990b. Die Duisburger Altstadt von den Anfängen bis in die Neuzeit, in G. TROMNAU ed. 1990, 66–86

KRAUSE, G. 1990c. Zur Geschichte der archäologischen Forschung in Duisburg, in TROMNAU, G. ed., Führer zur archäologischen Denkmälern in Deutschland 21, Duisburg und der untere Niederrhein, 24–29

KRAUSE, G. 1992. Stadtarchäologie in Duisburg, in: KRAUSE, G. ed., *Stadtarchäologie in Duisburg 1980–1990*. Duisburger Forschungen 38, Duisburg, 1–65

KRAUSE, G. 1994. Archäologische und naturwissenschaftliche Untersuchungen im Bereich der Duisburger Altstadt, mit Beiträgen von H. BERKE, R. GERLACH, K. – H. KNÖRZER, J. MEURERS-Balke, in *Germania* 72, 529–579

KRAUSE, G. 1994a. Pottery Sequences of the 13th to 16th centuries from Duisburg, Lower Rhine, in: Assembled Articles I, *Symposium on Medieval and Postmedieval Ceramics*, Nijmegen 2 and 3 September 1993, Nijmegen, 153–169

KRAUSE, G. 1994b. Museum Rescue-Archaeology in Duisburg, the Lower Rhineland, in: *Museum Archaeology in Europe*. Proceedings of a conference held at the British Museum 15-17th October 1992. The Museum Archaeologist vol. 19 (The Society of Museum Archaeologists) = Oxbow Monograph 39, 49–75

KRAUSE, G.1997. Archaeological evidence of medieval shipping from the Old Town of Duisburg, Lower Rhineland, in: *Travel Technology and Organisation in medieval Europe*. Papers of the 'Medieval Brugge 1997' Conference, Volume 8, 101–116

KRAUSE, G. 1998. Vergangenheit ohne Zukunft? Archäologische Zeugnisse aus Duisburg-Huckingen und dem Duisburger Süden von den Anfängen bis ins Industriezeitalter, Duisburg

KRAUSE, G. 1999. Duisburg, Lower Rhineland. The Harbour and the Topography of the Town from the Merowingian Period to c. 1600, in: Jan Bill (ed.), *Maritime topography and the Medieval Town*. Papers from the 5th International Congress on Waterfront Archaeology in Copenhagen 14.16 May 1998. PNM Studies in Archaeology and History vol. 4, Kopenhagen, 99–108

KRAUSE, G. 2002. Duisburg and its environs at the confluence of Rhine and Ruhr from the Late Antiquity to the Industrial Age – Essential aspects of its development according to archaeological and historical sources, in *Medieval Europe* Basel 2002. 3rd international conference of medieval and later archaeology Basel 10–15. September 2002. Preprinted Papers volume 2, 155–165

KRAUSE, G. 2003. Duisburg als Handels- und Hafenort im Mittelalter und der frühen Neuzeit, in *Mitteilungen der deutschen Gesellschaft für Archäologie des Mittelalters und der Neuzeit* 14, 2003, 30 – 42

KRAUSE, G. 2004. Stadtarchäologie in Duisburg gestern und heute. Von den Schwierigkeiten bei der Suche nach den Wurzeln unserer städtischen Zivilisation, in: *Schild von Steier*, Kleine Schriften 20, Graz, 117–135

KÜHNEL, H. 1985. *Alltag im Spätmittelalter*, Graz (2nd edition)

LAUX, F. 1982. Der Lüneburger Schweinetopf: Ein Gefäß der bürgerlichen Küche des 17. Jahrhunderts, in Bremen 1982, 123–132

LEESE, M. N., HUGHES, M. J. H. & CHERRY, J. 1986. A scientific study of N. Midlands medieval tile production, *Oxford Journal of Archaeology*, 5, No. 3, 355–370

LEHNEMANN, W. 1976. Die Fayancemanufaktur Telgte, *Keramos*, 72 (May 1976), 45–54

LEHNEMANN, W. 1978. *Irdentöpferei in Westfalen: 17. bis 20. Jahrhundert*, Schriften der Volkskundlichen Kommission Westfalen 24, Münster

LEHNEMANN, W. ed. 1980. *Töpferei in Nordwestdeutschland*, Beiträge zur Volkskultur in Nordwestdeutschland 3, Münster

LEHNEMANN, W. 1982. Fayencemanufakturen zwischen Rhein und Weser, *Keramos* 96 (March 1982), 65–78

LEMOINE, C., WALKER, S. & PICON, M. 1982. Archaeological, geochemical and statistical methods in ceramic provenance studies, in J. S. OLIN & A. D. FRANKLIN eds, *Archaeological Ceramics*, Washington, 57–64

LEXINGTON 1985. *Unearthing New Englands Past: The Ceramic Evidence*, Museum of our National heritage, Lexington, MA

L'HOUR, M., LONG, L. & RIETH, E. 1989. *Le Mauritius. La Mémoire Engloutie*, Grenoble

L'HOUR, M. & RICHEZ, P. 1990. An 18th century French East Indiaman: the Prince de Conty (1746), *International Journal of Nautical Archaelogy* 19:1, 75–79

L'HOUR, M. *et al.* 1990. The wreck of an "experimental" ship of the Oost-Indische Companie: the Mauritius (1609), *International Journal of Nautical Archaeology* 19.1, 63–73

LIEBGOTT, N.-K. 1972. *Kakler. Hovedtraek af kakkelovens historie ca. 1350–1650*, Nationalmuseet, Copenhagen

LIEBGOTT, N.-K. 1978. Danske Fund af Montdateret Keramik ca. 950–1450, *Arkaeologisk-historisk raekke*, 18, Nationalmuseet, Copenhagen

LIGHTLEY, R. A. 1976. An 18th century Dutch East Indiaman found at Cape Town, 1971, *International Journal of Nautical Archaeology* 5:3, 305–316

LIPPERHEIDE, B. 1961. *Das rheinische Steinzeug und die Graphik der Renaissance*, Berlin

LOBBEDEY, U. 1968. *Untersuchungen mittelalterlicher Keramik vornehmlich aus Südwestdeutschland*, Arbeiten zur Frühmittelalterforschung 3, Berlin

LÖBERT, H. 1980. Das keramische Inventar einer Abfallgrube des 16. Jahrhunderts aus Göttingen. Studien zum Handel, zur Funktion und sozialgeschichtlichen Interpretationen frühneuzeitlicher Keramik, *Zeitschrift für Archäologie des Mittelalters* 8, 7–45

LOCKETT, T. A. 1982. Salt-glazed stoneware, in T. A. LOCKETT & P. A. HALFPENNY eds 1982, 35–52

LOCKETT, T. A. & HALFPENNY, P. A. eds 1982. *Stonewares and Stone Chinas of Northern England to 1851*, City Museum & Art Gallery, Stoke-on-Trent

LOCKETT, T. A. & HALFPENNY, P. A. eds 1986. *Creamware & Pearlware*, City Museum & Art Gallery, Stoke-on-Trent

London 1968. *Pictures & Drawings*, Wallace Collection Catalogues, London

London 1976. *Art in Seventeenth Century Holland*, The National Gallery, London

London 1988. *The Harold Samuel Collection. 17th century-Dutch Painting*, Barbican Art Gallery, London

LULEY, H. 1990. Ausgrabungen im Schloss Brake, in HELLENKEMPER *et al.* 1990, 318–325

LUNG, W. 1955–6. Die Ausgrabungen nach-karolingischer Töpferöfen in Paffrath, Gem. Bergisch Gladbach, Rheinisch-Bergischer Kr., *Bonner Jahrbücher*, 155/156, 355–371

LUNSINGH-SCHEURLEER, D. F. 1970. *Wits delfts*, Lochem

LUNSINGH-SCHEURLEER, D.F. 1973. Invloed en navolging van het Chinese Wan Li-en Overgangs-porselein op Nord-Nederlandse majolica, *Mededelingenblad vrienden van de nederlandse ceramiek*, 60, Pt. 3, 7–21

LUNSINGH-SCHEURLEER, D. F. 1975. *Delfts Blauw*, Bussum

LUNSINGH-SCHEURLEER, T. Th. 1976. The Dutch at the tea-table, *Connaisseur* 193, No. 776 (Oct. 1976), 85–93

MARSDEN, P. 1985. *The Wreck of the Amsterdam*, London

MAYER, O. E. 1977. Fünfundzwanzig Jahre Grabungen im Raerener Land, in H. HELLEBRANDT et al. 1977, 172–224

MCCARTHY, M. 1979. The pottery, in J. H. WILLIAMS, *St. Peter's Street Northampton. Excavations 1973–1976*, Northampton Development Corporation Archaeological Monograph 2, 151–240

McKendrick, N. 1982. Josiah Wedgwood and the commercialisation of the Potteries, in N. McKendrick, J. Brewer & J. H. Plumb eds, *The Birth of the Consumer Society. The Commercialisation of Eighteenth-century England*, London, 100–145

Medieval Pottery Research Group, in prep. *Guidelines for the processing and publication of medieval pottery*

Mellor, M. 1984. The Pottery, in T. G. Hassall, C. E. Halpin & M. Mellor, Excavations in St. Ebbe's, Oxford, 1967–1976: Pt .II, *Oxoniensia*, XLIX, 211–219

Mennell, S. 1988. *Die Kultivierung des Appetits. Die Geschichte des Essens vom Mittelalter bis heute*, Frankfurt am Main

Metzger, M. 1900. Lübecker Ofenkacheln der Renaissancezeit. Eine Studie, in *Das Museum in Lübeck, Festschrift zur Erinnerung an das 100 jährige Bestehen der Sammlungen der Gesellschaft zur Beförderung gemeinnütziger Tätigkeit*, Lübeck, 125–152

Meurers-Balke, J., Knörzer, K.-H., Glasmacher, H.-A., Berke, H., Gerlach, R., Tegtmeier, U. 1999. Ein spätmittelalterlicher Brunnen in der Duisburger Niederstraße, in *Bonner Jahrbücher* 199, 347–396

Meyer-Heisig, E. 1954. *Mit Drehscheibe und Malhorn*, Germanisches Nationalmuseum, Nuremberg

Mielke, H.-P. 1977. Zur Typologie und Datierung gotischer Nischenkacheln mit dem Mainzer Rad, *Mainzer Zeitschrift* 71/72, 149–157

Mielke, H.P. 1981a. Von der Ofenkachel zum Kachelofen. Keramische Ofenelemente am Flussystem der Weser, in H.-P. Mielke ed., *Keramik an Weser, Werra und Fulda*, Schriften des Mindener Museums für Geschichte, Landes- und Volkskunde, Kunstgeschichtliche Reihe 1, Lübbecke, 107–114

Mielke, H.- P. 1981b. Ein hessischer Hafner und sein Werk: Hans Bermann, *Kunst in Hessen und am Mittelrhein* 21, 23–52

Mielke, H.-P. 1983. Handelswege und Umschlagplätze für Ofenkeramik, in *Beiträge zur Keramik 2*, Hetjens-Museum, Düsseldorf, 59–61

Mielke, H.- P. 1989. Langlebigkeit gotischer Kacheln am Niederrhein, in J. Naumann ed. 1989, 83–84

Millett, M. 1987. A Question of Time? Aspects of the future of pottery studies, *Bulletin of the Institute of Archaeology* 24, 99–108

Milz, J. 1982. Untersuchungen zur mittelalterlichen Stadtmauer von Duisburg. Mit einem Beitrag über die archäologischen Funde, in Krause G. ed., *Vor- und Frühgeschichte des unteren Niederrheins*. Rudolf Stampfuß zum Gedächtnis. Quellenschriften zur westdeutschen Vor- und Frühgeschichte, 135–171

Milz, J. 2005. Duisburger Topographie im 16. Jahrhundert. Duisburger Forschungen 52

Mohrmann, R. E. 1985. Wohnen und Wohnkultur in nordwestdeutschen Städten im Spätmittelalter und in der frühen Neuzeit, in Braunschweig 1985, 513–525

Moorhouse, S. 1981. The medieval pottery industry and its markets, in D. W. Crossley ed. *Medieval Industries, Council for British Archaeology* Research Reports 40, 96–125

Moorhouse, S. 1982. The pottery, in J. R. Hunter, Medieval Berwick-uponTweed, *Archaeologia Aeliana*, 5th Ser. 10, 99–123

Moorhouse, S. 1983a. The medieval pottery, in P. Mayes & L. A. S. Butler, *Sandal Castle Excavations 1964–1973*, Wakefield Historical Publications, Wakefield, 83–212

Moorhouse, S. 1983b. Documentary evidence and its potential for understanding the inland movement of medieval pottery, *Medieval Ceramics* 7, 45–87

Moorhouse, S. 1986. The non-dating uses of medieval pottery, *Medieval Ceramics* 10, 85–124

Moulin, L. 1988. *Augenlust & Tafelfreude. Essen und Trinken in Europa. Eine Kulturgeschichte*, Antwerp

Müller, G. & Wentscher, J. 1981. Ein Töpferofen vom Raerener Typ in Langerwehe, in *Ausgrabungen im Rheinland 1979/80*, Führer des Rheinischen Landesmuseums Bonn 104, 207–209

Müller, J. 1992. Zur Baugeschichte der Stadtmauer am Innenhafen und am Springwall, in Krause G. ed. *Stadtarchäologie in Duisburg 1980–1990.* Duisburger Forschungen 38, Duisburg, 463–519

Müller, P. 1988. Neue Bodenfunde aus Wesel, in J. Naumann ed. 1988, 153–157

Munich 1986. *Sammlung Fritz Thyssen. Ausgewählte Meisterwerke*, Bayerisches Nationalmuseum, Munich

Naumann, J. ed. 1988. *Keramik vom Niederrhein. Die Irdenware der Duppen- und Pottbäcker zwischen Köln und Kleve*, Veröffentlichungen des Kölnischen Stadtmuseums 4, Cologne

Naumann, J. ed. 1989. *Keramik vom Niederrhein und ihr internationales Umfeld. Internationales Keramik-Symposium in Duisburg*, Düsseldorf und Neuss 1988, Beiträge zur Keramik 3, Hetjens-Museum, Düsseldorf

Naumann, J. *et al.* 1988. Keramik vom Niederrhein, *Weltkunst* 19, 2802–2808

Neu, S. 1990. Zwei spätmittelalterliche Töpferofen an der Severinstrasse, in S. Wirth ed. 1990, 37–48

Neuss 1986. *Von Pieter Breughel bis Gerrard Terboch. Niederländische Meister aus eigenem Bestand und Rheinischem Privatbesitz*, Clemens-Sels Museum, Neuss

New York 1975. *The Secular Spirit: Life and Art at the End of the Middle Ages*, Metropolitan Museum of Art, New York

Nienhaus, H. 1989a. Selterswasserkrüge – Möglichkeiten und Grenzen der Altersbestimmung, *Keramos* 123 (January 1989), 71–84

Nienhaus, H. 1989b. Keramische Bruchstücke ersetzen schriftliche Dokumente, *Keramos* 126 (October 1989), 47–60

Nobis, G., Ninov, L. 1992. Zur Haustierwelt des Mittelalters. Nach Studien an Tierresten aus der Altstadt von Duisburg, in Krause, G. ed. Stadtarchäologie in Duisburg 1980-1990, Duisburger Forschungen 38, 1992, 237-294

Noël Hume, I. 1989. The wells of Williamsburg. Colonial time capsules, *Colonial Williamsburg Archaeological Series* 4, Williamsburg

Nottebrock, J. 1926. Die Aachener-Frankfurter Heerstraße in ihrem Verlauf von Aachen bis Sinzig, *Bonner Jahrbücher* 131, 245–284

Nuremberg 1952. *Deutsche Kunst und Kultur im Germanischen Nationalmuseum*, Germanisches Nationalmuseum, Nuremberg

Nuremberg 1984. *Aus dem Wirtshaus zum Wilden Mann. Funde aus dem mittelalterlichen Nürnberg*, Germanisches Nationalmuseum, Nuremberg

Ocklenburg, U 1997. Ein spätmittelalterlicher Töpferofen aus Brühl. In: *Archäologie im Rheinland* 1996, Köln/Bonn, 136-138.

Ohm, Schmitt & Brockmeier, 1971. Die Langerwehe Keramik, Töpfereimuseum Langerwehe, *RWE-Verbund Werkszeitschrift*, 76 (October 1971)

Oost, T. 1988. Het archeologisch onderzoek in 1982, in *750 jaar Gasthuis op't Elzenveld 1238–1988, Het St. Elisabethziekenhuis te Antwerpen.* Brussels

Orton, C. R. 1975. Quantitative pottery studies. Some progress, problems and prospects, *Science and Archaeology*, 16, 30–35

Orton, C. R. 1977. Studying the City's pottery, *The London Archaeologist*, 3, No. 4 (Autumn 1977), 100–105

Orton, C. R. 1979. Dealing with the pottery from a 600 acre urban site, in M. Millett ed., *Pottery and the Archaeologist*, Institute of Archaeology Occasional Papers, 4, University of London, 61–71

Orton, C. R. 1980. *Mathematics in Archaeology*, Cambridge

Orton, C. 1982a. The Excavation of a Late Medieval Transitional Pottery Kiln at Cheam, Surrey, *Surrey Archaeological Collections*, 73, 49–92

Orton, C. 1982b. Pottery evidence for the dating of the revetments, in G. Milne & C. Milne, *Medieval waterfront development at Trig Lane, London*, Transactions of the London and Middlesex Archaeological Society, Special Paper, 5, 92–99

Orton, C. 1985. Diffusion or Impedance – Obstacles to innovation in medieval ceramics, *Medieval Ceramics*, 9, 21–34

Orton, C. 1986. Quantification of pottery assemblages, *West Midlands Research Group Newsletter* 9 (October 1986), 15-17

Orton, C. 1987. The "Envelope": Un nouvel outil pour l'etude morphologique des ceramiques, in J. Chapelot et al. eds 1987, 33–41

Orton, C. 1988. Post-Roman Pottery, in P. Hinton ed., *Excavations in Southwark 1973–76, Lambeth 1973–79*, London and Middlesex Archaeological Society & Surrey Archaeological Society Joint Publication 3, 295–364

Orton, C. & Pearce, J. 1984. The Pottery, in A. Thompson et al. 1984, 34–68

Pabst, A. 1889. *Kunstvolle Thongefässe aus dem 16.–18. Jahrhundert. Sammlung des Freiherrn Albert von Offenheim*, Köln, Berlin

Päffgen, B. 1995. Spätmittelalterliche Töpfereifunde aus Langerwehe, Kreis Düren, in *Ein Land macht Geschichte.* Archäologie in Nordrhein-Westfalen. Begleitbuch zur Landesausstellung, Mainz, 339–343

Panhuysen, T. A. S. M. 1984. *Maastricht staat op zijn verleden*, Stichting Historische Reeks Maastricht, Maastricht

Peacock, D. P. S. 1982. *Pottery in the Roman World*, Harlow

Pearce, J. E. 1981. Chinese Porcelain, in J. Maloney ed., *The contents of a late 18th century pit at Crosswall, City of London, Transactions of the London and Middlesex Archaeological Society*, 32, 159–182

Peremans, P. 1986. Archeologica op de kreukenstukken en de Markttafferleren van Joachim Beuckelaer, in Ghent 1986, 53–60

Philadelphia 1984. *Masters of Seventeenth-Century Dutch Genre Painting*, Philadelphia Museum of Art, Philadelphia

Platt, C. & Coleman-Smith, D. 1975. *Excavations in Medieval Southhampton 1953–1969*, 2, *The Finds*, Leicester

Price, R. & Muckelroy, K. 1974. The second season of work on the Kennemerland site, 1973. An interim report, *International Journal of Nautical Archaelogy*, 3:2, 257–268

Price, R. & Muckelroy, K. 1979. The Kennemerland site. The fifth season, 1978. An interim report, *International Journal of Nautical Archaelogy*, 8:4, 311–320

Prieur-Pohl, J. 1989. Die Stadt Wesel. Wesel als Hansestadt, in Hamburg 1989, 222–224

Rackham, B. 1926. *Early Netherlands Maiolica with Special reference to the Tiles at the Vyne in Hampshire*, London

Rackham, B. 1939. A Netherlands Maiolica Vase from the Tower of London, *Antiquaries Journal* 19, 285–290

Radomérsky, P. 1968. Zur Datierung von Siegburger Steinzeug mit Hilfe eines Mainzer Schüsselpfennigs, *Forschungen und Berichte* 11, Staatliche Museen zu Berlin, Berlin, 35–38

Rech, M. 1979. Ergebnisse der Ausgrabungen in Burg Brüggen, Kr. Viersen, *Bonner Jahrbücher* 179, 565–611

Rech, M. 1982. Mittelalterliche Keramik der Töpfereien um Elmpt und Brüggen aus der Sammlung Franz Janssen, Brüggen, *Zeitschrift für Archäologie des Mittelalters* 10, 147–169

Redknap, M. 1987. *Mayenerware and Eifelkeramik: The Roman and medieval pottery industries of the West German Eifel*, University of London, Ph.D. Diss.

Redknap, M. 1988. Medieval pottery production at Mayen: recent advances, current problems, in D. R. M. Gaimster et al. eds 1988, 3–37

Redman, C. L. 1978. Multivariate artefact analysis: A basis for multidimensional interpretation, in C. L. Redman et al. eds, *Social Archaeology. Beyond Subsistence & Dating*, New York, 159–172

Redman, C .L. 1986a. *Qsar es-Seghir. An Archaeological View of Medieval Life*, London

Redman, C.L. 1986b. Methods used to compare Islamic ceramic assemblages from northern Morocco, in *II Coloquio Ceramica Medieval del Mediterraneo Occidental*, Toledo 1981, Ministerio de Cultura, Madrid, 11–19

Reichmann, Ch. 1982. Ausgrabungen in einem Linner Haus, *Die Heimat* 53, Krefeld, 35–44

Reichmann, Ch. 1988. Das Haushaltsgeschirr des Syndikus Kupers um 1784, in J. Naumann ed. 1988, 125–134

Reichmann, Ch. 1989. *Festtagsschüsseln vom Niederrhein*, Museum Burg Linn, Krefeld

Reichstein, H. 1992. Vogelknochen aus mittelalterlichen Siedlungsabfällen in Duisburg, in Krause, G. ed. *Stadtarchäologie in Duisburg 1980–1990*, Duisburger Forschungen 38, 306–315

Reineking-von Bock, G. ed. 1966 *Rheinische Töpferkunst*, exhibition catalogue Frechen, Cologne

Reineking-von Bock, G. 1970. Steinzeug – Nachahmung, Nachbildung oder Fälschung, *Keramos* 49 (July 1970), 3–66

Reineking-von Bock, G. 1980. Verbreitung von rheinischem Steinzeug, *Lübecker Schriften für Archäologie und Kulturgeschichte* 4, Bonn, 115–119

Reineking-von Bock, G. 1981. Die Bedeutung Kölns für das rheinische Steinzeug im 16. Jahrhundert, *Weltkunst* 17 (September 1981), 2358–2361

Reineking-von Bock, G. 1986. *Steinzeug*, Kataloge des Kunstgewerbemuseums Köln, Bd. 4, Cologne

Reineking-von Bock, G. 1989. Steinzeug in Raeren, *Keramos*, 125 (July 1989), 87–106

Renaud, J. G. N. 1952. Middeleeuwse gebruiksvoorwerpen, Spangen (ZuidHolland), *Berichten van de Rijksdienst voor het Oudheidkundig Bodenonderzoek* 3, 53–62

Renaud, J. G. N. 1959a. Aardewerkvondsten van het Klooster Mariendael, *Berichten van de Rijksdienst voor het Oudheidkundig Bodenonderzoek* 9, 199–224

Renaud, J. G. N. 1959b. Laat-middeleeuws aardewerk met ornament in sgraffito, *Berichten van de Rijksdienst voor het Oudheidkundig Bodenonderzoek* 9, 225–237

Renaud, J. G. N. 1959c. Voorlopers van "Delfts" uit opgravingen, *Berichten van de Rijksdienst voor het Oudheidkundig Bodenonderzoek* 9, 238–244

Renaud, J. G. N. 1989. Vijftig jaar slibkras-aardewerk, *Mededelingenblad nederlandse verenigung van vrienden van de ceramiek* 134, No. 2, 4–12

Ressing, H.-H. 1989. Frankfurter Fayencen aus der Zeit des Barock, *Mededelingenblad nederlandse vereniging van vrienden van de ceramiek* 134, No. 2, 13–18

Ricke, H. 1987. Glas des Mittelalters und der frühen Neuzeit, in E. Baumgartner ed., *Glas des späten Mittelalters. Die Sammlung Karl Amendt*, Kunstmuseum Düsseldorf, Düsseldorf, 11–22

Rinaldi, M. 1989. *Kraak porcelain: A Moment in the History of Trade*, London

Roehmer, M. 1998. *Burg Friedestrom in Zons.* Mittelalterliche Keramik und Baubefunde einer rheinischen Zollfestung. Mit Beitr. v. B. Hollack, M. Kunter u. F. Siegmund. Rheinische Ausgrabungen 42, Köln/Bonn

Roehmer, M. 2001. *Steinzeug.* In H. Lüdtke u. K. Schietzel, Handbuch zur mittelalterlichen Keramik in Nordeuropa. Mit Beiträgen von A. Falk, T. Kemke et al. Schriften des Archäologischen Landesmuseums 6, Neumünster 465-535

Röntgen, R. E. 1989. Die Nachahmungen und Verfälschungen des Strohblumenmusters, in Hamburg 1989, 80–81

Rotterdam 1973. *Verdraaid goed gedraaid. Verzameling H. J. E. van Beuningen*, Museum Boymans-van Beuningen Rotterdam, Rotterdam

Ruempol, A. & Garthoff-Zwaan, M. 1988. *Communicerende Vaten. Beeldtaal van silbversiering* op *laat-middeleeuws aardewerk in de Nederlanden*, Museum Boymans-van Beuningen, Rotterdam

Ruempol, A. P. E. & van Dongen, A.G.A. 1991. *Pre-industrial Utensils 1150–1800*, Museum Boymans-van Beuningen, Rotterdam

Ruppel, Th. 1988. Spuren der Duisburger Fayencemanufaktur, in Th. Ruppel et al., *Beiträge zur Duisburger Stadtarchäologie. Zwei Jahre Modellprojekt "Stadtgeschichte"*, Niederrheinisches Museum der Stadt Duisburg, Duisburg, 142–144

Ruppel, Th. 1989. Ausgrabungen im Duisburger Stapelviertel, in *Archäologie im Rheinland 1988*, Rheinisches Amt für Bodendenkmalpflege, Bonn, 110–111

Ruppel, Th. 1991a. Siegburg, Aulgasse Nr. 8 – Die Ausgrabungsergebnisse im Überblick, in A. Korte-Böger ed. 1991, 15–28

Ruppel, Th. 1991b. Zur Brandschatzung der Aulgasse während des Truchsessischen Krieges. Historische Überlieferung und archäologische Spuren, in A. Korte-Böger ed. 1991, 59–63

Sarfatij, H. 1979. Münzschatzgefäße in den Niederlanden I: Die Periode 1190–1566, *Berichten van de Rijksdienst voor het Oudheidkundig Bodenonderzoek* 29, 491–526

Sauer, S. 1988. Ein reichhaltig verfüllter Brunnenschacht vom Gelände des mittelalterlichen Gasthauses, *Neusser Jahrbuch für Kunst, Kulturgeschichte und Heimatkunde*, 1988, 33–39

Sauer, S. 1989. Ein frühneuzeitlich verfüllter Marktbrunnen, in *Archäologie im Rheinland 1988*, Rheinisches Amt für Bodendenkmalpflege, 152–153

Sauerlandt, M. 1928. Über Rheinische Steinzeugkrüge mit englischer Goldschmiedefassung, in P. Clemen ed., *Karl Koetschau von seinen Freunden und Verehrern zum 60. Geburtstag am 27. März 1928*, Kunstverein für die Rheinlande und Westfalen, Düsseldorf, 67–83

Schama, S. 1988. *The Embarrassment of Riches. An Interpretation of Dutch Culture in the Golden Age*, London

Scheil, E. 1977. *Fayencen in der Malerei des Mittelalters*, Diss., Munich

Schiffer, M. B. 1987. *Formation Processes of the Archaeological Record*, Albuquerque

Schilling, L. 1991. Katalog, in V. Burhenne et al. 1991, 90–140

Schnall, U. 1989b. Zur Binnenschiffahrt im Mittelalter, Hamburg, 592–593

Schneider, N. 1989. *Stilleben. Realität und Symbolik der Dinge. Die Stillebenmalerei der frühen Neuzeit*, Cologne

Scholten, F. 1989. Frankfurt revisited, *Mededelingenblad nederlandse verenigung van vrienden van de ceramiek* 134, No. 2, 19–23

Scholten-Neess, M. 1975. Vierzehn Ofenkacheln, *Rheydter Jahrbuch* 11, 131–137

Scholten-Neess, M. 1979. Duisburger Töpferfamilien, *Duisburger Forschungen* 27, Duisburg, 28–35

Scholten-Neess, M. & Jüttner, W. 1971. *Niederrheinische Bauerntöpferei 17.– 19. Jahrhundert*, Werken und Wohnen. Volkstümliche Untersuchungen im Rheinland 7, Düsseldorf

Schulz, C. 1990. Keramik des 14. und 16. Jahrhunderts aus der Fronerei in Lübeck, *Lübecker Schriften für Archäologie und Kulturgeschichte* 19, 163–264

Schütte, S. 1985. Bürgerliches Hausgerät des Hoch- und Spätmittelalters in Nordwestdeutschland, in Braunschweig 1985, 545–568

Schwarz, J. 1984. *Das Langerweher Töpfergewerbe in der Vergangenheit*, Töpfereimuseum Langerwehe, Langerwehe

Segal, S. 1983. *Niederländische Stilleben von Breughel bis van Gogh*, Amsterdam

Segal, S. 1988. *A Prosperous Past. The Sumptuous Still-Life in the Netherlands 1600–1700*, The Hague

Sheaf, C. & Kilburn, R. 1988. *The Hatcher Cargoes. The Complete Record*, Oxford

Siegmund, F. 1994. Jülich. Scherben und Schichten zu den Feuersbrünsten des 15. und 16. Jahrhunderts in M. Perse ed., Beiträge zur Jülicher Archäologie III. *Jülicher Geschichtsblätter* 62 (1994) 131–184

Siepen-Koepke, M. 1990. *Untersuchungen des mittelalterlichen Burggrabens der Burg Uda, Grefrath, Kr. Viersen*, Lecture to congress of Nordwestdeutscher Verband für Altertumsforschung e. V., Duisburg 1990

Sievers, J. 1908. *Pieter Aertsen. Ein Beitrag zur Geschichte der niederländischen Kunst im 16. Jahrhundert*, Kunstgeschichtliche Monographien 9, Leipzig

Smart Martin, A. 1989. The role of pewter as a missing artefact: consumer attitudes toward tablewares in late 18th-century Virginia, *Historical Archaeology* 23, No. 2, 1–27

Smetánka, Z. 1969. K Morphologii Českých Středověkých Kachlů, (Zur Morphologie der böhmischen mittelalterlichen Kacheln), *Památky archeologické* 60, 228–264

Soechting, D. ed. 1976. *Archäologie eines Bauernhofes*, Führer des Regionalmuseums Xanten 2, Xanten

Soffner, A. 1987. Keramik, in M. Untermann 1987, 414–434

Solon, M. L. 1892. *The Ancient Art of Stoneware of the Low Countries and Germany or "Gres de Flandres" and "Steinzeug"*, London

Spiegel, H. 1980. Über die Entwicklung des historischen Steinzeugs am Beispiel des Westerwälder Steinzeugs, *Beiträge zur Keramik* 1, Hetjens Museum, Düsseldorf, 4–19

Stanbury, M. 1974. *Batavia Catalogue*, Department of Maritime Archaeology, Western Australia Museum, Perth

Steinbring, B. 2001. Ein Keramikkopf aus Erberich, Gem. Eschweiler-Lohn, Kr. Aachen. In: E. Pohl, U. Recker u. C. Theune, *Archäologisches Zellwerk.* Beiträge zur Kulturgeschichte in Europa u. Asien. Festschrift H. Roth, Rahden/Westf., 609–613

Stenuit, R. 1974. Early relics of the VOC trade from Shetland. The wreck of the flute Lastdrager lost off Yell, 1653, *International Journal of Nautical Archaeology*, 3:2, 213–256

Stephan, H.-G. 1980a. Zur Typologie und Chronologie von Keramik des 17. Jahrhunderts im Oberweserraum, in W. Lehnemann ed. 1980, 69–124

Stephan, H.-G. 1980b. Überlegungen zur wirtschafts- und sozialgeschichtlichen Interpretation archäologischer Fundmaterialien des späten Mittelalters und der Neuzeit. Am Beispiel ausgewählter Fundkomplexe des 16. und 17. Jahrhunderts aus Göttingen und Höxter, *Lübecker Schriften für Archäologie und Kulturgeschichte*, 4, 120–131

Stephan, H.-G. 1981. Werra-Keramik und Weserware: Zentren der Renaissancekeramik im Werraland und an der Oberweser, in H.-P. Mielke ed. 1981, 69–90

Stephan, H.-G. 1982. Die mittelalterliche Keramik in Norddeutschland (1200–1500), in Bremen 1982, 65–122

Stephan, H.-G. 1983. The developmemt and production of medieval stoneware in Germany, in P. Davey & R. Hodges 1983 eds, 95–120

Stephan, H.-G. 1987a. *Grossalmerode. Ein Zentrum der Herstellung von technischer Keramik,* Steinzeug und Irdenware in Hessen, 1, Glas- und Keramik Museum, Grossalmerode

Stephan, H.-G. 1987b. *Die bemalte Irdenware der Renaissance in Mitteleuropa. Ausstrahlungen und Verbindungen der Produktionszentren im gesamteuropäischen Rahmen*, Forschungshefte Bayerisches Nationalmuseum, 12, Munich

Stephan, H.-G. 1987c. Keramikproduktion und -handel in Nordwesteuropa 1350–1650, *Zeitschrift für Archäologie des Mittelalters* 14/15, (1986/1987) 153–165

Stephan, H.-G. 1988. Diskussionsbeitrag zur Abgrenzung und Definition mittelalterlicher deutscher Steinzeuggruppen, in Gaimster *et al.* eds 1988, 81–117

Stephan, H.-G. 1990. Review of I. Unger ed. 1988, *Post-Medieval Archaeology*, 24, 238–40

Stephan, H.-G. 1991. Neue Forschungen zur Werraware der Renaissance. Unter besonderer Berücksichtigung der Verbindung zu den Niederlanden und der frühen Malhornware des Rheinlandes, in V. Burhenne *et al.* eds 1991, 69–85

Stoepker, H. 1986. *Graven naer het Kasteel van Tilburg*, Bijdragen tot de Studie van het Brabantse Heem, Deel 29, Waalre

Strauss, K. 1968. Der Kachelofen in der graphischen Darstellung des 15. und 16. Jahrhunderts, *Keramos*, 39 (June 1968), 22–37

Strauss, K. 1972. *Die Kachelkunst des 15. und 16. Jahrhunderts in Deutschland, Österreich, der Schweiz und Skandinavien*, 2, Basel

Strauss, K. *Die Kachelkunst des 15. bis 17. Jahrhunderts in europäischen Ländern*, 3, Munich

Streeton, A. 1982. Medieval ceramics in South-East England: a regional research strategy, *Medieval Ceramics*, 6, 21–32

Strunk-Lichtenberg, G. 1975. Die Beschaffenheit des Scherbens, in B. Beckmann 1975, 345–349

Sweetman, P. D. 1981. Some late seventeenth to late eighteenth-century finds from Kilkenny Castle, *Proceedings of the Royal Irish Academy*, Section C, 81, 10, 249–266

Tauch, M. 1988. Das Zeichen IHS auf niederrheinischer Keramik, in J. Naumann ed. 1988, 383–390

Tegtmeier, U. 2002. Hölzer aus den Stadtkerngrabungen in Duisburg. Archäologische und botanische Untersuchungen. *Archaeo-Physika* 14, Mainz

ter Molen, J. R., Ruempol, A. P. E. & van Dongen, A. G. A. 1986. *Huisraad van een molenaarsweduwe. Gebruiksvoorwerpen uit een 16de-eeuwse boedel-inventaris*, Museum Boymans-van Beuningen, Rotterdam

THIER, B. 1993. *Die spätmittelalterliche und neuzeitliche Keramik des Elbe-Weser-Mündungsgebietes.* Ein Beitrag zur Kulturgeschichte der Keramik. Probleme der Küstenforsch. im südlichen Nordseegebiet 20, Oldenburg

THIER, B. 1999. Des Schomaker Ampts kroese to Munster. Trinkgefäße Münsteraner Gilden und Bruderschaften aus Siegburger Steinzeug. *Westfalen* 77, 1999, 207–247.

THIJSSEN, J. R. A. M. 1981. *Pan huisvuil tot museumstuk. Vondsten uit een afvalput aan de Nonnenstraat,* Nijmegen Museum Commandnderie van Sint Jan, Nijmegen

THIJSSEN, J. R. A. M. 1985. De analyse van 17e- en 18-eeuws aardewerk uit vondstcomplexen van het Waterlooplein te Amsterdam, *Bulletin KNOB* 84, No. 2 & 3 (June 1985), 113–119

THIJSSEN, J. R. A. M. 1989. Stadtkernarchäologie und niederrheinische Keramik in Nijmegen, in J. NAUMANN ed. 1989, 6–14

THIJSSEN, J. R. A. M. ed. 1991. *Tot de Bodem Uitgezocht. Glas en ceramiek uit een beerput van de "Hof van Batenburg" te Nijmegen, 1375–1850,* Stichting Stadsarcheologie Nijmegen, Nijmegen

THIJSSEN, J. R. A. M. *et al.* 1984. *Een burgerfamilie in de Smidstraat 1760–1840,* Stichting Stadsarcheologie Nijmegen, Nijmegen

THOMAS, T. 1977. *Villeroy und Boch 1748–1930,* Rijksmuseum Amsterdam, Amsterdam

THOMPSON, A., GREW, F. & SCHOFIELD, J. 1984. Excavations at Aldgate, 1974, *Post-Medieval Archaeology,* 18, 1–148

THORNTON, P. K. 1978. *Seventeenth-Century Interior Decoration in England, France and Holland,* New York/London

TICHELAAR, P. J. *Fries tinglazuur aardewerk,* Fries Museum, Facetten 12, Leeuwarden

TIETZEL, B. 1980. *Fayence I,* Kataloge des Kunstgewerbemuseums Köln, 9, Cologne

TITE, M. S. 1972. *Methods of Physical Examination in Archaeology,* London

TOWNSEND, C. D. 1983. Rheinisches Steinzeug aus dem englischen Segelschiff Mary Rose, *Keramos,* 102 (October 1983), 55–60

TREUE, W. 1973. Ostasiatische Porzellan- und Wedgwood-Importe in Deutschland im 18. Jahrhundert, *Keramos,* 59 (January 1973), 17–27

TROMNAU, G. ed. 1990. *Duisburg und der untere Niederrhein zwischen Krefeld, Essen, Bottrop und Xanten,* Führer zu archäologischen Denkmälern in Deutschland, 21, Stuttgart

UNGER, I. 1983a. *Kölner Ofenkacheln vom 14. Jahrhundert bis um 1600,* Universität Bonn, Phil. Diss.

UNGER, I. 1983b. Das Kölner Kachelbäckerhandwerk des 16. Jahrhunderts, *Beiträge zur Keramik,* 2, Hetjens-Museum, Düsseldorf, 52–58

UNGER, I. ed. 1988. *Kölner Ofenkacheln. Die Bestände des Museums für Angewandte Kunst und des Kölnischen Stadtmuseums,* Kölnisches Stadtmuseum, Cologne

UNGER, I. 1991. Ein Kachelbäcker und ein Kachelfund aus der Kölner Kartause, in W. SCHAFKE ed., *Die Kölner Kartause um 1500,* Kölnisches Stadtmuseum, Cologne, 345–358

UNTERMANN, M. 1987. Schloss Bloemersheim, Gem. Neukirchen-Vluyn, Kr. Wesel. Bauuntersuchungen und Grabungen anlässlich der Bergschaden Prophylaxe im Jahr 1983, in *Beiträge zur Archäologie des Rheinlandes,* Rheinische Ausgrabungen, 27, 294–436

UNTERMANN, M. 1990. Die Markthalle am Alten Markt, in G. TROMNAU ed. 1990, 173–177

UNTERMANN, M. 1992. Der Baukomplex der Markthalle am „Alten Markt" in Duisburg, in KRAUSE, G. (ed.) *Stadtarchäologie in Duisburg 1980-1990,* Duisburger Forschungen 38, 393–450.

VAN BASTELAER, D.-A. 1885. *Les grès wallons, grès- cérame orné de l'ancienne Belgique ou de Pays-Bas, improprement nommés grès Flammands,* Mons & Brussels

VAN DAM, J. D. 1982. *Geleyersgoet en Hollands porceleyn ontwikkelingen in de nederlandse aardewerk-industrie 1560–1660,* Mededelingenblad nederlandse vereniging van vrienden van de ceramiek 108, No. 4

VAN DAM, J. D. 1988. *Nederlandse tegels,* Utrecht/Antwerp

van Dam, J. D. 1991. Portuguese and Dutch faience. Comments on a catalogue and four articles, *Mededelingenblad nederlandse vereniging van vrienden van de ceramiek* 142, No. 2, 37–38

Vandenberghe, S. & Raffo, R. 1987. Het oudheidkundig bodemonderzoek in het Mechelse in 1980 en 1981, *Handelingen van de Koninklijke Kring voor Oudheidkunde, Letteren en Kunst van Mechelen*, 85, 244–283

Vandenbulke, Lic. V. & Groeneweg, G. 1988. The stoneware stock of Jan-Peterss and Cornelis-de-Kannemann: two merchants of Rhenish pottery at Bergen-op-Zoom (NL) during the 2nd quarter of the 16th century, in D. R. M. Gaimster *et al.* eds 1988, 343–357

van der Pijl-Ketel, C. L. ed. 1982. *The Ceramic Load of the Witte Leeuw (1613)*, Rijksmuseum Amsterdam, Amsterdam

van Gangelen, H. & Lenting, J. J. 1985. Enkele voorbelden van minder bekend Duits loodglazuuraardewerk onder de Bourtanger bodem bodemvondsten I & II, *Antiek* 19, No. 8 (March 1985), 458–465

van Gangelen, H. & Lenting, J. J. 1986. Groninger Schotels van loodglazuuraardewerk met silberversiering (ca. 1600), *Antiek* 20, No. 6 (January 1986), 338–347

van Loo, J. 1984. Jan Allers, Schippers en handelaar in aardewerk te Nijmegen en Culemborg uit de late zestiende en vroege zeventiende eeuw, *Antiek* 19, No. 1, 57–74

van Loo, J. 1986. Pieter van den Ancker en Jan op de Kamp, handelaren in frechense kruiken omstreeks het drede kwart van de 17e eeuw, *Antiek* 21, No. 1, 22–29

van Loo, J. 1989. Johan Aldersz de Veer "de Jonge", "kannecooper/beytelschipper" uit Dordrecht in de zeventiende eeuw, *Antiek* 23, No. 7, 383–390

van Vlierberghe, K. & Denissen, S. 1982. Het Steengoed, in T. Oost ed., *Van Nederzetting tot Metropol. Archeologisch-historisch onderzoek in de Antwerpse binnenstad*, Volkskundemuseum, Antwerp, 73–79

Verhaeghe, F. 1983. Medieval pottery production in coastal Flanders, in P. Davey & R. Hodges ed. 1983, 63–94

Verhaeghe, F. 1987. La céramique en Flandre (XIIIe-XVe siècle): quelques aspects de l'évolution et de la concurrence, in J. Chapelot, et al. eds 1987, 203–225

Verhaeghe, F. 1988. Post-medieval pottery research in Flanders and in the Waasland, in F. Verhaeghe & M. Otte eds, *Archéologie des Temps Modernes*. Actes du Colloque International de Liege (23–26 avril 1985), Études et recherches archéologiques de l'Université de Liège 26, Liège, 227–326

Verhaeghe, F. 1991. An aquamanile and some thoughts about ceramic competition with quality metal goods in the Middle Ages, in E. Lewis ed., *Custom and ceramics. Essays presented to Kenneth Barton*, Wickham, 25–61

Verheyen, E. 1966. *Duisburg*, Die Denkmäler des Rheinlandes, Düsseldorf, 10–12

Verhoeven, A. A. A. 1998. *Middeleeuws gebruiksaardewerk in Nederland* (8ste-13de eeuw). Amsterdam Arch. Stud. 3, Amsterdam

Vey, H. & Kesting, A. 1967. *Katalog der niederländischen Gemälde von 1550 bis 1800 im Wallraf-Richartz-Museum*, Kataloge des Wallraf-RichartzMuseum 3, Cologne

Vince, A. G. 1977. Some aspects of pottery quantification, *Medieval Ceramics* 1, 63–74

Vince, A. G. 1981a. Recent research on post-medieval pottery from the City of London, *The London Archaeologist* 4, No. 3 (Summer 1981), 74–81

Vince, A. G. 1981b. The medieval pottery industry in southern England: 10th to 13th centuries, in H. Howard & E. Morris eds, *Production and Distribution: A Ceramic Viewpoint, British Archaeological Reports* International Series 120, Oxford, 309–322

Vince, A. G. 1985. Saxon and medieval pottery in London: a review, *Medieval Archaeology* 29, 25–93

Vince, A. G. 1989. Review of P. Hinton ed. 1988, *Medieval Ceramics* 13, 55–56

Vince, A. & Egan, G. 1981. The Contents of a late 18th century pit at Crosswall, City of London, *Transactions oft the London and Middlesex Archaeological Society* 32, 159–182

Vlierman, K. & Kleij, P. 1990. *Ceramiek uit de inventaris van een Klein 17de eeuws vrachtschip in zuidelijk Flevoland*, Corpus Middeleeuws Aardewerk (C. M. A.) 5, Amersfort

von Falke, O. 1898a. Kölnische Hafnergeschirre, *Jahrbuch der Königlich-Preussischen Kunstsammlungen* 19, Heft 4, 1–11

von Falke, O. 1898b. Kölnische Steinzeugkrüge, *Kunst und Kunsthandwerk*, Österreichisches Museum für Kunst und Industrie 1, 54–59

von Falke, O. 1899. Kölnisches Steinzeug, *Jahrbuch der Königlich-Preussischen Kunstsammlungen* 20, Heft 1, 30–53

von Falke, O. 1908. *Das Rheinische Steinzeug*, Berlin, (2nd edition, Osnabrück, 1977)

von Roden, G. 1984. *Geschichte der Stadt Duisburg. Das alte Duisburg von den Anfängen bis 1905*, Duisburg

Vyner, B. & Wrathmell, S. eds 1987. *Studies in Medieval and Later Pottery in Wales presented to J. M. Lewis*, University College, Cardiff

Wahlöö, C. 1974. En grann ugn, *Kulturens årsbok*, 1974 Lund, 13–32

Wahlöö, C. 1976. *Keramik 1000–1600 i svenska fynd*, Archaeologica Lundensia, 6, Lund

Walcher von Molthein, A. 1909. Die deutschen Keramiken der Sammlung Figdor II, *Kunst und Kunsthandwerk*, Österreichisches Museum für Kunst und Industrie 12, 301–362

Walz, R. 1984. Wirtschaft und Verkehr, in Cleves 1984, 109–118

Wastfelt, B., Gyllensvard, B. & Weibull, J. 1990. *Ostindiefararen Gotheborgs porslinslast*, Wiken

Weatherill, L. 1988. *Consumer Behaviour and Material Culture in Britain 1660–1760*, London

Weber, C. 1988. Ausgrabungen auf dem Großen Markt in Wesel, in *Archäologie im Rheinland 1987*, Rheinisches Amt für Bodendenkmalpflege, Bonn, 147–149

Weber, C. 1989. Ausgrabungen auf dem Großen Markt in Wesel II, in *Archäologie im Rheinland 1988*, Rheinisches Amt für Bodendenkmalpflege, Bonn, 103–105

Wegner, H.-H. 1981. Eine mittelalterliche Keramikbrennanlage in Xanten, *Bonner Jahrbücher*, 181, 437–447

Weisser, M. 1980. *Porzellan- und Steingutfabrik Ludwig Wessel, Bonn-Poppelsdorf*, Katalog zur Ausstellung Volkskunst im Wandel, 2, Führer und Schriften des Rheinischen Freilichtmuseums und Landesmuseums für Volkskunde in Kommern, 12, Cologne

White, G. L. 1997. Ein Töpferofen des Hochmittelalters aus Langerwehe. In: *Archäologie im Rheinland* 1996 (1997) 134–136

Wilson, T. 1987. *Ceramic Art of the Italian Renaissance*, British Museum, London

Wilson, T. ed. 1991. *Italian Renaissance Pottery.* Papers written in association with a colloquium at the British Museum, British Museum, London

Wingood, A. J. 1982. Sea Venture: An interim report on an early 17th century shipwreck lost in 1609, *International Journal for Nautical Archaeology*, 11.4, 333–347

Wirth, S. ed. 1990. *Mittelalterliche Gefäßkeramik. Die Bestände des Kölnischen Stadtmuseums*, Kölnisches Stadtmuseum, Cologne

Wishart, D. 1978. *Clustan User Manual*, Edinburgh

Wishart, D. 1982. *Clustan User Manual*, Supplement to the 3rd Edition, Edinburgh

Wolters, Ch. 1988a. Das Rechnungsbuch des Töpfers Heinrich Nobis aus Sonsbeck, Kr. Wesel, in D. R. M. Gaimster *et al.* eds 1988, 201–219

Wolters, Ch. 1988b. Die Töpferfamilie Nobis in Sonsbeck. Dokumente zur Spätzeit des Töpferhandwerks am Niederrhein, in J. Naumann ed. 1988, 227–236

Wustenhoff, H. 1989. A collection of Dutch excavated pewter, *Journal of the Pewter Society*, 7, No. 1 (Spring 1989), 8–12

Yentsch, A. 1990. Minimum vessel lists as evidence of change in folk and courtly traditions of food use, *Historical Archaeology*, 24, No. 3, 24–53

Zoller, D. 1980. Keramische Bodenfunde vom frühen Mittelalter bis zum 17. Jahrhundert im Nordoldenburger Geestgebiet, in W. Lehnemann ed. 1980, 9–66

# Appendix 1

## Concordance of principal contexts from Duisburg containing post-medieval pottery (Key to Plan 2)

| Nr. | Site Name | Context Nr. | Inv. Nr. | Status |
|---|---|---|---|---|
| 1. | Alter Markt | 45 | 82:31 | Build-up levels trench 1 & 2 |
| | | 28 | 83:31/0 | " |
| | | 45 | 82:32 | " |
| | | 32 | 86:5 | Cellar complex 4 |
| | | 25 | 88:25 | Cellar complex 5/6 |
| | | 27 | 82:35/28 | Build-up levels trench 6 |
| 2. | Salvatorkirche | 26 | 55:2K | Finds scatter |
| | | 50 | 61:54a | Finds scatter |
| 3. | Alte Post | 47 | 63:73a | Brick-lined latrine |
| 4. | Dreigiebelhaus | 46 | 77:22 | Midden levels & brick-lined latrine |
| 5. | Minoritenkloster | 36 | 84:52 | Midden levels |
| 6. | C & A | 42 | 84:6/62 | Brick-lined latrine |
| 7. | C & A | 43 | 84:6/65 | Brick-lined latrine |
| 8. | C & A | 41 | 84:6/Grube34 | Pit group |
| 9. | Innenhafen | 37 | 84:7/34 | Brick-lined latrine |
| 10. | Innenhafen | 38 | 84 :7/37 | Midden level over cellar floor |
| | | 39 | 84:7/4b | Midden level |
| | | 40 | 84:7/4c | Midden level |
| 11. | Abteistraße | 44 | 1987 | 3 sm. pit groups |
| 12. | Minoritenkloster | 23-24 | 89:25 | Stone-built latrine building |
| 13. | Niederstraße | 20 | 89:17 | Brick-lined latrine |
| 14. | Niederstraße | 21 | 89:18 | Brick-lined latrine |
| 15. | Niederstraße | 22 | 89:20 | Well, reused as refuse pit |
| 16. | Niederstraße | 29 | 87:29 | Pit group |
| 17. | Niederstraße | 30 | 87:52 | Pit group |
| 18. | Schwanenstraße | 14 | 85:135/3 | Pit group |
| 19. | Schwanenstraße | 3-6 | 85:135/5a-d | Brick-lined latrine |
| 20. | Schwanenstraße | 7-13 | 85:135/15 a-g | Brick-lined latrine |
| 21. | Schwanenstraße | 1 | 85:135/16 | Pit group |
| 22. | Schwanenstraße | 2 | 85:135/17 | Midden levels |
| 23. | Schwanenstraße | 19 | 86:1/3 | Pit group |
| 24. | Schwanenstraße | 18 | 86:1/16 | Brick-lined latrine |
| 25. | Schwanenstraße | 17, 34 | 86:2 | Brick-lined latrine |
| 26. | Schwanenstraße | 15, 16 31, 33 | 86:4a-b | Brick-lined latrine |
| 27. | Schwanenstraße | 35 | 86:10/23 | Well group |

# Appendix 2

## Pottery information table: stratified & associated groups of pottery from the Duisburg Altstadt

### **Context 1**: Duisburg Schwanenstraße 85:135/16 (Pit group)
Date: c. 1450–1485 (coin dated 1449–76, Friedrich I of Rhineland-Palatinate)

| Ware | min./form | % ware | Fig. |
|---|---|---|---|
| Ia.3 | 1 x tripod pipkin | 5 % | 1.10 |
| Ia.6 | 3 x bowl | 19 % | 1.6–8 |
| | 1 x jar | | |
| Ia.7 | 1 x tripod pipkin | 5 % | 1.9 |
| Ia.8 | 5 x tripod pipkin | 47 % | 1.3–5 |
| | 1 x skillet | | 1.2 |
| | 4 x bowl | | 1.1 |
| Ib.1 | 1 x tripod pipkin | 5 % | |
| II.1 | 1 x lid | 5 % | 1.13 |
| II.2 | 2 x beaker | 9 % | 1.12 |
| II.6 | 1 x ointment pot | 5 % | 1.11 |
| Total: | 21 vessels | | |

### **Context 2**: Duisburg Schwanenstraße 85:135/17
Date: c. 1450–75 (midden)

| Ware | p/a | Fig. |
|---|---|---|
| Ia.3 | 1 x tripod pipkin | |
| Ia.5 | 1 x tripod pipkin | 2.1 |
| Ia.6 | 1 x bowl | 2.2 |
| II.2 | 2 x beaker | |
| Total: | 5 vessels | |

### **Context 3**: Duisburg Schwanenstraße 85:135/5a (Brick-lined latrine bottom fill a)
Date: c. 1425–75

| Ware | min./form | % ware | fig. |
|---|---|---|---|
| Ia.6 | 1 x tripod pipkin | 12.5 % | 3.6 |
| Ia.8 | 1 x pipkin | 12.5 % | |
| II.1 | 3 x jug/bottle | 37.5 % | 3.1-3 |
| II.2 | 1 x jug | 37.5 % | |
| | 1 x beaker | | 3.5 |
| | 1 x drinking jug | | 3.4 |
| Total: | 8 vessels | | |

### **Context 4**: Duisburg Schwanenstraße 85:135/5b (Brick-lined latrine fill b)
Date: c. 1600–1670

| Ware | min./Form | % ware | Fig. |
|---|---|---|---|
| Ib.5 | 2 x dish | 3 % | 4.7–8 |
| Ic.1 | 17 x tripod pipkin | 46 % | 7.11–12 |
| | 4 x porringer | | |
| | 11 x bowl | | 7.13–19 |
| | 1 x jug | | |
| | 1 x dish | | 7.23 |
| Ic.3 | 14 x tripod pipkin | 24 % | 7.1-4, 7–8 |
| | 3 x porringer | | 7.5–6,9 |
| | 1 x dish | | 4.6 |

| | | | |
|---|---|---|---|
| Id.1 | 3 x plate (intrusive) | 4 % | 7.20-22 |
| II.4 | 2 x beaker | 3 % | 4.1-2 |
| II.9 | 1 x jug | 4 % | 4.3 |
| | 2 x tankard | | 4.4-5 |
| III.1 | 1 x plate | 11 % | 5.3 |
| | 3 x dish | | 5.1, 4-5 |
| | 3 x tile | | 6.5-7 |
| | 1 x porringer | | 5.2 |
| III.2 | 1 x dish | 1 % | 6.2 |
| III.3 | 3 x plate | 4 % | 6.1, 3-4 |

Total 74 vessels

### **Context 5**: Duisburg Schwanenstraße 85:135 (Brick-lined latrine fill c)
Date: c. 1670–1700

| Ware | min./form | % ware | Fig. |
|---|---|---|---|
| Ic.1 | 1 x tripod pipkin | 4 % | 8.10 |
| Ic.3 | 3 x tripod pipkin | 11 % | 8.8-9 |
| Ic.4 | 1 x dish | 15 % | 8.5 |
| | 1 x dish | | 4.9 |
| | 1 x dish | | 12.1 |
| | 1 x tripod pipkin | | 8.6 |
| Id.4 | 1 x chamber pot | 7 % | 8.12 |
| | 1 x tripod pipkin | | 8.13 |
| II.9 | 1 x tankard | 4 % | 8.7 |
| III.1 | 2 x dish | 7 % | |
| III.2 | 6 x plate | 26 % | |
| | 1 x jug | | |
| III.3 | 2 x plate | 26 % | 8.1-2 |
| | 2 x lobed dish | | 8.4 |
| | 1 x tankard | | 8.3 |
| | 1 x ointment pot | | |
| | 1 x tea-bowl | | |

Total: 27 vessels

### **Context 6**: Duisburg Schwanenstraße 85:135/5d (Brick-lined latrine upper fill d)
Date: c. 1700–1750

| Ware | min./form | % ware | Fig. |
|---|---|---|---|
| Ic.3 | 2 x tripod pipkin | 5 % | 9.1-2 |
| Ic.4 | 1 x dish | 20 % | 9.3 |
| | 6 x tripod pipkin | | 9.4-6, 8-9 |
| | 1 x porringer | | |
| Id.1 | 1 x dish | 13 % | 9.3 |
| | 4 x tripod pipkin | | |
| Id.2 | 1 x dish | 2.5 % | |
| Id.4 | 2 x tripod pipkin | 15 % | 9.12 |
| | 1 x cauldron | | 9.11 |
| | 2 x lid | | 9.10, 14 |
| | 1 x jug | | 9.16 |
| Id.7 | 1 x pipkin | 2.5 % | 9.15 |
| II.9 | 1 x jug | 5 % | 10.1 |
| | 1 x tankard | | 10.2 |
| III.2 | 1 x dish | 7 % | 10.4 |
| | 1 x plate | | 10.9 |
| | 1 x ointment pot | | 10.6 |
| III.3 | 2 x dish | 20 % | 10.3, 5 |
| | 3 x saucer | | 10.10, 11, 13 |
| | 3 x tea-bowl | | 10.12, 14, 15 |
| III.4 | 2 x dish | 5 % | 10.7, 8 |
| IV.2 | 1 x tea-bowl | 2.5 % | 10.16 |
| IV.3 | 1 x saucer | 2.5 % | 10.17 |
| Total: | 40 vessels | | |

### **Context 7**: Duisburg Schwanenstraße 85:135/15a (Brick-lined latrine bottom fill a)
Date: c. 1425–75

| Ware | min./form | % ware | Fig. |
|---|---|---|---|
| Ia.3 | 1 x tripod pipkin | 8 % | 11.9 |
| Ia.4 | 1 x cup | 8 % | 11.5 |
| Ia.6 | 1 x jar | 8 % | |
| Ia.7 | 1 x jug | 8 % | 11.6 |
| Ia.8 | 4 x pipkin/chamber pot | 50 % | 11.1, 4 |
| | 1 x tripod pipkin | | 11.3 |
| | 1 x lid | | 11.2 |
| II.1 | 1 x drinking jug | 18 % | 11.7 |
| | 1 x jug | | 11.8 |
| Total: | 12 vessels | | |

### **Context 8**: Duisburg Schwanenstraße 85:135/15b (Brick-lined latrine, fill b)
Date: c. 1600–1650

| Ware | min./form | % ware | Fig. |
|---|---|---|---|
| Ib.5/Ic.4 | 5 x dish | 4 % | 12.3-5, 7 |
| | 2 x porringer | | 12.2 ,6 |
| Ic.1 | 55 x tripod pipkin | 64 % | 15.9 |
| | 11 x porringer | | 15.10 |
| | 18 x bowl | | 15.7 |
| | 1 x chamber pot | | 15.8 |
| | 7 x dish | | 15.1-3 |
| | 1 x tripod colander | | 15.6 |
| | 9 x cauldron | | |
| | 1 x jug/handled jar | | 15.5 |
| | 2 x lid | | 15.11-12 |
| Ic. 2 | 1 x dish | 0.5 % | 15.4 |
| Ic. 3 | 3 x dish | 20 % | 14.1-2 |
| | 5 x porringer | | 14.3, 7, 8 |
| | 23 x tripod pipkin | | 14.4-6 |
| | 1 x colander | | 14.10 |
| II.8 | 1 x jug | 2.5 % | 15.13 |
| | 2 x small bottle | | 15.14-15 |
| | 1 x handled jar/jug | | 15.17 |
| II.9 | 1 x flagon (d. 1633) | 0.5 % | 15.16 |
| III.1 | 7 x dish | 7 % | 13.3-6 |
| | 1 x plate | | |
| | 2 x porringer | | |
| III.3 | 1 x plate | 0.5 % | 14.11 |
| IV.1 | 2 x dish | 1 % | 13.1-2 |
| Total: | 163 vessels | | |

### **Context 9**: Duisburg Schwanenstraße 85:135/15c (Brick-lined latrine fill c)
Date: c. 1700

| Ware | min./form | % ware | Fig. |
|---|---|---|---|
| Id.1 | 7 x plate | 56 % | 16.1 |
| | 2 x porringer | | |
| Id.4 | 1 x brazier | 6 % | 16.2 |
| III.3 | 3 x saucer | 32 % | 16.3-4 |
| | 1 x tea-bowl | | |
| | 1 x bowl | | |
| IV.3 | 1 x saucer | 6 % | 16.5 |
| Total | 16 vessels | | |

### **Context 10**: Duisburg Schwanenstraße 85:135/15d (Brick-lined latrine fill d)
Date: c. 1675–1725

| Ware | min./form | % ware | Fig. |
|---|---|---|---|
| Ic.3 | 1 x tripod pipkin | 1.5 % | |
| Id.1 | 3 x dish | 12 % | 17.3 |
| | 1 x plate | | 17.2 |
| | 1 x porringer | | 17.5 |
| | 2 x tripod pipkin | | |
| Id.2 | 2 x dish | 5 % | 17.1 |
| | 1 x plate | | 17.4 |
| Id.4 | 1 x cauldron | 23 % | 19.1 |
| | 1 x lid | | |
| | 6 x bowl | | |
| | 5 x tripod pipkin | | 19.2, 3 |
| | 1 x pipkin | | 19.4 |
| Id.8 | 2 x lid | 6.5 % | 19.5 |
| | 2 x tripod pipkin | | |
| II.9 | 13 x jug | 23 % | 19.6, 7 |
| | 1 x chamber pot | | |
| III.1 | 1 x dish | 1.5 % | 18.1 |
| III.2 | 1 x salt | 8 % | 18.3 |
| | 4 x plate | | 18.2 |
| III.3 | 1 x dish | 15 % | 18.8 |
| | 2 x plate | | 18.4, 5 |
| | 1 x bowl | | 18.12 |
| | 3 x saucer | | 18.6, 7, 11 |
| | 1 x tea-bowl | | 18.9 |
| | 1 x tile | | 18.10 |
| IV.2 | 2 x tea-bowl | 3 % | 18.13,14 |
| IV.3 | 1 x saucer | 1.5 % | 18.15 |
| Total: | 61 vessels | | |

**Context 11**: Duisburg Schwanenstraße 85:135/15e (Brick-lined latrine fill e)
Date: 1725–1750

| Ware | min./form | % ware | Fig. |
|---|---|---|---|
| Ic. 3 | 3 x tripod pipkin | 8 % | |
| Id.1 | 5 x dish | 31 % | 20.4-5, 21.1-2 |
| | | | 22.1 |
| | 4 x plate | | 21.3-6 |
| | 3 x tripd pipkin | | 22.2-4 |
| Id.2 | 3 x plate | 8 % | 20.1-3 |
| Id.3 | 2 x plate | 8 % | 22.6-7 |
| | 1 x chamber pot | | 22.5 |
| Id.4 | 6 x bowl | 26 % | |
| | 3 x tripod pipkin | | 22.8-10 |
| | 1 x tea-bowl | | 22.11 |
| II.9 | 1 x chamber pot | 2 % | 23.4 |
| II.10 | 1 x tea-bowl | 2 % | 23.5 |
| III.3 | 3 x plate | 13 % | 23.1-2 |
| | 2 x tea-bowl | | 23.3 |
| IV.2 | 1 x tea-bowl | 2 % | |
| Total: | 39 vessels | | |

**Context 12**: Duisburg Schwanenstraße 85:135/15f (Brick-lined latrine fill f)
Date: c. 1750–1775

| Ware | min./form | % ware | Fig. |
|---|---|---|---|
| Id.1 | 1 x porringer | 14.3 % | 24.2 |
| Id.2 | 1 x dish | 14.3 % | 24.1 |
| Id.4 | 1 x tripod pipkin | 14.3 % | 24.3 |
| II.9 | 1 x chamber pot | 14.3 % | 24.4 |
| III.3 | 1 x tea-bowl | 14.3 % | 24.6 |
| IV.3 | 1 x tea-bowl | 14.3 % | 24.5 |
| IV.4 | 1 x saucer | 14.3 % | |
| Total: | 7 vessels | | |

**Context 13**: Duisburg Schwanenstraße 85:135/15g (Brick-lined latrine fill g)
Date: c. 1775–1800

| Ware | min./form | % ware | Fig. |
|---|---|---|---|
| Id.1 | 10 x dish (1 x d. 178-) | 30 % | 25.9, 17 |
| | 1 x tripod pipkin | | |
| | 2 x porringer | | 25.18, 19 |
| Id.3 | 1 x dish | 2 % | |
| Id.4 | 5 x bowl | 16 % | |
| | 1 x platter | | 25.8 |
| | 1 x storage jar | | |
| Id.8 | 1 x tripod pipkin | 2 % | |
| Id.10 | 1 x teapot | 2 % | 25.7 |
| II.5 | 4 x storage jar | 9 % | 25.1 |
| II.9 | 1 x jardiniere | 2 % | 25.2 |
| II.11 | 1 x mineralwater bottle | 2 % | 25.3 |
| III.5 | 2 x tea-bowl | 11 % | 25.14 |
| | 1 x saucer | | |
| | 1 x plate | | |
| | 1 x lid | | |
| IV.2. | 2 x tea-bowl | 5 % | 25.11, 15 |
| IV.3 | 2 x tea-bowl | 7 % | 25.16 |
| | 1 x saucer | | 25.10 |
| IV.4 | 1 x cup | 5 % | 25.13 |
| | 1 x saucer | | 25.12 |
| V.1 | 1 x cup | 7 % | 25.4 |
| | 1 x saucer | | 25.5 |
| | 1 x punch bowl | | 25.6 |
| Total: | 44 vessels | | |

**Context 14**: Duisburg Schwanenstraße 85:135/3 (Pit group)
Date: c. 1600–1675

| Ware | min./form | % ware | Fig. |
|---|---|---|---|
| Ic.1 | 2 x cauldron | 44 % | 30.3 |
| | 8 x tripod pipkin | | 30.1, 2, 4, 5 |
| | 1 x pipkin | | 30.6 |
| | 2 x skillet | | |
| | 1 x chamber pot | | 30.12 |
| | 6 x bowl | | 30.15 |
| | 3 x lid | | 30.8-10 |
| | 2 x porringer | | |
| | 1 x dish | | 30.14 |
| | 1 x brazier | | 30.11 |
| Ic.3 | 2 x dish | 8 % | 29.1, 2 |
| | 2 x tripod pipkin | | 29.3 |
| | 1 x porringer | | 29.4 |
| Ic.4 | 1 x tripod pipkin | 4 % | |
| | 1 x porringer | | 29.13 |
| II.4 | 1 x beaker | 2 % | 26.1 |
| II.5 | 1 x storage jar | 2 % | |
| II.8 | 1 x handled jar/jug | 6 % | 26.2 |
| | 2 x ointment pot | | |
| | 1 x chamber pot | | 26.9 |
| II.9 | 3 x jug | 12 % | 26.2, 3, 5 |
| | 1 x pipkin | | 26.6 |
| | 1 x drug jar | | 26.7 |
| | 1 x porringer | | |
| | 1 x feeding bottle | | 26.8 |
| III.1 | 2 x dish | 10 % | 27.1, 3 |
| | 1 x plate | | 27.2 |
| | 1 x drug jar | | 27.3 |
| | 2 x tile | | 27.4, 5 |
| III.2 | 2 x lobed dish | 6 % | 28.5 |
| | 1 x saucer | | 28.6 |
| | 1 x jug | | |
| III.3 | 2 x plate | 6 % | 28.1, 2 |
| | 1 x lobed dish | | 28.3 |
| | 1 x saucer | | 28.4 |
| Total: | 61 vessels | | |

**Contexts 15, 31, 33**: Duisburg Schwanenstraße 86:4a (Brick-lined latrine fill a)
Date: c. 1450–1525

| Ware | min./form | % ware | Fig. |
|---|---|---|---|
| Ia.3 | 4 x tripod pipkin | 19 % | 31.1-2 |
| 46.1 | | | |
| Ia.6 | 1 x pipkin | 5 % | 31.3 |
| Ia.7 | 1 x bowl | 5 % | 31.4 |
| Ia.8 | 1 x tripod pipkin | 14 % | |
| | 1 x pipkin | | |
| | 1 x bowl | | |
| II.1 | 1 x drinking jug | 5 % | |
| II.2 | 2 x drinking jug | 28 % | 46.6 |
| | 3 x beaker | | 46.7 |
| | 1 x mug | | 46.5 |
| II.6 | 2 x mug | 9 % | 46.2 |
| Ib.1 | 2 x tripod pipkin | 14 % | 46.8-9 |
| | 1 x pipkin/jug | | 46.10 |
| Total: | 13 vessels | | |

**Context 16**: Duisburg Schwanenstraße 86:4b (Brick-lined latrine fill b)
Date: c. 1585–1650

| Type | min./form | % type | Fig. |
|---|---|---|---|
| Ib.1 | 2 x chamber pot | 4 % | 31.10 |
| | 1 x pipkin/jug | | 31.11 |
| | 1 x jar | | 31.12 |
| Ib.5/Ic.4 | 4 x dish | 5 % | 32.1-4 |
| | 1 x porringer | | 32.6 |
| Ib.6 | 1 x dish | 1 % | 32.5 |
| Ic.1 | 26 x bowl | 58 % | 33.3, 5-7 |
| | 2 x cauldron | | 34.1-2 |
| | 6 x pipkin | | 33.2 |
| | 12 x tripod pipkin | | 34.3, 6, 8 |
| | 9 x tripod pipkin with hollow handle | | 34.9-11 |
| | 2 x tripod skillet | | 34.12-13 |
| | 2 x lid | | 34.4 |
| | 1 x jar/pipkin | | |
| | 1 x chamber pot | | 33.1 |
| | 1 x jug | | 33.2 |
| | 1 x tripod colander | | 34.7 |
| Ic.3 | 3 x tripod colander | 18 % | |
| | 3 x ointment pot | | 32.7 |
| | 12 x tripod pipkin | | |
| | 2 x tripod pipkin with hollow handle | | |
| Id.4 | 1 x dish | 1 % | 33.8 |
| II.4 | 1 x beaker | 2 % | 31.8 |
| | 1 x jug | | |
| II.5 | 1 x storage jar | 1 % | 31.9 |
| II.8 | 2 x Bartmann jug | 3 % | 31.5, 7 |

| | | | |
|---|---|---|---|
| | 1 x chamber pot | | 31.6 |
| II.9 | 2 x jug | 4 % | |
| | 1 x chamber pot | | |
| | 1 x bottle | | |
| III.2 | 2 x tankard | 2 % | 33.10-11 |
| III.3 | 1 x lobed dish | 2 % | |
| | 1 x dish | | 33.9 |
| Total: | 108 vessels | | |

**Context 17, 34**: Duisburg Schwanenstraße 86:2 (Brick-lined latrine, built on a wooden ring, felling date 1534)
Date: c. 1580–1640

| Ware | min./form | % ware | Fig. |
|---|---|---|---|
| Ib.1 | 1 x porringer | 1 % | |
| Ib.2 | 1 x dish | 1 % | 36.11 |
| Ib.5 | 1 x dish | 2.5 % | 35.1 |
| | 1 x porringer | | 35.5 |
| Ic.1 | 1 x lamp | 73 % | |
| | 4 x dish | | 36.12-15 |
| | 1 x cup | | 37.9 |
| | 2 x porirnger | | 37.10 |
| | 2 x chamber pot | | 37.5 |
| | 3 x pipkin | | 37.8, 13 |
| | 16 x tripod pipkin | | 37.2, 6, 11, 14, 23 |
| | 3 x tripod pipkin with hollow handle | | 37.12 |
| | 6 x cauldron | | 37.1 |
| | 13 x bowl | | 37.16-22 |
| | 2 x tripod skillet | | 37.7 |
| | 1 x storage jar | | 37.3 |
| | 1 x jar | | 37.15 |
| | 1 x salt | | 46.11 |
| Ic.3 | 2 x tripod pipkin | 2.5 % | |
| Ic.4 | 3 x dish (1 x d. 1639) | 5 % | 35.2-3 |
| | 1 x tripod pipkin | | 35.4 |
| II.3 | 1 x jug/pitcher | 5 % | 36.1 |
| | 1 x drinking jug (d. 1598) | | 36.2 |
| | 1 x tankard | | 36.6 |
| | 1 x beaker | | 36.3 |
| II.6 | 1 x jug | 1 % | 36.4 |
| II.8 | 2 x Bartmann jug | 4 % | 36.8-9 |
| | 1 x chamber pot | | |
| II.9 | 1 x jug | 5 % | 36.7 |
| | 2 x chamber pot (inc. 1581) | | 36.5, 10 |
| Total: | 77 vessels | | |

**Context 18**: Duisburg Schwanenstraße 86:1/16 (Brick-lined latrine)
Date: c. 1700

| Ware | min./form | % ware | Fig. |
|---|---|---|---|
| Ic.3 | 2 x tripod pipkin | 5 % | |
| Id.1 | 1 x dish | 7 % | |
| | 2 x tripod pipkin | | 38.4 |
| Id.2 | 2 x plate | 5 % | 38.5-6 |
| Id.4 | 6 x tripod pipkin | 26 % | 38.10-12 |
| | 1 x lid | | 38.7 |
| | 1 x storage jar | | |
| | 3 x bowl | | |
| Id.8 | 1 x tripod pipkin with hollow handle | 2 % | 38.8 |
| II.9 | 1 x jug (toy) | 2 % | 38.9 |
| III.1 | 1 x dish | 2 % | |
| III.2 | 1 x bowl | 5 % | 38.1 |
| | 1 x porringer | | 38.2 |
| III.3 | 7 x plate | 46 % | 39.1-5 |
| | 4 x tea-bowls | | 39.10 |
| | 5 x saucer | | 39.6-7 |
| | 1 x jug/vase | | 39.9 |
| | 3 x dish | | |
| Total: | 43 vessels | | |

**Context 19**: Duisburg Schwanenstraße 86:1/3 (Pit group)
Date: c. 1750–1775

| Ware | min./form | % ware | Fig. |
|---|---|---|---|
| Id.1 | 1 x plate | 40 % | 40.1 |
| | 3 x dish | | 40.3-4 |
| Id.2 | 1 x dish | 10 % | 40.2 |
| Id.4 | 1 x tripod pipkin | 30 % | 41.2 |
| | 1 x storage jar | | 41.1 |
| | 1 x bowl | | 41.3 |
| Id.8 | 1 x chamber pot | 10 % | 41.4 |
| III.3 | 1 x plate | 10 % | 40.5 |
| Total: | 10 vessels | | |

**Context 20**: Duisburg Niederstraße 89:17 (Brick-lined latrine)
Date: c. 1500–1615

| Ware | min./form | % ware | Fig. |
|---|---|---|---|
| Ia.11 | 1 x stove-tile | 7 % | |
| Ia.12 | 1 x stove-tile | 7 % | |
| Ib.1 | 1 x porringer | 7 % | |
| Ib.5 | 1 x dish | 7 % | 42.6 |
| Ib.8 | 3 x stove-tile | 19 % | |
| X.1 | | | |
| Ic.1 | 1 x porringer | 7 % | |
| Ic.4 | 1 x porringer | 7 % | 42.5 |
| Ic.5 | 2 x dish | 13 % | 42.7-8 |
| II.3 | 1 x drinking jug | 19 % | 42.1 |
| | 2 x beaker | | 42.2-3 |
| II.4 | 1 x tankard | 7 % | 42.4 |
| Total: | 15 vessels | | |

**Context 21**: Duisburg Niederstraße 89:18 (Brick-lined latrine)
Date: c. 1450–1600

| Ware | p / a | Fig. |
|---|---|---|
| Ib.5 | 1 x dish | 43.8 |
| II.2 | 4 x jug | 43.1-4 |
| | 1 x drinking jug | 43.5 |
| II.3 | 2 x jug | 43.6-7 |
| | 1 x costrel | 43.9 |
| Total: | 9 vessels | |

**Context 22**: Duisburg Niederstraße 89:20 (Well, reused as refuse pit), for fuller publication of the whole complex see Meurers-Balke et al. 1999
Date: c. 1450–1525

| Ware | min./form | % ware | Fig. |
|---|---|---|---|
| Ia.8 | 1 x tripod pipkin | 22 % | |
| | 1 x basket | | 44.4 |
| | 1 x bowl | | |
| Ia.12 | 2 x stove-tile | 14 % | |
| Ib.1 | 1 x tripod pipkin | 22 % | |
| | 2 x dish | | |
| Ib.3 | 1 x dish | 14 % | |
| | 1 x plate | | 44.3 |
| II.1 | 1 x jug | 7 % | |
| II.2 | 1 x jug | 14 % | 44.1 |
| | 1 x drinking jug | | 44.2 |
| II.7 | 1 x mug | 7 % | |
| Total: | 14 vessels | | |

**Context 23**: Duisburg Minoritenkloster 89:25 (Stone-built latrine building adjoining bastion, lower fill), see Müller 1992, 511, 503, fig. 18 and 512, fig. 19.
Date: c. 1450–1550

| Ware | p/a |
|---|---|
| Ia.8 | 1 x pipkin/chamber pot |
| | 3 x lid |
| | 2 x salt |
| Ib.1 | 2 x bowl/pancheon |
| II.2 | 3 x jug |
| II.3 | 1 x jug |
| II.7 | 1 x jug |

**Context 24**: Duisburg Minoritenkloster 89:25 (Stone built latrine building adjoining bastion, upper fill of midden levels)
Date: c. 1550–1700

| Ware | p/a |
|---|---|
| Ia.12 | 3 x stove-tile |
| Ic.1 | 1 x tripod pipkin |
| Ic.4 | 1 x dish |

| | | |
|---|---|---|
| Id.1 | 1 x dish | |
| II.3 | 1 x jug | |
| II.9 | 2 x jug | |

**Context 25**: Duisburg Alter Markt 88:25 (Cellar complex 5/6)
Date: c. 1450

| Ware | p/a | Fig. |
|---|---|---|
| Ia.8 | 1 x lid | 44.5 |
| | 1 x salt | 44.6 |

**Context 26**: Duisburg Burgplatz (Salvatorkirche) 55:2K (scattered finds)
Date: c. 1475–1525

| Ware | p/a | Fig. |
|---|---|---|
| II.6 | 1 x figurine | 44.7 |

**Context 27**: Duisburg Alter Markt 82:35/28 (removed latrine fill, trench 6=market hall cellar 2)
Date: c. 1525–1550

| Ware | p/a | Fig. |
|---|---|---|
| II.3 | 1 x jug/flagon | 44.8 |
| II.7 | 1 x jug | 44.9 |

**Context 28**: Duisburg Alter Markt 83:31/0 (Stray finds, trenches 1& 2)
Date: c. 1750

| Ware | p/a | Fig. |
|---|---|---|
| Id.3 | 1 x dish | 44.10 |

**Context 29**: Duisburg Niederstraße 87:29 (Pit group)
Date: c. 1450–1590

| Ware | p/a | Fig. |
|---|---|---|
| Ia.3 | 1 x tripod pipkin | |
| Ia.2 | 1 x drinking jug/baby feeder (or beaker, drawn) | |
| Ia.5 | 1 x colander | 45.3 |
| Ia.8 | 1 x tripod pipkin | |
| Ia.12 | 2 x stove-tiles | |
| Ib.1 | 1 x tripod pipkin | |
| Ic.1 | 1 x porringer | |
| II.2 | 1 x jug | |
| | 1 x costrel | |
| II.3 | 1 x jug | 45.1 |
| | 1 x tankard | 45.2 |
| II.8 | 1 x tankard | |
| | 1 x jug | |
| | 1 x large pitcher | |
| II.1 | 2 x bottle | |
| | 1 x very large str. jar | |
| Total: | 18 vessels | |

**Context 30**: Duisburg Niederstraße 87:52 (Pit group; lower level)
Date: c. 1450–1550 (Coin date: 1454–90 Matthias I, Hungary)

| Ware | min./form | % ware | Fig. |
|---|---|---|---|
| Ia.7 | 8 x bowl | 6 % | |
| Ia.8 | 1 x dripping pan | 7 % | |
| | 6 x pipkin | | |
| | 2 x bowl | | |
| | 1 x jug/bottle | | 45.4 |
| Ia.9 | 1 x bowl | 5 % | |
| | 2 x tripod pipkin | | |
| | 2 x tripod skillet | | |
| Ia.11 | 13 x stove-tile | 9 % | Ia.12 |
| | 3 x stove-tile | 1.5 % | |
| Ib.1 | 12 x chamber pot/pipkin | 43 % | 45.12 |
| | 1 x cauldron | | |
| | 4 x bowl | | |
| | 35 x tripod pipkin | | |
| | 7 x dish | | |
| | 3 x porringer | | |
| | 5 x lid | | |
| | 1 x pipkin (two handles) | | 45.13 |
| Ib.3 | 1 x dish | 1.5 % | 45.14 |
| | 2 x porringer | | 45.5, 7 |
| II.1 | 8 x jug | 6 % | |
| | 2 x costrel | | |
| II.2 | 10 x jug | 12 % | |
| | 2 x drinking jug | | |
| | 4 x costrel | | |
| II.3 | 3 x jug | 4 % | |
| | 1 x drinking jug | | 45.8 |
| | 1 x drinking cup | | |
| II.5 | 4 x jug | 2 % | |
| II.6 | 3 x jug | 2 % | 45.11 |
| | 1 x mug | | |
| II.7 | 2 x jug | 1 % | 45.9-10 |
| II.8 | 6 x jug | 5 % | |
| III.2 | 1 x ointment pot | 0.5 % | 45.15 |
| Total: | 158 vessels | | |

**Context 31** (86:10/13): part of Context 15 (86:4a)

**Context 32**: Duisburg Alter Markt buildings 86:5 (Cellar complex 4)
Date: c. 1400–1475

| Ware | p/a | Fig. |
|---|---|---|
| II.2 | 1 x jug | 46.3 |
| Ia.8 | 1 x cup/salt | 46.4 |

**Context 33** (86:10/16): part of Context 15 (86:4)

**Context 34** (86:10/26-27): part of Context 17 (86:2)

**Context 35**: Duisburg Schwanenstraße 86:10/23 (Part of well group 86:1/23/0)
Date: c. 1525

| Ware | p/a | Fig. |
|---|---|---|
| II.7 | 1 x jug | 46.13 |

**Context 36**: Duisburg Minoritenkloster 84:52 (Monastic site, midden levels with no internal stratification; coin William II., duke of Jülich 1387–1393)
Date: c. 1350–1450

| Ware | sherd | % | EVE | % | Fig. |
|---|---|---|---|---|---|
| Ia.1 | 147 | 8 | 5.01 | 13 | 48.3, 4 |
| Ia.3 | 29 | 1.7 | 2.64 | 7 | 48.1, 2 |
| Ia.7 | 4 | 0.2 | 0.05 | 0.1 | 48.6-9 |
| Ia.12 | 2 | 0.1 | – | – | 48.10 |
| II.2 | 1300 | 73 | 21.65 | 56 | 47.1-31 |
| Residual | 233 | 13 | 6.86 | 18 | |
| Intrusive | 72 | 4 | 2.32 | 6 | |
| Total: | 1787 | | 38.53 | | |

**Context 37**: Duisburg Innenhafen 84:7/34 (Brick-lined latrine)
Date: c. 1425–1525

| Ware | min./form | % ware | Fig. |
|---|---|---|---|
| Ia.1 | 2 x jug | 7 % | |
| Ia.3 | 2 x tripod pipkin | 7 % | |
| Ia.6 | 2 x storage jar | 17 % | 49.1, 4 |
| | 2 x bowl | | 49.5, 6 |
| | 1 x jar/chamber pot | | 49.2 |
| Ia.7 | 1 x pipkin | 10 % | 49.9 |
| | 2 x bowl | | |
| Ia.8 | 2 x tripod pipkin | 13 % | 49.7; 50.1 |
| | 2 x bowl | | 50.8 |
| Ib.1 | 2 x dish/pancheon | 20 % | 50.5-6 |

| | | | |
|---|---|---|---|
| | 1 x storage jar | | 50.7 |
| | 3 x jar/ pipkin | | 50.8-10 |
| II.1 | 2 x jug | 13 % | |
| | 2 x beaker | | 50.2 |
| II.3 | 2 x beaker | 10 % | |
| | 1 x jug | | 50.3 |
| II.5 | 1 x beaker | 3 % | 50.4 |
| Total: | 30 vessels | | |

**Context 38**: Duisburg Innenhafen 84:7/37 (Rubbish level over cellar floor)
Date: c. 1400–1475

| Ware | min./form | % ware | Fig. |
|---|---|---|---|
| Ia.1 | 2 x jug | 6 % | |
| | 1 x jar | | |
| Ia.2 | 1 x drinking jug | 6 % | |
| | 1 x tripod pipkin | | 52.10 |
| | 1 x pilgrim horn | | |
| Ia.2/Ia.3 | 1 x cup/ drinking jug | 2 % | 52.11 |
| Ia.3 | 2 x tripod pipkin | 12 % | 52.7 |
| | 2 x dripping pan | | |
| | 1 x cup | | 52.8 |
| | 1 x lid | | 52.9 |
| Ia.4 | 1 x cup/ porringer | 2 % | 52.12 |
| Ia.6 | 1 x storage jar | 20 % | 51.1 |
| | 1 x jar | | 51.10 |
| | 7 x bowl | | 51.2-6, 8-9 |
| | 1 x colander | | 51.7 |
| Ia.7 | 1 x pipkin | 4 % | 51.12 |
| | 1 x tripod pipkin | | 51.13 |
| Ia.9 | 2 x dripping pan | 10 % | 51.15 |
| | 1 x tripod pipkin | | |
| | 2 x lid | | 51.14 |
| Ia.10 | 2 x jar | 4 % | 51.11 |
| Ia.12 | 2 x stove-tile | 4 % | |
| Ib.3 | 1 x porringer | 2 % | 52.14 |
| II.1 | 3 x jug | 6 % | |
| II.2 | 1 x costrel | 18 % | 52.1 |
| | 1 x drinking bowl | | 52.4 |
| | 2 x jug | | 52.3, 6 |
| | 2 x drinking jug | | 52.2, 5 |
| | 1 x beaker | | |
| | 1 x marble | | |
| | 1 x mug | | 52.13 |
| II.3 | 2 x beaker | 4 % | |
| Total: | 50 vessels | | |

**Context 39**: Duisburg Innenhafen 84:7/4b (Rubbish level over cobbling, immediately outside medieval buildings)
Date: c. 1400–1750

| Ware | p/a | not drawn |
|---|---|---|
| Ia.3 | 1 x dripping pan | |
| Ia.6 | 2 x bowl | |
| Ib.1 | 3 x tripod pipkin | |
| | 1 x dish | |
| Ic. 1 | 2 x tripod pipkin | |
| | 1 x dish | |
| Ic. 3 | 1 x tripod pipkin | |
| Id.1 | 1 x dish | |
| II.2 | 2 x jug | |
| II.8 | 2 x jug | |
| II.9 | 1 x jug | |
| | 1 x tankard | |
| III.3 | 1 x dish | |

**Context 40**: Duisburg Innenhafen 84:7/4c (Cobbling level immediately outside medieval buildings)
Date: c. 1400–1500

| Ware | p/a | not drawn |
|---|---|---|
| Ia.1 | 2 x jug | |
| Ia.3 | 1 x tripod pipkin | |
| Ia.6 | 1 x bowl | |
| II.1 | 2 x jug | |
| II.2 | 2 x drinking jug | |
| | 1 x jug | |
| | 1 x costrel | |
| II.3 | 2 x beaker/drinking jug | |

**Context 41**: Duisburg C & A site 84:6 Grube 34 (Pit group)
Date: 1500–1580

| Ware | min./form | % ware | Fig. |
|---|---|---|---|
| Ib.1 | 1 x tripod storage jar | 100 % | 53.2 |
| | 1 x casserole | 53.1 | |
| | 1 x cup | | 53.4 |
| | 1 x chamber pot/ pipkin | 53.5 | |
| | 1 x skillet | | 53.5 |
| | 2 x tripod pipkin | | 53.3 |
| | 1 x porringer / handled bowl | | 53.7 |
| Total: | 8 vessels | | |

**Context 42**: Duisburg C & A site 84:6/62 (Brick-lined latrine)
Date: 1550–1680 (lowest fill with vessel glass d. (1)573)

| Ware | min./form | % ware | Fig. |
|---|---|---|---|
| Ib.1 | 2 x bowl with pouring lip | 27 % | 55.1-2 |
| | 2 x pipkin | | 55.3, 11 |
| | 3 x chamber pot | | 55.4-6 |
| | 2 x tripod pipkin with hollow handle | | 55.9; 56.1 |
| | 1 x cauldron | 55.8 | |
| | 1 x tripod storage jar | | 55.10 |
| | 1 x storage jar | | |
| Ib.2 | 5 x dish | 11 % | 54.1-5 |
| Ib.3 | 3 x porringer | 7 % | 56.6, 11, 12 |
| Ic. 1 | 1 x bowl | 21 % | 55.7 |
| | 3 x tripod pipkin with hollow handle | | 56.2-4 |
| | 1 x skillet | | 56.5 |
| | 4 x pipkin | | 56.7–10 |
| Id.1 | 1 x dish | 2 % | |
| Id.2 | 1 x dish | 2 % | 56.19 |
| Id.12 | 1 x dish | 2 % | 56.18 |
| II.3 | 2 x jug/ bottle | 7 % | 56.20–22 |
| | 1 x drinking jug | | 56.21 |
| II.9 | 1 x chamber pot (d. 1677) | 2 % | 56.23 |
| III.2 | 2 x plate | 5 % | 56.24, 25 |
| III.3 | 1 x dish | 7 % | 56.13 |
| | 1 x plate | | |
| | 1 x saucer | | 56.17 |
| IV.2 | 3 x tea-bowl | 7 % | 56.14–16 |
| Total: | 44 vessels | | |

**Context 43**: Duisburg C & A site 84:6/65 (Brick-lined latrine)
Date: c. 1650–1690

| Ware | min./form | % ware | Fig. |
|---|---|---|---|
| Ic. 3 | 1 x jug | 8 % | 57.8 |
| Id.4 | 1 x brazier | 30 % | 57.9 |
| | 1 x chamber pot | | 57.6 |
| | 1 x jug | | 57.7 |
| Id.12 | 1 x bowl | 8 % | 57.5 |
| II.8 | 1 x Bartmann jug | 8 % | 57.10 |
| II.9 | 1 x jug | 8 % | 57.11 |
| III.3 | 2 x dish | 30 % | 57.1, 2 |
| | 1 x jug | | 57.4 |
| III.5 | 1 x plate | 8 % | 57.3 |

Total: 11 vessels

**Context 44**: Duisburg Abteistraße 87:47 (aggregate of three adjacent small pit groups)
Date: c. 1745–1775

| Ware | min./form | % ware | Fig. |
|---|---|---|---|
| Id.1 | 1 x pipkin/chamber pot | 9 % | 59.11 |
| | 3 x dish | | |
| | 1 x porringer | | |
| Id.3 | 1 x chamber pot | 2 % | |
| Id.4 | 4 x bowl | 11 % | |
| | 1 x storage jar | | |
| | 1 x brazier | | 59.10 |
| Id.9 | 1 x teapot | 5 % | |
| | 1 x lid | | 59.6 |
| | 1 x sugar-bowl | | 59.7 |
| Id.10 | 1 x small jug | 2 % | |
| Id.11 | 1 x bowl | 2 % | 59.8 |
| II.5 | 1 x storage jar ("Baare") | 2 % | |
| II.9 | 2 x storage jar | 11 % | |
| | 1 x small jug | 59.13 | |
| | 1 x jug | | |
| | 1 x tankard | | |

| | | | |
|---|---|---|---|
| | 1 x porringer | | 59.12 |
| II.11 | 3 x mineralwater bottle | 5 % | |
| III.3 | 8 x plate | 17 % | |
| | 1 x dish | | 59.9 |
| | 1 x chamber pot | | |
| IV.2 | 1 x teabowl | 2 % | |
| IV.3 | 2 x saucer | 7 % | |
| | 2 x teabowl | | |
| V.1 | 3 x dish | 25 % | 59.1 |
| | 3 x plate | | 59.2 |
| | 4 x teabowl | 59.4 | |
| | 2 x saucer | | 59.5 |
| | 1 x sugar-bowl | | |
| | 1 x chamber pot | | 59.3 |
| Total: | 56 vessels | | |

**Context 45a**: Duisburg Alter Markt Trenches 1 & 2 82:31 (Aggregate of build-up levels 3c-d on market place; see Gaimster 1986a)
Date: c. 1700–1800

| Ware | eve | % ware | Fig. |
|---|---|---|---|
| Id.1 | 14.41 | 29.6 % | 60.1-5 |
| Id.2 | 0.20 | 0.4 % | |
| Id.3 | 1.42 | 3.0 % | |
| Id.4 | 5.35 | 11.0 % | |
| Id.5 | 0.12 | 0.2 % | |
| Id.6 | 0.42 | 0.9 % | |
| Id.7 | 0.20 | 0.4 % | |
| Id.8 | 2.00 | 4.0 % | |
| Id.9 | 0.08 | 0.2 % | |
| Id.12 | 0.10 | 0.2 % | |
| II.9 | 4.47 | 9.0 % | 61.1-2, 4-6 |
| II.10 | 1.00 | 2.0 % | |
| II.11 | 8.80 | 18.0 % | 61.3 |
| II.12 | 0.50 | 1.0 % | 62.10 |
| III.3 | 6.87 | 14.1 % | 62.1-7 |
| III.5 | 0.58 | 1.2 % | 62.8 |
| IV.2 | 0.21 | 0.4 % | 62.11-12 |
| IV.3 | 1.10 | 2.3 % | 62.13 |
| V.1 | 0.80 | 1.6 % | |

Total: 48.63 eve

**Context 45b**: Duisburg Alter Markt / 82:32
Date: c. 1775–1800

| Ware | p/a | Fig. |
|---|---|---|
| II.13 | 1 x teapot (marked EDMUND BIRCH) | 58.13 |

**Context 46**: Duisburg Dreigiebelhaus 77:22 (Midden levels & brick-lined latrine on nunnery site)
Date: c. 1575–1775

| Ware | p/a | |
|---|---|---|
| Ib.1 | 2 x tripod pipkin | not drawn |
| Ic.1 | 3 x tripod pipkin | |
| | 2 x bowl | |
| Ic.4 | 1 x tripod pipkin | |
| | 1 x porringer | |
| Id.1 | 2 x porringer | |
| Id.4 | 1 x jug | |
| | 2 x tripod pipkin | |
| Id.8 | 2 x tripod pipkin | |
| II.4 | 1 x tankard | |
| II.5 | 1 x storage jar | |
| II.8 | 1 x bottle | |
| II.9 | 2 x jug | |
| | 2 x tankard | |
| | 1 x storage jar | |
| II.11 | 1 x mineralwater bottle | |
| III.2 | 1 x chamber pot | |
| | 1 x ointment pot | |
| III.3 | 3 x dish | |
| | 2 x saucer | |
| | 2 x teabowl | |
| | 2 x jug | |
| IV.2 | 2 x saucer | |
| IV.3 | 2 x saucer | |
| | 1 x teabowl | |
| V.1 | 1 x plate | |

**Context 47**: Duisburg Alte Post 63:73a (Brick-lined latrine)
Date: mixed

| Ware | p/a | Fig. |
|---|---|---|
| Ic.4 | 1 x tripod pipkin | 58.2 |
| Id.8 | 1 x ointment pot | 58.3 |
| III.1 | 1 x plate | 58.1 |

**Context 48**: Duisburg Niederstraße 88:14 (Pit group)
Date: mixed assemblage

| Ware | p/a | Fig. |
|---|---|---|
| III.6 | 1 x plate | 58.4 |

**Context 49**: Duisburg Alter Markt 84:4 (Stray finds found during watching brief)
Date: mixed assemblage

| Ware | p/a | Fig. |
|---|---|---|
| III.6 | 1 x plate | 58.5 |
| | 1 x dish | 58.6 |

**Context 50**: Duisburg Burgplatz 61:54a (Scattered finds)
Date: c. 1700–1775

| Ware | p/a | Fig. |
|---|---|---|
| II.9 | 1 x storage jar | 58.7 |
| | 4 x jug | 58.8-10, 12 |
| | 1 x porringer | 58.11 |

**Context 51**: Duisburg Kuhstraße 87:2/28 (Brick-lined well)
Date: c. 1500–1550

| Ware | p/a |
|---|---|
| Ib.7 | 3 x stove-tile |

**Context 52**: Duisburg Schwanenstraße 86:6/29 (Stray find)
Date: c. 1550–1560

| Ware | p/a |
|---|---|
| Ib.7 | 1 x stove-tile |

**Context: 53**: Duisburg Niederstraße 90:22
(Wasters of the Becker faience manufactory; see Ruppel, 1988)
Date: working 1764–87

| Ware | forms |
|---|---|
| III.6 | plates, teabowls, dishes |

# Appendix 3

## Pottery information table: stratified & associated groups from the Duisburg hinterland & Lower Rhine sites

**Context 54**: Duisburg-Hamborn 87:29d (Abbey site, destroyed 1587; upper fill of brick-lined latrine)
Date: c. 1575–1587

| Ware | p/a | Fig. |
|---|---|---|
| Ib.1 | 1 x tripod pipkin | |
| Ib.5 | 1 x porringer | 63.3 |
| III.3 | 1 x "Bartmann" jug | |

**Context 55**: Duisburg-Hamborn 87:29c (Abbey site, destroyed 1587; 2nd fill of brick-lined latrine)
Date: c. 1550–1587

| Ware | p/a | Fig. |
|---|---|---|
| Ib.1 | 2 x cauldron | |
| III.3 | 1 x sm (oil) jug | 63.2 |
| | 1 x flagon | 63.1 |

**Context 56**: Duisburg-Hamborn 87:29b (3rd fill of brick-lined latrine)
Date: c. 1500–1550

| Ware | p/a |
|---|---|
| Ib.1 | 1 x tripod pipkin |

**Context 57**: Duisburg-Hamborn 87:29a (Bottom fill of brick-lined latrine)
Date: c. 1400–1500

| Ware | p/a |
|---|---|
| II.1 | 2 x drinking jugs |
| II.2 | 1 x drinking jug |

**Context 58**: Duisburg-Meiderich, Haus Hagen (Niederrheinisches Museum) (Moated manor site, sample trench through moat; see Hofius 1982)
Date: c. 1400–1500

| Ware | p/a | Hofius Fig. |
|---|---|---|
| Ia.6 | 4 x bowl | 1,4,5,6 |
| | 1 x globular jar | 2 |
| Ia.7 | 1 x jar with thumbed base | 3 |
| Ia.12 | 1 x niche-tile | 9 |
| II.1 | 1 x drinking jug | 8 |
| II.2 | 1 x jug | 7 |
| II.6 | 1 x jug | 10 |

**Context 59**: Duisburg-Ruhrort, Kasteelstraße (77:26) (Rubbish pit adjacent to site of Ruhrort fortified customs house; see Hofius 1982)
Date: c. 1550–1800

| Ware | p/a |
|---|---|
| Ib.1 | 1 x dish |
| | 1 x tripod pipkin |
| Ib.8 | 3 x stove-tile |
| Ic.1 | 1 x porringer |
| | 1 x chamber pot |
| Ic.3 | 1 x tripod pipkin |
| Id.1 | 16 x dish |
| | 5 x plate |
| | 1 x brazier |
| | 1 x sm jug |
| Id.2 | 1 x dish |
| Id.3 | 5 x dish |
| | 4 x plate |
| | 1 x porringer |
| | 1 x chamber pot |
| | 1 x colander |
| | 1 x jug |
| | 1 x tripod pipkin |
| Id.4 | 1 x bowl |
| | 1 x tripod pipkin |
| Id.8 | 1 x tripod pipkin |
| II.3 | 1 x drinking jug |
| | 1 x tall beaker |
| | 1 x flagon |
| | 1 x tankard |
| | 1 x jug |
| II.6 | 1 x storage jar |
| II.8 | 1 x "Bartmann" jug |
| II.9 | 1 x plate |
| II.10 | 1 x cup |
| | 1 x saucer |
| III.1 | 5 x dish |
| III.3 | 18 x plate |
| | 1 x dish |
| | 1 x bowl |
| | 1 x jug |
| | 3 x saucer |
| | 7 x tea-bowl |
| III.5 | 2 x dish |
| | 8 x plate |
| | 2 x saucer |
| | 4 x tea-bowl |
| IV.2 | 2 x saucer |
| | 6 x tea-bowl |
| | 1 x plate |
| | 1 x bowl |
| | 1 x jug |
| IV.3 | 1 x saucer |
| IV.4 | 1 x saucer |
| | 1 x tea-bowl |
| V.1 | 1 x plate |
| | 6 x tea-bowl |
| | 6 x saucer |

**Context 60**: Krefeld-Linn, Margaretenstraße 32 (Museum Burg-Linn) (Cellar assemblage sealed by flood of 1740; Reichmann 1982; 1988)
Date: c. 1700–1740

| Ware | min./form | % Ware | Fig. |
|---|---|---|---|
| Id.1 | 28 x dish | 27 % | 64.1-7 |
| | 2 x dish with horizontal handles | | |
| | 2 x plate | | |
| | 1 x dish with footring | | |
| | 2 x large jug | | |
| | 4 x tripod pipkin | | |
| | 3 x porringer | | 65.11 |
| | 1 x beaker | | 65.12 |
| Id.2 | 13 x dish | 8 % | 64.8-17 |
| Id.3 | 2 x plate | 2 % | |
| | 1 x dish | | |
| | 1 x bowl | | |
| Id.4 | 23 x bowl | 28 % | 66.7-13, 15-18 |
| | 2 x pancheon | | 66.5-6 |
| | 4 x cauldrons | | |
| | 1 x brazier | | |
| | 2 x colander | | 66.4 |
| | 1 x basket | | |
| | 6 x large jugs | | 66.1 |
| | 1 x storage jar | | |
| | 1 x kettle | | 66.3 |
| | 1 x lid | | 65.14 |
| | 2 x tripod pipkin | | 65.15; 66.2 |
| | 1 x skillet | | |
| Id.5 | 6 x bowl | 6 % | 66.14, 15 |
| | 1 x pipkin | | |
| | 2 x pancheons | | |
| | 1 x storage jar | | |
| Id.12 | 5 x dish | 4 % | 65.7-10 |
| | 1 x tripod pipkin | | 65.13 |
| II.5 | 1 x storage jar | 0.5 % | |
| II.8 | 1 x "Bartmann" jug | 0.5 % | |
| II.9 | 8 x tankard (various) | 12 % | 65.2-3 |
| | 9 x jug (various) | | 65.1 |
| | 1 x porringer | | |
| | 1 x chamber pot | | |

| | | | | |
|---|---|---|---|---|
| II.10 | 1 x saucer | | 1 % | 65.5 |
| | 1 x tea-bowl | | 65.4 | |
| II.11 | 8 x mineralwater bottle | | 5 % | |
| III.1 | 1 x dish with central Boss | 2 % | 65.6 | |
| | 2 x dish | | | |
| III.3 | 4 x plate | | 4 % | |
| | 3 x saucer | | | |
| Total: | 162 vessels | | | |

**Context 61**: Krefeld-Linn, Margaretenstraße 32 (Museum Burg Linn) (Cellar assemblage sealed by flood of 1784; see REICHMANN 1982; 1988)
Date: c. 1740–1784

| Ware | min./form | % Ware | Fig. |
|---|---|---|---|
| Id.1 | 26 x dish | 21 % | 67.1,3 -14; 68.1-4 |
| | 1 x dish with footring | | 67.2 |
| | 19 x plate | | 67.15-19; 68.5-6 |
| | 1 x bowl | | |
| | 5 x porringer | | 69.1-3 |
| | 3 x tripod pipkin | | |
| Id.2 | 3 x dish | 1 % | |
| Id.3 | 3 x dish | 1.5 % | 68.8-10 |
| | 1 x tripod pipkin | | |
| Id.4 | 7 x lid | 25 % | |
| | 12 x storage jar | | 69.14-15 |
| | 9 x tripod pipkin | | 69.6-9 |
| | 4 x tripod pipkin | | 69.12 |
| | 19 x bowl | | 69.16 |
| | 4 x tripod colander | | 69.11 |
| | 6 x large jugs | | 69.5 |
| | 1 x cauldron | | 69.13 |
| | 4 x sm jug | | |
| | 1 x tripod spouted jug | | |
| Id.5 | 1 x small jug | 2 % | 69.10 |
| | 2 x pancheons | | 69.4 |
| | 2 x bowl | | |
| Id.10 | 1 x teapot | 0.5 % | |
| Id.12 | 3 x dish | 1 % | 68.7 |
| II.5 | 2 x storage jars | 1 % | 72.8, 11 |
| II.8 | 3 x "Bartmann" jug | 1.5 % | |
| | 1 x chamber pot | | |
| II.9 | 1 x porringer | 13 % | 72.7 |
| | 1 x globular bottle | | |
| | 13 x jug (various) | | 72.1-2 |
| | 11 x tankard (various) | | 72.3-6 |
| | 3 x chamber pot | | |
| | 5 x storage jars | | |
| II.10 | 1 x saucer | 0.5 % | 72.12 |
| II.11 | 6 x mineralwater bottle | 2.5 % | 72.9-10 |
| III.1 | 2 x dish | 1 % | 70.8 |
| III.3 | 1 x bowl | 23 % | 70.6 |
| | 34 x plate | | 70.1-5 |
| | 14 x saucer | | 71.1-6, 8 |
| | 11 x tea-bowl | | 71.7,9-14 |
| IV.2 | 5 x saucer | 3.5 % | 71.15 |
| | 4 x tea-bowl | | 71.18-20 |
| IV.3 | 3 x saucer | 3 % | 71.16-17 |
| | 4 x tea-bowl | | 71.21-23 |
| Total: | 263 vessels | | |

**Context 62**: Oberhausen-Holten, "Gemeindehaus" (Private collection) (Fill under building of 1775)
Date: c. 1600–1775

| Ware | p/a | Fig. |
|---|---|---|
| Ic.1 | 10 x tripod pipkin | |
| | 1 x pipkin | |
| | 4 x chamber pot | |
| | 2 x porringer | |
| | 1 x brazier | |
| | 14 x bowl | |
| | 2 x cauldron | |
| | 1 x dish | |
| Ic.3 | 1 x tripod pipkin | |
| Ic.4 | 6 x dish | 63.4 |
| | 1 x porringer | 63.5 |
| Id.1 | 1 x tripod pipkin | |
| | 2 x dish with footing | |
| | 1 x porringer | |
| | 8 x dish | |
| Id.2 | 2 x dish | |
| Id.8 | 1 x plate | |
| II.3 | 1 x drinking jug | |
| II.8 | 1 x "Bartmann" jug | |
| II.9 | 3 x jug | |
| | 1 x tankard | |
| III.1 | 1 x dish | |

**Context 63**: Oberhausen-Holten, "Pfarrhaus" (Private collection) (Fill beneath building of 1775)
Date: c. 1500–1775

| Ware | p/a |
|---|---|
| Ia.2 | 1 x pilgrim horn |
| Ia.11 | 1 x niche-tile |
| Ia.12 | 1 x niche-tile |
| Ib.1 | 2 x tripod pipkin |
| | 1 x dish |
| | 1 x casserole |
| Id.1 | 22 x dish |
| | 3 x plate |
| | 1 x porringer |
| | 1 x tripod pipkin |
| Id.2 | 4 x dish |
| Id.4 | 1 x large jug |
| | 2 x brazier |
| | 1 x cauldron |
| | 3 x bowl |
| II.3 | 1 x flagon |
| II.10 | 1 x saucer |
| II.11 | 1 x mineralwater bottle |
| III.1 | 1 x dish |
| III.3 | 2 x dish |
| | 1 x saucer |
| IV.2 | 1 x tea-bowl |

**Context 64**: Düsseldorf Altstadt, Dammstraße 1988 (Hetjens-Museum) (Watching brief & recovery of finds)
Date: c. 1400–1800

| Ware (p/a) | |
|---|---|
| Ib.1 | II.1 |
| Ic.1 | II.2 |
| Ic.4 | II.3 |
| Id.1 | II.7 |
| Id.2 | II.8 |
| Id.3 | II.9 |
| Id.4 | III.3 |
| Id.6 | IV.2 |
| Id.9 | V.1 |
| Id.12 | |

**Context 65**: Düsseldorf Altstadt, Rheinort 1989 (Stadtmuseum) (Rubbish pit 86, trench E; see BECKERS & SIEGMUND 1990 40–49)
Date: c. 1400–1475

| Ware | p/a |
|---|---|
| Ia.3 | 1 x tripod pipkin |
| Ia.6 | 1 x tripod colander |
| II.2 | 4 x jug |
| | 3 x drinking jug |
| | 1 x drinking bowl |

**Context 66**: Düsseldorf Altstadt, Rheinort 1989 (Stadtmuseum) (Wooden barrel re-used as waste container, trench E; see BECKERS & SIEGMUND 1990, 40–49)
Date: c. 1500–1650

| Ware | p/a |
|---|---|
| Ia.10 | 1 x jar |
| Ib.1 | 1 x pancheon |
| | 1 x tripod pipkin |
| Ib.2 | 1 x dish with footring |
| Ic.1 | 1 x tripod pipkin |
| | 1 x chamber pot |
| Ic.4 | 1 x porringer |

| | |
|---|---|
| II.1 | 1 x jar with thumbed base |
| II.3 | 1 x drinking jug |
| II.4 | 2 x beaker |
| II.8 | 2 x "Bartmann" jugs |
| III.1 | 1 x dish |

**Context 67**: Düsseldorf Altstadt, Rheinort 1989 Stadtmuseum) (Pit group, Rheinort No. 10; see Beckers & Siegmund 1990, 56-62)
Ware: c. 1675–1725

| Type | p/a |
|---|---|
| Ic.3 | 10 x tripod pipkin |
| Id.4 | 1 x brazier |
| | 1 x pancheon |
| | 1 x tripod pipkin |
| | 1 x skillet |
| II.9 | 1 x handled jar ("mustard pot") |
| | 1 x jug |
| | 1 x chamber pot |
| III.2 | 1 x lobed dish |
| | 2 x plate |
| III.3 | 1 x dish |
| | 1 x saucer |

**Context 68**: Düsseldorf Altstadt, Rheinort 1989 (Stadtmuseum) (Various contexts Rheinort Nr. 10,12,14; see Beckers & Siegmund 1990, 32–38)
Date: c. 1565–1575

| Ware | p/a |
|---|---|
| Ib.8 | 7 x stove-tile |

**Context 69**: Neuss, Mühlenstraße, 1972 & 1984 (Clemens-Sels-Museum) (Pit group in precinct of Minoriten monastery; see Tauch ed. 1984, 1821; Hupka 1988, 90-91; 1990, 21)
Date: c. 1400–1475; context associated with destruction caused by Burgundian War of 1474/5

| Ware | forms |
|---|---|
| Ia.2 | miniature cauldrons |
| | beakers |
| | money boxes |
| | pilgrim horns |
| Ia.3 | tripod pipkins |
| | deep bowls with footring |
| | dripping pans |
| Ia.7 | bowls |
| II.1 | jugs (various) |
| II.2 | jugs (various) |
| | beakers |
| | drinking bowls |
| | costrels |
| | lavabos |
| II.6 | beakers |
| | mugs |

**Context 70**: Neuss, Rheinwallgraben/Rheinstraße (RLMB) (Trench 1; see Hupka 1986 (for stove-tiles); 1988, 91–92)
Date: c. 1400–1550

| Ware | form | |
|---|---|---|
| Ia.2 | jugs | |
| Ia.3 | tripod pipkins | |
| | dripping pans | |
| | skillets | |
| Ia.7 | bowls | |
| Ia.8 | tripod pipkins | |
| Ia.12 | niche-tiles | (Hupka 1986, Fig.4) |
| II.1 | jugs | |
| | bottles | |
| II.2 | drinking jugs | |
| | beakers | |
| | jugs (various) | |
| II.3 | jugs | |
| | storage jars | |
| II.6 | jugs | |
| | mugs | |
| | tripod pipkins with hollow handle | |
| Ib.1 | tripod pikins | |
| | dripping pans | |
| | porringers | |
| Ib.3 | dishes | |

**Context 71**: Neuss, Markt 32 (Clemens-Sels-Museum) (Brick-lined well assemblage; see Sauer 1989)
Date: c. 1600–1800 (well constructed after 1586 destruction)

| Ware | forms |
|---|---|
| Ic.1 | dripping pans |
| | tripod pipkins |
| Ic.3 | tripod pipkins |
| Id.1 | dishes |
| | plates |
| Id.2 | dishes |
| II.8 | spouted pitchers |
| | "Bartmann" jugs |
| II.9 | tankards |
| | jugs |
| III.3 | plates |

**Context 72a**: Neuss, Büchel/Glockhammer (Clemens-Sels- Museum) (see Hupka 1988, 97–98, Fig. 3–4)
Date: c. 1725–1750

| Ware | forms |
|---|---|
| Id.1 | dishes |
| | tripod pipkins |
| | chamber pots |
| Id.6 | cauldrons |
| Id.5 | bowls |
| Id.4 | various |
| Id.12 | plates |
| | dishes |

**Context 72b**: Neuss, Oberstraße 21/23 (Clemens-Sels-Museum) (Well group; see Hupka 1989, 22)
Date: c. 1575–1700

| Ware | forms |
|---|---|
| Ib.1 | casseroles |
| Ic.1 | pipkins |
| | bowls |
| Ic.3 | porringers |
| | tripod pipkins |
| | dishes with thumbed rims |
| Ic.4 | dishes |
| II.6 | jugs |
| | beakers |
| II.9 | jugs |
| III.1 | dishes |
| III.3 | dishes |
| | plates |

**Context 73**: Cologne, Apostelnstraße 52, 1979 (Kölnisches Stadtmuseum, 1980/78 & 79) (Well assemblage)
Date: c. 1500–1550

| Ware | forms |
|---|---|
| Ib.1 | pancheons |
| | pipkins |
| | tripod pipkins |
| | shallow jars |
| | porringers |
| | sugar moulds |
| | bowls |
| Ib.2 | dishes |
| Ib.3 | dishes |
| | shallow jars |
| | porringers |
| II.7 | various jug/mug forms |

**Context 74**: Wesel, Magermannstraße (RLMB) (Pit group, c. 2 m in front of W. profile of trench; see Müller, 1988)
Date: c. 1580–1640

| Ware | min./form | % ware | Müller Fig. |
|---|---|---|---|
| Ib.1 | 6 x tripod pipkin | 10 % | |
| | 1 x dish | | |
| Ib.2 | 1 x dish | 1.5 % | |

| | | | |
|---|---|---|---|
| Ib.3 | 2 x tripod pipkin | 3 % | |
| Ib.5 | 1 x dish | 3 % | |
| | 1 x porringer | | 1.1 |
| Ib.9 | 3 x bowl | 4 % | |
| Ic.1 | 1 x cauldron | 20 % | |
| | 3 x storage jar | | |
| | 8 x tripod pipkin | | |
| | 1 x skillet | | |
| | 1 x bowl | | |
| Ic.3 | 1 x tripod pipkin | 1.5 % | |
| Ic.4 | 1 x porringer | 6 % | 2.1 |
| | 2 x dish | | |
| | 1 x tripod colander | | |
| II.1 | 1 x jug | 1.5 % | |
| II.2 | 1 x jug | 1.5 % | |
| II.3 | 1 x flagon | 1.5 % | |
| II.4 | 3 x flagon (d. 1577) | 11 % | |
| | 2 x jug | | |
| | 2 x tankard (Schnelle) | | |
| | 1 x beaker | | |
| II.5 | 1 x storage jar | 1.5 % | |
| II.8 | 1 x "Bartmann" jug | 1.5 % | |
| II.9 | 3 x jug (various) | 6 % | |
| | 1 x chamber pot | | |
| III.1 | 2 x dish | 3 % | |
| III.2 | 1 x lobed dish | 1.5 % | |
| III.3 | 11 x plate | 21 % | |
| | 2 x ointment pot | | |
| | 2 x dish | | |
| V.1 | 1 x tea-bowl | 1.5 % | |
| Total: | 70 vessels | | |

**Context** 75: Wesel, Magermannstraße (RLMB) (Pit group, c. 6m in front of S. profile of trench; see MÜLLER 1988)
Date: c. 1580–1620

| Ware | min./form | % ware | Müller Fig. |
|---|---|---|---|
| Ib.1 | 6 x tripod pipkin | 21 % | |
| | 1 x pancheon | | |
| | 1 x porringer | | |
| | 5 x chamber pot | | |
| Ib.3 | 1 x porringer | 1.5 % | |
| Ic.1 | 11 x tripod pipkin | 35 % | |
| | 1 x pipkin | | |
| | 1 x pancheon | | |
| | 2 x porringer | | |
| | 4 x chamber pot | | |
| | 3 x cauldron | | |
| Ic.2 | 3 x dish | 5 % | |
| Ic.4 | 3 x porringer | 7 % | 2.1 |
| | 1 x dish | | |
| II.1 | 1 x jug | 3 % | |
| | 1 x beaker | | |
| II.2 | 1 x drinking jug | 1.5 % | |
| II.3 | 1 x jug | 1.5 % | |
| II.4 | 1 x flagon | 7 % | |
| | 1 x jug | | |
| | 2 x drinking jug | | |
| II.8 | 6 x jug | 16 % | |
| | 3 x "Bartmann" jug | | |
| | 1 x chamber pot | | |
| IV.1 | 1 x dish | 1.5 % | |
| Total: | 62 vessels | | |

**Context** 76: Wesel, Magermannstraße (RLMB) (Latrine pit in front of W. profile of trench; see MÜLLER 1988)
Date: c. 1580–1620

| Ware | min./form | % ware | Müller Fig. |
|---|---|---|---|
| Ib.5 | 2 x dish | 13 % | 2.4 |
| | 1 x porringer | | |
| Ib.8 | 5 x stove-tile | 21 % | |
| Ic.1 | 4 x tripod pipkin | 21 % | |
| | 1 x skillet | | |
| Ic.3 | 2 x tripod pipkin | 16.5 % | |
| | 2 x dish | | |
| Ic.4 | 1 x salt | 16.5 % | |
| | 3 x dish | | 1.2 |
| II.8 | 1 x chamber pot | 4 % | |
| III.1 | 2 x dish | 8 % | |
| Total: | 24 vessels | | |

**Context** 77: Wesel, Magermannstraße (RLMB) (E. brick-lined feature, lower fill; see MÜLLER 1988)
Date: c. 1500–1580

| Ware | min./form | % ware |
|---|---|---|
| Ia.1 | 1 x jug | 7 % |
| Ib.1 | 1 x skillet | 40 % |
| | 1 x bowl | |
| | 1 x dripping pan | |
| | 2 x tripod pipkin | |
| | 1 x dish | |
| Ib.3 | 2 x dish | 13 % |
| II.1 | 2 x jug | 13 % |
| II.4 | 2 x jug | 20 % |
| | 1 x drinking jug | |
| II.6 | 1 x mug | 7 % |
| Total: | 15 vessels | |

**Context** 78: Wesel, Magermannstraße (RLMB) (Brick-lined shaft, 2nd fill; see MÜLLER 1988)
Date: c. 1550–1625; coin date: 1609–1624 (silver coin of Cleves)

| Ware | min./form | % ware | Müller Fig. |
|---|---|---|---|
| Ia.12 | 2 x niche-tile | 2 % | |
| Ib.1 | 4 x tripod skillet | 13 % | |
| | 2 x pancheon | | |
| | 1 x bowl | | |
| | 1 x dish | | |
| | 1 x tripod pipkin | | |
| | 1 x chamber pot | | |
| | 1 x jug | | |
| Ib.5 | 1 x porringer | 2 % | |
| | 1 x dish with footring | | 1.4 |
| Ib.7 | 6 x stove-tile | 8 % | |
| Ib.9 | 2 x bowl | 2 % | |
| Ic.1 | 1 x skillet | 46 % | |
| | 3 x porringer | | |
| | 1 x jug | | |
| | 6 x bowl | | |
| | 1 x chamber pot | | |
| | 19 x tripod pipkin | | |
| | 1 x tripod colander | | |
| | 3 x cauldron | | |
| | 1 x storage jar | | |
| | 4 x tripod skillet | | |
| Ic.2 | 1 x dish | 1 % | |
| Ic.4 | 1 x porringer | 8 % | |
| | 2 x bowl | | |
| | 2 x dish | | |
| | 1 x dish with pinched feet | | |
| Ic.5 | 2 x dish1 | 2 % | 2.3, 2.5 |
| II.1 | 2 x jug | 2 % | |
| II.2 | 2 x drinking jug | 2 % | |
| II.3 | 1 x drinking jug | 1 % | |
| II.4 | 1 x jug | 2 % | |
| | 1 x drinking jug | | |
| II.6 | 1 x jug | 1 % | |
| II.8 | 1 x chamber pot | 5 % | |
| | 1 x ointment pot | | |
| | 1 x jug | | |
| | 1 x "Bartmann" jug | | |
| II.9 | 2 x jug | 2 % | |
| III.1 | 1 x porringer | 1 % | |
| Total: | 87 vessels | | |

**Context** 79: Wesel, Magermannstraße (RLMB) (Pit group before centre of S. trench profile; see MÜLLER 1988)
Date: c. 1580–1620

| Ware | min./form | % ware |
|---|---|---|
| Ib.1 | 1 x tripod pipkin | 11 % |
| | 1 x pipkin | |
| Ic.1 | 1 x pancheon | 62 % |
| | 2 x cauldron | |
| | 1 x jug | |
| | 6 x tripod pipkin | |
| | 1 x bowl | |
| II.3 | 1 x flagon | 5 % |
| II.6 | 1 x jug (d. 1595) | 5 % |
| II.8 | 1 x jug | 17 % |

| | |
|---|---|
| | 1 x chamber pot |
| | 1 x handled jar |
| Total: | 18 vessels |

**Context 80**: Wesel, Magermannstraße (RLMB) (finds concentration in front of N. section of W. trench profile; see MÜLLER 1988)
Date: c. 1600–1770

| Ware | p/a |
|---|---|
| Ib.1 | 1 x encrusted beaker |
| | 1 x dish |
| Ic.1 | 2 x cauldron |
| Ic.2 | 1 x dish |
| Ic.3 | 1 x ointment pot |
| | 1 x dish |
| | 3 x tripod pipkin |
| Ic.4 | 1 x porringer |
| Id.1 | 1 x dish |
| | 1 x chamber pot |
| Id.4 | 1 x chamber pot |
| II.8 | 1 x storage jar |
| II.9 | 3 x jug |
| | 1 x chamber pot |
| II.14 | 1 x teapot |
| III.1 | 5 x dish |
| | 1 x porringer |
| | 1 x drug jar |
| III.2 | 3 x plate |
| | 1 x bowl |
| III.3 | 2 x dish |
| | 4 x plate |
| | 1 x ointment pot |
| IV.3 | 2 x bowl |

**Context 81a**: Wesel Magermannstraße (RLMB) (various contexts/stray material)
Date: c.1750–1775

| Ware | p/a |
|---|---|
| V.1 | various plain, coloured forms |

**Context 81b**: Wesel Magermannstraße (RLMB) (Cleaning of well head)

| Ware | p/a |
|---|---|
| Ia.12 | 2 x stove-tile |

Context 82: Burg Uda, Grefrath (Gemeinde Grefrath) (current excavations of this moated castle site; trench across moat; see SIEPEN-KOEPKE, 1990)
Date: c. 1600–1650 (site destroyed during 30 Years War)

| Ware | forms |
|---|---|
| Ib.1 | tripod pipkins |
| Ic.4 | dishes |
| | dishes with footrings |
| II.3 | various |

Context 83: Xanten hinterland fieldwalking survey 1983 (RLMB) (see GAIMSTER 1984)
Date: c. 1400–1800

| Ware | ware |
|---|---|
| Ic.1 | II.1 |
| Id.1 | II.2 |
| Id.3 | II.3 |
| Id.4 | II.5 |
| | II.8 |
| | II.9 |
| | II.11 |

Context 84: Haus Mormter, Xanten, fieldwalking survey 1985 (Niederrheinisches Museum) (Moated manor house, fieldwalking survey, unpublished)
Date: c. 1400–1800

| Ware | ware | ware |
|---|---|---|
| Id.1 | II.1 | III.3 |
| Id.3 | II.2 | IV.3 |
| Id.4 | II.3 | IV.4 |
| | II.8 | |
| | II.9 | |
| | II.11 | |

# Appendix 4

## Pottery information table: post-medieval ceramics published in excavation reports from the Lower Rhineland

Context 85: Neuss, Oberstraße/Michaelstraße (Clemens-Sels Museum) (Brick-lined well; material unquantified; see SAUER 1988)
Date: c. 1400–1500

| Ware | forms | Sauer Fig. |
|---|---|---|
| Ia.2 | beakers | 5.5 |
| Ia.3 | tripod pipkins | 5.1, 3, 4, 7 |
| Ia.5 | tripod pipkins | 5.10, 12, 14 |
| Ia.6 | glob. jars | 4.8 |
| Ia.8 | cauldron | 5.17 |
| Ia.12 | stove-tile | 5.9 |
| II.1 | jugs | 4.1-2 |
| | jars | 4.4 |
| | costrels | 4.3 |
| | flagon | 4.5 |
| II.2 | costrel | 3.1 |
| | beakers | 3.3-8 |
| | drinking jugs | |
| | drinking bowls | 3.10-11 |
| | mugs | 3.12 |
| | jugs | 2.1-5 |

**Context 86**: Neuss, Klarissenstraße 12 (Clemens-Sels Museum) (Cellar fill; see GIERTZ, 1988)
Date: c. 1600–1650

| Ware | forms | Giertz Fig. |
|---|---|---|
| III.1 | dish | cover pl. |

**Context 87a**: Bonn, Kapuzinerkloster (RLMB) (Latrine complex; see KESSELRING-POTH 1989)
Date: c. 1700–1750

| Ware | forms | K.-P. Fig. |
|---|---|---|
| Ic.3 | tripod pipkins | |
| Id.3 | dishes | |
| Id.12 | dishes | 1-4 |
| | bowls | |

Context 87b: Bonn, Universitätsgebäude (RLMB) (Pit group; see Barfield *et al.* 1963)
Date: c. 1575–1625

| Ware | forms | Barfield Fig. |
|---|---|---|
| Ib.1 | tripod pipkins | 17.3, 4, 6 |
| Ib.2 | dishes | 16.6 |
| Ib.3 | tripod pipkins | 17.5 |
| Ic.1 | cauldrons | 17.1 |
| | porringers | 16.9 |
| Ic.2 | dishes | 16.5 |
| Ic.3 | dishes | 16.4 |
| | porringers | 16.8 |
| II.3 | jugs | 16.1 |
| | beakers | 16.2 |
| | | Pl. 46.1-3 |
| II.9 | beakers | Pl. 46.4 |

Context 88: Aachen, Domhof 8 (Rheinisches Amt für Bodendenkmalpflege) (Brick-lined well, re-used as latrine; see Franzen & Päffgen 1989)
Date: c. 1700–1800

| Ware | forms |
|---|---|
| II.9 | various |
| IV.2 | plates |
| | saucers |
| | tea-bowls |

Context 89: Aachen, Domhof 8 (Rheinisches Amt für Bodendenkmalpflege) (Courtyard levels; see Franzen & Päffgen 1989)
Date: c. 1600–1650

| Ware | forms |
|---|---|
| Ic.3 | porringers |
| | colanders |
| | tripod pipkins |
| | dishes |
| | bowls |
| | cauldrons |
| | pancheons |
| II.3 | various |
| II.6 | various |
| II.9 | various |
| III.1 | dishes |

Context 90: Bocholt town centre, various sites by Archäologische Gruppe Bocholt (see Bocholt 1987 Cat. 57–64)
Date c. 1400–1700

| Ware | forms | Cat. No. |
|---|---|---|
| Ia.6 | bowls | 14 |
| Ib.1 | porringer | 35 |
| Ib.9 | bowl | 45, 46 |
| Ic.1 | skillet | 41 |
| Ic.3 | tripod pipkins | 42 |
| Ic.4 | dish | 48 |
| Id.1 | dishes | 50, 52 |
| Id.2 | dish | 51 |
| Id.4 | jug | 57 |
| | tripod pipkins | 54, 56 |
| | brazier | 60 |
| II.2 | jugs | 23, 27 |
| | beakers | 25 |
| | drinking jugs | 22 |
| II.3 | drinking jugs | 26 |
| II.4 | beakers | 32, 33 |
| | tankards (Schnelle) | 30, 31 |
| II.6 | mug | 34 |
| II.8 | "Bartmann" jug | 38 |
| II.9 | jugs | 39 |
| | bottles | 59 |
| II.11 | mineralwater bottles | 58 |
| III.1 | dishes | 47 |
| III.3 | dishes/plates | 49 |

**Context 91**: Stürzelberg, Neuss, Rhein-Uferstr. 15a, 1973 (Clemens-Sels-Museum) (see Hupka, 1988)
Date: c. 1600–1700

| Ware | form | Hupka Fig. |
|---|---|---|
| Ic.3 | lavabo | 3, 4.1 |

Context 92: Nievenheim, Neuss, Salvatorstr. 20, 1977 (Clemens-Sels-Museum) (see Hupka, 1988)
Date: c. 1650–1700

| Ware | form | Hupka Fig. |
|---|---|---|
| Ic.3 | tripod pipkin | |
| | dishes | |
| | porringer | 5.2 |
| Ic.1 | tripod pipkins | 6.2 |
| Ic.4 | dishes | 6.1 |

Context 93: Haus Gelinde, Rheinberg, Kreis Wesel (RLMB) (Moated farmhouse; trench across motte & moat; see Hackspiel 1982)
Date: c. 1700–1850

| Ware | form | Cat. No. |
|---|---|---|
| Ic.3 | tripod pipkins | |
| Id.1 | dishes | Ir. 7-9 |
| | plates | Ir. 2-5 |
| | porringers | Ir. 25 |
| | tripod pipkins | Ir. 27-28 |
| | spouted jugs | Ir. 20 |
| Id.2 | dishes | Ir. 10-12 |
| | plate | Ir. 1,6 |
| | shaving bowl | Ir. 30 |
| Id.3 | chamber pots | – |
| Id.4 | cauldrons | Ir. 13 |
| | tripod pipkins | Ir. 14 |
| | storage jars | Ir. 15, 32 |
| | spouted jars | Ir. 16 |
| | jugs | Ir. 18 |
| | pipkins | Ir. 21-23 |
| | bowls | Ir. 31 |
| | colanders | Ir. 33 |
| | braziers | Ir. 34-35 |
| | ointment pots | Ir. 24 |
| Id.10 | coffee pot | Ir. 19 |
| II.8 | "Bartmann" jug | Sz. 3 |
| II.9 | jugs | Sz. 1,2 |
| | tankards | Sz. 8 |
| | storage jars | Sz. 5 |
| | chamber pots | Sz. 7 |
| | spouted jugs | Sz. 6 |
| | porringers | Sz. 11 |
| | plates | Sz. 10 |
| | ointment pots | Sz. 9 |
| | lidded jars | Sz. 12 |
| III.2 | plates | F. 13 |
| III.3 | plates | F. 3, 6, 10, 11, 14-18 |
| | saucers | F. 7,8 |
| | tea-bowls | F. 1, 2, 5 |
| III.4 | plates | F. 19, 20 |
| IV.2 | saucers | P. 3 |
| | tea-bowls | P. 1, 2, 4, 5 |
| IV.3 | tea-bowls | P. 6 |
| V.1 | tea-bowls | Sg. 1-4 |
| | saucers | Sg. 2 |
| | plates | Sg. 8, 9 |

| | | | |
|---|---|---|---|
| N. B. | Ware I | 72 % | by sherd count |
| | II | 4.5 % | |
| | III | 7.7 % | |
| | IV | 2.25 % | |
| | V | 5.4 % | |

**Context 94**: Schloss Bloemersheim, Kreis Wesel (RLMB) (Excavation of foundations of this moated site, see SOFFNER 1987)
Date: c. 1400–1800

| Ware | forms | Soffner Pl. |
|---|---|---|
| Ia.5 | tripod pipkins | 86.K3 |
| Ia.8 | lids | 86.K5, K6 |
| Ib.1 | cauldrons | 86.K7 |
| Ib.3 | bowls | 87.K65-67 |
| Ic.3 | dishes | 89.K57 |
| Ic.4 | dishes | 94.K77, K79 |
| Id.1 | dishes | 91; 92.K82; 94; 95 |
| Id.2 | dishes | 90.K70 |
| II.2 | beakers | 87.K87, K88 |
| II.6 | jugs | 87.K90 |
| II.7 | mugs | 87.K91 |
| II.9 | bottles | 90.K94 |
| | jugs | 90.K.93, 95, 92.K96 |
| | chamber pots | 90.K63 |
| III.3 | saucers | 90.K97 |

**Context 95**: Burg Brüggen, Kreis Viersen (Latrine pits on moated castle site; see RECH 1979)
Date: c. 1400–1700

| Ware | forms | Rech Fig. |
|---|---|---|
| Ia.6 | bowls/pancheons | 9.1, 2, 7; 10.1 |
| | jars | 9.3, 4, 6, 8, 9 |
| II.1 | jugs | 10.5-7 |
| II.2 | jugs | 10.2-4 |
| | beakers | 12.6 |
| II.4 | jugs | 12.8 |
| Ib.1/Ic.1 | pipkins | 12.9, 11, 12 |
| | storage jars | 12.10 |
| | tripod pipkins | 13.3 |
| Ic.4/Id.1 | porringers | 13.1 |
| II.9 | jugs | 13.4 |
| | tankards | 13.2 |

# Appendix 5

## Pottery information table: examples of Lower Rhine earthenwares found in Cologne

### Kölnisches Stadtmuseum, Cologne (KSM)

| Ware | form | inv. nr. | publication |
|---|---|---|---|
| 1. Ia.3 | tripod pipkin | KSM 1971/511 | |
| 2. Ia.3 | bowl | KSM 1971/493 | |
| 3. Ia.3 | bowl | KSM 78,1115.4 | |
| 4. Ib.3 | deep bowl | KSM 1971/512 A | |
| 5. Ib.1 | casserole | KSM 79, 2400.9 | |
| 6. Ib.3i | beaker | KSM E. 2014 | Schilling 1991, 68 |

### Museum für Angewandte Kunst, Cologne

| Ware | form | inv. nr. | publication |
|---|---|---|---|
| 7. Ia.3 | deep bowl | E. 3340 | |
| 8. Ia.3 | deep bowl | E. 3385 | |
| 9. Ia.3 | pilgrim horn | E. 3397 | |
| 10. Ia.3/Ib.3 | "Ring-beaker" | E. 1854 | Reineking-von Bock (=R-vB) 1966, 214 |
| 11. Ia.3/Ib.3 | "Ring-beaker" | E. 2319 | R-vB 1966, 214 |
| 12. Ia.3/Ib.3 | "Ring-beaker" | E. 2319a | R-vB 1966, 215 |
| 13. Ia.6 | bowl/pancheon | E. 4475 | |
| 14. Ib.1 | jug/ pipkin | E. 3337 | |
| 15. Ib.1i | pedestal beaker | E. 1914 | R-vB 1966, 221 |
| 16. Ib.1 | beaker | E. 50 | R-vB 1966, 219 |
| 17. Ib.3 | beaker | E. 49 | R-vB 1966, 220 |
| 18. Ib.1 | "bear-jug" | E. 1515a | |

### Rheinisches Freilichtmuseum Kommern (Traubert Collection)

| Ware | form | inv. nr. | publication |
|---|---|---|---|
| 19. Ib.2 | dish | 64/1104 | Schilling 1991, 11 |
| 20. Ib.2 | dish | 66/76 | Schilling 1991, 13 |
| 21. Ib.3 | dish | 74/51 | Schilling 1991, 14 |
| 22. Ib.3 | dish | 74/43 | |
| 23. Ib.3 | dish | 74/44 | |
| 24. Ib.2 | dish | 74/42 | |
| 25. Ib.2 | dish | 74/48 | |
| 26. Ic.3 | dish | 65/66 | Schilling 1991, 4 |
| 27. Ic.3 | dish | 74/47 | Schilling 1991, 7 |
| 28. Ic.4 | dish | 65/5 | Schilling 1991, 22 |

### Museum Boymans-van Beuningen, Rotterdam

| Ware | form | inv. nr. | publication |
|---|---|---|---|
| 29. Ia.3 | tripod pipkin | F. 1893 | Rotterdam 1973, 436 |
| 30. Ib.1 | casserole | F. 1424 | Rotterdam 1973, 437 |
| 31. Ib.1 | jug/pipkin | F. 844 | Rotterdam 1973, 441 |
| 32. Ib.1 | tripod pipkin | F. 1176 | Rotterdam 1973, 444 |
| 33. Ib.1 | tripod pipkin with hollow handle | F. 1743 | Rotterdam 1973, 442 |
| 34. Ib.1 | cauldron | F. 2442 | Rotterdam 1973, 443 |
| 35. Ib.3 | cup | F. 1897 | Rotterdam 1973, 438 |
| 36. Ic.3 | bowl | F. 1566 | Rotterdam 1973, 439 |
| 37. Ic.3 | ointment pot | F. 2951 | Rotterdam 1973, 445 |
| 38. Ia.3 | tripod pipkin | F. 1463 | Hurst *et al.* 1986, 192 |
| 39. Ib.3i | bird-whistle | F. 3360 | Hurst et al. 1986, 355 |
| 40. Ib.1i | beakers (encrusted) | F. 2465<br>F. 2435 | Hurst et al. 1986, 357, 359 |
| 41. Ib.1i | (encrusted) jug | F. 1802 | Hurst et al. 1986, 360 |
| 42. Ib.3 | puzzle jug | F. 5668A | Hurst et al. 1986, 351 |
| 43. Ib.3 | pilgrim horn | F. 2954 | Hurst et al. 1986, 353 |

# Appendix 6

## Dated shipwrecks containing rhenish pottery & imports found in the Lower Rhine region

### A. Rhenish stoneware

1. 1545
The Mary Rose, Solent, Portsmouth, England
Wares: II.6, II.7
(TOWNSEND 1983)

2. 1609
Le Mauritius, Gulf of Guinea
Wares: II.8
(L'HOUR et al. 1989, 176–177)

3. 1609
The Sea Venture, Bermuda
Wares: II.8
(Wingood 1982)

4. 1613
VOC Witte Leeuw, St. Helena
Wares: II.3, II.8
(van der Pijl-Ketel ed, 246–248)

5. 1629
VOC Batavia, Wallabi Islands
Wares: II.8, II.9
(Stanbury 1974)

6. 1653
VOC Lastdrager, Yell, Shetland Islands
Wares: II.8
(Stenuit 1974, 239–243)

7. 1656
VOC Vergulde Draeck, Western Australia
Wares: II.8, II.9
(Green 1977, 95–151)

8. 1664
VOC Kennemerland, Lerwick, Shetland
Wares: II.8
(Foster & Higgs 1973, 297–298; Price & Muckel roy 1974, 216; Price & Muckelroy 1979, 315

9. 1676
The Kronan, Öland Sound, Sweden
Wares: II.8, II.9
(Kalmar 1990)

10. 1677
Dutch galliot Kvitsøy, Stavanger, Norway
Wares: II.8
(Andersen 1974, Fig. 3)

11. 1749
VOC Amsterdam, Hastings, Sussex, England
Wares: II.8, II.9, II.11
(Marsden 1985, 128)

12. 1752
VOC Geldermalsen, Bintan, South China Sea
Wares: II.8, II.9, II.11
(Jörg 1986, 53)

13. 1770
HMS Swift, Puerto Deseado, Argentina
Wares: II.9
(pers. comm. M.N. Arias Incolle)

14. 1778
HMS Orpheus, Portsmouth, Rhode Island, N. America
Wares: II.9, II.11, II.12, II.14
(Lexington 1985, 87–95)

15. 1779
The Defence, Penobscot Bay, Maine, N. America
Wares: II.11
(Lexington 1985, 96–98)

## B. Oriental Porcelain

1. 1609
Le Mauritius, Gulf of Guinea
Wares: IV.1
(L'Hour et al. 1989, 136–173)

2. 1613
VOC Witte Leeuw, St. Helena
Wares: IV.1
(van der Pijl-Ketel ed. 1982, 46–142)

3. 1645
Hatcher Collection, South China Sea
Wares: IV.1, IV.2
(Harrison 1984; Curtis 1985; Sheaf & Kilburn 1988, 13–80)

4. 1738
The Sussex, Bassis da India, Indian Ocean
Wares: IV.2
(Bousquet et al. 1990, Fig. 3)

5. 1745
The Götheborg, Gothenburg, Sweden
Wares: IV.2, IV.3
(Wästfelt et al. 1990)

6. 1746
The Prince de Conty,
Wares: IV.2
(L'Hour & Richez 1990)

7. 1752
VOC Geldermalsen, Bintan, South China Sea
Wares: IV.2, IV.3
(Jörg 1988; Sheaf & Kilburn 1988, 81–162)

8. 1776
VOC Nieuw Rhoon, Cape Town, South Africa
Wares: IV.2
(Lightley 1976)

9. 1778
HMS Orpheus, Portsmouth, Rhode Island, N. America
Wares: IV.2
(Lexington 1985, 87–95)

## C. NL Faience

1. 1677
Dutch galliot Kvotsøy, Stavangar, Norway
Wares: III.3
(Andersen 1974, Fig. 7 & 8)

## D. English finewares

1. 1770
HMS Swift, Puerto Deseado, Argentina
Wares: II.12, II.14, V.1
(pers. comm. M. N. Arias Incollé)

# Appendix 7

## Selected list of contemporary graphical sources depicting post-medieval ceramics

### *I. 15th to 17th-century Interiors*

#### A. Living interiors / Dining scenes

Sources — wares

1.
Hieronymus Bosch (c. 1450–1516) — II
"The Marrige at Cana"
Mus. Boymans-van Beuningen,
Rotterdam
Bosing 1987, p. 23

2.
Dieric Bouts (1410/20–75) — II
"Christ in the House of the Pharase
Simon"
Staatl. Mus. Preuss. Kulturbesitz, Berlin
Cat. Nr. 533A

3.
Dieric Bouts (1410/20–75) — II
"The Last Supper"
Kunstmuseum, Basle
Cat. Nr. 656

4.
Jan Mostaert (1472/3–1555/6) — II
"The Holy Family at a Meal"
Wallraf-Richhartz-Museum, Cologne
Cologne 1987, p.49

5.
Jan Mostaert (1472/3–1555/6) — I II
"Jozef duidt de dromen van de
bakker" (c. 1495)
Maritshuis, The Hague
Clevis & Kottman 1989, 25

6.
Gerard David (1450/60–1523) — II
"The Marriage of Cana"
Louvre, Paris
Friedlander 1956, Pl. 128

7.
Gerard David (1450/60–1523) — II
"Madonna & Child"
Coll. v. Panwitz, Haarlem
Scheil 1977, Cat. 128

8.
Jan van Eyck (d. 1441) — II
(Turin Book of Hours)
"Birth of St. John the Baptist" (c. 1400)
Museo Civico, Turin
Friedländer 1956, Pl. 22;
Chatelet 1988, Pl. 15

9.
Master of Catherine of Cleves — I
(c. 1435–40)
(The Hours of Catherine of Cleves)
"Death of a Rich Man"
Pierpont Morgan library, N. Y.
Chatelet 1988, Pl. 43

10.
Master of Catherine of Cleves (c. 1435–40) — II
(The Hours of Catherine of Cleves)
"The Holy Family"
Pierpont Morgan Library, N. Y.
Chatelet 1988, Pl. 47

11.
Master of the Altar of St. Bartholomew, — II
Cologne (c. 1480–95)
"The Marriage of Cana"
Musee des Beaux Arts, Brussels
Haedecke 1983, Fig.94

12.
Jacob Corneslisz. van Oostzanen — II
(1470–1533)
"The Last Supper" (1514)
Mus. Boymans-van Beuningen, Rotterdam
Ruempol & van Dongen 1991, p. 283

13.
Pieter Aertsen (1508–1575) — II
"Christ in the House of Martha
& Mary" (1553)
Mus. Boymans-van Beuningen, Rotterdam
Ruempol & van Dongen 1991, p. 285

14.
Pieter Aertsen (1508–75) — I II
"Peasant's Room" (1556)
Mus. Mayer van den Bergh, Antwerp
Antwerp 1978, Cat. 43

15.
Joachim Beuckelaer (c. 1533–75) — I II
"Christ in the house of Martha &
Mary" (1568)
Galerie Hoogsteder, The Hague
Ghent 1986, Cat. 715.

16.
Jan Dwart van Groningen — II
(Before 1500–after 1535)
"The Marriage of Cana"
Bodemuseum, Berlin
Cat. Nr. 1927

17.
Pieter Huys (c. 1519–1581) II
"The Bagpipe player"
Bodemuseum, Berlin.
Cat. Nr. 693

18.
Toe Beocup (16th century) II
"The Last Supper"
Gemeentelijk Mus. Kampen
Clevis & Kottman 1989, 43

19.
Jodocus van Winghen (1544–1603) II
"The fat couple" (1593)
Mus. Boymans-van Beuningen, Rotterdam
ter Molen et al. (eds) 1986, Cat.150

20.
Gerrit van Honthorst (1590–1656) II
"The Concert" (c. 1625)
Galleria Borghese, Rome
Philadelphia 1984, Cat.49

21.
Pieter de Hooch (1629–1648) II
"Woman Drinking with Soldiers" (1658)
Louvre, Paris
Philadelphia 1984, Cat.52

22.
Johannes Vermeer (1632–1675) III
"Girl with Wineglass" (c. 1658–60)
S. M. P. K., Gemäldegalerie, Berlin
Philadelphia 1984, Cat. 116

23.
Gerard Dou (1613–75) I II
"Woman eating Porridge" (c. 1632–37)
Private Collection
Philadelphia 1984, Cat. 53

24.
Gerard Dou (1613–75) II
"A Seated Woman making Lace"
H. Samuel Collection
London 1988, Cat. 18

25.
Pieter de Hooch (1629–after 1684) II
"The Mother" (c.1659/60)
Staat. Mus Preuss Kulturbesitz
Gemäldegalerie, Berlin
Philadelphia 1984, Cat. 55

26.
Jan Steen (c. 1625/6–1679) I II III
"The Christening Feast" (1664)
Wallace Collection, London
London 1968, P 111

27.
Jan Steen (1625/6–1679) II III
"Prayer before the Meal" (1660)
Private Collection
Philadelphia 1984, Cat. 102

28.
Jan Steen (1625/6–1679) I II
"A Peasant Family at Meal-time" (c. 1665)
National Gallery, London
Cat. 2558

29.
Gerard ter Borch (1617–81) III
"Woman Peeling Apples" (c. 1660)
Kunsthist. Museum, Gemäldegalerie, Vienna
Philadelphia 1984, Cat. 14

30.
Jacob Ochtervelt (1634–82) II
"The Lemon cutter"
Bayerisches Nationalmuseum, Munich
Munich 1986, Cat. 9

31.
Quiringh van Brekelenkam (c. 1620–68) II
"A Woman asleep with a Bible on her
lap" (c. early 1660s)
National Gallery, London
Cat. 2550

32.
Q. van Brekelenkam (c. 1620–68) I II III
"Grace before the meal"
Mus. Boymans-van Beuningen,
Rotterdam
Ruempol & van Dongen 1991, p. 190

33.
Adriaen van Ostade (1610–85) I
"Interior of a Peasants Cottage" (1668)
Her Maj. Queen Elizabeth II, London
Philadelphia 1982, Cat. 91.

34.
Nicolaes Verkolje (1673–1746) II III
"The household of Beslikte Swaatje"
Mus. Boymans-van Beuningen,
Rotterdam
Ruempol & van Dongen, p. 296

## B. Kitchen & Cellar scenes

1.
Hans Wertinger (c. 1465/70–1533) I
"December " in calender-series
Germ. Nat. Mus., Nuremberg
Brandl 1984, Fig. 4

2.
J. van Coninxloo (1489–1545) I
"Het mirakel van de gebroken Zeef"
Koninklijk Mus. eumoor Schone
Kunsten, Antwerp
ter Molen et al. (eds) 1986, Fig. 20

3.
Pieter Breughel The Elder (1525–69) I
"De vette keuken" (engraving 1563)
Mus. Boymans-van Beuningen, Rotterdam
ter Molen et al. (eds) 1986, Cat. 149

4.
Pieter Breughel The Elder (1525–69) — I
"De magere keuken"
Mus. Boymans-van Beuningen,
Rotterdam
ter Molen et al. (eds) 1986, Cat. 148

5.
Jacob Matham (1571–1631) — I II
"Kitchen scene"
Mus. Boymans-van Beuningen,
Rotterdam
ter Molen et al. (eds) 1986, Cat. 147

6.
Pieter Aertsen (1508/9–1575) — I III
"De pannekoekebackerij" (1560)
Mus. Boymans-van Beuningen,
Rotterdam
ter Molen et al. (eds) 1996, Fig. 109

7.
Pieter Aertsen (1508/9–15775) — I II
"Kitchen scene" (1572)
Royal Painting Gallery,
Copenhagen
Sievers 1908, Pl. 29

8.
Joachim Beuckelaer (1533–1573) — I II
"Keuken" (1570)
Museum voor Schone Kunsten, Ghent
Ghent 1986, Cat. 11

9.
Anonymous (after Beuckelaer) — I II
"Kitchen scene"
Galerie Saint-Luc, Brussels
Ghent 1986, Pl. 28

10.
Wolffaert — II III
"Kitchen table"
Stedelijk Museum Vander Kelen-Mertens,
Liege
Peremans 1986, Pl. 48

11.
S. Netherlands School — II IV
"Cook with provisions" (c. 1630–40)
Wallraf-Richartz Museum, Cologne
Vey & Kesting 1967, Cat. 2345

12.
Joachim A. Uytewael (1566–1638) — I II
"Kitchen scene" (1605)
Bodemuseum, Berlin
Cat. Nr. 2002

13.
A. van de Venne (1589–1662) — I II
Kitchen scene
Museum Boymans-van Beuningen,
Rotterdam
Ruempol & van Dongen 1991, p. 289

14.
Cornelis Jacobsz. Delff (1571–1643) — I
"The Housekeeper"
Museum Boymans-van Beuningen,
Rotterdam
Ruempol & van Dongen 1991, p. 292

15.
Pieter van den Bosch — I II
"The young cook"
Kunstmuseum, Basle
Inv. Nr. 919

16.
Johannes Vermeer (1632–1675) — I II
"The Kitchen Maid"
Rijksmuseum, Amsterdam

17.
Nicolaes Maes (1643–1693) — I II III
"A Woman scraping Parsnips" (1655)
Nat. Gallery, London
Cat. Nr. 207

18.
Nicolaes Maes (1643–1693) — I II
"The Eavesdropper" (1655)
H. Samuel Collection, London
London 1988, Cat. 38

19.
Nicolaes Maes (1643–1693) — I II III
"Woman Plucking a Duck" (c. 1655–56)
Philadelphia Museum of Art
Philadelphia 1984, Cat. 65

20.
David Teniers (1610–90) — I
Kitchen with still life & slaughtered
Ox (1640s)
Priv. Collection, N. Y.
Klinge 1982, Cat. 23

21.
Renier Covijn (17th century) — I II III
Kitchenmaid
Dordrechts Museum
Clevis & Kottman 1989, 63

C. Display & Ornament

1.
Memling (c. 1430/40–94) — II
"Annunciation" (1482)
Private Collection, N. Y.
Friedländer 1949, p. 35

2.
Hans Holbein The Elder — II
(c. 1465–1524)
"Throned Virgin" (1499)
Germ. Nat. Museum, Nuremberg
Nuremberg 1952, p. 90

3. IV
Gonzales Coques (1614–84)
Interior scene (c. 1600)
Musee d'Art et d'Histoire, Geneva
Thornton 1978, Fig. 232

4. III
Jan Miense Molenaer (1610–68)
"Woman at her Toilet" (1633)
Toledo Museum of Art
Philadelphia 1984, Cat.20

5. III
Quirijn van Brekelenkan (1620–68)
"Interior of a Tailor's shop" (1653)
Worcester Art Museum, Mass
Philadelphia 1984, Cat. 18

6. II III
Quirijn van Brekelenkan (1620–68)
"Woman Combing a Child's Hair" (1648)
Stedelijk Museum, Leiden
Philadelphia 1984, Cat.17

7. III
Pieter de Hooch (1629–84)
"Lady, Child & Maidservant" (1650s)
H. Samuel Collection, London
London 1988, Cat. 34

8. III
Pieter de Hooch (1629–84)
"Woman nursing an Infant" (c.1658–60)
Fine Arts Museum of San Francisco
Philadelphia 1984, Cat. 54

## *II. 16th to 17th-century Genre scenes*

### A. Market Scenes

1.
Joachim Beuckelaer (c. 1533–75) I
"The Greengrocers's Wife" (1565)
Museum Mayer van den Bergh, Antwerp
Antwerp 1978, Cat. 49

2.
Joachim Beuckelaer (c. 1533–75) I
"Poultry market" (1570)
Museum voor Schone Kunsten, Ghent
Ghent 1986, Cat. 10

3.
Pieter Aertsen (1508–75) I II
"Meat stall" (1551)
University of Uppsala
Sievers 1908, Pl. 8

4.
Pieter Aertsen (1508–75) II
"Game seller"
Herzogl. Museum, Brunswick
Sievers 1908, Pl. 5

5.
Pieter Aertsen (1508–75) I
"Market scene" (1550s)
Suermondt Museum, Aachen
Grimme 1963, Cat. 114

6.
Jan Steen (1626–79) I
"The Poultry Yard"
Mauritshuis, The Hague
London 1976, Cat. 105

### B. Festivals

1.
Pieter Breughel The Elder I
(active 1550/1–1569)
"The Peasant Dance"
Kunsthistorisches Museum, Vienna
Grossmann 1973, Pl. 134

2.
Pieter Breughel The Elder I
(active 1550/1–1569)
"The Wedding Feast"
Kunsthistorisches Museum, Vienna
Grossmann 1973, Pl. 129

3.
Pieter Aertsen (1508–75) I II
"Peasant festival" (1550)
Kunsthistorisches Museum, Vienna
Sievers 1908, Pl. 6

4.
Pieter Aertsen (1508–75) II
"Egg Dance" (1557)
Rijksmuseum, Amsterdam
Sievers 1908, Pl. 21

5.
Jan Steen (1626–79) I II
"The Egg Dance" (c. 1675)
Apsley House, London
London 1976, 108

### C. Tavern scenes

1.
Adriaen Brouwer (1605/6–38) I II
"Inn with Drunken Peasants"
Rijksmuseum, Amsterdam
Klinge 1982, Cat. 1

2.
Adriaen Brouwer (1605/6–38) I II
"The Smokers"
Private Collection
M. Klinge 1982, Cat. 3

3.
David Teniers (1610–90) I II
"Le bonnet vert"
Thyssen-Bornemisza Collection
Klinge 1982, Cat. 15

4.
David Teniers (1610–90) I II
"Smokers at an inn" (1641)
Private Collection
Klinge 1982, Cat. 20

5.
David Teniers (1610–90) I II
"Dice & skittle players"
Private Collection
Klinge 1982, Cat. 26

6.
David Teniers (1610–90) I II
"Man & woman playing cards"
Richard Green Gallery, London
Klinge 1982, Cat. 29

7.
David Teniers (1610–90) I II
"Carpenters playing cards" 1661
Priv. Collection
Klinge 1982, Cat. 46

8.
Abraham Diepraam (1622–70) I II
"Barroom" (1665)
Rijksmuseum, Amsterdam
Philadelphia 1984, Cat. 30

9.
Adriaen Ostade (1610–85) I II
"The Backgammon Players"(1674)
H. Samuel Collection, London
London 1988, Cat. 49

10.
Jan Steen (1625/6–79) I II III
"Beware of Luxury" (1663)
Kunsthistorisches Museum, Vienna
Philadelphia 1984, Cat. 104

11.
Jan Steen (1625/6–79) I II
"The Interior of an Inn"
National Gallery, London
Cat. Nr. 5637

12.
J. M. Molenaer (c. 1610–68) I II
"The Musicians"
Art Gallery & Museum, Glasgow
Glasgow 1961, Cat. 385

## *III. 16th to 17th-century Still Life scenes*

1.
Pieter Aertsen (1508–75) II III
"Christ at the House of Mary
and Martha" (1552)
Kunsthistorisches Museum, Vienna
Münster 1979, Fig. 193

2.
Follower of P. Aertsen I II
Still life
Musee des Beaux-Arts, Brussels
Bergström 1956, Pl. 20

3.
Ludger tom Ring d. J. (1522–84) II
"Bouquet of flowers in ceramic vase"
Westfälisches Landesmuseum, Münster
Münster 1979, Fig. 165

4.
Unknown master II
Objects in a cupboard (1538)
Kroller-Müller Museum, Otterlo (NL)
Segal 1988, Pl. 1.6

5.
Ambrosius Bosschaert The Younger II
(1609–1621)
Still life
Private Collection
Bergström 1956, Pl. 5

6.
Ambrosius Bosschaert The Elder IV
(1573–1621) Panel
Sofdeborg Castle, Stockholm, Sweden
Bergström 1956, Pl. 44

7.
Frans Badens (1571–1618) II
Untitled (c. 1600–1630)
Private collection
Segal 1988, Pl. 51

8.
Johannes Baers (d. 1641) IV
Fruit still life
Clemens-Sels-Museum, Neuss
Neuss 1986, Cat. 3

9.
Osias Beert (1580–1624) IV
"Still life with cherries &
strawberries" (1608)
Staatl. Mus. Preuss. Kulturbesitz, Berlin
Schneider 1989, p. 97

10.
Peter Binoit (c. 1590–1632) II
Untitled
Private collection
Segal 1985, Cat. 26

11.
Follower of Breughel The Younger II
"Bouquet of flowers in stoneware vase"
Wallraf-Richartz-Museum, Cologne
Vey & Kesting 1967, Cat. 2860

12.
Jan Breughel The Younger (1601–78) II IV
"Still life with fruit, flowers and
jug on a table"
H. Samuel Collection, London
London 1988, Cat. 11

13.
Pieter Claesz (1597/98–1661) II IV
Panel (1621)
Private collection
Bergström 1956, Fig. 100

14.
Pieter Claesz (1597/98–1661) IV
Panel (1627)
Rijksmuseum, Amsterdam
Bergström 1956, Fig. 104; van Thiel 1975

15.
Pieter Claesz (1597/98–1661) I II
Still life panel (1636)
Hermitage, Leningrad
Dresden 1983, Cat. 32

16.
Jan Davidsz De Heem (1606–84) IV
"Pronk Still life with a World
Map" (1640)
Louvre, Paris
Segal 1988, Cat. 8.2

17.
Jan Davidsz. De Heem (1606–84) IV
Untitled
Museum Boymans-van Beuningen,
Rotterdam
Segal 1988, Cat. 39

18.
Jan Davidsz. De Heem (1606–84) IV
"Fruit still life"
Rheinisches Landesmuseum, Bonn
Bonn 1936

19.
Pieter De Ring (1615–60) IV
Still life
Private collection
Segal 1988, Cat. 43

20.
Gillis Jacobsz. van Hulsdonck II
(1582–1647)
"Still life with stoneware jug & 2
Roemers" (c. 1640–50)
Private collection
Grimm 1988, Pl. 8

21.
Georg Flegel (1566–1638) II
"Still life with beetle" (1635)
Wallraf-Richartz-Museum, Cologne
Erichson-Firle & Vey 1973, Cat. 2824

22.
Georg Flegel (1566–1639) II
Still life
Private collection
Segal 1988, Cat. 4

23.
Georg Flegel (1566–1639) II
"Still life with fruit & bouquet of
flowers" (early 17th century)
Private collection
Münster 1979, Fig. 222

24.
Georg Flegel (1566–1639) IV
"Dessert-still life" (early 17th century)
Alte Pinakothek, Munich.
Schneider 1989, p. 91

25.
Georg Flegel (1566–1639) II
"Peach branch in a jug" (c. 1630)
Hessisches Landesmuseum, Darmstadt
Grimm 1988, Pl. 131

26.
Nicolaes Gillis (c. 1580–1632) IV
Still life (1601)
Private collection
Bergström 1956, Fig. 89

27.
Nicolaes Gillis (c. 1580–1632) II IV
"Laid table" (1612)
Private collection
Münster 1979, Cat. 213

28.
Willem Claesz. Heda (c. 1594–1679/82) II
Still life
Museum Mayer van den Bergh, Antwerp.
Antwerp 1978, Cat. 21

29.
Willem Claesz. Heda (c. 1594–1679/82) IV
"Still life with Nautilus cup" (1649)
Staatliches Museum, Schwerin
Grimm 1988, Pl. 70

30.
Willem Claesz. Heda (c. 1594–1679/82) II
"Still life with overturned jug" (1644)
Worcester Art Museum, Mass.
Grimm 1988, Pl. 72

31.
Jan Jansz. Treck (1606–1652) IV
"Still life with a pewter flagon
and two Ming bowls" (1649)
National Gallery, London
Cat. Nr. 4562; Segal 1988, Cat. 36

32.
Willem Kalf (1619–93) IV
Still life (1653/4)
Hermitage, Leningrad
Dresden 1983, Cat. 86; Grimm 1988, Pl. 103

33.
Willem Kalf (1619–93) — IV
Still life (1678)
Statens Museum for Kunst, Copenhagen
Bergström 1956, Cat. 231

34.
Cornelis Mahu (1613–89) — II
"Still life with glass goblet &
stoneware jug" (1648)
Staatl. Mus. Preuss. Kulturbes., Berlin
Berlin 1978, Cat. 944

35.
Clara Peeters (c. 1583–1657) — II II
"Dessert-Still life" (1597)
Alte Pinakothek, Munich
Schneider 1989, p. 94

36.
Clara Peeters (c. 1583–1657) — II
"Pronk goblet, flowers and shells"
(1612)
Staatliche Kunsthalle, Karlsruhe
Segal 1988, Cat. 4.8

37.
Clara Peeters (c. 1583–1657) — I II IV
Still life (1612)
Private collection
Segal 1988, Cat. 8

38.
Clara Peeters (c. 1583–1657) — II
"Still life with Lobster" (1612)
Kunstmuseum, Poltawa
Dresden 1983, Cat. 124

39.
Clara Peeters (c. 1583–1657) — II IV
Still life (1612)
Private collection
Segal 1983, Cat. 24

40.
Clara Peeters (c. 1583–1657) — II III
"Still life with flowers" (1612)
Museo del Prado, Madrid
Münster 1979, Cat. 221

41.
H. van Ravesteyn (1638–91) — II IV
Still life (1667)
Private collection
Spriggs 1966, Pl. 69a

42.
H. van Ravesteyn (1638–91) — I II
Smoking still life (c. 1664)
H. Samuel Collection, London
Klein 1957, Fig. 19; London 1988,
Cat. 56; Grimm 1988, Pl. 78

43.
Frans Snyders (1579–1657) — IV
Still life
Kon. Museum voor Schone Kunsten,
Ghent
Segal 1983, Fig. 21

44.
Pieter van Anraadt (1635–78) — I II
"Still life with jug & beer glass"
(1658)
Mauritshuis, The Hague
The Hague 1984, Cat. no. 1
Grimm 1988, Pl. 90

45.
Abraham van Beyeren (1620–90) — IV
"Still life with a silver ewer" (1660s)
Toledo Museum of Art, Toledo
Segal 1988, Cat. 9.4

46.
Abraham van Beyeren (1620–90)
Still life (1655) — III IV
Worcester Art Museum, Worcester
Bergström 1956, Cat. 198

47.
Abraham van Beyeren (1620–90)
"Still life with fruit and dead game" — II IV
Private collection
Apollo, June 1989, p. 57

48.
Floris van Dijk (1575–1651)
Panel (1610) — II IV
Private collection
Bergström 1956, Cat. 92

49.
Floris van Dijk (1575–1651)
Still life — II IV
Private collection
Segal 1983, Cat. 7

50.
Hans van Essen
Panel (c. 1610) — I II
Private collection
Bergström 1956

51.
Floris van Schooten (w. 1612–55)
Still life (1617) — IV
Private collection
Bergström 1956, Pl. 11

52.
Joris van Son (1623–67)
"Fire" (1656) — II IV
Private collection
Segal 1988, Fig. 8.8

| | | | |
|---|---|---|---|
| 53.<br>Juriaen van Streek (c.1632–87)<br>Still life<br>Private collection<br>SEGAL 1983, Cat. 52 | | III | IV |
| 54.<br>Adriaen van Utrecht<br>"Still life with parrot" (1636)<br>Royal Museum, Brussels<br>Münster 1979, Cat. 229 | | | IV |
| 55.<br>Adriaen van Utrecht<br>"Fruit still life with lobster"<br>Ashmolean Museum, Oxford<br>GRIMM 1988, Pl. 121 | | III | |
| 56.<br>Balthasar van der Ast (1593/94–1657)<br>Still life<br>Private collection<br>SEGAL 1983, Cat. 12 | | | IV |
| 57.<br>Gottfried von Wedig<br>Still life (1639)<br>Wallraf-Richartz-Museum, Cologne<br>ERICHSON-FIRLE & VEY 1973, Cat. 3163 | II | | |

# Appendix 8

## Figures: Concordance of Ware-types and forms by context

| Fig. Nr. | Ware-code | Form-type |
|---|---|---|
| 85:135/16 Duisburg, Schwanenstraße (context 1) | | |
| 1.1 | Ia.8 | bowl |
| 1.2 | | skillet |
| 1.3 | | tripod pipkin |
| 1.4 | | tripod pipkin |
| 1.5 | | tripod pipkin |
| 1.6 | Ia.6 | bowl with pouring lip |
| 1.7 | | bowl with pouring lip |
| 1.8 | | bowl with pouring lip |
| 1.9 | Ia.7 | tripod pipkin |
| 1.10 | Ia.3 | tripod pipkin |
| 1.11 | II.6 | ointmet pot |
| 1.12 | II.2 | beaker |
| 1.13 | II.1 | lid |
| 85:135/17 Duisburg, Schwanenstraße (context 2) | | |
| 2.1 | Ia.5 | tripod pipkin |
| 2.2 | Ia.6 | bowl with pouring lip |
| 85:135/5a Duisburg, Schwanenstraße (context 3) | | |
| 3.1 | II.1 | jug / bottle |
| 3.2 | | jug |
| 3.3 | | jug |
| 3.4 | II.2 | drinking jug |
| 3.5 | | beaker |
| 3.6 | Ia.6 | tripod pipkin |
| 85:135/5b Duisburg, Schwanenstraße (context 4) | | |
| 4.1 | II.4 | beaker |
| 4.2 | | beaker |
| 4.3 | II.9 | jug |
| 4.4 | | tankard |
| 4.5 | | tankard |
| 4.6 | Ic.3 | dish |
| 4.7 | Ib.5 | dish |
| 4.8 | | dish |
| 4.9 | Ic.4 | dish with loop handles (85:135/5c) |
| 85:135/5b Duisburg, Schwanenstraße (context 4) | | |
| 5.1 | III.1 | dish |
| 5.2 | | porringer |
| 5.3 | | plate |
| 5.4 | | dish |
| 5.5 | | dish |
| 85:135/5b Duisburg, Schwanenstraße (context 4) | | |
| 6.1 | III.3 | plate |
| 6.2 | III.2 | dish |
| 6.3 | III.3 | plate |
| 6.4 | | plate |
| 6.5 | III.1 | tile |
| 6.6 | | tile |

| | | |
|---|---|---|
| 6.7 | | tile |
| **85:135/5b Duisburg, Schwanenstraße (context 4)** | | |
| 7.1 | Ic.3 | tripod pipkin |
| 7.2 | | tripod pipkin |
| 7.3 | | porringer |
| 7.4 | | tripod pipkin |
| 7.5 | | tripod pipkin |
| 7.6 | | porringer |
| 7.7 | | tripod pipkin |
| 7.8 | | tripod pipkin with hollow handle |
| 7.9 | | porringer |
| 7.10 | Ic.1 | bowl |
| 7.11 | | tripod pipkin with hollow handle |
| 7.12 | | tripod pipkin with hollow handle |
| 7.13 | | bowl |
| 7.14 | | bowl |
| 7.15 | | bowl |
| 7.16 | | bowl |
| 7.17 | | bowl |
| 7.18 | | bowl |
| 7.19 | | bowl |
| 7.20 | Id.1 | plate |
| 7.21 | | plate |
| 7.22 | | plate |
| 7.23 | Ic.1 | dish |
| **85:135/5c Duisburg, Schwanenstraße (context 5)** | | |
| 8.1 | III.3 | plate |
| 8.2 | | plate |
| 8.3 | | tankard |
| 8.4 | | lobed dish |
| 8.5 | Ic.4 | dish |
| 8.6 | | tripod pipkin |
| 8.7 | II.9 | tankard |
| 8.8 | Ic.3 | tripod pipkin |
| 8.9 | | tripod pipkin |
| 8.10 | | tripod pipkin |
| 8.11 | Ic.1 | tripod pipkin |
| 8.12 | Id.4 | chamber pot |
| 8.13 | | tripod pipkin |
| **85:135/5d Duisburg, Schwanenstraße (context 6)** | | |
| 9.1 | Ic.3 | tripod pipkin |
| 9.2 | Ic.3 | tripod pipkin |
| 9.3 | Ic.4 | dish |
| 9.4 | | tripod pipkin |
| 9.5 | | tripod pipkin |
| 9.6 | | tripod pipkin |
| 9.7 | Id.2 | dish with horizontal loop handles |
| 9.8 | Ic.4 | tripod pipkin |
| 9.9 | Ic.4 | tripod pipkin |
| 9.10 | Id.4 | lid |
| 9.11 | | tripod pipkin |
| 9.12 | | tripod pipkin |
| 9.13 | | tripod pipkin |
| 9.14 | | lid |
| 9.15 | Id.7 | pipkin with pouring lip |
| 9.16 | Id.4 | jug |
| **85:135/5d Duisburg, Schwanenstraße (context 6)** | | |
| 10.1 | II.9 | jug |
| 10.2 | | tankard |
| 10.3 | III.3 | lobed dish |
| 10.4 | III.2 | lobed dish |
| 10.5 | III.3 | plate |
| 10.6 | III.2 | ointment pot |
| 10.7 | III.4 | dish |
| 10.8 | | dish |
| 10.9 | III.2 | plate |
| 10.10 | III.3 | saucer |
| 10.11 | | saucer |
| 10.12 | | tea bowl |
| 10.13 | | saucer |
| 10.14 | | tea-bowl |
| 10.15 | | tea-bowl |
| 10.16 | IV.2 | tea-bowl |
| 10.17 | IV.3 | saucer |
| **85:135/15a Duisburg, Schwanenstraße (context 7)** | | |
| 11.1 | Ia.8 | pipkin |
| 11.2 | | lid |
| 11.3 | | tripod pipkin |
| 11.4 | | pipkin |
| 11.5 | Ia.4 | cup |
| 11.6 | Ia.7 | jug |
| 11.7 | II.1 | drinking jug |
| 11.8 | | jug |
| 11.9 | Ia.3 | tripod pipkin |
| **85:135/15b Duisburg, Schwanenstraße (context 8)** | | |
| 12.1 | Ic.4 | dish (85:153/5c) |
| 12.2 | Ib.5 | porringer |
| 12.3 | | dish with horizontal loop handles |
| 12.4 | | dish |
| 12.5 | | dish |
| 12.6 | | bowl / porringer |
| 12.7 | | dish |
| **85:135/15b Duisburg, Schwanenstraße (context 8)** | | |
| 13.1 | IV.1 | dish |
| 13.2 | | dish |
| 13.3 | III.1 | dish with footring |
| 13.4 | | dish |
| 13.5 | | dish |
| 13.6 | | dish |
| **85:135/15b Duisburg, Schwanenstraße (context 8)** | | |
| 14.1 | Ic.3 | dish |
| 14.2 | | dish |
| 14.3 | | porringer |
| 14.4 | | tripod pipkin |
| 14.5 | | tripod pipkin |
| 14.6 | | tripod pipkin |
| 14.7 | | porringer |
| 14.8 | | porringer |
| 14.9 | | tripod pipkin with hollow handle |
| 14.10 | | colander |
| 14.11 | III.3 | plate |
| **85:135/15b Duisburg, Schwanenstraße (context 8)** | | |
| 15.1 | Ic.1 | dish |
| 15.2 | | dish with footring |
| 15.3 | | dish |
| 15.4 | Ic.2 | dish |
| 15.5 | Ic.1 | pipkin |
| 15.6 | | tripod colander |
| 15.7 | | bowl |
| 15.8 | | chamber pot |
| 15.9 | | tripod pipkin with hollow handle |
| 15.10 | | porringer |
| 15.11 | | lid |
| 15.12 | | lid |
| 15.13 | II.8 | jug |
| 15.14 | | bottle |
| 15.15 | | bottle |
| 15.16 | II.9 | flagon, d. 1633 |

| | | |
|---|---|---|
| 15.17 | II.8 | handled jar |
| 85:135/15c Duisburg, Schwanenstraße (context 9) | | |
| 16.1 | Id.1 | plate |
| 16.2 | Id.4 | brazier / ash bin |
| 16.3 | III.3 | saucer |
| 16.4 | | saucer |
| 16.5 | IV.3 | saucer |
| 85:135/15d Duisburg, Schwanenstraße (context 10) | | |
| 17.1 | Id.2 | dish |
| 17.2 | Id.1 | plate |
| 17.3 | | dish |
| 17.4 | Id.2 | plate |
| 17.5 | Id.1 | porringer |
| 85:135/15d Duisburg, Schwanenstraße (context 10) | | |
| 18.1 | III.1 | dish |
| 18.2 | III.2 | dish |
| 18.3 | | salt |
| 18.4 | III.3 | plate |
| 18.5 | | plate |
| 18.6 | | saucer |
| 18.7 | | saucer |
| 18.8 | | dish |
| 18.9 | | tea-bowl |
| 18.10 | | tile |
| 18.11 | | saucer |
| 18.12 | | bowl |
| 18.13 | IV.2 | tea-bowl |
| 18.14 | | tea-bowl |
| 18.15 | IV.3 | saucer |
| 85:135/15d Duisburg, Schwanenstraße (context 10) | | |
| 19.1 | Id.4 | cauldron |
| 19.2 | | tripod pipkin |
| 19.3 | | tripod pipkin |
| 19.4 | | pipkin |
| 19.5 | Id.8 | lid |
| 19.6 | II.9 | jug |
| 19.7 | | jug |
| 85:135/15e Duisburg, Schwanenstraße (context 11) | | |
| 20.1 | Id.2 | plate |
| 20.2 | | plate |
| 20.3 | | plate |
| 20.4 | Id.1 | dish |
| 20.5 | | dish |
| 85:135/15e Duisburg, Schwanenstraße (context 11) | | |
| 21.1 | Id.1 | dish |
| 21.2 | | dish |
| 21.3 | | plate |
| 21.4 | | plate |
| 21.5 | | plate |
| 21.6 | | plate |
| 85:135/15e Duisburg, Schwanenstraße (context 11) | | |
| 22.1 | Id.1 | dish |
| 22.2 | | tripod pipkin |
| 22.3 | | tripod pipkin |
| 22.4 | | tripod pipkin |
| 22.5 | Id.3 | chamber pot |
| 22.6 | | plate |
| 22.7 | | plate |
| 22.8 | Id.4 | tripod pipkin |
| 22.9 | | tripod pipkin |
| 22.10 | | tripod pipkin |
| 22.11 | | tea-bowl |
| 85:135/15e Duisburg, Schwanenstraße (context 11) | | |
| 23.1 | III.3 | plate |
| 23.2 | | plate |
| 23.3 | | tea-bowl |
| 23.4 | II.9 | chamber pot |
| 23.5 | II.10 | tea bowl |
| 85:135/15f Duisburg, Schwanenstraße (context 12) | | |
| 24.1 | Id.1 | dish |
| 24.2 | | bowl / porringer |
| 24.3 | Id.4 | tripod pipkin |
| 24.4 | II.9 | chamber pot |
| 24.5 | IV.3 | tea-bowl |
| 24.6 | III.3 | tea-bowl |
| 85:135/15g Duisburg, Schwanenstraße (context 13) | | |
| 25.1 | II.5 | storage jar |
| 25.2 | II.9 | jardiniere |
| 25.3 | II.11 | mineralwater bottle |
| 25.4 | V.1 | tea-cup |
| 25.5 | | saucer |
| 25.6 | | bowl |
| 25.7 | Id.10 | teapot |
| 25.8 | Id.4 | dish |
| 25.9 | Id.1 | dish |
| 25.10 | IV.3 | saucer |
| 25.11 | IV.2 | tea-bowl |
| 25.12 | IV.4 | saucer |
| 25.13 | | tea-cup |
| 25.14 | III.5 | tea-bowl |
| 25.15 | IV.2 | tea-bowl |
| 25.16 | IV.3 | tea-bowl |
| 25.17 | Id.1 | dish (d. 178_) |
| 25.18 | | porringer |
| 25.19 | | porringer |
| 85:135/3 Duisburg, Schwanenstraße (context 14) | | |
| 26.1 | II.4 | beaker |
| 26.2 | II.8 | handled jar |
| 26.3 | II.9 | jug |
| 26.4 | | jug |
| 26.5 | | jug |
| 26.6 | | pipkin / spouted pitcher |
| 26.7 | | drug jar |
| 26.8 | | feeding bottle |
| 26.9 | II.8 | chamber pot |
| 85:135/3 Duisburg, Schwanenstraße (context 14) | | |
| 27.1 | III.1 | dish |
| 27.2 | | plate |
| 27.3 | | drug jar |
| 27.4 | | tile |
| 27.5 | | tile |
| 27.6 | | dish |
| 85:135/3 Duisburg, Schwanenstraße (context 14) | | |
| 28.1 | III.3 | plate |
| 28.2 | | plate |
| 28.3 | | dish |
| 28.4 | | dish |
| 28.5 | III.2 | lobed dish |
| 28.6 | | saucer |
| 85:135/3 Duisburg, Schwanenstraße (context 14) | | |
| 29.1 | Ic.3 | dish with footring |
| 29.2 | | dish with footring |
| 29.3 | | tripod pipkin with hollow handle |
| 29.4 | | porringer |
| 85:135/3 Duisburg, Schwanenstraße (context 14) | | |
| 30.1 | Ic.1 | tripod pipkin |

| | | |
|---|---|---|
| 30.2 | | tripod pipkin |
| 30.3 | | cauldron |
| 30.4 | | tripod pipkin with hollow handle |
| 30.5 | | tripod pipkin |
| 30.6 | | pipkin |
| 30.7 | | porringer |
| 30.8 | | lid |
| 30.9 | | lid |
| 30.10 | | lid |
| 30.11 | | brazier |
| 30.12 | | chamber pot |
| 30.13 | Ic.4 | porringer / bowl |
| 30.14 | Ic.1 | dish |
| 30.15 | | bowl |
| 86:4a Duisburg, Schwanenstraße (context 15) | | |
| 31.1 | Ia.3 | tripod pipkin |
| 31.2 | | tripod pipkin |
| 31.3 | Ia.6 | pipkin |
| 31.4 | Ia.7 | bowl |
| 86:4b Duisburg, Schwanenstraße (context 16) | | |
| 31.5 | II.8 | "Bartmann" jug |
| 31.6 | | chamber pot |
| 31.7 | | bottle |
| 31.8 | II.4 | beaker & handle of jug |
| 31.9 | II.5 | storage jar |
| 31.10 | Ib.1 | pipkin / chamber pot |
| 31.11 | | pipkin |
| 31.12 | | jar |
| 86:4b Duisburg, Schwanenstraße (context 16) | | |
| 32.1 | Ib.5 | dish |
| 32.2 | | dish |
| 32.3 | | dish |
| 32.4 | | dish |
| 32.5 | Ib.6 | dish with pulled feet |
| 32.6 | Ib.5 | porringer / bowl |
| 32.7 | Ic.3 | ointment pot |
| 86:4b Duisburg, Schwanenstraße (context 16) | | |
| 33.1 | Ic.1 | chamber pot |
| 33.2 | | pipkin |
| 33.3 | | bowl |
| 33.4 | | bowl |
| 33.5 | | bowl |
| 33.6 | | bowl |
| 33.7 | | bowl |
| 33.8 | Id.4 | dish |
| 33.9 | III.3 | dish |
| 33.10 | III.2 | tankard |
| 33.11 | | tankard |
| 86:4b Duisburg, Schwanenstraße (context 16) | | |
| 34.1 | Ic.1 | cauldron |
| 34.2 | | cauldron |
| 34.3 | | jug / storage jar |
| 34.4 | | lid |
| 34.5 | | cauldron |
| 34.6 | | tripod pipkin with hollow handle |
| 34.7 | | colander |
| 34.8 | | tripod pipkin with hollow handle |
| 34.9 | | tripod pipkin with hollow handle |
| 34.10 | | tripod pipkin with hollow handle |
| 34.11 | | tripod pipkin with hollow handle |
| 34.12 | | skillet |
| 34.13 | | skillet |
| 86:2 Duisburg, Schwanenstraße (context 17) | | |
| 35.1 | Ib.5 | dish |
| 35.2 | Ic.4 | dish (d. 1639) |
| 35.3 | | dish with footring |
| 35.4 | | tripod pipkin |
| 35.5 | Ib.5 | porringer |
| 35.6 | Ic.4 | dish |
| 86:2 Duisburg, Schwanenstraße (context 17) | | |
| 36.1 | II.3 | flagon |
| 36.2 | | drinking jug (d. 1598) |
| 36.3 | | beaker |
| 36.4 | II.6 | jug |
| 36.5 | II.9 | chamber pot (d. 1581) |
| 36.6 | II.3 | tankard |
| 36.7 | II.9 | jug |
| 36.8 | II.8 | "Bartmann" jug |
| 36.9 | | bottle |
| 36.10 | II.9 | chamber pot |
| 36.11 | Ib.2 | dish |
| 36.12 | Ic.1 | dish |
| 36.13 | | dish |
| 36.14 | | dish |
| 36.15 | | dish with footring |
| 86:2 Duisburg, Schwanenstraße (context 17) | | |
| 37,1 | Ic.1 | cauldron |
| 37.2 | | tripod pipkin |
| 37.3 | | storage jar |
| 37.4 | | chamber pot / jug |
| 37.5 | | chamber pot |
| 37.6 | | tripod pipkin |
| 37.7 | | skillet |
| 37.8 | | jug / handled jar |
| 37.9 | | cup |
| 37.10 | | porringer |
| 37.11 | | tripod pipkin |
| 37.12 | | tripod pipkin with hollow handle |
| 37.13 | | pipkin |
| 37.14 | | chamber pot |
| 37.15 | | bowl |
| 37.16–22 | | bowl |
| 37.23 | | jar / pipkin |
| 86:1/16 Duisburg, Schwanenstraße (context 18) | | |
| 38.1 | III.2 | bowl |
| 38.2 | | porringer |
| 38.3 | Ic.3 | tripod pipkin |
| 38.4 | Id.1 | tripod pipkin |
| 38.5 | Id.2 | plate |
| 38.6 | | plate |
| 38.7 | Id.4 | lid |
| 38.8 | Id.8 | tripod pipkin with hollow handle |
| 38.9 | II.9 | jug (toy) |
| 38.10 | Id.4 | tripod pipkin |
| 38.11 | | tripod pipkin |
| 38.12 | | tripod pipkin |
| 86:1/16 Duisburg, Schwanenstraße (context 18) | | |
| 39.1 | III.3 | plate |
| 39.2 | | plate |
| 39.3 | | plate |
| 39.4 | | plate |
| 39.5 | | plate |
| 39.6 | | saucer |
| 39.7 | | saucer |
| 39.8 | | saucer & marks |
| 39.9 | | vase |
| 39.10 | | tea-bowl |
| 86:1/3 Duisburg, Schwanenstraße (context 19) | | |

| | | |
|---|---|---|
| 40.1 | Id.1 | plate |
| 40.2 | Id.2 | dish |
| 40.3 | Id.1 | dish |
| 40.4 | | dish |
| 40.5 | III.3 | plate |
| **86:1/3 Duisburg, Schwanenstraße (context 19)** | | |
| 41.1 | Id.4 | storage jar |
| 41.2 | | tripod pipkin |
| 41.3 | | bowl |
| 41.4 | Id.8 | chamber pot |
| **89:17 Duisburg, Niederstraße (context 20)** | | |
| 42.1 | II.3 | drinking jug |
| 42.2 | | beaker |
| 42.3 | | beaker |
| 42.4 | II.4 | tankard |
| 42.5 | Ic.4 | porringer |
| 42.6 | Ib.5 | dish |
| 42.7 | Ic.5 | dish |
| 42.8 | | dish |
| **89:17 Duisburg, Niederstraße (context 21)** | | |
| 43.1 | II.2 | jug |
| 43.2 | | jug |
| 43.3 | | jug |
| 43.4 | | jug |
| 43.5 | | drinking jug |
| 43.6 | II.3 | flagon |
| 43.7 | | jug |
| 43.8 | Ib.5 | dish with footring |
| 43.9 | II.3 | costrel |
| **89:20 Duisburg, Niederstraße (context 22)** | | |
| 44.1 | II.2 | jug |
| 44.2 | | drinking jug |
| 44.3 | Ib.3 | plate |
| 44.4 | Ia.8 | basket |
| **88:25 Duisburg, Alter Markt (context 25)** | | |
| 44.5 | Ia.8 | lid |
| 44.6 | | salt |
| **55:2K Duisburg, Burgplatz (context 26)** | | |
| 44.7 | II.6 | figurine |
| **82:35/28 Duisburg, Alter Markt (context 27)** | | |
| 44.8 | II.3 | flagon |
| 44.9 | II.7 | "Bartmann" jug |
| **83:31/0 Duisburg, Alter Markt (context 28)** | | |
| 44.10 | Id.3 | dish |
| **87:29 Duisburg, Niederstraße (context 29)** | | |
| 45.1 | II.4 | "Bartmann" jug |
| 45.2 | II.4 | tankard ("Schnelle") |
| 45.3 | Ia.5 | colander |
| **8:52 Duisburg, Niederstraße (context 30)** | | |
| 45.4 | Ia.8 | jug |
| 45.5 | Ib.3 | porringer |
| 45.6 | Ia.9 | bowl |
| 45.7 | Ib.3 | porringer |
| 45.8 | II.3 | drinking jug |
| 45.9 | II.7 | "Bartmann" jug |
| 45.10 | | jug |
| 45.11 | II.6 | jug |
| 45.12 | Ib.1 | chamber pot |
| 45.13 | | pipkin with two handles |
| 45.14 | Ib.3 | dish |
| 45.15 | III.3 | ointment pot |
| **86:10/13 Duisburg, Schwanenstraße (context 31)** | | |
| 46.1 | Ia.3 | tripod pipkin |
| 46.2 | II.6 | mug |
| **86:K4 (86:5) Duisburg, Markt buildings (context 32)** | | |
| 46.3 | II.2 | jug |
| 46.4 | Ia.8 | bowl / salt |
| **86:10/16 Duisburg, Schwanenstraße (context 33)** | | |
| 46.5 | II.2 | mug |
| 46.6 | | drinking jug |
| 46.7 | | beaker |
| 46.8 | Ib.1 | tripod pipkin with hollow handle |
| 46.9 | | tripod pipkin with hollow handle |
| 46.10 | | pipkin |
| **86:10/26–27 Duisburg, Schwanenstraße (context 34)** | | |
| 46.11 | Ia.8 | salt |
| 46.12 | | skillet |
| **86:10/23 (86:1/23/0) Duisburg, Schwanenstraße (context 35)** | | |
| 46.13 | II.7 | "Bartmann" jug |
| **84:52 Duisburg, Minoritenkloster (context 36)** | | |
| 47.1 | II.2 | costrel |
| 47.2 | | jug |
| 47.3 | | jug |
| 47.4 | | drinking jug / beaker |
| 47.5 | | jug |
| 47.6 | | jug |
| 47.7–17 | | drinking jug / beaker |
| 47.18 | | mug |
| 47.19–21 | | drinking jug / beaker |
| 47.22 | | beaker |
| 47.23–25 | | drinking jug / beaker |
| 47.26 | | drinking bowl |
| 47.27–30 | | drinking jug / beaker |
| 47.31 | | marble (toy) |
| **84:52 Duisburg, Minoritenkloster (context 36)** | | |
| 48.1 | Ia.3 | dripping pan |
| 48.2 | | bowl |
| 48.3 | Ia.1 | bowl |
| 48.4 | | bowl |
| 48.5 | | tripod pipkin |
| 48.6 | Ia.7 | bowl |
| 48.7 | | bowl |
| 48.8 | | bowl |
| 48.9 | | bowl |
| 48.10 | Ia.12 | stove-tile (niche-type) |
| **84:7/34 Duisburg, Innenhafen (context 37)** | | |
| 49.1 | Ia.6 | storage jar |
| 49.2 | | storage jar |
| 49.3 | Ia.8 | bowl |
| 49.4 | Ia.6 | storage jar |
| 49.5 | | bowl |
| 49.6 | | bowl |
| 49.7 | Ia.8 | tripod pipkin |
| 49.8 | | bowl |
| 49.9 | Ia.7 | pipkin |
| **84:7/34 Duisburg, Innenhafen (context 37)** | | |
| 50.1 | Ia.8 | tripod pipkin |
| 50.2 | II.1 | drinking jug |
| 50.3 | II.3 | flagon |
| 50.4 | II.5 | beaker |
| 50.5 | Ib.1 | pancheon |
| 50.6 | | pancheon |
| 50.7 | | storage jar |
| 50.8 | | jar |
| 50.9 | | jar |

| | | |
|---|---|---|
| 50.10 | | jar |
| **84:7/37 Duisburg, Innenhafen (context 38)** | | |
| 51.1 | Ia.6 | storage jar |
| 51.2 | | bowl |
| 51.3 | | bowl |
| 51.4 | | bowl |
| 51.5 | | bowl |
| 51.6 | | bowl |
| 51.7 | | colander |
| 51.8 | | bowl |
| 51.9 | | bowl |
| 51.10 | | bowl |
| 51.11 | Ia.10 | jar |
| 51.12 | Ia.7 | pipkin |
| 51.13 | | tripod pipkin |
| 51.14 | Ia.9 | lid |
| 51.15 | | dripping pan |
| **84:7/37 Duisburg, Innenhafen (context 38)** | | |
| 52.1 | II.2 | costrel |
| 52.2 | | drinking jug |
| 52.3 | | drinking jug |
| 52.4 | | drinking bowl |
| 52.5 | | drinking jug / beaker |
| 52.6 | | jug |
| 52.7 | Ia.3 | tripod pipkin |
| 52.8 | | cup / small bowl |
| 52.9 | | lid (reversed in fig.) |
| 52.10 | Ia.2 | tripod pipkin |
| 52.11 | Ia.2/3 | beaker |
| 52.12 | Ia.4 | cup |
| 52.13 | II.2 | mug |
| 52.14 | Ib.3 | porringer |
| **84:6/Grube 34 Duisburg, C & A (context 41)** | | |
| 53.1 | Ib.1 | casserole |
| 53.2 | | tripod storage jar |
| 53.3 | | tripod pipkin |
| 53.4 | | cup |
| 53.5 | | chamber pot |
| 53.6 | | skillet |
| 53.7 | | bowl with single vertical handle |
| **84:6/62 Duisburg, C & A (context 42)** | | |
| 54.1 | Ib.2 | dish |
| 54.2 | | dish |
| 54.3 | | dish |
| 54.4 | | dish |
| 54.5 | | dish |
| **84:6/62 Duisburg, C & A (context 42)** | | |
| 55.1 | Ib.1 | bowl with pouring lip |
| 55.2 | | bowl with pouring lip |
| 55.3 | | pipkin |
| 55.4 | | pipkin |
| 55.5 | | pipkin |
| 55.6 | | pipkin |
| 55.7 | Ic.1 | bowl |
| 55.8 | Ib.1 | cauldron |
| 55.9 | | tripod pipkin with hollow handle |
| 55.10 | | tripod storage jar |
| 55.11 | | pipkin |
| **84:6/62 Duisburg, C & A (context 42)** | | |
| 56.1 | Ib.1 | tripod pipkin with hollow handle |
| 56.2 | Ic.1 | tripod pipkin with hollow handle |
| 56.3 | | tripod pipkin with hollow handle |
| 56.4 | | tripod pipkin with hollow handle |
| 56.5 | | skillet |
| 56.6 | Ib.3 | porringer |
| 56.7 | Ic.1 | pipkin |
| 56.8 | | pipkin |
| 56.9 | | pipkin |
| 56.10 | | pipkin |
| 56.11 | Ib.3 | porringer |
| 56.12 | | porringer |
| 56.13 | III.3 | dish |
| 56.14 | IV.2 | tea-bowl |
| 56.15 | | tea-bowl |
| 56.16 | | tea-bowl |
| 56.17 | III.3 | saucer |
| 56.18 | Id.12 | dish |
| 56.19 | Id.2 | dish |
| 56.20 | II.4 | flagon |
| 56.21 | | drinking jug |
| 56.22 | | bottle |
| 56.23 | II.9 | chamber pot (d. 1677) |
| 56.24 | III.2 | plate |
| 56.25 | | plate |
| **84:6/65 Duisburg, C & A (context 43)** | | |
| 57.1 | III.3 | dish |
| 57.2 | | dish |
| 57.3 | III.5 | plate |
| 57.4 | III.3 | jug |
| 57.5 | Id.12 | bowl |
| 57.6 | Id.4 | chamber pot |
| 57.7 | | jug |
| 57.8 | Ic.3 | jug |
| 57.9 | Ic.1 | brazier |
| 57.10 | II.8 | "Bartmann" jug |
| 57.11 | II.9 | jug |
| **63:73a Duisburg, Schwanenstraße Alte Post (context 47)** | | |
| 58.1 | III.1 | plate |
| 58.2 | Ic.4 | tripod pipkin |
| 58.3 | Id.8 | ointment pot / ink pot |
| **88:14 Duisburg, Niederstraße (context 48)** | | |
| 58.4 | III.6 | plate |
| **84:0 Duisburg, Alter Markt (context 49)** | | |
| 58.5 | III.6 | plate |
| 58.6 | | dish |
| **61:54a Duisburg, Burgplatz (context 50)** | | |
| 58.7 | II.9 | storage jar |
| 58.8 | | jug |
| 58.9 | II.9 | jug |
| 58.10 | | jug |
| 58.11 | | porringer |
| 58.12 | | jug |
| **82:32 Duisburg, Alter Markt (context 45)** | | |
| 58.13 | II.13 | teapot |
| **A 1612 Niederrheinisches Museum reserve collection** | | |
| 58.14 | II.11 | mineralwater bottle |
| **87:47 Duisburg, Abteistraße (context 44)** | | |
| 59.1 | V.1 | dish |
| 59.2 | | plate |
| 59.3 | | chamber pot |
| 59.4 | | tea bowl |
| 59.5 | | saucer |
| 59.6 | Id.9 | lid |
| 59.7 | | bowl |
| 59.8 | Id.11 | saucer |
| 59.9 | III.3 | plate |

| | | |
|---|---|---|
| 59.10 | Id.4 | brazier |
| 59.11 | Id.1 | pipkin / chamber pot |
| 59.12 | II.9 | bowl |
| 59.13 | | jug |
| **84:31 Duisburg, Alter Markt (context 45)** | | |
| 60.1 | Id.1 | colander |
| 60.2 | | tripod pipkin |
| 60.3 | | porringer |
| 60.4 | | dish |
| 60.5 | | jug |
| **84:31 Duisburg, Alter Markt (context 45)** | | |
| 61.1 | II.9 | storage jar |
| 61.2 | | writing set |
| 61.3 | II.11 | mineralwater bottle |
| 61.4 | II.9 | bowl with double loop handles |
| 61.5 | | tureen |
| 61.6 | | flagon |
| **84:31 Duisburg, Alter Markt (context 45)** | | |
| 62.1 | III.3 | dish |
| 62.2 | | plate |
| 62.3 | | plate |
| 62.4 | | saucer |
| 62.5 | | saucer |
| 62.6 | | saucer |
| 62.7 | | plate |
| 62.8 | III.5 | tea-bowl |
| 62.9 | II.12 | plate |
| 62.10 | IV.2 | tea-bowl |
| 62.11 | | saucer |
| 62.12 | IV.3 | saucer |
| **87:29 Duisburg-Hamborn, Abtei (contexts 54, 55)** | | |
| 63.1 | II.3 | flagon |
| 63.2 | | bottle |
| 63.3 | Ic.1 | porringer |
| **Oberhausen-Holten, Gemeindehaus 1977 (context 62)** | | |
| 63.4 | Ib.5 | dish |
| 63.5 | | porringer |
| **Krefeld-Linn, Margaretenstraße 32 (context 60)** | | |
| 64.1 | Id.1 | dish with footring |
| 64.2–7 | | dish |
| 64.8 | Id.2 | dish |
| 64.9 | | dish |
| 64.10 | Id.1 | dish |
| 64.11 | Id.2 | dish |
| 64.12 | | dish |
| 64.13 | | plate |
| 64.14 | | plate |
| 64.15 | | dish |
| 64.16 | | plate |
| 64.17 | | dish |
| **Krefeld-Linn, Margaretenstraße 32 (context 60)** | | |
| 65.1 | II.9 | jug |
| 65.2 | | tankard |
| 65.3 | | tankard |
| 65.4 | II.10 | tea-bowl |
| 65.5 | | saucer |
| 65.6 | III.2 | dish with footring |
| 65.7 | Id.12 | dish (d. 1729) |
| 65.8 | | dish (d. 1719) |
| 65.9 | | dish |
| 65.10 | | dish |
| 65.11 | Id.1 | porringer |
| 65.12 | | beaker |
| 65.13 | Id.12 | tripod pipkin |
| 65.14 | Id.4 | lid |
| 65.15 | | tripod pipkin |
| **Krefeld-Linn, Margaretenstraße 32 (context 60)** | | |
| 66.1 | Id.4 | jug |
| 66.2 | | tripod pipkin |
| 66.3 | | kettle |
| 66.4 | | colander |
| 66.5–6 | | pancheon |
| 66.7–13 | | bowl |
| 66.14 | Id.5 | bowl |
| 66.15–18 | Id.4 | bowl |
| 66.19 | Id.5 | bowl |
| **Krefeld-Linn, Margaretenstraße 32 (context 61)** | | |
| 67.1 | Id.1 | dish |
| 67.2 | | dish with footring |
| 67.3–14 | | dish |
| 67.15–19 | | plate |
| **Krefeld-Linn, Margaretenstraße 32 (context 61)** | | |
| 68.1–4 | Id.1 | dish |
| 68.5 | | plate |
| 68.6 | | plate |
| 68.7 | Id.12 | plate |
| 68.8 | Id.3 | dish |
| 68.9 | | dish |
| 68.10 | | dish |
| **Krefeld-Linn, Margaretenstraße 32 (context 61)** | | |
| 69.1 | Id.1 | porringer |
| 69.2 | | porringer |
| 69.3 | Id.4 | porringer |
| 69.4 | Id.5 | pancheon |
| 69.5 | Id.4 | jug |
| 69.6 | | tripod pipkin & lid |
| 69.7 | | tripod pipkin |
| 69.8 | | tripod pipkin |
| 69.9 | | tripod pipkin & lid |
| 69.10 | | tripod pipkin with spout |
| 69.11 | | tripod colander |
| 69.12 | | pipkin |
| 69.13 | | cauldron with flat base |
| 69.14 | | storage jar |
| 69.15 | | storage jar |
| 69.16 | | bowl |
| **Krefeld-Linn, Margaretenstraße 32 (context 61)** | | |
| 70.1a–e | III.3 | plate |
| 70.2–5 | | plate |
| 70.6 | | bowl |
| 70.7 | Id.10 | teapot & lid |
| 70.8 | III.2 | dish |
| **Krefeld-Linn, Margaretenstraße 32 (context 61)** | | |
| 71.1–6 | III.3 | saucer |
| 71.7–14 | | tea-bowl |
| 71.15 | IV.2 | saucer |
| 71.16 | IV.3 | saucer |
| 71.17 | | saucer |
| 71.18 | IV.2 | tea-bowl |
| 71.19 | | tea-bowl |
| 71.20 | | tea-bowl |
| 71.21 | IV.3 | tea-bowl |
| 71.22 | | tea-bowl |
| 71.23 | | tea-bowl |

| Krefeld-Linn, Margaretenstraße 32 (context 60) | | |
|---|---|---|
| 72.1 | II.9 | jug |
| 72.2 | | jug |
| 72.3 | | tankard |
| 72.4 | | tankard |
| 72.5 | | tankard |
| 72.6 | | tankard |
| 72.7 | | porringer |
| 72.8 | II.5 | storage jar |
| 72.9 | II.11 | mineralwater bottle |
| 72.10 | | mineralwater bottle |
| 72.11 | II.5 | storage jar |
| 72.12 | II.10 | saucer |

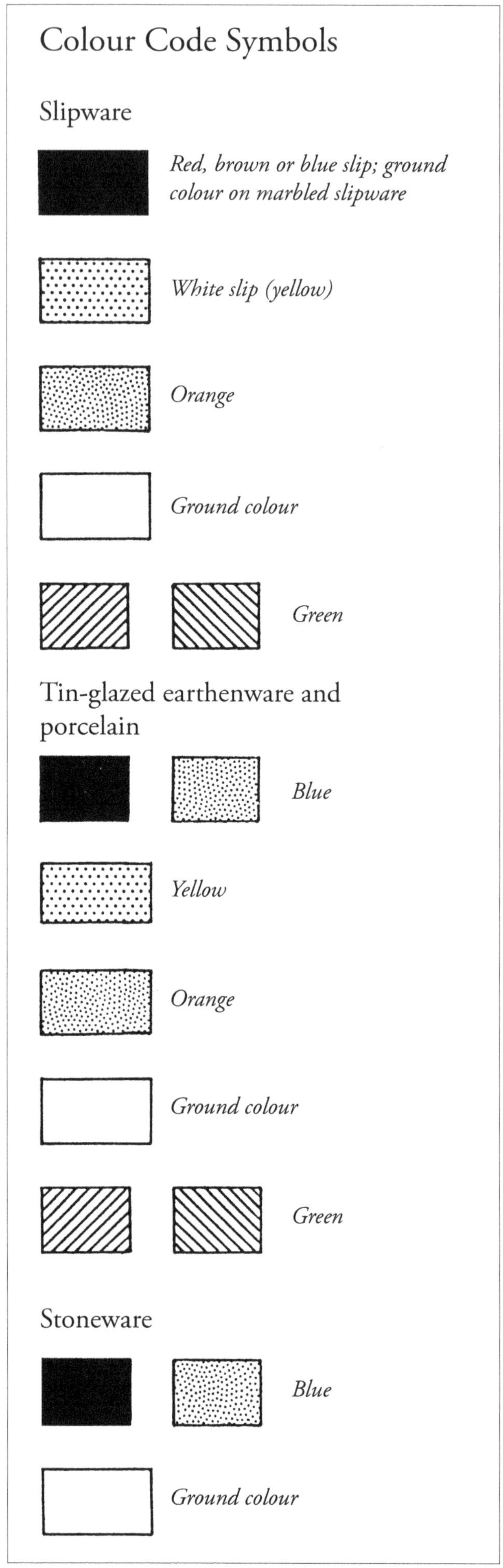

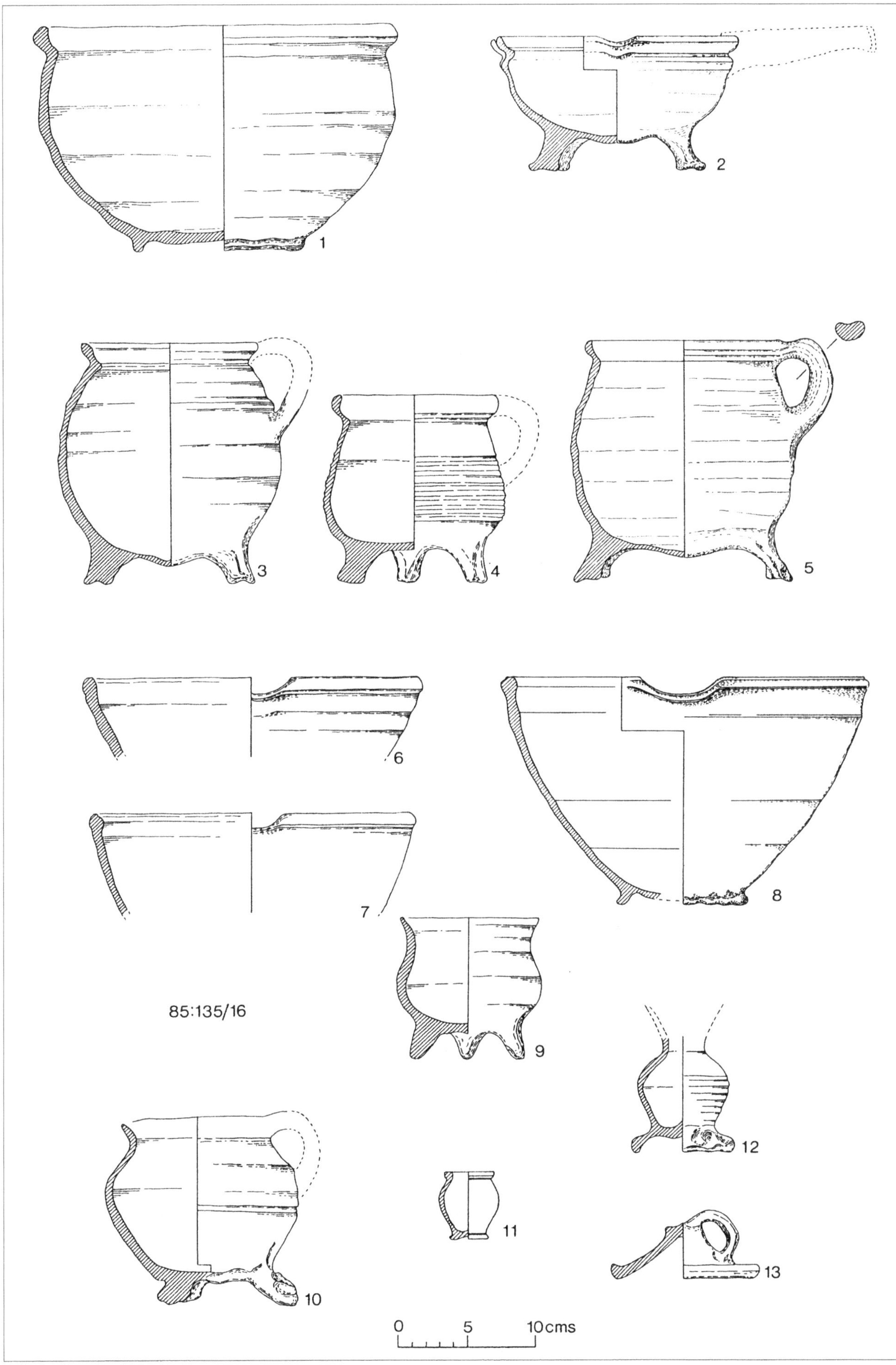


*Fig. 1 Pottery from Duisburg Schwanenstraße 85:135/16*

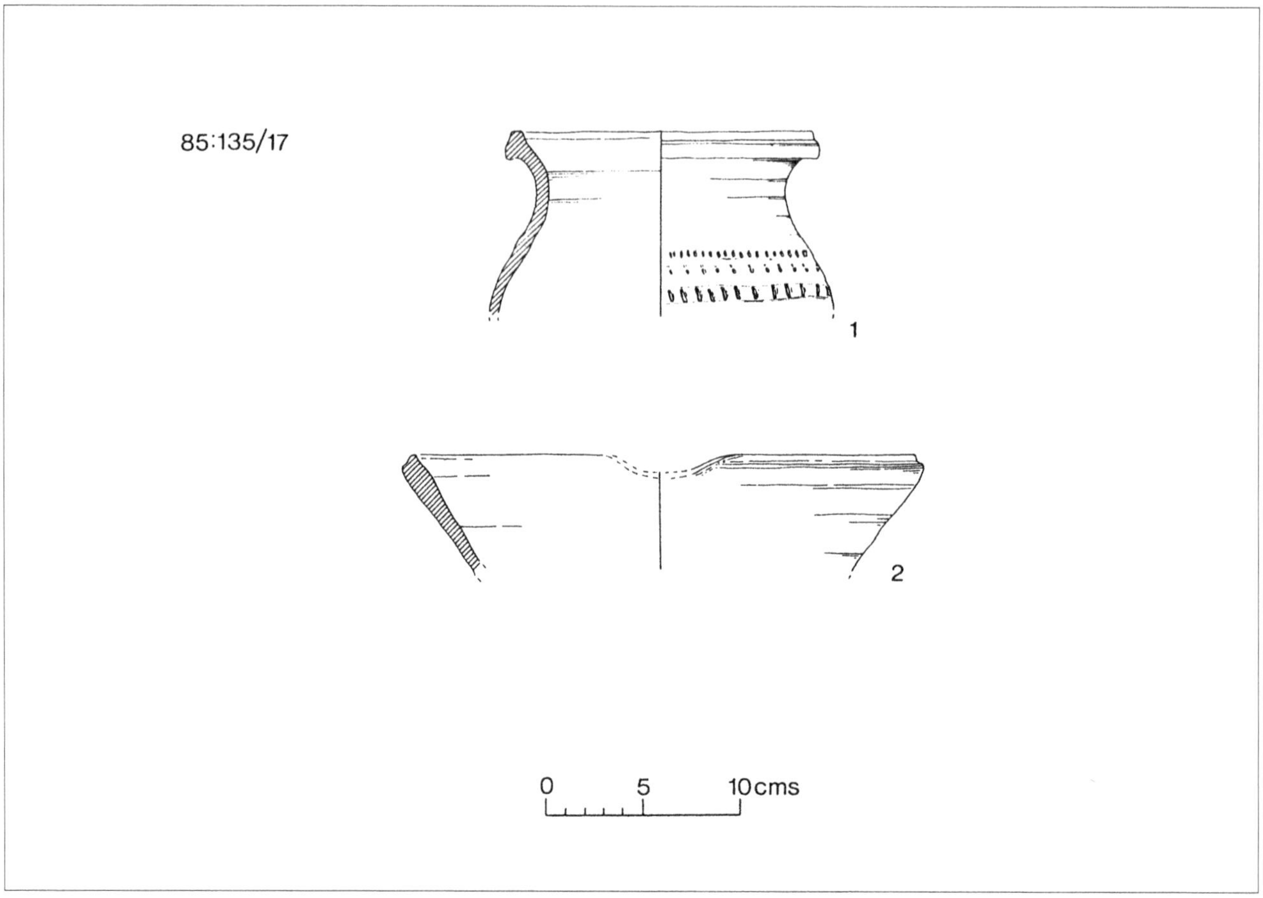


*Fig. 2 Pottery from Duisburg Schwanenstraße 85:135/17*

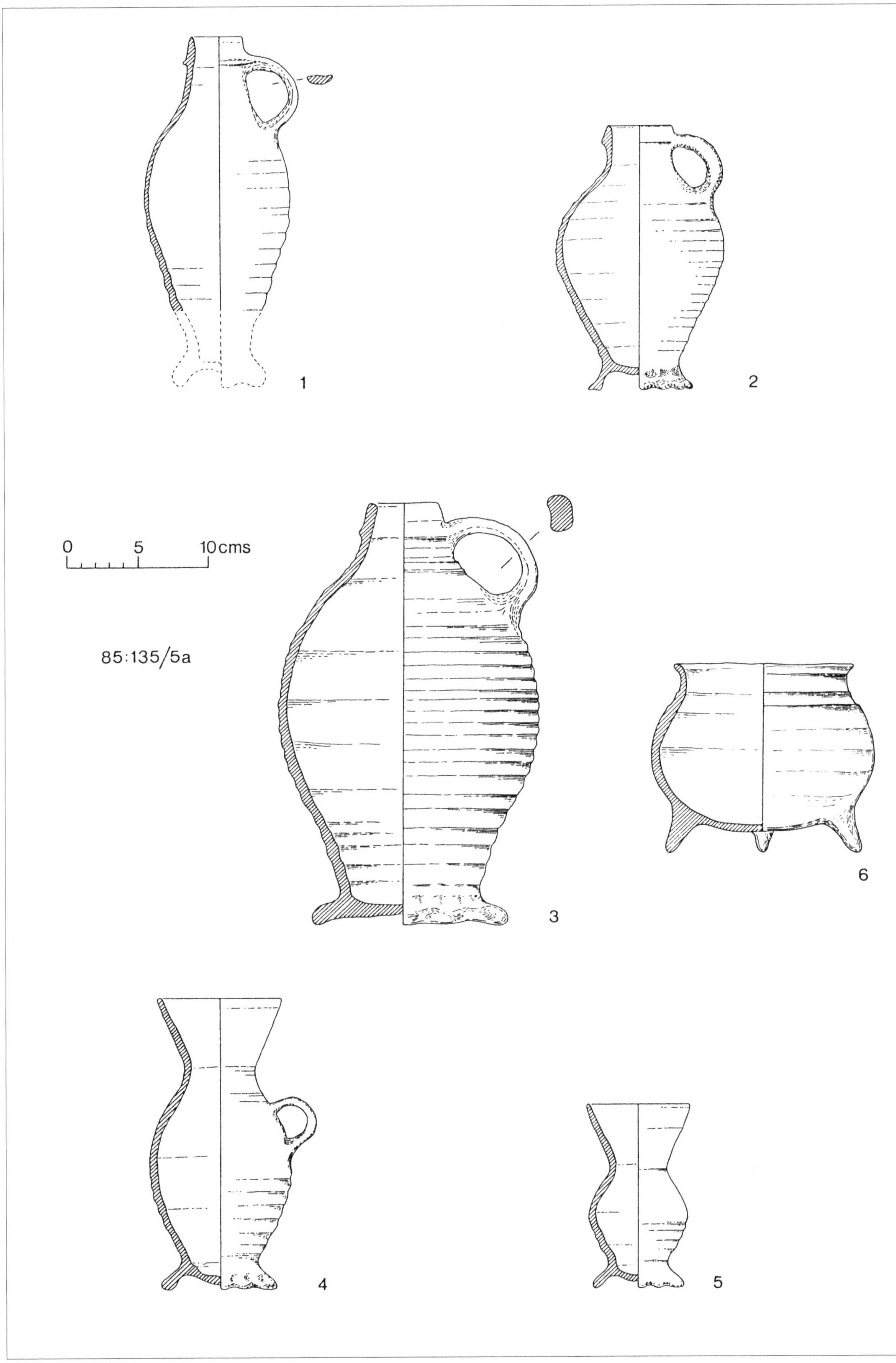


*Fig. 3 Pottery from Duisburg Schwanenstraße 85:135/5a*

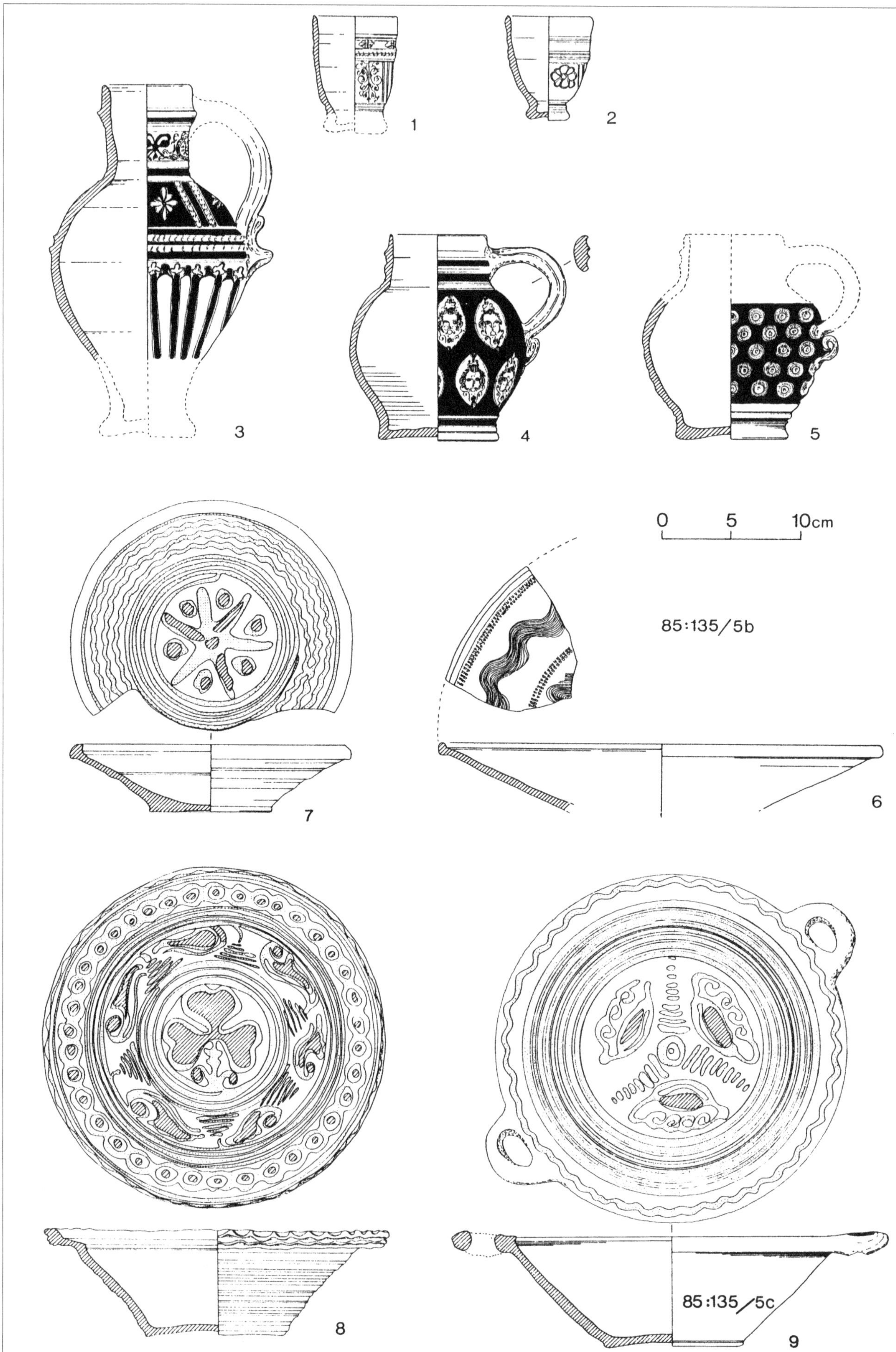


*Fig. 4 Stoneware & slipware from Duisburg Schwanenstraße 85:135/5b*

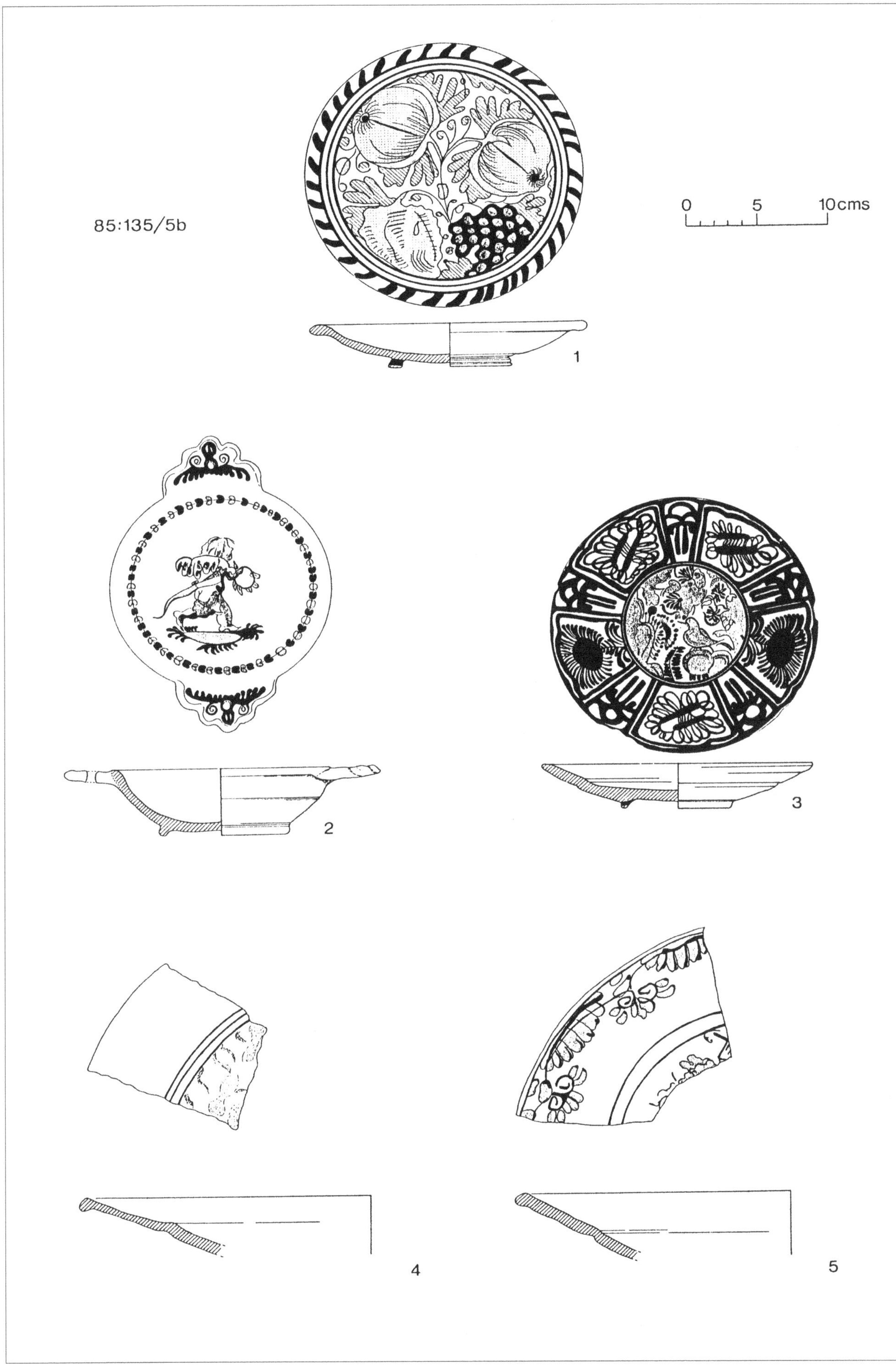


*Fig. 5 NL Maiolica from Duisburg Schwanenstraße 85:135/5b*

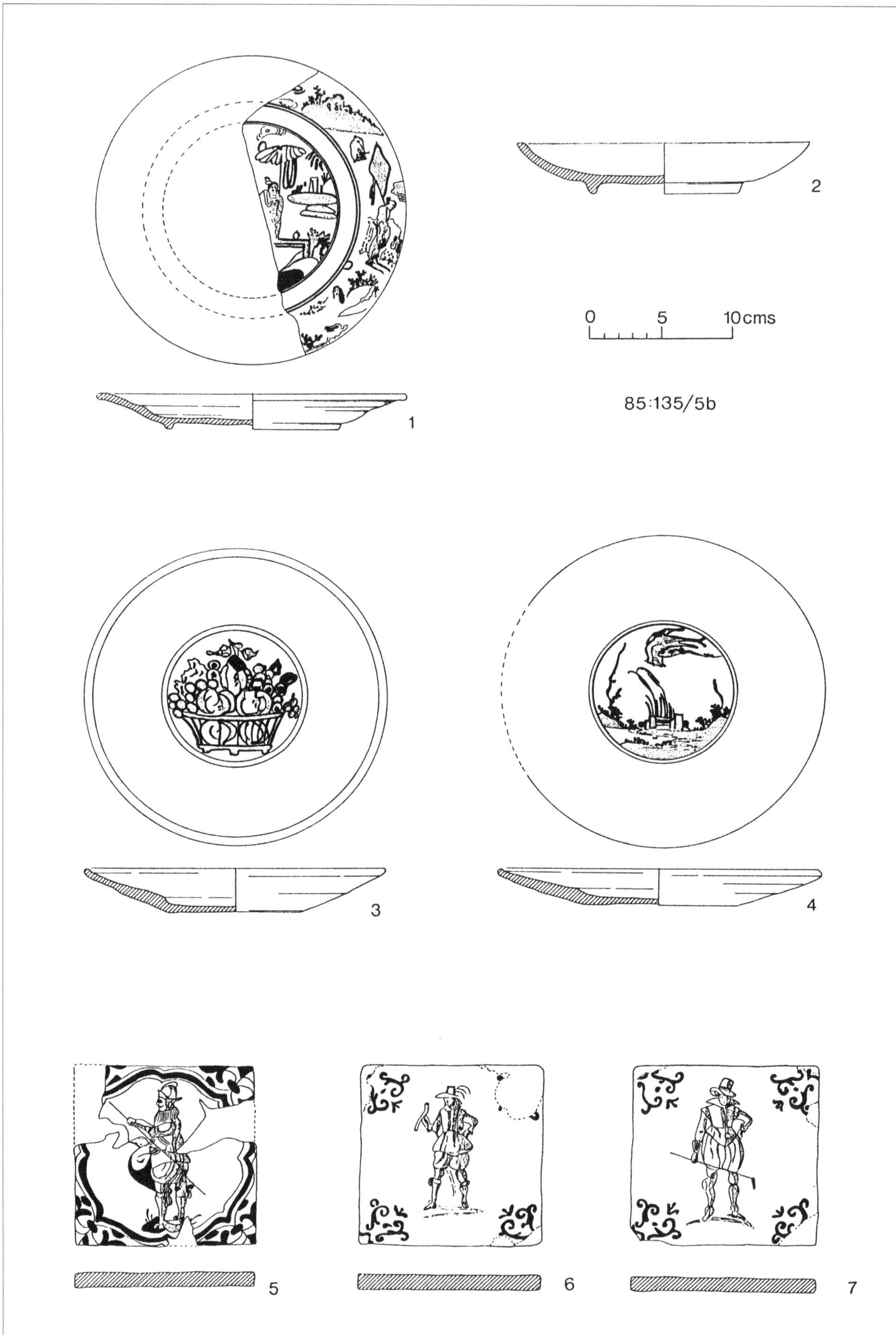


*Fig. 6 NL Faience & maiolica tiles from Duisburg Schwanenstraße 85:135/5b*

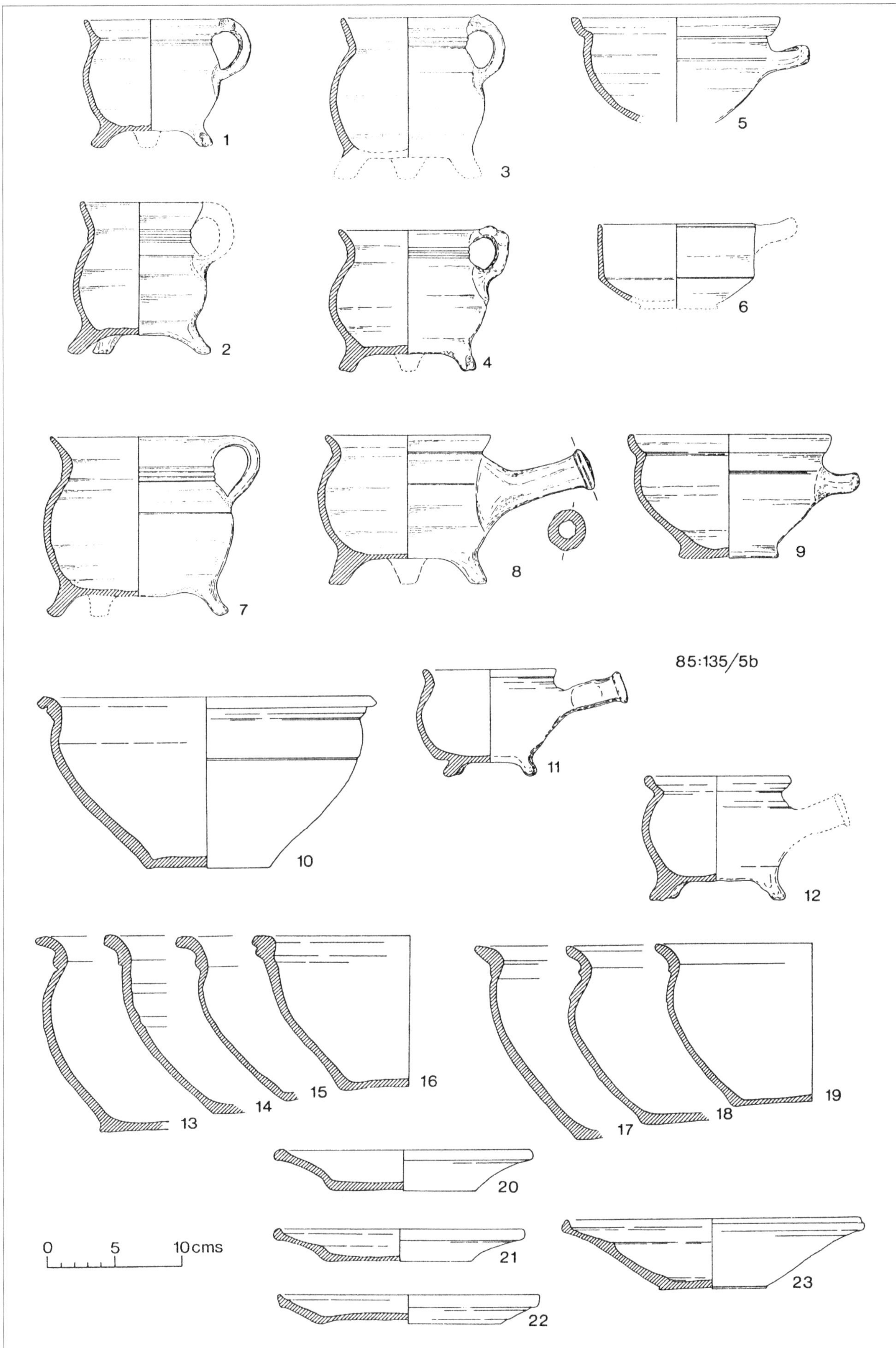


*Fig. 7 Whiteware & plain redware from Duisburg Schwanenstraße 85:135/5b*

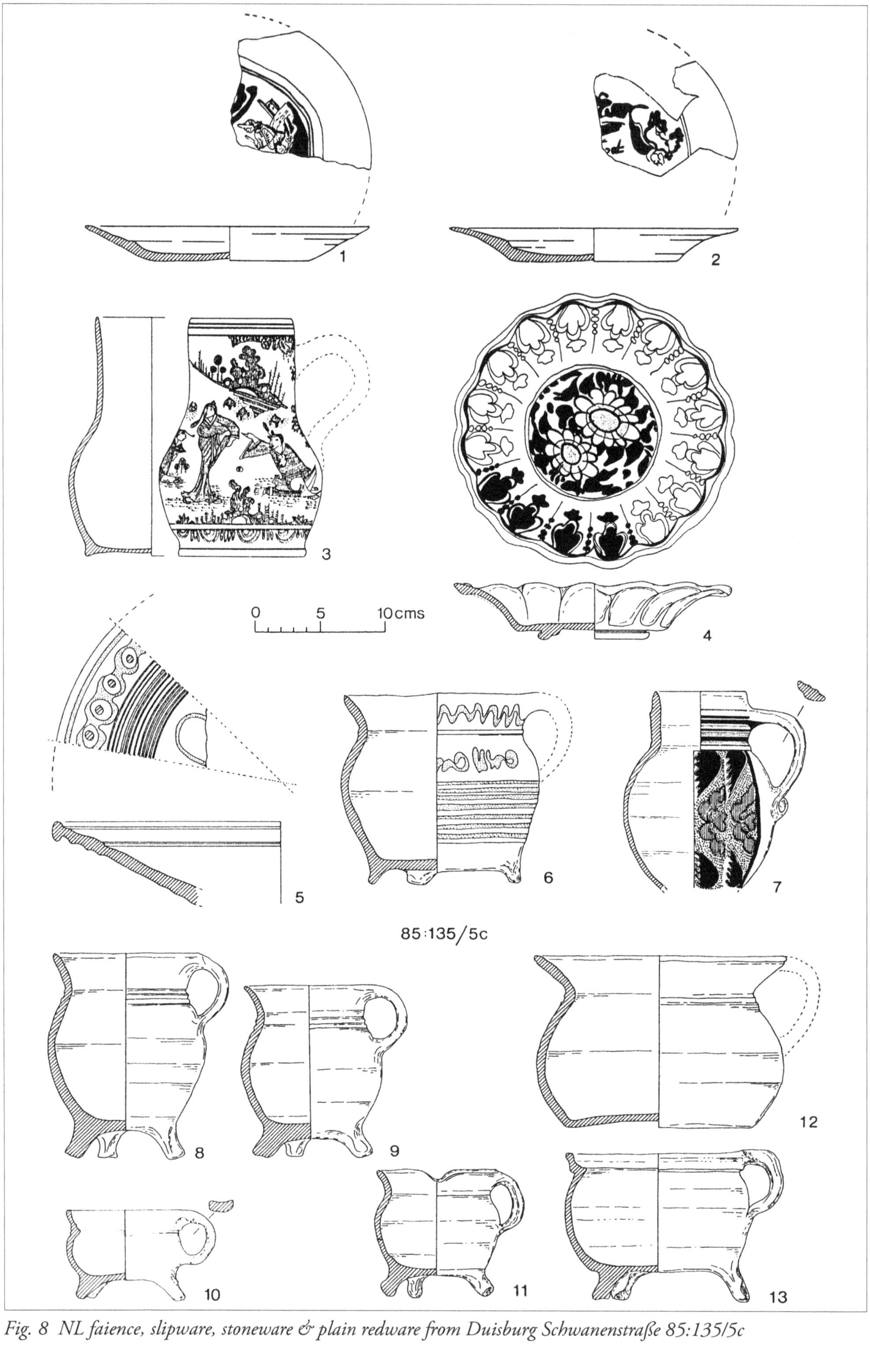


*Fig. 8 NL faience, slipware, stoneware & plain redware from Duisburg Schwanenstraße 85:135/5c*

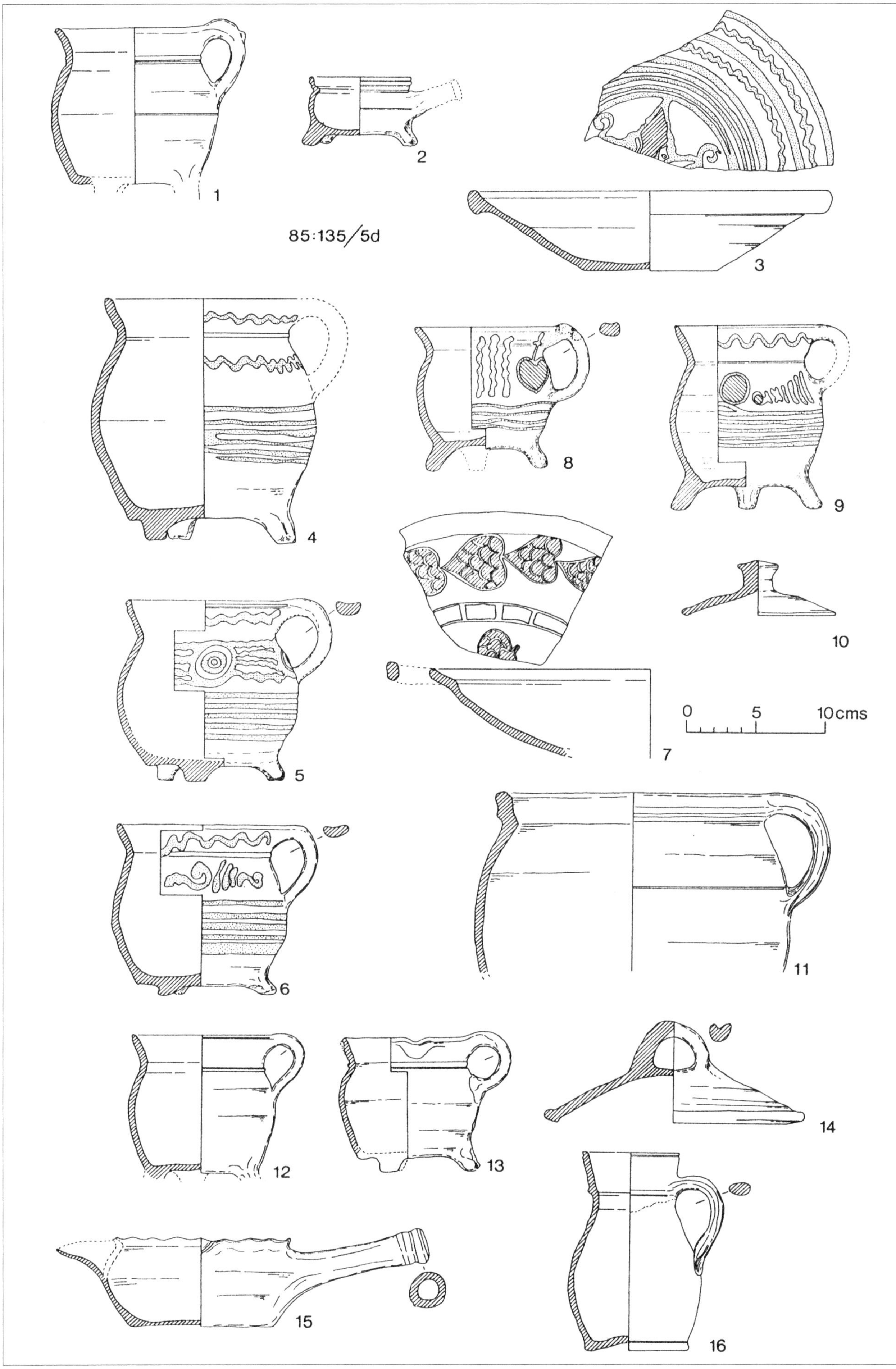


*Fig. 9 Slipware & plain redware from Duisburg Schwanenstraße 85:135/5d*

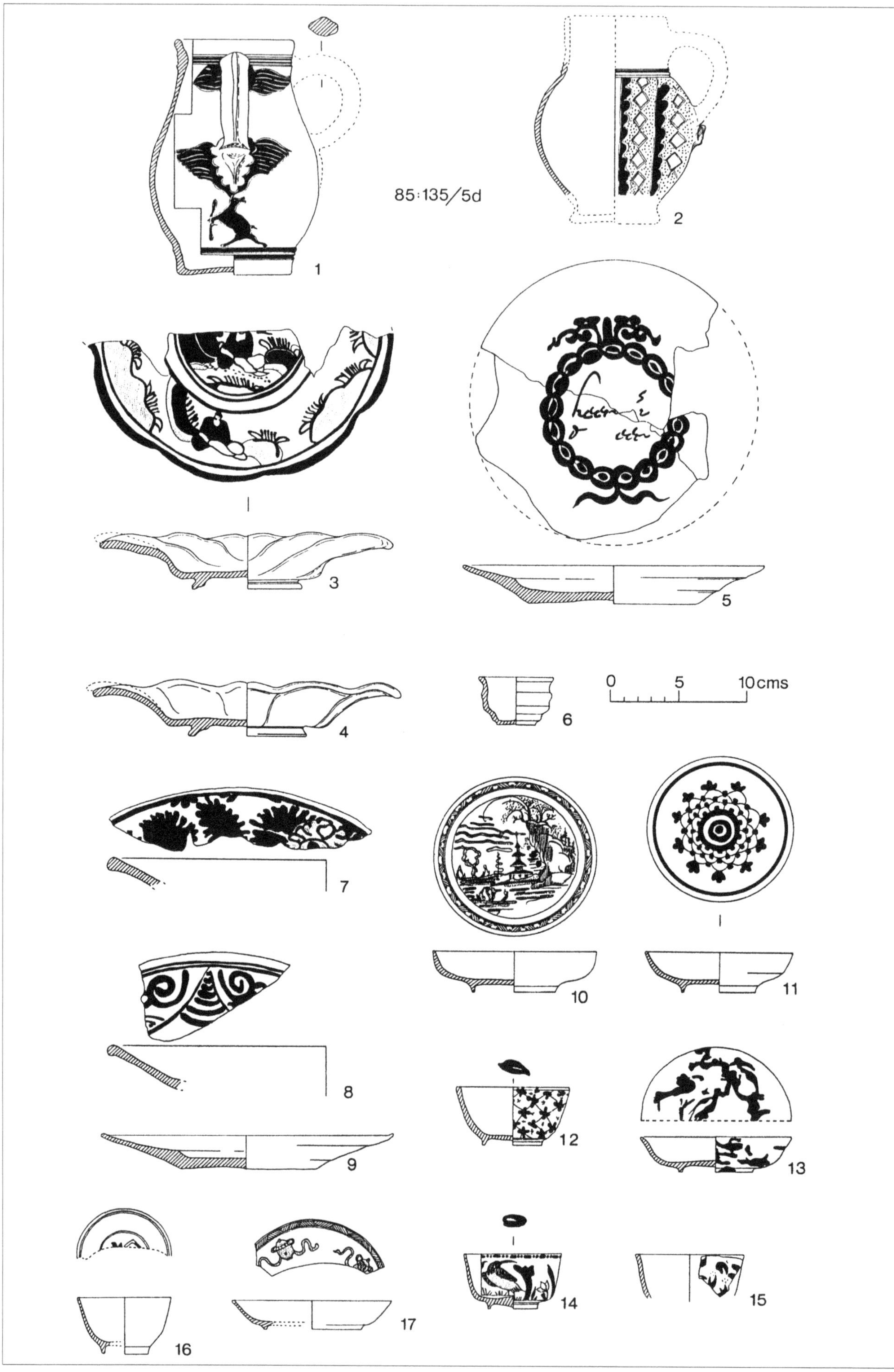


*Fig. 10 Stoneware, NL faience & porcelain from Duisburg Schwanenstraße 85:135/5d*

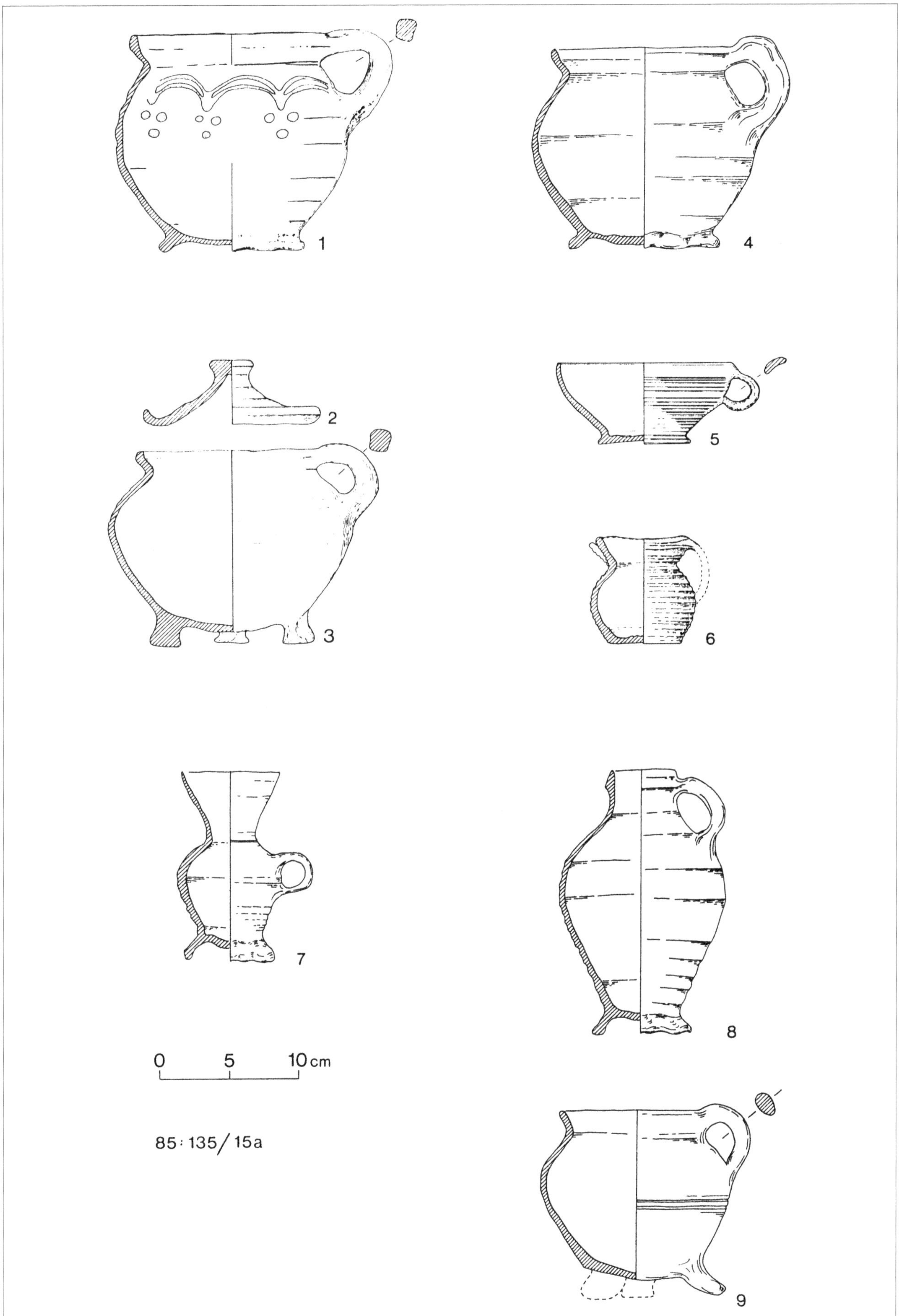


*Fig. 11 Pottery from Duisburg Schwanenstraße 85:135/15a*

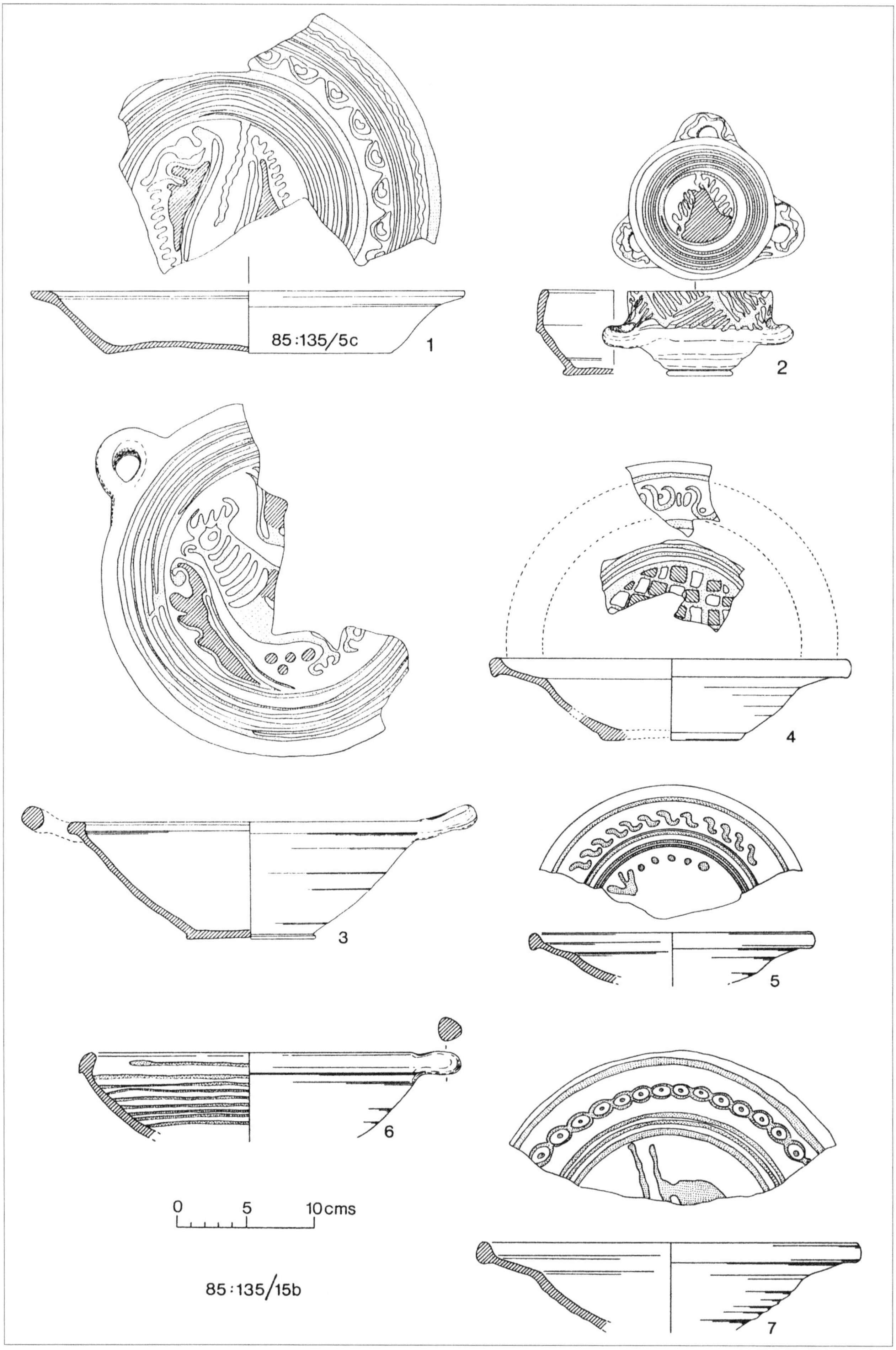


*Fig. 12 Slipware from Duisburg Schwanenstraße 85:135/15b*

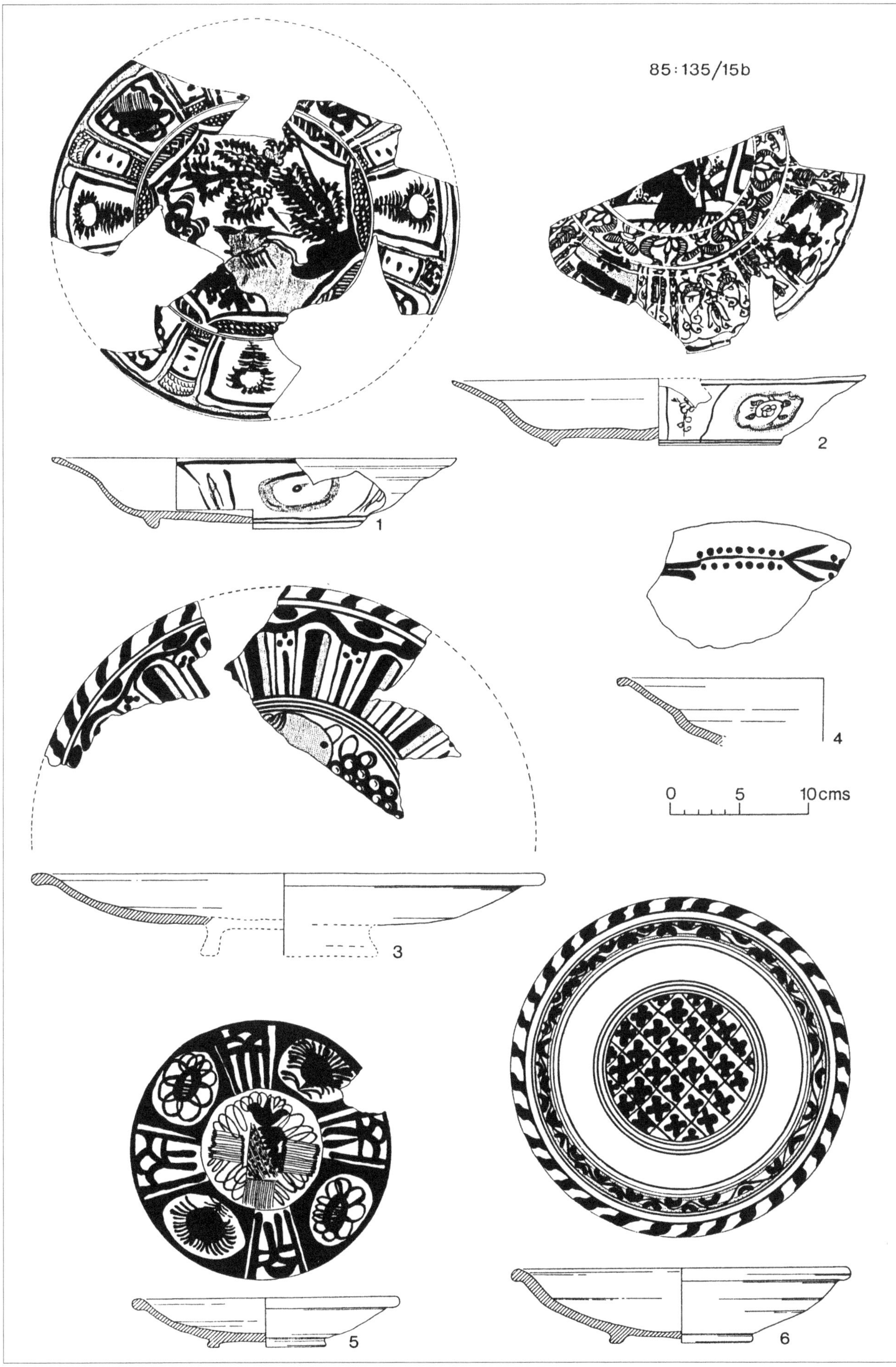


*Fig. 13 Oriental porcelain & NL maiolica from Duisburg Schwanenstraße 85:135/15b*

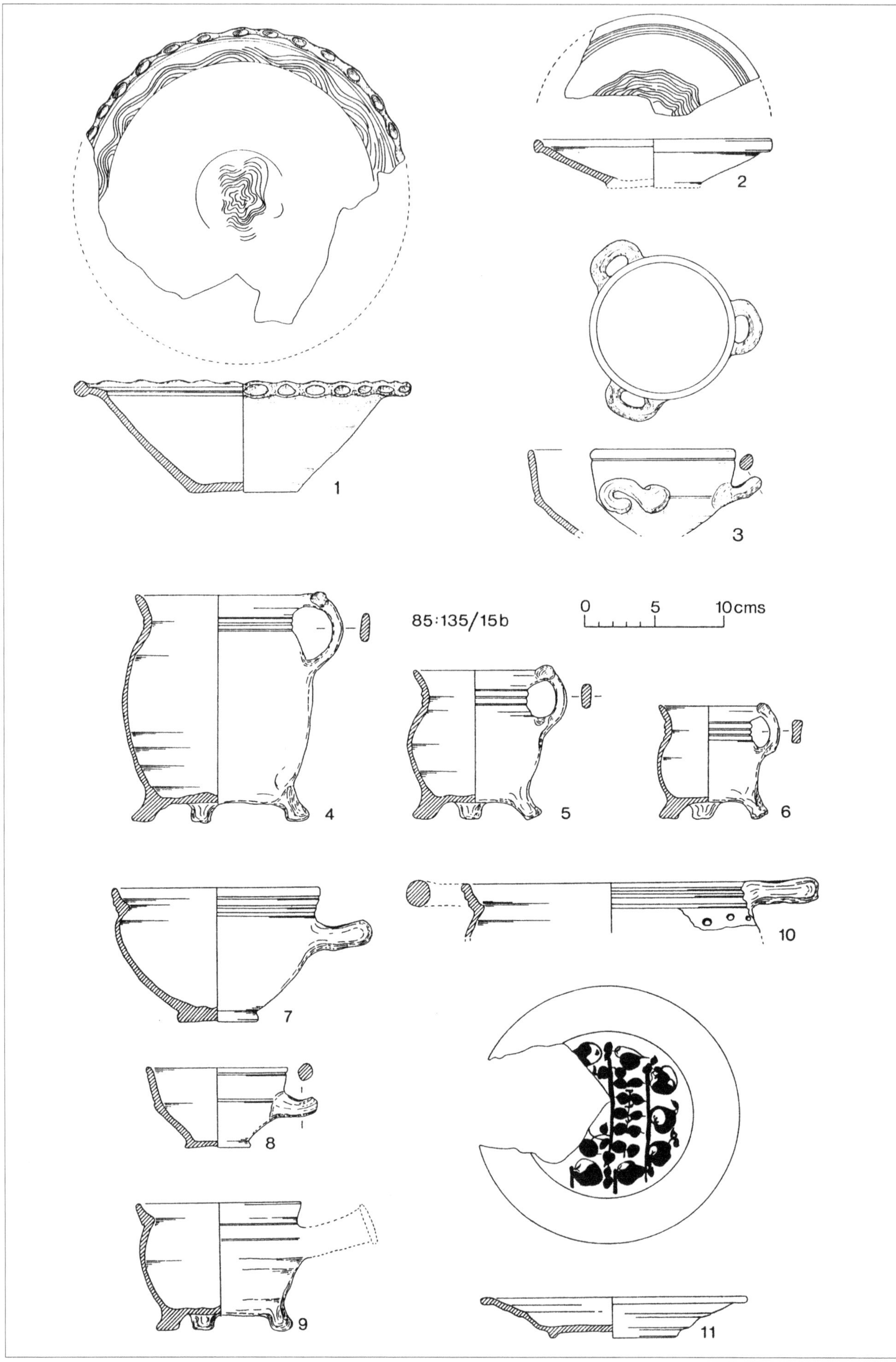


*Fig. 14 Whiteware & NL faience from Duisburg Schwanenstraße 85:135/15b*

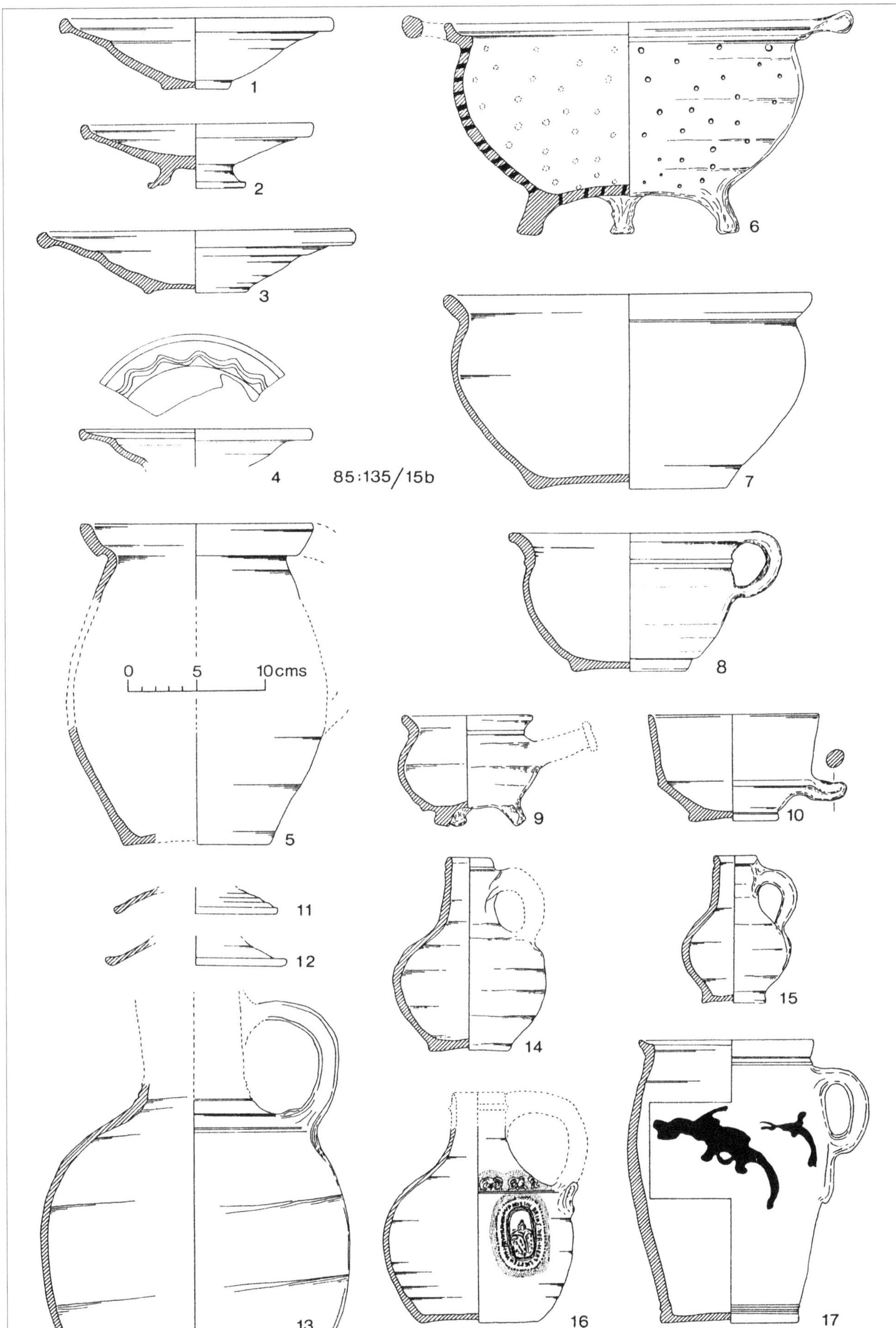


*Fig. 15 Plain redware & stoneware from Duisburg Schwanenstraße 85:135/15b*

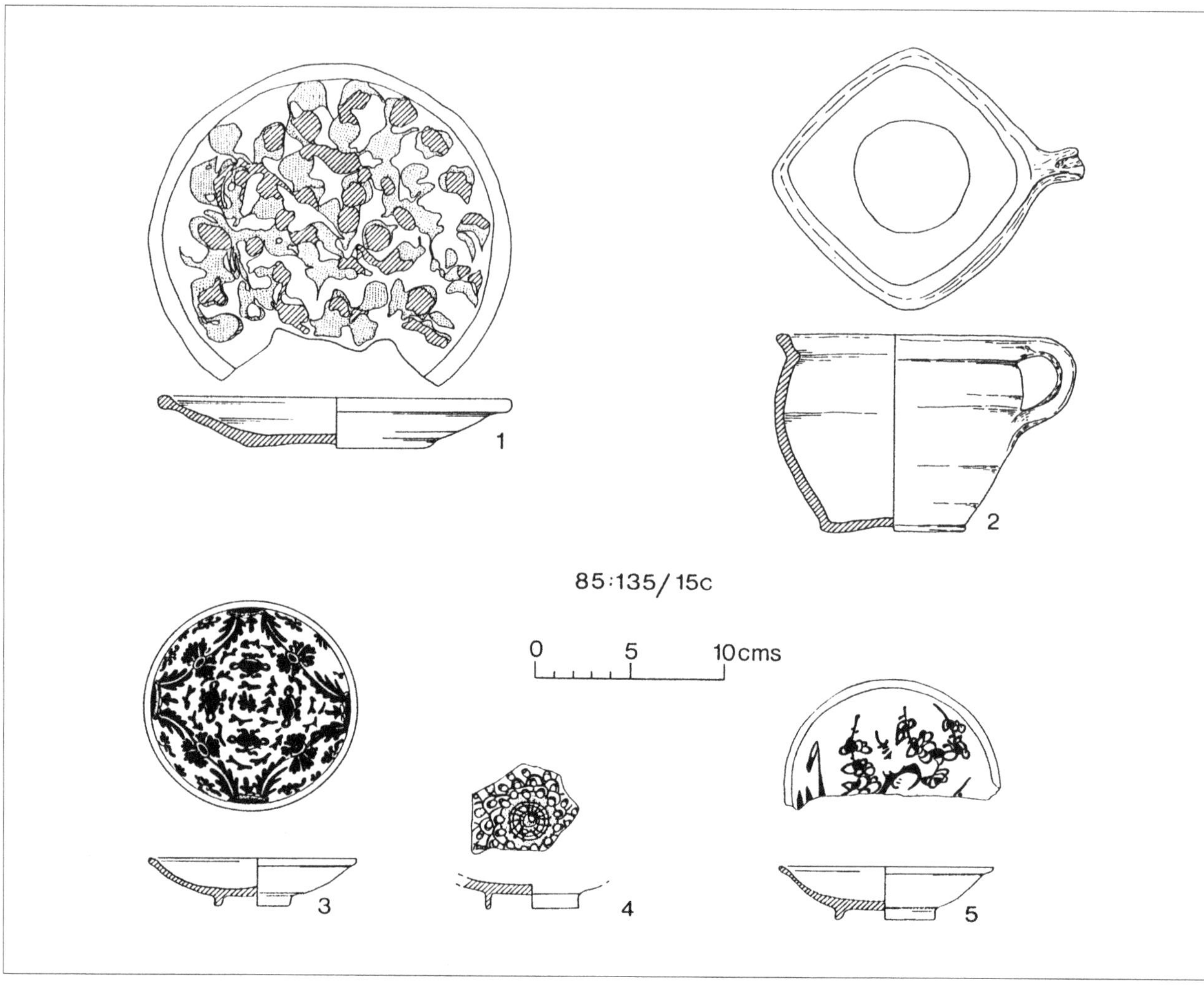


*Fig. 16 Slipware, plain redware & NL faience from Duisburg Schwanenstraße 85:135/15c*

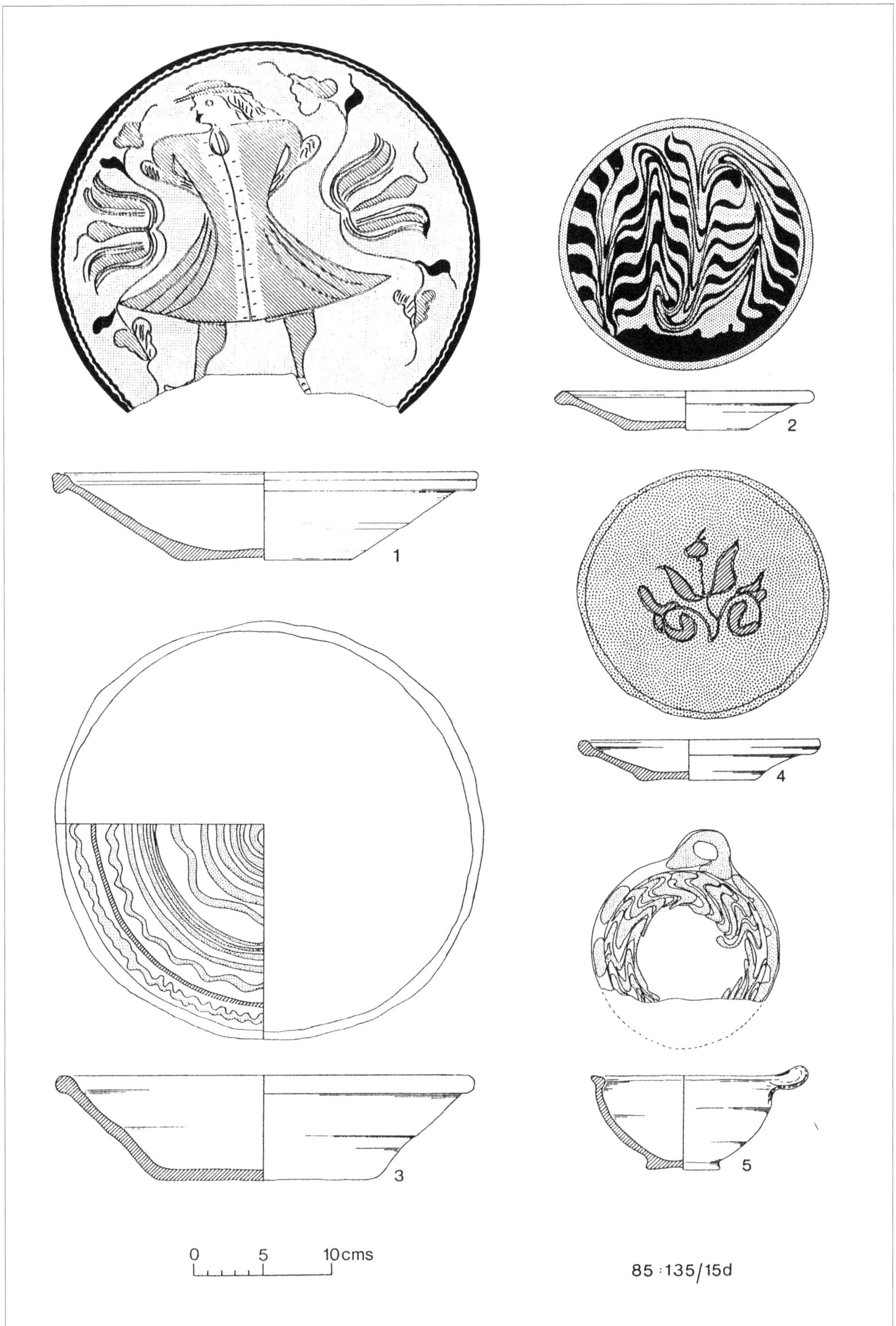


*Fig. 17 Slipware from Duisburg Schwanenstraße 85:135/15d*

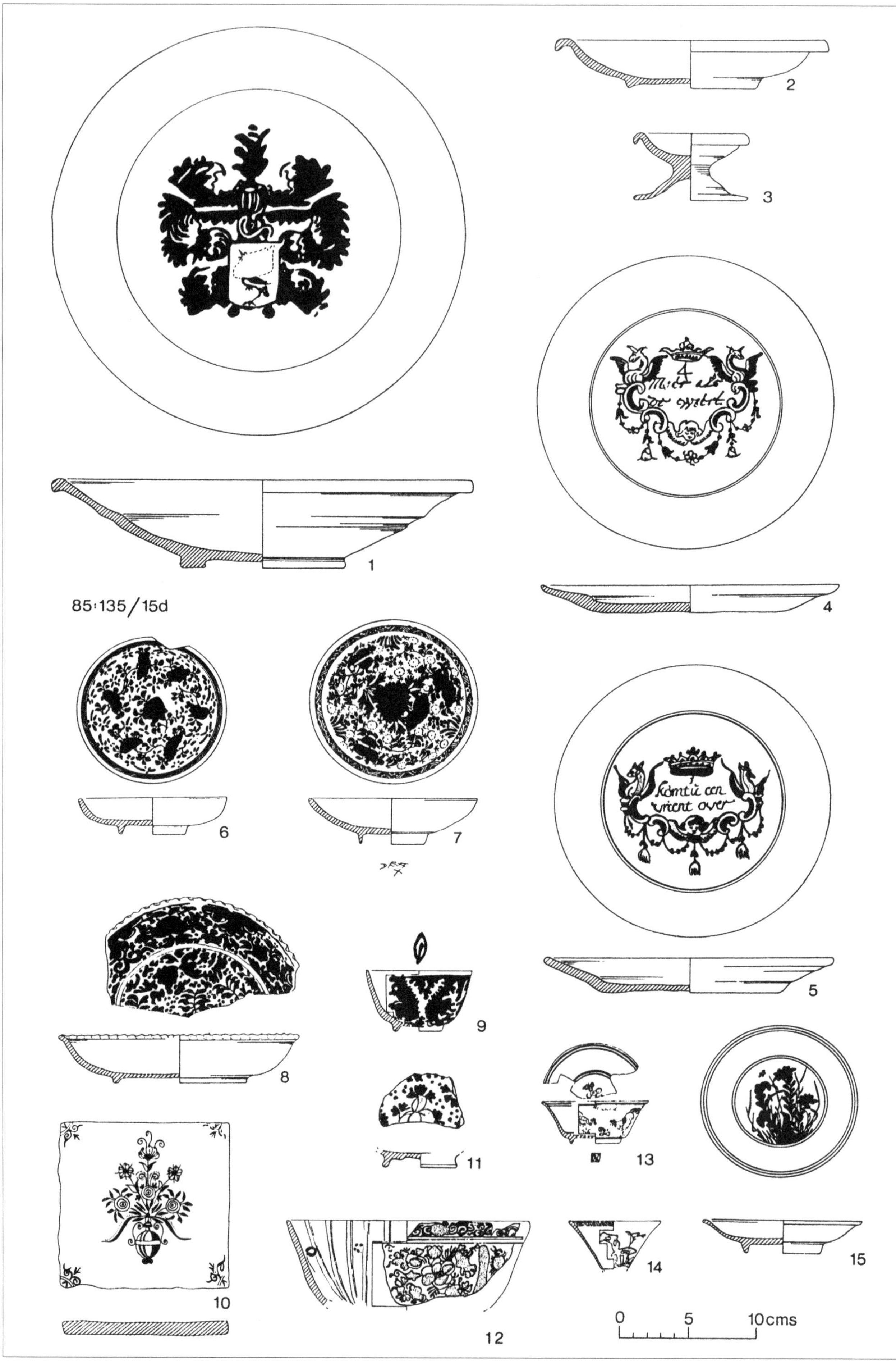


*Fig. 18 NL maiolica, NL faience, oriental porcelain from Duisburg Schwanenstraße 85:135/15d*

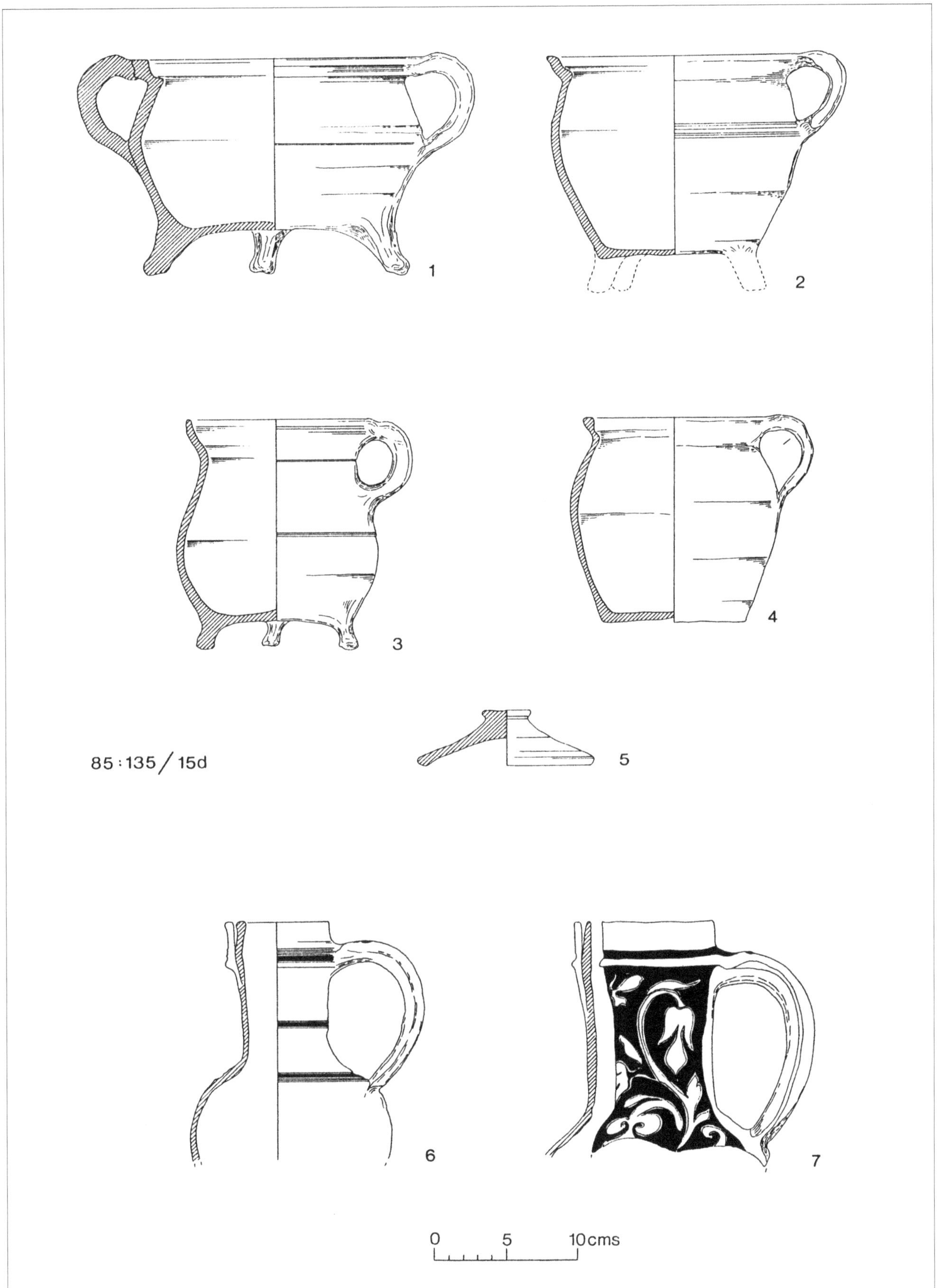


*Fig. 19 Plain redware & stoneware from Duisburg Schwanenstraße 85:135/15d*

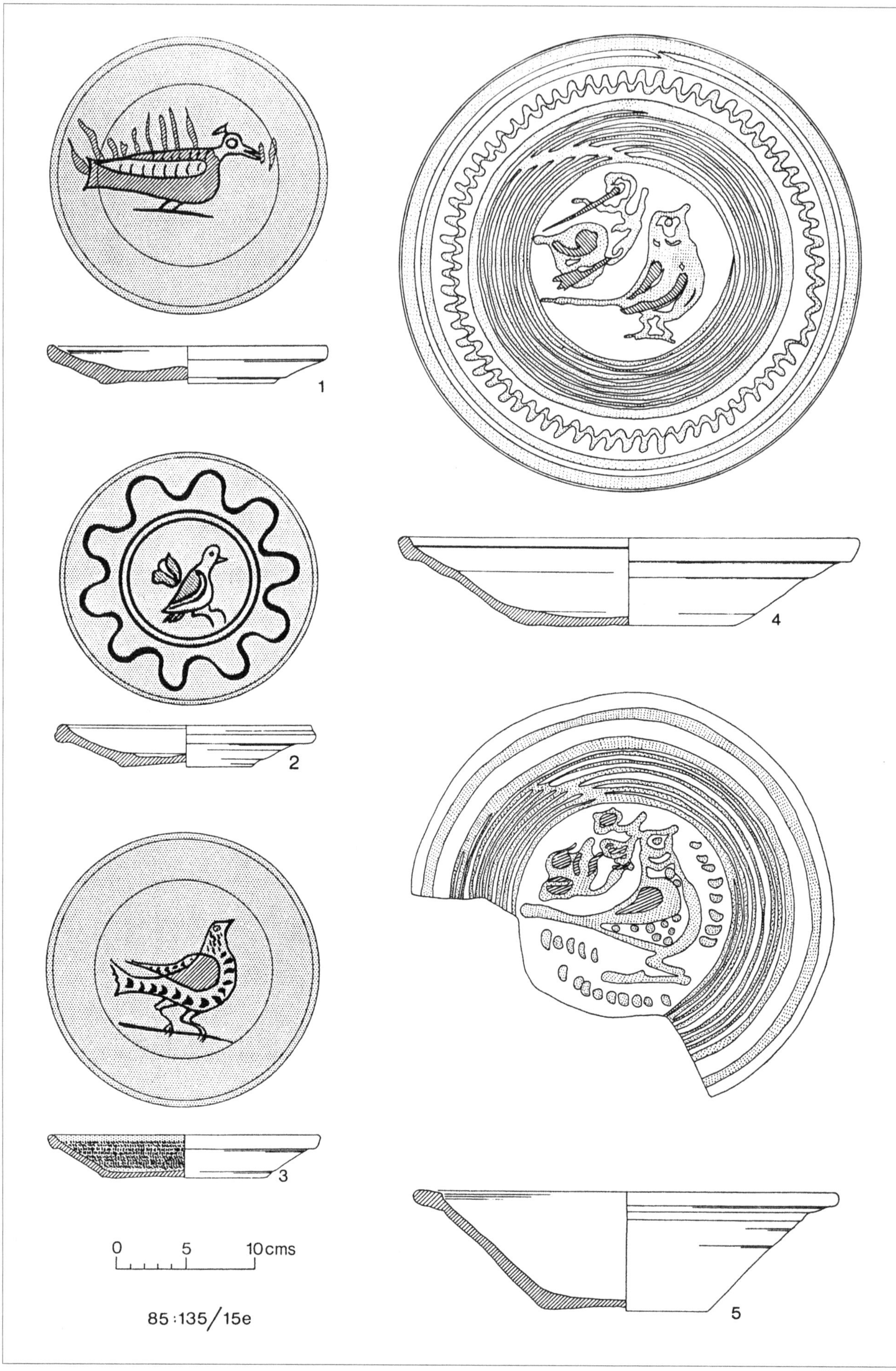


*Fig. 20 Slipware from Duisburg Schwanenstraße 85:135/15e*

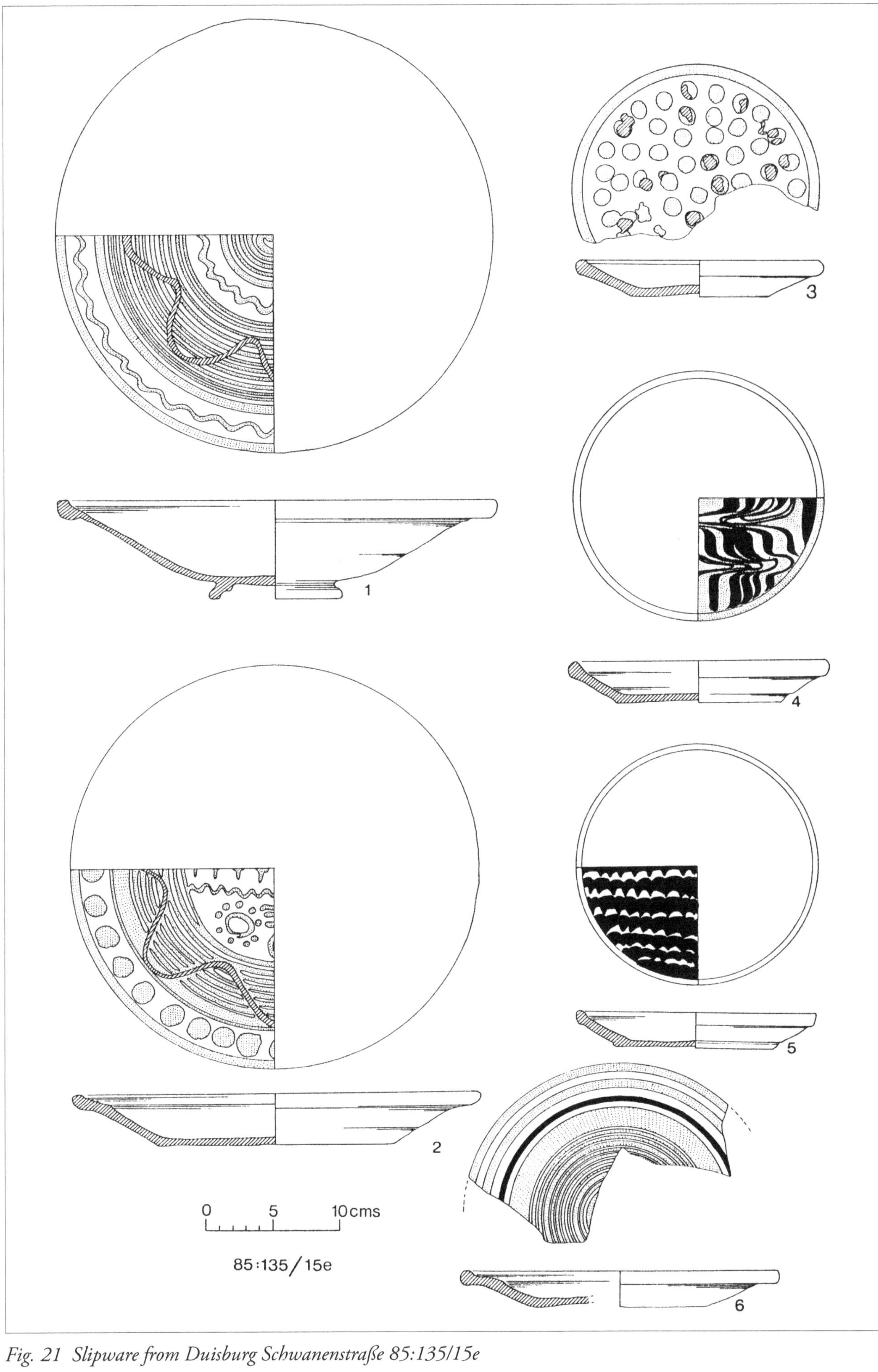


*Fig. 21 Slipware from Duisburg Schwanenstraße 85:135/15e*

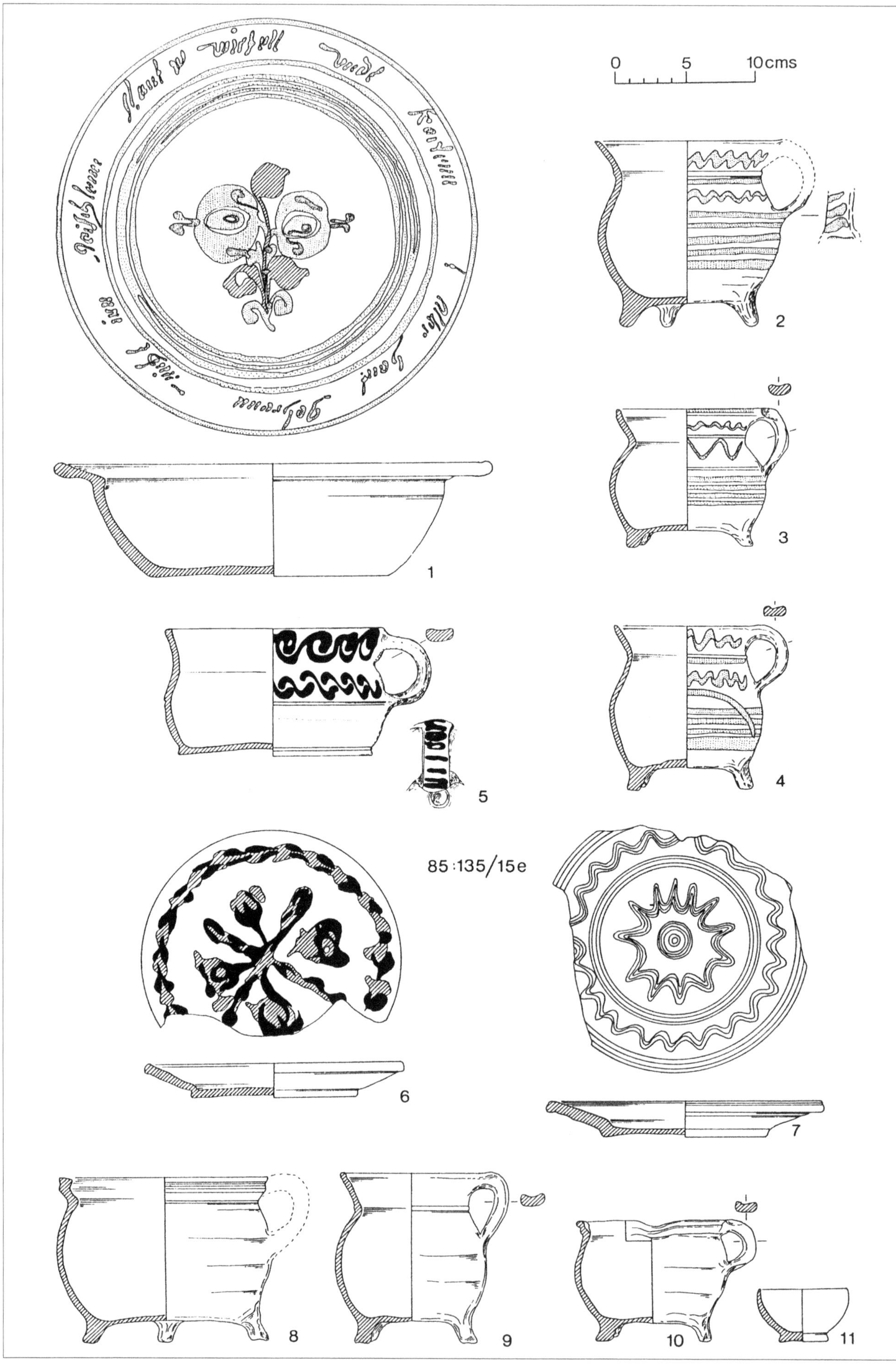


*Fig. 22 Slipware & plain redware from Duisburg Schwanenstraße 85:135/15e*

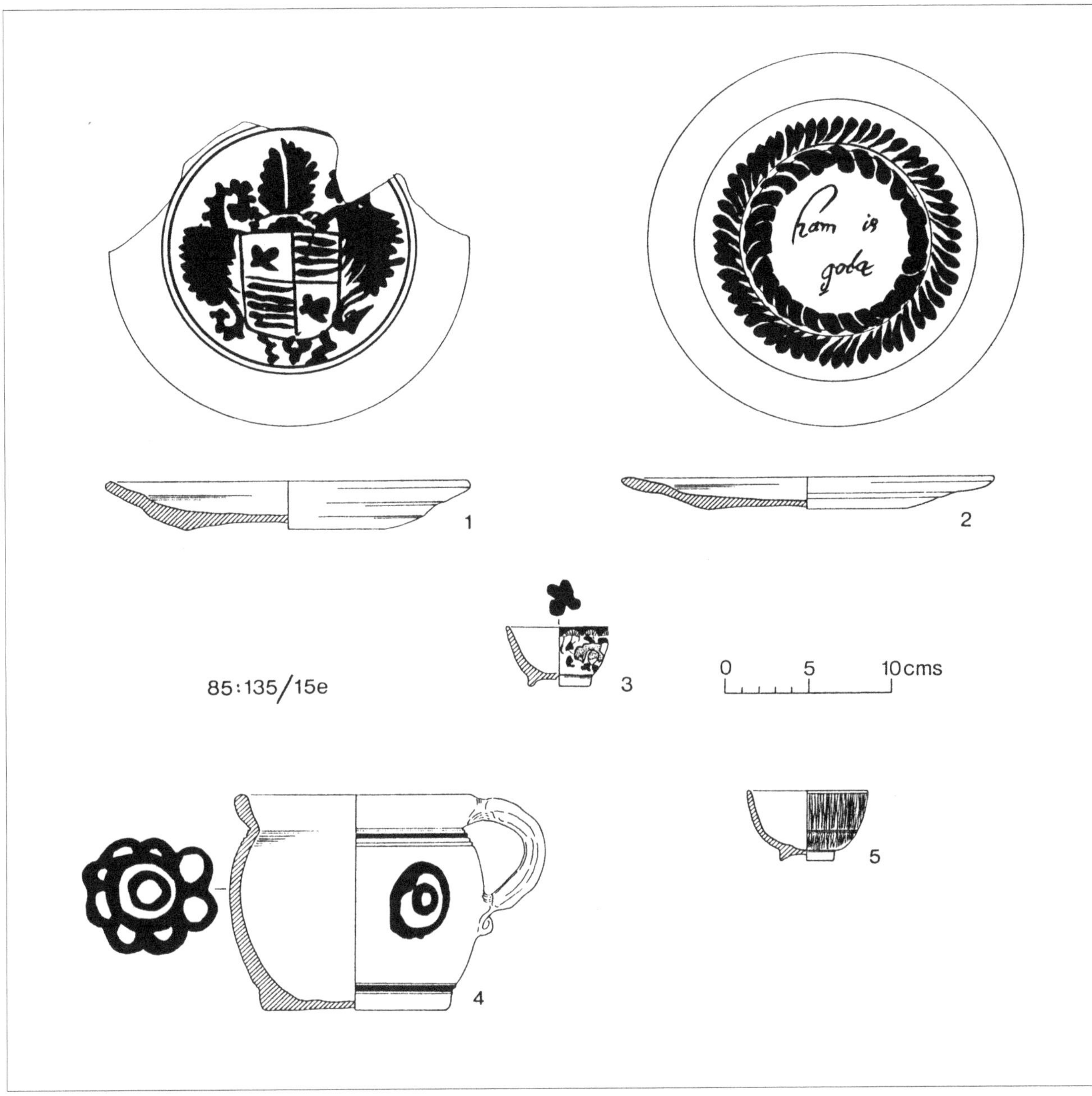


*Fig. 23 NL faience & stoneware from Duisburg Schwanenstraße 85:135/15e*

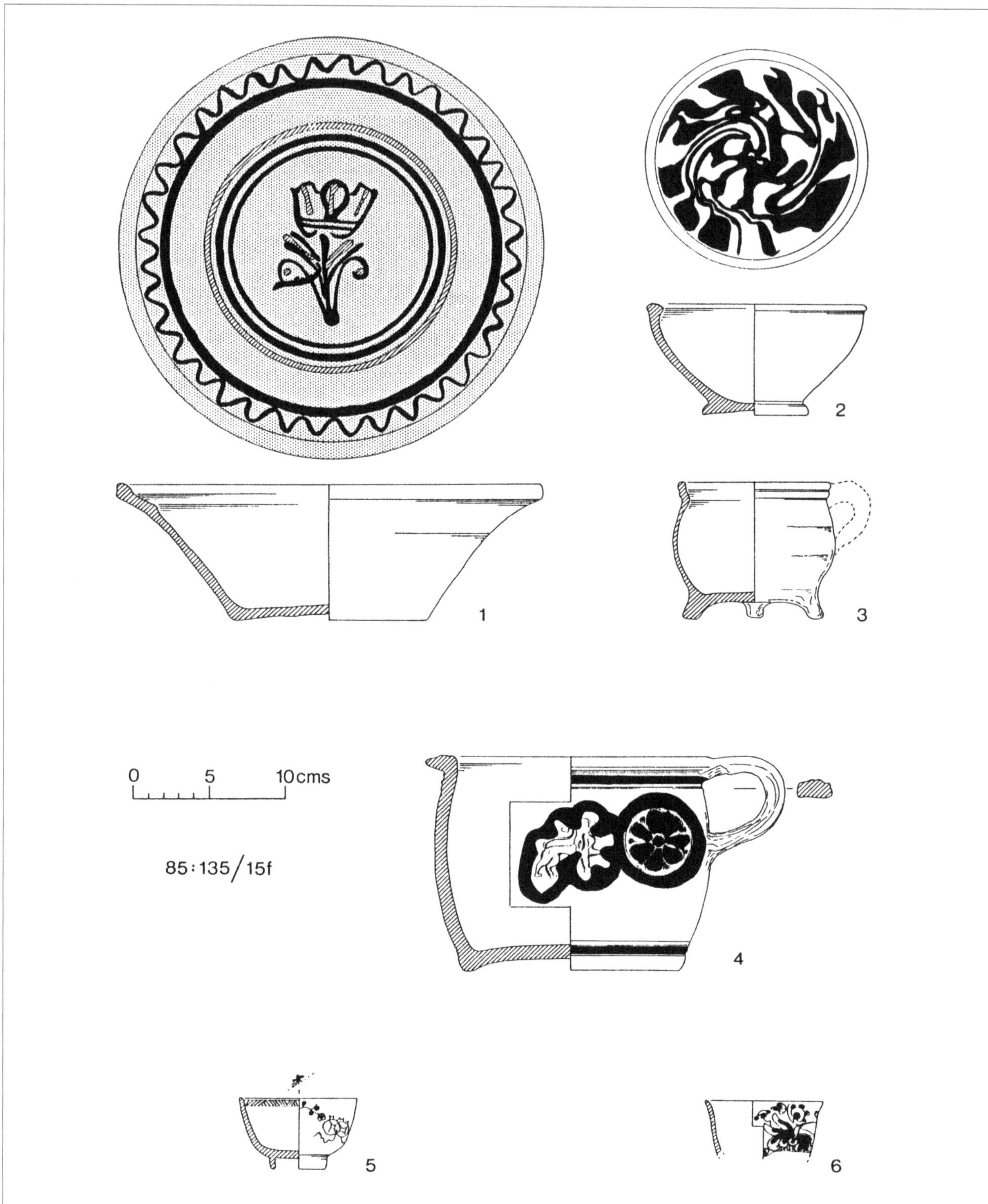


*Fig. 24 Slipware, stoneware & oriental porcelain from Duisburg Schwanenstraße 85:135/15f*

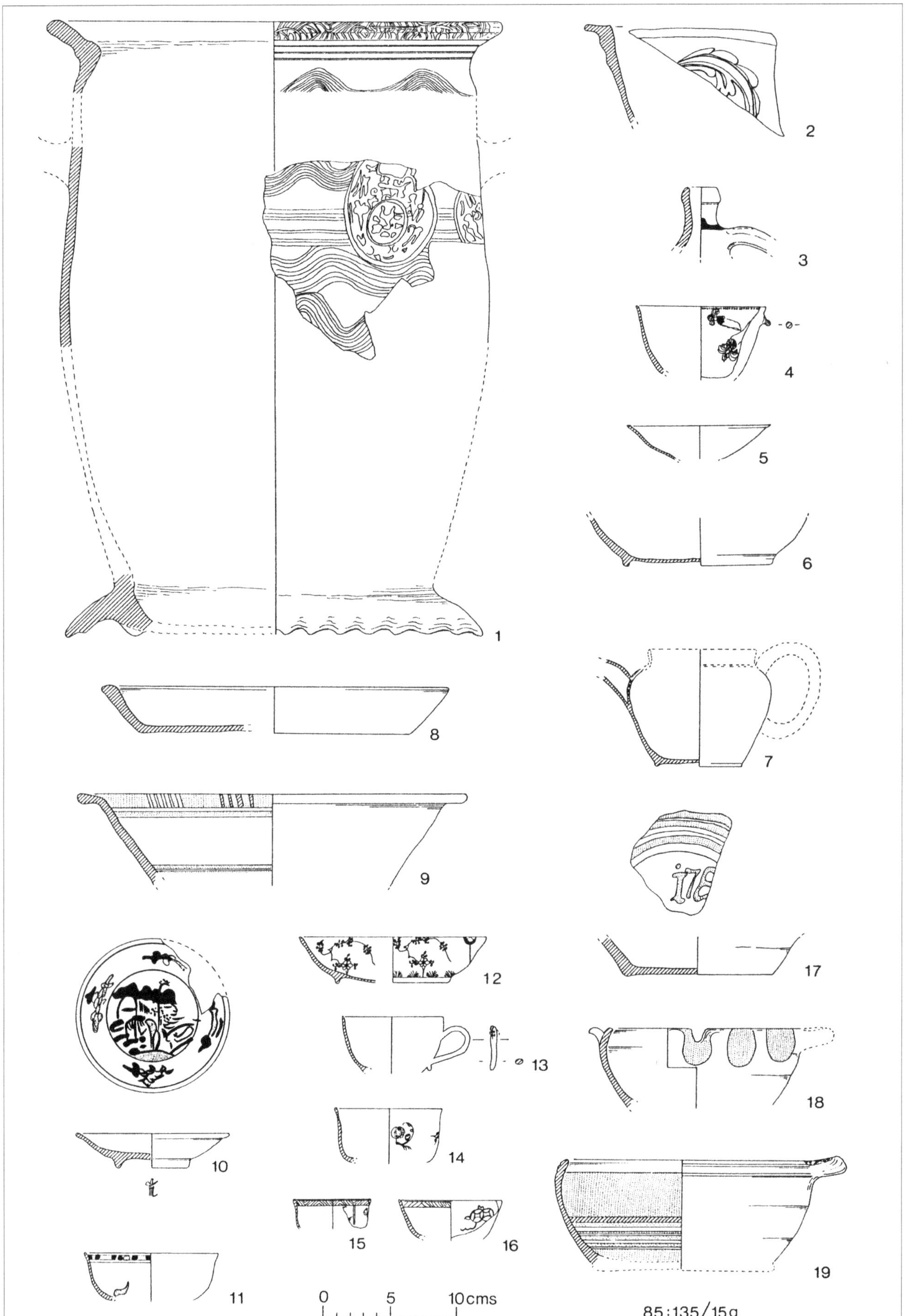


*Fig. 25 Stoneware, slipware, English finewares, Oriental & German porcelain from Duisburg Schwanenstraße 85.135/15g*

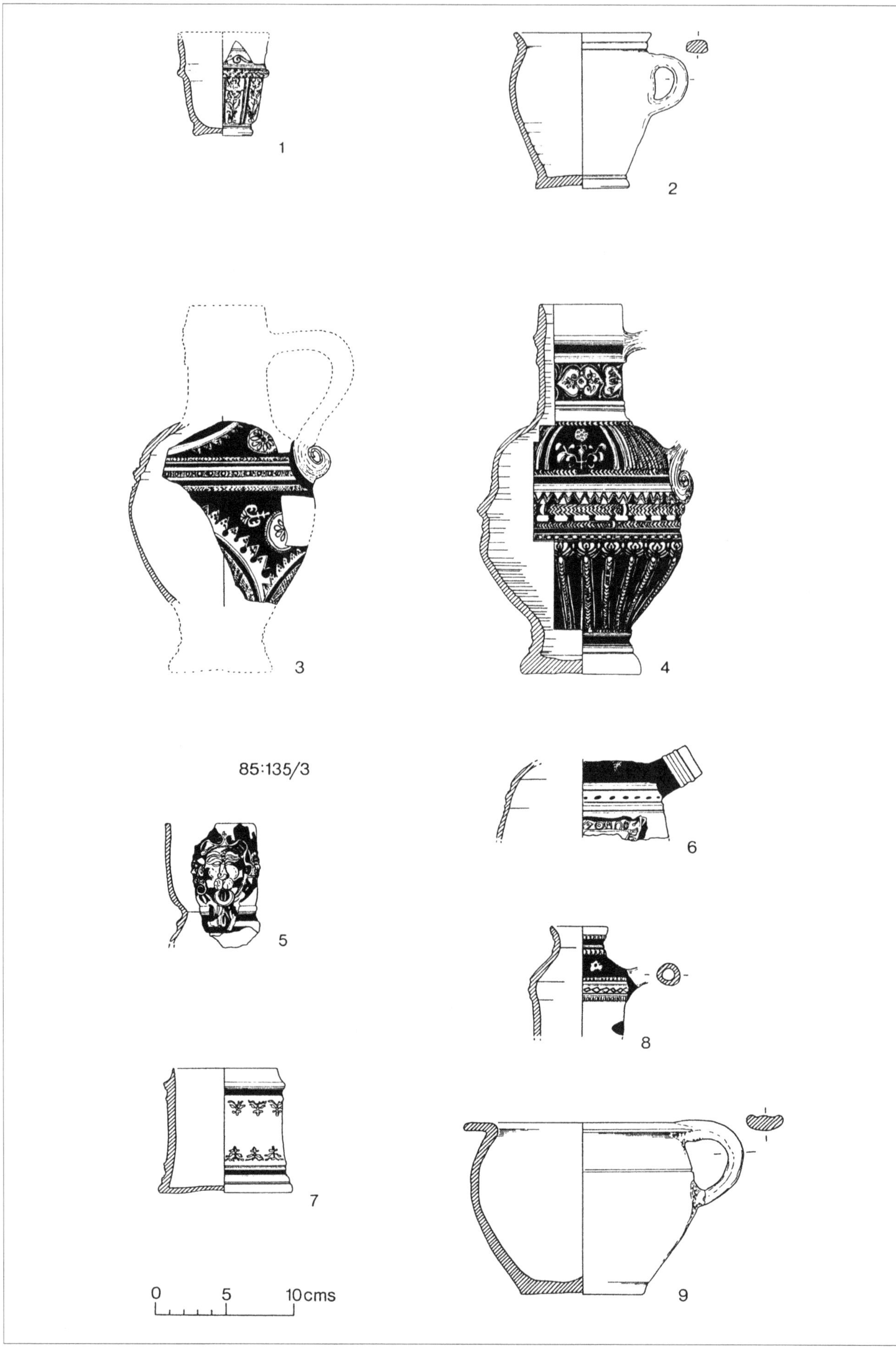


*Fig. 26 Stoneware from Duisburg Schwanenstraße 85:135/3*

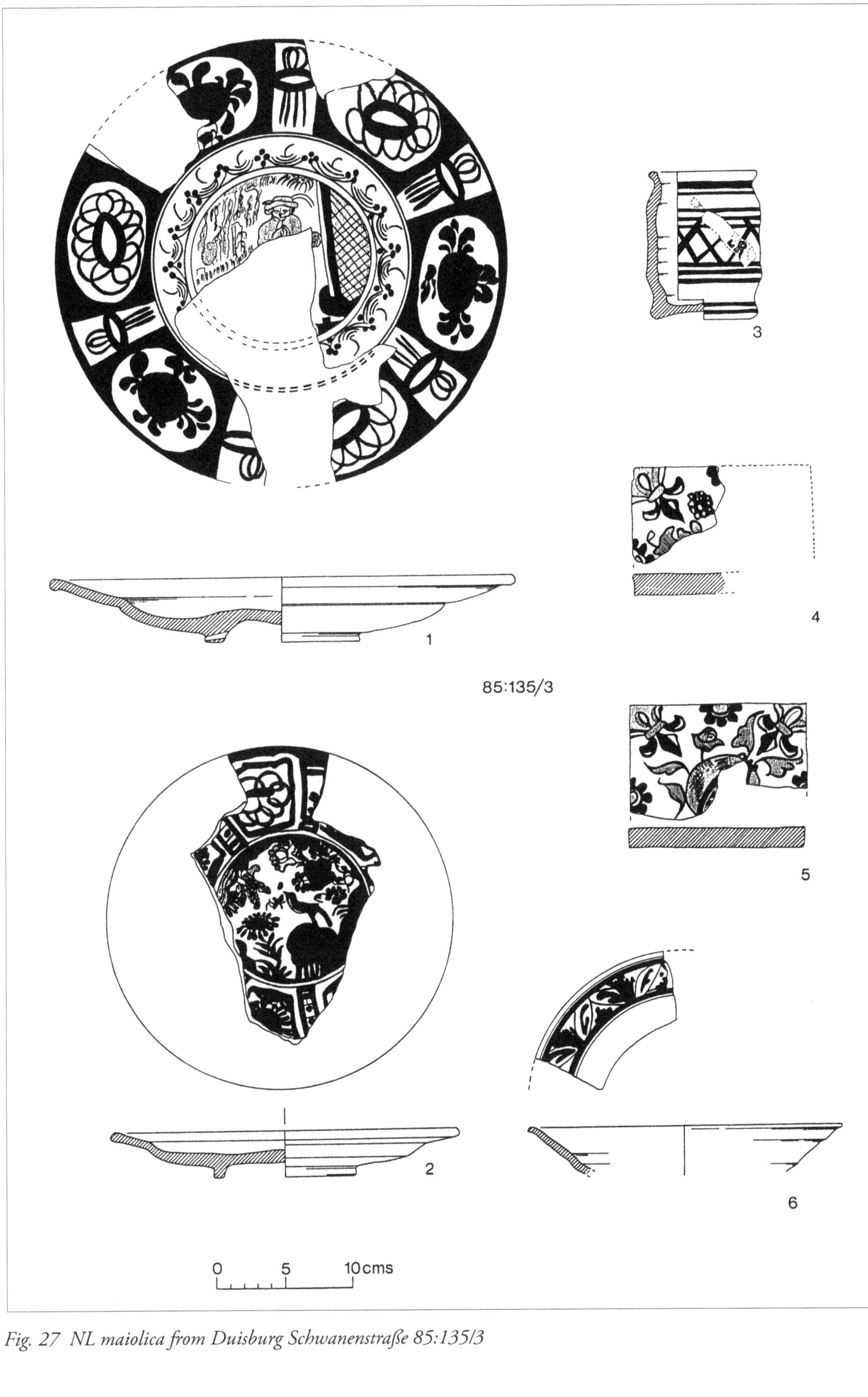


*Fig. 27 NL maiolica from Duisburg Schwanenstraße 85:135/3*

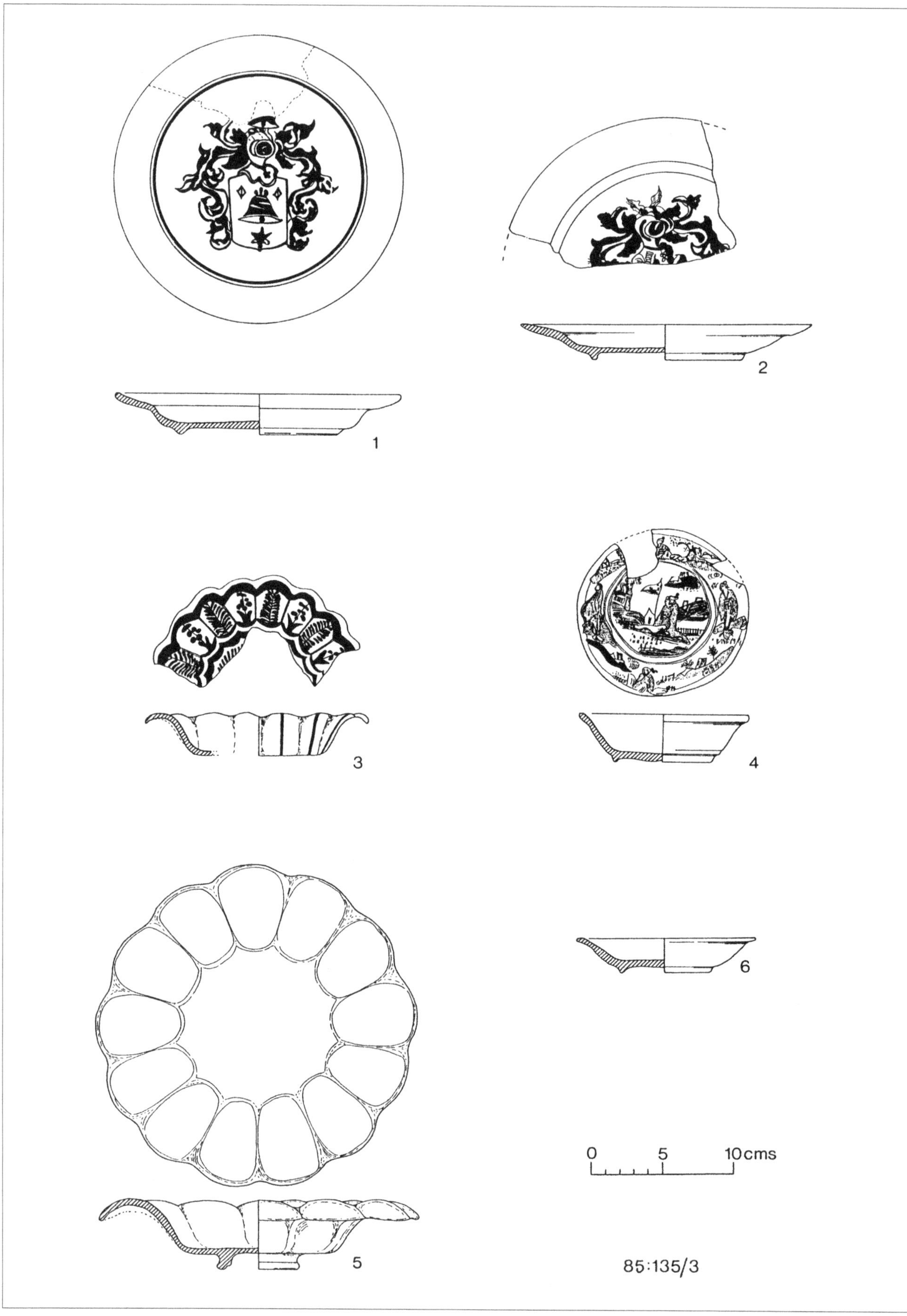


*Fig. 28 NL faience from Duisburg Schwanenstraße 85:135/3*

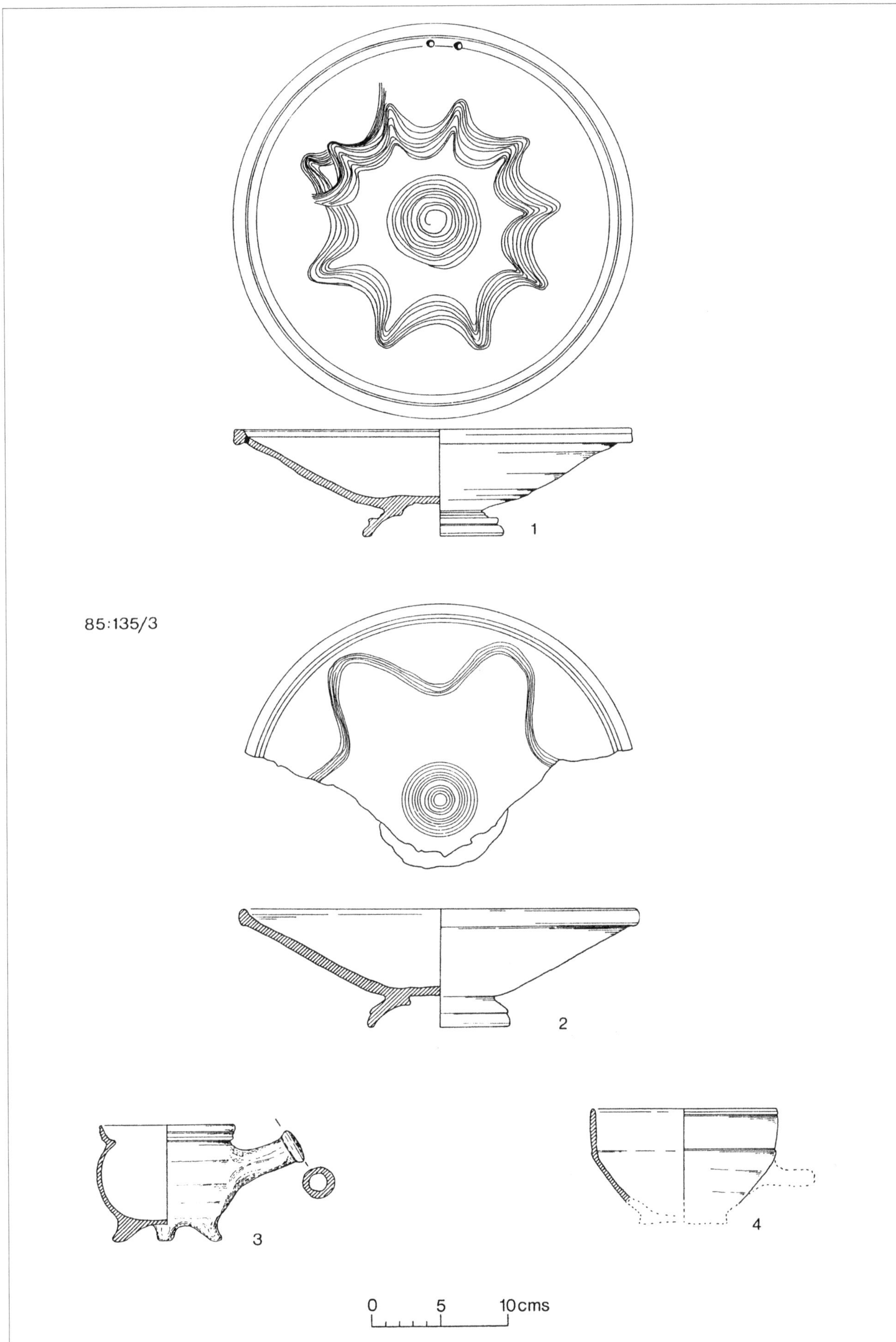


*Fig. 29 Whiteware from Duisburg Schwanenstraße 85:135/3*

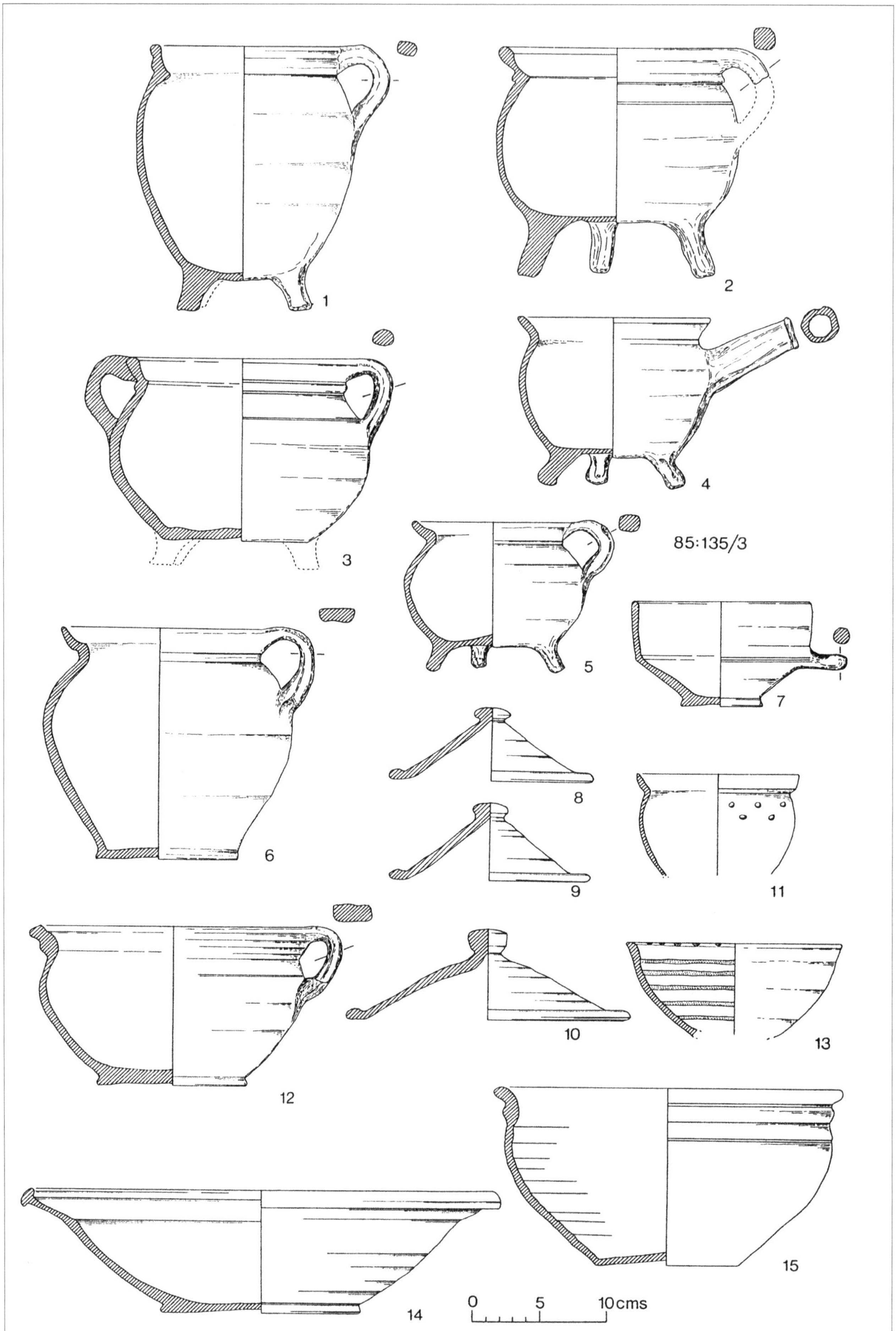


*Fig. 30 Plain redware from Duisburg Schwanenstraße 85:135/3*

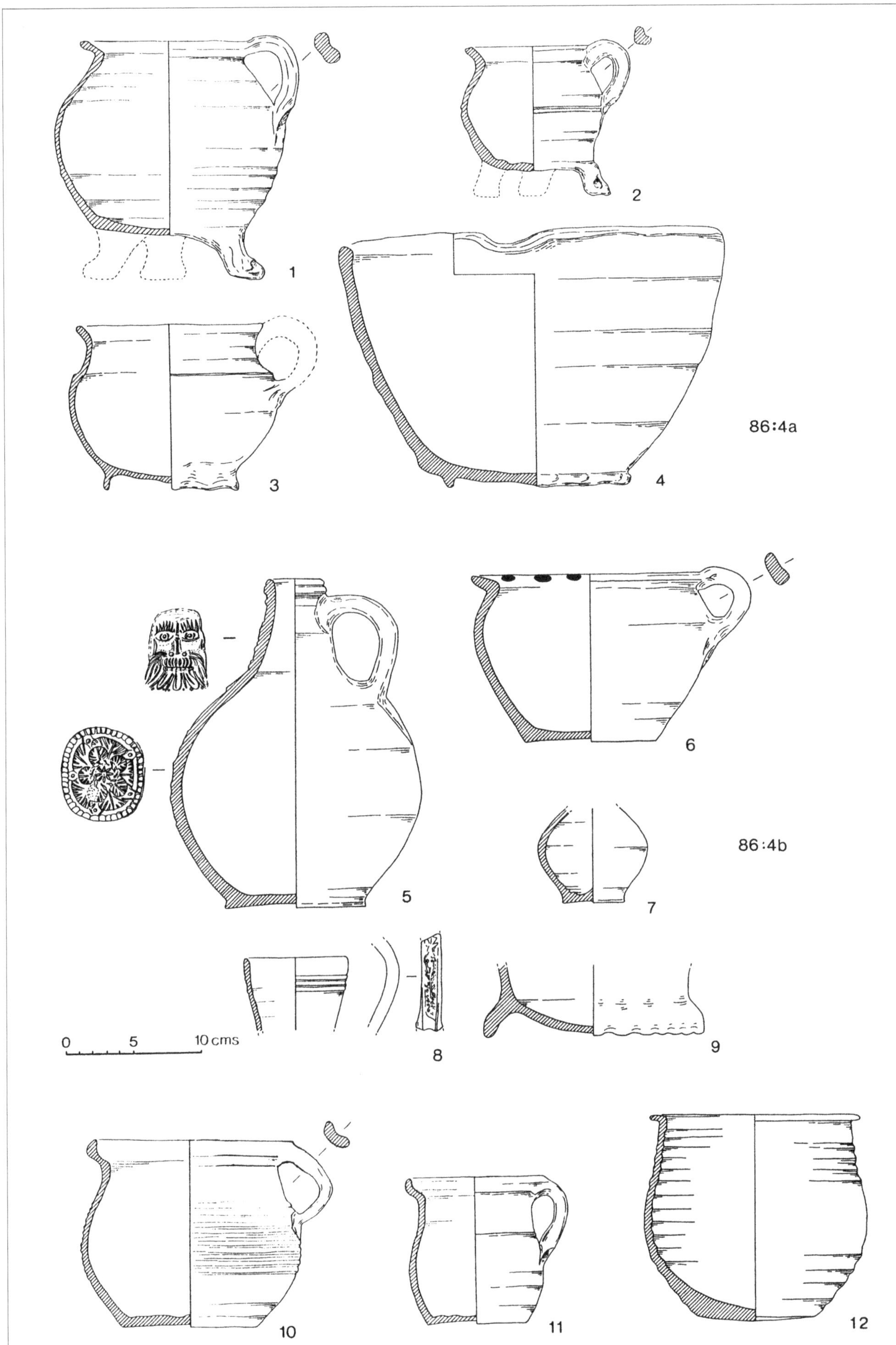


*Fig. 31 Pottery from Duisburg Schwanenstraße 86.4a; stoneware & redware from Duisburg Schwanenstraße 86:4b*

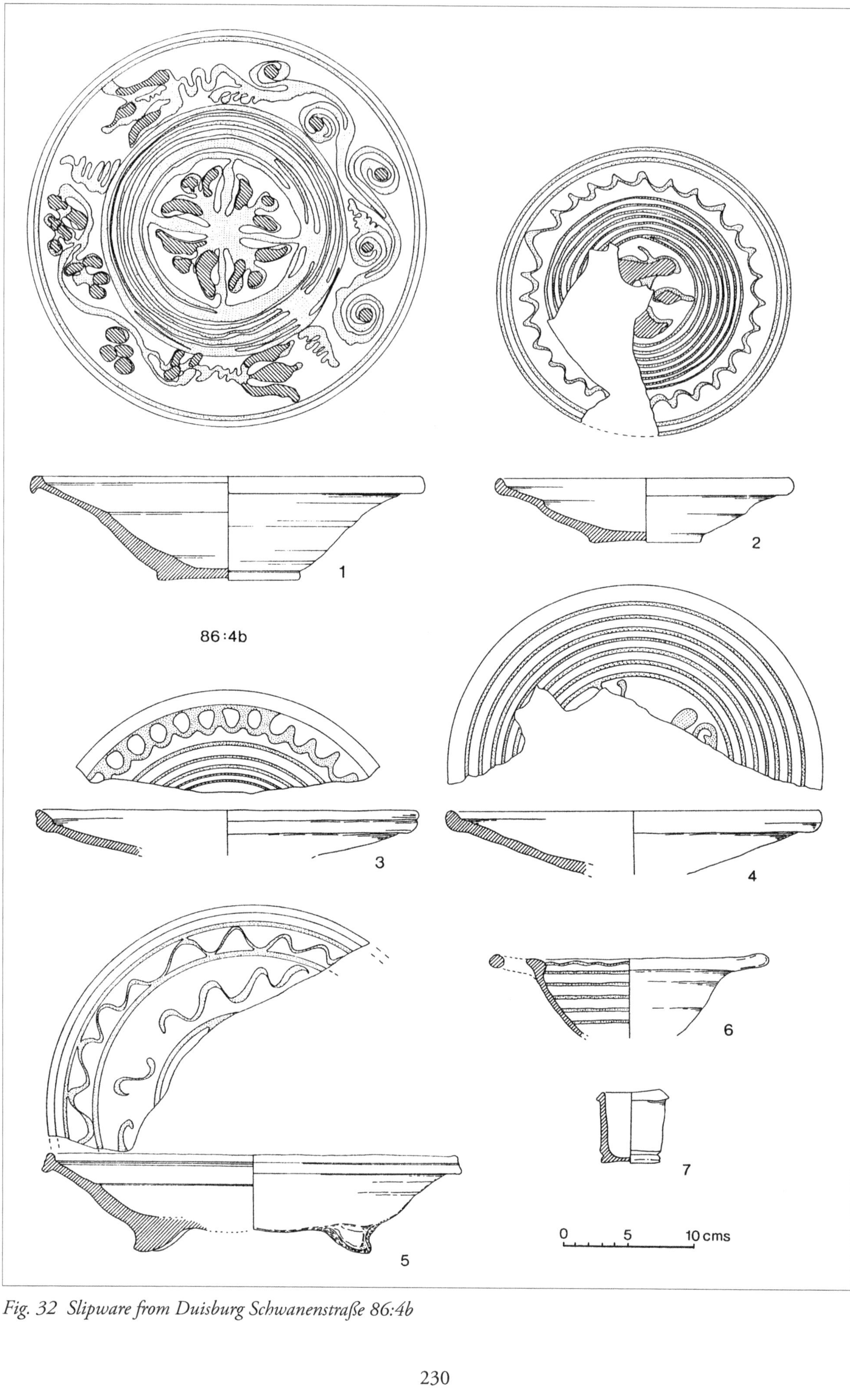


*Fig. 32 Slipware from Duisburg Schwanenstraße 86:4b*

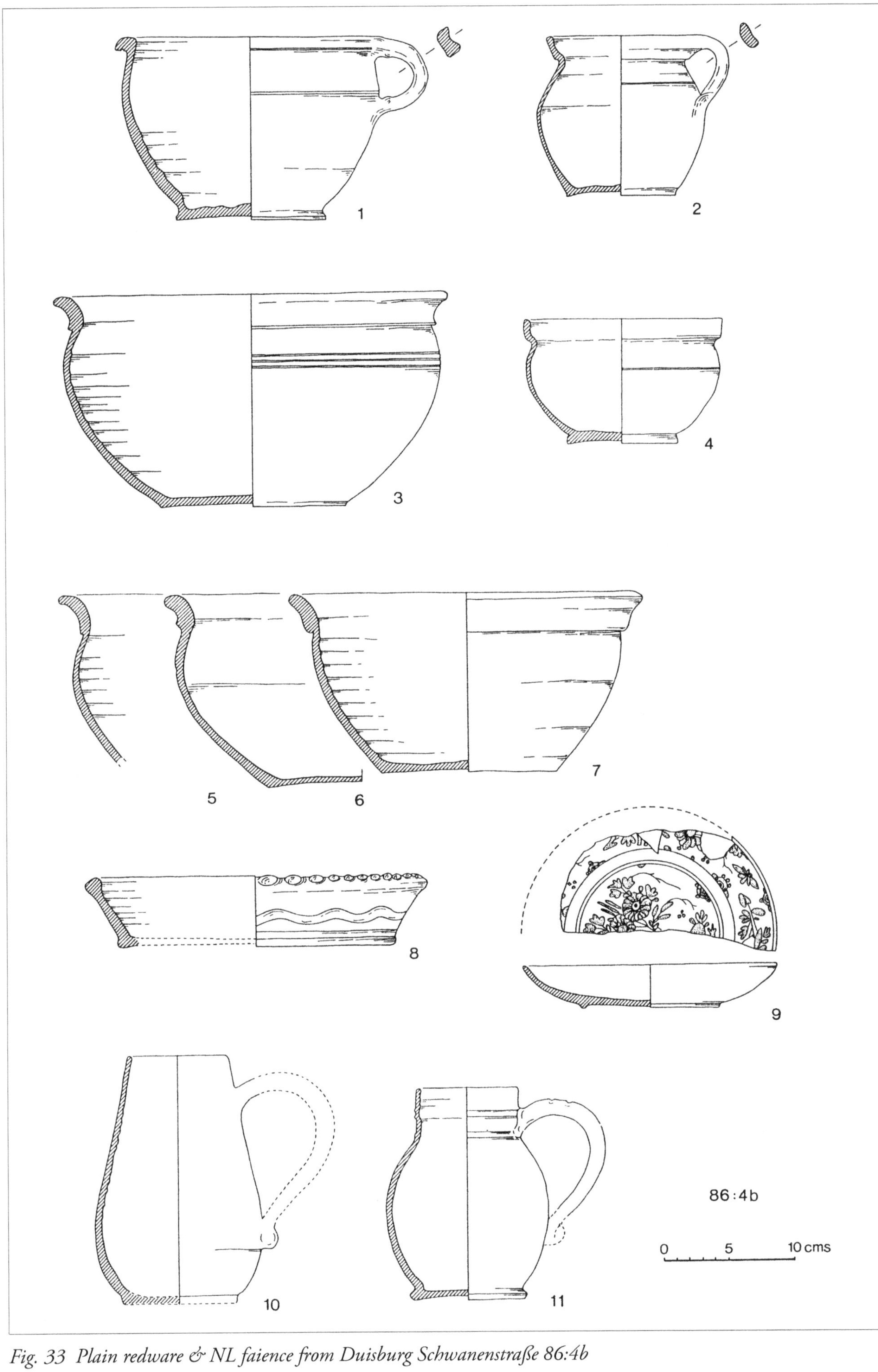


*Fig. 33 Plain redware & NL faience from Duisburg Schwanenstraße 86:4b*

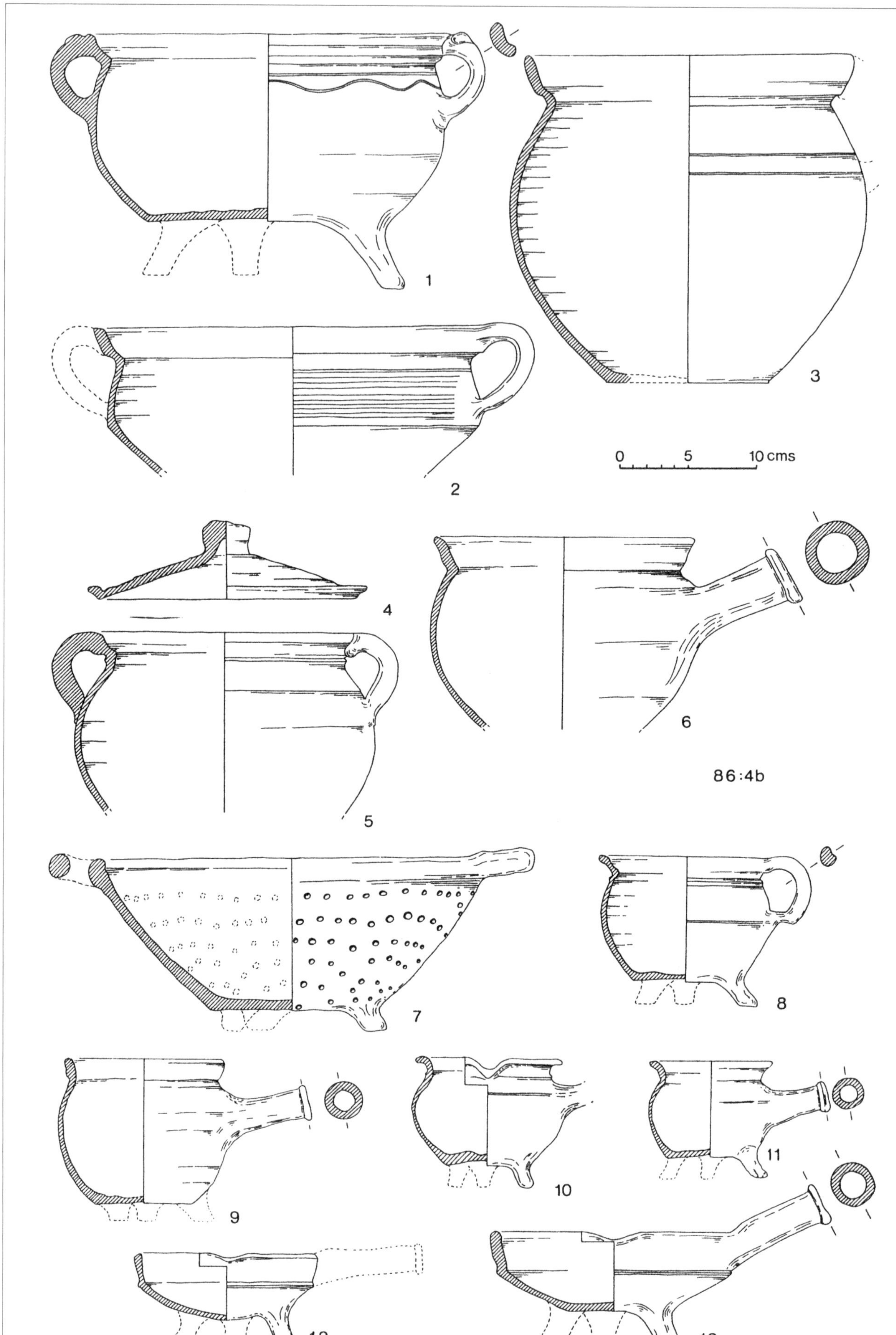


*Fig. 34 Plain redware from Duisburg Schwanenstraße 86:4b*

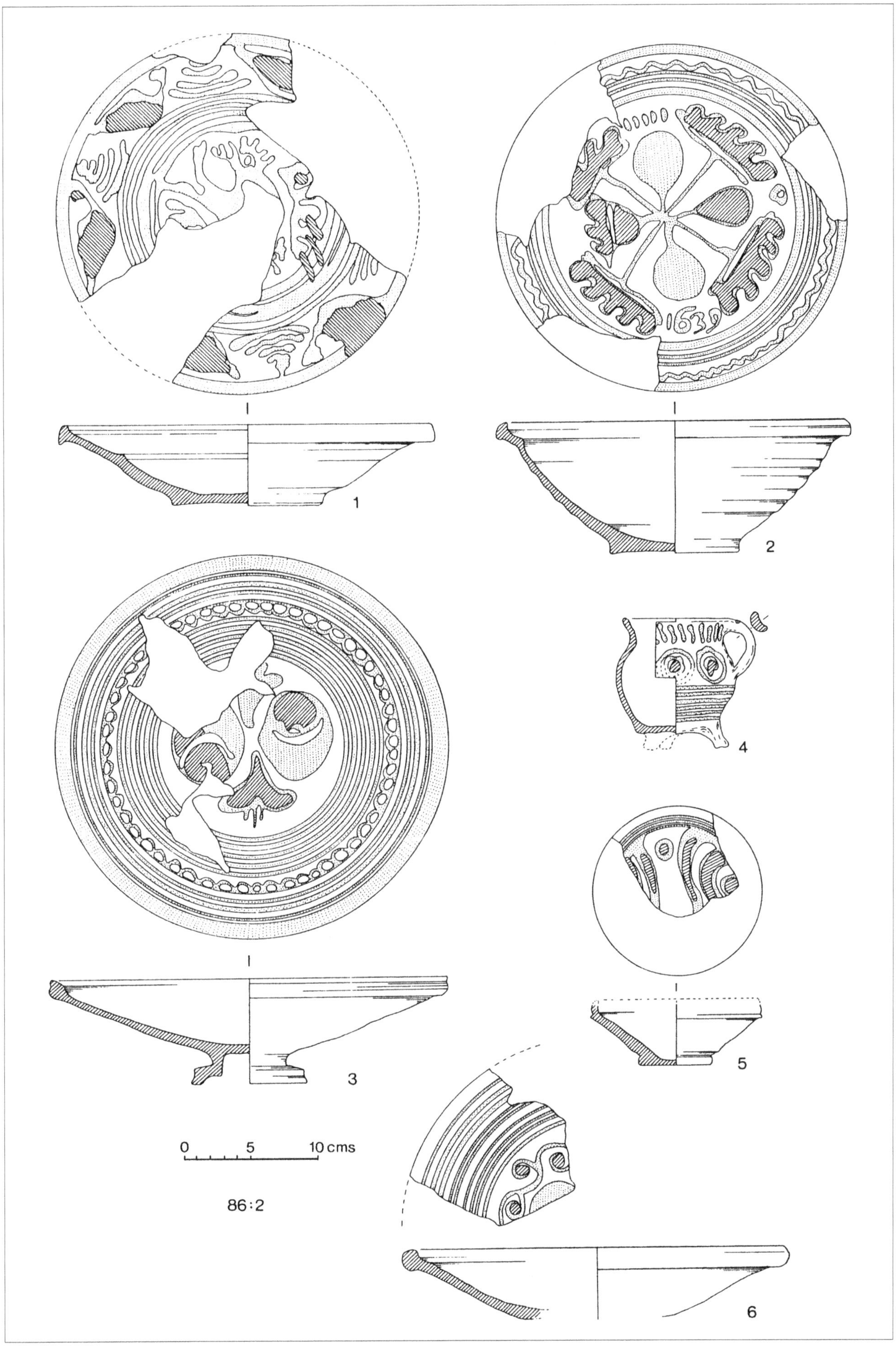


*Fig. 35 Slipware from Duisburg Schwanenstraße 86:2*

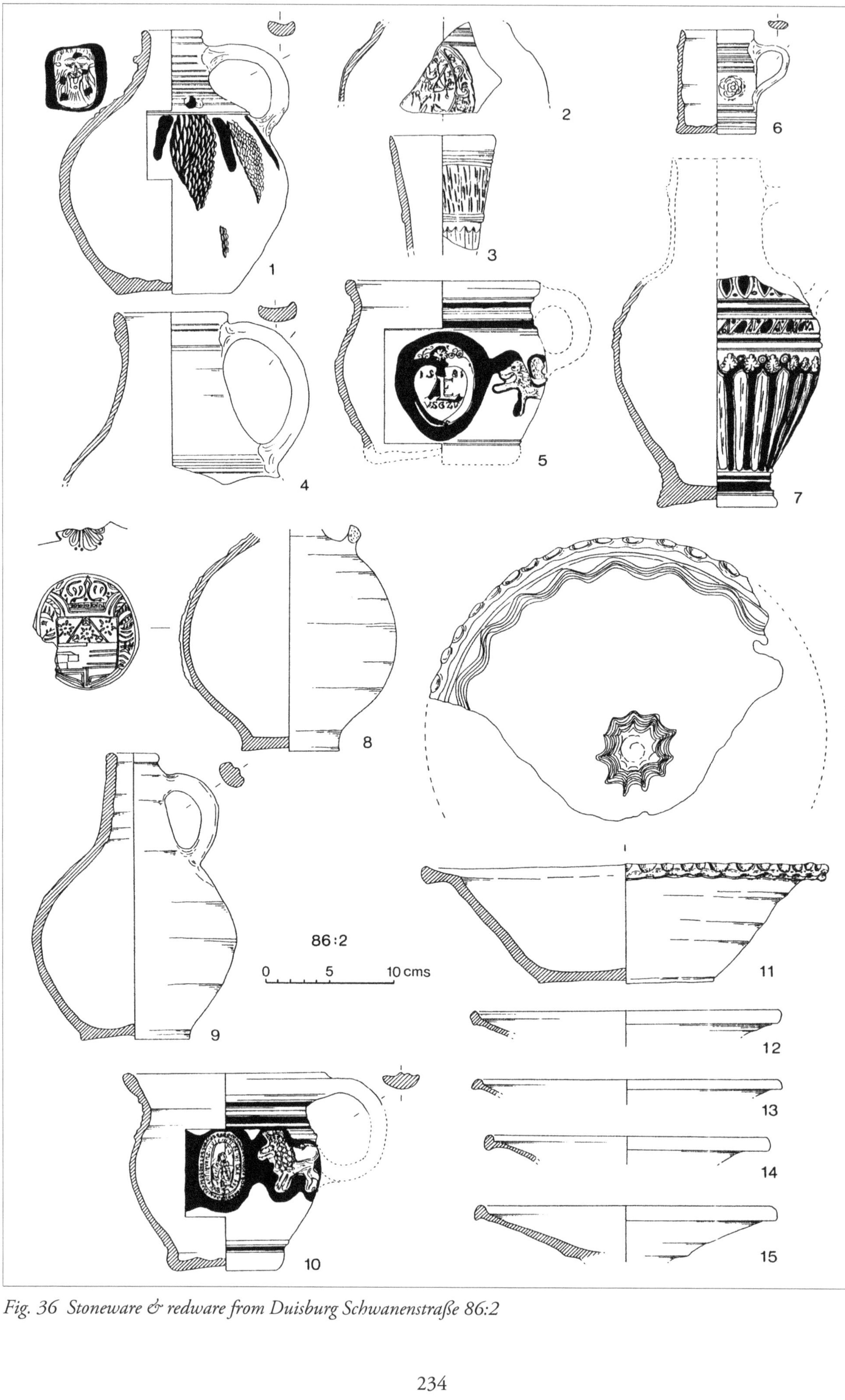


*Fig. 36 Stoneware & redware from Duisburg Schwanenstraße 86:2*

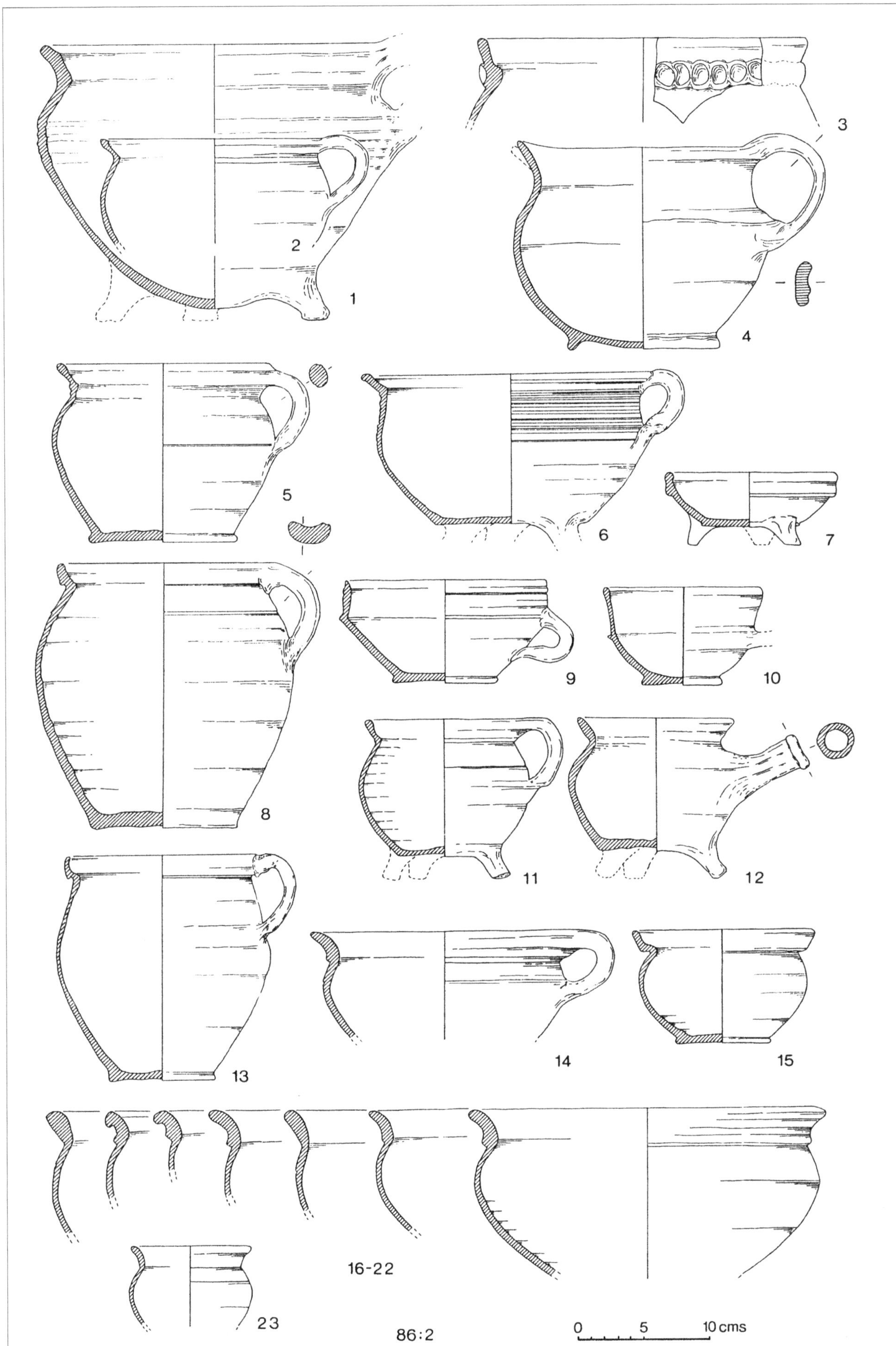


*Fig. 37 Plain redware from Duisburg Schwanenstraße 86:2*

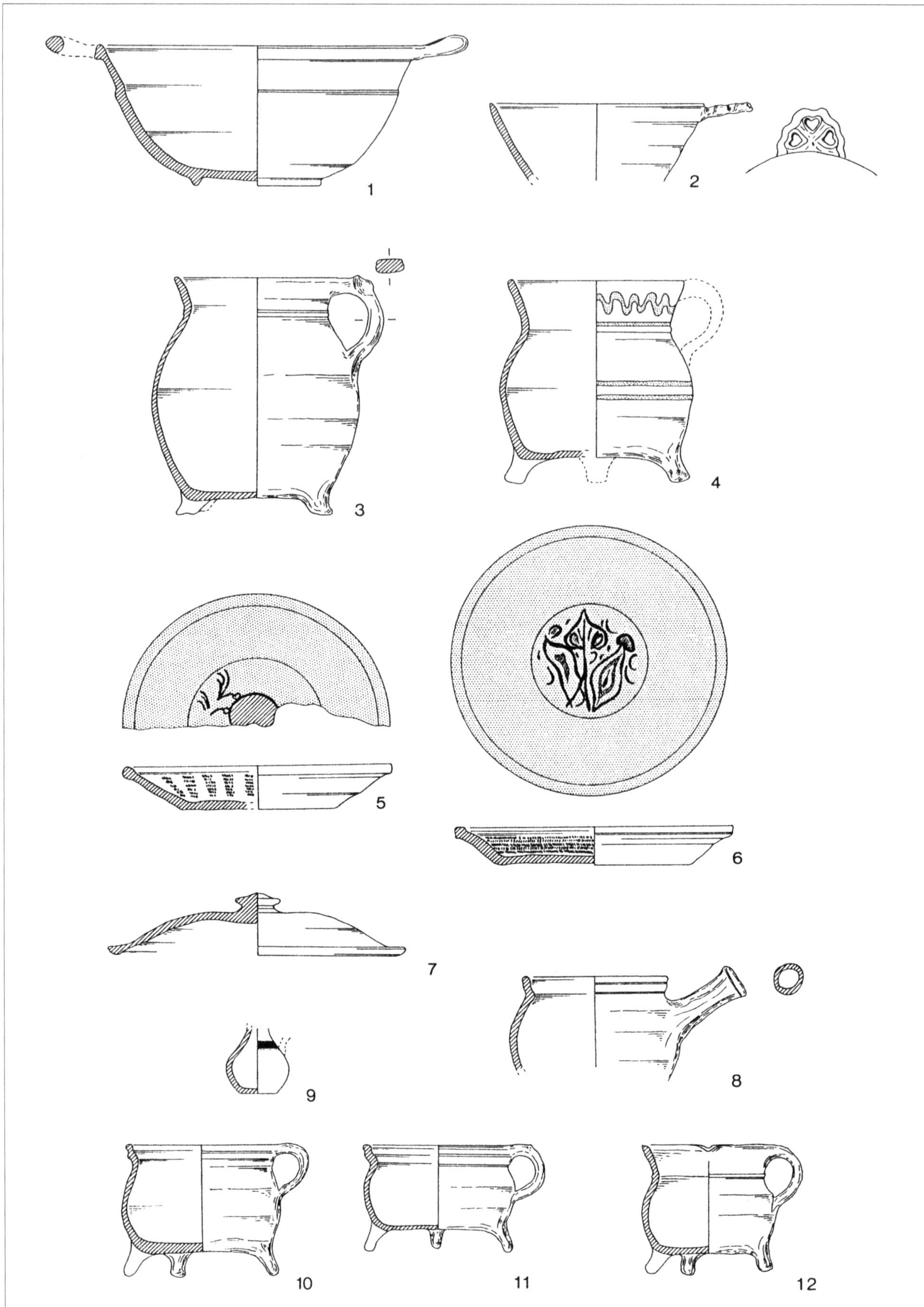


*Fig. 38 NL faience, slipware & plain redware from Duisburg Schwanenstraße 86:2*

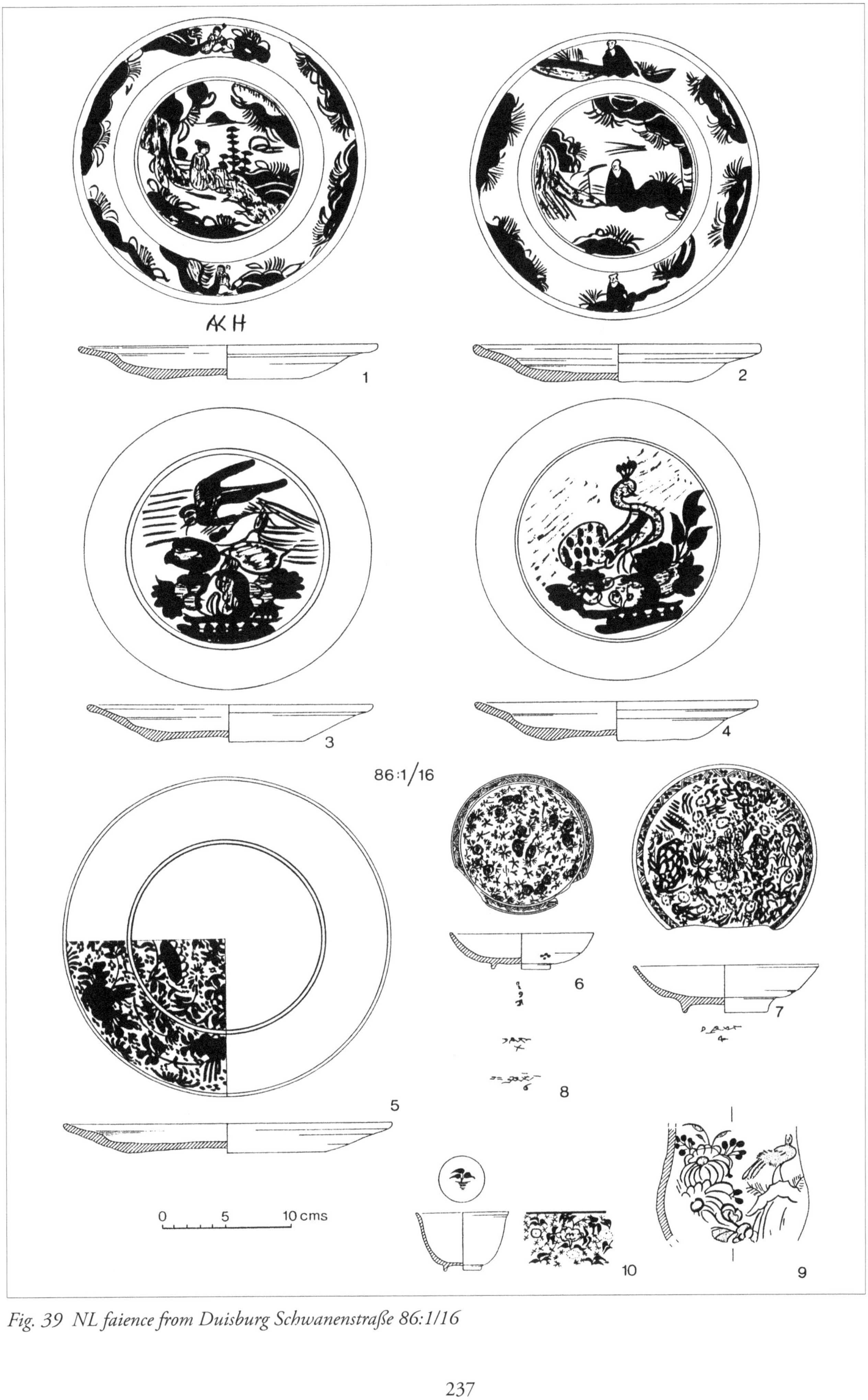


*Fig. 39 NL faience from Duisburg Schwanenstraße 86:1/16*

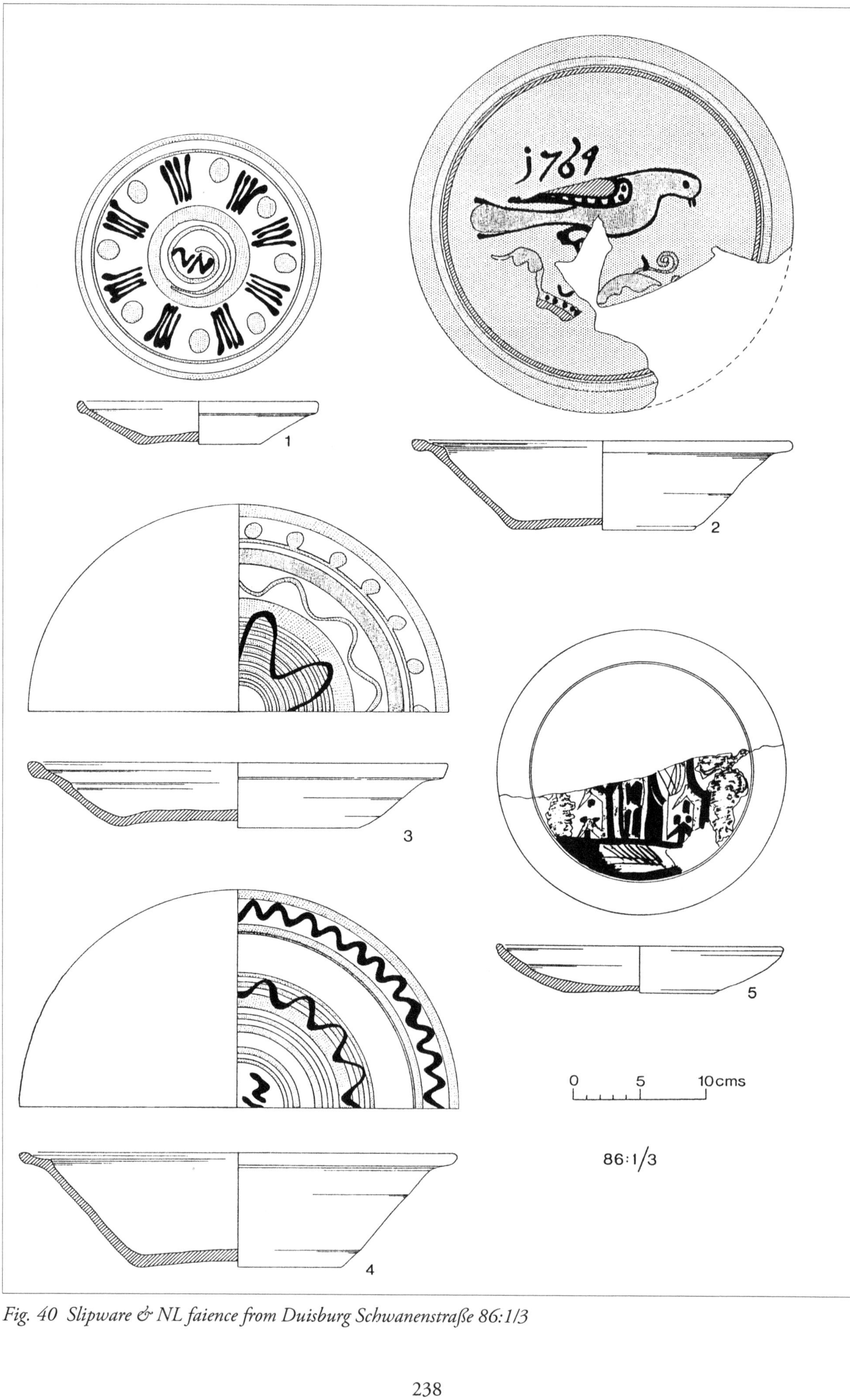


*Fig. 40 Slipware & NL faience from Duisburg Schwanenstraße 86:1/3*

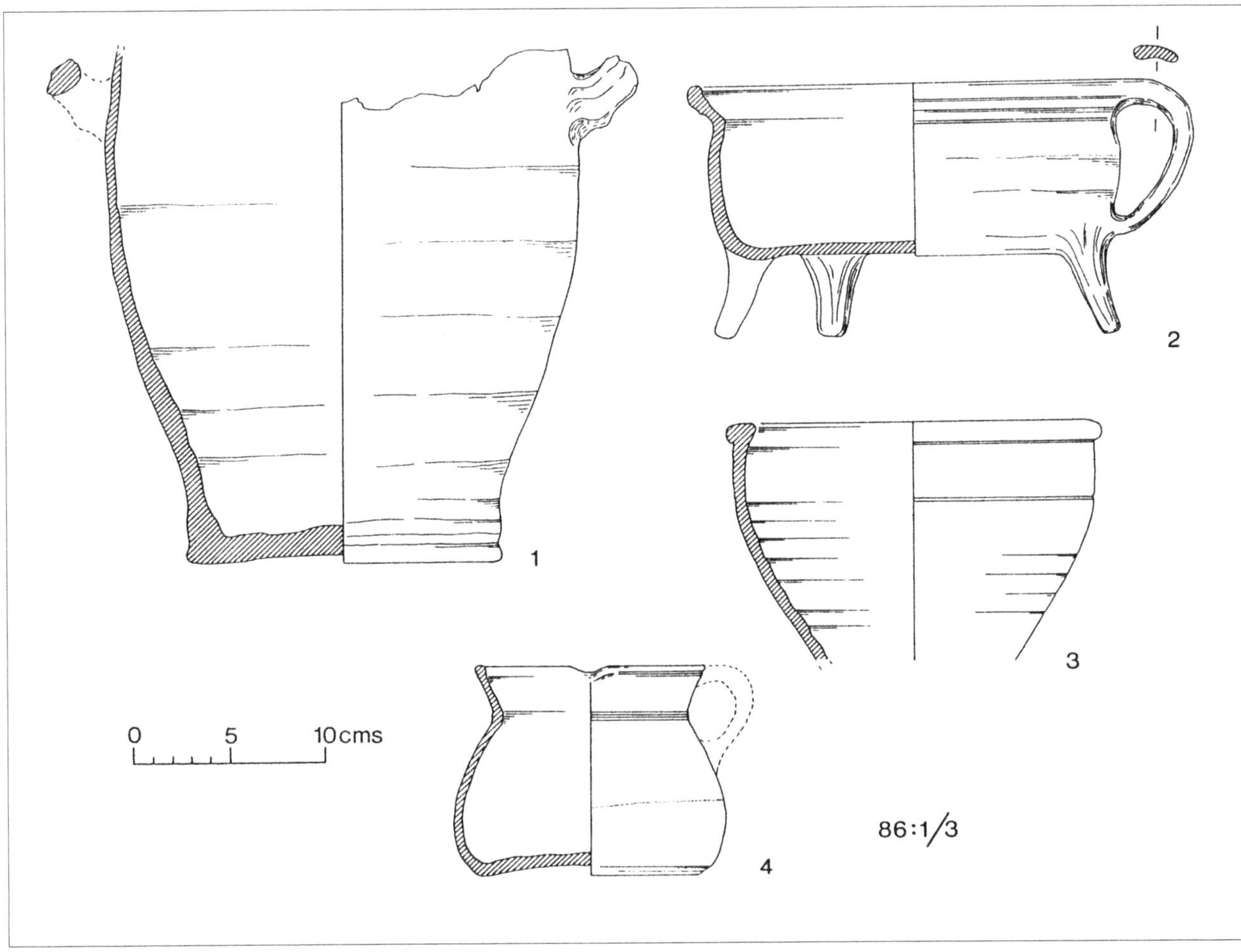


*Fig. 41 Plain redware from Duisburg Schwanenstraße 86:1/3*

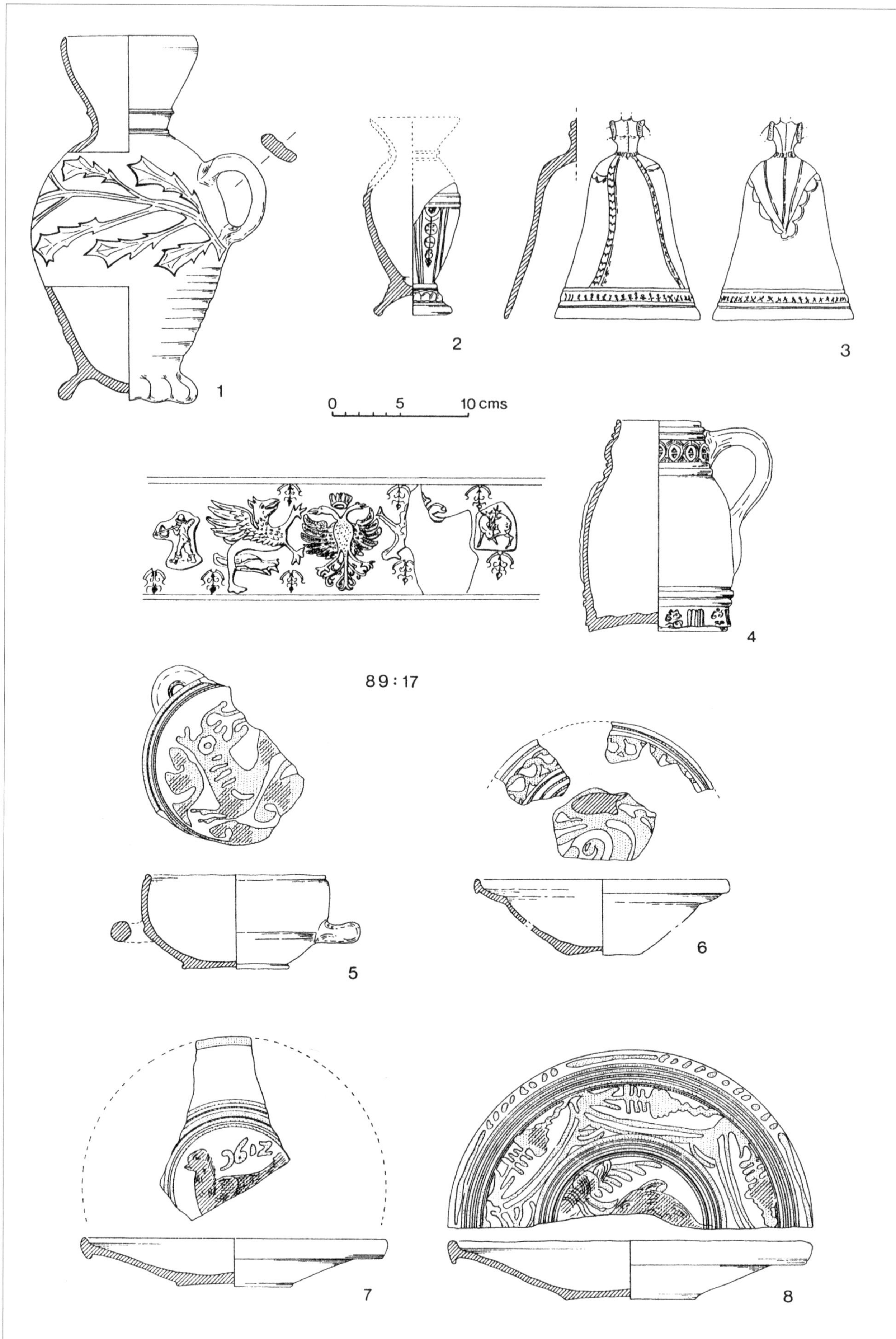


*Fig. 42 Stoneware & slipware from Duisburg Niederstraße 89:17*

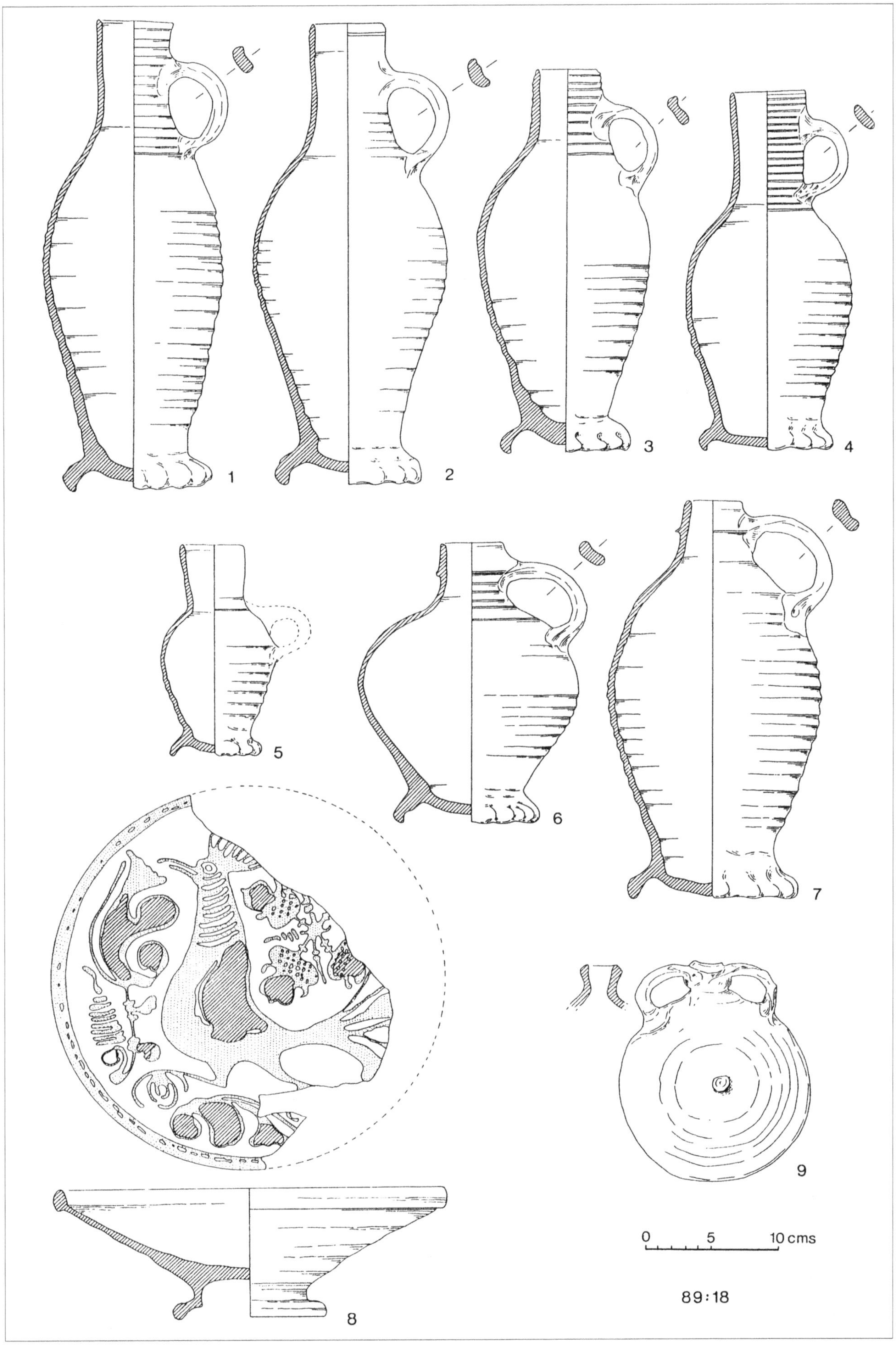


*Fig. 43 Stoneware & slipware from Duisburg Niederstraße 89:18*

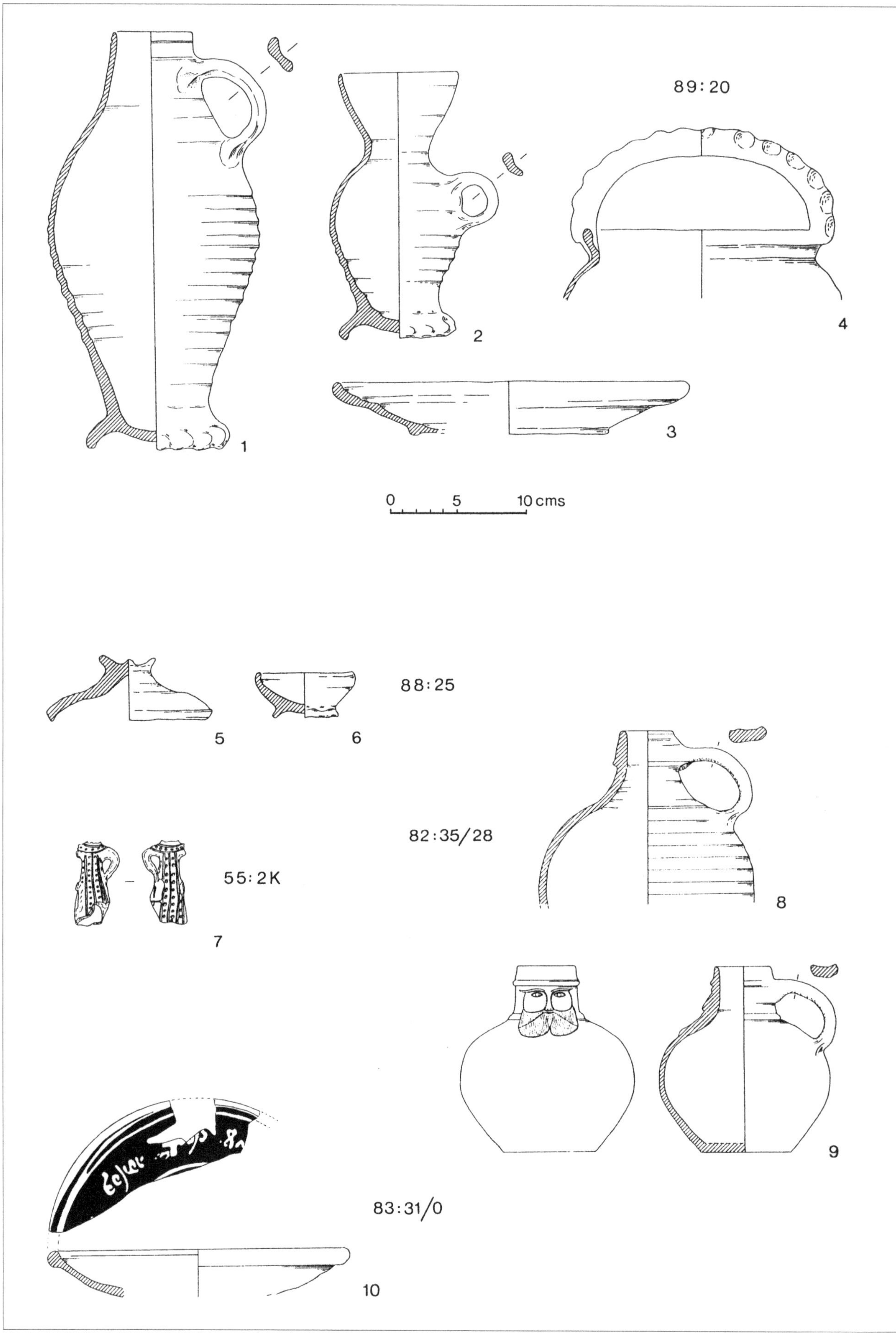


*Fig. 44 Stoneware, redware & slipware from Duisburg contexts 89:20, 88:25, 55:2K, 82:35/28 & 83:31/0*

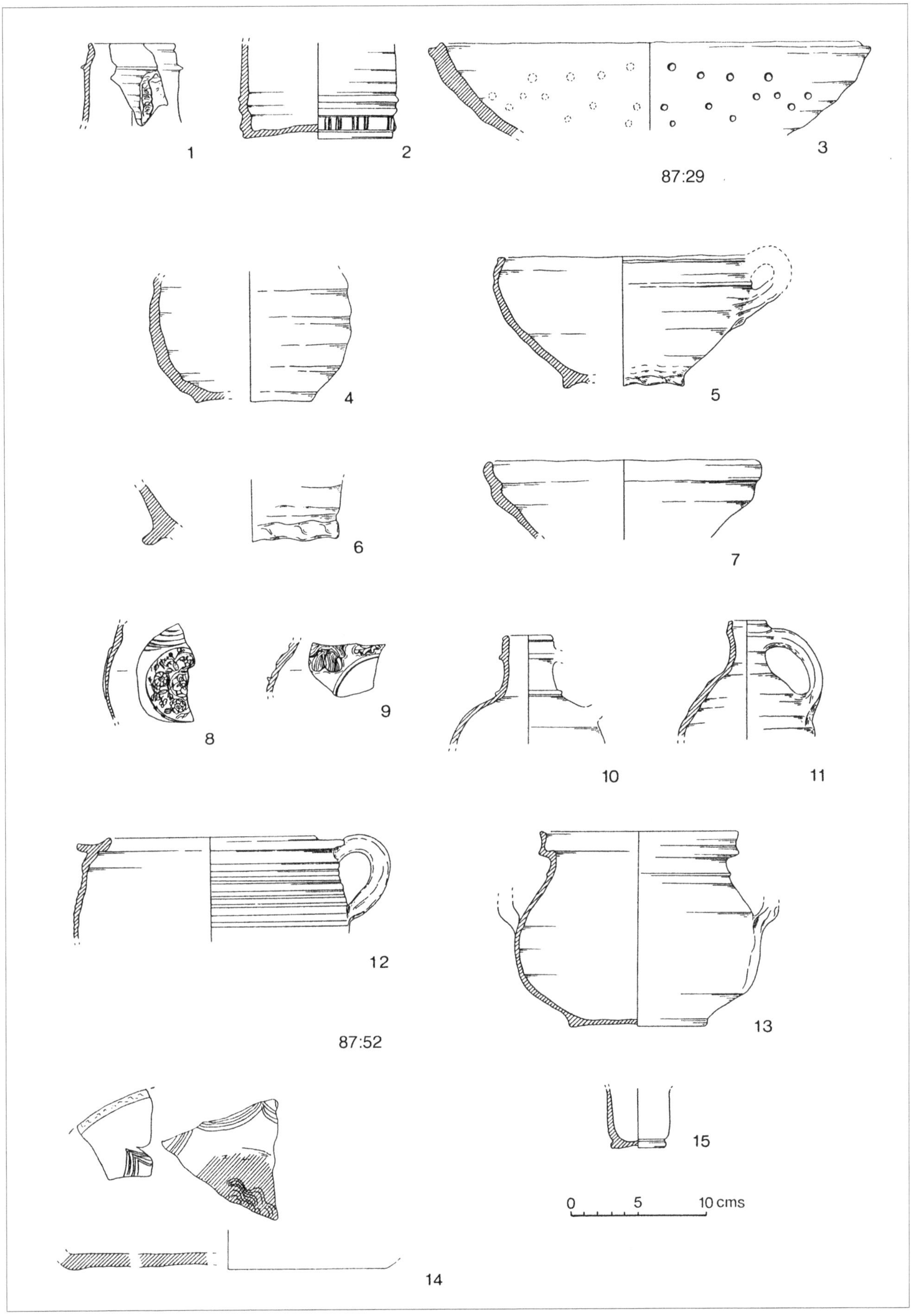


*Fig. 45 Stoneware & earthenware from Duisburg contexts 87:29 & 87:52*

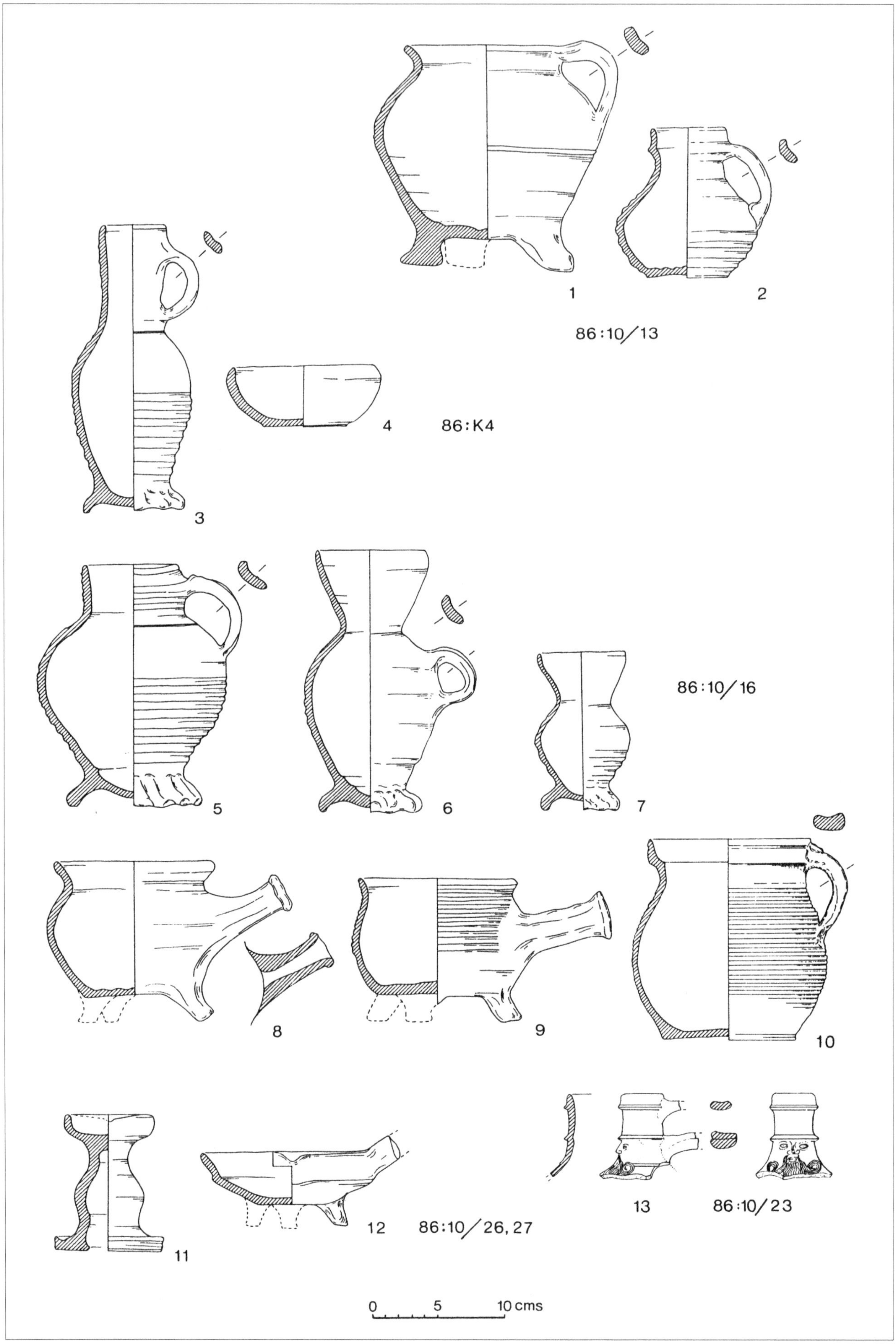


*Fig. 46 Earthenware & stoneware from Duisburg contexts 86:10/27, 86:K4, 86:10/16, 86:10/26,27 & 86:10/23*

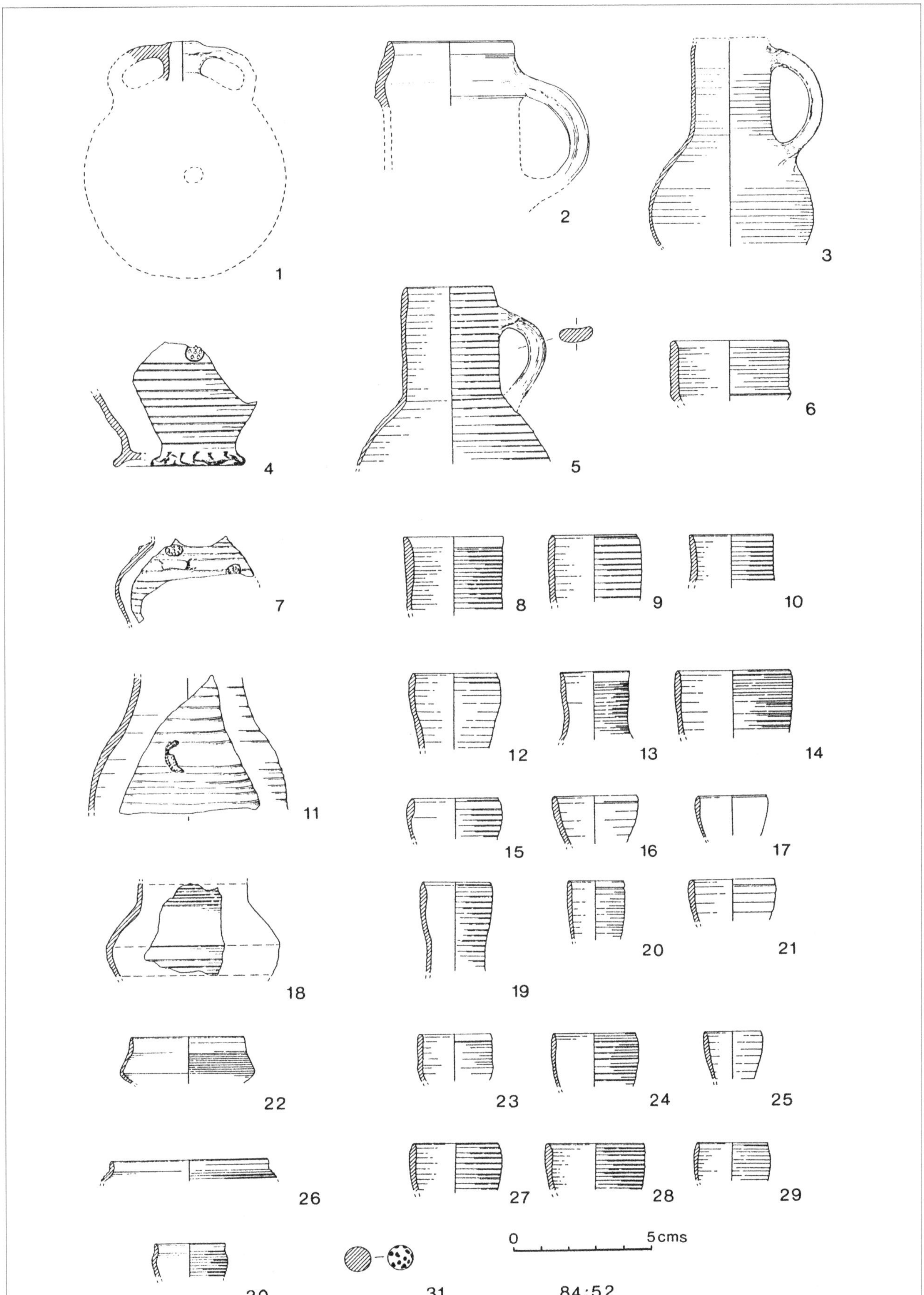


*Fig. 47 Stoneware from Duisburg Minoritenkloster 84:52*

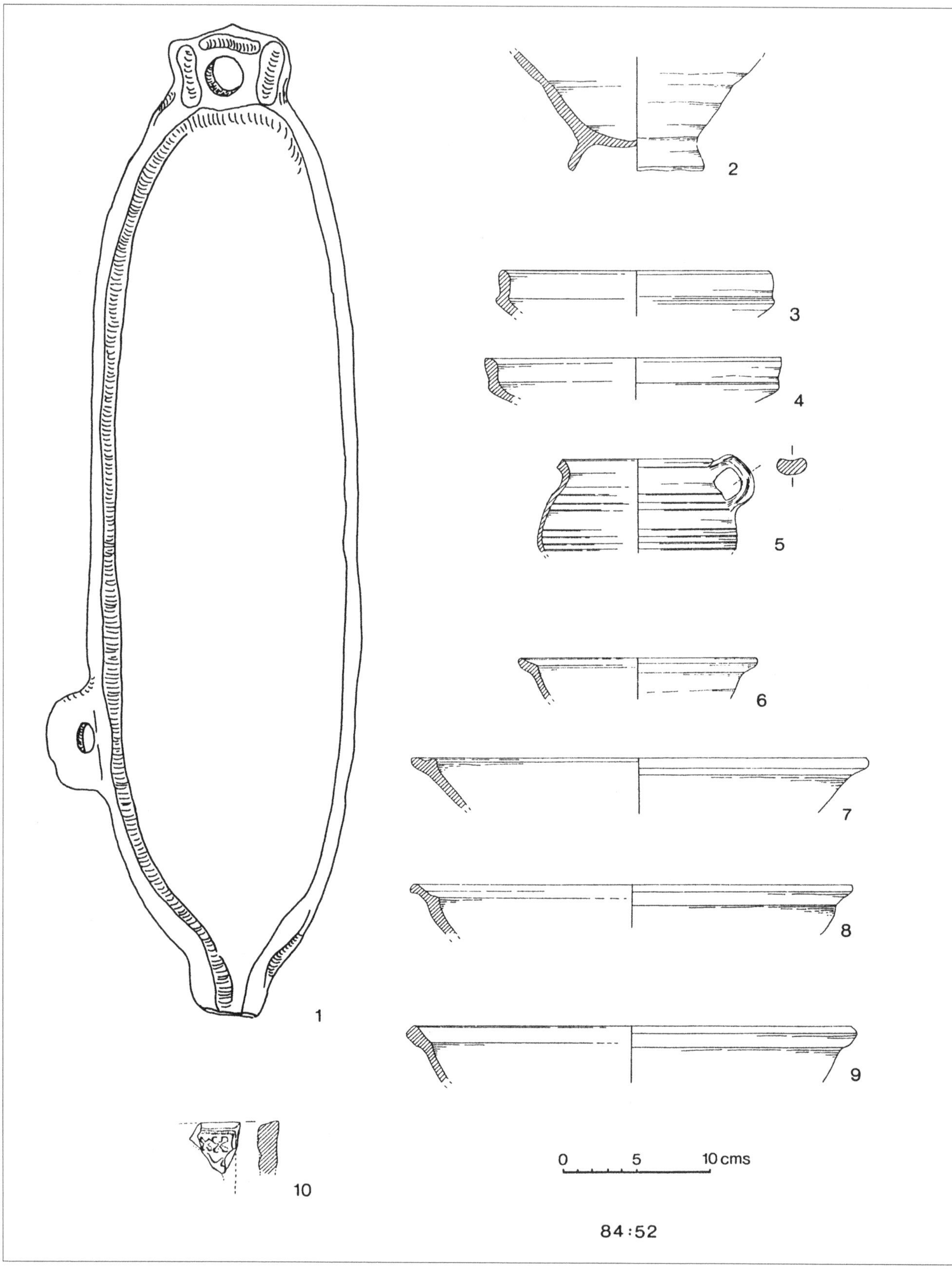


*Fig. 48 Earthenware from Duisburg Minoritenkloster 84:52*

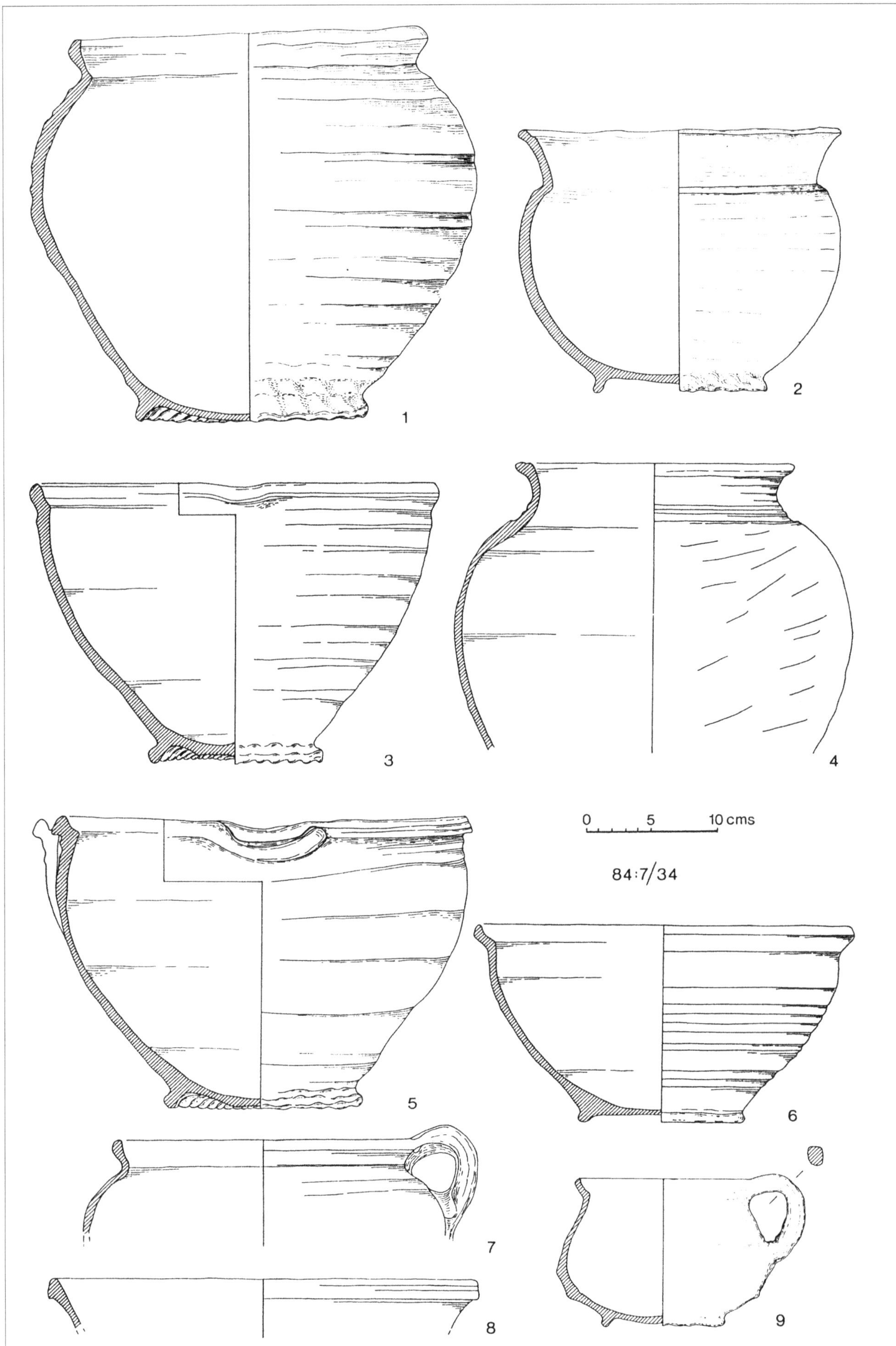


*Fig. 49 Greyware & redware from Duisburg Innenhafen 84:7/34*

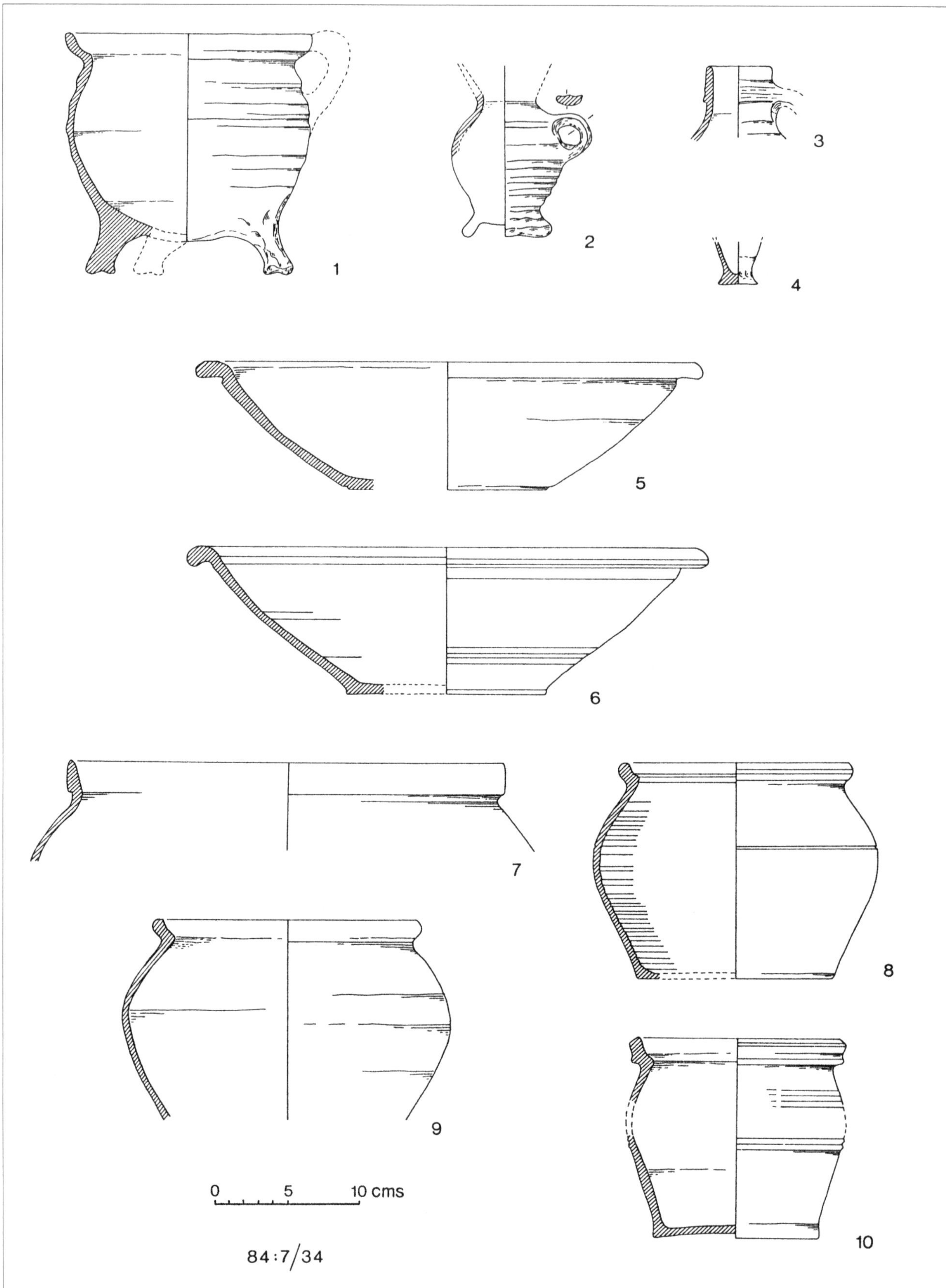


*Fig. 50 Redware & stoneware from Duisburg Innenhafen 84:7/34*

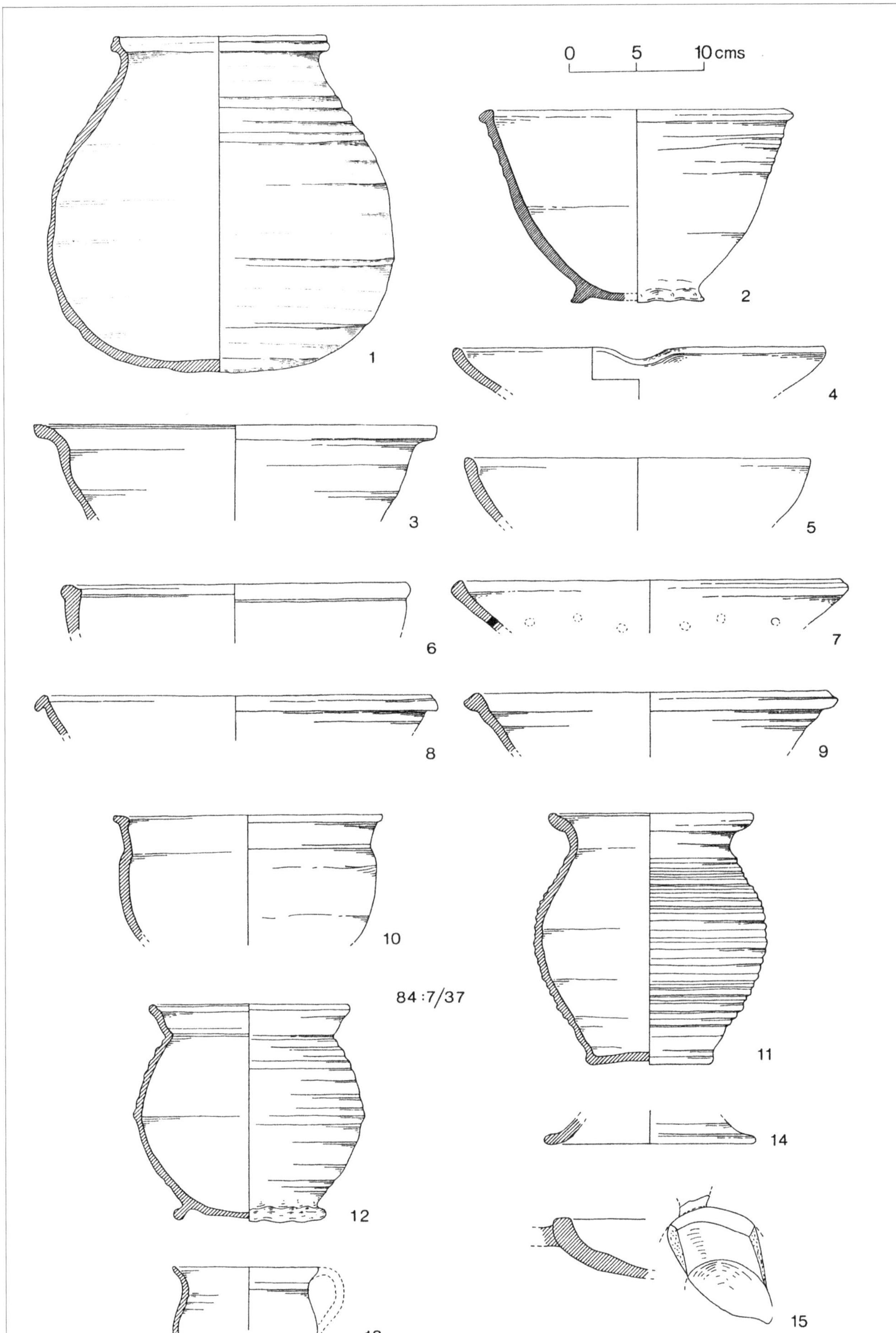


*Fig. 51 Greyware & redware from Duisburg Innenhafen 84:7/37*

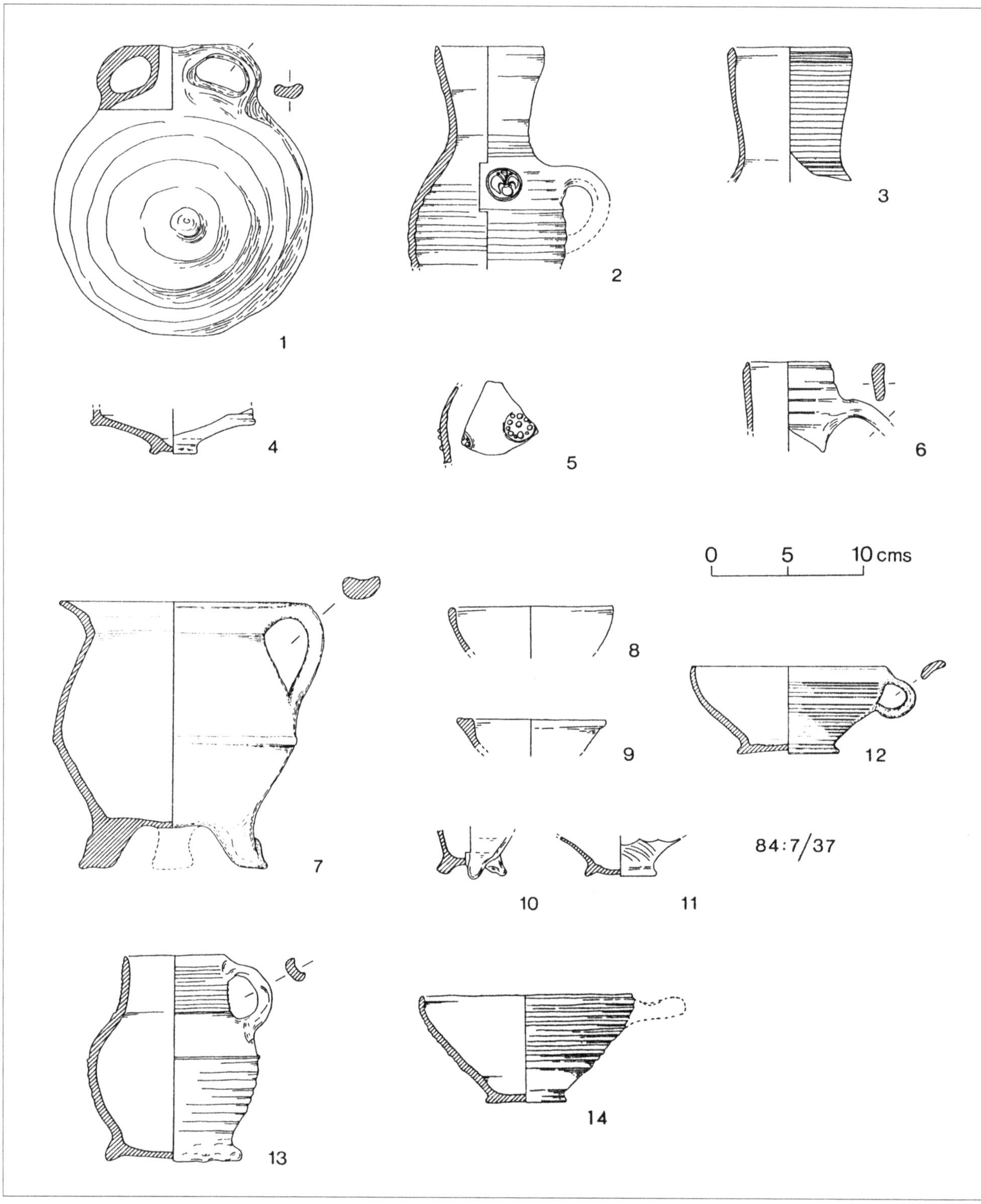


*Fig. 52 Stoneware & whiteware from Duisburg Innenhafen 84:7/37*

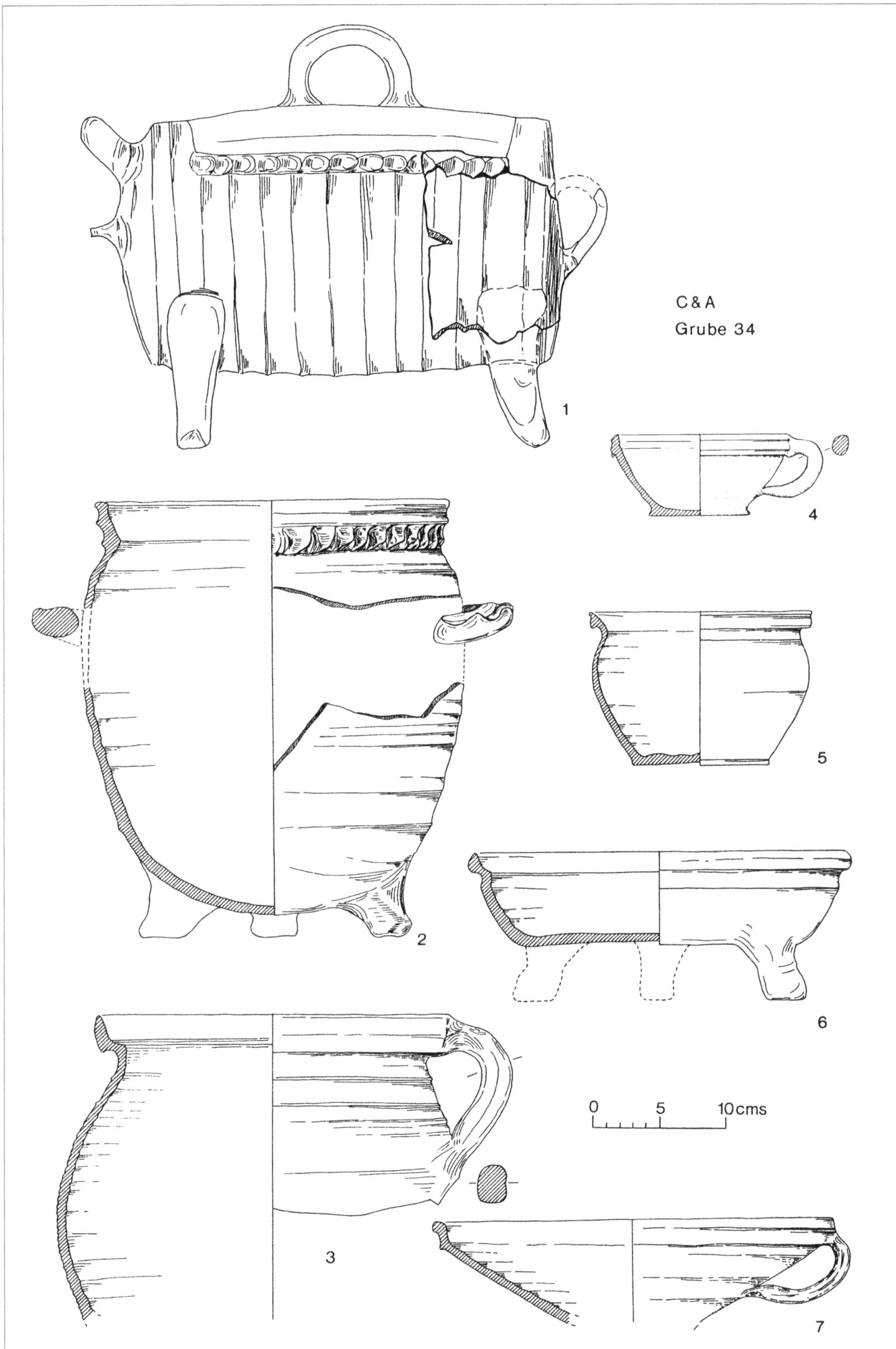


*Fig. 53 Redware from Duisburg C & A, Grube 34*

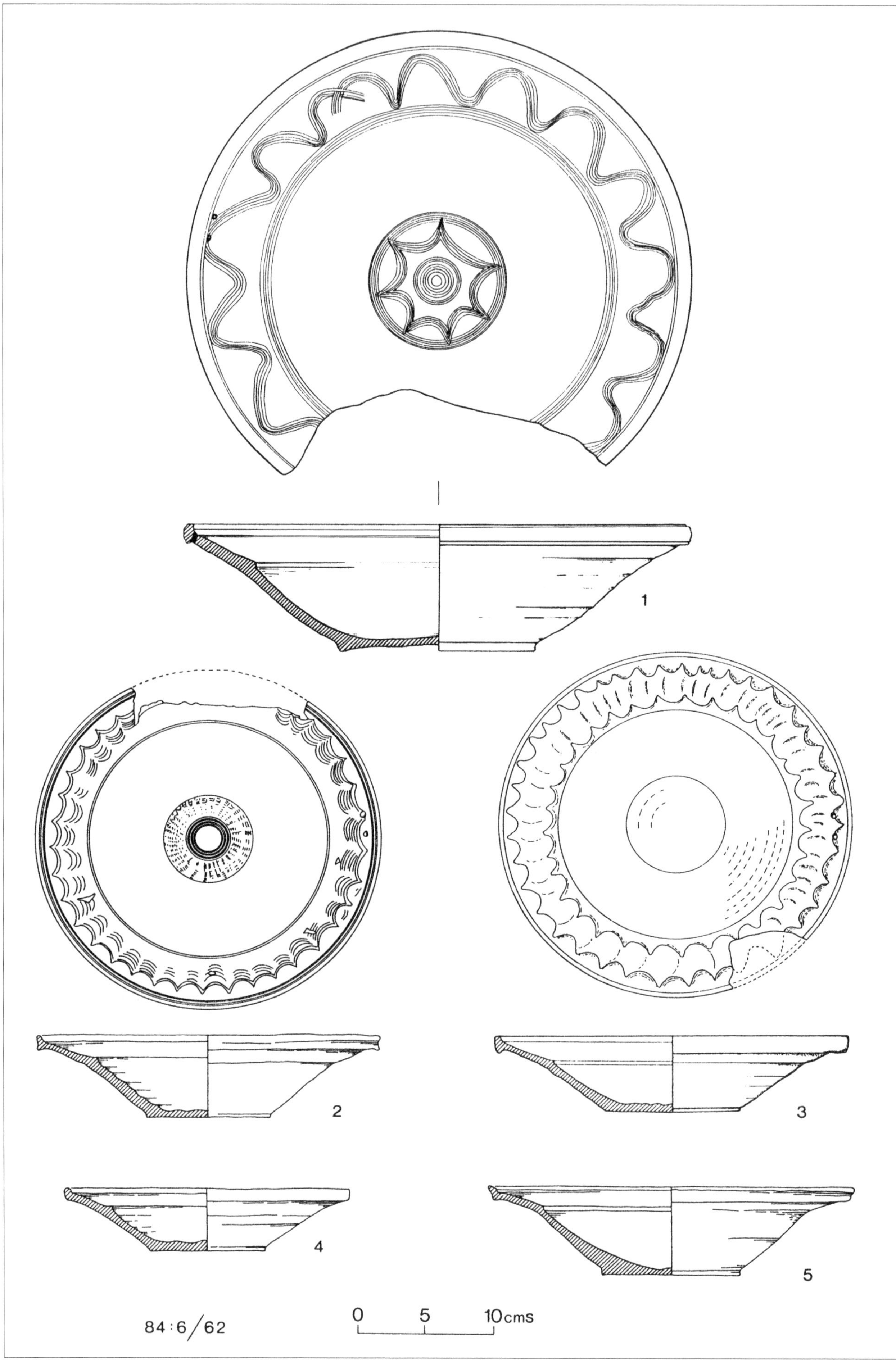


*Fig. 54 Incesed redware from C & A 84:6/62*

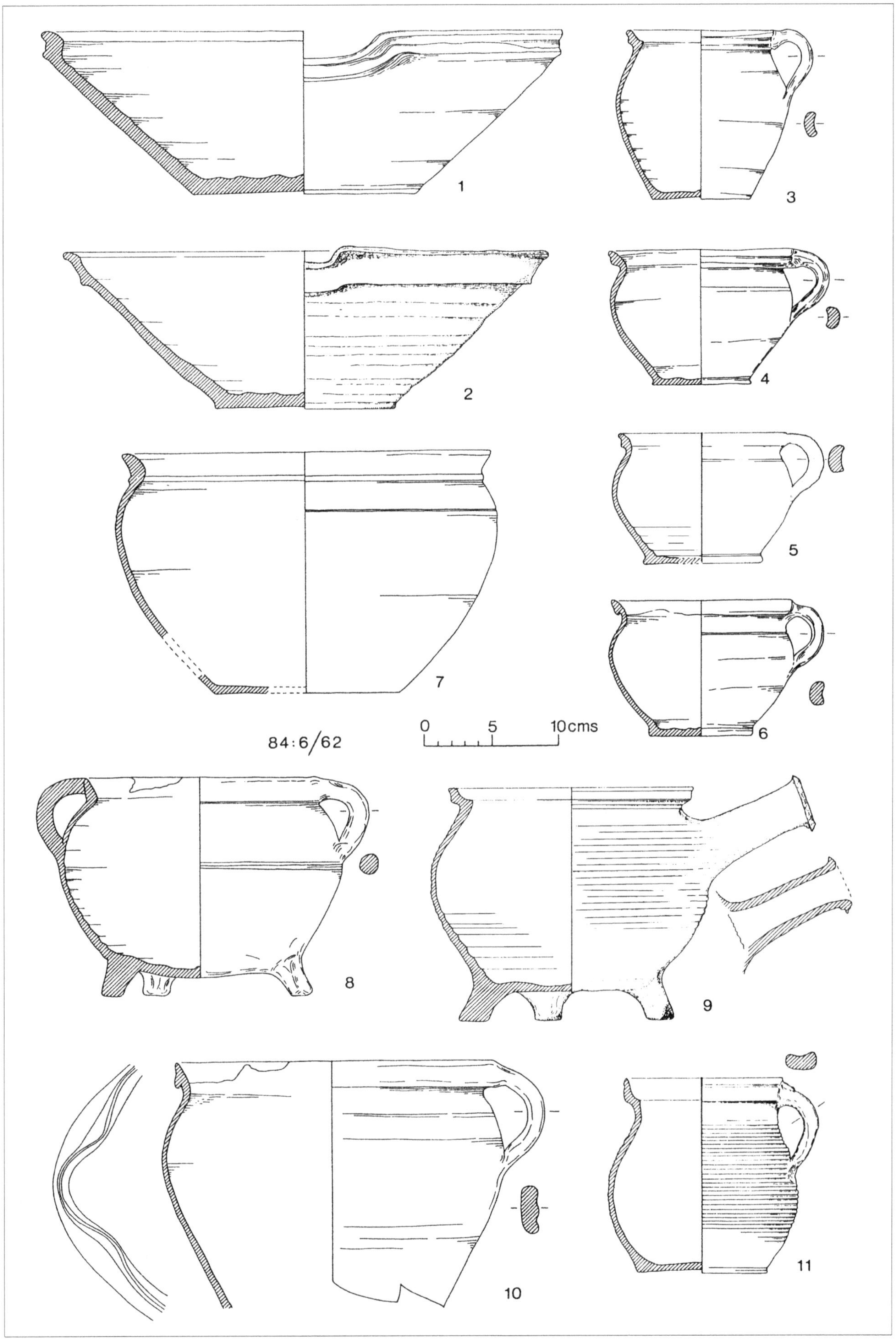


*Fig. 55 Redware from Duisburg C & A 84:6/62*

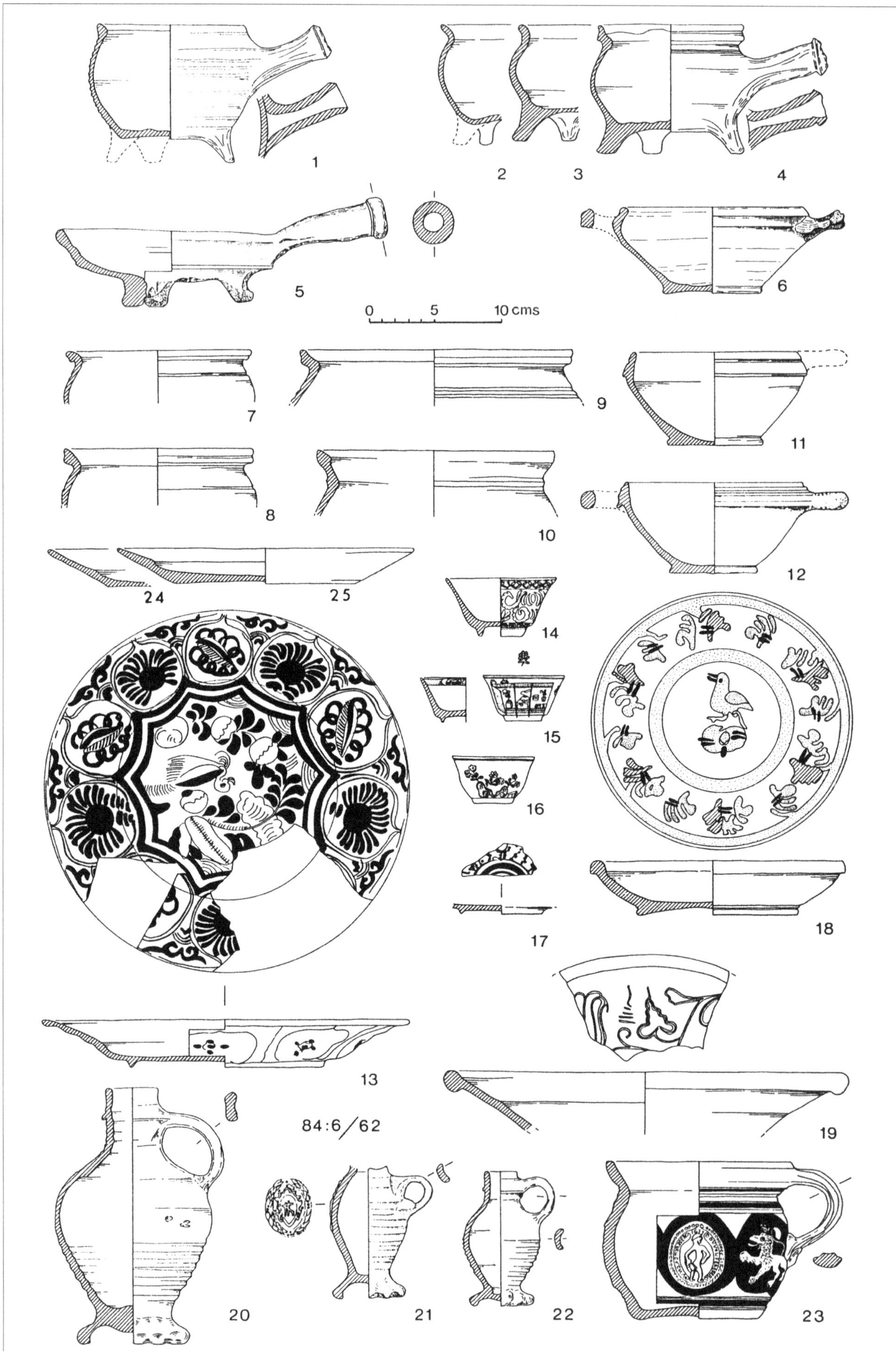


*Fig. 56 Redware, whiteware, NL faience, Oriental porcelain, slipware & stoneware from Duisburg C & A 84:6/62*

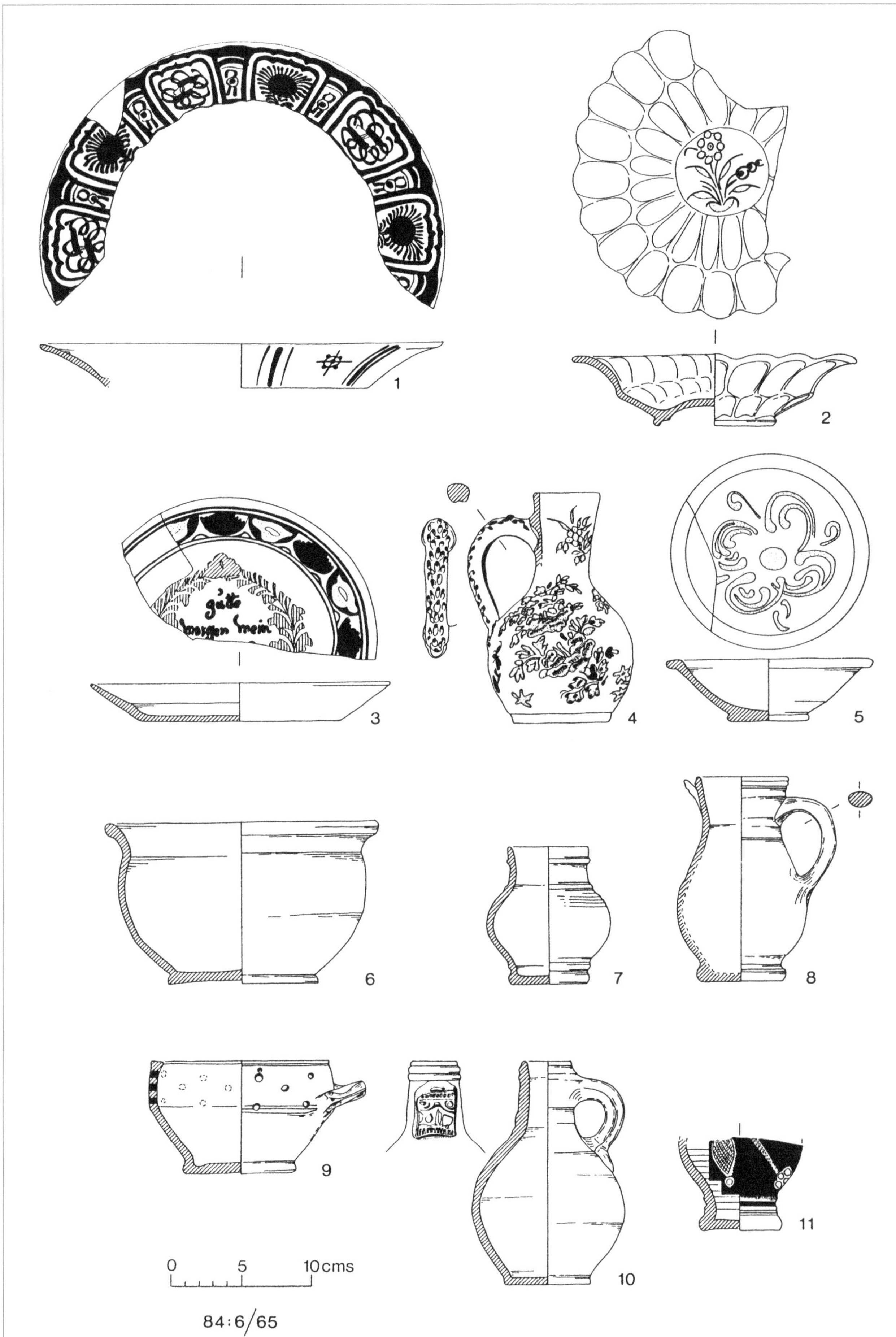


*Fig. 57 NL faience, slipware, plain redware & stoneware from Duisburg C & A 84:6/65*

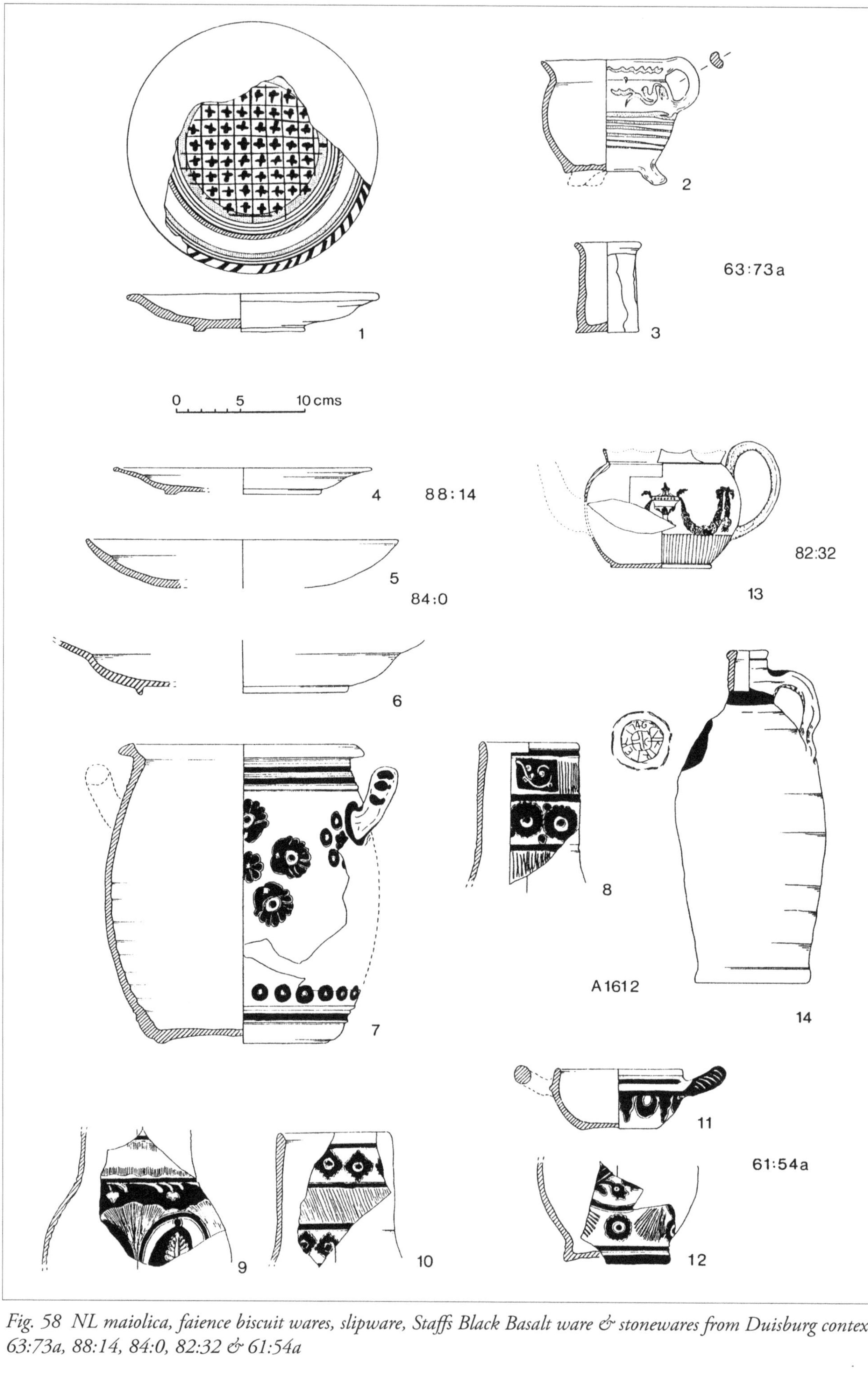


*Fig. 58 NL maiolica, faience biscuit wares, slipware, Staffs Black Basalt ware & stonewares from Duisburg contexts 63:73a, 88:14, 84:0, 82:32 & 61:54a*

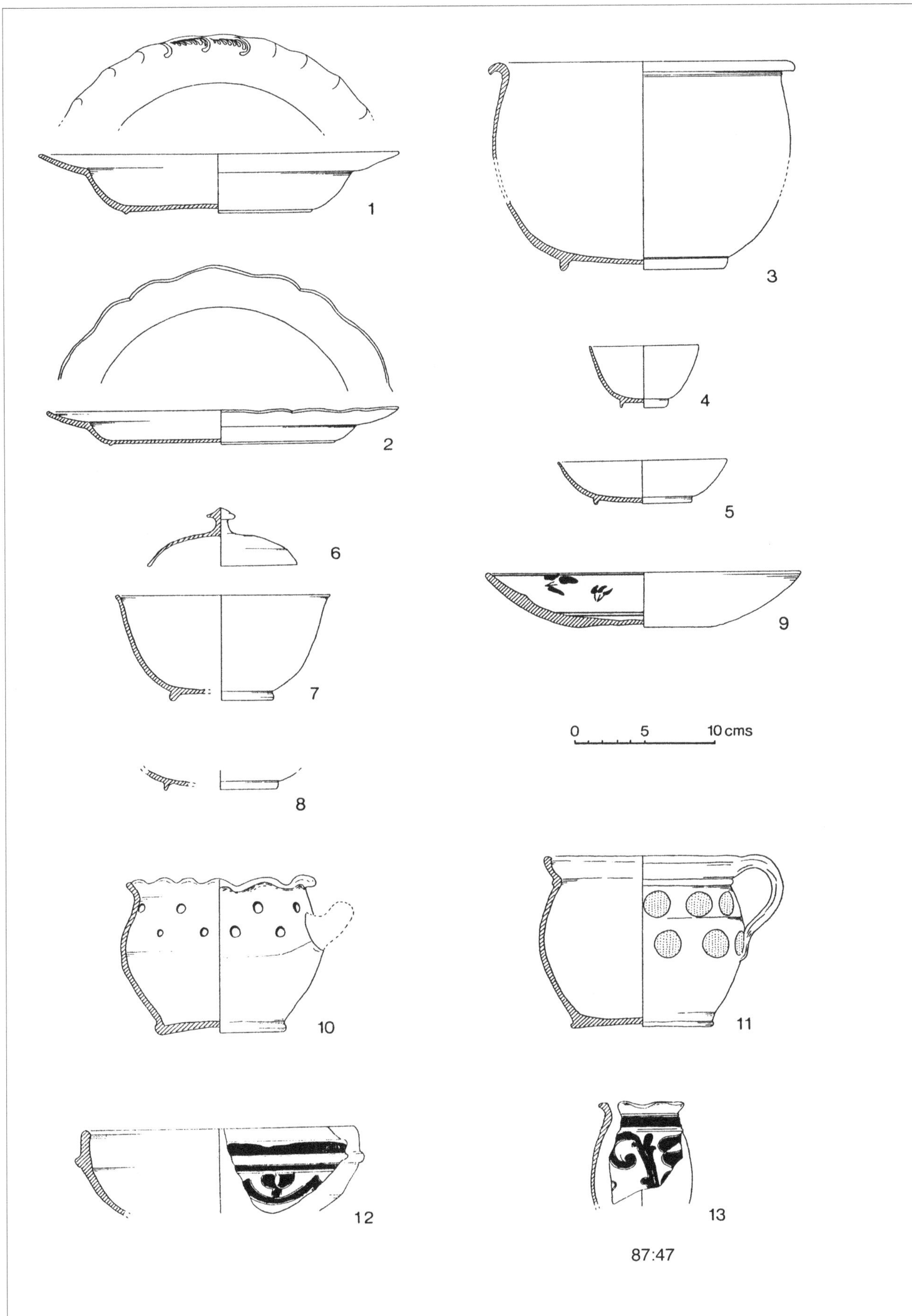


*Fig. 59 English finewares, NL faience, plain redware & stoneware from Duisburg Abteistraße 87:47*

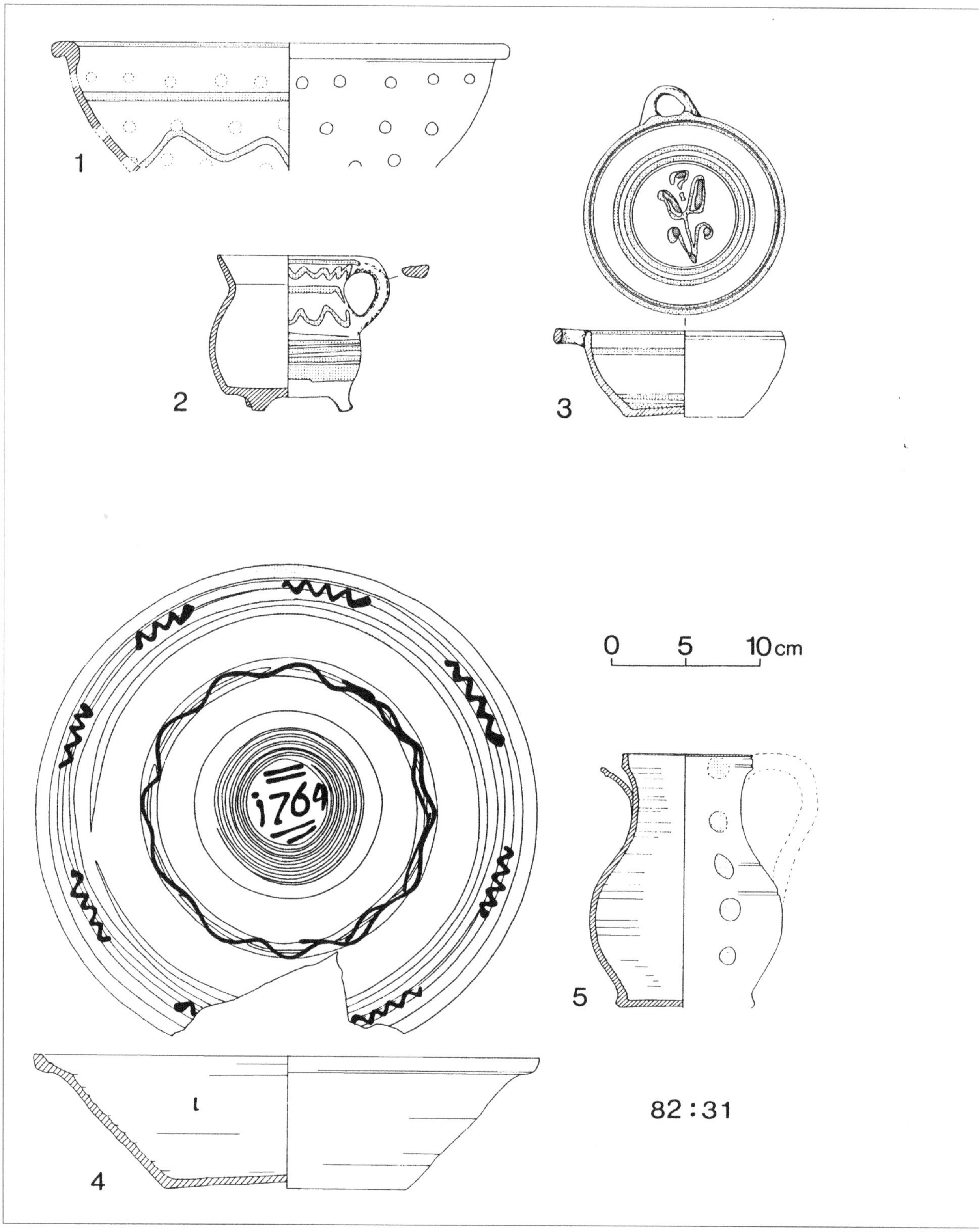


*Fig. 60 Slipware from Duisburg Alter Markt 82:31*

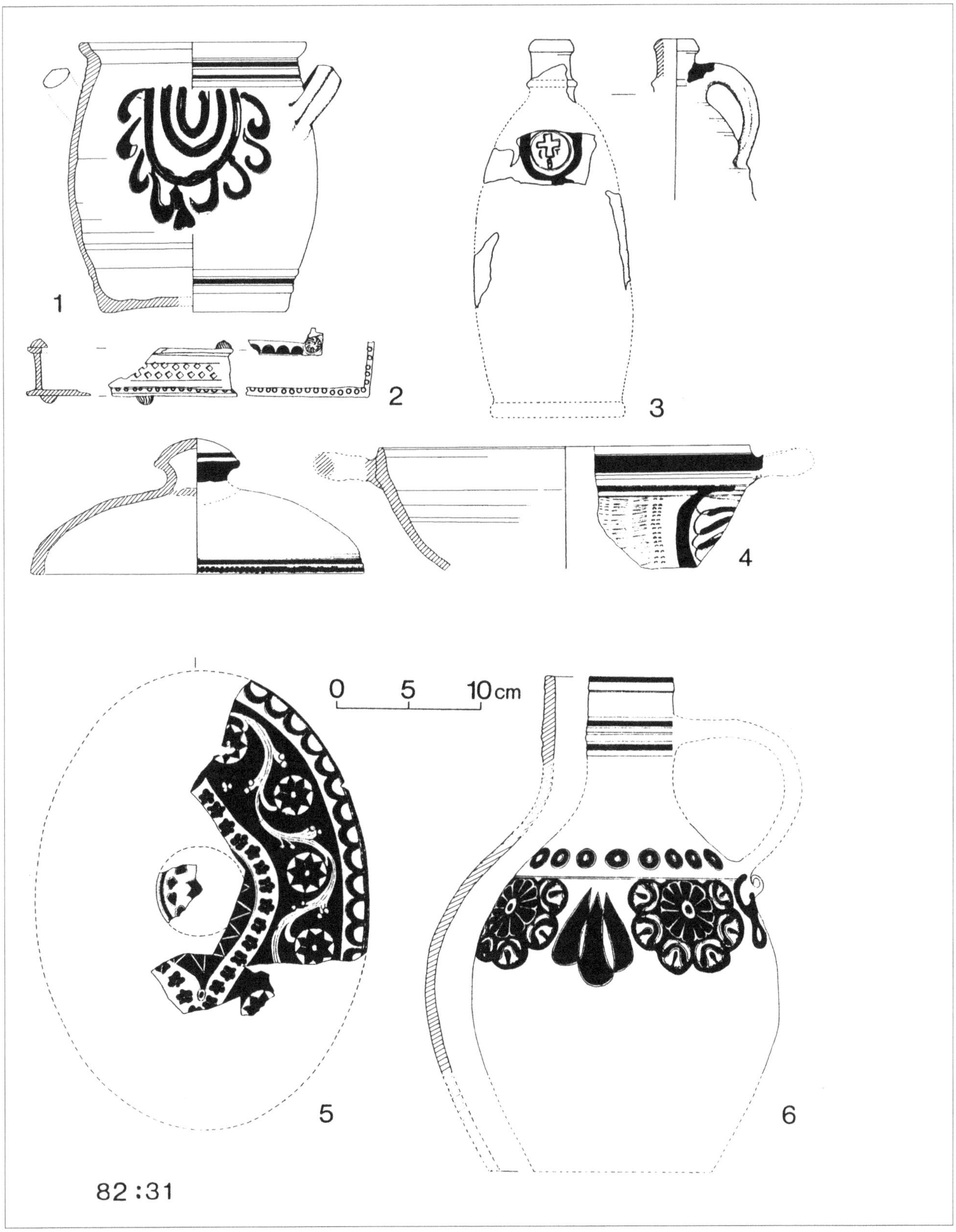


*Fig. 61 Stoneware from Duisburg Alter Markt 82:31*

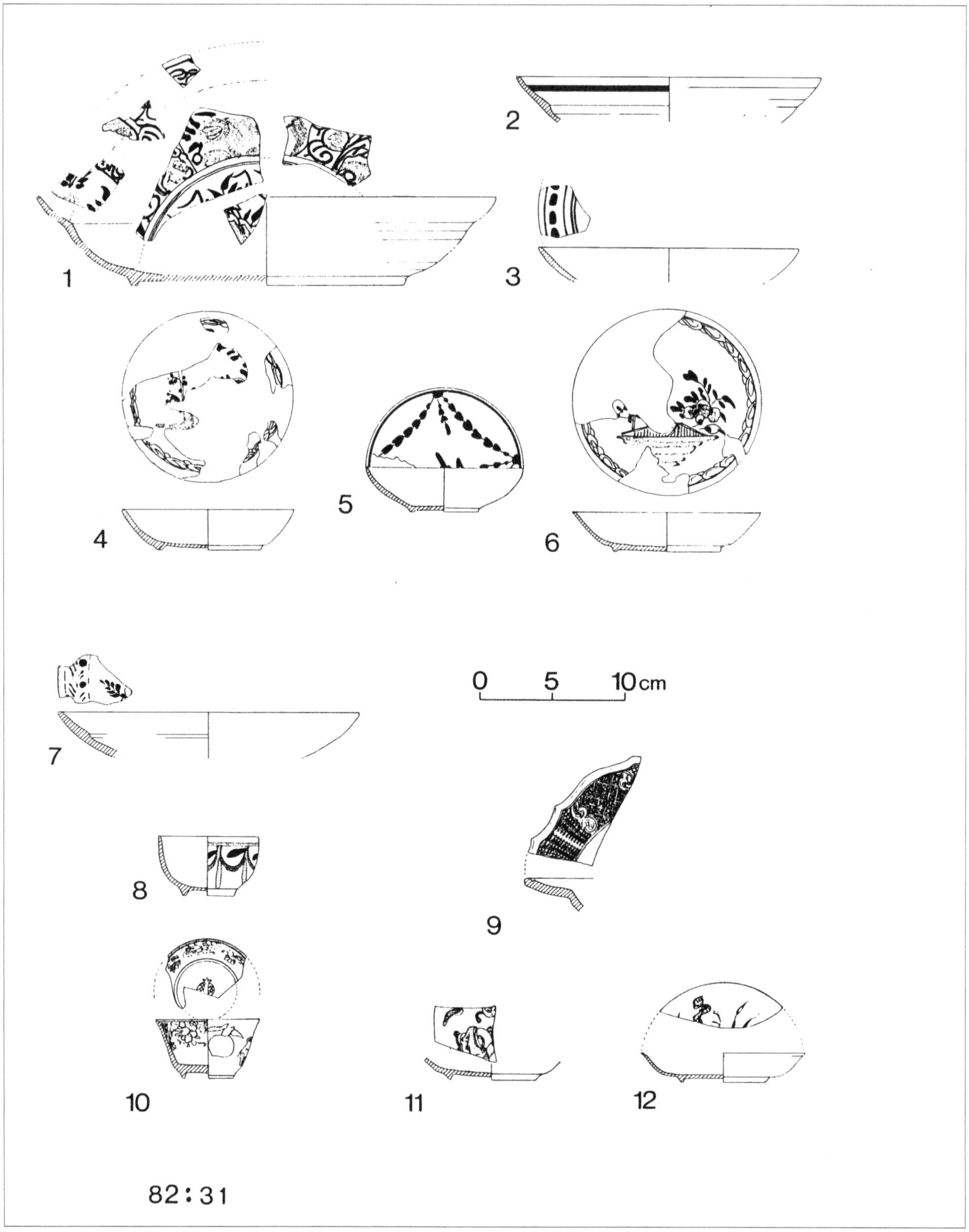


*Fig. 62 NL faience, English finewares & Oriental porcelain from Duisburg Alter Markt 82:31*

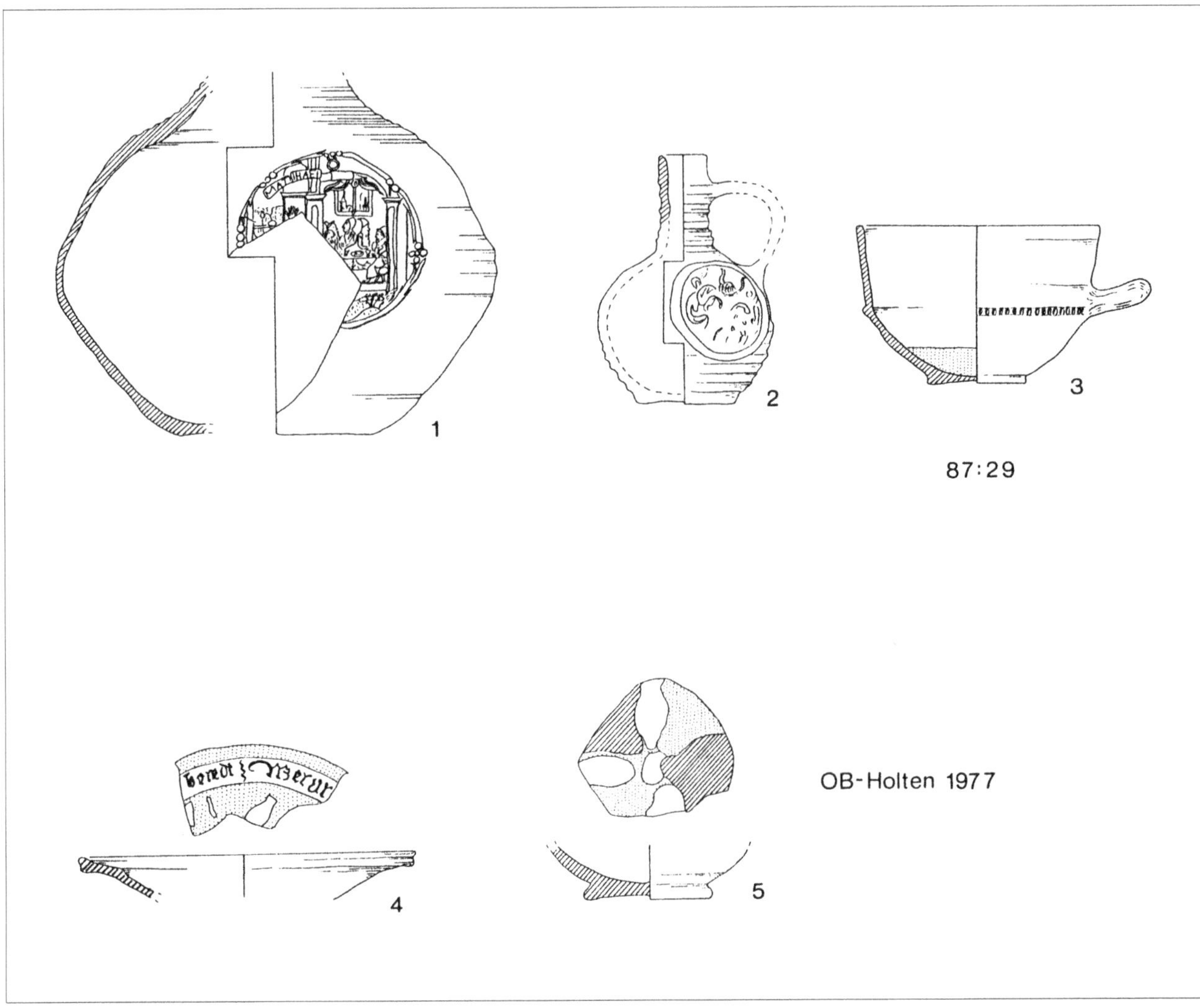


*Fig. 63 Stoneware & plain redware from Duisburg-Hamborn 87:29; slipware from Oberhausen-Holten 1977*

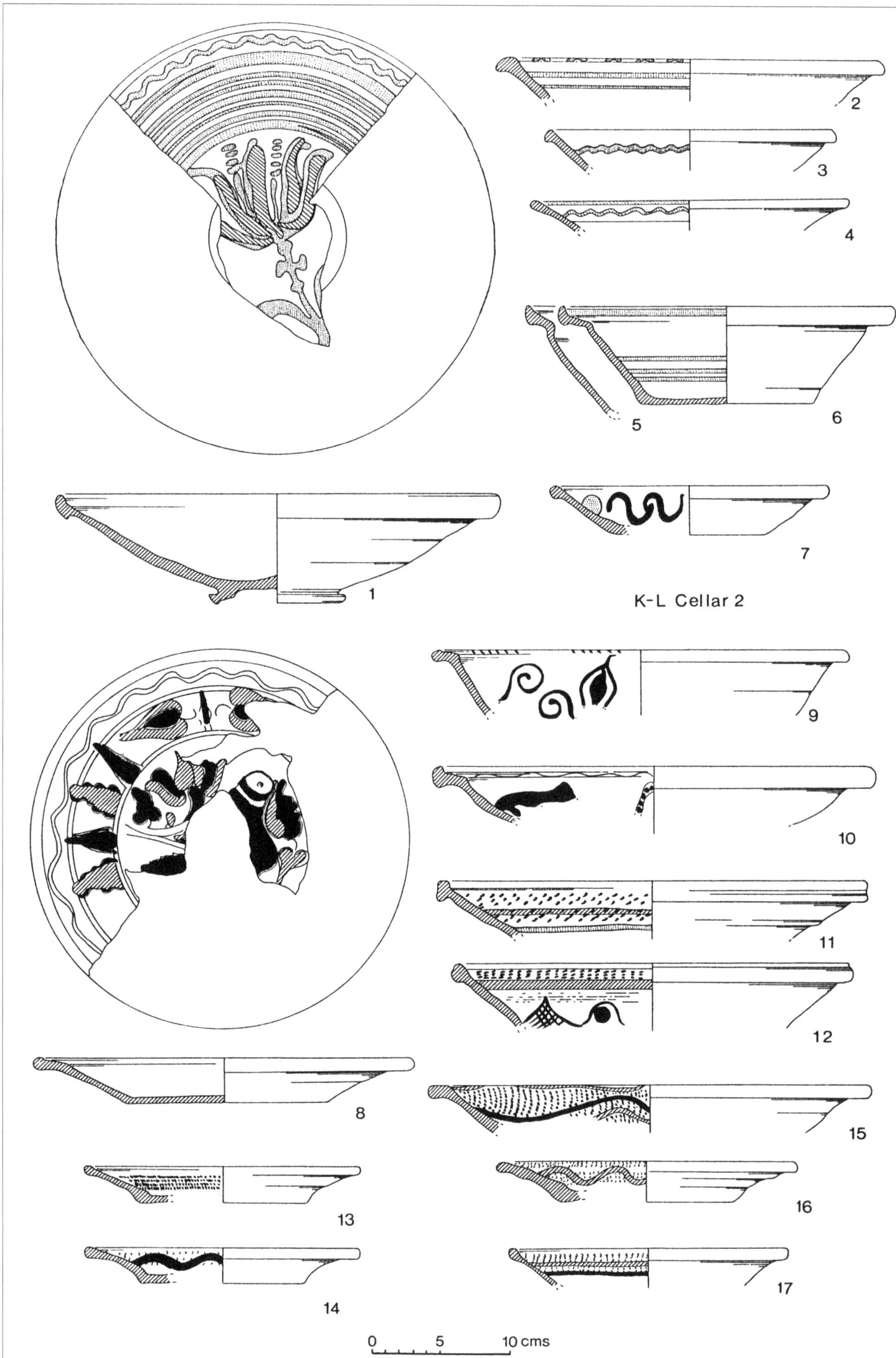


*Fig. 64 Slipware from Krefeld-Linn, Margaretenstraße 32, cellar 2*

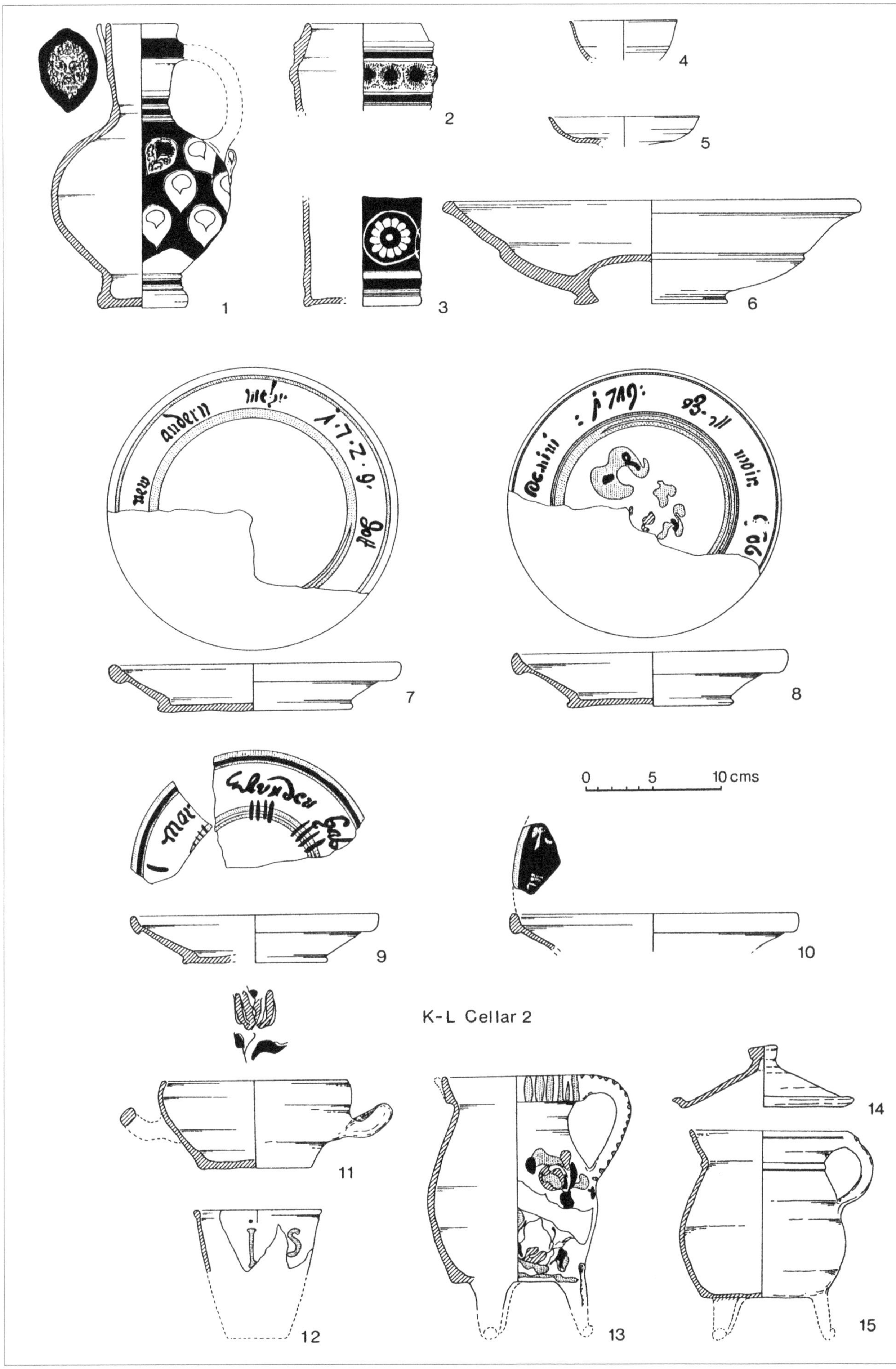


*Fig. 65 Stoneware, NL maiolica & slipware from Krefeld-Linn, Margaretenstraße 32, cellar 2*

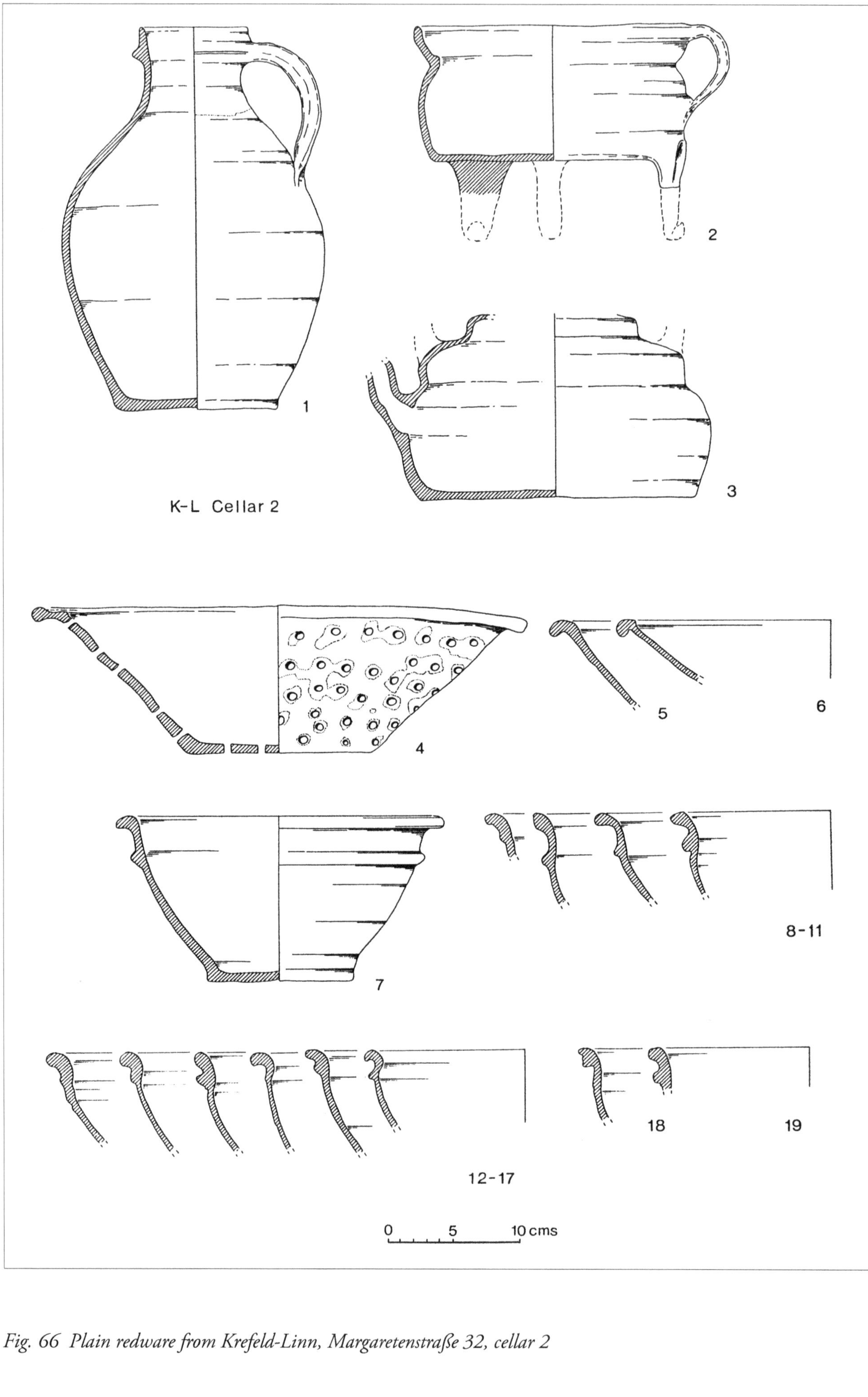


*Fig. 66 Plain redware from Krefeld-Linn, Margaretenstraße 32, cellar 2*

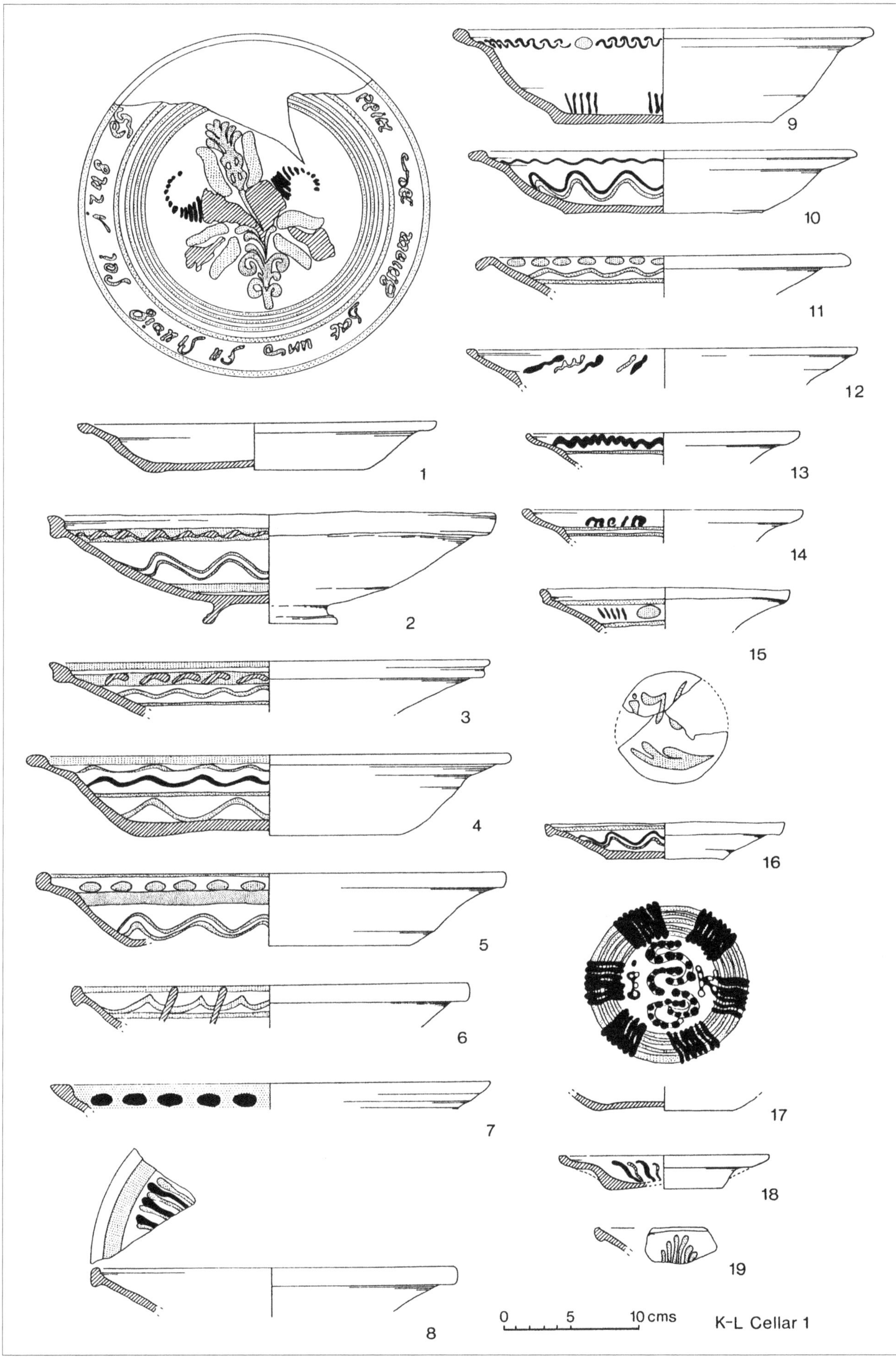


*Fig. 67 Slipware from Krefeld-Linn, Margaretenstraße 32, cellar 1*

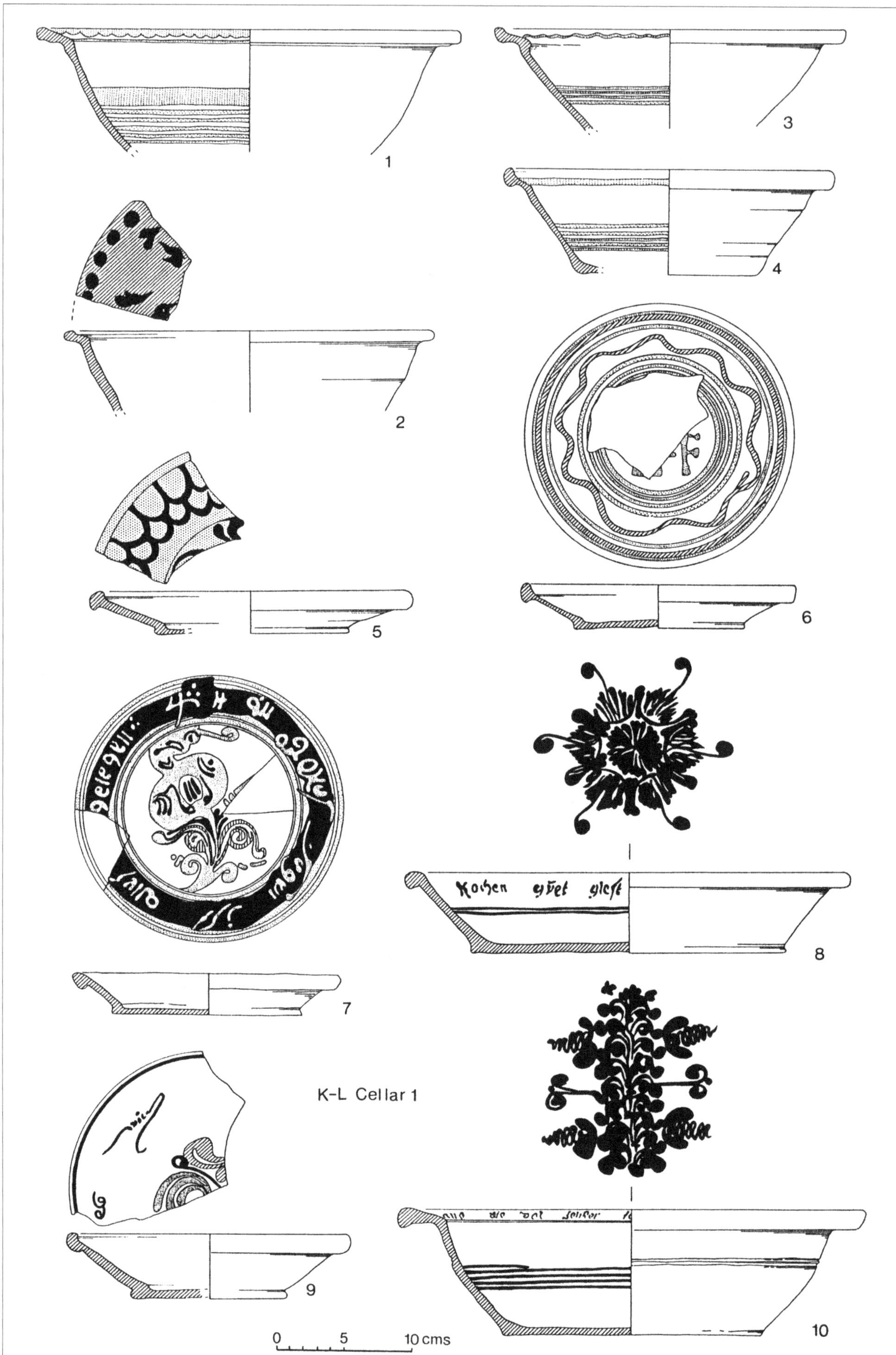


*Fig. 68 Slipware from Krefeld-Linn, Margaretenstraße 32, cellar 1*

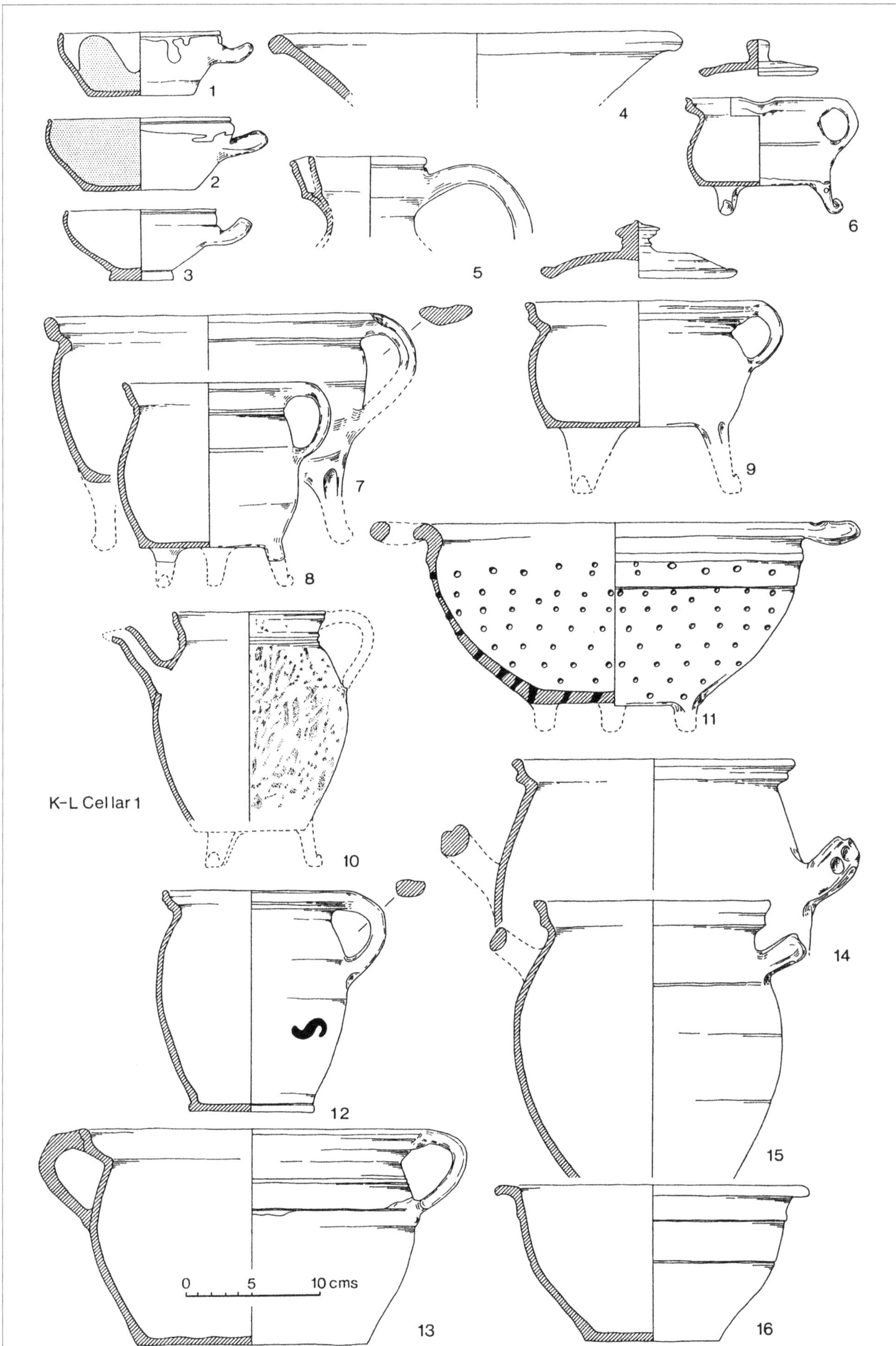


*Fig. 69 Plain redware from Krefeld-Linn, Margaretenstraße 32, cellar 1*

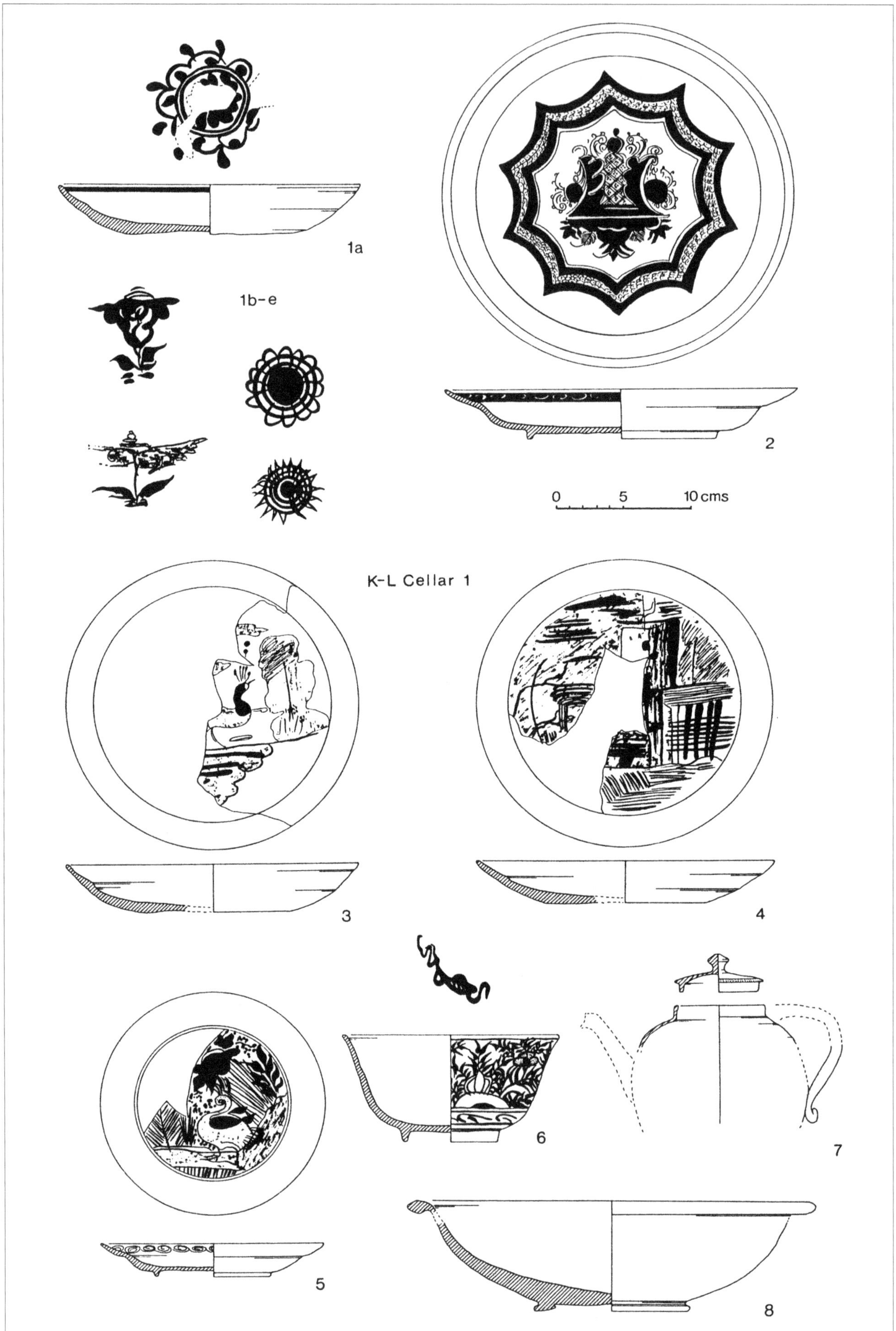


*Fig. 70 NL faience & Staffs earthenware from Krefeld-Linn, Margaretenstraße 32, cellar 1*

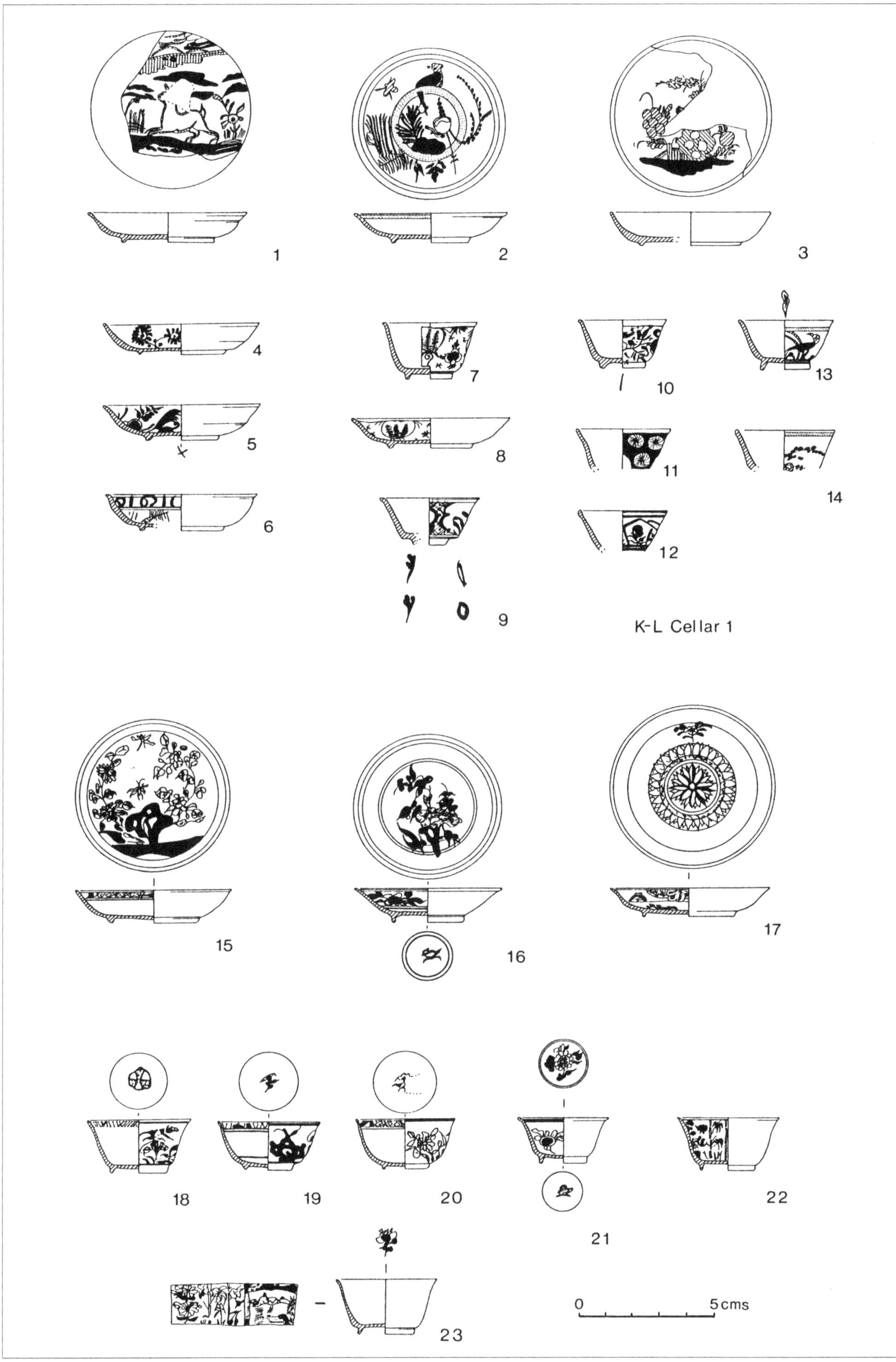


*Fig. 71 NL faience & Oriental porcelain from Krefeld-Linn, Margaretenstraße 32, cellar 1*

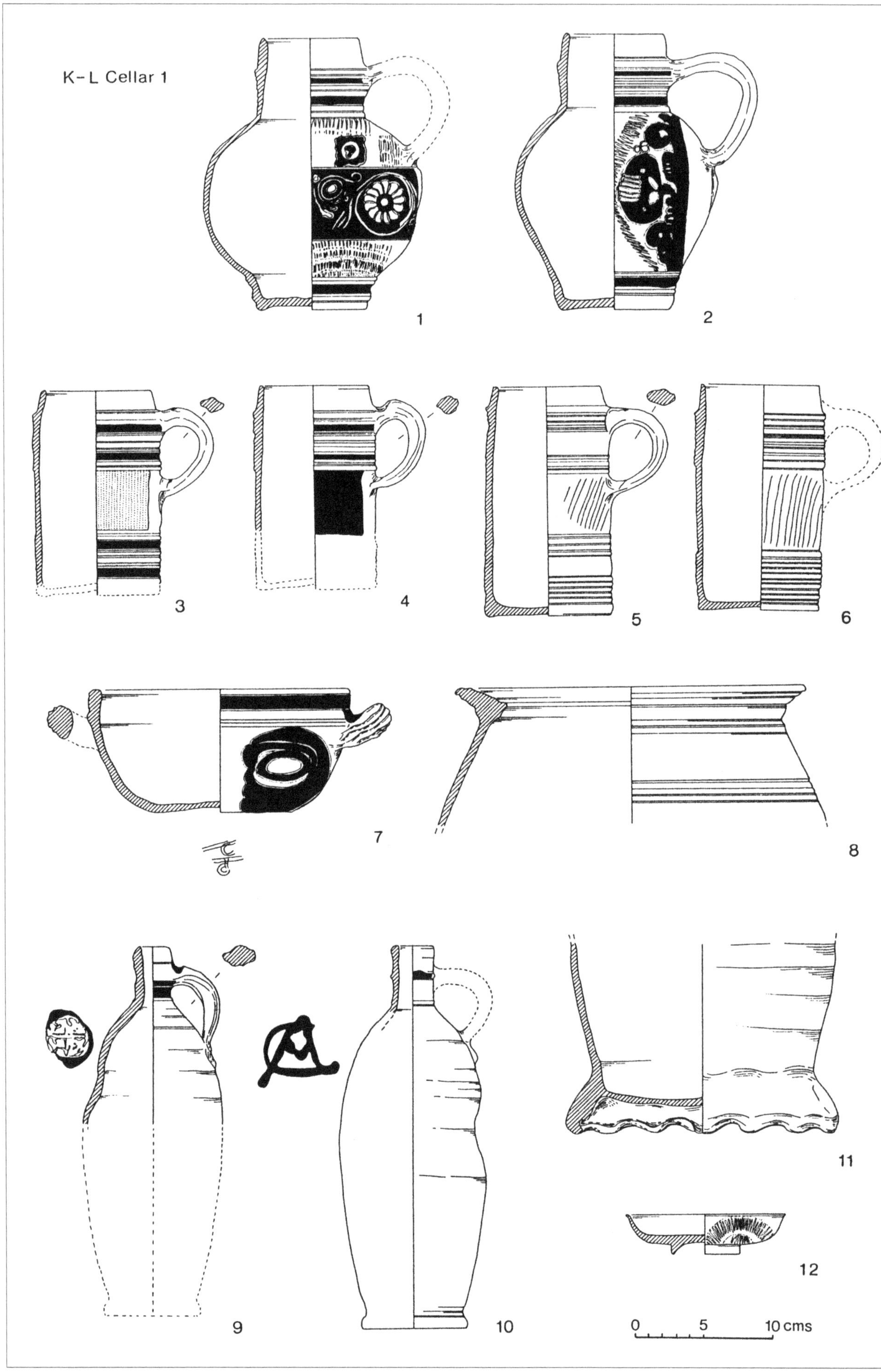


*Fig. 72 Stoneware from Krefeld-Linn, Margaretenstraße 32, cellar 1*

www.ingramcontent.com/pod-product-compliance
Ingram Content Group UK Ltd.
Pitfield, Milton Keynes, MK11 3LW, UK
UKHW061846041026
15591UKWH00015B/937

9 781841 719528